INDIAN TERRITORY 1861–1865

THE FORTS
THE BATTLES
THE SOLDIERS

Ethel Crisp Taylor

HERITAGE BOOKS
2010

HERITAGE BOOKS
AN IMPRINT OF HERITAGE BOOKS, INC.

Books, CDs, and more—Worldwide

For our listing of thousands of titles see our website at
www.HeritageBooks.com

Published 2010 by
HERITAGE BOOKS, INC.
Publishing Division
100 Railroad Ave. #104
Westminster, Maryland 21157

Copyright © 2010 Ethel Crisp Taylor

Other books by the author:
Shifting Winds of War: Indian Territory, 1861–1865

All rights reserved. No part of this book may be reproduced or transmitted in any form or by any means, electronic or mechanical, including photocopying, recording or by any information storage and retrieval system without written permission from the author, except for the inclusion of brief quotations in a review.

International Standard Book Numbers
Paperbound: 978-0-7884-3398-6
Clothbound: 978-0-7884-8486-5

This book is dedicated to the many family history researchers, whose "family stories" have passed down regarding an Indian Ancestor. That is a very hard search as Native American history was/is passed by word of mouth. There aren't any records of births, deaths, wills, land deeds and such by which white ancestors can be traced.

Over 22,000 Indian soldiers took part in this theater of the Civil War west of the Mississippi, which devastated the country and left many homeless, widows and orphans.

Before the war there were homes, schools, businesses, livestock, fields and crops. The once mighty Nations of the Southeast had been forcibly removed west of the Mississippi, their lands taken and came with nothing to Indian Territory. Many perished during the forced move west. But they rebuilt. After the War the Territory was a burned out battleground! In the 1890s, their lands were taken again, reducing them to 160 acres per person.

CONTENTS

Title Page	i
Copyright	ii
Dedication	iii
Table of Contents	v
Acknowledgements	ix
Introduction	xi
Part One, The Forts, 1861-1865	1
Fort Washita, IT	3
Fort Davis, IT	7
Fort Gibson, IT	8
Fort Towson, IT	10
Fort McCulloch, IT	12
Fort Arbuckle, IT	13
Fort Wayne, IT	16
Fort Smith, AR	17
Fort Cobb, IT	18
Fort Coffee, IT	19
Part Two, The Fights	21
Wilson Creek, MO	23
Round Mountain, Chusto-Talasah, Chustenalah, IT	24
Elkhorn Tavern (Pea Ridge) AR	26
Locust Grove, IT	30
Bayou Menard, IT	31
Maysville, AR	32
Honey Springs, IT	32
Perryville, IT	35
Backbone Mountain, IT	35
Middle Boggy, IT	36
Boggy Depot	37
Poison Springs, AR	39
Pleasant Bluff, IT	41
Massard Prairie, AR	42
First and Second Cabin Creek	43
Part Three, The Soldiers	45
Confederate Introduction	47
Confederate Units	49
Cherokee Units	51
1st Regiment, Cherokee Mounted Rifles	53
McDaniel's Company, 1st. Cherokee Mounted	

Rifles	71
1st Regiment, Cherokee Mounted Volunteers	73
2nd Regiment, Cherokee Mounted Volunteers	97
2nd Cherokee Artillery Company	113
Cherokee Mounted Rifles (Watie's Original)	115
Bryan's Battalion	125
Cherokee Regiment (Special Service)	127
Frye's/Scales' Battalion, Cherokee Cavalry	129
1st Squadron, Cherokee Mounted Volunteers, (Holt's)	133
Chickasaw Units	135
1st Regiment, Chickasaw Infantry	137
Shecoe's Chickasaw Battalion Mounted Volunteers	149
Choctaw Units	153
1st Regiment, Choctaw Mounted Rifles	155
Deneale's Regiment, Choctaw Warriors	167
Wilken's Company Choctaw Infantry	173
1st Regiment, Choctaw and Chickasaw Mtd. Rifles	175
Seminole Units	211
1st Regiment, Seminole Mounted Volunteers	213
Creek Units	227
1st Regiment, Creek Mounted Volunteers	229
1st Creek Mounted Rifles	263
2nd Creek Mounted Volunteers (Special Service)	271
1st Creek Regiment, Company H	275
2nd Regiment Creek Cavalry Volunteers	279
Small Miscellaneous Confederate Units	283
1st Battalion Chickasaw Cavalry	285
1st Battalion, Choctaw Cavalry (McCurtains)	285
3rd Regiment Choctaw Cavalry	285
1st Osage Battalion	285
2nd Regiment, Choctaw Cavalry	286
Cherokee Regiment Volunteer Cavalry	286
Choctaw Infantry	286
Cooper's Battalion, 1st Indian Brigade	287
Washington's Squadron	287
Union Troops	289
Union Introduction	291
1st Regiment Indian Home Guards	293
2nd Regiment Indian Home Guards	341
3rd Regiment Indian Home Guards	381
Indian Home Guard Discharges	413

Indian Home Guards Pension Applications	421
Indian Home Guard Pensions	427
Widows Pension Checks, Indian Home Guards	435
Cease Fire Treaty	439
Sale of Arkansas Cherokee Nation Land	441
Confederate States of America – Cherokee	447
Confederate States of America - Choctaw-Chickasaw	469
Confederate States of America – Creek	497
Confederate States of America – Seminole	521
Confederate States of America - Great Osage	541
Confederate States of America – Quapaw	555
Confederate States of America - Seneca, Shawnees	565
Confederate States of America – Comanche	581
Confederate States of America - Wichita, et. al.	591
Important Sites in Indian Territory	601
Resources	611

A special thank you goes to Michael Kelley, Colonel of Terrell's 37th Texas Cavalry, CSA, Re-enactment Unit. Colonel Kelley helped me list the specific military ranks and billets in the correct descending order.

He maintains a website, http://www.37thtexas.org/, with more than 100 pages. With 2000+ visitors per month, and 117 Web Awards, this site remains the largest, most visited War for Southern Independence re-enactor web site. Members are historians, professional and amateur, of many racial, ethnic, and religious backgrounds that are committed to a mission of historical research and documentation of Confederates of all races, ethnic origins and religions.

INTRODUCTION

"The only allies of the Confederacy, the five Indian Nations of the Creek, Cherokees, Seminoles, Choctaws and Chickasaws in the War Between The States, suffered a larger percent of losses than did any of the other states"
Confederate Memorial Hall
Oklahoma Historical Society
Dedicated to "The Forgotten Heroes 1861-1865"

In 1861 the area of present-day Oklahoma was known as "Indian Territory", populated by Sovereign Nations. About 60,000 Choctaw, Cherokee, Chickasaw, Creek and Seminole Indians resided in the Territory with 1,500 white men married to Indian women, and 10,000 Negro slaves. An estimated 2,500 Osage, Caddo, Wichita, Shawnee, and Delaware were part of the I. T. population and approximately 3,000 Comanche, Kiowa, Cheyenne and Arapaho were located in the western part of Oklahoma, the Texas panhandle, southeast Colorado and southwest Kansas. Of these people, 8,000 served the Union in the three Indian Home Guard Regiments and 15,000 plus served the Confederacy. Indian Territory supplied a larger percentage of her population to the cause, second only to Virginia, than any other Confederate state. Given the task of keeping invading Federal armies out of Texas, Indian Territory suffered more destruction and loss of civilian life than any state in the Confederacy. But the Indians held the line; the Federals were never able to reach the Red River.

Unlike the rest of the Confederacy, the Indian troops became more successful after July 1863. The majority of the Indian Division of the Army of the Trans-Mississippi was still in the field and undefeated in June, 1865.

Oklahoma has recovered from the Civil War era into a modern 21st century state now. The scars from the War are lost in the passage of time. Many of the battle sites are also lost. Although a list exists, many of them are only a memory in a book. Some have a small historical marker to designate what happened, but beyond the sign are green pastures, livestock, homes or towns. Some are covered by lakes and vacation spots. Most of the smaller sites are on private lands with no designations visible. Any remnants of the War in the territory are long gone, save the forts that are designated historical sites.

The soldiers that fought and died are also a faded memory. Many of their descendents do not know they served in the Union or

Confederacy, or of their sacrifices, deaths, victories or defeat. These soldiers that fought, died and survived have faded into obscurity over the 140 plus years since Brigadier General Stand Watie rode into Doaksville, Choctaw Nation that hot 23rd day of June, 1865 and signed the Treaty of Cease Fire with the United States of America. These are the "Forgotten Heroes, 1861-1865".

Some of the major sites, such as prominent forts, are now historical sites maintained by the federal or state governments. These host many visitors a year, with tours or re-enactments, as the public's knowledge and curiosity grows. The public is beginning to be aware that the Civil War did not just happen east of the Mississippi, it happened in Indian Territory also. The soldiers were not only white with ancestral lines stretching back to Europe, but were Native Americans, who's ancestral lines stretched back further into the mists of time than when the first white man sat foot on North American soil.

Oklahoma has a rich history that is only enhanced by the Nations that were put there against their will, but adapted, made it their home and fought for the principles they believed in. As more people research their family, they become aware they have an Indian ancestor. Now, this is a measure of pride and not hidden as so many of the great grandparents, great, great grandparents did, in order to survive in a white society.

The photos contained in this book belong to the author, except if otherwise noted.

The names of men that fought these battles are not known to people, just as the many nameless soldiers that fought the Civil War in the east. This book will bring to light the names of many of those soldiers, so their descendents can see them and know who they are. A number of the Confederate units' rosters have been lost. The remaining rosters have been used for this book. The three Union Indian Home Guard Regiments are listed, as are the available lists of the Union pensions that were applied for in 1871 at Tahlequah, Cherokee Nation.

The rosters of the troops that are listed in these pages were recorded by white soldiers. They recorded them as they did the white soldiers, such as "Smith, John", so you will find many of the native names could be reversed as to their actual translation. I do not know the various languages, so was unable to list the soldiers correctly.

Broadfoot Publishing may be able to assist in getting copies of your Union and Confederate Indian soldiers (if available), costs are less than the National Archives and faster to receive.

Part I

The Forts

1861 - 1865

Fort Washita, IT

Fort Washita was established in 1842 as the then southwestern most post in the United States. Beyond the borders to the south and west was the Republic of Texas which had recently won its independence from Mexico. The purpose of the post was to protect the Chickasaw and Choctaw Indians from the Plains Indians. For centuries the Plains Indians had used this area for hunting and were not happy with newcomers settling in the area.

At the outbreak of the Civil War in 1861, Federal troops under the command of Colonel William Emory pulled out of Indian Territory. Fort Washita was abandoned and quickly occupied by Texas Confederates.

Douglas Hancock Cooper was the U. S. Indian agent to the Choctaw and Chickasaw and had his office at Fort Washita. He was commissioned a Colonel of the Choctaw-Chickasaw Mounted Rifles, CSA.

The Fort Washita site was acquired by the Oklahoma Historical Society in 1962. It has belonged to the Colbert family, members of the Chickasaw Nation, since the Department of the Interior transferred it to them in 1870. The Society maintains the fort, reconstructing some of the buildings, developing the museum, and conducting tours at times through the year.

Remains of other buildings are visible as you tour the site. The current visitor's center was the Chaplain's quarters and contains the museum.

According to some park employees there have been reports, from some night tour visitors and reenactors; of restless spirits that inhabit some areas of the fort. In the years of the Fort between 1842 and 1861, a murder took place which may have given the fort its resident ghost.... or at least one of them.

The ruins are still said to be haunted today by this restless spirit, the ghost of a headless woman who has been dubbed "Aunt Jane".

The legend of the ghost is a strange one and is filled with numerous holes. No one really knows for sure how she died, although some say she was killed by thieves and others say by soldiers. No matter what happened, she was apparently beheaded in the process of her murder because she has been seen in the years following dressed in a white gown and walking about the fort with no head. The story says that Aunt Jane allegedly hid a large amount of gold somewhere on the grounds and her ghost is still looking for it. Needless to say, this part of the story has prompted many would-be treasure hunters to go out in search of the treasure... only to be frightened off by the ghost of Aunt Jane.

General Douglas Cooper's Cabin

Right - Reconstructed South Barracks, 120 feet long, 30 feet Wide, Orderly and Company rooms on top floor, kitchens, mess halls, food storage on 1st level.

1917.

West Barracks built 1856 -Upper floors contained company rooms, orderly rooms for sergeants. Ground floor was kitchens, mess rooms, food storage rooms. The Colbert family used it as home until it burned in

Old Post Cemetery (right) also has Colbert family members. Located north of post hospital (left)

West and a little north of the main gate is the Confederate Cemetery. There are over 200 unmarked graves of Confederate soldiers buried here and without a record of who they are.

Below - Layout of old Fort Washita

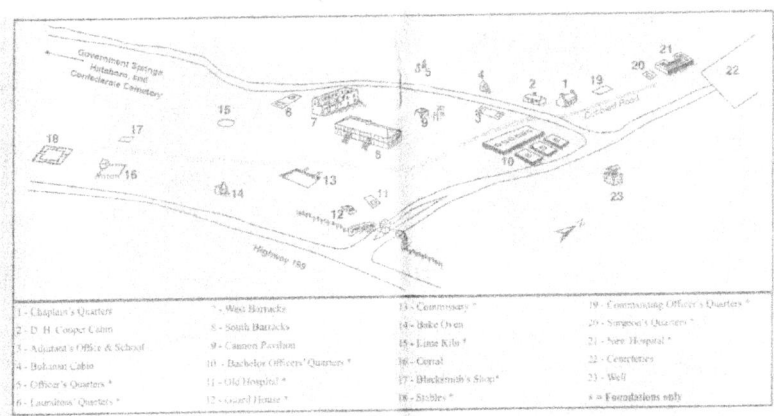

The "Bohanan Cabin", originally built near Durant by Edward Bohanan, was moved to the fort in 1990's. Bohanan was a teamster at the fort and during the war was a member of General Cooper's Indian Brigade. It is

similar to the cabins used by the officers. It is used for military re-enactments and living history demonstrations. Though it doesn't look it, the cabin is two-story.

According to female re-enactors that have stayed there during living histories, the cabin is home for other restless spirits. They have  reported sensations of being strangled and impressions of a hostile presence. None of the men who have stayed in the cabin have been bothered. The story of the Bohanans includes a husband being murdered, the widow marrying soon after to the man suspected of the crime and his untimely death soon after that.

The reconstructed barracks provides its own spirit visitations. Aunt Jane has been known to disassemble locks in the east room on the first floor. There has been reported a civil war soldier wearing a great coat on the second floor porch, pacing back and forth and  smoking. There have been reports of hearing a commotion sounding like a large group of soldiers up on that same porch, faint shapes seen, then footsteps coming down the stairs, only to fade away at the bottom

Every Halloween, members of a re-enactment group perform at Fort Washita telling ghost stories and leading a ghost hunt around the fort. Proceeds from this event are used to improve the site. It really is an enjoyable experience as there are many ghosts around that fort.

There has been other hauntings at the site that can be validated by the Oklahoma Historical Society and many other tales.

Left- The old wagon road to California passed thru Fort Washita. Right – The trail was worn so deep it is still visible just to the east of the old Post Cemetery.

Fort Davis, IT

Fort Davis was established November, 1861 by General Albert Pike and named for President Jefferson Davis who had been stationed in this region as a lieutenant in the US Army. Nearly $1,000,000.00 was spent on this post by the Confederates. Site is near the campus of Bacone Indian College one mile east of town.

In the second Federal invasion, Fort Davis was destroyed December 27, 1862 by Union troops, including the Third Indian Home Guard Regiment under Colonel W. A. Phillips. It was located just north of present day Muskogee on a hill overlooking the Arkansas River, opposite where the Grande and Verdigris Rivers enter.

After an exchange of fire, the outnumbered Southerners abandoned Fort Davis to the Union. Phillips burned the post and followed Watie and Cooper into the Creek Nation, burning the homes of Southerners along the way. All that is left is the monument erected by the Oklahoma Historical Society.

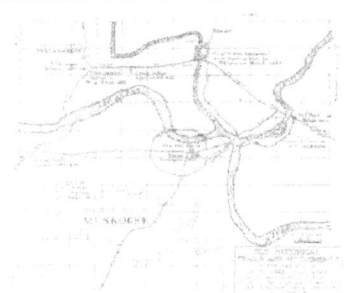

Old Historical Trails and Settlements in the vicinity of Muskogee, OK compiled from data furnished by Dr. Grant Foreman, old citizens and visible remains of the old trails and settlements. The circle is where Ft. Davis was located.

Fort Gibson, IT

At the beginning of the war, Fort Gibson was occupied by the Southern forces. In April, 1863, General Blunt sent Union forces, including the First, Second and Third Indian Home Guards to escort the Loyal Indians home to Indian Territory. A small force under Watie occupied Fort Gibson, which was attacked by the Second Home Guard and a detachment of the Sixth Kansas Cavalry. They literally drove the small detachment into the Grande River to swim for their lives. On April 13th, Colonel W. A. Phillips rode into Fort Gibson followed by his supply wagons and hundreds of Union Creeks and Seminoles, whose land was still in the hands of the Confederacy.

The fort was occupied by three thousand one hundred fifty Union soldiers. It was a good defensive position, sitting on a bluff overlooking the Grand River, near the intersection of the Arkansas River and the Texas Road, two main arteries for trade in the territory.

Post Hospital

Post Bakery

Powder Magazine – Commissary. The commissary is now the fort visitor center.

Right - Enlisted Men's Quarters

Adjutant's Office – Blacksmith shop, left

Commanding Officer's Quarters

Fort Gibson is maintained as a National Historic Site. Adjacent is the Fort Gibson National Cemetery. There are over 15,000 interments. Of the Union soldiers buried here the names of 156 are known and 2,208 are unknown. Many are dated back prior to the Civil War, being moved here from other abandoned forts, such as Forts Towson, Arbuckle and Washita.

Fort Towson, I. T.

At the beginning of 1865, the war in Indian Territory was at an end. Watie's troops were fighting a desperate holding action, and the most feared Confederates, Stand

Watie's Cherokee riders, were reported repeatedly to be preparing for a raid along the Neosho valley. Many dreaded the coming of spring, 1865, with its deadly military raids and terrifying guerilla raids.

Fort Towson, near the small town of Doaksville, Choctaw Nation, Indian Territory, became the focal point for the end in Indian Territory. April 9, 1865 brought the surrender of General Lee in Virginia. Lt. General Edmond Kirby-Smith surrendered the Trans-Mississippi Department, May 26, and one by one, the Indian Rebels surrendered their forces.

Above – View north

Above: wide angles old Fort Towson

Suttler's store

Left; Old Military Road

On a hot, muggy June 23, 1865, the proud and fiercely patriotic Brigadier General Stand Watie made the hardest ride of his life, no Yankee guns aimed at him, no sabers slashing at his body, no smell of gunpowder mixed with dust on a battlefield
(Below – Doaksville, ca 1850's)

With this ride, into the small town of Doaksville, Stand Watie signed a Treaty of Cease Fire with the United States. The last Confederate Field General officer, and the only American Indian to become a Brigadier General, to cease fire, with the full respect of his men and his enemies, turned his horse toward home. The ghostly Cherokee Braves flag rippled across the hot June sky, the battles, shouts of Pins and Rebel Indians screams of dying men and animals, Rebel Yells on a Southern charge were now alive only in memories and the dust that swirled in the wind.

Fort McCulloch, IT

Nail's Crossing .... 1.6 miles, where the Texas Road crossed the Blue River, named for a prominent Choctaw family. The Nail house is still standing--its logs held together firmly by the wooden pegs used in the original construction about 1847. Nearby is a family cemetery that has been well kept through the years. Fort McCulloch is on private property southwest of Kenefic, Oklahoma.

One of the interesting historic remains can be found in Bryan County near the old Nail's Crossing on the Blue River about ten miles north of Durant. On the south side of the river, and about two hundred yards from its banks is the well-defined outline of the redoubts and bastions built during the summer, 1862 by Texas, Arkansas and Indian Confederate troops. About a hundred yards or so to the right and left of the main fortifications are the remains of the arsenal pits, where the ammunitions were stored. Nothing of the headquarters or temporary buildings remain, all is overgrown with trees.

It is hard to realize after spending a day among the peaceful scenes along the river and near the fort and crossing, that this was once a place teeming with life and throbbing with activity. Nail's Crossing was on the military road that ran from Fort Gibson via Perryville (near present site of McAlester), Boggy Depot, Fort

Washita, into Texas and the Southwest. From 1850 on this was a much-traveled road, and thousands of adventurers, bound for homes in Texas, or for the gold fields of California crossed the Blue at Nail's as they pushed on to the unknown West. Remains of a dam are still to be seen, and bits of the cable of the ferry-boat, used in times of high water, and by those who preferred not to risk the ford, or the crude wooden bridge which generally spanned the stream at this point.

Courtesy: Southwest American Historical Artifact Research Association, Ft. Smith, Arkansas

Fort Arbuckle, I. T.

A carefully drawn and neatly lettered ground plan, obtained from the office of the Chief of Engineers, U. S. A., and probably made by Major Birch, reveals that the post was composed of a picket stockade with one blockhouse at the northeast corner. This blockhouse was 25 feet square, the lower half setting square with the fort and the upper half at an angle of 45 degrees. Inside were five log buildings, arranged around three sides of a

OLD FORT ARBUCKLE

parade sixty yards square.

On the north side was a double officers' quarters, each room 22 feet square with a six foot open space between. It was joined on the east by a kitchen of round logs which was connected to the quarters by a heavy stone chimney of the double-mouth variety.

On the East was a similar building for officers with the same type chimney, but the kitchen was not built. On the west the company quarters were of two 22 by 22 rooms of hewed logs connected by a double-mouth chimney. The round-log kitchen was separate, and had a stick-and-mud chimney.

The move to the new location was made in April 1851. Already almost every officer and man in the company had been ill with malarial fever, which gave an added reason for the change. Previous to evacuating Camp Arbuckle, Lieutenant Updegraff and Dr. Glisan went down and made a careful report on the topography of the proposed site, especially from the standpoint of sanitation and health.

The location was carefully chosen on the slopes of the Arbuckle Mountains (these were so named from the fort), at an elevation of five hundred feet above the Washita River, and four miles from that stream, near Wild Horse Creek. A never failing water supply was furnished by a limpid spring that gushed from the mountain side with power enough to run a mill, Dr. Glisan said. This spring still flows from the mountains, but like so many others, has lost much of its volume since the forests have been cut away and the fields reduced to cultivation. The fort received its name from the veteran General Matthew Arbuckle, who had recently died of the cholera at Fort Smith.

The new fort was constructed with considerable care. The buildings were erected in the shape of a rectangle, a line of barracks on either side, with commissary and quartermaster's quarters at one end, and the officers' quarters at the other.

Outside of the rectangle there was another long one-story building, suitably divided, and used as dispensary and steward's room hospital, and

NEW FORT ARBUCKLE

kitchen.

One hundred yards north of the commissary was the sutler's store. The houses were all well built of hewn logs, chinked with wood and clay, and had stone chimney

At the outbreak of the Civil War there were two companies of cavalry stationed at Arbuckle, while Colonel W. H. Emory at Fort Smith was in command of all the troops of the Territory. Fort Arbuckle was evidently not considered of much importance at this time, as Fort Cobb had already been constructed farther west, and Fort Washita commanded the lower reaches of the river of the same name.

It was hastily abandoned May 3, 1861, when Colonel Emory marched north accompanied by the garrisons of all the posts in this section. It was temporarily occupied by Texas troops who were pursuing Emory. Arbuckle played no part of any importance during the war, but was generally occupied by a portion of the Chickasaw forces. A section of the Chickasaw Battalion, one of the best known troops of cavalry furnished to the Confederacy by that Indian tribe, was stationed here in 1862.

In Vol. XI of the Chronicles of Oklahoma, Dr. James H. Gardner of Tulsa tells of a visit he made to the site of Old Fort Arbuckle some years ago. Its exact location was something that had slipped quietly out of the memories of all the old timers of the vicinity, but luckily he had learned that a very  old Creek, Lincoln Postoak, living some miles to the south, had been raised near the place. After Dr. Gardner and Dr. Grant Foreman had interviewed the aged Indian and established the accuracy of his memory concerning other events and conditions, Dr. Gardner and some other gentlemen took him to where he said the fort had been.

There, in the field of Bud Anderson, were the piles of stones and rubble that marked the location of the old chimneys, all arranged in a pattern which proved beyond doubt that it was the fort site.

The quarter section, range and township were carefully noted, and thus was a pin put in the historical map of Oklahoma to mark a place which, up to that time, the historians had only been able to point out with a "right about here" and a jab of the finger.

Postoak was able to point out the spot only because the old buildings had been used for many years after their abandonment as a military post. It seems that at one time there was a sort of trading post there, and without a doubt it was preserved for a while as a camping place of the wagoners who almost made a highway of the old Osage hunting trail as they passed on their way to California and other points west.

Fort Arbuckle, near the crossing of the Washita River, was built to protect the relocated Chickasaw Indians from the native plains tribes. The site is seven miles west of Davis on the south-side of Wild Horse Creek. Some of the structures of the old fort may still exist on private property. (In 2005, we searched for the location but found no evidence. – Ethel Taylor)

Fort Wayne, I. T.

Fort Wayne was established in autumn 1839 by Lt. Col. R.B. Mason and 1st Dragoons, U.S. Army, and named in honor of Gen. "Mad" Anthony Wayne and abandoned on May 15, 1842. Here in July 1861, Col. Stand Watie established a Confederate army post and organized the Cherokee Mounted Rifles.

On October 22, 1862, Cooper's Confederates were camped on Beatty's Prairie nearby, when General Blunt attacked them with his small advance force. In the following battle, both sides dueled with cannon. Reinforcements for Blunt arrived, outnumbering the Confederates. Confederate losses were 6 killed, 30 wounded and 26 missing. Blunt's forces had 5 killed, 5 wounded. They captured the Rebel artillery, flag, and burned Fort Wayne.

Scenes near Beatty's/Beattie's Prairie.

Fort Smith, AR

At Fort Smith National Historic Site you can walk where soldiers drilled, pause along the Trail of Tears, and stand where justice was served. The park includes the remains of two frontier forts and the Federal Court for the Western District of Arkansas.

The main entrance to the Visitor Center is located on the south end of the Barracks/Courthouse/Jail building. Exhibits in the visitor center focus on Fort Smith's military history from 1817 – 1871,

western expansion, Judge Isaac C. Parker and the federal court's impact on Indian Territory, U.S. Deputy Marshals and outlaws, Federal Indian policy, and Indian Removal including the Trail of Tears. Located on the grounds are the foundation remains of the first Fort Smith (1817-1824), the Commissary building (c. 1838) and a reconstruction of the gallows used by the federal court. A walking trail along the Arkansas River includes wayside exhibits on the Trail of Tears.

In July, 1864 General Cooper advanced on the strong Union force at Fort Smith, chasing the haying crew back to the fort. They pulled back to the Federal camp that had just been evacuated, where the Federals had left a tasty meal. They advanced with Texas artillery, but had to withdraw back into the territory.

In August, intelligence reached Watie that a large wagon train of supplies was loading to move to Fort Gibson. The prize was worth the risk.

On September 16, about 2000 troops and six artillery pieces moved out and crossed the Arkansas near the Creek Agency. At Flat Rock about two miles from the Grand River they found a large

Federal hay camp operation. They over ran the Union troops, sent them "each man for himself" scurrying back to Fort Gibson. The Rebels confiscated all the supplies, mules and ordinance left behind, and burned an estimated five thousand tons of hay. From prisoners taken at Flat Rock, Watie learned the large wagon train for Fort Gibson was coming from Fort Scott, Kansas instead of Fort Smith.

Fort Cobb, I. T.

In existence but a decade, from 1859 until 1869, this fort on the Washita River nevertheless had a colorful history. It and the adjacent Wichita Indian Agency were established to receive Indians relocated from Texas reservations, to protect them and the local Wichita from the Kiowa and Comanche, and to keep the latter from raiding into Texas. When the post and the agency were only 2 years old, the Union abandoned them.

In September 1862, rumor around Fort Cobb was that the Union sympathizing Indians were coming south to wipe out the Confederate officials at the agency. A cavalry of 196 Union Kickapoo, Delaware and Shawnee set out from Fort Leavenworth to attack the Confederates and the Southern sympathizing Indians at the agency. Although the Tonkawa fled the attack, they were followed and attacked along the Washita River. Approximately half the Tonkawa Nation was killed, including Chief Placido.

To clear the way for his 1868-69 offensive against the southern Plains tribes, General Sheridan ordered it reactivated in 1868 and the Fort Cobb Reservation (Kiowa-Comanche and Wichita Agencies) created as a refuge for all Indians in the area of the offensive who claimed to be peaceful, as well as for the Wichita and the Texas tribes that had returned from their temporary haven in Kansas. In December 1868, the month after Custer's victory in the Battle of the Washita, General Sheridan moved his headquarters to Fort Cobb. To hasten the capitulation of the Kiowa, he seized and threatened to hang Chiefs Satanta and Lone Wolf. The next March, the adobe and sandstone fort was abandoned after Fort Sill was established. He activated Fort Sill to replace Fort Cobb and transferred the Kiowa-Comanche Agency to the new fort.

There are no surface remains of the log-sod fort, on private property, but the cottonwood-lined site is comparatively undisturbed. A State marker is located one-half mile to the southwest.

The town was founded in 1899 one mile west of the fort site. Marker located on OK 9 east of town. (NOTE: Fort Cobb State Park has nothing to do with the historic fort.)

Fort Coffee, I. T.

Short-lived Fort Coffee (1834-38), a crude log post atop a high bluff at the Skullyville boat landing along the south bank of the Arkansas River about 3 miles north of the village, kept peace on the Choctaw lands and patrolled river traffic to prevent illegal trading. Located at Swallow Rock, it was a temporary post located in the Choctaw Nation on the Butterfield Overland Route, originally built to stop illegal whiskey shipments into Indian Territory.

From 1843 until the outbreak of the Civil War, Fort Coffee Academy, a school for Choctaw boys financed by the Choctaw Nation and administered by the Methodist Episcopal Church, occupied the fort buildings. Confederate troops moved into them in the Civil War and stayed until 1863, when Federal troops captured and burned them

Part Two

The Fights

1861-1865

Battle at Wilson Creek, MO

With the exception of the vegetation, the 1,750 acre battlefield has changed little from its historic setting, enabling the visitor to experience the battlefield in near pristine condition.

Photos courtesy National Park Service

The battle fought here on August 10, 1861, was the first major Civil War engagement west of the Mississippi River, involving about 5,400 Union troops and 12,000 Confederates, including about 1,000 Cherokee and Choctaw soldiers. Although a Confederate victory, the Southerners failed to capitalize on their success. The battle led to greater federal military activity in Missouri, and set the stage for the Battle of Pea Ridge in March 1862.

General Nathaniel Lyons

Wilson's Creek was also the scene of the death of Nathaniel Lyon, the first Union general to be killed in combat. At this battle just southwest of Springfield, Missouri, although General Lyons held the high ground, he was outnumbered. The Union fell back to Springfield. Wilson's Creek was the Bull Run of the west and its analogy to the first great battle in Virginia is remarkable. Casualties of all involved at Wilson's Creek were about 23 percent.

The Phillips/Patterson Cabin, built during the 1850's in what is now the town of Battlefield, Missouri, was moved to Wilson's

Creek National Battlefield in the 1970's. The cabin was placed on the site of the home of William B. Edwards and the headquarters of the Missouri State Guard Commander Major General Sterling Price. It has been restored to its 1861 appearance with funds donated by the Wilson's Creek National Battlefield Foundation. A formal dedication took place in September 2005.

Battles at Round Mountain, Chusto-Talasah, Chustenalah, IT

In August, a large gathering of large pro-union refugees from about 20 Nations joined the old Creek chief, O-Pothle-yahola, who opposed joining the Confederacy at his camp on the Deep Fork of the Canadian River near North Fork Town. O-Pothle-yahola began moving his people north to Kansas by November. He had more than 3,500 Indians including women and children and a fighting force of about 1,500 warriors. Most were Creek, but there were a few Seminole, including three Seminole war captains, Alligator, Holata Micco and Halleck Tustenuggee, armed with muzzle-loading shotguns, hunting rifles, knives, tomahawks, bow and arrow, spears and war clubs. The large number of wagons and stock they had meant they could not all travel together. They had to move in parallel columns, making their trail easy to follow.

Nearly 1000 Confederate troops set out from Fort Gibson after O-Pothle-yahola's group on November 15th. The weather had turned bitterly cold, both the soldiers and the refugees suffered. The first battle between the Loyals and the Confederates took place at a very nondescript place in Northern Creek County called Round Mountain. That location now is Lake Keystone.

Breaking away and crossing the cold Arkansas River during the night, the warriors caught up with the families at Chusto-Talasah on Bird Creek in Cherokee Country. Here they rested as the weather got colder. By December 9th, the Confederates caught up with them. The night before the battle, a large group of Col. John Drew's regiment slipped away with their weapons and joined O-Pothle-yahola's Loyals.

The Loyals moved on north after that battle, the Confederates catching up again on December 26th at Chustenalah on Shoal Creek. O-Pothle-yahola's rebellion was crushed. Of the nearly 9,000 Loyals from more than 20 Nations that followed him north, only about 6,000 survived to reach Kansas. Over the next four years, many more died from cold, malnutrition and disease

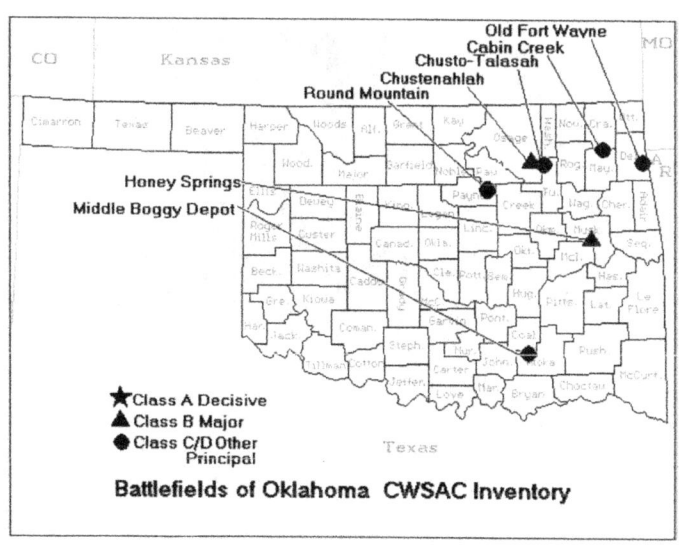

Battle of Elk Horn Tavern/Pea Ridge, AR

In late February 1862, Major General Curtis began moving his Federal troops south, following and harassing Gen. Sterling Price's Missouri Confederates, as they pulled back south out of Missouri. The stage was being set for the largest battle west of the Mississippi. All roads led now to Elkhorn Tavern (Pea Ridge to the Union).

Major General Earl Van Dorn sent orders out to Generals Price, McCulloch and Pike, Colonels Watie, Drew and McIntosh, to start moving their forces toward Fayetteville, timed to join Van Dorn's troops by March 7.

Generals that commanded the battle at Elkhorn Tavern.

Union

Gen. Franz Sigel Gen. Samuel Curtis

Confederate

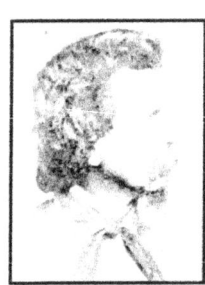  

Gen. Earl Van Dorn Gen. Albert Pike Gen. Sterling Price

Gen. James McIntosh,   Gen. Ben McCullock

(Generals' photos courtesy Oklahoma Historical Society, National Park Service, University of Arkansas, Little Rock, Archives.)

General Curtis' headquarters camp was to the east of Leetown, southwest of Elkhorn Tavern.

The Battle of Leetown began late morning March 7, 1862. About noon, regular units of the Confederate Cherokee began their first action outside Indian Territory. While Brig. General James McQueen McIntosh's brigade charged the Federals in a large field to the east, Pike drew his 1,000-man brigade and Colonel Sim's 150-200 Texans into a line near some woods as the 3-gun Union battery opened on the Confederate Column.

The Union guns of Elbert's Missouri Light Artillery opened fire into the wooded area where Watie and Drew's troops were. The range of the gunners was good but not deadly. Watie's troops  dismounted on the right flank of the Confederate line, on the left was Sim's Texans and in the middle were Welch's Texans, and Drew's still in the saddles. Pike ordered a charge by his full line. With war whoops and Rebel yells, the Cherokees and Texans erupted in the attack. Because of a popular but wildly inaccurate Currier and Ives Print, there is a persistent myth that the Cherokee that were in McIntosh's cavalry charge were dressed in war bonnets and other Plains Indian regalia. In fact, the Indians fought on their own in the woods bordering the west side of Foster's farm, some wore colorful turbans and other traditional Cherokee dress. Many wore the same mix of store-bought and homespun clothing as practically every other southerner in the Army of the West.

Here the Cherokee captured the Union "Shooting wagons", as

they called them.
Cannons across battle

site

The current Elkhorn Tavern is a reproduction by the National Park Service. As the original, it faces onto the old Telegraph Road.

Telegraph Road running past Elkhorn Tavern from the east

Surgical instruments of the time

Confederate Artifacts

Elkhorn Tavern.

Confederate Memorials at Elkhorn Tavern (Pea Ridge in the North)
These memorials lie to the south of

The memorials honor the Confederate Dead, General Ben McCullough, and General James McIntosh.

The Army of the Southwest (Union) lost 1,384 men at Pea Ridge – 203 killed, 980 wounded (of whom 150 later died) and 201 missing (presumably captured). Nearly half of the Federal casualties came from Carr's hard-fighting 4th Division.

The Army of the West (Confederate) lost hundreds of men to straggling and desertion during the campaign, especially during the retreat to Van Buren. The best estimate is that Van Dorn lost approximately 2,000 men in the battle, including 500 taken prisoner.

Battle at Locust Grove – Spavinaw Creek, IT

The skirmish site is located on the south edge of Locust Grove, near the south side of State Highway 33 (now US-412). The Oklahoma Historical marker is in the roadside park at Pipe Springs, on the east side of Locust Grove. The battlefield site is on the ridge, above the springs on the west and south.

On July 3, 1862, Colonel Watie's men, about 300-400, including Major Broke Arm and his Confederate Osage were camped near Spavinaw Creek when scouts brought word the Federals were headed their way. It became a running fight, as the Rebel troops galloped across the hot dry prairie.
Watie's troops split off in different directions, making it difficult for the Union troops to follow.

The same day, other Federal troops reached Colonel Clarkson's unfortified camp at Locust Grove. Colonel Weer's Union troops surrounded the camp before the Southerners knew they were there. They attacked just at daybreak. Watie had not had time to warn him.

Clarkson's force of about 300 men was so completely demoralized that they were unable to form a battle line, though gunfire continued in the woods all day. Colonel Clarkson surrendered the men that remained with him after the attack in the morning. Sixty wagons of ammunition and salt, sixty-four mule teams, and large quantities of provisions were captured by the Federals, together with 110 men who surrendered.

Bayou Menard Skirmish, IT

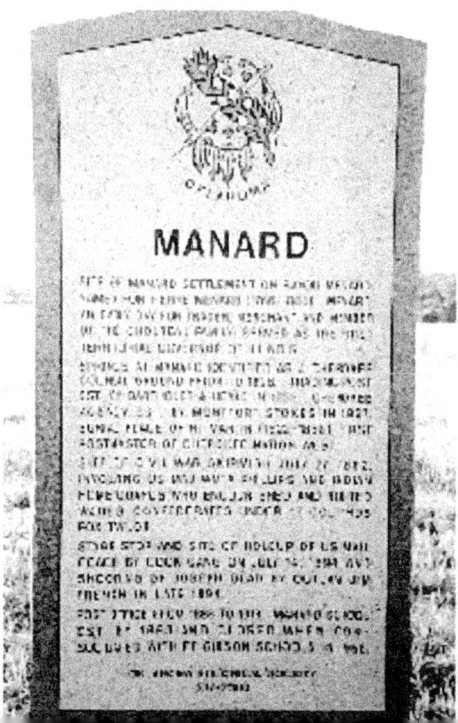

The Bayou Menard Skirmish, near the bridge across Bayou Menard, is located on the south side of U.S. Highway 62, about 7 miles east of Fort Gibson. In the first Federal effort to retake Indian Territory, Major William A. Phillips penetrated to a point about seven miles east of Fort Gibson. Here he met a force of Colonel Stand Watie's Confederates in a brief skirmish on July

27, 1862, taking twenty-five prisoners and killing and wounding about 100 men. Among the Confederate dead were a lieutenant colonel and three captains. Phillips was pleased with the conduct of his Indian forces in this skirmish. His only difficulty was in restraining their impetuous charge and in keeping back a reserve and guards for the wagons

Maysville Skirmish, AR

Battle of Maysville occurred on Oct. 22, 1862. While Gen. James Blunt was encamped on the old Pea Ridge battlefield, word came that Gen. Douglas Cooper and Col. Stand Watie's Indian Regiments were at old Fort Wayne across the line from Maysville. On Oct 20, he advanced his 2nd and 3rd brigades to Bentonville, AR. On Oct. 21, they moved toward Maysville. Crossing the prairie they found the Confederates lined up on the edge of some timber a quarter mile from the town. Before his superior force they retreated in disorder followed by the 6th Kansas cavalry and the 3rd Cherokee regiment for seven miles

Battle of Honey Springs, IT

Honey Springs was a Confederate camp and supply depot located 18 miles south of Fort Gibson, near present day Muskogee, in the Creek Nation. There was a frame commissary building, a log hospital; several brush arbors and hundreds of tents. Several springs supplied fresh water. By July 1863, it was the most important Confederate installation in Indian Territory and a prime target for General Blunt and his Union forces.

The Union forces came into sight on July 17. The Confederates had been fore-warned after a skirmish near Chimney Mountain between the Union leads and Confederate scouts during a rain shower. The scouts noticed a serious problem that could affect the upcoming battle; some of the gunpowder absorbed moisture from the damp weather and would not fire

The Battle of Honey Springs marked the end of large scale Confederate military resistance in Indian Territory. This battle has been referred to as the "Gettysburg of Indian Territory".

.Battlefield sites

Memorial erected to Five Civilized Tribes who fought at Honey Springs; Federal: First Indian Home Guards, (Cherokee); Second Indian Home Guards, (Cherokee): Confederate: First Choctaw Regiment; Second Choctaw Regiment; First Chickasaw and Choctaw Regiment; Cherokee Regiment; First Creek Regiment; Second Creek Regiment; Seminole Detachment.

Right: Monument erected by Daughters of the Confederacy, Texas Unit.

Below: Monument erected for Confederate Indians and Texas Troops

Honey Springs Battlefield is maintained by the Oklahoma Historical Society and the Friends of Honey Springs Historic Battle Site. Civil War re-enactments are held here.

Battle of Perryville, IT

After the battle of Honey Springs, began the deadly game of cat and mouse between the well armed Federals and the ragged Confederate troops.

In August, Blunt took his forces out again to pursue Steele, Cooper and Watie when he heard they were near Perrysville. The Rebel Commanders decided to make a stand, brought up their howitzers to cover the road and spread their forces behind what scant cover that was available. The outnumbered Confederates answered the attack, but Federal Artillery overcame them. Since Perryville was a supply depot, Blunt loaded all he could carry and burned the rest.

Perryville was originally the trading post of James Perry. By 1849 was one of the most important towns at the intersection of the Texas and California Roads. Many noted expeditions passed through on these routes. Colbert Institute, Methodist School for Chickasaws was established here in 1854.

Backbone Mountain Battle, IT

This battle site is located north of Pocolo, Oklahoma, along US 271. On Sept. 1, 1863, Confederates under Brig. Gen. W. L. Cabell ambushed a Union force commanded by Maj. Gen J. G. Blunt, but were driven off after a three hour battle. Later, on July 27, 1864, the Choctaw Battalion led by Capt. Jack McCurtain defeated a Federal cavalry force here.

Photos – Okla. Historical Society

Middle Boggy Skirmish, IT

About 20 miles from Fort Washita, the Southerners had a supply depot located along Boggy Depot near present day Atoka. Confederate forces were assigned to guard and protect the stage route and delivery road to Boggy Depot which was about 15 miles southwest of the outpost camp located near the spring. Phillips sent a detachment of 350 men and a section of howitzers under Maj. Charles Willets to seize the outpost.

Graves at Middle Boggy Cemetery

On February 9, Maj. Willets attacked the Confederate outpost, which had only about 90 men and no cannon. The Confederates were poorly armed and had no heavy weapons, fought hard in the battle that lasted about 30 minutes, in which 49 of their men were killed and others wounded.

By the time Lt. Col. John Jumper arrived, the Union had already pulled out, leaving destruction in their wake. Following their commander's orders of no prisoners, wounded Confederates had been butchered like hogs with their throats slit open. It is still unknown which unit these men belonged to, so therefore, their names are unknown. Fear of the arrival of more Confederate troops influenced the Federals to retire to Fort Gibson. The dead were buried one mile north of Atoka, Oklahoma on the west side of Boggy River, and 100 yards north of Hwy. 69.

In 1862 Colonel C. L. Dawson's 19th Arkansas Infantry was sent to assist the building of earthen works at Fort McCullouch. On their journey from Ft. Smith to Fort McCullouch, they were forced to stop at the Confederate Camp known as Middle Boggy due to an outbreak of measles. Many of those men died and ten were buried in the small burying ground on the north side of the Middle Boggy River. There were sandstones inscribed with the name of the soldier, along with his death date and the letters "CSA" set up to mark the graves. In 1988, members of the Atoka County Historical Society identified as many as they could of those buried there and new headstones were placed beside the old. Their research continues in the effort to identify all the soldiers who rest there

This cemetery was also a burial ground for travelers on the old Boggy Depot Road before and after the Civil War.

Local legend says that in 1872, when the MK&T railroad laid new tracks through the area, they crossed a portion of the old cemetery, destroying several of the Confederate graves.

Boggy Depot, IT

Boggy Depot was the early capitol of the Choctaw Nation. An act of Congress, March 8, 1857, made the Butterfield Overland Mail the first trans-continental service. This route ran across Indian Territory from Fort Smith Arkansas through Boggy Depot, as one of its' two post offices in the territory to Colbert's Ferry, southwest on the Red River.

Boggy Depot had a school, church, and a Masonic Lodge, chartered November 18, 1868 by the Grand Lodge of Arkansas.

During the Civil War, Boggy Depot was the major supply depot for the Confederate Troops operating in Indian Territory. Located along the Clear Boggy River in southwest Choctaw Nation, (now Atoka County, OK), it provided water and shelter for the troops and stock. The old oaks provided protection during the winter lulls in fighting, also providing wood for fires to cook and keep warm. Meadows among the oaks were grazed by the stock. Supplies from Texas were brought in.

During the last year of the fighting, as food grew scarce and the Territory became more devastated by the fighting, Indian families pushed into the Choctaw and Chickasaw Nations seeking refuge and protection. What food supplies and shelter that was available was shared, but the last winter was hard on all.

Boggy Depot

is now a historical site and state park. Traces of buildings of the former Choctaw capitol are marked by signs at their locations. In the still of the night, the winds whispering through the trees fill your thoughts with the sounds of 145 years ago. Listen close and you hear the sounds of the animals moving about, the low mutter of soldiers, the cries of the refugees, hungry in the night. (This is one of our favorite campgrounds in OK-Ethel Taylor)

(Photo site of Gov. Allen Wright home.)

Poison Springs Arkansas, AR

On March 23rd, 1864, Federal Major General Fredrick Steele left Little Rock AR with 13,000 men, 9,000 horses and mules, 800 wagons and 30 pieces of artillery for the beginning of the Red River Campaign. The aim was to capture Shreveport, Louisiana and open Texas up to Federal occupation. He was harassed by the Confederates all the way.

Twenty-three days after Little Rock, the Union army arrived at Poison Springs, located 10 miles west of Camden on Ark. 76. A concentration of Confederates in southwest Arkansas had forced the Union trek to the east. Heavy rain and mud were partially to blame for the slow movement, which caused supplies to become dangerously low. When the Federals arrived on April 15, they found the Confederate troops had withdrawn.

On April 17, General Steele received word the Federal forces advancing northward in Louisiana with needed supplies were retreating. Further complicating matters, Steele also learned Confederate loyalists had either moved or destroyed most of a massive stockpile of corn he'd planned to ransack. The Union General then sent a force of 200 wagons; a detachment of 500 African American infantrymen, 195 cavalry troops and an artillery detachment to get what supplies remained.

It didn't take long for a scout under Confederate Brigadier General John S. Marmaduke, whose men were camped near Camden, to notice the wagon train. Marmaduke suggested to his superior, Confederate General Sterling Price, an ambush be set.

During the night, the Union wagon train was reinforced by 400 soldiers Steele sent from Camden, as approximately 1,500 Confederates prepared to attack the Union troops from both sides of the blocked road. The attack on April 18 began near a place the locals call Poison Spring. When the battle ended, the Union force of more than 1,100 had been reduced to 800.

Another 80 Federals were killed as they clawed their way back to Camden through the bottomlands. Fewer than 20 Confederates were killed in the victory that kept much-needed supplies from enemy hands. This ended the Red River Campaign.

Pleasant Bluff, I. T.

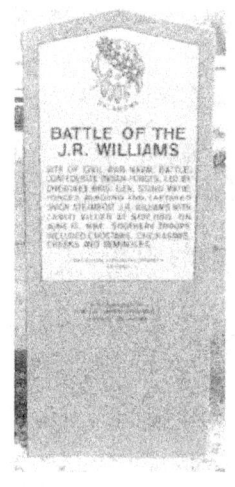

Union forces were hard pressed the summer of 1864 to protect wagon trains and hay stations. All supplies had to be brought in as the war had destroyed the Territory north of the Arkansas, after two Federal invasions, foraging by Confederates and thefts by swarms of bushwhackers.

June, 1864, brought a rise to the Arkansas River so supplies for Fort Gibson could be sent by boat from Fort Smith. There were no Federal outposts between Fort Gibson and Fort Smith along the Arkansas, the country was open and the river easily accessed at almost any place for forty to fifty miles. Federal outposts could not be kept out over ten to fifteen miles for fear of constant danger of attack.

The steam ferryboat, J. R. Williams was loaded with a cargo of commissary goods, quartermaster supplies, and some sutler goods for the troops at Fort Gibson. Lieutenant G. W. Houston, quartermaster of the Fourteenth Kansas Cavalry and captain of the boat was ordered to take the supplies upriver. There was an escort of twenty-six men from the Fourteenth, but no cavalry support along the south bank.

Arkansaw River

Confederate Indian forces, led by Cherokee Brig. Gen. Stand Watie, forced it aground on a sand bar and captured the Union Steamboat J. R. Williams' cargo valued at $120,000 on June 15, 1864. Southern troops included Choctaws, Chickasaws, Creeks, and

Seminoles. Upon hearing their scouts' reports the Federals were coming, they loaded what they could carry and burned the rest.

Massard Prairie, AR

Massard Prairie Battlefield is located .1 mile west of the corner of Red Pine Road and Morgan's Way at Fort Smith. This was the site of the 6th Kansas Cavalry Regiment's camp, attacked by Stand Watie's Confederates on July 27, 1864. The events leading to the battle developed quickly in late July of 1864. A significant body of Confederate troops was then operating in Indian Territory just west of the Arkansas border garrison town of Fort Smith. The commander of this force, Brigadier General Douglas H. Cooper, learned from scouts that four

companies (about 200 men in all) of the Sixth Kansas Cavalry lay in an open grove of trees along a small stream or branch near Fort Smith.

The Federal camp was arranged by company around a central parade ground and mess area. They had evidently picked the position because it offered access to water and tree shade adjacent to the extensive prairie where they were grazing a herd of horses

Deciding to launch an immediate attack, General Cooper ordered

General Gano and 500 of his men to be ready to move by 3 p.m. on the afternoon of the 26th of July.

The Confederates attacked and their repeated rushes against the Federals finally forced them to give way. Driven for some two and one-half miles across the prairie, the Union soldiers began to either surrender or were surrounded and captured. Of the 200 Federal soldiers in camp when the battle began, 10 were killed, 17 wounded and 117 (including two officers) were captured. The Confederates, meanwhile, reported losses of 7 killed, 26 wounded and one missing. They also reported the capture of 200 Sharps rifles, 400 six-shooters, horses, sutler's stores, camp equipment and more

Cabin Creek Battles, First and Second, I. T.

By July, 1862, Col. Phillips was becoming concerned about his precarious position at Fort Gibson. Supplies were needed badly. Cooper's forces of 5,000 outnumbered the Federals holding the fort. Blunt sent reinforcements and supplies, with a strong force south. Confederate scouts kept Stand Watie informed of its progress. On July 1, Watie's force of about 2,000 met the wagon train at the ford at Cabin Creek. In this battle, Watic's troops were out gunned and forced to flee.

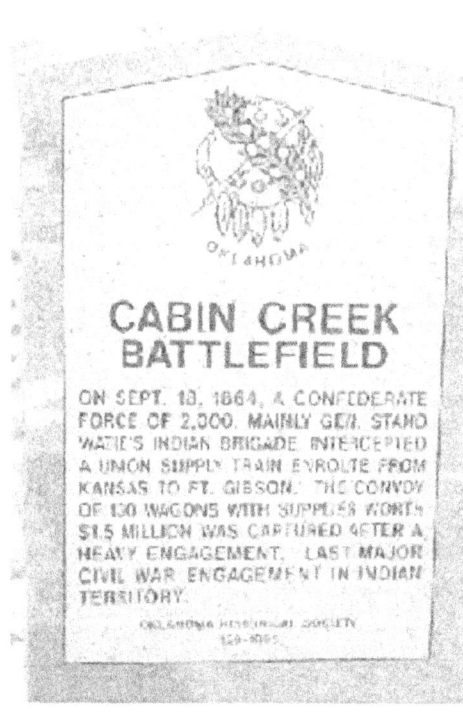

In September, 1864, this earlier loss was revenged. Another much needed wagon train was on its way to Fort Gibson. General Watie and General Richard Gano, Fifth Texas Brigade head of it and planned to meet it. The train reached the Cabin Creek crossing on

September 18, with over 1,000 Union troops to guard over 400 wagons and 1,800 horses and mules. The 2,000 Southerners opened up that early morning with shoulder weapons and artillery. By 9:00 a.m., the Federals had been driven from the field, leaving their wagon train, dead and wounded. The Rebels burned the disabled wagons along with about 3,000 tons of hay, and killed the crippled animals. They salvaged the stores of 710 mules and 130 wagons, loaded them heavily with clothing, raw food stuffs, ammunition. Nothing usable was left. The train headed south with more than $1,500,000, in 1864 dollars.

    Confederate forces were Brig. General Stand Watie's 1st Indian Brigade, Brig. General Richard M. Guano's Texas Cavalry Brigade and part of Howell's Battery. Union forces were Captain Henry Hopkins 2nd Kansas Cavalry and detachments of the 6th and 14th Kansas Cavalry, 2nd and 3rd Indian home Guards.

Part Three

The Soldiers

Confederate Introduction

The following pages contain the rosters/muster rolls of the Indian troops that exist. Many of the Confederate rosters do not exist. The ones I have found total over 20,000 soldiers in both Union and Confederate. Some of the smaller units were either a part of a larger one, or at some point absorbed into one. A few of the units involved only show one or two soldiers. These miscellaneous units are posted at the back of this section. The reader will notice some of the officers' names will be followed by the designation, "F & S". This shows those officers as the "Field and Staff" officers of that regiment.

There are thousands across the USA that grew up with the 'family legend' of Indian blood. They are not tribal members, yet they seek to find that ancestor, knowing if they do find him/her it will substantiate that family legend but will in all likelihood not get them a membership in the Nation. They search for their own reasons. These are the "mixed bloods", numbering in the hundreds of thousands across the country. They have no connections with the federally recognized Nations/Tribes, though they share the blood.

What is difficult about researching their Indian lines is documentation. In Native culture, the family lines are oral and passed down. There are no written records of early ancestors that can be traced, such as court records, land records, census, church records and others that document the European ancestors. Early tribal records are non existent, except in the cases where for various reasons the Indians are listed on government lists such as the Removal lists. Other documents, such as treaties, show only the few directly involved.

On some of the existing records, the Indian may be listed with his/her tribal name, phonetic spelling of the name or listed with their white name. Some also chose a first name and used their Indian name as a last name. That also makes tracking down a particular ancestor difficult.

That is the reason behind this book. This is only one small area of the country where many tribes were brought. This is only one small theater in the Civil War. These soldiers are the unknown participants in an era of two wars, a civil war within the civil war, a piece of history that has been forgotten, if known, or completely unknown.

CONFEDERATE UNITS

Cherokee Units

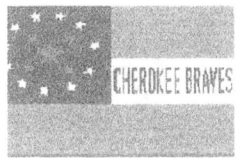

CSA flag 2 red stripes, 1 white
Blue field, large star, red, for Cherokee, surrounded by
4 smaller red stars for Choctaw, Creek, Chickasaw, Seminole
circled by 11 white stars for the Confederate States

 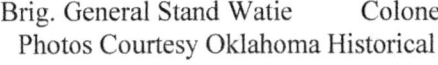

Brig. General Stand Watie   Colonel John Drew
Photos Courtesy Oklahoma Historical Society

1st Regiment, Cherokee Mounted Rifles

This Regiment, AKA Drew's Regiment and 1st Regiment Cherokee Cavalry, was organized October 4, 1861 at Park Hill, Cherokee Nation. It was originally the 2nd Regiment Cherokee Mounted Rifles. Chief John Ross established this Regiment and gave it the name 1st Regiment Cherokee Mounted Rifles, which had been Stand Watie's original regiment. Many of this regiment were full blood Cherokee, many were members of the Keetoowah Society. Many deserted to join the Union Indians and by July 8, 1862, for all practical purposes, this regiment was disbanded. Colonel Drew and approximately 400 of his troops, mostly the mixed bloods, were assimilated into the remaining Cherokee Regiments

Drew, John	F&S	Colonel
Ross, William P.	F&S	Lieutenant Colonel
Evans, James P.	F&S	Surgeon
Carden, Joseph W.	F&S	Assistant Surgeon
Downing, Lewis	F&S	Chaplain
Kerr, Frederick A.	F&S	Commissary of Subsistence
Vann, James S.	F&S	Adjutant
Vore, Israel G.	F&S	Quartermaster
Pegg, Thomas		Major
Ross, Wilt P.		Lieutenant Colonel
Benge, Pickens M.	K	Captain
Davis, John P.	C	Captain
Fields, Richard	F	Captain
Hicks, Edward R.	H	Captain
Hicks, Jefferson D.	A	Captain
Hildebrand, Isaac N.	D	Captain
Little, Bird		Captain
McDaniel, James		Captain
Pike, Albert	I	Captain
Sanders, Nicholas B.	B	Captain
Scraper, George W.	G	Captain
Vann, James	E	Captain
Benge, Anderson	A	First Lieutenant
Benge, George	K	First Lieutenant
Fish, Nathan	H	First Lieutenant

Fish, Nathaniel	H	First Lieutenant
Foster, Samuel	I	First Lieutenant
Hewbanks, William	H	First Sergeant
Henry, Jesse	G	First Lieutenant
Smith, Eli	E	First Lieutenant
Smith, Samuel H.	C	First Lieutenant
Springston, George	D	First Lieutenant
Stop Watt,		First Lieutenant
White, Catcher	B	First Lieutenant
Young, John	F	First Lieutenant
Ah mer cher ner,	A	Second Lieutenant
Baldridge, Broom	F	Second Lieutenant
Bear Meat, John	I	Second Lieutenant
Chuwee, Joseph	G	Second Lieutenant
Crabgrass, Smith	K	Second Lieutenant
Deerinthewater, Josiah	B	Second Lieutenant
Downing, Samuel	H	Second Lieutenant
Drew, Charles	C	Second Lieutenant
Drowning Bear, Noah		Second Lieutenant
Fogg,	E	Second Lieutenant
Hawkins, Lacy	A	Second Lieutenant
Little Red,	I	Second Lieutenant
Little Redbird,	I	Second Lieutenant
Ross, George W.	H	Second Lieutenant
Runaway, Samuel	D	Second Lieutenant
Russell, Ezekiel	D	Second Lieutenant
Sanders, George O.	B	Second Lieutenant
Scraper, Arch	G	Second Lieutenant
Sky Yah too Kah,		Second Lieutenant
Star Deer in the water,	C	Second Lieutenant
Trotting, Wolfe	K	Second Lieutenant
Webber, William	F	Second Lieutenant
Chicken Torter, Christie	E	Third Lieutenant
Chickentoater, Christy	E	Third Lieutenant
Brewer, Thomas	C	First Sergeant
Cahnohaytat at quah,	I	First Sergeant
Daugherty, John	G	First Sergeant
Hair, Wilson	B	First Sergeant
James, Mill		First Sergeant
Josiah,	A	First Sergeant
Mills, William	F	First Sergeant
Ross, Thomas	K	First Sergeant

Name	Co.	Rank
Tahnie Walkingstick,	E	First Sergeant
Tyger, Wheeler	D	First Sergeant
Adams, George	B	Sergeant
Baldridge, James	B	Sergeant
Bat, Puppy	K	Sergeant
Bird,	K	Sergeant
Boar, George	I	Sergeant
Boggs, John	B	Sergeant
Buckskin, Jess	A	Sergeant
Cah se lahwie, Proctor		Sergeant
Crawford, Robert	F	Sergeant
Even, John	C	Sergeant
Flute Fox Skin,	B	Sergeant
Frog,	A	Sergeant
Hair, John	H	Sergeant
Handle, Dempsey	F	Sergeant
Hawk, Alex		Sergeant
Hendricks, Willis	H	Sergeant
Jackson, -	K	Sergeant
Jumper, Mills		Sergeant
Kas Knu ne, Man Killer	E	Sergeant
Peter, -	H	Sergeant
Proctor, Johnson	G	Sergeant
Rogers, John	A	Sergeant
Ross, Allen	H	Sergeant
Scorn, Edward	E	Sergeant
Scraper, William	G	Sergeant
Sebolt, John	K	Sergeant
Seven, George	D	Sergeant
Sevier, Bushyhead	C	Sergeant
Shell, -	G	Sergeant
Smith, George	E	Sergeant
Smith, Jesse	D	Sergeant
Stagger,	I	Sergeant
Sunday, William		Sergeant
Sweet Cow,	D	Sergeant
Tadpole, Ely	I	Sergeant
Tadpole, Joshua	I	Sergeant
Tah ker Yer Wolf,	D	Sergeant
Tarrapin, Striker	F	Sergeant
Terapin, Nelson	G	Sergeant
Tony, George	C	Sergeant

Towie, John	A	Sergeant
Walkingstick, Levi	E	Sergeant
Watts, Thomas	C	Sergeant
Yellow, Jacket	F	Sergeant
Ah le cher,	A	Corporal
Ah le cher,	E	Corporal
Bird,	E	Corporal
Broom	E	Corporal
Cahlor nu hay oke,	B	Corporal
Cal le tol ter,	C	Corporal
Catcher, Ellis	I	Corporal
Cheewah, Stahtaw	F	Corporal
Chu nog hur kee,	I	Corporal
Ellis, James	K	Corporal
Ellis, Samuel	K	Corporal
Fawn, Killer	C	Corporal
Flying, Bird		Corporal
French,	H	Corporal
Gritts,		Corporal
Gunpile, Ned	F	Corporal
Hammer, James	C	Corporal
Larchy, John	D	Corporal
Leach,	B	Corporal
Little Allen,	K	Corporal
McCoy, Creek	F	Corporal
Moses, -	D	Corporal
Murphy, Saturday	H	Corporal
Peach Watts,	B	Corporal
Pickup, James		Corporal
Powel, -	D	Corporal
Pritchet, Umahhooge	G	Corporal
Ootah ne yau cah,		Corporal
Ootah tay gee skee,	I	Corporal
Otter Scraper,	G	Corporal
Rogers, Alexander	C	Corporal
Scraper, Henry H.	G	Corporal
Seed, Catcher	B	Corporal
Still, Cook	E	Corporal
Stoples, Charles	F	Corporal
Tah ner yes ky,	A	Corporal
Tah yes Ky,	A	Corporal
Tar che che Nick,	G	Corporal

Name	Co.	Rank
Ter Nah ee,	D	Corporal
Ticke Eater,	I	Corporal
To cher la ner,	A	Corporal
Vann, Joseph	K	Corporal
Wind, David	H	Corporal
Baldridge, Wilson	B	Bugler
Bear Paw,	G	Bugler
Bird, Chopper	E	Bugler
Buffalo,	C	Bugler
Ellis, William	K	Bugler
Fox, Jack	A	Bugler
Grease, George	H	Bugler
Myers, John		Bugler
Rogers, John	H	Bugler
Tle yer ker,	D	Bugler
Evans, Walter N.	H	Hospital Steward
Blackfox, Ezekiel	G	Blacksmith
Christie, Watt	E	Blacksmith
Fish, Levi		Blacksmith
Green, William	F	Blacksmith
Sker Kee My,	D	Blacksmith
Tucker, John	B	Blacksmith
Bushyhead, Henry	G	Farrier
Chambers, William	E	Farrier
Childers, Daniel		Farrier
Falling, Pot	A	Farrier
Guess, George	C	Farrier
Path Killer,	B	Farrier
Rogers Silk,	K	Farrier
Tanner,	D	Farrier

Privates

Name	Co.	Name	Co.
A tun hee,	C	Ae tor he,	H
A wie,	E	Ah Sah lah tee skie,	G
A-to-la he,	B	Ah gah yah skie,	F
Adam, (A Creek)	K	Ah hool ota ke, Pouch	I
Adam,			
Ah hur too kat,	I	Ah lay oh ie,	F
Ah ker loo ker,	A	Ah le kee w nah	
Ah kil lu ne gah,	E	soo zee,	G
		Ah le whe ter,	A

Ah mah soo yah tee cah- cah husky,	I		Bear Paw,	C
Ah mi ye har,	H		Bear Sitting down, Cornelius	G
Ah na ne yeh skie,	G		Beaver, Hicory	
Ah nee chee,	E		Beaver, Lewis	K
Ah sto le ter, John	A		Beavertail, Jim	H
Ah taw hee, Ah Coo wah	D		Beavertoater, Ahlechel	G
Ah tsade hie,	F		Beeff, John	
Ah yun too kah,			Bell, Samuel	
Ahquahta, Kie	D		Ben, Alex	K
Ahque che, Charles	G		Bend, About	E
Aleck,	F		Benge, John	F
Allbones, Watt	A		Benge, Ned	H
Ar chil lar,	F		Benge, Richard	K
Ar le cha,	H		Big, Arch.	I
Archiller, Peach Eater	K		Big, Bullett	E
Archy,	A		Big, Jack	A
Ark tae hae skie,	H		Big Feather Chu wa	
Art lan se ne,	H		Big Flather chu wa loo kee,	I
Ashes, Joseph	C		Big Foot, Arch	E
Ashhopper, Joseph	E		Big Head, Daniel	I
Ashhopper, William	E		Big Head, Daniel	I
Ave, Vann	H		Big Road,	D
Ave Tah le yas Kie,	K		Big Sides,	H
Bagg, James	C		Bigfoot, Arch	E
Baldridge, Ave	A		Biggs, Nichols	B
Baldridge, Columbus	B		Bigjack, Joseph	A
Baldridge, Jesse	B		Bird, Baldridge	G
Baldridge, Jesse	K		Bird, Chopper	A
Baldridge, Samuel	K		Bird, Grapes	K
Baldridge, Weeting	B		Bird, Sanders	H
Baldrige, Dick	C		Birdtail, James	C
Baldrige, Ned	C		Black, Little Terapin	G
Ballow, Jeff	I		Black Haw, Pettet	B
Barbara, David	C		Black Haw,	A
Bark,	C		Black Haw,	D
Bat, Frank	A		Black Haw,	E
Beamer, Arch	D		Black Haw Crawfish,	I
Beamer, West	H		Blackcoat, James	F
Bean, Charles	H		Blackfox, Henry	A

Blacksmith,	I
Blair, Lewis	K
Blanket, George	H
Blue, Proctor	E
Bluebird, Luke	H
Board, Jack	B
Boggs, Shoeboots	B
Boling, Buck	F
Bottle, Joseph	I
Bottle, Judge	I
Bottle,	B
Bowen, James	E
Bowles, Dick	I
Bowles, Tah lar lor	I
Bowls, James	C
Bowls, John	C
Bowls, Johnson	C
Bread, Oo nur we ya lie	E
Brewer, Jesse	A
Broad, Christy	K
Broom, Arch	F
Broom, Bear	F
Broom, Richard	F
Brown, Bill	K
Brush, George	F
Buck, John	A
Bull,	C
Bullfrog, Dave	D
Bullfrog, George	D
Bullfrog, Koowee Skooure	I
Bullfrog, Moses	D
Bullfrog, Robin	C
Bullfrog, Wilson	G
Bullfrog,	H
Bump, Bill	K
Bunch, Rabbit	E
Bunch ne cow ie,	E
Burgess, John	C
Burntwood, Daniel	F
Butler, George	F
Cade, William	H
Cah le ger,	K
Cah lie okai wee,	G
Cah sar he la,	
Cah see lowie, Dick	I
Cah see lowie, Ezekiel	I
Cah soo yoh kie, Gritts	C
Cah tahyal tah,	H
Cahlornuhayskie, Pasoozorkie	B
Cahlornuhayskie, Trolohtaynte	B
Cahnaysoolayski Johe,	I
Cahquahter or Havy,	D
Cahtur tahtu, Terrapin	B
Camrol, Jack	A
Canoo, Budman	C
Car Sah tah,	H
Car nos gah,	F
Car ter oo yorlor choo he,	H
Car ter oot Sunnah,	H
Catchem, Moses	
Catcher, Ben	I
Catcher, Man Killer	B
Catfish, Jack	H
Cay noo gee kee ner,	I
Cha loo ky,	A
Chahyahnur Doochistah,	G
Chambers, Walker	F
Char ne way nohwily,	B
Charles, Dick	G
Charles,	
Che, Squyah Weaver	B
Che lah Ke te hee,	F
Che lah che lah,	F
Che nah que,	B
Che ne que,	C
Che quah, Kie	E
Chee Stay cha,	B
Chee Stoo, (Rabbit)	H
Chee lo ter ta Hy,	D
Chewa looky, Bill	

Chewie,			Chuweskah,	
Chicken, Cock	D		Ahdahketohee	G
Chicken, Lewis	F		Chuyah skil kee,	F
Chicken, Rider	A		Clay, Henry	B
Chicken, Samuel	F		Cloud, Samuel	B
Childers, Napoleon			Cloy See Nah	
Childers, Robert P.			Hummingbird,	B
Chillee,	F		Coffee,	G
Cho wail cer,	I		Cold Weather, Jack	B
Chocktaw, John	C		Cold Weather,	D
Choo Kah later,			Coldman, John	C
Thompson	E		Coley, Six Killer	K
Choo le Stee le, Tom	H		Colston, Bat	D
Choo noo lur hus-ky,	E		Colston, Daniel	B
Chooke yah, Skie	E		Colston, Sam	
Chool Squah loo tah,			Colston, William	C
Ned	I		Columbus,	K
Chool Squalootah,			Coming, Deer	H
White Bird	I		Coming Deer, Peter	K
Choon Stortie,			Coo los tah,	F
Leguoyah	I		Coolahchie, Nick	D
Choonstoo			Coon,	F
teechanaywotayski,	B		Corn Tassel	D
Christie, Allen	A		Corn Silk, Dick	G
Christy, Arch	E		Cornass, Daniel	B
Christy, Dick	B		Cornsilk, Joseph	F
Christy, James	E		Cornsilk, Spirit	D
Chu, Chu	B		Cornsilk, Thomas	F
Chu, Wee	A		Crawfish,	D
Chu Stoo lu,	E		Crawler, Proctor	K
Chu caw mer der,	F		Crawler,	E
Chu he tler, Joseph	A		Crawling, Dick	E
Chu lis quit ty,	I		Crawling Snake, Clark	D
Chu lix, Sie	E		Creek, Arch	B
Chu loe csgee, Wolf	G		Creek, Billy	F
Chu lu ya skie,	E		Creek, Charles	K
Chu nu lis ke,	G		Creek, David	K
Chu wae lu kee,	H		Creek, George	B
Chu wo yee,	G		Cree k, Jim	B
Chuglater, Moses	K		Creek, Jim	K
Chuleshwie, George	E		Creek, Samuel	K
Chuwalooke, Dane	D		Crittendon, Andrew	G

Name	Col	Name	Col
Crying Bear,	A	Draging, Jess	E
Crying Bear,	I	Draging Canoe,	E
Crying Wolfe,	D	Dreadful Water,	H
Cryingbird, David	F	Dreadful water, George	
Cul Kah los kee,	B	Drinker,	E
Cul cur Cos kee,	H	Drinking, Proctor	K
Culcayer, Smith	A	Driving out,	K
Culstuhim, Sky	D	Dropper,	F
Curteesuttee Ostahneeyartah,	I	Drumfish (Creek),	K
		Drunk,	C
Cut his head off,	C	Dry, Peter	G
Daniel,	E	Dry, Squirrel	G
Darke,	F	Dry, Water	C
Daugherty, David	H	Duck, Dave	A
Davidson,	A	Duck, Dick	
Davis, John	D	Duck, John	E
Davis,	D	Duck, Stephen	
Dee gee, Mee	F	Duvall, David	F
Deer Head, James	B	Duvall, Rogers	F
Deer in the water,	K	E char chy,	D
Deerhead, John	F	E nov le,	H
Deerinthewater, Tahchehoostah	B	Ecoo wee, Wolf	D
		Ecow ee, Kah von Kee ly	D
Dew, Watt	F		
Dick, Henry	H	Eetah Kur Stahsiqusyah,	I
Dick, Isaac	D	Elah we,	F
Dick, Richard	B	Ellis, Peter	K
Dirt Eater,	A	Elno, Ca Kay No Tos Ky	D
Dirt Eater Beg Mush,	I	Elow ie, Oote terahie	I
Dirt Hunter,	C	Elow ie,	A
Dirt Pott,		Elow ie,	D
Dirt Thrower,	K	Ely, Ah nee tah Kay yah	I
Dirteater Ahcortayskie,	I	Emory, Peter	F
Diver, Harris	E	England, Joseph	D
Dog in the Bush, Moses	B	Enor Ca Te Kus Key,	D
Dogwood, Jesse		Enoy C skon nah dah hee,	G
Dogwood, Joseph	E		
Dollar, Alex	E	Etan tes skie,	E
Dorchester, Chenehque	B	Ever Sought,	K
Downing, George	I	Falling, Dick	
Downing, Johnson	I	Falling, Jesse	A
Downing, Mink	K	Falling,	

Fawn, Head	K		Halcomb, Samuel	K
Fielding, Watt	G		Hammer, John	
Fields, Daniel	F		Hammer,	K
Fields, Thomas	F		Hanging Honey, Ooo	
Fields, Wiley	D		che shie lah	B
Firethrown, Henderson	E		Harnage, Thomas	B
Fish, John	F		Harris, William	C
Flute, John	B		Hatchet, Jacob	H
Flyingnundahee,	G		Hatchett, John	H
Foreman, Alexander	C		Hatchett, Tom	H
Foreman, Arch	D		Hawk, Dick	H
Foreman, George	H		Hawk, John	H
Fox, Mouse	A		Hawk, Lacey	I
Fox, Screech Owl	K		Hawk, Lewis	I
Frog, Tee Las Kie	E		Hawk Nettlecarrier,	E
Frog Jaw, Jesse			He Sar tas Kee,	D
Gah dah oo ne gah			Heavy,	D
hah nah,	F		Henry, Arch	G
Gee Surwohyec, Archilla			Henry, Thomas	C
Girl Catcher, Tom			Hicks, Crawler	F
Girth, Watt	D		Hiding Man Tu	
Glass, Judge	C		cabwohle nee	G
Glory, Dick	E		Hiding Man te cab ne	
Glory, Moses			ye skie	G
Gnat,			Hilderbrand, Joseph	A
Gobbler, Jack			Hogg, George	I
Going Back, Lewis			Hogshooter, Nelson	D
Going Snake,	E		Hogshooter,	A
Gone in the water,	F		Hogskin, Jim	A
Good Money,	K		Hogtoter,	E
Grapes,			Holmes, David	K
Graves, Oowa Coo Kee	C		Holt, Ely	K
Greece,	C		Hood, Barrow	K
Griffin, Jack	C		Hoppe, Daniel G.	B
Griffin, Joseph	C		Horn, Thompson	F
Grimmitt,	E		Horn, William	H
Gritts, Jim			Horsefly, Watt	D
Gritts, Westly	H		Housebig, Jackson	G
Go-back,	H		Houston,	I
Grubbs, Nelson	I		Humming Bird,	F
Gunrod, Robert			Hummingbird Six	
Ha ne,	F		Killer	I

Hummingbird Watt	K		Kee loh Ste,	D
Hungry,			Kee nah tu Kah,	C
Ice, Jack	B		Keenah, Daniel	I
Ice, John	H		Keener, Joe	I
Is Sar gur or, Breather	K		Keener, Ned	D
Isaac,	A		Ker na Soo tie,	A
Isaac,	E		Ker ne too,	A
Isaac,	D		Ker lur Soo Kee sky,	A
Israel, Philip	H		Ketchum too nie,	F
Jack Rabbit	G		Kickup, Punkin Pile	I
Jack, oo sa nah lee	E		Kiley, Archy	A
Jackson, Walter	C		Killah ne gah, Sam	K
Jackson, Wily	C		Kille arch, E.	G
Jackson,	C		King Fisher, William	I
James, -	D		Koo we skoo we, George	H
James, Dutchy	B		Koo wee skoo wee, John	I
James, Tobaco Will	K		Koo wee skoo wee,	I
Jessee, (A Creek)	F		Kuh lee Skuywie, Moses	B
John, Adam	I		Kuh lee Skuywiee,	
Johnson, Alex	E		Joseph	B
Johnson, Good Money	I		Kur la nes Ky,	A
Johnson, Jack	C		Kur lee tah Coon,	I
Johnson, Jack	D		Lacey,	
Johnson,	A		Langy, Martin	C
Josiah,	D		Lar, Kin ee	H
Joss ee,	K		Larchy, Chenahque John	I
Judge, Otter	F		Lawrie,	E
Jumper, Creek	B		Le to wade,	F
Jumper, Jack	C		Leaf,	
Jumper, Stitch	C		Lee, James	K
Jumper,	H		Left, Hand	
Jumper,	K		Lewis,	K
Juwayne, Dahgurdohsee	G		Little, Bird	G
KahNahlela,	A		Little Bird, William	B
KahmerSetayski,			Little Bird,	
Stephan	B		Little Dave,	A
Kahnuchchie,	E		Little Deer,	H
Kahselahw'e,	E		Little Dick,	
KakNowSosKee,	D		Little Girl,	
Kay, Skene ny			Little Jess,	C
Kaynoo, Rising Fawn	I		Little Jesse,	H
Ke lar ne gah, Aaron	G		Little Jim,	

Little Peter,	A	Moses,	H
Little hair Big Mush,	I	Mouse, Adam	A
Lizzard, Rider	F	Murphy, Comings	
Lizzard,	C	Murphy, Tiecahtohskie	B
Love, Alex	D	Mush, Henry	I
Love, Johnson	C	Mush, Lewis	E
Lovely, Rogers	F	Mush,	C
Low Cat,	F	Mush Rat, William	E
Lowry, John	F	Muskrat, Johnson	G
Lucy, Oo nay cur sen	B	Nah che ah,	
Lying, Fish Dai gur gah	G	Nah hoo lar,	A
Manning, Cherokee	H	Nah yoi take,	C
Manning, Lahchee	I	Ne ler ca yer,	A
Martin, Ah lee che	B	Ned, John Jacob	G
Martin, Jackson	B	Nedson, Ben	K
Martin, Jackson	B	Nedson,	K
Matier, John	H	Nelson,	F
Matlear, Richard	K	Nettlecarra, Ned	E
Matoy, Robin	C	Nick,	A
Mawking Crows		Nick,	F
May, Reynolds		Noisy Dahskekedehe,	G
McCoy, Thomas	F	Noisy Water, Nick	B
McKinsie, Dave		Noname, Dollars	E
McKinsie, Jack		Nowife, Andrew	B
McLamore,	H	Oak Ball,	G
McLane, Looney	B	Oakball, Ned	G
Meat, Thomas	C	Ohtahnaheesky	
Meigs, Henry	H	Nuryankahar,	I
Mellon Musk,	K	Old Buffalo,	C
Messenger,	G	Old Horse,	A
Middlestriker, Roly	K	Old Rabbit,	
Miller, Andrew	A	Oo Kil e Soo,	I
Milles, George		Oo Skur tur ne chy,	E
Mink,	C	Oo Squah loo gah,	E
Mister, Billy	F	Oo Stil hy, Joseph	K
Mole, Ned	K	Oo Wal tay, Samuel	B
Money Crier	K	Oo che loo tie,	A
Money Crier, James	F	Oo chee Tee hee,	I
Money Hunter	I	Oo har lu ge,	G
Moses, George	E	Oo her loo ky,	D
Moses, Jack	G	Oo kah hah ter,	A
Moses,	E	Oo kee lah ny,	I

Name	Code
Oo la Whatee,	A
Oo lan So ner,	E
Oo le stoo wah lah whe dah	G
Oo lee stoo, Stephen	G
Oo lor nah stee skie,	K
Oo ne che chu, Kestie	I
Oo ne tler,	A
Oo ner chos ty,	A
Oo no la te ka lee sky,	A
Oo ston Aner,	C
Oo tah he tah,	F
Oo tar tlor hee ter,	D
Oo te sah tah,	H
Oo wa loo kie Bighead	C
Oo wa yer Lut tie,	I
Oo wah wor See ty,	D
Oo way te,	D
Oo yor se stah che yah tuhah	B
Oo yor ter,	A
Oohahloo ke, Davis	D
Ook tay rie Wolf,	I
Ookees quawter,	A
Ool Skun nie,	C
Ool ce now ee,	D
Oolahhey at Corn Silk	K
Ooloh nah ste skie noo chah we,	G
Ooluyheeyahtah, Tahneemohteyse	B
Oon Clau e sur,	H
Ooo war numkee, Ben	H
Oot chay lur nur Sequoyah,	I
Ootah ne yunter,	D
Oote Sah tuh, Dave	H
Ootla noh tuer,	E
Ootuttie, Moses	H
Oowa lo kee, John	C
Oowa loo kee,	C
Oowahkah, Lewis	I
Oowarlay skie,	I
Oowarnunke, George	H
Oowor ser tie skelley,	I
Orcha gee sky,	E
Osage, Samuel	B
Ottor,	C
Packenham, Bear Meat	I
Packenham, Dave	A
Packing, Tom	I
Panther, John	D
Parch Meal,	I
Path Killer,	K
Path Killer,	
Patrick, James	H
PeachEater, George	E
Peacheater, John	K
Peel, Robert	
Peter, William	
Pettit, Levy	K
Pheasant, -	
Picket, -	F
Piddy, Jim	C
Pidid, James	C
Pig, John	
Pigeon, -	
Pigeon, Josiah	E
Poo Bear, -	B
Poor Boy, Eli	B
Poor Boy, Samuel	B
Porham, Davissy	C
Post, Silk	K
Pot kicker, -	
Potatoe, Thomas	
Pott, Ely	K
Pott, George	F
Pott, Thomas	D
Pottatoe, John	
Potts, Isaac	B
Pouch, Charles	I
Pritchett, George	B
Pritchett, Jack	E
Pritchett, John	E

Pritchett, Mike	H	Roeoe, David	A
Proctor, Adam	G	Rogers,	D
Proctor, Arch	G	Rope, Camrol	A
Proctor, Isaac	K	Rosin,	F
Proctor, John	E	Ross, Jonah J.	G
Proctor, Joseph	E	Ross, Oliver	K
Proctor, Peter	K	Round, Major	F
Pumpkin, Ben	A	Rounder,	D
Pumpkin, Charlie	G	Rowe, French	E
Pumpkin, Jesse	D	Rowe, Jack	C
Punkin Pile, Mose	I	Rowe, Levi	E
Punkinpile, William	I	Runabout,	A
Queen, -	H	Runabout,	F
Quinton, Daniel	K	Runabout,	H
Quinton, Lewis	K	Runaway, Person	D
Rabbit, Andrew	E	Runner, Chekele	G
Rafter, Jaybird	H	Sah Nah Ne, -	K
Raincrow, Arch	H	Sah ne Le kin Nie, -	E
Raincrow, Jim	H	Salt, -	F
Raincrow, Tony	F	Sam, Jack	
Rat, David	F	Samuel, -	F
Rat, John	G	Sanders, Dave	B
Ratcliff, Richard	C	Sanders, James	H
Ratcliffe, John	B	Sanders, John	C
Ratling Goard Rider	D	Sanders, John G.	C
Red Bird, Daniel	A	Sanders, Joseph	I
Red Bird,	C	Sanders, Mitchell	G
Red Bird,	F	Sanders, Sar Ke Yah	H
Red Bird,	G	Sap Sucker, -	K
Redbird, Jack	G	Saturduy, Vann	A
Redbird, Jesse	G	Sau ny,	D
Ridge, John	F	Scott, Alex	E
Ridge, John	G	Scott, Edward	E
Ridge,	K	Scott, Harry	I
Ridge chu we skah,	G	Scraper, -	F
Riley, John	B	Scraper, Buck	C
Riley, Samuel	B	Scraper, John	F
Robber,	F	Scud dis,	I
Robin,	H	Se que ah, -	K
Robin Young Duck,	G	Sea lol le, Bill	
Robinson, Richard	H	Seckeomey	
Rock Thrower,	C	Teecahlorhay Nah,	I

Secowie, Charles	A		Soap, John	C
See cah we, -	G		Soap, Nick	E
SeguoyahTahleyes kie,	I		Soap Kahnoo le Skee,	G
Sequoyah, -	D		Soap Toy oo Nese,	G
She Rain, Jack	K		Soap ooyahokah mo tie,	G
Shell, Jesse	G		Soldirr, James	K
Sherain, Leap	G		Soldum,	F
Short Arrow, Ned	B		Something, John	
Simmons, Arch	F		Soo, Chy	A
Simmons, Jess	C		Soo Wa Ky,	D
Simmons, Watt	F		Spaniard, Davis	1 G
Simmons, William	C		Spears, Arch	A
Simmons, Wilson	F		Spears, Bird	F
Simon, -			Spears, Stephen	1 B
Sit noo wa kic,	E		Spears, Wilson	F
Sitting on Bridge,	D		Spike, Alick	D
Sittingbare Fishing Hawk,	G		Spiller, Ned	D
			Spirit,	A
Sittingdown, Tom	I		Spirit,	K
Sittingdown, Wilson	K		Spirit,	F
Sitwwa Ky, Johnson	A		Spirit Sam,	I
Six	A		Spirit Vann,	K
Six Killrskiyatoo Ka,	E		Spring Spring,	K
Skahlol, Allen			Spunk, -	A
Skahyahtoogah Sahlegoo War,	G		Squah ne char,	G
			Squah ta le chy,	A
Skalol, Tom			Squirel, John	A
Skilp, -	C		Squirrel, Samuel	F
Skon tah hee, Lewis	B		Squirrel, Watt	G
Skon tah hee, Moses	B		Squirrel,	C
Slarch, Snail	D		Squirrel,	D
Slop, Wiley	D		Squirrel Clicken,	F
Small Dirt,	C		Stand, Arch	E
Small Dirt,	K		Standing, Buck	
Smith, Isaac	A		Starr, Ezekiel	C
Smith, John	F		Starr, John	D
SmithTahchai Kes,	C		Starr, Squirrel	C
Smoke, John	G		Starr, Whitekiller	E
Smoker, Gordon	C		Ste he Kee,	G
Snail, Simon	D		Stee ny Soo Wah tee,	G
Snake Track,	D		Steelum,	D
Soap, Aaron	E		Stephen,	G

Still, Josiah	C		Tah chur See, Jack	G
Stinson, Charley			Tah chur see Tah lah	G
Stinson, William			Tah gah che gee sy	
Stop Storekeeper,			Tah law se Redbird	H
Stop skon tah hee,			Tah le eus Ky Scraper	E
Storekeeper, James	D		Tah ne nah la	E
Su Wah tie,	G		Tah ne no li, David	G
Su ate, Tom			Tah ne no li sken tahee	G
Su iva Kie,	K		Tah ne yes Kie	C
Su wa Kie, Dick	G		Tallow, Jim	
Su wa Kie, Ezekiel	I		Tallow, Mays	H
Su way Kie Wor Sortie,	I		Tan chu lae Ner	H
Sul la tee skie,	E		Tanner, Aaron	D
Sul te skie,	E		Tanner, Jack	D
Sun ne coo yoh,	H		Tanner, Sequoyah	D
Sun too le,	E		Tanner Clow yer Kee,	D
Sunday, Tah ne yee sky	B		Tar los se	C
Sunday Hogtoter,	E		Tassel,	C
Sut tee cah Scoutie,	B		Tassel Ah hur Mah,	B
Sut tu hah, Joe	D		Taylor, Bill	
Sweet Water,	C		Taylor, Jim	
Swimmer, Alex	E		Taylor, John	
Swimmer, Jesse	E		Te Kah tos Kee, Joseph	A
Swimmer, Joe	F		Te Ke che Ah hur Nah	G
Swimmer, Joseph	K		Te cah noo le Cloud	B
Swimmer, Ool			Te cul Kel	C
Skewe Ney	I		Te sar Tah ske	D
Swimmer, Rider	K		Teacher, Smith	F
Swimmer,	E		Teacher	F
Swimmer,	F		Tee Ker ne Ye sky	A
Swimmer,	H		Tee Kin ee Mouse	D
Ta Ker Na Se ull	A		Tee Sah skie	F
Tabb, Lewis	F		Tee Say skie	B
Tadpole, David	I		Tee Ser Ne he	A
Tadpole, John	I		Tee ca tos Kee	D
Tae lus kie, Daniel	I		Tee cah nee Ye skie	E
Tah Ker yer oo			Tee hee, Charles	B
cha looty	D		Tee hurnee skie	
Tah Nowie Squirrel,	G		Tahlie Stayskie	I
Tah Yool Sin ee	D		Tee lah ski ske Stop,	G
Tah cah Soh Kah			Tee lah ski ske Tar	
Tee Ke chee	B		che chee	G

Tee lah ski ske Twister	G		Triplett, William	B
Tee sah tar skie Musk Mellon,	G		Tuck Se	H
			Tucker, David	
Tee see Yor kee			Tucker, Jerry	H
Tee soo Yoh gue, Bill	G		Tucker, Levi	
Teetah Nur Sue, Allick	G		TunSuylee, James	B
Tet Yer ner skie	E		Tur ne nall le	
Theodore, Jeremiah	G		Turnee see, Johnson	I
Thirsty Tyger	D		Turnohwailahne	G
Thomas	G		Turnover, Davis	D
Thomas	K		Turnover, Isaac	D
Ti e skie	H		Turnover, Tyeskie	I
Tie Ye skie	D		Twister	C
Tie Yes kie			Tyeall, James	
Timpson, Ned	H		Tyer, Mouse	D
Tlo yer ker	A		Tyer	
Tlos tah ner	E		Ul tee skeh	H
To nah yoh			Ulla teesky	K
Tom	A		Ur tah ol tah	
Tom	D		Uttahwohoki, Seontie	B
Ton a tae ton e	H		Vann, Clemm	K
Too che	H		Vann, Jesse	E
Too lees tee	D		Vann, Jesse	F
Too nah wee	G		Vann, Josiah	K
Too nie	C		Wagoner, John	E
Too nie ah	C		Wah Jah gee	K
Toonie, George	B		Wahheyuske Blanket	H
Toonie, William	G		Wahtartoo Kar, William	
Tooquah tah, Ned			Waktie	A
Toosewae e tah	A		Walker -	A
Toowohnaenertoo quarlah	G		Walker, Edmond	B
			Walker, George	F
Tor chu lay nah	B		Walker, Ground Squirrel	G
Tor yen nee see			Walker, John	F
Towie, John	D		Walker, William	H
Townsend, Loo Ney	A		Walking, Wolf	K
Toyartuseechee, Walooke	B		Walkingstick, John	E
			Walnut, -	F
Toye Sie Ne	E		Washington, -	H
Tracker,	F		Water, Killer	C
Tracking Wolf, David	G		Watt, -	E
Treasurer	D		Watts, Anotchiecreek	B

Watts, Charles	B	Yellow Reader	I
Watts, Johnson	C	Yellowhammer, Suwakey	G
Watts, Walter	B	Yorter, Lewis	A
Weedy Field	K	Young Beaver	C
Whitekiller, Davison	G	Young Beaver	D
Whitepath, Isaac	C	Young Bird	D
Whitewater, -	C	Young Bird	E
Wild Hog	B	Young Bird	K
Wild Cat, Weeley	B	Young, Charles	H
Wild Cat, Yahola	K	Young Deer	A
William, Sour John	I	Young Deer	
Wilson	A	Young Duck	A
Wilson	E	Young Duck	
Wind, Chockram	A	Young, Josiah	F
Wolf, Nelson	D	Young Pig	
Wolfe, James	E	Young Pigeon	A
Wolftracker,	A	Young Puppy	B
Woman Killer	I	Young Squirrel	F
Womankiller,	E	Young Squirril Flopper	I
Woodall, George		Young Tassel	
Woodall, Osceola		Young Terrapin	K
Wool, Stephen	E	Young, Thomas	F
Wor Saw tie	D	Young, William	F
Writer	D	Young Wolf	D
Ya ho la, James	K	Young Wolfe	A
Yah hoo lah	A	Young Wolfe	H
Yahnah oola San tah	E	Young Jr., John	F
Yahola, Sampson	K	Youngbird, Isaac	G
Yahola, Sr	K	Youngbird, Tah Nowie	I
Yahola, Thomas	K		
Yal Sutch ee	D		

McDaniel's Company
1st Cherokee Mounted Rifles

McDaniel, James	Captain
Proctor, Big sky Yah Wie	First Lieutenant
Stop, Watt	First Lieutenent
Drowning Bear, Noah	Second Lieutenant
James, Will	First Sergeant
Proctor, Cah se Lah wie	Sergeant
Hawk, Alex	Sergeant
Jumper Mills	Sergeant
Sunday, William	Sergeant
Flying Bird	Corporal
Gritts	Corporal
Oo Tah Ne Jan cah	Corporal
Pick Up Money	Corporal
CHilders, Daniel	Farrier
Myers, John	Bugler

Privates

Adam	Gee Sur Who Gee Archilla
Ah Yun Tuka	Girl Catcher, Tom
Beeff, John	Glary, Moses
Bell, Samuel	Gnat
Cah sar he la	Gobbler, Jack
Charles	Going Back, Lewis
Chewa Looky, Bill	Grapes
Chewie	Gritts, Jim
Childers, Napolean	Gunrod, robert
Childers, Robert	Hammer, John
Colston, Sam	Hungary
Dirt, Pott	Kay Skene Ny
Dogwood, Jesse	Lacey
Dreadful Water, George	Leaf
Duck, Dick	Left Hand
Duck, Stephen	Little Bird
Falling	Little Dick
Falling, Dick	Little Girl
Fish, Levi	Little Jim
Frogjaw, Jesse	Mawking, Crows

McKinsie, Dave
McKinsie, jack
Mills, George
Murphy, Coming
Nah Che Ah
Old Rabbit
Path, Killer
Peel, Robert
Peter, William
Pheasant
Pig, John
Pigeon
Potatoe, Thomas
Pot Kicker
Pottatoe, John
Sam, Jack
Sca Lol Le, Bill
Simon
St ney
Shah Lol, Allen
Ska Lol, Tom
Something, John
Standing Buck
Stinson, Charley
Stinson, William
Stop, Skon tah Hee

Stop, Storekeeper
Su Ate, Tom
Tah Gah Che Sy
Tallow, Jim
Taylor, Bill
Taylor, Jim
Taylor, John
Tee See Yor Kee
Tie Yes Kie
To Nah Yoh
Too Qua Tah, Ned
Tor Yeu Nee See
Tucker, David
Tucker, Levi
Tur Ne Nall Le
Tyeall, James
Tyer
Ur Tah Ol Tah
Wah Tar Too kar, William
Woodall, George
Woodall, Osceala
Young Deer
Young Duck
Young Pig
Young Tassell

1st Regiment, Cherokee Mounted Volunteers

This unit designation changed to 1st Regiment about December, 1862, after Drew's regiment had disbanded. It was the combined troops from Watie's Regiment Cherokee Mounted Rifles and the 2nd Cherokee Mounted Volunteers.

Watie, Stand	F&S	Colonel,/ Brig. General
Adair, Tom P.	F&S	Colonel
Taylor, Thomas F.	F&S	Lieutenant Colonel
Boudinot, E.C.	F&S	Major
Thompson, Joseph F.	F&S	Major
Anderson, Thomas T.	F&S	Adjutant
Watie, Charles	F&S	Adjutant
Adair, George W.	F&S	Quartermaster
Thompson, Johnson	F&S	Acting Quartermaster
Taylor, Ready	F&S	Quartermaster Sergeant
Foreman, H. Lincoln	F&S	Sergeant Major
West, George	F&S	Sergeant Major
Adair, W.T.	F&S	Chief Surgeon
Fields, Rich	F&S	Surgeon
Polson, William D.	F&S	Surgeon
Trott, Ben	F&S	Hospital Steward
Compere, E. L.	F&S	Chaplain
Ricker, William	F&S	Chief Bugler
Martin, Rich F.	F&S	Commissary of Subsistence
Ware, Samuel K.	F&S	Acting Commissary of Subsistence
Bell, J.M.	D	Lieutenant Colonel
Parks, Robert C.	B	Lieutenant Colonel
Alberty, B.W.	I	Captain
Butler, James L.	G	Captain
Buzzard,	A	Captain
Coodey, D. R.	C	Captain
Fields, Dumplin O.	D,F	Captain
Foreman, Alexander	C,E	Captain
Fry, M.C.	I	Captain
Frye, M.C.	I	Captain
Howland, Erasmus J.	G,D	Captain
Howland, Erastus J.	G,D	Captain

Johnson, George W.	I	Captain
Johnson, John	K	Captain
Kind, H. G.	G	Captain
Lowery, Charles	E,C	Captain
Mayes, J.T.	H	Captain
Parks, Thos. J.		Captain
Smallwood,	F	Captain
Spears, John	F H	Captain
Starr, George H.	G	Captain
Stuart, James	H,K	Captain
Thompson, James H.	K	Captain
Tinnin, Hugh	A	Captain
Wisner, Benjamin B.	D	Captain
Alexander, William V.	I	First Lieutenant
Benge, James	I	First Lieutenant
Brewer, Perry	C	First Lieutenant
Brown, John W.	C	First Lieutenant
Buzzard Flapper, M.	B	First Lieutenant
Catterson, John W.	H,K	First Lieutenant
Coody, Joseph	H	First Lieutenant
Cunningham, J. T.	A	First Lieutenant
Daniel, W.A.	E,C	First Lieutenant
Daniels, W.A.	E,C	First Lieutenant
Foster, John	H	First Lieutenant
Gott, John	G	First Lieutenant
Hillburn, F. M.	D	First Lieutenant
Knight, J. S.	D	First Lieutenant
Lynch, J.M.	D,G	First Lieutenant
McCoy, J.C.	F	First Lieutenant
McGhee, T.J.	E	First Lieutenant
McKisick, D.R.	H	First Lieutenant
Sandrin, H.	K	First Lieutenant
Su a gee, Wilson	A	First Lieutenant
Turner, William H.	F	First Lieutenant
Watie, Cherles E.	2B	First Lieutenant
Boudinot, William P.	E,C	Brevet Second Lieutenant
Ingle, Joseph	A	Senior Second Lieutenant
Baldridge, B.	I	Second Lieutenant
Barnes, William	I	Second Lieutenant
Barns, William	I	Second Lieutenant

Name	Company	Rank
Boon, D. Priestly	D	Second Lieutenant
Boone, D.P.	D	Second Lieutenant
Bussey, George W.	K	Second Lieutenant
Fields, Johnson O.	F	Second Lieutenant
Forrester, Henry	B	Second Lieutenant
Green, Matthew	H,K	Second Lieutenant
Gunter, Samuel H.	I	Second Lieutenant
Hick, J. C.	C	Second Lieutenant
Kitch, Tee-hee	F	Second Lieutenant
Kitchen, tu hu	F	Second Lieutenant
McLaine, JohnK.	C	Second Lieutenant
McLane, John K.	C	Second Lieutenant
McMullen, J.W.	I	Second Lieutenant
Raper, J.A.	D	Second Lieutenant
Roper, J.A.	D	Second Lieutenant
Smith, Edward	1 C	Second Lieutenant
Snoddy, George	H K	Second Lieutenant
Swiney, Lafayette	K	Second Lieutenant
Teehee, Ketchee	H	Second Lieutenant
Vann, E.	B	Second Lieutenant
Wofford, Alexander	G	Second Lieutenant
Woodall, Charles M.	A	Second Lieutenant
Woseta, Stand	E	Second Lieutenant
Evons, William	A	Junior Second Lieutenant
Hornet, Wilson	F	Junior Second Lieutenant
Lahay, Antoine	D	Junior Second Lieutenant
Barlow, John T.	K	Third Lieutenant
Childers, John	I	Third Lieutenant
Daniel, J.W.	B	Third Lieutenant
Crossland, R.	C	Third Lieutenant
Diver, John	A	Third Lieutenant
England, P.	D	Third Lieutenant
Falkner, D.	I	Third Lieutenant
Foreman, William	E	Third Lieutenant
Pheasant, Richard	2 C	Third Lieutenant
Wilkerson, Thomas	G	Third Lieutenant
Kell, John T.	H,G	Lieutenant
Llafet, Thos. F.	K	Lieutenant
Mayes, W.H.	G	Lieutenant

Name	Company	Rank
Rogers, C.V.	G	Lieutenant
Ross, John F.	K	Lieutenant
Adair, William P.		Assistant Quartermaster
Carter, Benjamin W.	G,B	Quartermaster Sergeant
Edmondson, Charles E.	H,K	Ordnance Sergeant
Harlin, George W.	B,D	Ordnance Sergeant
Moore, Allcut	A,C	Ordnance Sergeant
Moore, Olcutt	A,C	Ordnance Sergeant
Root, Thomas A.	G,D	Ordnance Sergeant
Tyger, Mark	F	Ordnance Sergeant
Walker, John E.	2 I	Ordnance Sergeant
Morgan, Mont	C	Sergeant Major
Morgan, R.M.	C	Sergeant Major
Adair, H.M.		First Sergeant
Anderson, John C.	K	First Sergeant
Bevert, Larkin	F,D	First Sergeant
Brewer, W.S.	C	First Sergeant
Hildebrand, M. W.	F	First Sergeant
Hilderbrand, M.	F	First Sergeant
Meyers, W.	J	First Sergeant
Parrott, William P.	E	First Sergeant
Patten, Patrick	A	First Sergeant
Rider, A.	B	First Sergeant
Ross, Stephen B.	K	First Sergeant
Sanders, Ellis	I I	First Sergeant
Ussrey, William	I	First Sergeant
Weaver, Lewis	1F	First Sergeant
Webber, Chas.	D	First Sergeant
Adair, B.F.		Sergeant
Beck, Rutherd D.	G	Sergeant
Beovert, Lorkin	D,F	Sergeant
Beyers, Nick	I	Sergeant
Bird, Coffee B.	B	Sergeant
Black Haw,	F	Sergeant
Blake, J.M.	D	Sergeant
Blake, James W.	G,D	Sergeant
Blankenship, William	A	Sergeant
Blevons, Mike	A	Sergeant
Bryant, Joseph V.	BDC	Sergeant
Burns, John	K	Sergeant
Butler, M.	I	Sergeant
Byers, Nicholas	I	Sergeant

Name	Company	Rank
Campbell, G. W.	C	Sergeant
Cawood, William	H,A	Sergeant
Chicken, Manners	H	Sergeant
Chicken, Manny	F,H	Sergeant
Chicken, Maurning	F,H	Sergeant
Choo wo loo ky,	F	Sergeant
Cochran, John	F	Sergeant
Coffelt, Thomas W.	K	Sergeant
Collins, William	G	Sergeant
Colston, William	B	Sergeant
Cook, E. B.	B	Sergeant
Critendon, W.	B,D	Sergeant
Crittenden, Wellington	B,D	Sergeant
Croslin, J.	I	Sergeant
Cross, Barr	F	Sergeant
Davis, W.H.	H	Sergeant
Davis, William	C	Sergeant
Dick, Ellis	E	Sergeant
Eby, Thomas	H,K	Sergeant
Feelin, Smokee	H	Sergeant
Feilem, Smoke	H	Sergeant
Ferr, Ignatius A.	G	Sergeant
Fivekiller, Jack	H	Sergeant
Foreman, Charles	I	Sergeant
Freshower, Joseph	DC	Sergeant
Glenn, Lewis	E,B	Sergeant
Handle, Dempsy	E	Sergeant
Huss, Daniel	A	Sergeant
King, Benjamin	CEI	Sergeant
King, John	G	Sergeant
Kirk, G.W.	F,G	Sergeant
Kirk, George	F,G	Sergeant
Lowery, Henry	G	Sergeant
Lowrey, John	I,E	Sergeant
Lowry, John	I,E	Sergeant
Lu ya tah,	F	Sergeant
Martin, Joseph L.	D	Sergeant
McCoy, R.M.	E	Sergeant
McCrary, William	I	Sergeant
McGhee, John	E	Sergeant
McPhaille, Samuel	A	Sergeant
McPherson, Alex	F	Sergeant

Moore, David	A,C	Sergeant
Moore, John	A,C	Sergeant
More, David	A,C	Sergeant
More, John	A,C	Sergeant
Neal, George W.	K	Sergeant
Paterson, W.	J	Sergeant
Patten, J.M.	H	Sergeant
Pharr, W.L.	2 A	Sergeant
Pigeon, Logan	1A	Sergeant
Reese, Johnson	G	Sergeant
Rodgers, John C.	K	Sergeant
Schrinscher, John	2 G	Sergeant
Sidna, Levi	H	Sergeant
Smith, Joseph	2 C	Sergeant
Smoke, Feelom	2 H	Sergeant
Squirrel, William	A	Sergeant
Alexander, John	G,H	Corporal
Allen, H.	D	Corporal
Baucum, Ezekiel	1 K	Corporal
Bean, Cornelius	CGJ	Corporal
Bell, J.M.	G	Corporal
Benge, R.	I	Corporal
Blevins, Luke	E,C	Corporal
Blevons, Ransom	A	Corporal
Bowlin, John	A	Corporal
Borland, George	H	Corporal
Brodie, John M.	K	Corporal
Buffington, George	H	Corporal
Buffington, Jonathan	G	Corporal
Buffinton, Jonathan A.	G	Corporal
Bullfrog,	F	Corporal
Buzzard, Moses	A,B	Corporal
Byers, Charles	I	Corporal
Childers, Samuel	I	Corporal
Coudy, Sam	B	Corporal
Coxe, Tom	F	Corporal
Deer, John	D,B	Corporal
Elliott, Wal A.	H	Corporal
Fields, Johnson	D,H	Corporal
Fool, Dick	C,E	Corporal
Fool, Richard	C,E	Corporal
Foreman, Elias	H	Corporal

Foreman, Lewis	B	Corporal
Foreman, Worcester	F	Corporal
French, Henry	G	Corporal
Givins, Jonas	K	Corporal
Green, William	A	Corporal
Griffin, William	E	Corporal
Hammer, Peter	A,B	Corporal
Hays, John	C	Corporal
Jailor, Ned	E	Corporal
Johnson, Jr., Benjamin	I	Corporal
Kinny, Jay	D	Corporal
Langly, L.	I	Corporal
Marcum, Carter	D	Corporal
Maxfield, Madison	E	Corporal
Mayer, Richard T.	H	Corporal
McCrarry, Napoleon	K	Corporal
McEntire, John	K	Corporal
McFields, M.	J	Corporal
Miller, D.	C	Corporal
Mitchell, George	I	Corporal
Mush, Ezekiel	A	Corporal
Newton, John W.	I	Corporal
Ool ok lea tah,	F,H	Corporal
Ools Kelley atah,	F,H	Corporal
Olds kelly Atah,	F,H	Corporal
Palmer, Samuel	E,C	Corporal
Parmer, Sam	E,C	Corporal
Pigeon, Edward	1A	Corporal
Pigeon, Jack	2C	Corporal
Pigeon, Ned	1A	Corporal
Reese, William	C	Corporal
Riley, P.A.	C	Corporal
Robins, Benjamin	G	Corporal
Rockshirt,	E,C	Corporal
Ross, George W.	K	Corporal
Russel, Joseph	G K	Corporal
Salt, Face	E C	Corporal
Sanders, David		Corporal
Sanders, J.	J	Corporal
Scott, Jack	A C	Corporal
Scott, William	E	Corporal
Sides, George		Corporal

Sixkiller, Arch	1 I	Corporal
Smith, William A.	2 D	Corporal
Smoke, George	F	Corporal
Starr Jr., J.M.	G	Corporal
Su-a-gee, Davis	A	Corporal
Sutton, T.		Corporal
Suaki, Davis	A	Corporal
Tex tas kee,	E	Corporal
Thomas, Thomas C.	F,G	Corporal
Vance, Richard	D	Corporal
Vann, William	B	Corporal
Walker, Steven	1E	Corporal
Webster, Daniel	H	Corporal
Wingfield, James	D	Corporal
Wright, John	G	Corporal
Lafet, Thomas F. S.	K	Orderly
Fisk, Francis H.	G	Drillmaster, Assistant Surgeon
Polson, Jasper		Hospital Steward
McCandless, William A.	D	Chief Bugler
Bean, William	G	Musician
Brower, James	D,K	Musician
Tinnin, James Preston	A	Musician
Johnson, R.M.		Wagonmaster
Lipe, Oliver W.	G	Acting Commissary of Subsistence
Lynch, Peter G.	H,B	Acting Commissary of Subsistence
Starr, J.M.		Forage Master

Privates

Abbacrumbie, B.F.	A	Adair, George		
Abbacrumbie, H.	A	Adair, George	I	
Abbacrumbie, John	A	Adair, James	C	
Abercrombie, B.F.		Adair, James	G	
Abercrombie, H.V.		Adair, Jesse	G	
Abercrombie, J.L.		Adair, John	M.	
Abercrombie, John		Adams, John		
Achords, William		Ah mi yoo ah,		
Acords, William		Ah-mar-yah,		
Adair, George		Ahnetawnohah,		

Name	Code	Name	Code
Aiken, John		Bean, Jeff	C
Alberty, A.J.		Bear, Grease	B
Alberty, Andrew		Beargrease, James	C
Alberty, Eli S.		Bearpaw, John	H
Alberty, George W.		Bears, George W.	1 K
Alberty, Jesse		Bearspaw, John	H
Alberty, John W.		Beck, Caleb	B
Alexander, Robert	I	Beck, Eaekiel	2 B
Allen, E.D.	D	Beck, Jeffrey	B
Anderson, James		Beck, Joseph	G
A,FAnderson, T.F.	H	Beck, Samuel	G,B
Ar lee cher,	F	Beck, Surry	G,B
Ar quier,	A	Bell, Eli	K
Ar see nee,	F	Bell, F.	I
Arch, Robinson	F,H	Bell, George	D
Archilla, D.	D	Bell, J.	D
Arluly, Ice	B	Bell, J.B.	G
Arsee nee, Daniel	F	Bell, Jack	I
Arsee nee, George	F	Bell, James M.	G
Arsena, G.	D	Bell, John	D
Aubry, J.T.	J	Benge, Benjamin	B
Aue,	F	Benge, Riddle	I
Awe,	F	Benge, Stand	C
Bacon, Bailey	G	Benge, William	I
Bacon, Thomas	G	Bennett, Simp	C
Badger, J.	I	Berket, D.	B
Baker, Levi	K	Berket, J.	BB
Baldface, Arch	F,H	Bethell, Chester	I
Baldridge, George	I	Beyers, Charles	I
Baldrige, G.	I	Big, Elk	I
Baldrige, W.	I	Big, Otterlefter	I
Ballface, Arch	F,H	Big Elk,	I
Ballridge, William	A	Bird, H.	I
Bark, William Wert	F	Bird,	E
Barker, Adam	K	Black, W.C.	G
Barns, Alex	C	Black Bird,	B
Baugh, Bevert	D	Blaylock, H.	B
Baugh, Levert	D	Bledsoe, Joseph	D
Bawcum, Gilbert A.	K	Blevens, G.T.	A
Beair,	I	Blevins, Elijah	C
Bean, Anderson	G	Blevins, Isham	K
Bean, Bruce	C		

Blister,	A,C	Campbell, Charles	G
Blue Bird,	F	Campbell, Hugh	I
Boats, John	B	Campbell, John	E
Bob, Robert	H	Campbell, John	I
Boggs, D.	J	Campbell, John C.	K
Bomaster, Henry	A	Campbell, W. W.	I
Boot, John	B	Campean, John	K
Bottoms, Newton	A	Canda, R.	G,I
Bowland, William	I	Canda, Sam	B,I
Bowlin, William	A	Candy, Jack	C,E
Bradshaw, J.H.	A	Candy, John	C,E
Brady, Charles	F	Candy, Reese	B,I
Bredris, Enoch O.	K	Candy, Samuel	B,I
Brewer, George W.	C	Candy, Thos.	D
Brewer, James	E	Candy, Jr., John	CD,I
Brewer, Jesse	F	Canoe, George	I
Brewer, John	C	Carey, E. D.	C
Brewer, T.F.	C	Carey, R. T.	E
Briches,	I	Carey, Ross	C
Brickey, John	A	Carpenter, Charles	B,D
Bright, John	G	Carpenter, J.	D
Bright, Samuel	C,E	Carpenter, Simon	D
Brock, Sherod	A	Carroll, Thomas	K
Bryant, Andrew J.	K	Carter, George	I
Bryant, Francis	K	Carter, Jefferson	I
Bryant, Samuel W.	K	Carvell, William W.	D
Bucher, Daniel	I	Cat, Samuel	F
Buck, Mose	C	Cawood, Thomas	A
Buck,	E	Chambers, George	I
Buck,	I	Chambers, Henery	H
Buck,	F	Chambers, James	G
Bullfrog, Mouse	A	Chambers, John	G
Bulsnake,	B	Chambers, Maxwell	G
Burgess, John	E	Chambers, William	G
Burns, Emmons F.	M	Chandler, Joseph	K
Burwisgarner, John	H	Char-ye-tee-he,	B
Butler, Knox	G	Chastain, M. M. C.	K
Butler, William	I	Chastane, John S.	K
Buzzard, John	A,B	Chastane, Joseph C.	K
Buzzard, Thompson	A	Chastane, William M.	K
Cabbage,	H	Chastine, J. T.	A
Callahan, James	I	Che nar chee,	B

Che ner mee,	C,A	Cockram, Alexander	D
Che-nar-chy,	B	Cockram, Charles	D
Che-now-em,	C	Cockrum, Lewis	A,F
Chenarshe,	B	Coker, J. R.	G
Chewalukee,	B	Coldwell, J. J.	I
Chewe,	I	Coleman, Abraham S.	K
Chips,	B	Collier, William H.	E
Cho-chucker,	A,B	Colston, Charles	G,B
Cho-er-chucker,	A,B	Colston, James	B
Choctaw, J.	I	Compton, A. W.	A
Choon se ye,	F	Connon, Lewis	C
Choowalooga, Daniel	H	Connor, Caleb	E,C
Choowalooga,	H	Connor, William	E
Chostain, J. F.	A	Connor, Jr., William	E
Chouton, Geers	D	Conseen, David	H
Christa, Thomas	I	Conseen, Frank	H
Christy, Thomas	I	Coody, Archibald	D
Chronoohaga, Peterson	H	Cook, Elias	D
Chu wa lu ke,	I	Coon, Alexander	G,H
Chu war no sky,	E,C	Coon, D.	B
Chuwarnoshy,	E,C	Coon, Jess	B,F
Clahyerhah,	H	Coon, Ketcher	B,H
Clark, G.W.	G	Copeland, Alexander	A
Clay, Daniel	I	Copeland, Richard	A
Clay, Hair	I,F	Cordery, Lewis	G
Clayton, J.W.	I	Cordery, Wilson	G
Cloud, Rider	B	Corn Tassel	A,C
Clynes, Cornelius	G	Corner, Jack	H
Clynes, Joseph	G	Couch, Charles	B,F
Coalman, A. S.	K	Coudy, John	B
Coat, John	A	Coudy, Thomas	B
Coats, George	D,I	Countryman, George	A
Coats, Henry	A	Countryman, John	A
Coats, John	A	Coupland, Richard	A
Coats, John S.	F,D	Cox, F.	D
Cochram, Allick	D	Coyl, William	K
Cochran, George	F	Crabtree, John	K
Cochran, Lewis	A,F	Cramp, Breeches	E,B
Cochran, Samuel	F	Cramp, Harry	E,B
Cochrane, Wm.	F	Cramp, Ned	B
Cochron, William	A,F	Cramp, Riddle	E,B
Cockeram, William	A,F	Cramp, Watt	A,B

Cramp, Jr., Broom	B	Dickey, A.J.	A
Cramp, Sr., Broom	B	Dickson, J.M.	J
Craven, John	K,D	Dirt Thrower,	B
Cravens, John	K,D	Dobbins, Charles	F
Crawfish, Jessee	B,D	Dobbins, George	F
Crawford, Virgil	G	Doghead, John	B,C
Cricket,	A,B	Doghead Che now se,	A,C
Crittend, H.	E	Dogwood, Jesse	I,E
Crittenden, Henry	C	Doherty, Ely	D
Cittendon, George	G	Downing, James	A
Cromwell, John	A	Downing, James	I
Crow, J. W.	I	Downing, Looney	D,I
Crowfish, Jesse	B,D	Downing, Wesley	H
Crutchfield, Luther	B	Downing, William	F
Culquetak,	B	Drake, James	A
Cummings, Wilson	E	Dreadful Water,	H
Cunlly, Thomas	D	Drew, Henry	G
Cunningham, Lewis	A,B	Drum, George	E
Curtis, James C.	K	Duch, John	E
Danel, R.	B	Dunbean, Lige	F
Daniel, John	C	Duncan, G.W.	E
Daniel, Squirrel	C	Duskey,	C
Daniel, T.W.	E	Earbot, Henery	H
Daniels, J.W.	G	Edmondson, Branerges	H,I
Daniels, M.D.	C	Edwards, Enick	K
Dannenberg, William	G	Eldridge, Jefferson	I
Daucleerty, C.	J	Elliot, Thomas W.	D
Davis, David	A,F	Elliott, A.	D
Davis, George W.	H,K	Elliott, James	D,I
Davis, James	F	Ellott, Coock	I
Davis, James	G	Elloutt, Coock	I
Davis, John	A,C	England, Lowery W.	K
Davis, Lemiel J.M.	K	England, M.	D
Davis, Mitchel	H	Evans, Edward	A
Dawson, Joseph	I	Falkner, C.C.	I
De car tos ky,	C	Fallem, Robert	H
Deerinthewater, John	G	Fallen, George	G,H
Deerinthewater, Scott	G		
Denis, Westley	A	Fallen, Jesse	G,H
Denton, David	A	Fallen, Joseph	D
Denton, John	G	Falling, Edward	E
Dgen, John	K	Falling, John	C

Name	Code	Name	Code
Farley, L.L.	E	Foster, James	G
Fauling, Ned	F	Fox, Hiram	I
Federick, Frank	I	Fox, Jack	H
Feelem, Charles	F,H	Francis, John	J
Feeling, Charles	H	Franks, Newton	K
Fields, Cherokee	F,H	Frazer, J.J.	K
Fields, James	A	Frazer, Joseph	K
Fields, James S.	A	Fredrick, Frank	I
Fields, Moses	A	Freshower, W.	D
Fields, Richard	A	Frizell, Daniel	K
Fields, Robert	F,H	Frizell, Henry J.	K
Fields, Thomas	B,H	Frizell, James T.	K
Fields, Walter	I,E	Furgerson, J.	B
Fike, R.S.	G	Gafford, Jess	I
Fike, Robt.	G	Gafford, John	I
Finley, Reuben	E	Gah Skernee,	A
Fish, John	E	Galyan, Randolph	H
Fish Tail,	B	Garberinao, S.	E
Fisher, Benjamin	G,E	George, (Indian)	F
Flack, Jerdon O.	H	Gholston, Mathew	A
Flecher, John C.	A	Gholston, W.M.	A
Flopper, M.B.	F	Gillespie, Jo	E
Flye, James H.	C	Girty, Simon	C,E
Flying, Push	F	Glass, B.	J
Flying,	B	Glass, Nelson	F
Fodder, George	F,H	Goard, R.R.	F
Fodders, George	F,H	Gonzales,	I
Foling, John	C	Goree, James L.	K
Fool, William	C,E	Gott, George S.	G
Foreaman, R.J.	F,G	Gott, William	G
Foreman, Amos	F	Gourd, T.R.	G
Foreman, Daniel	I	Grady, John	H
Foreman, George	G	Grass, Hoper	A,C
Foreman, J.A.	I,E	Grass, Jack	E,C
Foreman, John	I,E	Greene, A.	E
Foreman, P.B.	C,E	Greese, B.	B,B
Foreman, R.J.	F,G		
Foreman, Return	G	Greese, J.B.	B
Foreman, Spencer	B,D	Grey, Stan	H
Foreman, Stand	H	Griffin, R.	G
Foster, Benjamin	G	Griffith, Joe	I
Foster, Henry	G	Griffon, R.	G

Grigg, William	K	Hemstead, Oden	C
Grimmett, John	I	Henderson, B. F.	E
Grits, William	H	Hendren, W. H.	I
Groves, Alex	F	Hensley, John	EFC
Groves, Jack	F,F	Hensly, John	EFC
Groves, James	F,F	Henson, James	B
Groves, Luyatah	F	Hickey, B. B.	C,G
Guage, T.		Hickey, Beany	G
Guess, Joseph	I	Hickey, Bevely	C,G
Guest, G.	I	Hicks, A. V.	I
Guest, Joe	I	Hicks, Charles	C
Gunter, John	I	Hicks, John	I
Guset, R.	I	Hicks, Looney	E
Hair, Jeff	J	Hicks, N.	I
Hair, John	F,H	Hicks, Rufus	I
Hair, Samuel	F,H	Hickup, John	C
Hale, William W.	D	High,	A,B
Haley, Jackson	E	Hildebrand, Brice	G
Half Breed, James	C,E	Hildebrand, James	G
Halfbred, Steval	H	Hildebrand, M.	C
Halfbreed, Stand	F	Hildebrand, S.	C
Hall, John	I	Hildebrand, Thomas	F
Hampsing, Oden	G	Hilderbrand, James	G
Hampsing, Oelle	G	Hilderbrand, 1st John	F,H
Hampton, S.	I	Hilderbrand, 2nd John	F
Hansard, William B.	D	Hill, Henry L.	D,K
Harbin, George	D	Hillon, Charles	CED
Haris, W.	B	Hog to ter,	E
Harlin, John B.	I	Hogner, Walker	E
Harlin, Mitchel	D	Hogtoter, Bat	E
Harmage, R.	I	Hogtoter, Sunday	E
Harman, Charles	I	Holland, Richard	A
Harmon, Charles	I	Holt, Moses	I
Harris, Bird	B	Holymonk,	E
Hatchet, Edward	F	Hongry, James	I
Hatchet, Ned	F	Hood, Ellis	B
Hawk, William	I	Horn, Jeremiah	G
Hawk,	E,C	Hornet, Peter	F
Headrick, Joseph	F,H	Hornett, Peter	F
Headrick, William	H	Horse Fly,	F
Hedrick, Joe	H	Horsefly, James	A
Hedrick, Wm.	H	Horsefly,	A

Horton, Andrew C.	H		Jones, Wilburn	E
Horton, Christopher C.	A		Jumper, Charles	F
Horton, Pleasant P.	H		Justice, George	A,B
Hosmer, C.	C		Justice, Jack	E
House, George W.	K		Justice, John	A,B
House, Henry	I		Justice, John	C,E
Howell, William	A		Justice, Singer	C,E
Hoyt, Milo	H		Kanard, Robert	D
Hubbard, Thomas	B,G		Kaskoo me hee,	K
Hubird, T.	B,G		Keese, Andrew	H
Hufman, James W.	K		Keith, Elija	A
Hughes, John	H		Kell, Daniel O.	D,K
Hughs, George	I		Kell, Joseph	K
Hughs, T.	B		Kell, L.	D
Hughs, Thompson	B		Kell,	G,H
Humphrey, J.	E		Kelley, Isaac G.	I,K
Hurt, Winfield Scott	K		Kelley, J.G.	H,K
Ice, Arluly	B		Kelly, J.C.C.	A
Ingle, John	A		Ketcher, John	B
Ingram, Syl'r.	A		Ketcher, Sloman	H
Isbell, C.C.	A		Ketchum, John	1A
Isbell, G.W.	A		Ketchum,	D
Isbell, George	A		Ketchup, John	B
Ivy, Thomas	E		Keys, J.M.	C,G
Jackson, Benjamin H.	K		Keys, James	C,G
Jackson, John	C,G		Keys, William	C
Jackson, T.J.	E		Kickup, John	E
Jackson, Thomas	K		Killer, Rider W.	G
Jackson,	C		Kimbal, Robert	D
Jefferson,	E.C		Kineannon, John A.	K
Jerolds, Robert	C		King, Thomas	A
Johnson, Andrew	G		Kinkade, William A.	I
Johnson, Ellis	A		Kirk, Francis	I
Johnson, Nickolas	I		Kitcher,	E
Johnson,	E		Knight, Robert Q. R.	D
Jones, Charles F.	K		Knight, Thomas	D
Jones, Drew	C		Knightkiller, H.	E,C
Jones, J.	D		Lacy, William	I
Jones, Jackson	F		Lafabre, Thomas	F
Jones, James	K		Lafabre, Watie	A,F
Jones, Joab	A		Lahay, A. E.	D
Jones, Squire	A		Landrena, David	C

Landrom, J. P.	D,G	Lowry, Edward	F
Landrom, John	K	Lowry, Walker	K
Landrum, H. T.	G	Lowry, William	I
Landrum, Hiram	G	Loyd, John	K
Landrum, J. P.	D,G	Lozier, Charles	G
Landrum, Joseph	D,G	Lu hu, Daniel	F
Langford, Aaron T.	K	Lynch, Cicero L.	K
Lankford, A. T.	K	Lynch, Joe	G
Lasley, George	E	Maness, James N.	K
Latta, Allen	C,G	Mann, R.J.	G
Latta, Felix	H	Mann, Robert J.	G
Latta, Felix G.	H	Manning, Wooster	B
Lattee, Allen	C,G	Marcum, Jacob	D
Laugh at, Mush	A,B	Markham, G.	D
Le sqi na lah,	F	Marrs, Huston H.	H,K
Lea, Maston D.	K	Marshall, William	C
Leake, Jesse	C	Martin, Alexander L.	I,K
Lewis, Wash	C	Martin, B. Flopper	F
Lige, John	F	Martin, G.W.	A
Linder, John	C	Martin, H.T.	E
Linder, Julius	C	Martin, John	G
Lindsey, Edward J.	K	Martin, W.G.	A
Lindsey, William M.	K	Matlock, Nathaniel	A
Linzy, Martin	H	Matohe, John	G
Lipe, D. W. C.	I	Matoy, Willaim	G
Lipe, J. G.	C	Maxfield, J.W.	E
Lisenbe, Charles	E	May, Thomas	A
Lisenbe, Eli	E	McCandliess, A.	I
Lisenbe, G. W.	E	McCarthy, Jeremiah	K
Little, Johnson	I	McCoy, C.K.	E
Liver,	I	McCoy, Smith	E
Lizzard, James	E	McDaniel, John	I
Lofobare, Watie	C,F	McDaniel, Joseph	I
Long, Allen	K	McDaniel, L.	B
Long, John	H	McDaniel, Rob	J
Looney,	F	McDanil, Jail	J
Loree, Johnson	H	McDonall, William	I
Losier, Chas.	G	McFaden, Charles	A
Loux, Henry	A	McFaden, Filbert	A
Love, Daniel	F	McFaden, Marshall	A
Love, Ezekiel	F	McFaden, R.H.	A
Lowery, Ned	F	McFaden, Thomas	A

McGeehe, Elijah	K		Morrow, G.T.	I
McGhee, D.L.	E		Moses,	E
McLaughlin, Andy	G		Mouse, -	C,E
McLaughlin, D.	D		Mouse, Isaac	C,E
McLaughlin, James	G		Murphey, Alexander	I
McLoughlin, George	B		Murphy, Alex	I
McNair, David H.	G		Murphy, High	F
McNair, John	D		Murphy, John	H
McNelly, W.	C		Murphy, P.	B
McPherson, H.	B		Muskra, Wilson	A,F
McPherson, John	F		Muskrat, J.	D
McPherson, S.	B		Muskrat, James	A,B
McReynolds, James A.	K		Muskrat, Wilson	A,F
Meadows, George W.	K		Na hee, T.T.	
Meadows, William D.	K		Nance, John W.	K
Meek, Jacob	K		Nave, D.R.	I
Melton, Edward	E		Nave, S.D.	E
Melton, Moses	E		Nevins, John	G
Mertier, E.	J		Nicco Jack,	F
Michell, Henry	A		Nice Jack,	F,F
Michell, Reece	A		Nicey,	E,C
Mike,	F		Nickojack,	F,F
Miller, A.J.	C		Nicky,	E,C
Miller, Andrew	C		Nidever, Mark	J
Miller, Calvin	B,G		Nightkiller, Henry	E,C
Miller, G.W.	B,G		Nivens, M.D.	C
Miller, George	G,C		Noisywater, Judge	H
Miller, Jack	C		O'Brien, John	A
Miller, Jeff	F		Obrian, Peter	K
Miller, John	F,C		Om wah-nick-kee,	D
Miller, Lewis	F,H		Osey, Tom	F
Miller, Thomas	C		Otterlifter, James	I
Miller, Warren	F		Owens, Arch	A,B
Miller, Wash	G		Owens, George	B
Monkers, J.K.	H		Owens, Ice	A,B
Monkey,	B		Owens, Lewis	B
Moore, C.H.	C		Owl,	C
Moore, Isaac	B		Pack, Shory	B
Moore, James	B		Painter, John	A
Morgan, William	K		Palmer, Jack	J
Morris, George	E		Palmer, John	D
Morris, O.	D		Palmer, Levy	D

Panders, Calvin	G	Price, R.D.B.	1 I
Paris, John	B,G	Prichet, C.	J
Parres, Bryant	G	Proctor, Isaac	2H
Parres, Green	G	Proctor, James	2F
Parres, John	B,G	Proctor, Nelson	2B
Parres, Moses	G	Pumpkinpile, Ketcher	2H
Parris, Henry	I	Pumpkinpile, Ned	2H
Patrick, William	C	Rabbit, John	F,H
Patten, James	H	Ragsdale, Joel	
Patten, Samuel	H	Ragsdale, Thomas	I
Payton, William M.	K	Ramsey, L.C.	G
Peck, William H.	2 D	Ransom, Jacob N.	K
Pennel, Alonzo W.	2 K	Rat, W.M.	E
Peter, -	A	Ratcliff, Rose	G
Peters, Michael	1 K	Ratley, Wallace	E
Petete, Ples	1 C	Rattlin Gord	E,C
Petite, Charles	1 I	Rattling Gourd	B
Pettit, Charles	1 I	Rattling Gourd	E,C
Pettit, Marcus	2 I	Rattlingourd,	D
Pettit, Moster	2 I	Ray, John	K
Pettit, Pleasant	1C	Reader, Elias	E,C
Pettitt, T.	J	Reagdale, Thomas	I
Pheasant, James	I	Reckes, W.	B
Pheasant, Stealer	1 G	Red Bird,	H
Phillips, P.M.	2A	Reding, William	C
Phillips, William	2D	Reede, C.C.	I
Pigeon, Alfred	2B	Reese, Andrew	G
Pigeon, Eane	1A	Reese, B.N.	I
Pigeon, Foster	2B	Reese, George	G
Pigeon, Jesse	1A	Reese, Rody	I
Pigeon, John	1A	Renolds, George	C
Pippin, William J.	2 K	Rhea, John G.	A
Plantain, John `	2G	Richardson, L.C.	I
Polson, John W.	2G	Rider, T.L.	B
Polston, Joseph	1C	Ridge, Herman	D,G
Pool, John	J	Ried, C.C.	I
Posey, Pinckney	1K	Riley, Harrison	I
Preston, C.H.C.	1E	Riner, John	K
Price, Amos	1 I	Roach, William	B,I
Price, B.H.	1 I	Robbinson, Francis	D
Price, John	2 I	Roberts, Columbus	H
Price, Marcus L.	2K	Roberts, Richard M.	K

Roberts, William	D		Scott, Bill	2C	
Robertson, Arch	F,H		Scott, Jesse	E	
Robinson, Arch	F,H		Scott, Js	E	
Rodgers, William	E,C		Scott, Moses	AC	
Rogers, Ira	C		Scott,	2 H	
Rogers, James	C		Scotte, John	2 H	
Rogers, John	F		Scraper, -	EC	
Rogers, Joseph	D		Scraper, Ahlee chah	FE	
Rogers, Lewis	J		Scraper, Alexander	I	
Rogers, N.	D		Scraper, Luke	EC	
Rogers, T.L.	G		Scruggs, James H.	2 K	
Rogers, Thos.	G		Scruggs, William T.	2 K	
Rogers Jr., William	E,C		Se cow wee,	F	
Rogers Sr., William	E,C		Se cowee, C.	DH	
Root, Martin	B,D		Seven, Filds	J	
Ross, A.S.	D		Sexton, John	G	
Ross, Andrew	H		Sexton, T. J.	A	
Ross, Daniel	H		Shanenu,	2 H	
Ross, James M.	K		Shanklin, William	2 K	
Ross, Thomas J.	D		Shaw, Henry	2 G	
Rotramble, A.J.	H		Shaw, J. H.	2 G	
Rottenman,	C		Shell, -	C	
Rotting Goat,	E,C		Shelton, James K.	2 K	
Rowe, James	F		Shoeboot, Morrison	EC	
Royce, A.W.W.	D		Shoemake, W. N.	E	
Runabout,	F,E		Shoock, James	J	
Runaway, Frank	D,F		Short, Thom	A	
Runway, F.			Short, Tom	2 B	
Rush, Clemons	K		Silk, Levi	2 H	
Russel, Elisha	1H		Silk, Moses	2 H	
Russell, Jesse	2E		Simmons, Haney	2 I	
Russell, William	2A		Simmons, James	J	
Sagar, Samuel	A		Simmons, T.B.	2 I	
Sanders, Calvin	H		Sixkiller, Samuel	1 G	
Sanders, Henry A.	K		Skilky, Lewis	2 E	
Sanders, Isaac	1 I		Slolts, John	2 K	
Sanders, N.	J		Slolts, Sims	2 K	
Sanders, Thomas			Small Wood,	2 F	
Sanders, Watson	G,H		Smallwood, John	1G	
Sanders, William	J,H		Smallwood, Joseph	1 G	
Sanders, Sr, Isaac	2 I		Smith, Arch	2F	
Scales, J. A.	C		Smith, Coon	2 F	

Smith, David	2 K	Starr, Henry	C
Smith, E.G.	1 E	Starr, Thomas	G
Smith, Frank	C	Starr, Walter	G
Smith, H.L.	1 C	Stealer,	E
Smith, Jackson	1 G	Stealer,	F
Smith, John	2 E	Stephens, Spencer S.	K
Smith, John J.	J	Still, Jack	D
Smith, John L.	2 K	Stoner, E.P.	A
Smith, S.B.	2 G	Stotts, Sims	K
Smith, Samuel	1 C	Stour, Rogers	A
Smith, Stand	2C	Stover, R.	D
Smith, Thomas	2 E	Strickler, A.T.	
Smith, Thomas	2 F	Strickler, W.C.	
Smith, Thomas	2 F	Studefant, John	A
Smith, William	2 I	Studevant, John C.	G
Smoker, Mark	I	Studwan, Martin B.	G
Snider, Mitchel P.	HK	Sturdifan, John	A
Softshell Turtle,	2 E	Stute, Sam	E
Soldier, James	2 C	Sumerfield, Aheat	B
Solloman, Gerrald	H	Sumerfield, West	A,F
Solomon,	A	Summerfield, Joseph	A,B
Somerfield, Arquier	2 B	Summerfield, West	A,F
Sooter, Eli B.	1 H	Sutherland, J.A.	B
Sooter, William L.	H	Swimmer, J.	B,D
Sour, John	AC	Swimner, Jacob	B,D
Southerland, H.	1 D	Swindel, Christopher	K
Spaniard, A.M.	1 C	Ta looke, Sam	C
Spaniard, Mike	C	Tabb, Mose	F
Speaker,	1 C	Tah ner ees ky,	C
Spears, Archibald	BD	Tah ske gat eehe,	B
Spears, Joseph	2 H	Tah ske ke te hee,	C
Spencer, James	1 B	Tah skee ge tekee,	A,E
Spoon, James	K	Tah skee gee te hee,	A,E
Springfrog, James	G	Tahmuwee, Wm.	H
Squa ta lee chee,	1 F	Tahunee, Ben	H
Squirl, James	1 A	Tahunwell, Henery	H
Squirrel, Tough	1A	Tahuwee, Henry	H
Squirrel, Toyah	1A	Takes tas ker,	C
Squirrel, Tozah	1A	Takstas kee, George	C
Squta lee chee,	1F	Tangleson, George	G
Standing Man,	I	Tapp, Joseph	C
Star, Joseph	D	Tappin, Joseph	E

Name	Code	Name	Code
Tassel, Charles	G	Timpson, Owalar	E
Tasssel, N.	I	Timpson, Samuel	E,C
Taylor, Ezekiel	H	Timpson, Sandy	E,C
Taylor, Robert		Timpson, Sunday	E,C
Taylor, Samuel	K	Timpson, Walker	C
Taylor, T.F.	G	Tincup, James	C
Taylor, W.	B	Tincup, Jase	C
Tcah wah te ski,	I	Tincup, Jesse	E,C
Te cu we skey,	A,E	Tiner, Seburn	G
Te eksar,	H,D	Tinker, John	C
Teacher, James	A,B	Tinney, J.W.	D
Teche, Daniel	H	Tinney, T.A.	D
Techee, George	H	Tobacco, John	A,B
Techee, John	H	Tohunee, William	H
Techee, Stephen	H	Tom	
Teco he ste skee,	E	Toney, Levi	H
Tee te na hee,	C	Tony, George	B,D
Teeche, Daniel	H	Tony, L.	B,H
Teeche, George	H	Too ni ee,	F
Teeche, Tom	H	Towell, John	F,H
Teechee, John	H	Tracker,	2E
Teechee, Stephen	H	Trentham, Zachariah T.	K
Teehee, Tom	H	Trott, James J.	C
Terrapin, Shell	B,C	Trott, Jim	J
Thomas, Johnson	F,G	Trott, T.B.	I
Thomas, Nicholas	D	Tucker, Elijah	B
Thomas, Peter	D	Tucker, G.	B
Thomasson, Zimarah	A	Tucker, Levi	I
Thompson, Hughs	B,F	Turk, Hiram	K.
Thompson, Joseph L.	K	Turnover, Joseph	E
Thompson, Joseph N.	K	Turnover,	B
Thompson, Samuel W.	K	Turpen, John	G
Thompson, William	C	Turquah, George	B
Thompson,	J	Tyger, Looney	E
Thorn, Jasper	I	Tyner, A.	B
Thornton, John	G	Tyner, A.C.	B
Thornton, Oceola	B,D	Ul te Skee,	E
Thornton, Walter	E	Usery, D.C.	I
Thornton, William	G	Usery, Isaac	I
Timberlake, Dick	D,B	Usery, James	I
Timpson, Bear	E,C	Usery, John	I
Timpson, Clay	J	Usery, Philip	I

Usery Jr., William	I		Watts, Tom	1C
Vann, C.	B		Weaver, George	2E
Vann, D.W.	D		Webber, C.T.	1D
Vann, David	H,B		Webber, O.	D
Vann, Ephraim	F		Weir, Webster	2C
Vann, Flopper	B		Welch, James	2B
Vann, Joh L.	H		West, G.R.	2G
Vann, John	C		West, John	2G
Vann, Joseph	F		West, John W.	1C
Vann, Joseph	H		West, Jonathan	2D
Vann, Joshua	H		West, William M.	2G
Vann, Tahtanor	H,B		Whale, Stephen	2H
Vann, Yahtawnah	H,B		Wheeler, Isaac	2 I
Vestal, J.W.	E		Wheeler, J.C.	2G
Vicory, Wilb	C		Wheeler, Samuel	I
Vincent, James H.	K		White, D.S.	2A
Voluntine, William	K		White, David	2D
Wa-loo-ker, -	A		White, F.M.	2A
Wa-tuc-coo, -	1A		White, James	A
Wadkins, Henry N.	K		Whitekiller, Rider	G
Wagoner, George W.	K		Whitmire, Stephen	G
Waldron, Uriah	D		Whittemore, A.C.	1H
Walker, -	1A		Whortle, Berry	1F
Walker, -	2H		Wicked, Jesse	I
Walker, George	2D		Wicked, William	I
Walker, Hogner	2E		Wickit, John	2H
Walker, J.O.	1B		Wiggington, James	2K
Walking, Wolf	1I		Wilburn, Benjamin C.	G
Waluka,	C		Wilcox, A. F.	H
War tucker, -	F		Wiley, Squirrel	E
War war, Ceta	E		Wiley,	C
Ward, George	J		Wilkerson, H.	D
Ward, Samuel	A		Wilkerson, Hill	E
Warford, John	2D		Wilkerson, John	F
Waseat, Joseph	1E		Wilkerson, Riley	I
Waster, Benjamin	2C		Williams, Jonathan	H
Wastuck, L.	J		Willis, John N.	K
Wastuck, Thomas	1 I		Wilson, Bird	J
Waters, R.	J		Wilson, John	
Watie, Saladin	1D		Wingfield, George	D
Watt, Johnson	2H		Wisner, Samuel	D
Watts, Thomas	1C		Wo chot he,	M

Wocester, S.	J		Woseta, Jonce	E	
Wofford, Robert	G		Wright, B. F.	D	
Wolf, Duck	B		Wright, Caleb	E	
Womac, W. C.	B		Wright, William	A	
Woodall, Abraham	H		Wrinkle,	I	
Woodard, George	A		Yandel, Samuel D.	K	
Woodard, R. B.	A		Yates, George	I	
Woods, Leonard	G		York, John	K	
Woods, Wilson	B		Yost, J. D.	K	
Woodward, Boot	B		Yost, James	K	
Woodward, George	C		Young, Andrew	I	
Woodward, Ned	A		Young, Bird	E	
Woofe, Jesse	G				
Woolfe, Jesse	G				
Work,	A				
Woseta, Jo.	E				

2nd Regiment, Cherokee Mounted Volunteers, (Adair's Regiment, Cherokee Mounted Rifles)

This regiment was formed near Fort Davis in July, 1861. It served under Watie's Command. Most of Watie's command were mixed bloods. Originally it was part of 1st Cherokee Mounted Rifles. Because of the social and economic connections between the regiments officers and citizens of neighboring states, the organization contained white recruits from northwestern Arkansas and southwestern Missouri. Watie's Regiment would remain completely faithful to him and the Confederacy serving the duration of the war.

It was reformed 3 February 1863 at Prairie Springs, Creek Nation (winter camp of Indian Cavalry Brigade, 15 miles southeast of Fort Gibson), by the consolidation of Bryan's 1st Battalion, Cherokee Partisan Rangers, and five companies attached to Watie's 1st Cherokee Mounted Volunteers.

Adair, William P.	F&S	Colonel
Bell, James M.	F&S	Lieutenant Colonel
Eubanks, William	F&S	Captain
Mays, Joel B.	F&S	Acting Quartermaster
Timberlake, A.W.	F&S	Quartermaster Sergeant
Adair, Walter T.	F&S	Surgeon
Colley, Thomas M.	F&S	Surgeon
Payden, Harrison J.	F&S	Assistant Surgeon
Dun, W.C.	F&S	Assistant Surgeon
White, Robert	F&S	Assistant Surgeon
Corn, E. L.	F&S	Chaplain
Martin, Richard F.	F&S	Acting Commissary of Subsistence
Brewer, O.H.P.	F	Lieutenant Colonel
Bryan, J.M.		Major
Hammack, T.P.	A,E	Major
Hammock, Porter	A,E	Major
Vann, John	I	Major
Acridge, William H.	G	Captain
Adair, E.M.	D,K	Captain
Alberty, B.W.	B	Captain
Brewer, Geo. W.		Captain
Harden, J. R.	C	Captain

Hardin, J. R.	C	Captain
Holt, C.H.		Captain
Holt, Charles		Captain
Martin, Joseph L.	D	Captain
Miller, John	E,A	Captain
Patton, D.C.	E	Captain
Phagan, J.W. -		Captain/Acting Quartermaster
Shannon, W. H.	H	Captain
Shannon, William H.	H	Captain
Wafford, Alexander	D	Captain
Bell, J.M.	B	First Lieutenant
Benge, James	D	First Lieutenant
Burge, James	B	First Lieutenant
Brewer, Tho. F.	F	First Lieutenant
Flinn, T.D.	A,E	First Lieutenant
Hendren, W. H.	C	First Lieutenant
Hendron, W. H.	C	First Lieutenant
McGhee, T.J.	G	First Lieutenant
Miller, Robt.		First Lieutenant
Pickler, Jessee F.	H-A	First Lieutenant
Scales, Joab A.	F	First Lieutenant/Adjutant
Spencer, J.W.T.	D	First Lieutenant
Spencer, John W.	1 D	First Lieutenant
Taylor, William M.	HAC	First Lieutenant
Wlaker, Cary	I	First Lieutenant
Beck, R.D.	F	Brevet Second Lieutenant
Brewer, W.S.	F	Second Lieutenant
Brewer, Wm. S.	F	Second Lieutenant
Collins, William	K,D	Second Lieutenant
Davis, J.P.	I	Second Lieutenant
Drew, Charles	I	Second Lieutenant
Falkner, D.M.	B	Second Lieutenant
Folker, D.M.	B	Second Lieutenant
Forkner, David	B	Second Lieutenant
Kell, L.R.	D	Second Lieutenant
Kell, Lewis	D,B	Second Lieutenant
Lewis, A. G.	H,A	Second Lieutenant
McGee, Albert	G	Second Lieutenant
McGhee, A.S.	G	Second Lieutenant
Percifield, M.	C	Second Lieutenant

Piercifield, Marlin	C	Second Lieutenant
Rodgers, Lewis	G	Second Lieutenant
Vanhoy, J.F.	A	Second Lieutenant
Vanhoy, J.S.	A	Second Lieutenant
Vann, D.R.	K	Second Lieutenant
Mayers, William	B	Third Lieutenant
McCrary, Jonathan	K	Third Lieutenant
McCravy, John	K	Third Lieutenant
Ballinger, A. G.	C	Lieutenant
Ballinger, Archiles	C	Lieutenant
Ballinger, A. G.	C	Lieutenant
Ballinger, Archiles	C	Lieutenant
Condon, M. C.		Lieutenant/Drillmaster
Dickson, J. Mc.	E	Lieutenant
Greenway, Andrew J.	D	Lieutenant
Greenway, Andrew J.	D	Lieutenant
McCall, L.A.	E	Lieutenant
Miller, Jack		Lieutenant
Miller, R.A.	E	Lieutenant
Berk, J.W.	D	Sergeant Major
Burk, J.W.	D	Sergeant Major
Lindsay, Walter	H	Sergeant Major
Baxter, William	C	First Sergeant
Bean, Mark	K	First Sergeant
Bearert, James	A	First Sergeant
Denton, B.F.	H	First Sergeant
Hewbanks, William	B	First Sergeant
Hubanks, William	B	First Sergeant
Mason, John	C	First Sergeant
McCoy, J.C.	I	First Sergeant
Nevins, M.S.	F	First Sergeant
Preston, C.H.C.	G	First Sergeant
Shannon, J. L.	H	First Sergeant
Adair, R.B.	K	Sergeant
Butlar, Huy	B	Sergeant
Cannon, L. J.	A	Sergeant
Canon, L. J.	A	Sergeant
Chambers, William	B	Sergeant
Coodey, W. S.	I	Sergeant
Dick, Ellis	G	Sergeant
Drew, William H.	K	Sergeant
Eallett, W.A.	D	Sergeant

Elliott, W.A.	D	Sergeant
Gailey, Joseph	E	Sergeant
Godard, J.W.	H	Sergeant
Guiss, T.C.	I	Sergeant
Hanks, C.J.	I	Sergeant
Hayes, John	F	Sergeant
Heffington, James	G	Sergeant
Henderson, William	G	Sergeant
Lee, John	B	Sergeant
Lewis, G. W.	H	Sergeant
Mayes, R.T.	K	Sergeant
McBride, W.D.	H	Sergeant
McClatchey, J.L.	H	Sergeant
McCoy, S.W.	I	Sergeant
McDaniel, R.R.	D	Sergeant
McDaniel, Robert	D	Sergeant
Miller, R.F.	H	Sergeant
Patton, J.D.	E	Sergeant
Patton, James	E	Sergeant
Plemmons, S.J.B.	C	Sergeant
Porter, J.C.	F	Sergeant
Russell, A. Mc	C	Sergeant
Shannon, H. J.	H	Sergeant
Stringfield, E.P.	A	Sergeant
Thompson, William	E	Sergeant
Vann, David	F	Sergeant
White, J.G.	A	Sergeant
Wilson, W. F.	C	Sergeant
Wilkinson, J. W.	E	Sergeant
Wilkinson, Jasper	E	Sergeant
Williams, George	E	Sergeant
Payne, William P.	F	Ordnance Sergeant
Allen, Huston	D	Corporal
Bateston, N. S.	H	Corporal
Bell, J.S.	B	Corporal
Booth, John L.	A	Corporal
Bowls, James	I	Corporal
Buchannan, George	E	Corporal
Clark, H.J.	A	Corporal
Davis, M.W.	C	Corporal
Divine, A.	K	Corporal
Dowing, George	I	Corporal

Name	Company	Rank
Downing, George	I	Corporal
Elleatt, George	D	Corporal
Elliott, George	D	Corporal
Galyean, Noah	E	Corporal
Graham, Silas	A	Corporal
Harlen, John	B	Corporal
Haslet, F. M.	C	Corporal
Haslet, G. W.	C	Corporal
Hastings, John W.	E	Corporal
Hicks, Nathan	B	Corporal
Hinam, William	B	Corporal
Hynam, William	B	Corporal
Isgrigg, William	H	Corporal
January, B.F.	C	Corporal
Johnson, James	K	Corporal
Kettle, John	I	Corporal
Keys, William	F	Corporal
Love, James	H	Corporal
Minor, W.R.	A	Corporal
Phillips, John	C	Corporal
Rhotramelle, A.J.	E	Corporal
Rhotramelle, James H.	E	Corporal
Shook, James	B	Corporal
Shields, William	G	Corporal
Sims, B.F.	G	Corporal
Smith, J.A.	K	Corporal
Snake Gerty,	I	Corporal
Solomon, Jarad	E	Corporal
Spaniard, A.M.	1 F	Corporal
Steel, Samuel	G	Corporal
Thompson, William	F	Corporal
Tinker, J.E.	F	Corporal
Vann, John	K	Corporal
Walker, James	H	Corporal
Ward, Van	G	Corporal
Fair, S.T.	C	Adjutant
Payden, M.J.	H	Assistant Surgeon
Marrs, Frank	H	Hospital Steward
Marrs, J.F.	H	Hospital Steward
Walker, H.L.	C	Drillmaster

Burgess, T.O.	H	Bugler

Privates

Acorn, James	B	Baker, J.C.	E
Adair, G.W.	K	Baker, James	E
Adair, George	K	Baker, Lewis	E
Adair, J.M.	K	Balard, Marcus	B
Adair, John	B	Ballard, Markus	B
Adair, John B.	B	Ballard, Samuel	D
Adair, John R.	F	Ballou, William	E
Adams, Anderson	A	Banks, John	E
Adkins, S.	A	Barbery, David	I
Agnew, W.S.	B	Barbery, Peter	I
Ah lee cho,	I	Bark, Wert	D
Alberty, A.	K	Barnes, Henry	F
Alberty, Eli	B	Barnes, James	F
Alberty, Ely	B	Badman,	I
Alberty, G.A.	H	Bailey, A.	DHK
Alberty, Geo.	K	Baily, A.	DHK
Alberty, J.	K	Bain, A.J.	K
Alberty, J.C.	B	Baker, C.W.	E
Alberty, J.T.	B	Baker, J.C.	E
Alberty, John	B	Baker, James	E
Alburty, George	B,K	Baker, Lewis	E
Alison, James	D	Balard, Marcus	B
Allerson, James	D	Ballard, Markus	B
Allick,	G	Ballard, Samuel	D
Anderson, A.J.	K	Ballou, William	E
Andrew, L.	K	Banks, John	E
Andrews, William	A	Barbery, David	I
Applegate, James	F	Barbery, Peter	I
Arnold, George	I	Bark, Wert	D
Arnold, William	I	Barnes, Henry	F
Ashes, Joseph	I	Barnes, James	F
Austin, Elijah	E	Barnett, F. M.	C
Austin, W.B.	E	Barnett, Marion	B
Badman,	I	Bartlet, J. B.	H
Bailey, A.	DHK	Baugh, L.	D
Baily, A.	DHK	Baxter, WilliamA	
Bain, A.J.	K	Beale, Albert	E
Baker, C.W.	E	Beaman,	I

Bean, J.E.		K	Bowls, George		I
Bean, J.M.		K	Bowls, John		I
Bean, Jefferson		F	Bowls, Johnson		I
Bean, R.B.		F	Bowls, P.O.		I
Beans, William		A	Bowls, Samuel		I
Beares, William		A	Bradley, John		C
Beaver, Alleck		G	Bradshaw, A.		K
Beaver, John		G	Branie, Eli		C
Beavert, William		F	Brannock, C.W.		E
Beck, Elis		F	Breshirs, David		G
Beck, Jesse		F	Brewer, I.		K
Beck, Joseph R.		A	Bridges, John		C
Bell, G.T.		H	Brisco, J.E.		
Bell, James		H	Brisco, James		C
Bell, John		D	Britches,		B
Bell, Louis		H	Brovohill, G.W.		C
Benge, Mc.		B	Brown, H.N.		C
Benge, Samuel		F	Brown, J.J.		C
Bennette, Joseph		H	Brown, Jacob		A,H
Benton, J.S.F.		C	Brown, R.B.		A
Bergan, Logan		E,C	Brown, W.J.		C
Bigby, B.F.		K	Brown, William		F
Bigby, B.F.		K	Broyhill, G.W.		C
Bigby, B.J.W.		H	Bryant, Sam		D
Bigby, B.J.W.		H	Buck, Gerty		I
Bigby, J.L.		K	Buck, Girty		I
Bigby, J.L.		K	Buckett, James		C
Bigby, Thomas		K	Buffington, William		B
Bigby, Thomas		K	Bullfrog, Robert		I
Binge, R.		B	Burgess, G.W.		H
Blair, J.		B	Burgess, J.W.		H
Bledsaw, Joseph		G	Burgess, T.H.		H
Bledsoe, Alonzo		G	Burgess, W.W.		H
Bledsoe, Joseph		G	Burgin, G.P.		C
Blevins, Burrel		G	Burgin, Logan		E,C
Boatwrite, W.J.		C	Burgin, Merrit		C
Boggs, Richard		F	Bushyhead, D.C.		H
Boggs, Wilson		F	Butler, M.		B
Boling, Jackson		G	Butler, William		B
Boling, John		G	Byers, George		H
Bowers, Lewis		F	Cadwell, Jackson		G
Bowling, Jackson		G	Cagle, S.		K

Cah la ho yah,	I	Crain,	I
Campbell, Samuel	F	Crane, William	B
Canoe, George	B	Crawford, Virgil	D
Carl, T. R.	C	Cridington, Chs.	B
Carr, William	A	Cridington, James	B
Carrybare,	I	Critenden, George	H,K
Carter, B. W.	H	Critenden, John	K
Carter, J. R.	F	Crittenden, George W.	H,K
Cate, Nose	I	Crittenden, John	K
Catron, Lafayette	F	Crittendon, George	H,K
Cham,	A	Crittenton, James	B
Chambers, B.	D	Crofford, Verge	D
Chambers, L. D.	B	Cross, John	I
Chandler, James	K	Crossland, Samuel	F
Choat, George	D	Crump, J. S.	D
Chote, George	D	Crump, John S.	D
Chouch, Samuel	D	Cunningham, C.	B
Citaha, Chas.	C	Daniel, William	B
Citaha, Geo.	C	Dannenberg, J.H.	K
Clark, J.H.	A	Daugherty, John	K
Clay, W.E.	A	Daugherty, W.	C
Clayton, J.W.	A	Daugherty,	B
Clayton, Samuel	E	Daughtry, W.V.	H
Clines, C. W.	B	Davis, Cornelius	H
Clynes, C. W.	B	Davis, Frank M.	D
Clynes, Eli	B	Davis, Henry	F
Coats, George	D	Davis, William H.	K,D
Cogswell, David	D	Dawson, Joseph	B
Coker, Randolph J.	D	DeArman, Huston	F
Colbert, William C.	F	Delaney, John	H
Colby, L. W.	B	Delany, James	H
Coldwell, B.	H	Denton, G.O.	H
Coleman, John	I	Denton, Marke	B
Comings, J. W.	H	Denton, T.S.	C
Condon, Michael	G	Derrett, M.	A
Coody, Arch	F	Dick, Isaac	G
Cook, L. R.	A	Divine, C.	K
Cordry, C.	B	Divine, R.	K
Cordry, Seburn	B	Dohtry, W.V.	H
Couch, S. M.	D	Dority, Washington	C
Cox, Alfred	H	Dowing, Joseph	I
Craig, James	A	Downing, David	I

Downing, Edward	I		Finley, John	H
Downing, Joseph	I		Finley, Ruben	A
Downing, T.J.	A		Finly, R.	A
Downing, Walter	B		Fisher, A	K
Downnin, T.J.	A		Fisher, Benjamin	K
Drake, J.W.	H		Fisher, George	K
Duck, John	G		Fitswaters, A.W.	H
Dunagan, T.J.	H		Fitswaters, Henry	H
Dunagan, W.H.	H		Flyaway,	I
Dunham, Sanford	A		Foil, R.	K
Dupreest, William	D		Foils, Robert	K
Edon, James	A		Ford, H.M.	A
Edward, Robert	A		Foreman, E.	K
Edwards, E.	A		Foreman, Elias	H
Edwards, John	E		Foreman, S.J.	I
Edwards, Richard	E		Foreman, Samuel	B
Edwards, S.	C		Foreman, William	B
Eleson, S.C.	A		Forman, Samuel	B
Eliott, O.P.	A		Forman, William	B
Elip,	G		Francis, John	D
Elleatt, Arch	D		Frasier, George	G
Eller, J.M.	C		Frazier, J.D.	D
Ellick,	G		Frisley, George	B
Elliott, Archey	D		Gafford, Allen	B
Ellip,	G		Gafford, Jesse	B
Elms, E.O.	A		Gage, Jefferson	D
Elms, William M.	A		Gailey, Augustus	E
Evins, William	C		Gailey, Lucien	E
Fair, E.F.	C		Gailey, Warren	E
Fair, G.F.	C		Galyean, Randolph	E
Fargo, C.	B		Galyean, Riley	E
Farley, L.L.	G		Garrett, J.H.	A
Few, John	B		Gholson, George	E
Fields, A.	K		Gholson, John	C
Fields, Ezekiel	G		Gilley, F.M.	C
Fields, G.W.	G		Given, M.	C
Fields, George	G		Gnat,	I
Fields, Henry	G		Godard, William R.	A
Fields, James	G		Gordon, Alex	K
Fields, Mathew	G		Gorgers, James	A
Fields, Thompson	G		Gott, George	F
Fiew, John	B		Gracen, Burk	E

Graham, G.B.	C		Hayes, William	F
Graham, Green B.	C		Hayward, Jackson	C
Graham, J.B.	C		Henry, J. C.	G
Graham, J.T.	C		Henry, Joseph	G
Graham, Seabron S.	A		Henson, James	D
Graham, William	A		Hestang, M. M.	E
Gray, J.C.	H		Hicks, Andrew	B
Gray, Nelson	C		Higden, J. S.	C
Gray, W.S.	H		Hilderbrand, Mike	F
Greer, T.B.	H		Hilderbrand, Reece	F
Grey, Nelson	C		Hilderbrand, Stephen	F
Griffin, Jack	I		Hill, B. P. F.	F
Griffin, Jackson	H		Hisaw, J. H.	K
Griffin, Richard	D		Hisaw, J.H.	K
Grimsley, J.B.	H		Hodge, Jackson	H
Guilliams, William	H		Hodge, Oliver	H
Gun Rod, Driver	B		Hogue, Erastus S.	F
Guthrie, C.P.	K		Hollin, M.	B,K
Guthrie, Calvin	K		Hollond, M.	B
Hadley, Thomas	G		Holstetler, Stephen	I
Hagan, Shadrach	E		Holt, David	E
Halcomb, G.G.	A		Holt, James Henry	E
Hallon, M.	B,K		Homan, Jonathan	H
Hammack, W.R.	A		Honea, W.W.	G,C
Hanks, R.T.	F		Hood, Henry	B
Hardcastle, J. F.	C		Hood, James	F
Hardwick, F. E. P.	C		Horn, J.D.	D
Hardwick, G. A.	C		Horn, Jerry	K
Hardwick, G. R.	C		Hosmer, Clinton	F
Harlin, Dewite	B		Hosmer, Solomon	F
Harmon, B. H.	C		House, Henry	D
Harmon, James	C		Howdershell, U.M.	E
Harmon, Z. M.	C		Howdyshell, H.M.	E
Harris, Daniel	I		Howrz, D.J.	A
Harris, Elijah	I		Hubbard, Newton	F
Harris, R. D.	I		Huffman, H.F.	H
Hart, J. B.	C		Hughs, A.B.	H
Harvey, O. H.	A		Hughs, J.L.	A
Harvy, O. H.	A		Hughs, S.H.	A
Haslet, J. G.	C		Hunter, Juni	G
Hastings, W. A. T.	C		Hurley, E.R.	C
Hatchet, Ned	D		Ingland, Pinson	G

Inlow, John	F		Lawson, J. H.	A
Jackson, Carroll	G		Leaf,	I
Jackson, J.H.	G		Lee, Arch	B
Jackson, T.J.	G		Lee, James	F
Jackson, Walter	I		Lee, Thomas	B
James, G.W.	A		Leiver,	B
January, J.C.	C		Lewis, Newton	H
Jeffres, M.N.	C		Linder, E. O.	F
Johnson, D.R.	C		Linder, Julius	F
Johnson, I.	K		Lindsley, Waldemar	
Johnson, J.B.	K		Lite, John	B
Johnson, James	A		Liver,	B
Johnson, T.	A		Lizzenbe, Charles	G
Johnson, W.T.	A		Lizzenbe, G. W.	G
Jones, G.M.	H		Lizzenby, Ely	G
Jones, G.W.	A		Lonagin, R. D.	A
Jones, Wilbern	G		Looney, William	F
Jones, William	K		Loux, Henry	C
Jordan, John	F		Love, George	H
Katcherside, W.H.	H		Lovelace, T.A.	H
Kell, John	F		Lovett, Archibald	F
Kelly, J.H.	K		Lovett, James	F
Kelly, J.L.	A		Lovett, John	F
Kelly, Jasper	H		Low, H.	K
Kerskerluskie,	B		Lowrey, George W.	F
Kerskuluski,	B		Lucus, William	F
Kettle, Rainer	I		Lybe, William L.	A
Killian, Jesse	H		Mackey, A.	K
Kindrick, O.	A		Maloy, Henry	A
Kingcade, W.A.	G		Maloy, John	A
Knight, A.	B		Maloy, R.M.	A
Knight, R. W.	B		Maloy, William	A
Knight, Richard	B		Marcum, A.	A
Kuskerlesky,	B		Marshall, Thomas	G
Lamar, J. R.	K		Marshall, W.B.	G
Landrun, H. T.	D		Marshall, William	F
Langley, L.	B		Martin, Alman	F
Langly, L.	B		Martin, John	F
Lastley, Joe V.	F		Math,	G
Latta, Allen	D		Mathes, John A.	G
Latty, T. J.	E		Matoy, John	K
Latty, William	E		May, James	E

May, John	E		McPherson, Hughy	F
Mayes, James	H,K		McPherson, John	K
Mayfield, S.E.	K		McPherson, John V.	K
Mayfield, Walker	B		McPherson, S.	H,K
Mays, G.W.	B		McPhierson, Silus	H,K
McCall, James	C		McWhorter, William	A
McCartey, Timothy	H		Meece, J.H.	A
McClure, G.W.	H		Meice, James	A
McCord, Samuel	H		Millboy,	I
McCoy, John A.	I		Miller, A.	K
McCracken,	B		Miller, B.F.	A
McCracken,	B		Miller, Calvin	H
McDaniel, J.P.	A		Miller, Daniel	G
McDaniel, Joel	B		Miller, W.W.	K
McDaniel, John	I		Mills, J.L.	G
McDaniel, Joseph	F		Millsap, W.R.	H
McGarah, C.M.	A		Millsop, W.F.	H
McGarah, William	A		Milton, William	I
McGee, James	K		Mitchel, James	G
McGhee, David	G		Moor, Gerrn	A
McGhee,	G		Moore, D.F.	A
McGilliam, Wiley	H		Moore, James R.	A
McGuilliams, W.	H		More, James	G
McHeard, Richard	B		More, Solomon	G
McHerd, R.	B		Morgan, James	K,D
McKiney, Peter	H,D		Morgan, Joseph	H
McKisick, Greer	E		Morris, John	F
McLain, Calvin	F		Morris,	G
McLain, John	F		Mosely, John	F
McLain, Joseph	F		Mosier, A.C.	E
McLaughlan, David	D		Moulder, A.J.	A
McLaughlan, E.C.	D		Mush,	I
McLaughlin, David	D		Musrat, Joseph	G
McLaughlin, E.C.	D		Musrat, Wilson	G
McLaughlin, William	D		Neal, Richard	I
McMurphy, P.	K		Newton, H.A.	H
McMurtry, John	G		Nidiffer, Marcus	C
McMurtry, Joseph	G		Nidiffer, Moses	C
McNair, D.O.	A		Nivens, M.D.	F
McNair, John	D		Noblet, William	C
McNite, T.C.	H		Null, James	K,H
McNully, G.W.	D		O'Riley, John	I

Odle, J.S.	C		Pouch, Thomas	G
Oo wa Sal lee,	I		Presley, Thomas	K
Ool Skinnee,	I		Pressley, J.	K
Oolscuntnie 2d,	I		Pressley, T.	K
Ore, James	F		Pressly, Joshus	K
Ore, Joseph	F		Price, H.B.	B
Pack, William S.	B		Ragsdale, John	B
Packe, W.S.	B		Ragsdale, John	H
Paden, A.T.	H,K		Raper, George	G
Paden, Ben	K		Reader, A.G.	C
Paden, William	K		Renfroe, Robert	C
Page, James E.	A		Reynolds, Anderson	F
Parmer, Jack	D		Rhotramelle, D.W.	E
Parrish, John T.	A		Rhotramelle, Henry	E
Pass, Edward	E		Rhotramelle, J.L.	E
Pate, Richard	B		Rhotramelle, William	E
Patrick, John	F		Riley, Johnson	F
Patton, Samuel	E		Riley, Joseph	I
Payden, Taylor	H,K		Riley, P.A.	I
Percifield, S.M	C		Riley, Randolph	F
Perry, Benjamin	G		Roach, William	D
Perry, Joseph	F		Roberts, B.F.	G
Person, William	E		Roberts, John	A
Persons, John	E		Roberts, Lewis	B
Petit, Levi	B		Roberts, Louis	B
Petit, Thomas	B		Roberts, M.H.	B
Pettett, William	F		Roberts, William	A
Pettit Jr., Thomas	B		Robertson, Joseph	G
Phillipps, John	A		Robinson, W.P	H
Phillipps, W.C.	A		Rogers, Charles	F
Phillips, J.H.	C		Rogers, J.L.	G
Phillips, William	C		Rogers, James	F
Pierce, John	C		Rogers, John	F
Pierce, L.D.	C		Rogers, John	F
Pierce, W.C.	C		Rogers, Joseph	D
Pierce, W.P.	C		Rogers, Joseph	G
Pigeon, -	B		Rogers, N.B.	D
Poage, David	G		Rogers, Napoleon	D
Poorbear, John	K		Rogers, Nelson	D
Pope, John	B		Rogers, T.L.	F
Porum, David	I		Ross, Andrew	B
Posey, Edward	E		Ross, Commador	B

Ross, John	G
Ross, S.	B
Runnels, Gid	I
Russell, J. B.	C
Rutledge, Little B.	A
Rutlege, Littleberry	A
Sa tan Kee, -	I
Sanders, C.	K
Sanders, Conelius	B
Sanders, George	B
Sanders, John	I
Sanders, Joshua	B
Sanders, Robert	B
Sanders, T. D.	I
Sanders, Wilson	B
Saunders, M. D.	H
Sawyers, Thomas	A
Schrimsher, John	G
Scott, Noah	F
Seabolt, David	B
Seabolt, George	K
Seabolt, Jerry	K
Sebolt, David	B
Setser, J. W.	C
Setser, W. A.	C
Seviers, John	F
Seymour, James	H
Shannon, F. M.	H
Shannon, James H.	H
Shepherd, William	F
Shervill, J. S.	A
Shotpouch, -	G
Simco, C.	B
Simco, Ganes	B
Simco, Josephus	B
Simpson, James	K
Small Dirt,	D
Smith, A.H.	H
Smith, Berton	H
Smith, Franklin	F
Smith, J.	A
Smith, Jack	D

Smith, James R.	A
Smith, John	H
Smith, Lemuel.J.W.	H
Smith, T.J.	H
Smoker, Gordon	I
Socer, Paul	F
Sooter, W.L.	C
Spanyard, John	B
Spanyard, William	1 B
Spirey, James F.	1 A
Spiry, James F.	A
Stancil, L.	B
Starr, C.	K
Starr, Charles	F
Starr, E.	K
Starr, Ellis	F
Starr, Ezekiel	F
Starr, Henry	F
Starr, James	I
Starr, James	K
Starr, W.	K
Steadman, John	I,F
Stedman, John	I,F
Steel, R.	K
Still, John	F
Stoneroad, Thomas	B
Stonroad, Thomas	B
Stonsil, Louis	B
Stool,	I
Stout, C.M.	K
Stout, John	K
Stout, W.W.	H
Stud, Gerty	I
Sturtevant, M.B.	F
Sunday,	I
Sunday,	I
Surwakee,	B
Suton, Ely	B
Suton, Joshua	B
Tassel, Bird	G
Tassel,	I
Taylor, J.N.	H,K

Taylor, John	H,K		Ward, J.W.	K,D
Taylor, Joshua	F		Ward, John	E
Taylor, William B.	B,K		Ward, Martin	G
Taylor,	I		Ward, Samuel	G
Thomas, F.	C		Ward, Samuel	H
Thomas, Floyd	C		Ward, Jr., William	E
Thomas, P.N.	E		Ward, Sr., William	E
Thomas, William T.	A		Warford, Richard	I
Thompson, R.H.F.	B		Warford, Robert	B
Thornsberry, Jackson	A		Warspeaker, William	I
Thornton, Calvin	B		Washington, George	F
Thornton, John J.	F		Waters, Robert	B
Thurman, A.J.	A		Watts, Thomas	I
Tickerneeskee, George	K		Weber, G.E.	A
Tickerneskee, George	K		West, F.B.	C
Timberlage, Ritchard	B		West, J.D.	K,C
Tobacco, J.D.	I		West, J.R.	C
Trevett, William	D		West, J.W.	C
Trott, T.B.	D		West, T.L.	C
Trout, George	G		West, W.R.	C
Tucker, Levi	D		West, William	A
Twister,	I		Whinery, A.J.	C
Tyner, Ruben	H		Whinery, C.	C
Tyner, Seborn	H		Whitacre, William	H
Vance, Richard	D		White, B.	A
Vane, Johnson	B		White, D.F.	C
Vann, Ephraim	D		White, Henry	A
Vann, Jesse	I		White, J.R.	A
Vann, Joe G.	D		White, J.W.	C
Vann, Johnson	B		White, N.	C
Vann, Johnson	F		White, Noah	C
Vann, Moses	I		White, Samuel	A
Vann, Webster	D		Wiate, Joseph	B
Vann, William	F		Wilkerson, Hill	G
Walken, Wolf	B		Wilkerson, William	G
Walker, -	B		Wilkins, Joseph	H
Walker, Calvin	K H		Wilkinson, J. M.	E
Walker, W.C.	K-H		Wilkinson, James	E
Walking, Wolfe	B		Wilkinson, William	E
Ward, Flem F.	E		Williams, Franklin	F
Ward, H.C.	E		Williams, H. C.	C
Ward, J.F.	E		Williams, John	K

Williams, Marion	E	Woods, J. C.	G
Williams, Moses	H,D	Woods, William	K,H
Williams, Samuel	E	Word, James	K,D
Wilson, J. C.	C	Wright, A. T.	A
Wilson, James H.	E	Wright, John	B
Wilson, W. E.	H	Wrinkel,	B
Winingham, H. L.	A	Wrinkle,	B
Winingham, W. C.	A	Write, John	B
Witt, F. N.	K	Wyatt, Joseph	B
Wolf, Andrew	B	Yancy, H.	K
Wolfe, Andy	B	Yarberry, Henderson	C
Wood, W. J.	K,H	Young, Otter	I

2nd Cherokee Artillery Company

This artillery company got their battery: three twelve pound howitzers and a 2.2.1 pound brass rifle, early in 1863. One twelve pounder was lost in Elk Creek after the battle of Honey Springs. And found by the Federals while searching for dead. Three other guns were added, but their sources are not known. One gun burst by over charging at the capture of the steamer, J. R. WILLIAMS, on June 15, 1864 and the others were surrendered to the United States at the close of the war.

Foreman, Alexander	Captain
Lee, Roswell W.	Captain:
Forrester, Henry	First Lieutenant
Gregg, J. W.	First Lieutenant
Taylor, William	Second Lieutenant
Lindsey, Riley Wise	Second Lieutenant
Reese, John,	Orderly Sergeant
Clark, Taylor	Orderly Sergeant
Vann, John R.	Orderly Sergeant

Privates

Alberty, George W.	Hicks, Charles
Arseena	Hurd, Richard
Bacon, Bailey	Ice Nitts
Bacon, John	Marshall, John
Baker, J. Riley	Ootlenowi
Barnard, Robert	Peter, Thomas
Benge, Samuel	Phillips, William
Bigby, Thomas	Polk, John
Bledsoe, Alonzo	Proctor, Isaac
Brower, James	Rider Cloud
Campreau, John	Seymore, James
Clark, J. Hilary	Silk, Lee
Crane, William	Smith, McCoy
Crittenden, James	Solomon, Ketcher
Deadrick, William	Taylor, William
Doghead, John	Walker, William Brush
Edwards, Cap	Wilkerson, James

Womack, William

Cherokee Mounted Rifles

This information is not complete. There are parts of Companies A - I, Cherokee Mounted Rifles. On July 12, 1861, Stand Watie received a commission from Brig Gen Benjamin McCulloch to raise a regiment. At a mass meeting of the southern sympathizers among the Five Civilized tribes held at Old Fort Wayne, Delaware District, in the Cherokee Nation, on July 27, 1861, organization of the First Cherokee Regiment began. After the twelve-month enlistment time expired, the regiment was reorganized around 12 July 1862 at Spavinaw Creek, Tahlequah District, for 2 years, with mostly new officers and many new men. Note that the companies were not reorganized separately, rather a set of new companies were formed and new officers elected, although the majority of the men continued in service from the first organization.

Watie, Stand		Colonel
Buzzard,		First Lieutenant
Saugee, Wilson		Second Lieutenant
Watie, Charles E.		Third Lieutenant
Forrester, Henry		Orderly Sergeant
Adair, Ephriam Martin	G	Captain
Alberty, Bluford West	I	Captain
Bell, James Madison	D	Captain
Brewer, Thomas Fox	C	Captain
Brewer. 0. H. P.	C	Captain
Coody, Daniel Ross	C	Captain
Johnson, George W.	I	Captain
Mayes, John Thompson	H	Captain
Parks, Robert Calvin	B	Captain
Spears, John	K	Captain
Starr, George Harlan	G	Captain
Thompson, James	L	Captain
Thompson, Joseph Franklin	E	Captain
Watie, Charles E.	A	Captain
Wofford, Alexander	G	Captain
Adair, Ephriam Martin	G	First Lieutenant
Benge, James	I	First Lieutenant
Brewer, 0. H. P.	C	First Lieutenant
Brewer, Thomas Fox	C	First Lieutenant

Name	Co.	Rank
Faulkner, David McNair	I	First Lieutenant
Foster, —	K	First Lieutenant
Gott, John	G	First Lieutenant
Lynch, Joseph Martin	D	First Lieutenant
McGee, Thomas Jefferson	E	First Lieutenant
McKizzick, Daniel	H	First Lieutenant
Starr, Joseph McMinn Jr.	G	First Lieutenant
Vann, Ephraim	B	First Lieutenant
Wright, John R.	G	First Lieutenant
Bell, John Martin	I	Second Lieutenant
Brewer, William Snow	C	Second Lieutenant
Buzzardflopper, Martin	B	Second Lieutenant
Catterson, William	H	Second Lieutenant
Crossland, Richard	C	Second Lieutenant
Faulkner, David McNair	I	Second Lieutenant
Lynch, Joseph Martin	G	Second Lieutenant
Raper, John A.	D	Second Lieutenant
Starr, Ezekial	G	Second Lieutenant
Wawaseet Stand,	E	Second Lieutenant
Weaver, Lewis	K	Second Lieutenant
Wofford, Alexander	G	Second Lieutenant
Bean, Mark	G	Third Lieutenant
Beck, Reliford	C	Third Lieutenant
Candy Reese	A	Third Lieutenant
England, Pinson	D	Third Lieutenant
Foreman, William Y. H.	E	Third Lieutenant
Hendron, William H.	H	Third Lieutenant
Johnson, Andrew Cummings	G	Third Lieutenant
O'Fields Dumplin	A	Third Lieutenant
Wilkerson, Thomas	G	Third Lieutenant
Wilkerson, Thomas	K.	Third Lieutenant
Adair, Hugh Montgomery.	D	Orderly Sergeant
Danenburg, John Henry	G	Orderly Sergeant
Daniel, William Adolphus	E	Orderly Sergeant
Eubanks, William	I	Orderly Sergeant
Forrester, Henry	A	Orderly Sergeant
Myers, William	I	Orderly Sergeant
Root, —	G	Orderly Sergeant
Scales, Joseph Absalom	C	Orderly Sergeant
Stewart, John	H	Orderly Sergeant
Vann, John R.	G	Orderly Sergeant

Privates

Adair, Benjamin Franklin	D		Beck, Jeffrey	C
Adair, George Washington	G		Beck, John	G
Adair, Hugh Montgomery	G		Beck, Joseph	G
Adair, James	G		Beck, Releford	G
Adair, Jesse M.	G		Beck, Samuel	E
Adair, Jesse	G		Beck, Surry Eaton	C
Adair, John Bell	G		Beck, Weatherford	C
Adair, John Bell	I		Bell, David Jarrette	D
Adair, Oscar Fitzaland	G		Bell, George	D
Adair, Rufus Bell	G		Bell, James	G
Adair, William Penn	D		Bell, John	D
Adair, Benjamin Franklin	G		Bell, John	G
Adams, John	D		Bell, Lucien Burr	A
Agnew, Walter Scott	I		Benge, Samuel	C
Alberty, Andrew	G		Bennett, Simpson G	C
Alberty, George W.	I		Bigby, Benjamin Jackson	G
Alberty, George	G		Bigby, James Lafayette	G
Alberty, Jesse Clinton	G		Bigby, Thomas W.	G
Alberty, Jesse Clinton	I		Blake, James	G
Alberty, John	G		Bledsoe, Joseph	E
Alberty, Joshua	G		Bledsoe, Lorenzo	E
Alexander, John	G		Bledsoe, Thomas	E
Arseenee,	D		Blevins, Luke	E
Bacon, Bailey	G		Boggs, Richard	C
Badger or Trott, James	I		Boggs, Wilson	C
Ballard, Archibald	A		Boot,	E
Ballard, William	H		Brewer, Richard	C
Baugh, John H.	I		Bright, Samuel	E
Beamer, Alexander	E		Brower, James	D
Bean, Cornelius	G		Brown, Bruce	C
Bean, John Ellis	G		Brown, John	G
Bean, Joseph McMinn	G		Brown, William Edwin	C
Bean, Mark	G		Brown, William Edwin	G
Bean, Pleasant	C		Buck, Moses	E
Bean, Russell	C		Buffington, George	H
Bean, William	G		Buffington, Jonathan	G
Beatty, William	C		Bumgarner, John W.	G
Beavert, William	C		Bumgarner, John W.	K
Beck, David McLaughlin	G		Burgess, Jesse Bean	C
Beck, Ellis	C		Burkett, David	B

Burkett, James	B
Burkett, James	E
Butler, James Leon	B
Butler, William	I
Byers, George	G
Byers, Nicholas I	G
Caldwell, Jack	E
Campbell, Charles H.	C
Carey, Edmond Duncan	A
Carey, Ross Thomas	E
Carselowry, James	G
Catron, Lafayette	C
Chambers, L. D.	I
Chambus, Lorenzo D.	C
Chandler, James	G
Choate, James	G
Chouteau, Gesseau	D
Chuwalooka	D
Chuwanosky	E
Clyne, Cornelius	G
Clyne, Cornelius	I
Clyne, Joel M. B.	G
Coats, Charles	D
Coats, John	D
Colby, James	I
Collins, James	G
Colston,	E
Condon, Michael	E
Conner, Caleb	E
Conner, Jr., William	E
Conner, Sr., William	E
Conseen, Frank	H
Coody, John	C
Corntassel	E
Cox, Thomas	D
Cramp, Broom	E
Cramp, Harry	E
Cramp, Ned	E
Cramp, Riddle	E
Crawford, Virgil	D
Crittenden, Charles	G
Crittenden, George Washington	G
Crittenden, Harry	G
Crittenden, James	G
Crittenden, Wellington	G
Cummings Woodville	G
Cunningham, Cicero M	I
Danenburg, John Henry	G
Danenburg, William	G
Daniel, Harmaduke	E
Daniel, Joshua	E
Daniel, Thomas	E
Daniel, William	G
Davis, David	D
Davis, George	G
Davis, John L.	H
Davis, John	E
Davis, John	G
Davis, Michael	H
Davis, William Henry	G
Deerhead, Nicholas	E
Denton, David	E
Denton, John	G
Devine, James	G
Dick, Ellis	E
Dick, Isaac	E
Dixon, Maxwell	H
Doghead, John	E
Downing, Watt	I
Drew, Charles	C
Drew, William Henry	G
Duck, John	E
Eaton, Harlin	G
Eaton, Richard	G
Eckridge, William	E
EDaniel, John Martin	E
Elam,	E
Elders, George	C
Elliott, Archibald	D
Elliott, George W.	D
Elliott, Walter	D
England, Martin	D

England, Mitchell	D		Graham, J. B.	H
Eubanks, William	G		Graham, John	H
Eubanks, William	I		Grasshopper	E
Fargo, Charles A.	I		Green, Ansel	E
Farley, L. L.	E		Griffin, John	G
Faulkner, John	I		Hadley, Thomas	E
Fawling, John	E		Hair, John	K
Ferguson, John	C		Hair, Samuel	K
Few, Buck	I		Hanks, Robert Taylor	C
Few, Ignacious	G		Harlan, "Oce"	G
Fields, Ezekiah ("Bud")	E		Harlan, John Brown	I
Fields, Ezekiah	E		Harlan, Mitchell	B
Fields, George Washington			Harmon, Benjamin	H
	E		Harmon, James	H
Fields, George	E		Harmon, Murphy	H
Fields, Richard	E		Harris, William	B
Fields, Seven	I		Harris, William	C
Fields, Thompson	E		Hastings, W. A. Y.	H
Fisher, Benjamin	G		Hawk, Stephen Gray	E
Fishtail, George Harlan	B		Hayes, John Q.	C
Foreman, Charles	I		Hazlett, Joseph	H
Foreman, Elias Gourd	G		Hazlett, William	H
Foreman, Samuel	G		Henry, Joseph	E
Foreman, Samuel	I		Hensley, John	E
Foreman, William R.	I		Hicks, David	C
Frayser, George	E		Hildebrand, Joseph Martin	C
Freshower, Henry	D		Hildebrand, Michael	C
Freshower, Joseph	D		Hildebrand, Reese	C
Freshower, Wallace	D		Hildebrand, Stephen	C
Gafford, Jesse	I		Hillian, Charles	E
Gafford, John	I		Hinman, John	I
Gallagher, Thomas	G		Hogan, John	H
Garbarina	E		Hgg, Oliver	G
George, George	G		Holcomb, E. G.	E
Glenn, Lewis	E		Hood, James	C
Golston, John	H		Horn, Jeremiah	G
Golston, Matthew	H		Horsefly, James	E
Gonzales, Dennis	G		Hosmer, Solomon	C
Goss, Benjamin Franklin	G		Howland, Erastus J.	G
Gott, George	G		Humphrey, James	E
Gott, William	G		Huss, Charles	A
Graham, Green	H		Inlow, Philip	G

Inlow, Sylvester	G		Lowrey, Charles	A
Jailer, Ned	E		Lowry, Charles	E
Johnson, Andrew	G		Lucas, William	C
Johnson, James	G		Marshall, Bee	E
Johnson, John Bean	G		Marshall, John	E
Johnson, Riley	C		Martin Butler	C
Jones, Drewry	E		Martin, Almon	C
Jones, Jackson	E		Mathis, John	E
Jones, James	E		Mayes, Joel Bryan	H
Jones, John	E		Mayes, Richard	G
Jones, Wilborn	E		Mayes, William Henry	H
Jordan, John W.	C		Mayfield, John Walker	G
Kagle, Shade	G		Mayfield, John Walker	I
Kell,	G		McCracken, William	I
Kell, Daniel O'Conner	D		McDaniel, Joel	I
Kell, John talala	D		McDaniel, Robert	D
Kell, Joseph	D		McDaniel, Robert	I
Kell, Lewis Ross	D		McGee, Albert	D
Ketcher, John	A		McGee, David	E
Keyes, James McDaniel	C		McGee, John R.	E
Killian, Jesse	G		McGee, Leander	E
Kincade, W. A.	E		McLain, John	C
Kirk, Charles	C		McLaughlin, David	D
Kirk, George	C		McPherson, Hugh	C
Lafabre, Watie	D		Miller, Alfred	G
Lafew, Benjamin	C		Miller, Andrew	E
Lamar, James	G		Miller, Daniel	E
Landrum, Proctor	D		Miller, John Martin	E
Langley, Lock	I		Miller, Joseph Gambold	E
Latta, Allen	C		Miller, Thomas	E
Latta, Diver	C		Montgomery Sturdivant,	C
Lewis, Gatz	G		Moore, David	A
Linder, John.	C		Moore, David	D
Linder, Julius Caesar	C		Moore, John	A
Lipe, Clinton	C		Moore, Ned	A
Lipe, John Gunter	C		Moore, Olcut	A
Lisenbe, Charles	E		Morgan, James	G
Lisenbe, Eli	E		Morgan, Joshua	G
Lisenbe, Washington	E		Morgan, Lone	G
Liver, Creek	I		Morgan, Mark	G
Lovett, Archibald	C		Morris, Albert	E
Lovett, John	C		Morris, Oliver	E

Mouse	E	Reynolds, Gideon	C
Neal, Richard	C	Rider, Alexander McCoy	B
Nightkiller, Henry	E	Rider, Alexander McCoy	I
Nivens, John	C	Riley, Johnson	C
Nivens, Marcellus	C	Riley, Joseph	C
Nivens, Moses	C	Riley, Joseph	C
Noisywater, George	G	Robards, Lewis	I
O'Fields, Dumplin	D	Rogers, James	E
O'Fields, Johnson	D	Rogers, John	C
Ogden, Emon	C	Rogers, Joseph	D
Oo-ni-quan-na	E	Rogers, Joseph	E
Ore, James	C	Rogers, Lewis	E
Osmond	C	Rogers, Napoleon	D
Pack, Shorey	I	Rogers, William	E
Palmer, Samuel	E	Rottenman	E
Parks, Thomas Jefferson	B	Saltface	E
Pate, Richard	I	Sanders, Calvin	G
Patrick, John Joshua	C	Sanders, Charles	G
Patrick, William	C	Sanders, Cornelius	I
Pettit, Frank	C	Sanders, David	G
Pettit, Thomas	I	Sanders, Isaac	I
Pheasant, Richard	E	Sanders, Joshua	I
Phillips, John	H	Sanders, Robert	I
Phillips, Sooter	H	Sanders, Watson	G
Phillips, William	H	Sanders, William	G
Pigeon, Creek	I	Sanders, Wilson	I
Pigeon, Jack	A	Scott, John	G
Pigeon, Jesse	A	Scott, Noah	C
Pigeon, Logan	A	Scott, Sterling	C
Pogue, David	E	Seabolt, George	G
Porter, John	C	Seabolt, Jeremiah	G
Preston, Dr. Charles H.	E	Seminole, John	I
Price, Amos	I	Sexton, John	G
Price, Berry	I	Shell	E
Price, John	I	Shepherd, William V.	C
Ratliff, Kiowa	D	Shields, John	E
Rattlinggourd, Dusky	E	Shields, William	E
Reader, Elias	E	Shirt, Rock	E
Reese, Andrew	G	Shoeboots, Morrison	E
Reese, George	G	Shoemaker, Runabout	E
Reese, Murray	G	Simco, Josephus	I
Reynolds, George	C	Simcon, Bose	I

Sixkiller, Samuel	G	Thornton, William H.	G
Smallwood, Joseph	G	Tiger, Looney	E
Smith, Flea	E	Timberlake, Allison	G
Smith, Frank	C	Timpson, Bear	D
Smith, John	G	Timson, Bear	E
Smith, Joseph	E	Tinker, John	C
Smith, Linder McCoy	C	Tinney, Thomas	D
Smith, Samuel (Buster)	C	Trott, Timothy	G
Smith, Stand	E	Trott, William Lafayette	G
Smith, Thomas	E	Trout, George Washington	E
Smith,	C	Tucker, James	H
Smoker, George	I	Tyner, Reuben R.	D
Snardy, George W.	H	Vanita, John	I
Sosa, Johnson	C	Vann, Cabbage	B
Spaniard, Andrew	C	Vann, Coon	B
Spaniard, Michael	C	Vann, Daniel Webster	C
Squirrel, Daniel	A	Vann, Daniel Webster	D
Squirrel, Jack	A	Vann, David R.	C
Stansel, Lewis	G	Vann, Henry	C
Stansil, John	I	Vann, Johnson	C
Stansil, Lewis	I	Vann, Joseph	K
Starr, Charles W	G.	Vann, William	C
Starr, Charles Washington	G	Vann, Yartunnah	B
Starr, Ellis	G	Vickery, John	G
Starr, Henry Clay	C	Vickery, Wilborn	C
Starr, James	C	Waite, Saladin	A
Starr, James	G	Walker, A. Daniel	B
Starr, John Walker	C	Walker, Stephen	E
Starr, Jr., Joseph McMinn	G	Ward, George, M.	E
Starr, Walter Adair	G	Ward, Vann	A
Steele, Samuel Tee-ge-ski	E	Ward, Vann	E
Stoneroad, Thomas	C	Waseeter	E
Stover, John Rogers	H	Waseeter, James	E
Sturdivant, John Calhoun	C	Waters, Andrew	I
Sturdivant, Martin Butler	G	Waters, Robert	I
Suagee, David	A	Watie, Saladin	D
Suagee, Stand	A	Wawaseet	E
Summerfield, Joseph	A	Webber, Charles	C
Taylor, Ezekieh	G	Webber, Charles	D
Tee-ge-ski	E	Webber, Charles	H
Thornton, John	G	West, James Polk	C
Thornton, Jolly	C	West, John Calhoun	C

West, John	H
West, Walter Adair	D
West, Walter Duncan	G
West, William M.	C
Whitekiller, Rider	C
Whitmore, Stephen	G
Wilborn, Benjamin C.	G
Wilkerson, Hill	E
Wilkinson, Hill	D
Williams, Moses	D
Wilson, James	H
Womankiller	E
Woodall, Thomas Jefferson	A
Wright, Franklin	D
Wyatt, Joseph	I
Yates, George	C
Yinney, John	D

Bryan's Battalion

By order of Brig Gen Douglas H Cooper, the battalion was, on February 3, 1863, consolidated with 5 companies attached to Watie's 1st Cherokee Mounted Volunteers to form the 2nd (Adair's) Cherokee Mounted Volunteers.

Among the miscellaneous Cherokees listed were John Vann, Provost Marshal, Canadian District, Cherokee Nation; B. Greycom, Company E. 2nd Cherokee Artillery; and S. J. Thompson of the Cherokee Battalion.

Bryan, Joel Mayes	Major
Waters, C. C.	Captain
Miller, John	Captain
Harden, John R.	Captain
Shannon, William	Captain
Hendron, William	First Lieutenant
Olay, J. R. Olay	First Lieutenant
Wilkerson, Jasner	First Lieutenant
Yeargain, James Chambers	Second Lieutenant
Love B. T.	Second Lieutenant
Patterson, J. C.	Second Lieutenant
Herron, Daniel	Third Lieutenant
Smith, S. C.	First Sergeant
Dillon, R.	Sergeant
Miller, B. F.	Sergeant
Banks, Mal	Orderly Sergeant
Bradley, J.	Corporal
Robinson, M.	Corporal
Sutton, T.	Corporal
VanClay, M.	Corporal

Privates

Baker, Charles	Blackwell, Robert
Baker, John	Booth, J. W.
Baker, Lewis	Brown, Wallace
Banks, George	Buchanan, George
Banks, John	Burns, H. F. B,
Bellows, A. A.	Burrows, James
Bellows, Charles	Burrows, Samuel

Burrows, Thomas
Cagel, Shade
Canard, Lindon
Caranay, John
Chappell, R. D
Clark, William
Clay, Henry C.
Copeland, David
Cordell, Jefferson
Crouch, Alex
Cunningham, J.M
Daugherty, Joseph
Davis, Frank
Davis, James
Davis, R. A.
Devine, Robert
Dreon, M. J.
Earp, Phillip
Edwards, John
Evans, Lewis
Evans, William
Fendle, W. C.
French, Daniel
Gailey, Augustus
Gailey, Joseph
Gailey, Lucien
Gailey, Warren
Gallion, Randolph
Gamble, Samuel
Gillett, Caleb
Green, G. W.
Greener, John
Grinder, William
Hammer/Hamner, H. A.
Havens, James
Hiser, Jacob M.
Holman, Thomas
Holt, David
Holt, George
Holt, Henry
Howard, William
Humphries, W. R.

Jasper, Neuton?Newton
Keen, R.
Latta, Matthew
Latta, William
Leeman, --------
Love, T. Jeff
Lukens, Henry
McCall, Alexander
McCullough, Thomas
Miner, Henry
Miner, William
Morris, J.
Nash, Van
Page, E. H.
Patterson, John
Patterson, W. F.
Patton, James
Reed, Daniel
Rosel, W. C.
Rotrammel, Henderson
Rotrammel, James
Rotrammel, John
Rotrammel, Wilson
Rozel, Peter
Russell, George
Russell, George
Shelton, George
Shelton, Joseph
Shelton, Samuel
Soap, Thomas
Strickler, A. T.
Strickler, W. C.
Sullivan, George
Taylor, Robert
Thomas, P. N
Thomas, Robert
Vinyard, Robert
Ward, George DeShields
Ward, Henry
Ward, William
Wilkerson, William

Cherokee Regiment, (Special Service) AKA Cherokee Partisan Rangers

Not much is known about this organization, which is mentioned in Brig Gen Douglas H Cooper's correspondence in March and May of 1865 and in a Federal report dated 23 Apr 65, then supposed to be at Fort Towson (in the southern Choctaw Nation), 300 strong. Joel M Bryan, who previously led the 1st Partisan Ranger Bn, was the commander. Captain John Miller led a company, and a Captain Owens another.

Shortly after the formation of the First Cherokee Mounted Rifles; Joel Mayes Bryan was authorized by Brig Gen Albert Pike to raise 100 men or more as partisan rangers during the summer of 1862. The company (A) was mustered in at Fort Davis, Canadian District, Cherokee Nation, July 20, 1862. Bryan proceeded to recruit another four companies, and was ordered by Maj Gen Thomas C Hindman to organize the force into a battalion, which was done September 13, 1862. Records indicate that the enlistment term was three years. This is only a partial roster.

Bryan, J.M.	Colonel
Miller, John	Captain
Clay, J.R.	First Lieutenant
Love, B.T.	Second Lieutenant
Patterson, J.C.	Second Lieutenant
Smith, S.C.	First Sergeant
Davis, R.A.	Sergeant
Dillon, R.	Sergeant
Miller, B.F.	Sergeant
Bradley, J.	Corporal
Robinson, M.	Corporal
Van Clay, M.	Corporal

Privates

Bellows, A.A.	Burrows, Samuel
Bellows, Charles	Burrows, Thomas
Blackwell, Robert	Cagle, Shade
Booth, J.W.	Canard, Lindon
Burns, H.F.B.	Caranay, John
Burrows, James	Chappell, R. D.
Burrows, John	Clay, Henry C.

Clay, W.G.
Cooper, John
Crouch, Alex
Cunningham, J. M.
Daugherty, Joseph
Davis, James
Divine, Andrew
Divine, Crockett
Divine, Robert
Dreon, M.L.
Dunman, E.
Earp, Philip
Evans, Lewis
Evans, William
Fendle, W.C.
French, Daniel
Green, G.W.
Greener, John
Hamner, H.A.
Havens, James
Holman, Thomas
Howard, William
Humphries, W.R.
Keen, R.

Leeman,
Love, T. Jeff
Marcum, A.
McCart, Henry
McCravy, John
McCullough, Thomas
Miner, Henry
Miner, William
Morris, J.
Nash, Van
Neuton, Jasper
Neuton, Lee
Page, E.H.
Patterson, John
Patterson, John
Patterson, W.F.
Reed, Daniel
Rozel, Peter
Rozel, W.C.
Soap, Thomas
Thomas, Robert
Van Clay, William
Waters, Samuel
White, James

Frye's – Scales' Battalion, Cherokee Cavalry

Shortly after the organization of the Second Cherokee Mounted Volunteers, Moses Frye organized a battalion and became its Major. He was succeeded by Joseph Absalom Scales.

Frye, Moses C.	Major
John Porum Davis	Captain
William Eckridge	Captain
Childers John	First Lieutenant
Drew, Charles	First Lieutenant
McGee, Thomas Jefferson	First Lieutenant
Alexander, William	Second Lieutenant
Gunter, John Edward	Second Lieutenant
McCoy, James Christopher	Second Lieutenant
Rogers, Lewis	Second Lieutenant
Hayes, John Q.	Third Lieutenant.
McGee, Albert McGee	Third Lieutenant
Preston, Dr. Charles H,	Orderly Sergeant
Neal, Richard	Orderly Sergeant
Evans John	Second Sergeant
Guess, Teesee	Third Sergeant
Campbell, Samuel	Fourth Sergeant.
Butler, Heavy	Fifth Sergeant
Downing, George	First Corporal
Poorbear, John	Second Corporal
Shepherd, Albert P.	Third Corporal.
Bowles, Thomas 0.	Fourth Corporal.

Privates

Applegate, James
Arnold, George
Ashes, Joe
Badger
Baldridge, Johnson
Barberry, David
Bashears, David
Beamer, John
Bertholf, Isaac W.
Bledsoe, Joseph

Bledsoe, Lorenzo
Bob, Robin
Bowles, George
Bowles, James
Bowles, Johnson
Bowles, Samuel
Broughil, George
Burkett, David
Butterfield, John
Cahlahhoola

Caldwell, John
Candy, Samuel
Carter, Thomas Jefferson
Crane, Chunarchur
Davis, David
Dick, Ellis
Dick, Isaac
Downing, David
Downing, Edward
Downing, Joseph
Duck, Dick
Duck, John
Ellis, Benjamin
Ellis, Lafayette
Fargo, Charles A.
Fields, Ezekial
Fields, Ezekial ("Bud")
Fields, George
Fields, George Washington
Fields, Henry
Fields, Matthew
Fields, Thompson
Flap
Flyingaway
Foreman, Stand
Frazier, George
Garves, Buffalo
Girty, Buck
Girty, Simon
Griffin, James
Griffin, William
Harlan, John Brown
Harris, David
Heffington, Samuel G.
Hicks, Nathan
Hunt, Scott
Jackson, Calvin
Jackson, Harvey
Jackson, Walter
Kettle, John
King, Benjamin
Kinkade, Samuel

Latta, Allen
Lisenbe, Charles
Lisenbe, Washington
Marshall, Bee
Martin, Hercules T.
Mathis, John
McCoy, Daniel
McCoy, W. S.
McGee, David A.
McLaughlin, David
McMurtrey, John
Miller, John
Moore, Solomon
Morris, Albert
Morris, George
Morris, Oliver
Muskrat, Wilson
Oolskunee
Oowa-looka
Ore, Joseph
Pogue, David
Price, John
Raper, George
Rogers, John L.
Rogers, Joseph
Sanders, Ellis
Sanders, Isaac
Satanka
Shepherd, Joseph
Shepherd, William
Shotpouch
Simms, Frank
Small Dirt
Smoker, George
Splitnose
Starr, Ellis
Starr, Ezekial
Starr, George
Starr, James
Sunshine, George
Ticanooly, William Stoven
Timberlake, Allison Woodville

Tobacco John
Trout, George Washington
Vann, David
Vann, Jesse
Vann, Monkey

Vann, Yartunnah
Walker, George Washington
Watts, Thomas
Williams, Reuben

1st Squadron, Cherokee Mounted Volunteers, (Holt's) Company A

This company was mustered in at Webber's Falls, Canadian District, Cherokee Nation, 12 December 62, for two years. The last record of the company is dated June 30, 1863, it probably was assigned to the 2nd Regiment as Company L after that date.

Holt, Charles H.	Captain
Baldridge,	Lieutenant
Morgan, R.M.	First Lieutenant
Alberty, John	Brevet Second Lieutenant
Baldrige, Squier	Second Lieutenant
Miller, John	Second Lieutenant
Gray, Stand	Sergeant
Reese, George A	Sergeant
Timpson, John A	Sergeant
Reid, Charles C.	Ordnance Sergeant
Alexander, A.	Corporal
Lea, Samuel	Corporal
Lowery, William	Corporal
Smith, Isaac	Corporal
Jones, Mathew	Blacksmith

Privates:

Alexander, Samuel Mc.
Ar le, Chia
Awsry, Thomas
Baldridge, Daniel
Baldridge, Jackson
Baldridge, Jefferson
Bear,
Boggs, Daniel
Butler, Martin
Byers, David
Byers, John
Carlisle, Stephen
Coleman, John
Coleman, William
Cueclaw, John
Deastead, James
Deerskin, George
Denton, John
Downing, David
Downing, George
Downing, Joseph
Eldridge, Jefferson
Elk, Rider
Good Money,
Hicks, David
Hicks, Rufus

Hindman, Frank
Holt, Walter
Horn, Jeremiah
Huff, Richard
Hugey, James
Ice, Nits
Jones, Charles
Lea, William
Lephin, Benjamin
Light, John
Lincoln, Abraham
Marshall, John
McIntosh, John
Melvin, John
Payne, Samuel
Plan, William
Plinn, William
Price, Amos
Price, B.H.
Price, Berry
Pritchard, George
Punkins, Dennis
Quintan, Joel
Quintan, Nathaniel
Quintan, Samuel
Ragsdale, Thomas

Rat, D.B.
Ratcliffe, Daniel
Reese, Andrew
Reese, Murray
Rivers, Frank
Scmitt, Arch
Seven, Fields
Shaughia,
Smallwood, Joseph
Smooker, George
Starr, James N.
Su wa Key,
Taylor, Ezekiel
Timpson, Clay
Ui Key Key Chi,
Warstuck, Joseph
Warstuck, Lewis
Warstuck, Thomas
Whitaker, Moses
Wicked, Jesse
Wicked, William
Winklesides, John
Winklesides, Palling
Winlklesides, Mink
Wittmeyer, Stephen
Wudwood,

Chickasaw Units

CSA Chickasaw Battleflag
Bright blue background with Chickasaw Seal in center

Brig. General Douglas Cooper　　**Winchester Colbert**
Commander　　　　　　　　　　**Governor, 1861-65**

1st Regiment, Chickasaw Infantry, (Hunter's Indian Volunteers)

Hunter, William L.	F&S	Colonel
Martin, Samuel H.	F&S	Lieutenant Colonel
Peters, William L.	F&S	Adjutant
Hays, Abram B.		Major
Gregg, Thaddeus		Captain
Hansell, William		Captain
Haynes, William		Captain
Kesner, John		Captain
McConnell, Franklin		Captain
McCord, David		Captain
Milam, Patterson		Captain
Minnis, John M.		Captain
Wallace, John P.		Captain
White, John T.		Captain
Blevins, John L.		First Lieutenant
Cowan, B. H.		First Lieutenant
Crosby, G. W.		First Lieutenant
Curtis, Henry		First Lieutenant
Grugitt, George		First Lieutenant
Hilliard, M. D.		First Lieutenant
Mitchell, George W.		First Lieutenant
Staden, George		First Lieutenant
Allison, Henry		Second Lieutenant
Callahan, E.		Second Lieutenant
Campbell, Charles		Second Lieutenant
Carmichael, John		Second Lieutenant
Fields, James M.		Second Lieutenant
Hamilton, Peter		Second Lieutenant
Hockett, Isaac		Second Lieutenant
Phipps, Joseph		Second Lieutenant
Sims, Horatio		Second Lieutenant
Smith, William H.		Second Lieutenant
Burgess, J.		Third Lieutenant

Cosby, H.	Third Lieutenant
Ferris, David	Third Lieutenant
King, Harvey	Third Lieutenant
Lynch, Amos	Third Lieutenant
Morrison, Calvin	Third Lieutenant
Nevils, D.F.	Third Lieutenant
Roberts, William C.	Third Lieutenant
Milam, Benjamin	Lieutenant
Munson, S. T.	Lieutenant
Carroll, H. T.	First Sergeant
McCra, David	First Sergeant
McGraw, J.	First Sergeant
Phelps, Thomas H.	First Sergeant
Reynolds, Absolom	First Sergeant
Roberts, Henry	First Sergeant
Roebuck, William	First Sergeant
Stewart, J.B.	First Sergeant
Tate, Hardin L.	First Sergeant
Williams, F. H.	First Sergeant
Bass, Henry	Sergeant
Blair, Wiley	Sergeant
Briggs, F.H.	Sergeant
Brisby, William R.	Sergeant
Caldwell, Nathan	Sergeant
Carroll, R.	Sergeant
Corvin, S.	Sergeant
Crisman, R.	Sergeant
Farmer, A.D.	Sergeant
Finley, T.	Sergeant
Harley, Scott	Sergeant
Hendertete, F. M.	Sergeant
Hinds, John T.	Sergeant
Howard, James	Sergeant
Jamison, Daniel	Sergeant
Johnson, John	Sergeant
Kron, Thomas	Sergeant
Lenoer, Abram	Sergeant
McGraw, Alexander	Sergeant
Norris, T.	Sergeant
Parker, Abram	Sergeant
Peters, Alfred	Sergeant
Reynolds, Alfred	Sergeant

Sheppard, J. W.	Sergeant
Taylor, Andrew	Sergeant
Terry, William	Sergeant
Vance, George	Sergeant
Ware, Harvey	Sergeant
Welsh, A.T.	Sergeant
Wightman, George	Sergeant
Adair, Jame	Corporal
Allen, William	Corporal
Ayrers, John	Corporal
Bennon, H.	Corporal
Brookin, F.	Corporal
Bryant, J.J.	Corporal
Campbell, George	Corporal
Carter, Abel	Corporal
Clark, William	Corporal
Cox, Abner	Corporal
Crabtree, J.	Corporal
Denton, D.H.	Corporal
Elliott, H.	Corporal
Garland, William	Corporal
Greme, Thomas	Corporal
Henson, Allen	Corporal
Hudson, T.	Corporal
Hunly, Prince	Corporal
Leonard, Thomas	Corporal
Patrick, James	Corporal
Robison, W.H.	Corporal
Rutherford, H.	Corporal
Sailor, Andrew	Corporal
Sanderson, J.	Corporal
Sarrio, John W.	Corporal
Simpson, A.T.	Corporal
Simpson, R.	Corporal
Smith, A.F.	Corporal
Smith, B.	Corporal
Smith, William	Corporal
Stroud, F.	Corporal
Sunatubba, F.	Corporal
Thomas, H.	Corporal
Trigg, A.	Corporal
Waddy, Dennis	Corporal

Whitakker, Henry
Whiteley, W.
Wilson, Richard
Wright, James C.

Corporal
Corporal
Corporal
Corporal

Privates

Peterson, Joel
Ablona, C.H.
Abracuna, James
Acker, Thomas
Adams, Daniel S.
Afanesa, R.
Afftata, James
Aikin, T.
Alderson, James
Alenander, P.
Alepps, James
Alexicoma, H.
Allen, H.
Almond, D.
Almond, H.
Almond, T.
Alob, T.
Alonamatubba, L.
Aloska, T.
Amafesta, G.
Amaffatatama, R.
Amahona, J.
Amalatub, Austin
Ambocona, H.
Amita, H.
Amos, Henry
Amy, John
Anamatubba, J.
Anderson, Solomon
Anoma, James
Apperly, Charles
Apperson, H.
Apuckee, Joe
Archy, J.
Arich, Henry

Arippa, H.
Armafilla, D.
Armstrong, George
Arper, T.
Arucha, J.
Asku, Benjamin
Astoba, H.
Astrogach, T.
Attala, J.E.
Attapaho, J.
Attonaha, Andrew
Austin, G.W.
Austin, James
Bachman, L.
Bailey, Ephaim
Baker, Hangron
Baker, Henry
Baker, Hilam
Baler, William
Balkfa, H.
Balorama, H.
Balow, V.
Bamasihs, L.
Banomy, H.
Barfoot, B.
Barker, F. M.
Barker, J.
Barker, William K.
Barlow, J.
Barlow, Thomas
Barny, William
Barraphano, S.
Barry, J.
Bascofa, E.
Baxter, W.L.

Bean, J.C.
Beekham, C.D.
Bellmona, H.
Bennett, R.S.
Benson, Caleb
Bentley, Lycurgus
Berry, J.
Berryman, S.
Beupa, F.
Bidges, H.
Bildo, James
Bird, J.K.
Black, T.V.
Bolivar, Henry
Bolufa, Henry
Bolufachubba, J.
Boncha, E.
Boneda, George
Bonja, N.
Bonnafano, Tim
Bontarala, H.
Bosalanthama, J.
Boska, James C.
Boskebo, John
Bouchanalla, F.
Bougue, F.
Bouser, H.C.
Boykin, Thomas
Brewster, J.
Brooks, Samuel
Brummett, E.
Bucks, William H.
Bumpuss, A.
Buncalaliah, T.
Bunnachubba, O.
Burgess, G.W.
Burgona, C.
Burho, R.
Burney, Caleb
Burney, Sampson
Burns, T.
Burny, G.W.

Burrell, James
Burrus, Argyle
Burrusson, H.
Bush, George
Bushong, William
Buster, John
Cadds, Abram
Cadmos, C.
Caffa eel,
Cahal, T.
Cajo, W.
Calapa, H.
Caldova, L.
Calebson, John
Callabans, H.
Callaway, F. M.
Callaway, James
Callaway, Oscar
Callaway, S.
Callopanotubba, H.
Callopata, H.
Calumachus, H.
Campbell, A.
Campbell, C. H.
Campbell, G. W.
Canallatubba, F.
Canona, William
Canter, A.
Caponaho, T.
Caracomo, H.
Caramaha, J.
Carga, Isam
Carmafano, O.
Carmaus, Abner
Carmoek, George
Carper, Henry
Carper, James
Carson, Francis
Carter, R. W.
Carter, S. C.
Carter, William E.
Cass, Stephen

Castaphano, R.
Caswell, Nicholas
Caswell, William
Catesby, H. B.
Catlett, James
Chapman, H.
Chichamaham, Nelson
Chofamaha, J.
Chubbamaha, T.
Chufa, Henry
Chufamicka, L.
Cimky, H.
Clark, David
Clark, G.
Coddo, Jim
Cofolapo, C.
Cola, George
Collins, H.
Collins, Micajah
Colopano, C.
Colquett, John
Colquett, T.
Colter, William
Coma, Thomas
Concha, S.
Concha, S.
Concufumaha, J.
Conecah, Henry
Confalipo, R.
Consa, F.
Coonawah, C.
Cooper, J. C.
Corbot, Allen
Corvina, S.
Costaphano, L.
Costatubba, M.
Cowan, David
Cowan, James
Cowan, Robert
Cowen, S. G.
Coweta, W.
Cowetena, T.

Cox, John B.
Cox, Stephen
Cubbamaha, A.
Cubby, F.
Cupoloba, E.
Dabney, R.
Daffy, B.
Dale, John
Danappa, R.
Danford, Abram
Darden, George W.
Darden, Philip
Davenport, J.Q.
Davidson, J.
Debask, H.
Debonapha, H.
Delano, D.
Deloma, Jim
Demos, T.
Dennison, John
Deshaba, E.
Deuman, Charles
Devine, H.
Dexter, H.
Dilrel, D.
Dishana, H.
Doane, James L.
Dodson, James
Doty, H.
Dougherty, William
Dowd, H.
Duma, J.
Dumfalado, S.
Durger, G.
Duscana, C.
Eagleton, James
Eanes, Richard
Early, J.
Eatherly, Joseph
Ebenebo, Jack
Echobo, G.
Echols, R.H.

Echols, William
Ecloma, J.
Edmonds, James
Eggleston, James
Elabow, M.
Elafa, C.
Elder, John
Eldridge, Jackson
Eldridge, John
Eldridges, Joseph
Elkins, George
Ellington, John H.
Ellis, Avery
Ellis, James
Ellis, John
Ellis, William
Elphamo, H.
Elseynamon, G.
Eltohena, C.
Emerson, A.P.
Emolana, C.
Emosano, Thomas
Enaraco, A.
English, W.
Enos, J.
Ensley, Enoch
Ensley, Joseph
Entaqueka, C.
Ephaluna, S.
Epperson, Harvey
Eska, H.
Eskridge, Abram
Eskridge, Julius
Esniho, Jerry
Estaphano, H.
Estaphono, D.
Estis, George W.
Estis, William
Eucharmo, L.
Evans, Johnathan
Everidge, Henry
Everly, J.

Fachena, S.
Fagaluka, G.
Faholo, A.
Fain, Russell
Faker, M.
Fallamatubba, B.
Fallobeno, H.
Fanoka, H.
Farlasa, T.
Farly, John
Farmer, John H.
FataSuka, K.
Ferrell, C.
Ferres, Julius
Ferris, Buck
Ferris, D.H.
Ferris, H.
Ferris, James
Foehema, E.H.
Folsom, H.
Foosha, T.
Ford, Thomas
Foster, Charles
Francis, F.T.
Francisco, Alexander
Franna, T.
Frazier, G.W.
French, Jacob
Fuller, A.
Fuquay, Henry
Fustamaha, E.
Gabona, E.
Gaines, Samuel
Gale, Andrew
Gallaghar, John
Gallawalk, F.
Gallona, C.
Ganaway, J.
Gano, H.
Gantt, Joseph
Gardner, Thomas
Garland, James

Garland, John
Garner, H.B.
Garnla, M.
Garrett, J.W.
Garrett, T.H.
Garrett, William
Garrison, P.
Garvin, Henry
Gassaphana, R.
Gaston, William
Gaut, William H.
George, H.
Gholson, Simon
Gibbs, William
Gibson, J.D.
Gill, J.
Givens, R.
Gofano, Elam
Goode, Sr., John
Grant, F.M.
Grant, H.
Grant, J.
Greene, Milton
Gregg, Henry
Gregg, Simon
Gregony, S.T.
Grevidge, J.
Grey, Peter
Gross, Henry
Grubb, A.
Gruff, Henry
Guepeno, C.
Gumka, N.
Hackett, John
Haden, James T.
Hadley, Rufus
Haffamatublee, G.
Haggerty, J.D.
Hale, Daniel
Hall, John C.
Hallamocona, D.
Haller, George

Halley, C.
Hammett, James
Hammott, A.
Hamon, J.T.
Hamon, R.
Hanamana, T.
Hannah, F.
Hansafa, H.
Hansell, George
Harcourt, Dennis
Harfoot, D.
Hargrove, Howell
Harmanapho, T.
Harmon, John
Harris, Wiley
Harrison, S. H.
Haster, J.
Hastopha, G.
Hauapa, T.
Hausell, John H.
Hawkins, H.
Hawser, W.
Heatherly, G.
Heloho, Ebenezer
Henderson, Samuel
Henritge, Paschal
Henry, John
Henson, C.
Herndon, E.
Hester, W.
Hettona, B.
Heuderlite, John
Hewark, D.
Hewsonalla, T.
Hicks, N.
Hicks, Robert
Higgins, C.
Hightower, G. W.
Hill, John
Hoback, J.
Hobrook, L.
Hobuck, A.F.

Hodge, B.F.
Hodges, Asa
Hodges, F.
Hogan, R.H.
Hogan, William L.
Hogston, H.E.
Holgee, H.
Holladay, Snitt
Hollinsworth, Henry
Homa, A.
Hone, L.
Hook, J.
Hook, Jesse
Hoover, Elisha
Hoover, J.
Hoover, L.
Horne, J.
Horrapego, L.
Houk, F.M.
Houndshell, L.E.
Houser, J.
Houston, D.
Howard, Joel
Howell, J.
Hudson, John W.
Hudson, Thomas
Huggins, William L.
Hullaphano, W.
Hulsta, Ed
Huma, C.
Hunlery, H.
Hunt, William
Hunta, John
Hurley, F.T.
Hyporta, S.
Hyson, Peter
Iapada, John
Ichahopha, H.
In Jabuno, D.
Incoma, F.
Jackson, John M.
Jackson, Johnathan

James, G.W.
James, S.
James, T.J.
James, William
Jenkins, Abram
Jenkins, James H.
Johnson, B.
Johnston, Micajah
Jonas, H.
Jones, George
Jones, Henry C.
Jones, Isaac
Jones, R.
Jones, Samuel C.
Jones, W.E.
Kachina, F.
Kahelo, M.
Kain, W.F.
Kalamda, H.
Kalmichuky, L.
Kampa, H.
Kann, L.
Kannika, J.
Keene, Jeremiah
Keller, Thomas
Kellumaha, H.
Kenneday, William
Kent, William
Kesley, C.M.
Kesner, Francis
Kesner, Nathan
Kickapa, H.
Kills, R.
King, A. P.
Kingsberry, P.
Kinsloe, William
Kinton, W.L.
Kluffka, H.
Knapp, C.
Kozart, A.
Kustamaha, H.
Labamementa, H.

Lafferty, W.
Laflore, G.
Lalamatubba, F.
Lamaha, T.
Lamb, Deadrick
Lamba, C.
Lambert, Samuel
Lamlana, H.
Lammeno, G.
Land, George
Langford, Wiley
Lano, Sim
Lanopiko, S.
Lanotubba, J.
Laphala, O.
Lappoo, H.
Lawrence, J.
Lazo, M.
Leitch, W.
Liggit, J.
Ligoba, F.
Ligoba, R.
Linder, Henry
Lonier, Joseph H.
Love, Washington
Luhfatah, G.
Lunatubba, F.
Lunatubba, G.W.
Lungreen, John
Lusta, L.
Maddox, William
Maffacela, K.
Magapola, F.
Mageno, H.
Maha, S.
Malona, Isom
Manalena, H.
Manicho, D.
Manly, F.T.
Manoroba, H.
Marcola, T.
Marrano, T.

Martin, Cassius
Martin, James
Martin, Theopolus
Mateleps, James
Mattaka, W.
Maun, Paralas
Mautabba, L.
Mautz, John H.
Maxwell, Peter
Mayaha, P.
McCann, J.
McCawba, L.
McClure, Thomas
McCord, Campbell
McCoy, James
McCoy, Lawrence
McGuire, John
McKelvey, Fletcher
McNabb, Arely
McNutt, J.
Meek, Joseph
Menesso, A.
Michoba, George
Migalasano, H.
Miltalemo, E.
Mingona, H.
Minnis, George
Minona, W.
Minter, Charles
Mixon, James
Mogans, H.
Mogridge, A.
Monolans, H.
Montgomery, James
Montieth, C.
Montrose, Alfonso
Moon, James
Moorfield, B.
Morgan, L.
Mulks, J.
Mulla, Henry
Munsey, D.

Munson, F.
Munsta, W.
Murphy, R.J.
Murray, James
Murray, John C.
Mustapha, E.
Muttakiddo, S.
Muttaphana, B.
Muxta, F.
Myler, J.M.
Nadome, J.
Naffans, W.
Nail, G.W.
Naloma, T.
Nappona, E.
Natubba, F.
Nelson, R.P.
Nelson, Wheeler
Newton, F.H.
Noble, John
Nonamatubba, C.
Noosatatah, L.
Norris, A.R.
Norton, H.
Nudkalah, D.
O'Brian, Nelson
Ogburne, J.
Oparke, G.
Ophana, E.
Ormond, John P.
Ortonatubba, E.
Osborne, William
Osgood, Greme
Overly, John
Page, W.
Pagget, Henry
Panahatche, M.
Panasago, P.
Panika, H.
Panola, H.
Panolapahah, J.
Pansy, W.

Papha, Luna
Paracliffa, S.
Parker, William
Patrick, Francis M.
Patrickson, John
Patton, Howell
Patton, James R.
Pauveska, Jim
Pendaluna, C.
Platomatubba, C.
Poloosa, A.
Polukta, T.
Poncha, Vinwa
Ponchena, T.
Pope, Walter
Posusa, D.
Puckett, Howell
Pumpka, S.
Quinby, W.T.
Raddo, F.
Rajomaha, S.
Rallaho, N.
Ramo, H.
Ramoge, John
Randall, Joseph
Rattler, H.T.
Renao, S.
Rice, H.
Richardson, Abner
Roach, George
Roamana, F.
Roapatome, D.
Rogens, F.M.
Rogers, William
Ronsephano, E.
Rosenbam, A.
Ross, John
Rossatubba, G.
Rout, Samuel
Rucker, Ambrose
Rucker, James
Rufa, H.

Ruffta, H.
Russama, L.
Sallaho, F.
Salopa, E.
Sameno, T.
Sands, J.
Sangho, H.
Simons, F.H.
Simpson, John
Sipata, H.
Smith, J.K.P.
Smith, James C.
Smith, James C.
Smith, William
Snafaliah, J.
Standifa, Alexander
Stinson, Gabriel
Stouffer, S.
Strain, Frank
Suhajah, H.
Sunnapah, G.
Tallaluk, J.
Tallequah, M.
Talmadge, S.
Talunatubba, M.
Talupa, H.
Tangipaho, E.
Tangipaho, G.
Tanner, W.
Taphano, C.
Tarper, Luna
Taylor, W.
Terrell, William
Thomas, Archy
Todd, James
Toncha, J.
Tullabouque, S.
Tullatubba, C.
Turner, Abram
Underwood, H.
Vance, John
Vanhoos, Sidney
Vasser, R.H.
Venable, J.C.
Vinson, F.
Wager, Simon
Walk, F.M.
Walker, J.Y.
Wallace, William C.
Walter, J.
Walton, William D.
Wana, George
Warren, James
Weennalufa, T.
Wichita, A.
Wilks, John
Williams, Joseph
Wilson, Allen T.
Winna, H.
Wisely, A.
Wisely, James
Wolff, S.
Wynn, James
Young, William

Shecoe's Chickasaw Battalion Mounted Volunteers

The largest surviving Chickasaw muster list is that for Shecoe's Chickasaw Mounted Volunteers, formed in October, 1864 by a reorganization of the 1st Battalion Chickasaw Cavalry (Mounted Volunteers).

Shecoe, Martin	F&S	Lieutenant Colonel
Nail, Jonathan	F&S	Major:
Campbell, M. H.	F&S	Major
Fisher, W. D. Fisher,;	F&S	Lieutenant, AAQM
Kingsberg, C. B.	F&S	Acting Quarter Master
Rennie, Alexander	F&S	Adjutant
Moore, J. H.	F&S	Surgeon
Cooper, David G.	F&S	ssistant Surgeon
Love, Henry	F&S	Ordnance Sergeant
Kingsberg, S. S.	F&S	Quarter Master Sergeant:
Gooding, C. E.	F&S	Sergeant Major:
Anderson, J. E.	F	Captain
Anderson, J.H.	F	Captain
Collins, Zach	F	Captain
Frazier, William,	C	Captain
Frazier, Wilson	C	Captain
James, G. D.	A	Captain
Keel, Booker	G	Captain
Martin, Walker	A	Captain
McCoy, A.	D	Captain
McGee, Isaac,	B	Captain
Miller, R.	D	Captain
Newberry, Lewis	E	Captain
Newbery, Lewis	D	Captain
Picey, Benson	G	Captain
Pikey, Benson	G	Captain
Walker Martin	A	Captain
Collins, Sam	F	First Lieutenant
Hawkins, Wilson	D	First Lieutenant
Keel, Overton	G	First Lieutenant
Killcrease, Simpson	I	First Lieutenant
Nail, Edward	A	First Lieutenant

Perry, Morgan	B	First Lieutenant
Alexander, Ephriam	D	Second Lieutenant
Brown, Josiah	D	Second Lieutenant
Columbus, A.	D	Second Lieutenant
Eskew, John E.	A	Second Lieutenant
Factor, Claborn	I	Second Lieutenant
Ishta	I	Second Lieutenant
Kehoe, B. A.	A	Second Lieutenant
Morrison, James S.	G	Second Lieutenant
Nehorter, : -------	F.	Second Lieutenant
Noah, John	F	Second Lieutenant
Percy, Charles P. H.	?	Second Lieutenant
Percy, Chas. F.H.		Second Lieutenant
Scotland, James	G	Second Lieutenant
Turley, James	A	Second Lieutenant
Eskew, John E.	A	Third Lieutenant
Bohanan, E.	A	Lieutenant
Fisher, W.D.		Lieutenant
Killcrease, Simpson	I	Lieutenant
Kingsbery, S.S.	A	Quartermaster Sergeant
Paul, John	A	1st Sergeant
Burney, Ben	A	Sergeant
Burney, Ben	A	Sergeant
Bussell, John T.	A	Sergeant
Lankford, Green	A	Sergeant
Lankford, Green	A	Sergeant
Martin, James	A	Sergeant
Martin, James	A	Sergeant
Merrill, Joseph D.	A	Sergeant
Wacacy, Zone	A	Sergeant
Wacacy, Zone	A	Sergeant
Coaehill, Absalom	A	Corporal
Cochil, Absalom	A	Corporal
Courtain, Richard	A	Corporal
Courtin, Richard	A	Corporal
Hensley, Robert L.	A	Corporal
Paul, John	A	Corporal
Reasenover, Jacob	A	Corporal
Reynolds, Thomas	A	Corporal

Privates

Appleton, F. R.	A		Ford, Thomas	A
Blair, Wesley	A		Garner, Robert	A
Blue, William D.	A		Garrison, A.J.	A
Bussell, John	A		George, William R.	A
Cain, Charles	A		Glover, Richard	
Calaway, Wesley	A			A
Caloway, Wesley	A		Griffith, Benjamin	A
Carroll, A. J.	A		Griffith, John	A
Casey, Zoue W.			Haines, Buck	A
Ceely, David			Harris, A. J.	A
Chaffin, W. R.	A		Hayes, Thomas	A
Chafin, W. R.	A		Hill, Thomas	A
Choat, G. W.	A		Homer, Frank	A
Choat, John	A		Jackson, G.H.	A
Choat, William	A		Johnson, Martin	A
Coaehill, Absalom	A		Keel, Booker	G
Cochran, William S.			Kemp, George	A
Cochran, Wm. S.			Kingsbery, S. S.	A
Collins, H. C.	A		Lewis, E. L.	A
Cooper, S. T.			Lewis, E. S.	A
Coutain, Richard	A		Linney, Perry	A
Crawford, Samuel F.	A		Miller, Robert	D
Crawford, Samuel	A		Mitchell, John	A
Davis, Mathew	A		Mondier, Peter	A
Degnoe, Narcissus	A		Moore, Loring	
Degraffenreid, James	A		Neal, Jehu	
Degraffenreid, V. M.	A		Neal, John	
Degraffenried, James	A		Nixon, George	A
Degraffenried, V.M.	A		Oliver, James C.	A
Degraftenreed, James	A		Philips, Joseph	A
Deneen, Nelson	G		Phillips, John	A
Dignoe, Narcissus	A		Ranier, Joseph	A
Doyal, Thomas	A		Ravier, Joseph	A
Doyle, Thomas	A		Reasonover, John	A
Drew, Judson	A		Rector, Banks	A
Eastman, B.F.	A		Rector, F.B.	A
Factor, Thomas	A		Sage, G. W.	A
Falkner, C.M.	A		Sage, J. W.	A
Faulkner, C.M.	A		Shuwonah, Sam	
Faulknerm, C. M.	A		Sinclair, William	A

Smith, A.J.	A		Wallace, Robt.	C
Smith, Stoffer	A		Welden, Frank	A
Staffer, Smith	A		Weldon, Frank	A
Stanton, William	A		Wheat, Samuel	A
Thompson, David G.	A		Wier, James	
Tiner, Jackson	A		Wies, James	
Tucker, Levi	A		Wiley, Jerome	A
Turley, B. F.	A		Wise, James	
Turner, A.J.			Woodlock, Edw.	A
Waldon, Thomas			Woodlock, Edward	A
Wallace, James			Wyrick, Jacob	A
Wallace, John			Wyrick, Jacon?	A
Wallace, Robert	G		Yale, Abner	A

Choctaw Units
Including 1ˢᵗ Regiment Choctaw & Chickasaw Mounted Rifles

CSA Choctaw Flag
Bright blue background, circle in white
With 2 arrows, bow and tomahawk

Colonel Douglas Cooper   Colonel Tandy Walker

Photos Courtesy Oklahoma Historical Society

1st Regiment, Choctaw Mounted Rifles

Harkins, D. F.	F&S	Lieutenant Colonel
Durant, Silvester	F&S	Major
Folsom, Sampson		Colonel
Fla tubbee,	A	Captain
Folsom, Martin	D	Captain
Gardner, Edmond	K	Captain
Gibson, John	B	Captain
Jones, Reson	E	Captain
Moor, Joseph	H	Captain
Moore, Joseph	H	Captain
Nelson, Coleman E.	G	Captain
Ok la bi,	F	Captain
Shemontah, -	B	Captain
Shemoter, -	B	Captain
Sinta Nowa (Walking Snake),	I	Captain
Thompson, Green W.	E	Captain
Wade, Alfred	C	Captain
Walking, Snake	I	Captain
Ward, Samuel		Captain
Allen, John W.	I	First Lieutenant
Chin O pa cha,	H	First Lieutenant
Chinup,	H	First Lieutenant
Clay, Henry	F	First Lieutenant
Cobbert, James	D	First Lieutenant
Colbert, James	D	First Lieutenant
Crowder, Martin S.	E	First Lieutenant
Austin, Lewis	F	Second Lieutenant
Brown, Milton	A	Second Lieutenant
Cher ta ho lah,	I	Second Lieutenant
Ellis, Thomas	D	Second Lieutenant
Fletcher, Harris		Second Lieutenant
Frazier, E.	G	Second Lieutenant
Frazier, Elis	B	Second Lieutenant
Frazier, Ross	B	Second Lieutenant
Fry, George	D	Second Lieutenant
Gardner, C.R.	E	Second Lieutenant
Hampton, Willis	B	Second Lieutenant
Harland, C.	I	Second Lieutenant

Lewis, Ben W.	G	Second Lieutenant
McKinney, Thompson	F,C	Second Lieutenant
Pisa ho tubbee, -	H	Second Lieutenant
Riddle, Jerry	H	Second Lieutenant
Sexton, Harris S.	I	Second Lieutenant
Simpson, William	K	Second Lieutenant
Debinport, B.	G	Third Lieutenant
Frazier, Harris		Third Lieutenant
Nano ma tubbee,	F	Third Lieutenant
Risner, George W.	E	Third Lieutenant
Ta Cubbee,	K	Third Lieutenant
Taylor, Josephus	D	Third Lieutenant
Tek O bee,	K	Third Lieutenant
Thompson, Washington	C	Third Lieutenant
Moseley, Luffey		Lieutenant
Tooley, J.S.	K	Lieutenant
Torley, J.J.	K	Lieutenant
Dwight, Timothy	E	First Sergeant
Edwards, Thomas	H	First Sergeant
Ellis, Thomas	D	First Sergeant
Harkins, Richard	K	First Sergeant
Perkins, Henry N.	I	First Sergeant
Polk, James K.	B	First Sergeant
Anirt, Safg		Sergeant
Atena, Ebenezer		Sergeant
Billy, Alexander	B	Sergeant
Carn, Enos	B	Sergeant
Carn, Washington	E	Sergeant
Cass, Lewis	H	Sergeant
Coleman, John	K	Sergeant
Esahiutubbee,	F	Sergeant
Frazier, Jackson	F	Sergeant
Hampton, Isaac	B	Sergeant
Hobbert, Nathaiel	D	Sergeant
Homma, Moses	G	Sergeant
Houston, Samuel H.	I	Sergeant
King, Asa	E	Sergeant
Lawechubbe,	D	Sergeant
Morris, Thomas	G	Sergeant
Okchaya, Stanford	D	Sergeant
Onto kan un tabi,	I	Sergeant
Smith, Paul	K	Sergeant

Name	Co.	Rank
Tahishtubee, Thompson	F	Sergeant
Taklantubbee,	F	Sergeant
Tyler, Wat	H	Sergeant
Waid, Simon		Sergeant
Washington, George	H	Sergeant
Welsh, T.H.	B	Sergeant
Abitish tay, A.	B	Corporal
Ah tuk low tubbi,	K	Corporal
Allen, Benjamin	E	Corporal
An chah tobbi,	K	Corporal
Baptieste, Robinson B.	I	Corporal
Billy, Johnson	B	Corporal
Bond, James	G	Corporal
Charley, Jacob	D	Corporal
Christy, Ebenezer	B	Corporal
Cowen, D. M.		Corporal
Dix, Johnston	H	Corporal
Durant, Cyrus D.	I	Corporal
Folsom, Jielf		Corporal
Frazier, Adam	G	Corporal
Hays, William	E	Corporal
Hommul, James	I	Corporal
Hotematabi, Lucas	I	Corporal
Hottimtambee,	I	Corporal
Imalhetubbe,	D	Corporal
Kobee, Ith	H	Corporal
Laurence, Silas		Corporal
Loman, John	F	Corporal
Luke, Anderson	H	Corporal
Meha, Lewis	K	Corporal
Mitchell, Steward	F	Corporal
Peabobys, Charles	H	Corporal
Pisatahi, -	E	Corporal
Robinson, Wilkin	D	Corporal
Teklombi, Solomon	K	Corporal
Thompson, Harrison	G	Corporal
Tims, Edward	G	Corporal
Wacum, Sam	D	Corporal
Wesley, Jackson	F	Corporal
Wilkison, Garland	E	Corporal
Winthrop, Benny		Corporal
Wolf, Silas	F	Corporal

Byrd, W.S.		Adjutant	
Edwards, Thomas		Acting Adjutant	
Clay, Joseph	F	Bugler	
Colb,	B	Bugler	
Shoate, John	F	Bugler	
Colbert, Lyman	H	Musician	
Folsom, William	E	Musician	
Hays, Jack	D	Musician	
James, John	G	Musician	
Thom, Ramsey	G	Musician	

Privites

Abel,	G	Apis An tobbi,	K
Abelauli,	I	Apistikuile,	F
Abitish teya,	G	Apo won tubbi,	K
Adams, John		Archabus,	G
Ah napocubbee,		Arfus, William	I
Ah nokubbee,		Armstrong, William	
Ahant,	G	Artaway, Jackson	I
Ahayo chubbee,	G	Ashomoo, Tubbin	C
Ahhokatribbee,		Atabbee,	G
Ainhbacho, Simpson	K	Atohcheya,	G
Akitana, William		Atoklamubbee,	F
Alberson, Wilson		Atoklumbee,	F
Alexander, Solomon	D	Attabbee,	G
Alfred, Anderson	B	Atukbubbee, Henry	F
Alfred,	B	Austin, Benjamin	F
Allen, Benjamin	K	Austin, Henry	G
Allen, James	E	Austin, Stephen	K
Allen, John	B	Bacon, Thomas	
Allen,		Bail, Alexander	E
Amby, Benjamin B.	I	Bain, William	H
Amos, John		Ball, Robinson	I
Anderson, Reason		Balon, Jones	E
Andrew, James	I	Barnes, Jesse	B
Anokehito,	F	Batice, Watson	G
Anotambee,	H	Battice, Joeson	G
Anowar tubbee,	B	Beams, Jacob	C
Anukwiatubbe, Silas	K	Beavers, Simon	
Apehubbee,	G	Belven, Feling	E
Apesautabi, Cyrus	I	Belvin, Sampson	E

Ben, Wallace	G		Charley, James	D
Benjamin,	I		Charley, Willis	D
Benton, Thomas H.	I		Charlison,	
Beteper,	B		Chillita, Isom	F
Bethibill, Polk	H		Chinubbee,	
Betts, Ramsy D.	E		Choate, Joel	G
Billi, Bat			Christy, Alexander	E
Billis, James			Chubby, Jonas	
Billry, Walis	E		Chukmabi, Martin	I
Billy, Allen	H		Chukmabi, Wilson	I
Bowling, Jacob	H		Chukmahi, Charles	E
Brashers, Jesse	D		Chukmahi, Jess	E
Brewer, Elijah	I		Chukunubbee, Martin	I
Brewer, Samuel	I		Chuta, Thomas C.	I
Brown, Able			Cintia no war,	I
Brown, Felix	E		Clark, William	H
Brown, Johnson			Clay, Esaias	K
Brown, Lyman	H		Cobb, Forrister	F
Bully, Wesley	E		Colbert, Cole	G
Burns, Burton	H		Colbert, Isom	
Burns, Robert	H		Colbert, Nelson	
Burris, Gabriel	G		Cole, Eastman	K
Burris, Jonas	K		Cole, Edmund	B
Burton, Thomas H.	I		Cole, Sampson	B
Byington, Charles	I		Collister, Wallace	G
Byington, Lewis	H		Collister,	G
Byington, Sam	E		Cornelius, Jack	I
Byington, Wallace	D		Cornelius, Willis C.	I
Cabi Pesa hi,	I		Cosbee, John	F
Calimin, Luis	E		Cotton, John	K
Calvin, Willis	E		Cravat, Sam	B
Carny, Parmer			Crosby, Alfuss	K
Cass, Alfred	H		Crowder, Thomas	E
Cater, Willis	D		Cubby,	
Ceasar,	D		Cunemonubbee,	
Chafa tombi,	K		Daily, John	E
Chafatonubbee,	H		Daily, Samuel F.	I
Chaffatubbee,			Daniels, Israel	H
Chafin, Kubbee	H		Davis, Bob	G
Charity, Logan	H		Davis, Esin	
Charles, Thomas	B		Davis, George	G
Charles,	G		Davis, Jeff	K

Davis, William			Forest, John B.	I
Davis, Wilson	G		Foss, Billy	F
Dinsmore, Cyrus	E		Foster, John	E
Durant, Elis	E		Franciway,	G
Durant, Robinson	K		Franklin, David	
Durant, Samuel	E		Franklin, David	A
Durant, Taylor			Franklin, William	H
Durant, William	K		Frazer, Campbell	K
Eastman,	K		Frazer, Eden	E
Eber no war tu bbee,	B		Frazer, Harris	E
Ebez on ubbee,	G		Frazer, Nicholas	K
Echap otu bbee,			Frazier, Isom	
Sesin	K		Frazier, Jackson	
Elehalah, Johnson			Frazier, John	
Elihohloya,	E		Frazier, Joseph	
Ellis,	K		Frazier, Nelson	H
Elou Caso,			Frazier, Samenta	G
Eokon, Israel			Frazier, Steward	G
Es ticki tobi,	K		Frazir, John	D
Everin, Aron	D		Frivna, William	
Everin, Wacum	D		Gardner, Calvin R.	E
Fareamaehubbee,	G		Gardner, Green W.	E
Farles,	G		Garland, Simpson	I
Farlis,			Garret, Iris	H
Farris, John	G		Gibson, Charles	K
Fartem, Alex A.	I		Gibson, David	F
Feilheurtubbee,	G		Gibson, George	K
Felix,			Gibson, John	I
Fennell, Dewit	K		Gipsens, Henry	
Fennell, Thomas	K		Gipson, Colman	
Fisher, George	H		Gipson, Davis	
Fitokla kin tobe,	K		Glezin, Anderson	I
Fletcher, Cheloam	F		Goins, Henry	E
Fletcher, Coleman	F		Good, Phillip	H
Folsom, Charley P.	I		Gore, William	D
Folsom, Corbby B.	I		Gowings, Henry	E
Folsom, Cornelus			Graham, Nat	F
Folsom, Cyres			Gravy, James	K
Folsom, Ellis W.	I		Green, Alexander	G
Folsom, Jack	H		Grubbs, Joseph G.	E
Folsom, Jackson	E		Ha li che,	K
Folsom, Nat	B		Hala bit tabi, Sam	I

Hala bit tabi,	I		Hotachubbee,	F
Hall, Robert	B		Hotiehubbee,	G
Hall, Simeon A.	I		Hotimabe, Samuel	G
Hall, Steven	H		Hotimonubbee,	G
Hall, William	B		Hotinlubbee,	D
Hampton, Abel	I		Hotombi,	K
Hampton, Benson	K		Hotton,	K
Hampton, Collin	H		Houston, Simeon	I
Hampton, Joe	G		Hoyoponohi,	
Hampton, Willi	H		Sampson	E
Hancock, Martin	H		Hudson, George	I
Hancock, Simmion	H		Hunder, Andrew	G
Hancock, Yollis	H		Hunter, William	D
Harison, James			Iban o wa tobi,	K
Harkin, William	G		Iemma Inteahtubby,	D
Harkins, George	E		Ikllana, Simon	G
Harris, David	F		Im a ha tubbee,	H
Harris, Thomas	G		Ima ha labbi,	K
Harrison, James	K		Imanatubbee,	H
Harwas,	G		Imonatubbee,	D
Hauston, Isaac	G		Into labi, John	I
Hawkin, Joel	H		Isaac, Tom	B
Hawley, Jinn	I		Isaac, William	G
Haylen,	K		Ishatubbee,	H
Henderson,			Ishtafamma, Moses	D
Henry,			Ishtanebbe,	D
Hikitubbee,	F		Ishtiatubbee,	G
Hittakanas,			Ishtonubbee,	H
Hittukanas,			Itahinnatubi,	E
Hobah,	E		Iy a kombi,	K
Holbertubbie, Charles	F		Iy abo kachachi,	K
Holmes, David	H		Iya Monabbi,	K
Holmes, Duncan	H		Iyak om bi,	K
Homa, Moses	E		Jackson, Jacob	G
Homer, Chubbee	B		Jackson,	H
Homer, Moses			Jackson,	
Homma, George	G		Jacob, John	D
Homma, James	D		James, Adam	
Homma, Solomon	D		James, Alexander	I
Hopai a tobe,	K		James, Billy	
Hoper ke tubbee,	B		James, Doctor	E
			James, Henry	E

James, Jack			Kemp, Joel	H
James, Sampson	G		Kemp, Milton	H
James, Warren	B		Kemp, Robert	
Jefferson, Isom			Key o Kerbee, Lewis	B
G			Keyubbee, John	H
Jefferson, Laimes	D		King, Jackson	E
Jefferson, Nicholas	H		King, Joseph	E
Jefferson, Thomas	H		Koba, Anderson	K
Jefferson, Wallace	G		Kota bi,	K
Jefferson, William	I		Kota cha bi,	K
Jefferson,	D		Ksom,	E
Jessee,	B		Lackleve, David	H
Jessie,	H		Lake, Cage	K
Jesy, James			Lake, Elijah	K
Joel, Hoper Za	B		Lapinubbee,	H
Joel, John	B		Lason,	H
Joel, Joseph	B		Lawintabi, Winter	I
Joel, Thomas	B		Lawson, John	E
John,	B		Leah, C. Chubbee	H
John,			Leflare, Harry	E
Johnson, John			Leflore, Edmund	G
Johnson, Phillip	D		Leflore, Isom	G
Johnson, Simeon	I		Leflore, Robert	G
Johnson,	D		Leflore, Sampson	D
Johnson,			Left, John	H
Jonas, Slone			Lewis, Ben	K
Jones, Barton	G		Lewis, Billy	G
Jones, Daniel	H		Lewis, Cornelius	I
Jones, Forbes	H		Lewis, James	D
Jones, Jerry	H		Lewis, Johnston	H
Jones, Peter	K		Lewis, Joshoua	G
Jones, Sampson	E		Lewis, Simon	I
Jones, Solomon	E		Lewis, Thompson	H
Jones, Stephen	K		Logan, James	E
Jones, Wallace	E		Lola, John	E
Jones, William	E		Loman, Wilson	F
Jones			Lorin, James C.	I
Joseph			Loring, Nat	B
Josey, Nicholas	I		Loring,	K
Josey,			Luis, Alexander	E
Kamihmihubbee,	G		Luis, John	E
Kane zo tubbee,	B		Magee, David	D

Mahombi,	K		Mossis,	
Makintabi, Jim	I		Mstabi, Mish	K
Makintabi,	I		Mullen,	
Manypany, Edmun	I		Murphy, Simon	K
Marshall,	K		Murphy, Stephen	K
Martin, Henry	E		Musicunney,	G
Martin, William	H		Nail, Sampson	E
Maytish, Omma	I		Nak ni ba na be,	K
McCann, Thomas	H		Nak niller,	G
McClure, Ellis	B		Nakishe, Lewis	K
McClure, Johnston	H		Nelson, Gooding	G
McCoy, Charles	H		Nelson, Isaac	G
McCoy, Jesse	H		Nelson, James F.	E
McCoy, Logan	H		Nelson, Naaman	G
McKee,			Nelson, Simon	G
McKenney,	G		Nelson, Thomas	G
McKer, Alexander	G		Nicholas, Isaac	E
McKiney,			Nicholas, Sampson	E
McLane, James	D		Nicholas, Willis	E
Mehatichi, Davis			Nicholas,	G
Mevnis, Peter	G		Nicholes, Adam	E
Michel, Johnston	H		Nita kambe, Joe	D
Michey, Thomas			Noah, Davis	E
Mihintayo,	K		Noatubbee,	G
Mikyotubbee,	D		Nokie,	
Milton, John	H		Oconer, Walita	I
Minta, Hombi	K		Oklafa Caya, Simon	K
Minta ho bi, -	K		Oklahomby, Impsy	K
Mintabi, Simon	I		Oklarmatubee,	F
Mintihanubbee,	G		Oklo tubbee,	H
Mintubbee,			Oktabi, John	E
Mishnatomby,			Onna homby, John	K
Missulave, Isom			Onna-hubbee,	G
Mitchell, Mark	F		Onto-Cubbee,	H
Moh ho nacha bi,	K		Opiomby,	
Morgin,	H		Ormond,	H
Morris, James	G		Oshta, Edmond	E
Morris, William	D		Ott, Sann	H
Morrison, James	B		Pah li tubbee,	G
Morrison, William	G		Pah she Stiya,	H
Mosely, Mieles	I		Pakonubbee, Tyron	I
Mosley, Simon			Pakshika, James	G

Parish, Billy	F		Robinson, John	H
Parlar,			Robinson, Sam	D
Parney, Robert	F		Robison,	F
Parson, Lenile P.	I		Rusel, Freeman	D
Partubbee,	F		Samson, Field	
Paser, William	B		Scot, Henry	H
Payne, Forris A.	F		Scott, Josiah	
Peer, Frank	H		Scott, Simon	
Peet, -	B		Sharkerbee, Wallace	B
Pentowa, Davis			Sharlubby, Carnelas	
Perkins, William	AI		Sho Nambi, -	K
Perry, Jefferson	H		Sho ter bee, John	B
Pesarhombee, -	F		Sho tubbee, Ben	B
Pesartubbee, -	F		Shoate, Charles J.	F
Peter, Isum	D		Shoate, Eli J.	F
Peter, Jefferson	B		Shorlubbee, William	
Peter, Lewis L.	I		Shumpa bubee,	G
Peter, Martin	F		Skane,	D
Peter, Simon	D		Smillis,	E
Phillistine, -	F		Smith, Solomon	I
Pickins, Mason	E		Snitcure,	
Pis a too kubbee,	K		Solomon, James	D
Pis ato Kobi, -	K		Solomon,	
Pisa Makintubbee, -	G		Speaker, John	D
Pisa hiabbee, -	G		Speaker, Wesley	D
Pisahambee, -	H		Stanaford, Davis	B
Pistok che, Morris	K		Stanton, John	G
Pope, Sampson	H		Stantubbee,	H
Potonabi, -	E		Steal, John	
Potts, Joel			Stephson,	E
Prime, Erenius			Steward, Robert	G
Pumkin, Thomas	F		Strawn,	
Pusley, David	G		Summy,	
Puter, Solomon	E		Ta hobbi,	K
Ramsey, Paul	I		Tally, Silas	E
Reaves, Henry	G		Tam a hin lubbee,	G
Reubun,	D		Tambbee, Greenwood	G
Riddle, Moses	H		Tamby,	B
Roberts, Amos	D		Tan u hah be,	K
Robertson, James	G		Tanampishtobbee,	F
Robertson, John	G		Tanampishtubbee,	
Robertson, Lewis	G		Thomas	F

Taney, William B.	I		Ubi, Stephen	E
Tarbin,			Uihpisah, Thomas	K
Taylor, Albert	H		Ulph pis a tobi,	K
Taylor, Alexander	E		Vhintubbee,	F
Taylor, Mozers	D		Wacum, John	D
Taylor, Siveeny	I		Wade, Silas	B
Taylor, Thompson	I		Wade, Simpson	I
Taylor, William M.	E		Walker, Jesse	G
Te Kobbi, Moses	K		Walker, Willington	I
Tee Ho Tubbee,	H		Wall, Edwin	G
Tek bombi, Silas	K		Wall, Rempsey	I
Tek bombo, George	K		Wall, Thomas	G
Thomas, Bob	H		Wallen, Elisha	K
Thomas, Washington	K		Wallis, James	
Thomas,	D		Wallis, William	
Thomas,			Walls, Samuel	
Thompson, Isam	H		Walsh, Freeman	G
Thompson, James	G		Wapiachie,	
Thompson, James	H		Ward, Oaintehie	I
Thompson, James	K		Warren, Thompson	K
Thompson, Jimson	H		Wash, Johnson	G
Thompson, John	F		Washington, Ben	E
Thompson, Sriaheka	K		Washington,	
Thompson, Wallis			Corneuliusn	H
Tillis, Jim	F		Washington, George	B
Tillman,	H		Washington, George	K
Tiner, Stephen			Washington, Thomas	H
Tisho Hombi,	K		Washington, Wallace	I
Tishohintubbee,	D		Wasistucyrous, -	E
To mol chubbi,	K		Waten, -	B
Tobly, Davis			Water, Falling	I
Tokchetubbee,	H		Watson, Marion	
Tom, Isam	F		Watson, Peter	I
Tone o tubbee,	H		Waye, Joseph	E
Tonubbee,	F		Webster, Allen	I
Totubbee,	G		Webster, Daniel	K
Tukobbi, William	K		Webster, Jackson	H
Turnbull, Daniel			Webster, Robert	K
Turner, James	B		Webster, Thomas	H
Turnup nowa,	E		Wesley, -	D
Tushakaruttah,			Wesley, Benjamin	F
Tushpartubbee,	H		Wesley, George	B

Wesley, George	H		Willison, Wallac	E
Wesley, Larsen	E		Wilson, Charly	
Wesley, William	F		Wilson, Edward	H
Wheat, Samuel	E		Wilson, Henry	D
Wheaton, Rufus			Wilson, James	K
Wile, Edman C.	I		Wilson, Stephen	
Wilkins, Morris	H		Wilson, William	H
William, Edmond	K		Wilson,	H
William, George	K		Winchester,	E
William, Issam	H		Winston, Charles	E
William, James	E		Worcester,	D
William, John	B		Wright, Thomas	
William, Lorin	K		Ya mih to bi,	K
William, Simon			Yahaponubbee,	H
William, Solomon	K		Yale, Abney	K
William,	H		Yark he tubbee,	B
William,			Yimi tohombi,	
Williams, William			Jackson	K
Willis, Almon	F		Yimnitubbee,	G
Willis, Dickson	F		Yoter bee, Ben	B
Willis, Simon S.	I		Zimmabbee, Lartin	G
Willis, Taysin	D			

Deneale's Regiment, Choctaw Warriors

Deneale, George E.	F&S	Colonel
Hamilton, J.E.	B	Captain
Hamilton, Simeon E.	B	Captain
Hamilton, Simon E.	B	Captain
Ho Tubbee,	D	Captain
Hudson, Washington	A	Captain
Shoat, Jack	C	Captain
Murray, James A. N.		Captain/Acting Quartermaster
Johnson, W.N.	C	First Lieutenant
Mooney, R.M.		First Lieutenant/Adjutant
Pitchlynn, Peter P.	A	First Lieutenant
Robison, Lewis	B	First Lieutenant
Speaker, George	E	First Lieutenant
Ubbey, Minton	D	First Lieutenant
Albertson, Moses	D	Second Lieutenant
Cravat, Willis	B	Second Lieutenant
Dyer, Alliston	A	Second Lieutenant
Philip, Willis	C	Second Lieutenant
Webster, Wilson	D	Second Lieutenant
Youhubbee,	C	Second Lieutenant
Capt, Shona	A	Third Lieutenant
Dibrell, William H.	B	Third Lieutenant
Dyer, James	A	First Sergeant
Billy, Willis	C	Ordnance Sergeant

Privates

Achicanon, Tubbee	C		Alleson,	B
Ah kan noon tubbee,	C		Allice,	E
Ahche tubbee,	B		Amet, G.W.	B
Ahchuckmata cubbee			Amos, Sam	D
Ahekatubbee,	B		Amos,	D
Ahnoontubbee, Kotah	B		Anderson, John	B
Alexander, Charles	C		Apesatubbee,	B
Alic,	E		Atucklontubbee,	C
Allen, Charles	C		Bacon, Silas	D
Allen, J.M.	D		Baldwin, Erastus E.	D

Bame, S. R.	D
Barthlet,	B
Batiss,	C
Battiss, Youhubbe	C
Bean, Aaron	D
Benjamin, Charles	B
Benjamin,	B
Besoluppass,	C
Billy, Alex	C
Billy, Lewis	A
Billy, Simon	D
Billy, Thomas	C
Bixin, Tubbee	C
Bob,	A
Bohannan, Stephen	D
Bond, Joseph	A
Bond, Willis	A
Brashears, Johnson	E
Browning, William	C
Bunyan, Washington	E
Burrass, William	E
Burress, Joel	B
Burress, John	B
Burress, Jonas	B
Burress, William	B
Byington, Alfred	A
Caneel, William	B
Canemahby,	A
Casen,	A
Cass, Noel	D
Cass, William	D
Ceder, Joel W.	D
Chabbee,	C
Charles,	C
Chaslin, Louie	C
Chaslin,	B
Chester, John	D
Chickasaw, Lewis	E
Chinna, Loos	C
Choat, Dickson	C
Christy, Jesse	A
Chuffahta kubby,	B
Chuffahtamby,	B
Clark, Adam	D
Colbert, Davis	A
Colbert, Jonas	A
Colbert, Solomon	A
Comemiah, Davis	C
Coneal, William	B
Cotah, Adison	D
Cotah, Chubby	B
Cotton, John	B
Crowder, Lewis	E
Crowder, Richard	B
Cushman, William	C
Cyrus,	B
Dana, Judah	A
David, Jimison	D
David, Jimson	C
Davidson,	E
Davis,	A
Day, Robert	B
Dibrell, James E.	E
Dibrell, Joseph B.	B
Dickson,	G
Dixon,	C
Donovan, Thomas	B
Durant, Dixon	D
Durant, Douglas	B
Durant, Jesse	D
Durant, Wallice	B
Dureant, Jesse	D
Dyer, Alison	C
Eah Makintubbee,	E
Eahhanubbe, Joseph	A
Eahmockintubbee,	A
Eahpulla,	A
Easman,	A
Easman,	B
Easman,	C
Easman,	D
Eb unubb e,	A
Ebanubbi,	A
Elalomatubbe,	A

Elalomatubbee,	C		Harris, Edmond	C
Elism, Solomon	E		Harris, Sam	E
Elliot, Harris	A		Harris, William	D
Elm, James	E		Harrison, John	A
Eno tamba,	A		Hill, Jackson	A
Faube, Pero	A		Hill, Jackson	E
Faube, Simo	A		Hillatubbee,	A
Fehana, Jackson	C		Ho Yubby,	D
Feobe, Simo	A		Holaway, Thomas	C
Field, Colbert	D		Holly, Cyrus	D
Fokelin, Tubby	C		Homah, Cornelius	A
Folansora, Luppass	C		Hopkin,	B
Folsom, David	B		Hotamba,	C
Forb, Lewis	A		Hotamby,	C
Forb, Lewis	E		Hotecubbee, Ballace	E
Foster, John	A		Hoteenlubby,	B
Foster, John	B		Hotekubbee, Attison	E
Foster, Logan	D		Hudson, Jackson	A
Foster, Scott	B		Hudson, Willis	B
Foul, Frank	D		Ibbahotubbee,	D
Frank, Adam	C		Ille hambe,	B
Frazier, Louie	D		Immonahby,	A
Frazier, Thomas	D		Immonon tubbee,	B
Freeman, Wat	A		Impolumma,	A
Gaines, Henry	B		Impslumma, Adam	A
Gardner, Noel	B		Impson,	B
Garland, Edmond	B		Impsy, Oklahamby	E
Gibson, Henry	E		Isaac, Alic	D
Godsea, Amanuel	B		Isaac, James	C
Gooding, H.L.	B		Ishcotubbee,	A
Green, Henry	D		Ishmahyahubbee,	E
Greer, Henry	D		Ishminbbee,	A
Gregory, Jessy	C		Ishshatubbee,	A
Halsey, Olen	B		Ishtayah, Cornelius	D
Hamba, Shona	E		Jack, James	C
Hamba, Willis	B		Jackson, Billy	C
Hamby, Meak	B		Jackson,	B
Hamilton, Cyrus	B		Jacob, Thomas	C
Hamilton, Thomas	B		James, Bob	A
Hann, Sam	A		James, David	B
Harkin, Joseph	D		James, Harris	C
Harris, Daniel	C		James, Joseph	D

James, Joseph	E		Josephkin,	A
James, Joshua	D		Joshua,	A
James, Laonds	B		Karnes,	D
James, Leonadus	B		Keneda, William	E
James, Silas	C		Kerney, John	D
James,	D		Kincge, James	C
Jamukentube,	D		Kinches, James	C
Jefferson, Thomas	A		Kotah, Chubbe	B
Jeremiah,	D		Kotah,	B
Jesse,	B		Kunomamba,	E
Jim, William	D		Lamby, Meah	
Jima,	D		Leak, John	A
John, Wesley	C		Leflore, Osbon	B
Johnson, James	C		Lewis, John	E
Johnson, Jo	D		Loaring,	E
Johnson, Peter	A		Loasing,	E
Johnson,	A		Logan,	C
Jones, Frank	C		Loman, Jackson	D
Jones, Logan	D		Loman, Pitman	C
Jones, Peter	A		Loman,	D
Jones, Solomon	E		Looee, James	C
Joseph,	B		Loshoha,	
Josephkin,	A		Loui,	A
Joshua,	A		Lowman, Pitman	E
Karnes,	D		Lui,	A
Keneda, William	E		Macket, Forest	B
Kerney, John	D		Mahatukaha,	A
Kincge, James	C		Makahby, Noel	E
Kinches, James	C		Maket, Forest	B
Kotah, Chubbe	B		Marshall, Calvin	D
Kotah,	B		Mason, James H.	D
Kunomamba,	E		Maurice,	C
Lamby, Meah	A		McCann, Benjamin	D
Leak, John	A		McCarley, Johnson	D
Leflore, Osbon	B		McClure, Joseph	A
Lewis, John	E		McClure, Milton	A
Loaring,	E		McConel, Thomas	D
Loasing,	E		McCuern, George	C
Jones, Logan	D		McDaniel, Morris	E
Jones, Peter	A		McGee, Gilbert	A
Jones, Solomon	E		McGould,	B
Joseph,	B		McKinny, Abner	C

McKolven, Mulin	A		Sampson, -	B	
Menger, Wilson	D		Sampson, -	D	
Mintihabbi, -			Sampson, Isaac	E	
Mishoontubby, Charles	B		Seabots, Chan	E	
Moore, Thomas	E		Sexton, Jackson	C	
Morgan, Moses	B		Shamby, Willis	C	
Morgan, Moss	E		Shaw, John	B	
Mucknatubbee, Thomas	B		Sho namba, -	A	
Mullens, John	B		Silas, -	B	
Mullins, John	B		Simma, -	C	
Muntubbee, -	B		Smith, Billy	C	
Nelson, Charles	C		Smith, C.	E	
Nock ish ta kubbe,	A		Smith, Gilbert	D	
Nock ish takubbe,	D		Smith, Stephen C.	D	
Nockishtacubby,	D		Smith, Stephen C.	D	
Nockna la nubbee,	B		Spuel, Samuel	B	
Noles, J.M.	C		Steward, Edmond	D	
Oak Lon Tubbee,	C		Steward, Silas	D	
Ocean, Billy	A		Stewart, C.	B	
Ochalentubbee,	A		Stocker, C.R.	D	
Oma, Losh	C		Sweney,	B	
Pa sa hubbee,	C		Talla, Simon	D	
Parish, Tony	D		Tallowacubbee,	A	
Peter, -	A		Tamby Theoth,	A	
Philip, James	C		Tautah, Joseph	A	
Pirahtubbee, -	E		Taylor, Jacob	A	
Pisahhamby, -	B		Taylor, James	A	
Pisahhonubbee, -	B		Taylor, Sam	A	
Pisahtakubbee, -	B		Taylor, Samuel	A	
Pisohubby, -	C		Tecklin,	B	
Pissallatubbee, Willis	B		Tesnah,	B	
PoShubbee, -	A		Thom, William	C	
Pushamataka, Johnson	D		Thomas, Simeon	E	
Raby,	D		Thomas,	B	
Roberts, Jackson	E		Thompson, Jack P.	B	
Robinson, Jackson	D		Thompson, Jake	A	
Robinson, Jones	D		Thompson, John	B	
Roller, Jesse	E		Thompson, John	E	
Sage, John	B		Thompson,	A	
Sam, -	C		Ticbamba, Silas	B	
Sam, Charles	E		Ticklantubbee,	E	
			Ticklin,	B	

Tiebamba, Silas	B		Watkin, Steven	D
Tike, Sam	D		Watkins, Eastman	D
Tishohamby,	B		Watson, Willie	E
Tishuah,			Webster, Daniel	E
Titheio tubbee,	E		Webster, Earman	D
Tohubby,	C		Webster, Thomas E.	E
Tom, William			William, Bill	B
Tomihintubby,	C		William, Edmond	A
Towantabbee,	A		Williams, James	C
Tubbee, Ho.			Williams, John	B
Tubbee, Sam	C		Williams, Sampson	E
Tubby, Bizen			Williams, Willis	D
Tubby, Fekelin			Willis, David	E
Vaughn, Hickman	B		Willis, George	C
Vaughn, Joseph	B		Willis, James	C
Vaugn, Willis	A		Willis, John	D
Wade, Edward	D		Willis, John W.	B
Wakayomebe,	A		Willis,	A
Wakayonube,	A		Wilson, John	B
Wall, James	A		Wilson, William	A
Wallis, -	A		Wilson,	B
Ward, Colonel	L		Yimmie,	C
Ward, Folsom	E		Yohtah, Gilbert	D
Warren, Solomon	D		Yutah,	B
Watkin, Simpson	D			

Wilken's Company, Choctaw Infantry

Wilkins, John	Captain
Gage, Joseph	First Lieutenant
McCan, Simpson	Second Lieutenant
Mulitubbee, John	Second Lieutenant
Mullen, James	First Sergeant
Alexander, James	Sergeant
Thomas, Celestie	Sergeant
Williams, Hollins	Sergeant
Carnry, William	Corporal
Ekatubbee, James	Corporal
Elatubbee, James	Corporal
McCurtain, Kemper	Corporal
Sam, Jackson	Corporal
Henry, Matthew	Musician
Maurice, Johnson	Musician

Privates

Adam, John	Hancock, William
Ahho to tubbee	Harlin, Lewis
Alomolubbee	Hayes, Henry
Bascum, Henry	Hayes, Lyon
Billy, Alex	Hochubbee, ----
Billy, Jackson	Hullotubbee
Browning, William	Humbee, --------
Cherokee, --------	Hush co char
Choate, Thomas	Ionubbee, -------
Colbert, Jamerson	Ish to chubbee
Colbert, Thomas	Ish to nubbee
Colbert, Wallis	Jackson, Robin
Coleman, Joseph	James, Billy
Compillubbe	James, Collin
Cricklin, James	James, Isom
Davis, Charles	James, Silas
Davis, James	Jefferson, Billy
Dotson, Joseph	Johnson, Maurice
Franklin, Benjamin	Johnson, Willis
Frazier, Dickson	Jones, William
Frazier, Jackson	Latubber, Mosho
Halubbee, -------	Latubber, Nosho

Lewis, Isaac
Lewis, William
Logan, Jamieson
Loshomy, -------
Luce, John B.
McAllester, Elijah
McAllister, Elijah
McDaniel, Johnson
Mulitubbee, John
Mullen, James
Myer, Lewis
Ola hau cha
Ola haucha,
Paine, John
Payne, John
Peter, Thomas
Peter, Wilson
Phillip, James
Piotabbee
Pisahbohubbee

Pisahochubee, -
Sah co
Sah Co, -
Simeon, -
Talapoose, John
Taylor, Harrington
Taylor, Harrison
Thomas, Celestie
Tin lubbee
Tubbee
Wade, Pickens
Washington, George
Washington, James
Wilkins, William
William, Jackson
Willis, James
Willis, John
Wilson, James
Wilson, John
Wright, Allen

1st Regiment, Choctaw and Chickasaw Mounted Rifles

Cooper, Douglas H.	F&S	Colonel
Lee, Roswell W.	F&S	Colonel
Leflore, Mitchell	F&S	Major
Loering, Samson	F&S	Major
Stewart, Charles F.	F&S	Sergeant Major
Cooper, Jr., Douglas H.	F&S	Adjutant
Alexander, Samuel G.	F&S	Adjutant
Wooten, William H.	F&S	Quartermaster
Miner, F.W.	F&S	Assistant Quartermaster
Leflore, Campbell	F&S	Assistant Quartermaster
Morris, F.W.	F&S	Assistant Quartermaster
Rosser, William	F&S	Quartermaster Sergeant
Bond, Thomas J.	F&S	Surgeon
Cooper, David G.	F&S	Assistant Surgeon
Kearby, Edw. P.	F&S	Assistant Surgeon
Cass, William	F&S	Chaplain
West, Thomas	F&S	Bugler
Breedlove, Napoleon B.	F&S	Commissary of Subsistence
Thompson, James	F&S	Acting Commissary of Subsistence
Walker, Sandy		Colonel
Walker, Tandy		Colonel
Reynolds, Lemuel M.	E	Lieutenant Colonel
Riley, James	G	Lieutenant Colonel
Rilley, J.	G	Lieutenant Colonel
Benton, Thomas H.	B	Captain
Dewnt, E.	I	Captain
Dwight, Edward	I	Captain
Folsom, Ellis W.	D	Captain
Hall, Joseph R.	H	Captain
Ish kate ne homma,	K	Captain
Ish kits homa,	K	Captain
Iskitini, Homa	K	Captain
Jones, Willis	C	Captain
Krebbs, Alfred L.	H,F	Captain

Krebs, Alfred L.	H,F	Captain
Levi, John	E	Captain
Martin, John	K	Captain
Matubbee, Peter	D	Captain
Maytubbee, Peter		Captain
McClluse, William	C	Captain
McClour, William	C	Captain
McClure, William	C	Captain
McCurtain, Jackson	G	Captain
Nail, Adam	A	Captain
Perkins, D.	E	Captain
Perry, Bolin	G	Captain
Pitchlim, William B.	A	Captain
Pitchlynn, L.F.	H	Captain
Pitchlynn, William B.	A	Captain
Runddaly, L.	1 E	Captain
Stewart, Charles J.	H	Captain
Wade, Jerry	D	Captain
Welch, Otis G.	1 I	Captain
Young, Robert A.	K	Captain
Bobbly, J.	H	First Lieutenant
Carney, Albert	A	First Lieutenant
Daugherty, Matt	I	First Lieutenant
Edward, Simon	D,E	First Lieutenant
Folsom, Alfred	E,A	First Lieutenant
Folsom, Ebenezer	I	First Lieutenant
Folsom, Joel J.	K	First Lieutenant
Fowler, John	C	First Lieutenant
Hamilton, Simeon	C	First Lieutenant
Jones, Johnson	C	First Lieutenant
Matubbe, Peter	D	First Lieutenant
Maytubbee, Peter	D	First Lieutenant
Nail, Wilson	I	First Lieutenant
Shorey, Alfred	H	First Lieutenant
Ta hi cubbee,	D	First Lieutenant
Tahek obbee,	D	First Lieutenant
Thompson, James	H	First Lieutenant
Vaughn, Thomas	K	First Lieutenant
Wells, William J.	1K	First Lieutenant
Hubbard, Stephen		Senior Second Lieutenant
Boardman, Wallace	C	Second Lieutenant

Name	Co.	Rank
Boardman, Willis	C	Second Lieutenant
Carroll, Joseph A.	I	Second Lieutenant
Coker, John C.	I	Second Lieutenant
Cole, B.	K	Second Lieutenant
Cole, Richmond	K	Second Lieutenant
Curtain, M. M.	B	Second Lieutenant
Debrill, J.R.	C	Second Lieutenant
Diberill, Joseph	C	Second Lieutenant
Frasier, Kelley	A	Second Lieutenant
Frazier, Kelly	A	Second Lieutenant
Hampton, Wade N.	G,K	Second Lieutenant
Harper, Joshua R.	E	Second Lieutenant
Heard, Benjamin C.	B	Second Lieutenant
Irwin, Alexander D.	K	Second Lieutenant
Jackson, William F.	B	Second Lieutenant
James, Silas	A	Second Lieutenant
Jefferson, Thomas	H	Second Lieutenant
Jones, Tobias	H	Second Lieutenant
Jones, William Clayton	K	Second Lieutenant
Levi, Simeon	K	Second Lieutenant
Logan, John	C	Second Lieutenant
Lonney, Morris	G	Second Lieutenant
Lucas, Lyman	K	Second Lieutenant
Lucas, Milton	H	Second Lieutenant
McAfee, Abel	C	Second Lieutenant
McAfield, Abel	C	Second Lieutenant
McCurtain, Edmund	G	Second Lieutenant
McCurtain, J.	G	Second Lieutenant
Pitchlynn, E.D.	1E	Second Lieutenant
Pitchlynn, Ebenezer	1E	Second Lieutenant
Plaster, T.W.	K	Second Lieutenant
Riddle, Jerry	F	Second Lieutenant
Sexton, Jefferson	A	Second Lieutenant
Sexton, Nathan	G	Second Lieutenant
Sexton, W.	G	Second Lieutenant
Simon, B.N.	2 I	Second Lieutenant
Simon, Barnhart	2 I	Second Lieutenant
Strickland, Charles K.	A	Second Lieutenant
Suney, M.	D	Second Lieutenant
Thompson, Thomas J.	K	Second Lieutenant
Tobby, Samuel B.	D	Second Lieutenant
Tobly, Samuel B.	H	Second Lieutenant

Name	Co.	Rank
Toby, Samuel B.	H	Second Lieutenant
Wade, Summy	E	Second Lieutenant
Wells, Daniel	B	Second Lieutenant
William, Amos	I	Second Lieutenant
William, Charles J.		Second Lieutenant
Williams, Charles J.		Second Lieutenant
Wright, Jesse F.	I	Second Lieutenant
Wright, Leonard	D	Second Lieutenant
Baker, James Frank	1K	Junior Second Lieutenant
Johnson, William		Junior Second Lieutenant
Corwin, William	K	Third Lieutenant
Foster, Lewis	E	Third Lieutenant
Kettubbee, Hoper	F	Third Lieutenant
Lee, R. M.	D	Third Lieutenant
Loring, William	K	Third Lieutenant
McClure, Isaac	C	Third Lieutenant
Thompson, D.	C	Third Lieutenant
Belvin, Wilson	HH	Lieutenant
Fisher, David O.		Lieutenant
McCurtain, Mitchell	B	Lieutenant
Pisar ho tubbee, -	3 F	Lieutenant
Winship, David H.	H	Lieutenant
Wurship, David H.	H	Lieutenant
Milton, Davis	C	Sergeant Major
Colbert, Benjamin	E	First Sergeant
Cooper, William	F	First Sergeant
Field, Josiah	D,E	First Sergeant
Folsom, Tandy W.	H,D	First Sergeant
Fry, James	I	First Sergeant
Fry, William	E	First Sergeant
Gillett, Levi E.	K	First Sergeant
Hill, Jackson	H	First Sergeant
Levi,	D	First Sergeant
McCurtain, Houston	B	First Sergeant
Miffett, Nicholas	A	First Sergeant
Moffatt, Nicholas	A	First Sergeant
Patterson, Spencer	K	First Sergeant
Patton, Samuel P.C.	I	First Sergeant
Perry, Daniel	K	First Sergeant
Riggin, Henry C.	K	First Sergeant

Robison, John	K	First Sergeant
Stewart, Charles	C,E	First Sergeant
Stuart, Charles	C,E	First Sergeant
Van Osdel, Henry	A	First Sergeant
Van Osdol, Henry	A	First Sergeant
Wesley, Thompson		First Sergeant
Aberson, Stephen		Sergeant
Adam, John	A	Sergeant
Adams, John	A	Sergeant
Albertson, Stephen		Sergeant
Anotambi,	H	Sergeant
Anutambi,	H	Sergeant
Beames, Joel	I	Sergeant
Beams, Isam	D	Sergeant
Beams, Joel	C	Sergeant
Belvin, Thomas	H	Sergeant
Billy, James	H,D	Sergeant
Bliss, William	D,K	Sergeant
Bohannan, Edward	E	Sergeant
Boon, James	K	Sergeant
Bowman, Granville	K	Sergeant
Brown, Charles	C	Sergeant
Brown, Fielding	K	Sergeant
Byington, Simon	I	Sergeant
Byington, Thomas	I	Sergeant
Cole, Sampson	A	Sergeant
Camp, Amos	G	Sergeant
Cockrell, Simon		Sergeant
Collins, James	A	Sergeant
Darneil, James	H	Sergeant
Darniel, James	H	Sergeant
David,	E,H	Sergeant
Dearneal, James	H	Sergeant
Donivan, Thomas	E	Sergeant
Eyerkuntubbee,	K	Sergeant
Filieyutubi,	H	Sergeant
Filiyotobi,	H	Sergeant
Folsom, Albert	H	Sergeant
Foster, Joseph P.	K	Sergeant
Garland, L.D.	H	Sergeant
Garland, Leonidas	H	Sergeant
Geddes, James S.	K	Sergeant

Geddis, James S.	K	Sergeant
Goin, Isom	C	Sergeant
Going, Isan	C	Sergeant
Green, Lewis	A	Sergeant
Hamilton, Cyrus	C	Sergeant
Hancock, Robert	F	Sergeant
Harrison, Daniel		Sergeant
Havkunnoble,		Sergeant
Heiston, Felix S.	I	Sergeant
Henry, Eli		Sergeant
Holston, Lymen	K	Sergeant
Homah, Moses		Sergeant
Hommer, Robert	K	Sergeant
Hunter, Jackson	K	Sergeant
Jacob, Norris	C,D	Sergeant
Joel, William	K	Sergeant
Jonas, Gimson	H,K	Sergeant
Jones, Jimpson	H,K	Sergeant
Kemp, Amos	G	Sergeant
Kemp, Benjamin	E	Sergeant
King, Anderson	A	Sergeant
Lawetobbe,	K	Sergeant
Lewis, James	B	Sergeant
Loring, Thomas	K	Sergeant
Lowettubbee,	K	Sergeant
Lowetubbee,	K	Sergeant
Martin, Elijah	I	Sergeant
Martin, Lewis	I	Sergeant
Martin, William	F	Sergeant
Matubbe, Toney	D	Sergeant
Maytubbee, Tony	D	Sergeant
McCan, Sam	D	Sergeant
McCurtain, Allen	G	Sergeant
McFerrin, Jere	B	Sergeant
McKan, Sam	D	Sergeant
Minteehubbee,	B	Sergeant
Mintiehubbee,	B	Sergeant
Noahaya, Thompson	E	Sergeant
Payne, William H.	I	Sergeant
Perry, Gilbert	G	Sergeant
Pesalitabba, Johnson	1G	Sergeant
Reddick, William	K	Sergeant

Riddle, George W.	A	Sergeant
Riddle, Joseph	F	Sergeant
Sampson, Joel	3 E	Sergeant
Smith, John E.	1 K	Sergeant
Tanapaya, Jacob	C	Sergeant
Thomas, Joseph	D	Sergeant
Throckmorton, Robert M.	I	Sergeant
Tolbert, Nathan	C	Sergeant
Turner, John B.	K	Sergeant
Vawter, David M.	K	Sergeant
Waletubbee, -	2C	Sergeant
Walilubbe, -	2C	Sergeant
Watkins, Johnson	2C	Sergeant
Wilson, John	D	Sergeant
Adams, Joseph B.		Corporal
Ah cha la tabbee,		Corporal
Ahcholotubb,		Corporal
Allen, Samuel H.	D	Corporal
Anecha, James	A	Corporal
Bohanan, Julius	C	Corporal
Bohannan, Julius	C	Corporal
Brandy, Robert	G,K	Corporal
Burris, Vanburen	C	Corporal
Cage, Wilson	K	Corporal
Capen, John	I	Corporal
Cass, Alfred	K	Corporal
Colbert, Levi	E	Corporal
Ebahna...a,	C	Corporal
Fleming, John	F	Corporal
Fletcher, Moses	E	Corporal
Folsom, Ellis	H	Corporal
Forbis,	K	Corporal
Frazier, Sexton	D	Corporal
Graham, George	H	Corporal
Hampton, Isaac	H	Corporal
Heiston, Thornton B.	I	Corporal
Holmes, John	H	Corporal
Holtin, Coolidge		Corporal
Homes, John	H	Corporal
Hopakintobi,	K	Corporal
Humma, Moses	E	Corporal
Hunt, Wyatt N.	K	Corporal

Iklawaehubbee,	K	Corporal
Ilanontobi,	H	Corporal
Ilapishnowa,	H	Corporal
Jefferson, Joseph	E	Corporal
Kampe, Lubbee	A	Corporal
Kampelabi,	A	Corporal
Kampi labe,	A	Corporal
Kanimatubbee, Jackson	I	Corporal
Kanimonubbee,	I	Corporal
Kanimotubbee, Jackson	I	Corporal
Kanimubbee,	B	Corporal
Kemp, Josiah	A	Corporal
King, Tecumseh	F	Corporal
Lacy, Patrick H.	K	Corporal
Lewis, Thomas	B	Corporal
Liger, Billy	K	Corporal
Loman, Henderson	B	Corporal
Lyan, Charles S.	E	Corporal
Lyon, Charles S.	E	Corporal
McCurtain, Amos	I	Corporal
McCurtain, William	G	Corporal
McGilberry, Charles	H	Corporal
McKenney, John	H	Corporal
McKenny, John	H	Corporal
McKiney, John	H	Corporal
McKinney, John	H	Corporal
Nail, Benjamin	I	Corporal
Nathaniel, Abel		Corporal
Nolen,	G	Corporal
Pakommi,	H	Corporal
Parker, Johnson	G	Corporal
Parnubbee,	B	Corporal
Pasabbee, William	K	Corporal
Patterson, David	K	Corporal
Pattison, Sam	E	Corporal
Peter, John	2 I	Corporal
Pisar tubbee, -	2H	Corporal
Pissa tubbee, -	2H	Corporal
Pissartobbee, -	2H	Corporal
Ponobbi, William	2K	Corporal
Ponubbe, William	2K	Corporal
Pukummi, -	H	Corporal

Reynolds, James	E	Corporal
Rosser, William E.	K	Corporal
Sebolin, -	2 C	Corporal
Sha key, -	2 C	Corporal
Strickland, Daniel	I	Corporal
Strickland, John	I	Corporal
Ta Cubbee,	G	Corporal
Talapoose, Washington	H	Corporal
Talapose, Washing	H	Corporal
Taubbe, Jacob	D	Corporal
Tecubbee,	G	Corporal
Teubbee, Jacob	D	Corporal \
Thomas, Logan	H	Corporal
Thompson, Henry	B	Corporal
Thompson, Jimson	F	Corporal
Tiger, Billy	K	Corporal
Tom, Wesley		Corporal
Tucker, Levi	E	Corporal
Underwood, William P.	I	Corporal
Wade, James	A	Corporal
Walker, Richard	2C	Corporal
Washetuckney, -	2 I	Corporal
Washituckney, -	2 I	Corporal
White, Robert R.	1K	Corporal
White, Thomas W.	1K	Corporal
Williams, Napoleon B.	K	Corporal
Willis, Sexton	A	Corporal
Winlock, Silas	A	Corporal
Yak oh tambe,	C	Corporal
Hays, Joseph N.	K	Adjutant
Jones, Solomon R.	K	Adjutant
Henry, Timothy K.	K	Quartermaster Sergeant
McDaniel, James H.	K	Ordnance Sergeant
Colly, T. M.	H	Surgeon
Colley, Thomas M.	K	Surgeon
Cook, Walter J.	K	Assistant Surgeon
Cock, J. Walter	K	Assistant Surgeon
Harris, Edgar Poe		Contract Physician
Anositubbee, Thomson	K	Bugler
Anosituffe, Thompson	K	Bugler
Anusitobbi, Thompson	K	Bugler
Carter, Freeman W.	I	Bugler

May, William	K	Bugler
Reed, Thomas	L	Bugler
Strickland, Thomas W.	I	Bugler
Austin, Daniel	D,E	Musician
Buris, Elias	D,C	Musician
Burris, Elias	D,C	Musician
Burrows, Elias	D,C	Musician
Henderson, Thomas	C	Musician
McCarter, Solomon	E	Musician
Paxton, Benson	B	Musician
Fletcher, Thomas	I	Blacksmith
Frazier, Davis	I	Blacksmith
Loring, Sampson	K	Blacksmith
White, Jerry	H	Blacksmith
Stone, Thomas B.	K	Farrier
Wokum, Johnson	D	Wagoner
Yotubbee,	D	Wagoner

Privates

Abohlaabi,	A		Ah ne chubbee,	
Abohlaba,	A		Ah no bi,	
Abohlabe,	A		Ah no la tubbee,	G
Acha Kanle,			Ah no li,	
Achakanlet,	G		Ah no tam bee,	
Achayalabbee,			Ah took lan tubbee,	
Achohbby, Ed.			Aha ka tam ba,	
Achukmabbi,			Ahaiotobbe,	
Acker, Martin			Ahe kartom be,	
Actkinson, John D.	I		Ahe katambee,	
Adam, A			Aheka tam bbee,	
Adam, Isaac			Ahekatambee,	
Adam, William C.	G		Aherkar tambbee,	
Adams, Isaac			Ahka ni erubbee,	
Ah cha kan la,	G		Ahkarniubee,	
Ah cha kan li,			Ahnechabee,	
Ah char kanle,			Ahnechobbee,	
Ah chi a tubbee,			Ahni tambee,	G
Ah ho ban tubbee,			Ahnole,	
Ah ho yo tubbee,			Ahnubi,	
Ah kar ne ubbee,			Aho zo tubbee,	A
Ah kurni ubbee,			Ahotabe,	

Ahoyotabi,	A		Edmund	C
Ahoyotubbee,			Anderson,	E
Ahuklintobbe,			Anderson, S.H.	C
Jefferson			Anderson,	
Ahyo kutobbee,			Stephen C.	
Ahyokartubee,			Anderson,	
Ahyokatobie,			Stephen C.	
Ai a ka hubbee,			Anderson, Thomas	E
Ai ni tubbee,	A		Anderson, Thomas	E
Aiatahubbee,			Annumpahonabee,	C
Aiinintobe,	A		Annumpahonubbee,	C
Aikin, Peter	I.		Ano li chubbee,	B
Ainitabi,	A		Ano li chubbee,	B
Aishetabi,	A		Anolatubbee,	G
Aishitobe,	A		Anole,	H
Aius,			Anth la tubbee,	A
Aiyinitobi,			Anukfila,	H
Aiyinitubi,			Anukfilla,	H
Aiyishitobi,			Anumpahorsabbee,	C
Aiyo ka tubbee,			Anuttubbee,	I
Aiyus,			Apo to tubbee,	C
Akineyobbe,			Apototabbie,	C
Al moon tubbee,	G		Arbis,	H
Aladam, W.F.			Arfin,	E
Albertson, Austin			Arkarninbbee,	D
Albertson, Calvin	A		Arketubbee,	B
Alexander,	I		Arkoehartubbee,	B
Alexander,	I		Arkoek as tubbee,	B
Alexander, Joseph	DB		Arlabbee,	K
Alexander, Thomas	G		Arniett,	C
Alexander, Thomas	H		Arnit,	C
Alhitabi,	A		Arnolechubbee,	B
Alhitabi,	A		Arphin,	E
Alick, Gohwikileh	G		Artikitubbee,	B
Allen,	CA		Aryoka tubbee,	F
Allen, Lycurgus	E		Aryokartubbee,	F
Allerson, James T.	K		Atecktohwekeleh,	G
Allion, Danie	D		Atitubbee,	C
Allison, James T.	K		Atkinson, John D.	I
Almon tubbee,	G		Atoklanttabbee,	C
Amson, Sexton	A		Atop li tubbee,	A
Anchahubbee,			Atopletabi,	A

Attabi,	C		Battice, Robinson	H
Attobbee,	C		Battiee, McKenzie	H
Aucha tubbee,			Battiste, Gibson	G
Edmond	B		Battiste, Israel	D,E
Aya ta tubbie,	B		Bays, Joel	I
Ayosh A tubbee,	A		Bays, Joseph	1 I
Ayukpachi tubbee,	A		Beams, Elam	H
Ayukpachitabi,	A		Beams, Elijah	G
Bacon, Armstead			Beams, Thomas	F
Bacon, Charles	H		Beams, William	F
Bacon, Solomon	D		Bear, Jacob K.	I
Bacon, William	B		Beaver, Billy	D
Bahlum, Samuel	K		Bell, Daniel	F
Bailey, Abraham	K		Bell, Hampton	G
Baily, Abraham	1K		Bell, J.	D
Baily, T.B.	D		Bell, John T.	D
Bains, Willaim	D		Bell, W.H.	D
Baker, John	H		Bell, Westley	H
Baker, Lewis	K		Belvin, Gilbert	2 F
Baker, Solomon	F		Belvin, Griffin	F
Baley, Abraham	1K		Belvin, Jefferson	I
Ballard, Isaiah W.	I		Belvin, Jesse	H
Ballard, Robert V.	K		Ben,	E
Ballou, Thomas	K		Benjamin,	C
Ballow, Thomas	1 K		Benton, Alfred	E
Balwin, Griffin	H		Benton, Charles	B
Bane, S. R.	B		Benton, James H.	I
Barness, Jackson			Benton, Robert	G
Barnett, Elya	D		Benton, Thomas	K
Barnett, Hiram	D		Big, John	C
Barnstein, Julius	2 I		Big, John	I
Bars, Roberson	C		Biggs, Daniel U.	K
Bascomb, Benjamin	H		Biggs, Daniel U.	K
Bascome, Benjamin	H		Biggs, Thomas C.	K
Baseum, Benjamin	1 H		Biggs, Thomas C.	K
Basin,	B		Biley,	1E
Baskum, Benjamin	H		Bilinga, Willis	K
Batabbee,	G		Bilinka, Willis	K
Bates, N. E.	3 D		Billika, Willis	K
Bates, William P.	1 I		Billis, Thompson	K
Batiste, Gibson	G		Billy,	
Battice, Nicholas	HH		Billy,	E

Billy, Cornelius	K		Bowman, Dallas W.	K
Billy, Creek	H		Boyle, William	I
Billy, John	A		Boyles, William	I
Billy, John	C		Bradley, John M.	K
Billy, John	F		Bradley, John M.	K
Billy, John	H,D		Bradley, William R.	K
Billy, John	K		Bradley, William R.	K
Billy, Lyman	D		Brashears, William	D
Billy, Mutson	D		Braziers, Morris	C
Billy, Simon	K,H		Breadford, Elijah	K
Billy, Ubsen	K		Breashears, William	D
Billy, William	K		Brewer, Albert	
Bishop, George	D		Brewer, David	
Bliss, Thompson	I		Brewer, Isaac	D
Blue, William	G		Brewer, Nicholas	D
Board, Alexander	K		Brewster, William J.	I
Bobb,	K		Brown, Dallas	K
Bohani, Felin	A		Brown, David	G
Bohannin, Phelin	A		Brown, Dickson	I
Bohlum, Samuel	K		Brown, Dixon	I
Bohtabbee, Harkin	C		Brown, Edmund	H
Bohtubbee, Harkin	C		Brown, George H.	D
Bolen, Johnson	C		Brown, Harris	I
Bolin, Johnson	C		Brown, Jefferson	I
Bond, Alexander	C		Brown, Joshua	D
Bond, Isom			Brown, Rufus	I
Bond, Jonas	H		Browning, Edmond	H
Bond, Thomas	K		Browning, Edmund	H
Bond, Wesley	A		Bull, George W.	I
Bonette, Lewis	B		Bully, Dickson	E
Boot, Square	H		Bully, William	D
Boots, Esquare	H		Bun, Winchester	K
Boots, Esquire	H		Buris, Ben	D
Bosin,	B		Burn, Winchester	K
Botabi,	A		Burnam, Joseph	C
Botubbee,	A		Burnett, Louis	B
Bowers,			Burns, Ashley	K
Thomas Martin	K		Burris, Benjamin	C
Bowland, Billy	H		Burris, William	C
Bowlend, Billy	H		Burroughs, Ben B.	C
Bowles, James K.P.	I		Burrows, Ben	D
Bowls, James K.P.	I		Burrows, Benjamin B.	C

Burton, Thomas	K	Chafathekubbee,	K
Butler, Thomas F.	K	Chafatonubbee,	K
Byington, Gibson	C	Chafatunobbe,	E
Byington, Silas	F	Chaffatubbee,	I,C
Byngton, Gibson	C	Chaffitubbee,	I
Byrington, Silas	F	Chafish cubbee,	G,B
Cain, Joel	K	Chambers, William	K
Calbert, Jameson	G	Chapton, David	D
Caleb, Charles	K	Charfis cubbee,	G,B
Calhoun, John C.	G	Chark, Chark Jefferson	C
Callahan, Thomas	K		
Callihan, Thomas	K	Charles,	D
Calvin, Ephraim	A	Charles,	D
Calvin, Jasper	A	Charles, Eastman	H,D
Caminautubee,	H,D	Charleston, Thomas	K
Caminiantubbee,	H,D	Charley,	A
Camp, William	H	Chetah, Benjamin	C
Campbell, Nicholas	C	Chi che aney,	G
Candy, Summers	K	Chickaway,	G,B
Candy, Teams	E	Chickwa,	G,B
Cane, Jewel	K	Chickway,	G,B
Canimantobbee,	H,D	Chickwey,	G,B
Canimantobe,	H,D	Chipani,	A
Carmantubbe,	D	Chitto, Joseph	K
Carminantubbee,	D	Choate, Alexander	G
Carn, Simon	G	Choate, William	G
Carney, Allen W.	I	Chonoontah,	H
Carney, Billy	F	Chonunta,	H
Carney, Cornelius	D	Chriner, G. A.	F
Carroll, William W.	A	Chubbee, Charlis	G,B
Carson,	H,D	Chubbee, John	D
Carter, Robert	I,C	Chubbee, Samuel	B
Cartilley,	K	Chuckmubbee, Waymus	I
Cartilly,	K		
Carvell, William W.	A	Chumenta,	H
Cass, Lewis	F	Chunontah,	H
Cass, Maurice	H,D	Chuzlischubbee,	G,B
Cass, Morris	H,D	Clardy, Smith	K
Cass, Thompson	F	Clark, Frank J.	I
Cauldwell, George	H	Clark, Willis	K
Cauldwell, James	H	Clay, Simon	C
Cedar, Joel	H	Cline, Israel	I

Name	Code
Coachneauer, Edward	E
Coat, Phillip	F
Cobb, Gains	G
Cobb, Ganis	G
Cobb, McKinney	D,C
Coffee, Thomas	A
Colbert, Calvin	E
Colbert, Jackson	H
Colbert, James	
Colbert, James	E
Colbert, Jameson	G
Colbert, Jose	E
Colbert, Logan	E
Colbert, Morgan	A
Colbert, Samuel	A
Colbert, Silas	D,K
Colbert, William	B
Colbert, Wilson	A
Colburt, Jameson	G
Cole, Henry	E
Cole, John	D
Coleman, Joseph	F
Collin, Samuel	K
Collin, Simpson	I
Collins, David	B
Collins, Ellis	B
Collins, Isaac	I
Collins, Jackson	D
Collins, Jeremiah	H
Collins, Joseph	C
Collins, Nathan	B
Collins, Westley	C
Columbus, Martin	D
Con on ta shubbee,	G
Conner, John N.	K
Conner, William B.	K
Conway, Jackson	A
Conway, Logan	A
Coody, John	D
Cook, James F.	I
Cook, Joseph W.	F
Cooke, James F.	I
Cooke, Joseph W.	I
Cooper, Alfred	D
Cooper, D. H.	C
Cooper, David R.	I
Cooper, Henry	F
Cooper, Larfield	F
Cooper, Samuel	K
Copeland, Charles	K
Copland, Charles	K
Copter, Samuel	K
Cornelius, Doctor	C
Corney, George	H
Corney, John	H
Cosby, John	
Couch, Bizzel	I
Coward, William	K
Cox, Daniel L.	I
Cox, John	
Cravat, William	E
Cravet, Sila	I
Crawford, Alsbury R.	K
Crawford, Edwin T.	K
Crawford, Elsbury R.	K
Crite, Joseph	K
Crofford, Silas N.	I
Crouder, William J.	H,D
Crowder, William J.	H,D
Cubbee,	I
Curshah, Ellis	C
Curtis, Elias	C
Cushah, Ellis	C
Daily, Edmond	I
Daily, Edmund	I
Dale, Allen	D,E
Dana, Solomon	H
Daniel, Samuel	H,D
Darnell, John W.	K
Davenport, Charles C.	K
Davidson, John K.	K
Davis,	A

Davis,	B	Echabe,	C	
Davis, J. Russell	K	Echarpotubbee,	F	
Davis, James M.	I	Echubbee,	C	
Davis, Jefferson	K	Edmond,	B,H	
Davis, John	A	Edmund,	B,H	
Davis, Oklarbe	D	Edward, Lewis	E	
Davis, Russel J.	K	Eelachahumbee,	G	
Day, John	I	Eglinnatta, George	C	
Dean, William	K	Ela che hamba,	G	
Debrell, James	H	Ela hatubbee,	E	
Demas, Jackson		Ela pira tubbee,	E	
Dewette,	H	Elachahumbbee,	G	
Dewitte,	H	Elachatubbee,	C	
Dibbrell, James	H	Elachetubbee,	E	
Dibbril, James	H	Elafehnubbee,	K	
Diberill, James	H	Elah ha tubby,	E	
Dick, Martin	I	Elam,	D	
Dickson,	A	Elambee,	D	
Dickson,	H	Elanubbee,	B	
Dixon,	A	Elapimltubbee,	D	
Dow, L.B.	D	Elarpintubbee,	E	
Drew, Lemuel	E	Elematubbee,	A	
Dukes, Joseph	B	Elemitabi,	A	
Durant, Alexander	H	Elias, John	H,D	
Durant, Benjamin	H	Elliott, John	G	
Durant, Samuel	G	Elonubbee,	F	
Dwight, Johnathan	D	Elumbbee,	B	
Dwight, Joseph P.	A,C	Emah none tubbee,	C	
Dyer, James	E,I	Emahlitabee,	C	
Dyer, Willis	E,I	Emanotabee,	C	
Eah ha nubber,	G	Emm onotubbee,	C	
Eah ha tubbee,	G	Er pa tors tubbee,	E	
Eahan tubbee,	D	Erpa tun tubbee,	E	
Eakatubbee,	G	Eshobbe,	E	
Ealambe,	D	Esus,	E	
Eastman, James H.	A	Evans, James W.	I	
Eastman, Mont	D	Eyah ho nubbee,	A	
Easton, James H.	A	Eyah katubbee,		G
Eatambee, Sampson	D	Eyahanobe,		A
Ebahaka, Joslin	K	Eyahhatubbee,		G
Ebahnubbee,	C	Eyahmata, Stephen		I
Echabbee,	C	Eyahmataha, Stephen		I

Eyahonabi,	A	Folsom, Steanes W.	K
Eyahonubbee,	G	Folsom, Stephen	A
Eyarmonubbee,	B	Folsome, Starnes W.	K
Eyashahopaiye, Wilson	I	Folsum, Josiah	D
Eyashahopaiyi, William	I	Forbes,	H
Eyashahopaye, William	I	Forbis,	H
Eyashahopiye, William	I	Forbis,	I
Eyashahopiye, Wilson	I	Ford, James M.	K
Eyohmonubbee,	B	Forris,	I
Farris, Joseph	I	Forst, Tom	E
Fauler, Charles	E	Foster, Byington	I
Fechubbee,	F	Foster, Hopkin	H
Fechuble, Amos	I	Foster, John	
Fechubli, Amos	D	Foster, Joseph B.	K
Fellemahchubbee,	G	Foster, Josephus	K
Felumeche,	B	Foster, Lewis	D
Fiblummiche,	B	Foster, Ruben	K
Fichak, Jackson	C	Foster, Scott	H
Field, William	D	Foster, Simms	K
Fillamintubbee,	G	Foster, Timmies	K
Fillamuchubbee,	G	Foster, Tims	K
Fillemachubbee,	G	Frank, John	B
Fillimsentubbee,	G	Frank, William	B
Fillumin tubbee,	G	Franklin, Charles	K
Filmore, Gibson	D	Franklin, Harris	I
Fisher, Charles P.	G	Franklin, James	B
Fisher, Ellis	G	Franklin, Levi	K
Fisher, P. Charles	G	Franklin, Robert	C
Fisher, William	K	Franklin, William	K
Flint, Solomon	I	Frasier, Fletcher	A
Folsam, Edward	E	Frasier, Hickman	
Folsom, Alexander	A	Frasier, William	
Folsom, Arnold	D	Frazier, Aaron	H
Folsom, David	H	Frazier, Alexander	A
Folsom, Edward	E	Frazier, Daniel	I
Folsom, Harris	A	Frazier, Esus	I
Folsom, Joel	G	Frazier, Fletcher	A
Folsom, Joseph	I	Frazier, Johnson	I
Folsom, Josiah	D	Frazier, Sampson	K
Folsom, Levi	D	Frazier, William	K
Folsom, N.M.	K	Freeny, Frank	D
Folsom, Simon	I,A	Freeny, John	

Name	Col
Freney, Frank	D
Fry, Johnson	I
Fullumma,	K
Fullummi,	K
Fulsome, David	
Fulton, Samuel	
Gaines, Alexander	K
Gains, Alexander	K
Gains, John	D
Gardner, Lewis	A,C
Gardner, Simeon	A
Garey, S.H.	F
George, Israel	K
Gibson, Calvin	
Gibson, Coleman	I
Gibson, David	
Gibson, Henry	H
Gibson, Irvin W.	I
Gibson, Irwin W.	I
Gibson, James	
Gibson, Joseph	H
Gipson, Joseph	H
Goforth, Solomon	D
Goforth, William	
Goforth, William	D
Going, Stephen	C
Gooding, John	E
Gose, Felix	I
Graham, Phillip	H
Grant, Alas M.	K
Grant, Atlas M.	K
Grason, John	A
Graves, Edward	K
Grayson, James	G
Grayson, John	A
Greenwood,	D
Greenwood, Allen	E
Greenwood, Gibson	E
Greenwood, Harris	E
Greenwood, Hogan	E
Greenwood, Sesson	E
Gregg, John B.	D
Griffin, John	D
Griffith, Charles	G
Haiakonobi,	H
Haiarka, Lewis	H
Haiarkar, Lewis	H
Haiarkas, Lewis	H
Haikin, Wakaya	D
Haiokonubi,	H
Hait,	E
Halatubbee,	K
Hale, George	K
Hall, George	K
Hall, Gordon	I
Hall, James J.	K
Hall, James	H
Hall, Joseph I.	D
Hall, Joseph S.	H,D
Hall, Sampson	H
Hall, Sickum	E
Hall, Stephen	F
Hall, Wallis	E
Halley,	C
Hammock, Willoughby	I
Hampton,	C
Hampton, Wanice	H
Hancock, Cumelius	F
Hancock, William	F
Hannubbee,	E
Hanto, Joe	D
Hanya,	C
Harkin,	H
Harkin, James	D
Harkin, Jamison	D
Harkin, Joel	K
Harkin, Wiley	D
Harkin, William	D
Harkin, William	I
Harkin, Wilson	H
Harkines, Willis	K
Harkins,	H
Harkins, Joseph	H

Harkins, Newton	H		Helm, Theophilus	K
Harkins, Thomas	K		Hemakabee, William	I
Harkins, William	I		Hemakabi, William	I
Harkins, Willis	K		Hemokabbe,	K
Harkins, Wilson	H		Hemokabbi,	K
Harley, Silas	H		Henderson,	
Harlow, Elija	D		B. Charles	G
Harnubbee,	E		Henderson,	
Harper, Isaac N.	I		Charles B.	G
Harris, A. Sidney	K		Henderson, Jacob	K
Harris, E. Poe			Henderson, Richard	B
Harris, Gooding			Henter,	C
Harris, Joseph	B		Herrin, Ephraim	K
Harris, Lewis	E		Herris, Henry	K
Harris, Lewis	K		Herris, Joel	K
Harris, Solomon	G		Heustm, Sam	K
Harris, William F.	K		Heuston, Sam	K
Harris, William	H,K		Hiakar, Henry	H
Harrison,	H		Hiarka, Henry	H
Harrison, James M.	I		Hiarka, Lewis	H
Harrison, John	B		Hiarkar, Henry	H
Harrison, Malachi	I		Hiarkar, Lewis	H
Harrison, William H.	G		Hiarker, Lewis	H
Harwell, James E.	K		Hiasker, Henry	H
Haskin,	H		Hicks,	H
Haskin, Joseph	H		Hicks, William	E
Haueston, Isam	I		Hikvchi,	H
Havens, John	I		Himakambi, Lewis	C
Hawkins,	H		Himmakambee,	
Hawkins, Newton	H		Louis	C
Hawkins, Thomas	K		Hinka, Jimson	D
Hawkins, Wilson	H		Hinka, Jimson	D
Haynes, Marcus	I		Hlem, Theophilus	K
Hays, Loman	H		Hlepota,	K
Hays, Philip	K		Hliohtubbi, Bobb	K
Hays, Thomas	D		Hlopota,	K
Hayse, Loman	H		Hluputa, Joseph	K
Hayse, Philip	K		Ho pa kin tubbee,	D
Hayyah,	C		Ho tin lubbee,	I
Headly, Wilson	K		Hobert, Jerry	I
Heath, Benjamin A.	K		Hobert, John	I
Hekeantubbee,	G		Hodge, John H.	I

Hodges, Albest J.	I	Hopinabe,	A
Hodges, John H.	I	Hornsinger,	
Hodges, Thomas	I	Thomas F.	I
Hodges, William	D	Hotakubbee, Amos	A
Hoeha,	A	Hotambe, John	C
Hogan, Pisahonabe	C	Hotambee, John	C
Hoklitubbee,	I	Hotantubbee,	G
Hol lk a tu, Amos	A	Hotenlubbee,	I
Holekabi, Amos	A	Hotinlabee,	C
Holland Jr.,		Hotumbi, John	C
Spearman	K	Housa,	D
Hollis, William H.	I	House, James T.	K
Holmes,	A	Houston, John	D
Holmes, David	F	Houston, Sam	K
Holmes, Forbis	A	Howell, John	H
Holston, Aaron	I	Howell, P.P.	H
Holston, David	C	Howell, Peter	H
Homa, Joseph	C	Hoyopa, Hilbert	E
Homa, Ward	K	Hoyt,	E
Homah, Enoch		Hoyupa, Kelob	E
Hombi, Joseph	H	Hudson, George	B
Homer,	G	Hully,	C
Homes, Forbis	A	Humbly,	E
Homma, Elias	D	Humma, Edmund	E
Homma, Joseph	C	Humma, Levi	E
Homma, Robert	D	Humma, Martin	E
Homma, Ward	K	Humphreys,	
Hommer, Thomas	K	William Riley	K
Honey, Josepheus	E	Humphries,	
Hood,	C	William R.	K
Hood, James	C	Hunter, Allen	F
Hooper, Abel	I	Hunter, Joe	D
Hoosa,	D	Hunter, Joseph	
Hopa ka tubbee,	H	Hunter, Stilon	
Hopa kin tubbee,	A	Hunter, William	H,D
Hopaii, John	E	Hush to lubbee,	K
Hopakin to bi,	A	Hushtahlabbee,	K
Hoparkatobbee,	H	Hushtup, Isham	C
Hoparketobe,	H	Husten, John	D
Hoparketubee,	H	Huthtub, Isom	C
Hoparkin tubbe,	D	Hyle, Alfred	
Hoparkitobbee,	H	Ia kan tubbee,	C

Iah ho ka tubbee,	C		Illapahne,	A
Iah ko nubbee,	D		Illapishtiah, Moses	K
Iaho ko ttubbee,	C		Illapkshlanya, Moses	K
Iakanttubbee,	C		Illappambbee,	G
Iakombi,	H		Illehim ma chi,	C
Iatochobi,	H		Illihombi,	H
Iba o nabi,	A		Ilopoitubbee,	G
Iba o nubbee,	A		Ilth ko la cha,	G
Ibafohkalabi,	A		Ilthkolehoha,	G
Ibaheka, Jorsilame	K		Ilthkolihcha,	G
Ibahika, Juslyn	K		Ima ton tubbee,	A
Ibaiekbi, John	K		Imelobi,	H
Ibbakokatubbree,	A		Imilambi,	A
Ichaeotubbee,	A		Imilubi,	H
Ichapatabi,	A		Immahantubbee,	G
Ieshetubbee,	I		Immahautabbee,	G
Ihtonubbee,	K		Immahuma,	A
Ihttotubbee,	E		Immaithatubbee,	G
Iit tu tubbee,	E		Immathatubbee,	G
Ik il oka tubbee,	A		Immathla chubbee,	E
Ikania,	A		Immathla tubbee,	G
Ikilloketabi,	A		Imme lambee,	A
Iklannaotta, George	C		Immilabbi,	A
Ila ba tubbee,	I		Immilobbi,	A
Ilafehnobbi,	K		Immonabbe,	A
Ilafehnobbie,	K		Immonubbee,	A
Ilahekabbe,	K		Immonubbee,	E
Ilahika bbi,	K		Immonubbee,	
Ilaintibbee,	D		Jefferson	E
Ilanowur,	D		Imonabi,	A
Ilantubbee,	I		Impa tubbee,	E
Ilap ah ni,	A		Impartubbee,	E
Ilapahnobi,	H		Impson,	H
Ilapin tobbi,	K		Impson, Harrison	I
Ilapintobbe,	K		Imuton ta bi,	A
Ilawtubbee,	D		In la hubbee,	C
Illa ho tam bee,	C		In tal le Ky,	C
Illa ho ttumbee,	C		Inkania,	A
Illa ka nubbee,	K		Inlahabbee,	C
Illa pam be,	G		Innowatubbee,	I
Illa po nubbee,	D		Inshalahtubbee,	G
Illap pah cha,	E		Inshalihtubbee,	G

193

Inshalitubbee,	G		James, Allen	K
Intalikey,	C		James, Amos	C
Inthalehtubbee,	D		James, Collin	F
Iohkonubbi,	D		James, Dickson	I
Isam,	E		James, Dixon	I
Isam,	H,D		James, George	K
Isam, Robert	G		James, John	D
Ishseka, Solomon	D		James, John	H,E
Ishtahaka, Thomas	K,C		James, Jone	D
Ishtaheka, Thomas	K,C		James, Joshua	H
Ishtahuka, Thomas	K,C		James, Kobbe	E
Ishtaya, Cornelius	H		James, Lyman	K
Ishteahhonubbee,	K		James, Silas	F
Ishteka, Solomon	D		James, William	H,K
Ishteke tubbee,	G		Jefferson, Abnan	K
Ishtiahonabbee,	K		Jefferson, Henry	G
Isom,	H,D		Jefferson, Thomas	B
Isum,	H,D		Jefferson, Thomas	D
Isum, Robert	G		Jefferson, Thomas	D
Ittiyanitabee,	C		Jefferson, Thomas	E
Iuppa hubbee,	E		Jefferson, Thomas	F
Iuppe ubbee,	E		Jefferson, Thomas	K
Iyahambe, Amos	E		Jefferson, Timothy	C
Jackson,	A		Jeffrey, Joseph	E
Jackson,	D		Jeffry, Joseph	E
Jackson,	F		Jelette, Levi E.	K
Jackson, Durant	K,E		Jellett, Levi E.	K
Jackson, Edmond	H		Jenkins, Amon	I
Jackson, Edmund	H		Jerimiah,	H
Jackson, James B.	H		Joel,	H
Jackson, Loman	B		John, Impson	I
Jackson, William	G		John, Sam	K
Jacob,	I		John, Simpson	I
Jacob, Austin	I		John, Willis	C,K
Jacob, Gibson	G		Johnson,	
Jacob, Jack	C		Johnson,	A
Jacob, M.D.	C		Johnson, Collin	I
Jacob, M.E.	C		Johnson, David	D,E
Jacobs, Gibson	G		Johnson, Isaac	K
Jam, John	K		Johnson, John	I
James,	E		Johnson, Laron	K
James, -	H,D		Johnson, Lewis	E,K

Johnson, Philip	I	Kanontabe, William	C
Johnson, Samuel	C	Kanutubee, William	C
Johnson, William	I	Kartillier,	K
Jon, James	H,E	Kawasha, James	H
Jonas, Harris	C	Kemp, Milton	F
Jonas, Isaac	H	Kerbs, Robert	H
Jonas, Simon	C	Key, Frank	D
Jones, Billy	D	Keyubabe,	A
Jones, David	H	Keyuhbabi,	A
Jones, Frank	D	Killen, Robert	B
Jones, H.Cornelius	E	Kincade, Joseph	B
Jones, Harris	C	Kincaid, George	C
Jones, Isaac	H	Kincaid, Joseph	B
Jones, Isreal	H	King, Adam	K
Jones, Jr., Simon	C	King, Bob	K
Jones, L.	D	King, Boff	K
Jones, Lyman	B	King, Columbus	I
Jones, Noel	C	King, George	I
Jones, Sr., Simon	C	King, John	C
Jones, Thomas	B	King, John	I
Jones, Willis	C,K	King, Mitchell	G
Joseph,	H	King, Nelson	K
Josiah, Taylor	A	King, Peter	D
Judas,	I	King, Willis	K
Judson,	H	Kington, Robison	K
Juzon, Jackson	H	Koa, William	K
Kahlamba,	D	Koche tum bee,	A
Kamihtubbee, Alexander	I	Koe foney,	H
		Koe, Thomas	K
Kampillachubbee,	G	Koehatambe,	A
Kampittchubbee,	G	Kohlambe,	D
Kanaiayachobi,	H	Koifoney,	H
Kanalichubbee,	K	Koifony,	H
Kanayah chubbee,	G	Kolidge,	D
Kanimabee,	K	Krebbs, Johnson	F
Kanimantobi,	I	Krebs, Robert	H
Kanimontobi,	K	Kunemantubbee,	A
Kanimuntabi,	A	Kunne mantubbee,	H
Kaninchubi,	H	Kunneah chubba,	G
Kaniobbe, Thomas	E	Kunneo tubbee,	A
Kaniyotabi,	A	Kunoontambee, William	C
Kannayahchubbee,	G		

LaBaker, Lewis	D		Lewis, Moses	E
Lacy, John	E		Lewis, Page	G
Lacy, William D.	H		Lewis, Philip	H
Lafintabbee	C		Lewis, Silan	I
Lah fintubbee	C		Lewis, Stephen	E
Lane, John	E		Lewis, Thomas	D
Langston, James J.	I		Lewis, William	E
Lapishhomma,	D		Light, Amos	E
Larkin,	D		Likee, Sampson	E
Lasso,	C		Lockly, David	K
Latham, King	K		Loeman, Harkins	A
Lather, William	K		Logan, John	H
Lawaytubbee,	E		Logan, Sam	H
Lebaker, Lewis	D		Loma,	A
Lebukur, Lewis	D		Loma,	G
Lee, E. M.	E		Loman, Felix	K
Lee, Robert K.	K		Loman, Harkin	A
Lee, Thomas J.	K		Loman, Jackson	H
Lee, William Newton	K		Loman, Loring	K
			Loman, Watt	A
Leesoy, Arthur	A		Lomata, Kubbee	A
Leflare, Joel	E		Lomen, Felix	K
Leflore, Edmund	G		Lomen, Loring	K
Leflore, Joel	E		Lommah,	G
Leflore, John	K		London, Marcus L.	I
Leflore, Simeon	I		Long, Davis	A
Leflore, Sweeney	C		Long, John	H,D
Leflore, Thompson	D		Loring,	G
Leighton, Lorenzo D.	I		Loring, Austin	K
Lewis,	I		Loring, Eastman	I
Lewis, Ben	C		Loring, Loman	K
Lewis, Isiah	K		Loring, Sweal	E
Lewis, Isom	K		Losam, Christy	C
Lewis, James M.	G		Losan, Christy	C
Lewis, James O.	K		Loumar,	B
Lewis, James	E		Lovejoy, William W.	I
Lewis, James	H,D		Loving, John	G
Lewis, John F.	K		Lowatubbee,	E
Lewis, John T.	K		Lucas, Johnson	I
Lewis, John	K		Lucas, Jonas	I
Lewis, Joshua	D		Luma,	A
Lewis, M. James	G		Luma, Limmon	E

Lumar,	B	
Lumatukabi,	A	
Lumma, Limmon	E	
Lynch, James	D	
Lytle, William J.	I	
Ma kinla, James	I	
Mack in tubbee,	I	
Magie, Charles	K	
Mahambee,	C	
Mahola, John	E	
Maihobo, John	E	
Makintabi,	A	
Makobi, Noel	H	
Malelehabbee,	C	
Malhalli,	A	
Malis,	C	
Malone, John	K	
Mambee,	C	
Mambey,	C	
Marion, Thomas	E	
Markintabe,	C	
Marlin,	H	
Marlin, Silas	I	
Marlis,	C	
Marrison, John	H,D	
Mars,	C	
Marsh, Kilfot	E	
Martin, Ben	I	
Mash kokabbi,	K	
Mason, Irvin P.	K	
Mason, Irving P.	K	
Mass,	C	
Mathalli,	A	
Mathis, E.W.	D	
Mathis, J.F.	D	
Matubba,	C.	
Mayers, Jefferson	G	
Mayfield, George T.	I	
Maylone, John	K	
Maytubbee, Hogan	D	
Maytubbee, Moses		
McCain, William L.	K	
McCaine, William L.	K	
McCalister, Wilson	F	
McCan, James	K	
McCan, Watt	K	
McCann, Benja	H	
McCann, Charles	F	
McCann, Thomas	K	
McCassin, William	G	
McCasson, Samuel	G	
McCasson, William	G	
McClane, James	H	
McClenden, William B.	K	
McClish, George	A	
McClore, Samuel	K	
McClure, Adam	G	
McCollin, Jesse	I	
McConnell, Samuel	D	
McCoy, George Clark		
McCoy, John	A.	
McCullin, Jesse	I	
McCurtain, Johnson	G	
McCurtain, Partick	G	
McDaniel, John	K	
McDaniel, Thomas B.	K	
McDonld, Cauldwell	H	
McDowell, J.B.	F	
Mcfa, Amos	E	
McGahey, David C.	I	
McGee, George	H	
McGee, Harris	A	
McGee, James	E	
McGelbery, Nicholas	G	
McGilberry, Loui	A	
McGilberry, Nicholas	G	
McGilberry, Simpson	F	
McGilbury, Lewe	A	
McGilbury, Simpson	F	
McGowan, Davis	H	

McGowan, Tobias	H
McGowen, Davis	H
McGowen, Tobias	H
McGowon, Davis	H
McGowon, Tobias	H
McIlvene, Polk	K
McIlvne, Polk	K
McKain, William M.	K
McKee, Silas	B
McKenney, Watt	A
McKey, Ellis	G
McKinney, Morris	D
McKinney, Watt	A
McKlain, Holis	D
McLain, Hallis	D
McLean, James	H
McLendon, W.B.	K
McNoel, Histy	G
Me ha tam bee,	K
Me ha tambe,	C
Me ham be,	I
Me ham bee,	C
Me ham bi,	I
Me heo tubbee,	G
Me hin Cam bee,	C
Me ho chubbee,	B
Me she mahtubbee,	C
Me yah tubbee,	C
Meahshintubbee, Barn	C
Meahtubbee, David	
Measheya, Farbus	D,E
Meashintabbee, Ben	C
Meashiya, Forbis	D,E
Meashonubbee,	D
Mehahte kah, Bazil	C
Mehatika, Bazil	C
Mehyohtubbee,	C
Mehyotubbee,	G
Meirs, Jefferson	G
Melton, George	K
Meshantubbee,	H
Meshontarbbee, Aron	K
Meshontarbbee, Elias	K
Meyattubbee,	C
Mi hi Cambe,	C
Miashaya, Forbis	D,E
Miashintabee, Barn	C
Miashonabe,	C
Miashonubbee,	K
Miathonubbee,	D
Mickle, J.A.	D
Mihahtambee,	K
Mihinlohtabe,	A
Mihyoh chubbee,	B
Mike, John	H
Miki, John	H
Miller, George	D
Miller, Hutcherson	A
Milton, Philip	I,A
Miltree,	C
Minlehambbee,	B
Mintihumbbee,	B
Miottobbe, David	E
Mishaantubbee,	E
Mishamatubbee,	G
Mishe ma tubbee,	G
Mishemahtabee,	C
Mishihmahtobbee,	C
Mishontibbee,	H
Mishontobbi, Aaron	K
Mishontobbi, Isom	C
Mishontubbee,	H
Mishoontaba, Aaron	K
Mishoontaba, Elias	K
Mishoontaba, Isom	C
Mishoontahbe,	C
Mishoontubbee,	E
Mishoutabbee,	C
Mock, A tubbee	G
Mokintubbee,	A
Moncrief, Thomas	A

Monico, John	E		Nail, Jefferson	K
Monico, John	E		Nail, Josiah	I
Monroe, William	G		Nail, Samuel	I
Montahi,	A		Nail, William	K
Moore, Albert	B		Nak i ma sha,	A
Moore, Ewing	A		Nak nein tobbee,	H
Moore, G.P.	B		Nak ni chih,	A
Moore, James	E		Nak ni chubbee,	I
Moore, John Henry			Nak nun to bee,	H
Moore, Nephus	C		Nakey, Abi	A
Moore, Wesley	I,C		Nakis ho ubbe,	D
Moore, William	B		Nakishhoyobbe,	E
Moot, G.P.	B		Nakiyabi,	A
More, Albert	B		Naknichi,	A
More, Neol	E		Naknihobbi,	K
More, Wesley	I,C		Naknin tu bbee,	H
Morgan, Silas	F		Narkechi, John	B
Morholetabi,	A		Narkotubbee,	B
Moricks, J.J.	D		Narreymore,	
Morris,	I		Holden G.	K
Morris, Eugene S.	K		Narrymore,	
Morris, George	F		Holden G.	K
Morrison, John	E		Nath la homma,	K
Morrison, John	H,D		Neal, Tandy K.	
Morrison, Thomas	I			K
Morrison, William	E		Neale, Tandy K.	K
Moses, Daniel	K		Necko tubbee,	
Mosho li tubbee,	A			B
Mosholitabe,	A		Ned, John	D
Mude, Jery	C		Neely, James M.	I
Mul la le hubbee,	C		Nelson, Brown	I
Muletambe,	D		Nelson, Job	K
Mullatamba,	D		Nelson, Simon	B
Munroe, William	G		Nelson, Washington	D
Mustilles, -	I		Nemukarmbee,	
Mustillis,	I		Robert	E
Nahla, Homa	K			
Nahobi, Willis	H		Nenukinbbee,	
Nail,	D		Robert	E
Nail, Amos	A		Nerrymore,	
Nail, Harrison	I		Holden G.	K
Nail, Henry	A		Newson, Eugene	A

Newson, John	A		Oky a harmbbee,	K
Newton, Isaac	H		Oky an humbbee,	K
Newton, Lyman	I		Okyanhubbee,	G
Nicholas,	I		Okyea h hubbee,	G
Nickodemas,	D		Oliphant, Samuel M.	K
Nickodemus,	D		Olliphint, Samuel M.	K
Nickodemus,	I		Olttharchubbee,	E
No ko wa,	E		On hat tubbee,	G
No kow ah,	E		Ona hat tubbee,	K
Noah, Harris	H		Ona te chubbee,	A
Nockeche, John	B		Onabe,	C
Nockishmehubbee,	B		Onarhachubbee,	B
Nockishtmuhyubbee,	B		Onateehabi,	A
Noel,	H		Onchiubi,	H
Nok homma,	I		Onchivbi,	H
Nok humma,	I		Onhuttubbee,	G
Nok oho pa,	E		Onnaha tubbee,	K
Nokish ho yubbee,	D		Onnahecubbee,	B
Norris, Charles	H		Ontecubbee,	B
Novtabi, Samuel	K		Onteyahtubbee,	B
Nowatabbi, Samuel	K		Ontikubbee,	B
Nowatubbee, Samuel	K		Ontiyahtubbee,	B
Nuck na hubbee,	K		Opahni,	A
Nuk sho bli,	D		O'Quinn, Nathaniel J.	I
Nukohobbe,	D		Orphen, Stephen	A
Nutt, Stephen M.	K		Osborn, Cyrenius P.	I
Ok la chi,	A		Osborne, Cyrenius P.	I
Ok lash ubbee,	I		Pa laoh tubbee,	E
Okabe, Samuel	E		Pa subbee, Johnson	K
Okchaya, Willson	E		Pache, Willis	E
Okchiya, Moses	D		Packnayubbee,	G
Okchoya, Moses	D		Page, Stephen P.	K
Okehaya, Lewis	C		Page, William	H
Okla be, Davis	D		Paine, Walker C.	I
Oklaba, Davis	D		Panubbee,	B
Oklachukma,	G		Parker,	A
Oklachukmee,	G		Parker, James	C
Oklahambbee,	K		Parker, Moses	P
Oklahambee, Joseph	C		Parr, Leonard	K
Oklahambee, Wilkin	C		Pasabbee, Johnson	K
Oklaharmbbee,	K		Patten, Bryel	I
Oklashinta,	A		Pattern, Bryce	I

Name	Col	Name	Col
Patton, Bryce	I	Pike, Albert	3"D
Paul, John	K	Pike, James	3D
Paxton, John	A	Pinckney, William	2"H
Paxton, William	B	Pinkney, William	2H
Payne, Walker C.	I	Pis a tubbee, -	A
Peak, Junius	1 I	Pisa no ubbee, -	A
Pears, Franklin	K	Pisah no abi, -	A
Peas, Franklin	K	Pisaho cha,	C
Pehletubbee,	3 D	Pisahonabe, Hegan	2"C
Pen, Silas	2 K	Pisahonobi, -	2 H
Perry, Benjamin	G	Pisaiutubbee, -	2B
Perry, Calvin	2 H	Pisalitobi, Willis	H
Perry, Edward	2 B	Pisarhonubbee, -	2H
Perry, Farbis	2 B	Pisaryohtubbee, -	2B
Perry, Jackson	A	Pisatabi, -	A
Perry, Jefferson	K	Pisatobe, -	A
Perry, Lewis	K	Piser no yubbee, -	A
Perry, Nail	G	Pisotiyobbe, -	3E
Perry, Oliver	A	Pisottiyobbe, -	3E
Pesornoyubbee, -	A	Pissa ho cha, -	2C
Peter, Anderson		Pissa ho nubbee, -	2 H
Peter, Henry	3D	Pistambbee, -	G
Peter, Isaih	2D	Pistambee, -	G
Peter, James	2B	Pistambee, -	K
Peter, Jessamin	1E	Pisto kcha, -	2C
Peter, Joseph	3 E	Poche, Willis	1E
Peter, Joseph	A	Pope, Sampson	3F
Peter, Lewis	2D	Porter, Henderson	A
Peter, William	A	Posey, George W.	1K
Peter, Willis	2 D	Posy, George W.	1K
Petty, Hubbard C.	1 I	Potter, Sander	2D
Petty, Jonathan	1 I	Potter, Sanders	2D
Pexton, Jermiah	2 K	Prather, James M.	I
Phelon, -	2 C	Prewit, Elisha B.	1K
Philip, -	1 E	Price, John	1"I
Philip, Gooding	2 D	Price, Nail	3E
Philip, Horn	2 D	Price, William	1 I
Philips, R.D.	1K	Pruitt, Elisha B.	1K
Phillip, Horn	2D	Pucknayubbee, -	G
Phillips, Richard	1K	Pucknucktubbee, -	1E
Picken, Harris	2I	Push, Jackson	2K
Pierce, William H.	1K	Pusley, Edmund	A

Quincey, John	2B	Sakkie, Simpson	2 C
Quincy, John	2B	Sam, -	
Ragsdale, Samuel F.	K	Sam, Isaac	2 I
Rainey,	H	Sam, Jackson	3 F
Ray, Felix	K	Sam, James	2 B
Retorking, Remon	H	Sam, William	2 H
Rettigg, Paul	K	Sam, William	3 D
Rhodes, Frank T.	K	Sampson, -	2 I
Riddle, Edmond	H	Sampson, John	2 K
Riddle, Edmund	H	Samuel, -	2 K
Riddle, Isearrel	D	Sanders, James	3 D
Riddle, W.J.	A	Sargo, -	3 F
Risener, Jackson	E	Scott, Leundons	2 K
Risner, Jackson	E	Selby, Robert H.	I
Rissahocha,	C	Sempson, Gabriel	
Roach, Charles	I	Sexton, Charles	A
Robert,	E	Sexton, Gibson	G
Robert, Joseph	K	Sexton, Jackson	H
Robert, William	C	Sexton, Jacob	A
Robinson, Amos	K	Sexton, Willis	A
Robinson, James M.	I	Sha ka, -	2 K
Robinson, James W.	I	Shah kubbee, -	E
Robinson, James	A	Shakie, -	2 K
Robinson, Moses	D	Sharien, George W.	2 C
Robison, Amos	K	Sharkey, -	2 K
Robuck, Ephraim	D	Sharrin, W. George	2 C
Rockmore, Thomas J.	K	Shat ta wa,	A
Rodgers, Andrew J.	I	Sheco, Martin	E
Roebuck, Benjamin		Sheehee, Thomas J.	K
Rogers, Andrew J.	I	Shehee, Thomas J.	K
Rogers, Hezekiah R.	K	Sheman, -	3 E
Rondon, James	B	Shettawi, -	A
Roquemore, Thomas J.	K	Shield, James	3 D
Ross, Jackson	B	Sho noon ta, -	G
Roy, Felix	K	Shonontah, -	G
Sai ille tubbee, -	2 C	Shouter, Jackson	2 K
Sailitabee, Rias	2 C	Silby, Robert H.	I
Sailli tabbee, -	2 C	Simeon, -	2 D
Saint, Paul	3 E	Simmons, James	G
Sakey, Jim	2 C	Simon, James	2 B
Sakey, Simpson	2 C	Simon, Peter	2 H
		Simon, Peter	2 K

Simon, Peter	3 E		Stewert, Silas	K,H
Simon, Peter	H		Stocker, Charles	H
Simpson,	1 E		Stone, Sylvanus G.	K
Simpson, -	2 D		Sudduth, Samuel	I
Simpson, John	2 K		Sullivan, Tyson A.	K
Simpson, John	2 K		Sullivan, Tyson E.	K
Singer, Comodore	K		Summey,	A
Skegg, Henry	3 D		Sunney, Morris	D
Slaughter, -	2 B		Sunny,	C
Slawter, -	2 B		Sunny, Morris	D
Smallwood, William			Ta cha year,	E
Smith, Abel	A		Ta fa matubbee,	G
Smith, James	3 F		Ta ha,	C
Smith, Reuben	3 E		Ta ho ta,	E
Soap, James R.	K		Tabbe, William	B
Soap, Thomas H.	1 K		Taf ammontubbee,	G
Soape, Robert J.	1 K		Tahnehubbee,	C
Soape, Thomas H.	1 K		Tains,	H
Soben,	2 B		Talapoose, John	E
Sobin, -	2 B		Talapoose, Sampson	H
Soccy, Jim	2 C		Talbott,	B
Soccy, Simpson	2 C		Talbott, Nathan	A
Solomon,	2 D		Tallapoose, Sampson	H
Solomon, James	E I		Tallapouse, John	E
Sorrel, James	2 B		Tamalacha Sowell,	K
Southward, William	2 K		Tamolacha, Sowell	K
Southwood, William	2 K		Tan uh no ubbee,	C
Speaker, Doak			Tanatubbee, Adam	
Speaker, Thomas			Tandy,	H
Speaker, William			Taney,	E
Spring, Joseph			Tanihubbee,	H
Spring, Levi			Tannahubee,	H
Spring, William			Tannapnonobbee,	C
Stallcup, Charles	I		Tanubbee,	D
Stanton, Thomas	H		Tanubbee, Jackson	D
Stephen, John	C		Tarha,	C
Stephen, Samuel	K		Tashkabi, William	K
Stephen, Tandy	H		Taylor, David F.	H
Stephen, W.T.	H		Taylor, George W.	K
Stephens, Samuel	K		Taylor, Harrington	F
Stewart, Nicholas	I		Taylor, James T.	K
Stewart, Silas	K,H		Taylor, John	D

Taylor, Thomas	C		Thompson, John	E,K
Taylor, Walton	A		Thompson, Josiah	A
Tebo, James	A		Thompson, Levi W.	K
Tecumseh,	I		Thompson, Robert O.	I
Teho tubbee,			Thompson, William	A
Edmund	K		Thompson, William	I
Tekbonah,	I		Thomson,	H
Telly, Wilkison	I		Thornton, Jessie	
Temalicha, Wilson	K		Throckmorton,	
Ter shun a cha,	E		William E.	I
Ter shun a cher,	E		Thunder, Billy	D
Terril, Nicholas	H		Thurman, John R.	I
Terrill, Lyman	C		Tibbs, William	B
Thacher, Moses	D		Ticbuntubbee,	K
Thar tubbee,	E		Tick but tubbee,	A
Thebo, James	A		Tikbatabi,	A
Thishotubbi,	K		Tikbattabee,	C
Thomas,			Tikbonna,	I
Thomas,	H		Tiller, Cornelius	K
Thomas, Bob	F		Tilman,	F
Thomas, James	K		Timaheka,	
Thomas, Joseph	H		Thompson	C
Thomas, Peter	K,C		Timmahaka,	
Thomas, Wilson	C		Thompson	C
Thomas, Wilson	K		Timmaheka,	
Thomason, Amos	I		Thompson	C
Thomason, Davis	I		Tish ah ho tubbee,	K
Thomason, Ellis	I		Tisho,	C,E
Thomason, Joseph	I		Tishohinlubbee, John	
Thomason, Lamus	K		Tishotubbee,	K
Thomason, Laymis	K		Tittle, Adam E.W.	I
Thomes, Sam	K		To ah cho yer,	E
Thompson,	F		Tobley, David	A
Thompson,	H		Tohnotubbee,	K
Thompson,	H		Tohwekeleh, Alick	G
Thompson,	I		Toins,	H
Thompson, Allen	A		Tokko, Harrison	D,C
Thompson, Elam	A		Tolubbee,	F
Thompson, Elano	A		Tom, Billy	D
Thompson, Isaac	B		Tom, James	A
Thompson, James	B		Tom, Josiah	D
Thompson, James	F		Tom, Loman	I

Name	Code
Tom, Williamson	E
Tone,	E
Toonlah Yarn,	H
Toto bbee,	H
Totobee,	H
Totubbee,	H
Tucchetubbe,	K
Tudson, Josephus	
Tulapose, John	E
Tulapose, Sampson	
Turnbull, Simeon	
Turner, William	A.K
Tushkamba, William	K
Tushkambi, William	K
Tushkaya,	G
Tushkiyah,	G
Tushkoonta, Jonas	G
Tushkoonta, Thomas	G
Tushkoontah, Jonas	G
Tushkoyah,	G
Tushpahtubbee,	G
Tyler, John	D
Tyrrell, Nicholas	H
Tyrril, Nicholas	H
Tywell, Nicholas	H
Ubbee,	G
Uhlichobe,	A
Ulmer, John	D
Underwood, Watt	A
Vaughn, Joseph	A
Victor, Robert	H
Vinson, C.S.	E
Vore, Israel	K
Wabington, Horatio	EK
Wacom,	I
Wacum, Johnson	D,E
Wade, Billy	H,D
Wade, Blunt	A
Wade, Eastman	D
Wade, Jerry	A
Wade, Jerry	C
Wade, Jesse	H
Wade, Leonidas	G
Wade, Robinson	K
Wade, Silas	B
Wade, Washington	A
Wade, William L.	K
Wah kay ah,	D
Wakage, Aikin	D
Wakaigee, William	H
Wakaija, Davis	H
Wakaiya, Davis	H
Wakaiya, William	H
Wakaya, Davis	H
Wakayacha,	K
Wakiah, Davis	H
Wakiah, William	H
Walker, Harris	2C
Walker, Henderson	2H
Walla, tubbee	2C
Wallis, Dickson	3D
Wallitabee, Wesley	2C
Ward, Dixon	G
Ward, Logan	2B
Ward, Samuel	G
Ward, Silas	2B
Ward, Williston	2I
Ware, Edgar	3D
Warn, Johnson	2 I
Warren, -	H
Warren, -	H
Wart, Stephen	K
Washington, -	2H
Washington, Amos	2B
Washington, Arkortubb	3D
Washington, David	2B
Washington, George	2 I
Washington, George	K
Watkin, Jonas	2C
Watkin, Jones	2C
Watkin, Simon	3H
Watkins, John	3H
Watkins, Jones	2C

Watkins, Simon	3H		White, Norman	2 I
Watson, -	A		White, Reuben	2B
Watson, Billy	2I		White, Robert M.	1K
Watson, Harris	2I		White, Stephen	2 I
Wattis, -	G		Whortner, Dixon	2D
Watty, -	G		William,	D
Waykaya, William	2H		William, A. J.	A
Waytubbee, -	2K		William, Aaron	H
Weaver, Joseph	2 I		William, Abel	I
Webster, Daniel	1E		William, Amow	E
Webster, Eastman	2C		William, Charles	K
Webster, Francis	2 I		William, David	H
Webster, Johnson	3 E		William, David	I
Webster, Lorain	2D		William, Davis	F
Webster, Loring	2D		William, Eastman	
Webster, Samuel	2D		William, Horatio	D
Webster, Thomas	K		William, James	H
Wecom, -	2 I		William, John	A
Welimus, -	H		William, John	E
Wellington, Jesse			William, Raymon	I
Weshontarbbee, Isam	2C		William, Robinson	I
			William, Sampson	D
Wesley, -	A		William, Simon	C
Wesley, Davidson	A		Williams,	H
Wesley, Hayes	3F		Williams, Aaron	H
Wesley, John	2 I		Williams, Amon	E
Wesley, Sweeney	3E		Williams, Charles W.	D
Weslly, Sandy	K			
Wesly, Samuel	2K		Williams, Charles	K
Westley, -	A		Williams, David	E
Westley, Davidson	A		Williams, David	H
Westley, John	2 I		Williams, Enock	D
Westley, Sam	2K		Williams, Horatio	D
Weston, George W.	1K		Williams, James	H
Wetobbi, -	2K		Williams, John	E
Wetubbee, -	2K		Williams, Joshua H.	K
Whail, Wesley	1E		Williams, Sampson	H
Whale, Wesley	1E		Williams, Willis	H
Whartner, Dixon	2D		Willis,	C
Whertner, Dixon	2D		Willis,	K
White, Jonas	G		Willis, Amos	D
White, Lewis	G		Willis, James	K

Willis, John	B	
Willis, John	H	
Willis, John	K	
Willis, Levi	K	
Willis, Loman	I	
Willis, Moses	I	
Willis, Samuel	B	
Willis, Silas	K	
Willison,	H	
Willison, Job	E	
Willson, Job	E	
Wilson,	A	
Wilson,	B	
Wilson,	F	
Wilson,	H	
Wilson, Aaron	I	
Wilson, Albert	K	
Wilson, Austin	K	
Wilson, Dixon	D	
Wilson, Edward	K	
Wilson, James	K	
Wilson, John J.	K	
Wilson, John	D	
Wilson, John	K	
Wilson, John	K	
Wilson, Tom		
Wilson, W. W.	K	
Wilson, William	F	
Wilson, William	I	
Winder, John S.	K	
Winlock, Bazil		
Winster, Samuel	K	
Wintlock, Bazil	C	
Wobington, Horatio	EK	
Woh, Rayo	D	
Wolf, Quimer	B	
Wolf, Simon	B	
Woody, John	D	
Worbington, Horatio E.	K	
Worcester, Abel	A	
Worley, John W.	K	
Worly, John W.	K	
Wright, Aaron	K	
Wright, Alfred	I	
Wright, Cornelius	I	
Wright, Jarvis	A	
Wright, R. A.	D	
Wright, Simon	G	
Wright, William	D	
Yak oh tambi,	A	
Yakahpacha, William	E	
Yakapacha, Thomas	E	
Yan,	D	
Yantoon la, Lonlar	H	
Yantoonlah,	H	
Yarntoonlah,	H	
Yatatubbee,	C	
Yates, Reuben E.	I	
Yaw cah chay,	E	
Yearchaahpeycher, Thomas	E	
Yearchaahpeycher, William	E	
Yellow, Jim	H	
Yok ah tubbee,	C	
Yokah tam ba,	A	
Yokubbee,	G	
Yota, Thomas	G	
Yotah, Thomas	G	
You cha chay,	E	
You toon lah,	H	
Young, Alexander	I	
Young, B.	F	
Young, George W.	I	
Youngblood, Isaac D.	K	
Yount, Andrew J.	I	
Youta,	H	
Yutobbe,	K	
Yutobbi,	K	

Seminole Units

CSA Seminole Flag
Two Red and 1 white diagonal stripes,
Green field in upper left corner with white quarter moon
and 1 small red star

Lieutenant Colonel John Jumper
Oklahoma Historical Society

1st Regiment, Seminole Mounted Volunteers

Formerly First Battalion Seminole Mounted Volunteers; then First Regiment Seminole Mounted Volunteers. Unit was organized in September, 1861, with two companies: A and B. Mustered into service 21 November 1861 with three companies: A, B, and C. Companies D, E and F were added by January 1862. Original companies had enlisted for one year.

During May, 1862, it had 380 men present for duty. The unit served in the Department of the Indian Territory. Later the unit was assigned to D.H. Cooper's and Watie's Brigade, Trans-Mississippi Department. It served as scouts and raided the Federals in the Indian Territory and along the border. On 19 September, 1864, the battalion took 130 officers and men into the fight at Cabin Creek. One officer, 1st Lieutenant D.R. Patterson, was killed during this battle. The unit was surrendered by Brigadier General Stand Watie at Doaksville, Indian Territory, on 26 May 1865.

Jumper, John	F&S	Lieutenant Colonel
Cloud, George	F&S	Major
Burnes, W.W.	F&S	Assistant Surgeon
Dyer, Charles C.	F&S	Acting Quartermaster
Robertson, E.C.	F&S	Acting Commissary Sergeant
Routin, William H.	F&S	Acting Quartermaster Sergeant
Routon, William H.	F&S	Acting Quartermaster Sergeant
Rowton, W.H.	F&S	Acting Quartermaster Sergeant
Reed, David	F&S	Sergeant Major
Chitto, Tustenaggee		Captain
Chitto, Tustenaggee		Captain
Cloud, Thomas		Captain
Factor, James		Captain
Foosatchee, Cojokenny		Captain
Foshutchecocha co ne,		Captain
Fushatchie co chokna,		Captain
Hill, Sam		Captain

Osuc chee Harjo,	Captain
Robinson, William	Captain
Robison, William	Captain
Tulsee Yo Hola,	Captain
Tustanucogee,	Captain
Tut te nuk ochee,	Captain
Itsin Yo Hola,	First Lieutenant
McGirt, Daniel	First Lieutenant
Reed, John	First Lieutenant
Reid, John	First Lieutenant
Tustenucochee,	First Lieutenant
Washbourn, H.E.A. -	First Lieutenant
Compeer, Harper	Second Lieutenant
Compier, Harper	Second Lieutenant
Echo, Yohola	Second Lieutenant
Icho yahola,	Second Lieutenant
Johnson, Alex	Second Lieutenant
Johnston, Alec	Second Lieutenant
Klehomata, Fixico	Second Lieutenant
Ma ta coke,	Second Lieutenant
Mathee Cokee,	Second Lieutenant
McClish, Frazier	Second Lieutenant
Micco, Machasar	Second Lieutenant
Micco, Mu chase	Second Lieutenant
Nocose, Harjo	Second Lieutenant
Nocus, Harjo	Second Lieutenant
Nokfah, Harjo H	Second Lieutenant
Nokjah, Harjo	Second Lieutenant
Passuckee Yahola,	Second Lieutenant
Passuckee Yo Hola,	Second Lieutenant
Reed Sr., John	Second Lieutenant
Taylor, A.M.	Second Lieutenant
Thlarthlo Fixico,	Second Lieutenant
Thlothlo Fixico,	Second Lieutenant
Eufala, Tustanuggee	Third Lieutenant
Eufarvlaties te nukke,	Third Lieutenant
Itse Yaliola,	Third Lieutenant
Itse Yo ho la,	Third Lieutenant
McLish, Frazier	Third Lieutenant
Micco, Mu chasse	Third Lieutenant
Waxie, Emathla -	Third Lieutenant
Waxie, Imathla -	Third Lieutenant

White, John -	Third Lieutenant
Woxie, Emathla	Third Lieutenant
Aird, William	Lieutenant
Cat sar, Fixico	First Sergeant
Cotsa, Fixico	First Sergeant
Cotsa, Micco	First Sergeant
Fixico,	First Sergeant
Gibson, Fireman	First Sergeant
Meckks, Yoholah	First Sergeant
Micco, Yoholo	First Sergeant
Nokfuk, Harjo	First Sergeant
Passiec Harjo,	First Sergeant
Passuck Harjo,	First Sergeant
Passuggu Tom,	First Sergeant
Tallawah Micco,	First Sergeant
Ahallocogee,	Sergeant
Ahalock, Harjo	Sergeant
Billy, Harjo	Sergeant
Cabbitchee, Emathla	Sergeant
Cabichee, Emathla	Sergeant
Cabitch, Emathla	Sergeant
Cat chu chee,	Sergeant
Charley,	Sergeant
Charley,	Sergeant
Chisholm, William	Sergeant
Chisholm, William	Sergeant
Choeka,	Sergeant
Co Nip, Fixico	Sergeant
Cosa,	Sergeant
Fixico, Joe	Sergeant
Fus Harjo,	Sergeant
Gibson, Long	Sergeant
Holocta, Fixico	Sergeant
Its has, Harjo	Sergeant
Micco, Harjo N	Sergeant
Nehah, Yo ho la	Sergeant
Nocose, Emathla	Sergeant
Nocose, Harjo	Sergeant
Ocheesee Chopks,	Sergeant
Passuggu Harjo,	Sergeant
Sam, Charley	Sergeant
Tc coi ke,	Sergeant

Te ur ke,	Sergeant
Tommy, Tustanuggee	Sergeant
Tulwa Fixico,	Sergeant
Tulwa Harjo,	Sergeant
Ufal Tustemeggee,	Sergeant
Wecus in yohola, - -	Sergeant
Win, Leotty	Sergeant
Ac Chee, Yo Hola	Corporal
Ahallockochee,	Corporal
Ahtus, Yo Hola	Corporal
Alaloccochee,	Corporal
Alberta,	Corporal
Allos Yo ho la,	Corporal
Apiaka,	Corporal
Berryhill, Samuel	Corporal
Berryhill, Simon	Corporal
Bob, Tiger	Corporal
Chowasti, Micco	Corporal
Chowee, Emathla	Corporal
Chowoste, Micco	Corporal
Coches, Micco	Corporal
Condelle, Harjo	Corporal
Condul, Harjo	Corporal
Cotchillee,	Corporal
Cotsillochee,	Corporal
Cowee, Emathla	Corporal
Cowokots, Harjo	Corporal
Dusk, John	Corporal
Fook e lustee,	Corporal
Fox te tus te,	Corporal
Hadilat,	Corporal
Holatochee,	Corporal
Hotelgie, Harjo	Corporal
Its hasiochee,	Corporal
Its pas wochee,	Corporal
Itshus Yohola,	Corporal
Jacob, Frank	Corporal
Kle, Harjo	Corporal
Koker Lunder,	Corporal
Lunder Co Ker,	Corporal
McQueen, David	Corporal
Nocose, Harjo	Corporal

Nocus, Harjo	Corporal
Ochee Harjo,	Corporal
Ochis Harjo,	Corporal
Ok tiee Harjo,	Corporal
Okcherly ho la,	Corporal
Othle, Borin	Corporal
Sam, -	Corporal
Spanee, Harjo -	Corporal
Spybuck, Tom.	Corporal
Sunuckee Yo Hola,	Corporal
Tallawah Fuico,	Corporal
Talsee Micco,	Corporal
Tulsee Micco,	Corporal
Washington, Jim	Corporal
Yaha, Harjo	Corporal
Patterson, D.R.	Adjutant

Privates

Abeeka,
Abeekochee,
Ache huchee
Achehuchee, Fixico
Ah Alloe, Harjo
Ah chook ee,
Ah llak he,
Ah losk, Harjo
Aha, Micco
Ahal, Emathla
Ahalleck, Tustenuggee
Ahalloc, Tustanuggee
Ahallock, Fixuco
Ahalloco, Chee
Ahalock, Harjo Na
Ahbeeka,
Ahbeekochee,
Ahbiaikee,
Ahbiarkee,
Ahhahlock, Hopeza
Ahtus, Harjo
Ahulloc, Harjo
Aird, Alex

Ak ti as ce, Harjo
Aktiah chee, Harjo
Alabama,
Albamee,
Alberta, Chie
Alberta, Fixico
Alberta, Miccs
Alec,
Alpord,
Apathle, Emathla
Artus, Harjo
Artus, Hobier
Ashallos, Fixico
Atawai,
Bamee,
Barna, Chula
Barna, Julee
Barnee,
Barnee, Hlakko
Barnichula,
Bear,
Beaverstone, John
Beaverstone, Wison

Ben,
Ben,
Berryhill, John
Big Tom,
Big, George
Big, Jim
Billy,
Billy, Hagan
Blango, John
Bowlegs, William
Boyee, Hothle
Bruner, David
Bruner, Nathan
Bruner, Wilson
Buck Skin,
Buffalo Horn,
Burns, Burton
Burns, H.F.B.
Butcher, John
Butcher, Washington
Cabiche, Harjo
Cabichee, Fixico
Cabichee, Harjo
Cabichee, Yohola
Cabichu, Harjo
Cabit, Che si
Cabitch, Yo Hola
Cabitchee, Emathla
Cabitcher, Fixico
Cabitse, Harjo
Caboon,
Cadds, George
Cahmoty,
California,   ...
California, Beaverstone
Calmose, Emathla
Camp, Harjo
Canippe,
Canippe, Yohola
Canserd, Harjo
Carmotee,
Carson, Ne ha lo

Cat Sah ho muste,
Cat sar, Holwie
Cat sat, Hoth le poger
Catislee,
Catsa, Ya Hola
Catsar, Chopko
Catsar, Fixico
Catsar, Fixico chee
Catsur, Yohola
Ceopunichee,
Cesar,
Charlee,
Charlee,
Charlee, Chee
Charte, Jimmy
Charte, Jimmy
Che burnie,
Che burnie,
Che lok te, Harjo
Che lok te, Harjo
Che lokee, Harjo
Che lokee, Harjo
Che pa no, Lame
Che pa no, Lame
Che pah ne, Larne   F
Che pah ne, Larne   F
Chebarnichee,
Chebarnichee,
Cheburnie,
Cheburnie,
Cheesee,
Cheesee,
Cheeska,
Cheeska,
Cheskah,
Cheskah,
Chesse,
Chesse,
Chi is, Ka
Chi is, Ka
Chi si, Harjo
Chi si, Harjo

Chitto, Harjo
Chitto, Harjo
Chitto, Harjo
Chitto, Harjo
Choillee, Hakko
Choillee, Harjo
Chok, Charty Fixico
Chokote, Chopko
Cholokee, Harjo
Chopko, Ahalleck
Chopko, Ahalock
Chopko, Choka
Chotah,
Chowosti, Harjo
Choyo, Hola
Chu e mathlee,
Chu Osanah, Harjo
Chu, Emthla
Chu, Wastin Harjo
Chuillee,
Chuk cha dee,
Chuk nee Mik Koco,
Chulley,
Chully,
Cisepochee,
Clothlo, Harjo
Co Nep, Harjo
Co nup, Harjo
Cochus, Harjo
Cochus, Micco
Coe Harjo chee,
Coe, Harjo
Cofee,
Cohon, John
Colarnee,
Colattee,
Coleh, Mek
Coloctee,
Colomee,
Combigee,
Conippee, Emathla
Cooser, Micco

Corveh,
Cosa, Fixico
Cosa, Harjo
Cosa, Micco
Cosar, Micco
Coser, Fixico
Coser, Harjo
Cotsa, Chopko
Cotsa, Fixico chee
Cotsa, Hlakko
Cotsa, Homatta
Cotsa, Hulwee
Cotsa, Yo Hola
Cotsahho, Mattee
Cotsar, Holocta
Cow etah,
Cowee,
Cowee, Emathlochee
Cowokochee,
Cubbitchee, Fixico
Cubbitchee, Yo Hola
Cubbitchee, Yo Hola
Cubbitchochee,
Cubitchee, Yo Hola
Cummings, M.R.
Deleware,
Dickson,
Dotson, John
Dutch,
Dutichee, Cadds
Echo, Fixico
Echo, Harjo
Echuful wah,
Efah, Karjs
Elis Yo Hola,
Elis, John
Emath la Mik Ke,
Emathla, Hlakko
Emathla, Locko
Emathlochee,
Eufala, Harjo
Euneser,   B

217

Euno,
Factor, John
Factor, Tom
Fish, George
Foos Harjo,
Foos Narjo,
Foose yo ho la,
Foosuchee nehilous,
Fooswah chee,
Fox,
Freeman,
Fucke, Elusta
Fuckluste, Harjo
Fus Harjo,
Fus, Yo Hola
Fushatchee Harjo,
Fushatchie Harjo,
Fushatchie Neha Thlokke,
Fuswochee,
Gamble, Bob
Gambler, Robert
George Sammy,
George,
Georgy,
Gibson, Bowling
Gibson, John
Gilbert,
Gobler,
Greer, J.P.
Habahlee, Emathla
Habanise,
Habathlee, Ematha
Habicka, Harjo
Halberte, Harjo
Halberter,
Halberter, Fixico
Halberter, Harjo
Harjo Tacosar,
Hastings, J. M.
Hawkins, William
He ne hah chee,
He tir, Ochee

He we hah, Fixico
Hember, Micco   C
Hepi eka,
Hetch, Ka
Hickory, John
Hill, John
Hinihichee,
Hinihichee,
Hobiaka,
Hobiechee,
Hobieiethla,
Hobierchee,
Hobiochee,
Hobithlee,
Hoboithlee,
Holoctah, Harjo
Holoctucheechu,
Hombur, Mik Ko
Homer, John
Hood, James M.
Hood, Jim
Hotelgee, Harjo
Hotelgi,
Hothle boyee,
Hoto see,
Hotulgee,
Hotulgee, Harjo
Hotusee,
Houston, Sam
Iarpe cock,
Ibut,
Inclinisten, Emathla
Inclunissee, Emathla
Ispokoka, Harjo
Ispumie, Fixico
Istin chu yu,
It se Harjo gu,
Its Hars Nah,
Its Has, Fixico
Its has, Fixico
Its has, Harjo
Its, Fixico

Jack,
Jack,
Jack,
Jackson,
Jackson,
Jessee,
John,
John,
John, Ochee
Johnny,
Jonie, Joe
Jonie, Micco
Josee, Buck
Josiah,
Kanosie,
Kechi, Harjo
Key,
Killewa, Kibby
Kimimee, Harjo
Kimimi, Hays
Kis see. ...ito,
Kitchi, Ochilka
KleChummy, Yoholah
Klechummy, Yoholo
Klehomattee, Harjo
Ko oko gu, Harjo
Konippee,
Kooko chee,
Kotsa,
Kowokots, Emathla
Lahnego,
Lahta, Fixico
Lahta, Harjo
Landy, Coker
Lar la, Ka
Larnee,
Lecomton,
Lenah,
Lifthif, Harjo
Liftif, Harjo
Light Horse,
Lilka,

Lincy,
Lindah,
Linney, John
Linsey,
Lit tif, Firics
Litticher,
Littif, Harjo
Littif, Harjo
Little Bear,
Little Beaver,
Little Billy,
Little George,
Little Jack,
Little Joe,
Little Tom Fuctor,
Lo Chee Mee Chee,
Lo Chopka,
Logan,
Logan, John
Long Sam,
Long Tail,
Long, Jim
Lothee, Miccs
Ma ca see,
Mahachee,
Mahardy,
Majorlee,
Manokifka,
Manuck, John
Marthus, Cocker
Maytubby, John
McGirt, Alex
McKane, James
McLish, Alex
McQueen, Jesse
Me Char lee,
Meets, Ka
Metut wi Ke,
Miah Wepes, Cock
Micco chee,
Micco chee,
Micco,

Micco, Harjo
Micco, Harjo chee
Micco, Harjo N
Micco, Humper
Micco, Yo Hola
Micco, Yo Hola
Micco, Yohola
Micco, Yohola
Miggil, Cee
Mister, Cummings
Monday,
Monkey, -
Moses,
Mosey,
Mule,
Mulgas,
Munagee,
Muppee, Illecchee
Muppee, Illecha
Mut tif co,
Muttee,
Nah hi gee,
Nak to mie,
Naklahpiscah Harjo,
Nalus lusta,
Ne hah lock cochee,
Ne hi locko, Choko
Ne hi locko, Harjo
Ne po pa,
Nedurkio,
Neha locko yohola,
Neha locko, Fixico
Neha, Harjo
Neha, Hlakke Chopko
Neha, Hlakko Fixico
Nehah, Fixico
Nehah, Harjo
Nehah, Harjo gee
Nehi Yo Hola,
Nepochapko,
New upe tuck,
Noco, Leka

Noco, Se kee
Nocose Ille, Harjo
Nocose ko chopko,
Nocose, Ega
Nocose, Ega
Nocose, Egachopko
Nocose, Emathla
Nocose, Harjo
Nocose, Illee
Nocoseillee, Harjo
Nocus yohola,
Nocus, Eka
Nocus, Emathla
Nok, Harjo
Noklubissee,
Ocharchee Harjo,
Ochee Harjo,
Ochee Hlakko,
Ochee see Micco,
Ochee,
Oco se ka,
Octiarchee Fixico,
Octiarchee Fixico,
Octiarchee Harjo,
Octiarchee harjochee,
Octiarchee Yo Hola,
Octiarchee,
Ohulee Yohola,
Ok chi a see,
Ok fusk Harjo,
Okcheesee,
Okchun Emathla,
Okchun Holatta,
Okchussee,
Okelamee,
Okfuska Harjo,
Okfuska,
Okfuske Harjo,
Okfuskee,
Oklaithlee,
Okleebbissee Harjo,
Oklobbise Harjo,

Oklubisse Harjo,
Oklus Harjo,
Okson Emathla,
Oktiar chee,
Oktiarchee Fixico,
Olahhe ne ah,
Osah Fixico,
Osah he neha,
Osahe ne ha,
Osanah Harjo,
Oson Harjo,
Oson Holoclachee,
Osonwah,
Osuna Harjo,
Osuna Harjo,
Osunna Harjo,
Osunwah,
Pa ho kee,
Pa hose ne hah,
Paha Harjo,
Pahe Harjo,
Pahlee,
Pahose Emathla,
Pahose Fixico,
Pahose Harjo,
Pahsuckochee,
Palmer,
Pamosee,
Panassee,
Panischi,
Pano See,
Panosee,
Panosee,
Parscofer,
Passuck Tustenagga,
Passuckoohee,
Passuggee Tastanuggee,
Pauline, Sila
Peter, --
Picot ke, -
Pin Harp, -
Potatoes, -

Quapan, -
Rabbit,
Rhodes, Jacob
Ricketts, C.P. D
Rickits, Charles
Sacoon, -
Sage, George
Sagimga, -
Sahjimechee, -
Sahjimka, -
Saitigee, -
Sammy, -
Sammy, ...
Sampson No 2, -
Sampson, -
Sandulah, Harjo
Satgu Macha, -
Scarpeto, Owen
Semawakika, -
Sharty, Spybuck
Shawnee, Sam
Shoarke ep,   -
Showa, -
Siaga,
Simon, -
Simon, de lega-
Simpahlee,   -
Sin pah le,   -
Sinleetka, -   -
Sinleteka, -   -
Sinlitka, -   -
Skar, Owen   -
Skil i Wathre, -
Snake, -   -
Soat ka,   -
Sockill,   -
Spame, Fixico -
Spanee, Harjo -
Spaniard,   -
Spaniard, Ben -
Spaniard, John-
Spanish, Henry

Spybuck, Sampson
Squirle,
Stewart, George
Stewart, James
Stone Boar,
Sullivan, George
Sumiga,
Sundel Harjo,
Sundul Cah Harjo,
Suttah,
Swunok, Yohola
Ta co see Harjo,
Tah co Sah Harjo,
Tak eesom o,
Tallahassa,
Tallauah Harjo,
Tallawah Fuico,
Talmachus Harjo,
Talse Micco,
Talse Mico,
Talwahe Fixico,
Taycumath Cocker,
Taylor,
Taylor,
Taylor, John
Te ho yo kine,
Te Wayke,
Tecathlee,
Tecumseh,
Temahsee,
Temalth, Harjo
Temawe lah,
Tesekiah, Micco
Tesiah, Harjo
Tey Cumse cocker,
Teycumcpe,
Tharke to pah,
Tharthlo Harjo,
Thlanco ka,
Thlarthla Fixico,
Thlarwichee,
Thlothlo Harjo,

Thomson, John
Tiarchee Yo Hola,
Tiner, David
Tiner, George
To co ser Harjo,
To co ser Harjo,
To co ser Harjo,
To co sir,
To sarquash,
To wa,
Tobi, E.
Tocoser Fixico,
Tocoser, Emathla
Tolappi Hrajo,
Tom,
Tom, George
Tomassee,
Tommy Harjo,
Tommy Harjo,
Tommy,
Tommy, Tustanuegee
Tommy, Tustenuggee
Tomochee,
Tomochee,
Tomson,
Toney,
Tonkaway,
Tople,
Topley,
Tote kis Harjo,
Towaka,
Towi, Enah
Town,
Tuck Key,
Tuckey,
Tulwa mekko,
Tus Yahola,
Tusikiah Harjo,
Tuskiah Harjo,
Tuskiah Harjo,
Tuskiah Micco,
Tuslunuc Harjo,

Tustannugaee,
Tustenuc, Harjochee
Tustenuggee,
Tustunuc Harjo,
Tuswochee,
Ufala Harjo,
Wahloo,
Wahsix cocker,
Wak hah ge,
Wak ke,
Wak Se Harjo,
Wakee, Johnny
Walloo, -
Walscoos, Cocker
Washington, Thomas
Waxie, Harjochee
Wecus in ncha
Wecus, Harjo
William,
Wilson,
Wilson, Bill
Wilson, Bruner
Wissecarparwe,
Woatka, Harjo
Woatka, Yo he la
Wok, Harjo
Wolf,
Wolf,
Wotka, Fixico
Woxee, Holatta
Woxee, Holatta
Woxie, Harjo
Woxie, Harjo
Woxie, Hollattah
Woxie, Holoctah
Wright, George
Ya ha, Harjo
Ya la ha, John
Yah ha, Chopko
Yah ha, Harjo chee
Yah tana, Harjo
Yah tes, Kah
Yaha Yo, Hola
Yaha,
Yaha, Chopko
Yahal,
Yammy, Fixico
Yar Tomee,
Yokola Chopk, Micco
Yong, Man
Young, Panther

Creek Units

CSA Creek Flag
Two vertical red stripes, 1 white stripe
Square Green field in upper left corner with
White quarter moon, small red star

Colonel Daniel N. McIntosh
Oklahoma Historical Society

1st Regiment Creek Mounted Volunteers

McIntosh, D.N.	F&S	Colonel
McIntosh, William R.	F&S	Lieutenant Colonel
Derrysaw, Jacob	F&S	Major
Perryman, Joseph M.	F&S	Sergeant Major
Ross, Richard J.	F&S	Sergeant Major
Morrow, George	F&S	Quartermaster Sergeant
Clark, Isaac A.	F&S	Acting Quartermaster
Holmes, William M.	F&S	Acting Quartermaster
Hays, S. M.	F&S	Acting Quartermaster
Washbourne, G. M.	F&S	Acting Quartermaster
Washbourne, J.W.	F&S	Acting Quartermaster
Callahan, Samuel B.	F&S	Adjutant
Meyers, M.	F&S	Adjutant
Greepenkerl, Ferdinade	F&S	Surgeon
Che ko te, Samuel	B	Lieutenant Colonel
McHenry, James	H,D	Major
Brewner, Luney	L	Captain
Bruner, Lewner	L	Captain
Callahan, S. B.	K	Captain
Cully, Micco	C	Captain
Cully, Mikko	C	Captain
Fixico, Tarkinhar	1C	Captain
Foster, Abram	K	Captain
Hardage, Young	I	Captain
Harjo, Tulloaf	G	Captain
Harjo, Tulmachus	K	Captain
Harjo, Tustannck	D	Captain
Herrod, David	M	Captain
Hulputter, Micco	E	Captain
Jacobs, William	G	Captain
Kanard, Washington	H	Captain
Kannard, Wiley	M	Captain
Kenard, Washington	H	Captain
Kenard, Wiley	M	Captain
Kinnard, Wiley	M	Captain
McIntosh, William F.	C	Captain
Miller, Samuel	F	Captain

Severs, F. B.	B	Captain
Thlar ke ter,	A	Captain
Yah ho la,	D	Captain
Yarharla,	D	Captain
Yarharley,	D	Captain
Yarkinhar, Fixico	A	Captain
Ah far le, Hargo	A	First Lieutenant
Arfahle, Harjo	A	First Lieutenant
Arfar le, Harjo	A	First Lieutenant
Brown, John	D	First Lieutenant
Burgess, Jackson	B	First Lieutenant
Chus tu lee,	F	First Lieutenant
Chustullee,	F	First Lieutenant
Coo war sar, Harjo	G	First Lieutenant
Harjo, Tarcoosan	1C	First Lieutenent
Hotulkee, Harjo	B	First Lieutenant
It chas, Harjo	K	First Lieutenant
Its han, Harjo	K	First Lieutenant
Its hars, Harjo	K	First Lieutenant
Kannard, James	M	First Lieutenant
Kenard, James	M	First Lieutenant
Marshall, C.H.	C	First Lieutenant
Marshall, Chales	C	First Lieutenant
Ne ne, Har Yar	E	First Lieutenant
Nin me Haryer,	E	First Lieutenant
Nin ne har yar,	E	First Lieutenant
Nin ne hi ah,	E	First Lieutenant
Nocose, Yoholah		First Lieutenant
Nocus, Emarthla	E	First Lieutenant
Po ki tee, -	B	First Lieutenant
Po kita, -	B	First Lieutenant
Pokity, -	B	First Lieutenant
Tar nun po,	L	First Lieutenant
Ther wi key,	F	First Lieutenant
Tlur wi key,	F	First Lieutenant
Tocoser Harjo,	C	First Lieutenant
Tun nun po,	L	First Lieutenant
Vann, Martin	C	First Lieutenant
Vonn, Martin	C	First Lieutenant
Zakinhaw,	A	First Lieutenant
Adkins, Thomas		Second Lieutenant
Anderson, Robert	L	Second Lieutenant

Name	Co.	Rank
Atkins, Thomas	C	Second Lieutenant
Auster,	C	Second Lieutenant
Bare Arm,	E	Second Lieutenant
Berrihill, Pleasant	C	Second Lieutenant
Berryhill, Jim	F	Second Lieutenant
Berryhill, Pleasant	C	Second Lieutenant
Bown, Samuel	E	Second Lieutenant
Brewner, William	G	Second Lieutenant
Brown, Samuel	E	Second Lieutenant
Brown, Thomas	E	Second Lieutenant
Bruner, William	G	Second Lieutenant
Burgess, Toney	B	Second Lieutenant
Che ho, Jim	H	Second Lieutenant
Che par ney,	E	Second Lieutenant
Cheho, James	H	Second Lieutenant
Cowar sard, Harjo	G	Second Lieutenant
Cowas sart, Hachu	G	Second Lieutenant
Cowas sod, Harjo	G	Second Lieutenant
Es mot ti ye,	I	Second Lieutenant
Esmut, Eze	I	Second Lieutenant
Halputter, Hargo	A	Second Lieutenant
Halputtes,	A	Second Lieutenant
Harjo, Tommy	I	Second Lieutenant
Hulbutter, Harjo	A	Second Lieutenant
Hulputter, Hargo	A	Second Lieutenant
Hulputter, Harjo	A	Second Lieutenant
Kinnard, William	M	Second Lieutenant
Kowassart, Hays	G	Second Lieutenant
Lashley, Jack	G	Second Lieutenant
Lasley, Jack	G	Second Lieutenant
Lee, Richard	G	Second Lieutenant
Losley, Jack	G	Second Lieutenant
McIntosh, A.H.	G	Second Lieutenant
McIntosh, William	A	Second Lieutenant
Moore, John R.	K	Second Lieutenant
Moore, N.B.	K	Second Lieutenant
Nar tul li Key,	E	Second Lieutenant
Nater le Kee,	E	Second Lieutenant
No cos, Inka	E	Second Lieutenant
No cos, Inke	E	Second Lieutenant
No cus, Inka	E	Second Lieutenant
Ooter,	C	Second Lieutenant

Percival, William	F	Second Lieutenant
Pinehill, William	L	Second Lieutenant
Porter, John S.	1C	Second Lieutenant
Seaman, King	F	Second Lieutenant
Seamans, King	F	Second Lieutenant
Seman, King	F	Second Lieutenant
Simmons, W. King	F	Second Lieutenant
Smut ty ee,	I	Second Lieutenant
Sole, Joshua	H	Second Lieutenant
Soual, Joshua	H	Second Lieutenant
Soul, Joshua	H	Second Lieutenant
Soule, Joshua	H	Second Lieutenant
Suscooner,	H	Second Lieutenant
Tars Yie che,	M	Second Lieutenant
Thlars yech ee,	M	Second Lieutenant
Thle wallee Fixico,	B	Second Lieutenant
Thlewahle Fixico,	B	Second Lieutenan
Tuscooner,	H	Second Lieutenant
Water, Milon	F	Second Lieutenant
Winslett, David	H	Second Lieutenant
Woods, H. H.	B	Second Lieutenant
Woods, William H.	B	Second Lieutenant
Ya ka ley,	C	Second Lieutenant
Ya kin han,	A	Second Lieutenant
Co wac cochee,	C	Junior Second Lieutenant
Co wak cochee,	C	Junior Second Lieutenant
Kowakochee,	C	Junior Second Lieutenant
Harrison, Peter	M	Lieutenant
Hopwood, Robert	G	Lieutenant
Marshall, Lafayette	C	Lieutenant
Mellon, Water	F	Lieutenant
Mires, John	D	Lieutenant
Myers, John	D	Lieutenant
Passooner Harjo,	I	Lieutenant
Perryman, Joseph M.	H	Lieutenant
Perryman, Riley	H	Lieutenant
Waley, -	12	Lieutenant
Thlors Yicho,	M	Ensign
Alexander, Geore A.	G	First Sergeant

Berryhill, Mark	F	First Sergeant
Bruner, Louis	G	First Sergeant
Charlo, Harjo	H	First Sergeant
Clark, William	K	First Sergeant
Clinton, William M.	E	First Sergeant
Fisher, Richard	M	First Sergeant
Harjo, Charls	D	First Sergeant
Hujo, Charlo	H	First Sergeant
Ingrom, William	C	First Sergeant
No cus, Harjo	E	First Sergeant
Nocos, Harjo	E	First Sergeant
Perryman, Daniel	2C	First Sergeant
Steel, George	L	First Sergeant
Steele, George	L	First Sergeant
Stipka, Charles	B	First Sergeant
Tipkey, Charles	M	First Sergeant
Tom e ya ho la,	A	First Sergeant
Tommy Yarhola,	A	First Sergeant
Tommy zar ho la,	A	First Sergeant
Tommy,	B	First Sergeant
Tomny,	B	First Sergeant
Tomy yar hola,	A	First Sergeant
Wiley,	C	First Sergeant
Yar holar, Harjo	F,B	First Sergeant
Yar holer, Harjo	F,B	First Sergeant
Ah har lock co chee,	B	Sergeant
Ah lock fixico,	B	Sergeant
Aharlock, Fixico	B	Sergeant
Barnett, Chilly	M	Sergeant
Barnett, Toney	E	Sergeant
Brewner, Louis	G	Sergeant
Broun, Charley	E	Sergeant
Burgess, Edward	C,B	Sergeant
Burgess, John	B,I	Sergeant
Burgess, Joseph	C	Sergeant
Catcher, Harjo	D	Sergeant
Chark le chumper,	A	Sergeant
Charlack le chuppee,	A	Sergeant
Che kote yar holar,	K	Sergeant
Che navey,	A	Sergeant
Che pa noh,	A	Sergeant
Chipley, Carr	K	Sergeant

Cho cot te ya holo,	K	Sergeant
Cho ko te yoho lar,	K	Sergeant
Chu lah,	C	Sergeant
Churk le chunper,	A	Sergeant
Clarkle, Chumpar	A	Sergeant
Co we, Mathla	G	Sergeant
Conchar te tusternay,	B	Sergeant
Conchartee tustennggee,	B	Sergeant
Cos is ta,	F	Sergeant
Cos is tee,	F	Sergeant
Cot cha har chutche,	F	Sergeant
Cot cher har chutche.	Γ	Sergeant
Cotch ar, Harjo	H	Sergeant
Cousins, Pawney	F	Sergeant
Cuzzins, Pamy	F	Sergeant
Echo, Harjo	H,D	Sergeant
Echo, Hujo	H,D	Sergeant
Fife, Tally	L	Sergeant
Fo lecher,	L	Sergeant
Fos yo holer,	I	Sergeant
Fosya ho Car,	I	Sergeant
Frank, David	I	Sergeant
Fuch char la ke,	A	Sergeant
Fus ya hola,	I	Sergeant
Futch ar li key,	A	Sergeant
Futchar like,	A	Sergeant
Futchartekey,	A	Sergeant
Gentry, James	C	Sergeant
Hall, Joseph	C,I	Sergeant
Haney,	A	Sergeant
Harjo, Woatco	E	Sergeant
Hillis, Harjo	M	Sergeant
Holotta, Fixeco	M	Sergeant
Holotte, Fixico	M	Sergeant
Hotulke, Yahola	G	Sergeant
Hotulke, Yar hola	G	Sergeant
Hotulki, Yar hola	G	Sergeant
Isparhe cher,	K	Sergeant
Kanard, Harrison	H	Sergeant
Kannard, Harrison	H	Sergeant
Kar har thle che	D	Sergeant
Kattonna,	E	Sergeant

Marshall, Nicholas	M	Sergeant
Me te ta kee,	C	Sergeant
Me tee ca kee,	C	Sergeant
Micco, Pu ker	F	Sergeant
Miller, Joseph	F	Sergeant
Nar har thlo che,	D	Sergeant
Ne har hargo,	B	Sergeant
Ne har, Harjo	B	Sergeant
Ne ne chupper, Harjo	C	Sergeant
Nehar, Fixico	K	Sergeant
Neher thloe o chee,	D	Sergeant
Nehu thlo co chee,	D	Sergeant
Ninnechupper, Harjo	C	Sergeant
No cos elle,	L	Sergeant
Os che Tuster nugke,	E	Sergeant
Oso chee tus te nuggee,	E	Sergeant
Owsh tush te nuga,	E	Sergeant
Patten, John	G	Sergeant
Powell, William	G	Sergeant
Quegus, Harjo	B	Sergeant
Queques, Harjo	B	Sergeant
Reed, Jimsey	C	Sergeant
So litka,	F	Sergeant
So litker,	F	Sergeant
Soh let kar,	F	Sergeant
Soh lit kar, litkar	F	Sergeant
Ta lee chey,	I	Sergeant
Thlo ce,	E	Sergeant
Thlo see,	E	Sergeant
Thompson, James	D	Sergeant
Tiger, Robert	F	Sergeant
To le che,	L	Sergeant
Tulmo chussee,		Sergeant
Tutch ar li key,	A	Sergeant
Willingham, John	G	Sergeant
Willinghann, John	G	Sergeant
Wohar, Harjo	B	Sergeant
Ya ha, Harjo	C	Sergeant
Ya tappe,	C	Sergeant
Ya tu pe,	C	Sergeant
Ya tui chee,	C	Sergeant
Ya tuppu,	C	Sergeant

Yar tap pe,	C	Sergeant
Yoholar, Harjo	F,B	Sergeant
Yolke, Harjo	M	Sergeant
Porter, Pleasant		Quartermaster Sergeant
Davis, W.T.	B	Commissary Sergeant
Allen, W.H.	B	Ordnance Sergeant
Abraham,	G	Corporal
Arfa le, Hachn	A	Corporal
Artus, Micco	B	Corporal
Beaver, John	B,I	Corporal
Brewner, Jack	G	Corporal
Brown, Chepany	F	Corporal
Brown, Cheparney	F	Corporal
Brown, Chepary	F	Corporal
Bruner, George	G	Corporal
Bruner, Jack	G	Corporal
Burgess, Billy	F	Corporal
Burgess, Caesar	B,I	Corporal
Burgess, Peter	G	Corporal
Burgess, Zizer	H	Corporal
Captain, John	E	Corporal
Catcher, Homahte	K	Corporal
Catcher, Hujo	D	Sergeant
Cates, Jefferson	H	Corporal
Char lo tus tar, Nuggy	H	Corporal
Chis so,	F	Corporal
Chis soe,	F	Corporal
Chise, Harjo	A	Corporal
Chissey, Hargo	A	Corporal
Chissey, Harjo	A	Corporal
Cho cot to, Sam	H,D	Corporal
Chokottu, Sam	H,D	Corporal
Chular, Fixico	B,E	Corporal
Chulmer,	K	Corporal
Co li ke,	C	Corporal
Conip, Harjo chee	B	Corporal
Cosar, Harjo	M	Corporal
Cotcha, Homahte	K	Corporal
Cow o ck co chee,	B	Corporal
Cowacco chee,	B	Corporal
Cowe harjo,	C	Corporal
Crain,	E	Corporal

Echo, Hargo	A	Corporal
Echo, Harjo	A	Corporal
Elijah,	E	Corporal
Ema tul gee,	M	Corporal
Este C chee,	C	Corporal
Este le cher,	C	Corporal
Este li char,	C	Corporal
Fife, Benjamin	L	Corporal
Fog,	C	Corporal
Fos Harjo,	I	Corporal
Funke,	M	Corporal
Hanes, Lasley	H	Corporal
Haney,	C	Corporal
Hardage, Lewis	B,I	Corporal
Hardige, Lewis	B,I	Corporal
Hardrage, Louis	B,I	Corporal
Harjo,	K	Corporal
Hayne,	C	Corporal
Haynes, Lasley	H,D	Corporal
He chee,	C	Corporal
He ne e marthler,	M	Corporal
Hillis, Charver	K	Corporal
Hillis, Charver	K	Corporal
Ho lah tar, Fixico	M	Corporal
Ho lah tar, Fixico	M	Corporal
Hoshar tar ke,	L	Corporal
Hoshar tar ke,	L	Corporal
Hosputtarke,	L	Corporal
Hosputtarke,	L	Corporal
Isfarney, Harjo	K	Corporal
Jimme, Chupee	E	Corporal
Kanard, William	F	Corporal
Kat ti le nay,	E	Corporal
Kat ti ney,	E	Corporal
Kates, Jeff	H	Corporal
Ke omulke, Harjo	G	Corporal
Kennard, William	F	Corporal
Ki omulke, Harjo	G	Corporal
Kinnard, William	F	Corporal
Kiomel ke, Harjo	G	Corporal
Marcey,	K	Corporal
Marsee,	K	Corporal

Marsey,	K	Corporal
Masey,	A	Corporal
Masse,	A	Corporal
McKellup, John	H	Corporal
McKillop, John		Corporal
Meieter,	F	Corporal
Micco, Hutka	B	Corporal
Micco, Poekar	B	Corporal
Micco, Pooker	B	Corporal
Miller, Samuel	A	Corporal
Mims, John	K	Corporal
Mocco Pooker,	B	Corporal
Ne har yar hola,	B	Corporal
Nehar, Yoholah	B	Corporal
No ci Silly,	H	Corporal
No cos illy,	H	Corporal
No cos, Harjo	E	Corporal
No cus, Harjo	E	Corporal
No cusse ka,	D	Corporal
Nocas, Ekar	D	Corporal
Nocos elle,	H	Corporal
Nokos eker,	D	Corporal
Nokos, Eku	D	Corporal
Pahee Leiche,	F	Corporal
Par he Sei chee,	F	Corporal
Parnukee,	M	Corporal
Pars eekee,	M	Corporal
Payne, Easter	D	Corporal
Payne, Hester	D	Corporal
Perhos figico,	1C	Corporal
Phillip, -	H	Corporal
Pinharjo,	1C	Corporal
Poesey, Louis H.	G	Corporal
Posey, Lewis H.	G	Corporal
Posey, Louis H.	G	Corporal
Sa la like, -	A	Corporal
Sah luppe, -	L	Corporal
Sam, Che col to	H D	Corporal
Sam, Cho cottee	H D	Corporal
Sar luppee, -	L	Corporal
Se he che pi, -	2 C	Corporal
Se he chi pe, -	2 C	Corporal

Slannelle, -	A	Corporal
Smutiye, John	M	Corporal
Soc killer harjo,	1 C	Corporal
Soh lap pe,	L	Corporal
Soh ta la ke,	2 C	Corporal
Somme chi che,	H	Corporal
Thlar thlo Harjo,	B	Corporal
Thlar thlo ya ho la,	C	Corporal
Thue thlo Harjo,	B	Corporal
Tim kar,	G	Corporal
Tim ker,	G	Corporal
Tuskehenehar,	H	Corporal
Walker, Chales	G	Corporal
Wehi yo holah, -	B	Corporal
Wonter,	C	Corporal
Wot ko, Harjo	L	Corporal
Ar har loc, Harjo che	M	Musician
Ar pi ark hargo,	K	Musician
Arparark, Hargo	K	Musician
Arparark, Harjo	K	Musician
Barnett, Watty	M	Musician
Burgess, Tyler	B,I	Musician
Chullar harjo,	C	Musician
Coat ho hay,	E	Musician
Freeman, John	K	Musician
Hart ka,	C	Musician
Ho la tah,	A	Musician
Ho lar tao,	A	Musician
Holahtah,	A	Musician
Ne har, Fixico	M	Musician
No cos yar hola,	A	Musician
No cos zar hola,	A	Musician
No cus ya hola,	A	Musician
Pah has harjo chee,	B	Musician
Perryman, John W.	H	Musician
Perryman, Legus	H	Musician
Smith, George	G	Musician
Tomey, Larney	K	Musician
Tommeharjo,	C	Musician
Ward, William	2C	Musician
Landrum, H. T.	B	Chief Bugler
Efar, Emathla	L	First Bugler

Efar, Emerthla	L	First Bugler
Mat kar,	A	First Bugler
Meat kar,	A	First Bugler
Meatka,	A	First Bugler
Yarhola, Micco	B	First Bugler
Yoholar, Micco	B	First Bugler
Kiney, George	G	Second Bugler
Kinney, George	G	Second Bugler
Charley,	F	Bugler
Clinton, Charley	E	Bugler
Clinton, Chorley	E	Bugler
Co tah we,	E	Bugler
Downing, Watty	M	Bugler
Espokok yarh ola,	L	Bugler
Gah tah la na,	E	Bugler
Harthlon, Harjo	B	Bugler
Hlunthlon, Harjo	B	Bugler
Hulthin, Harjo	B	Bugler

Privates

A har lock,	F		Alge chi chee,	C
Aathle,	M		Allickee,	G
Abram,	M		Alllick,	G
Acly, Sandy	E		Anderson, David	L
Adam,	H		Anthla pe,	F
Adam,	M		Anthlah pe,	F
Ah co nin nay,	E		Appolla,	A
Ah Co Stun nay,	E		Ar be ker, Fixico	G
Ah ha lock,	F		Ar che yorhols,	M
Ah lock, Harjo	B		Ar co qua,	E
Ah mo li chu,	B		Ar cos ton nay,	E
Ah polahle nay,	E		Ar har loc yar holar,	K
Ah quan na,	E		Ar har lock fircico,	F
Ah quan ne,	E		Ar har lock,	F
Ah tel ay,	E		Ar har lock, Fixeco	F
Ah thle,	M		Ar har lock, Fixico	K
Aharlock, Harjo	B		Ar har lock, Yoholar	K
Al lut ter, Harjo	B		Ar har luck, Fixico	B
Alexander,	A		Ar har luck, Fixico	F
Alexander,	H		Ar har luck, Harjo	B

Ar her lark, Fixseco	F		Bartlett, John	K
Ar her lark, Yarholer	F		Battel, Jim	C
Ar ho vin na,	E		Bearfort, Lewis	M
Ar keilth ye,	F			
Ar le char,	G		Beauford, Lewis	M
Ar le cher,	G		Beaver, Alexander	M
Ar le chi che,	A		Beaver, David	A
Ar lee char,	G		Beaver, Jack	M
Ar pe Kar,	L		Beaver, Moses	F
Ar pek kar,	L		Bell, George	K
Ar quan na,	E		Bellow, Joseph	F
Ar quina,	E		Beney,	M
Ar ye mah har,	H		Benney,	A
Ar yi chi cha,	C		Benney,	B
Ar yi chi chee,	C		Benney,	C
Ar yo che,	H		Benney,	M
Archer,	C		Benny,	B
Archey,	C		Benny, -	B
Archeyarholar,	M		Berrihill, Robert	C
Archi,	A		Berryhill, James	B
Archi,	A		Berryhill, James	F
Archie,	A		Berryhill, William	F
Arharloc, Harjo	K		Big Tim,	E
Arharluck co che,	F		Biggs, Pompey	L
Arher lark o chee,	F		Biggs, Pompey	L
Arke thli ye,	F		Billey,	A
Arpar lar, Harjo	K		Billey,	C
Ars sey,	H		Billey,	E
Arth kil hi ye,	F		Billey,	H
Artus hopi ye,	L		Billey,	L
Aspberry, Daniel	B		Billoche,	G
Ass sey,	H		Billy,	A
Baker, Henry	F		Billy,	B
Bamnett, Dick	A		Billy,	E
Barnes, H. L. B.	G		Billy,	H
Barnes, L. B.	G		Billy,	K
Barnes, Lenard	G		Billy, Harjo	B
Barnett, Beaty	M		Blaylock, Henry	D
Barnett, Charle	E		Boatswin, John	M
Barnett, Timothy	E		Bolin, Goliah	E
Barnett, William	E		Boney,	M
Barns, L. B.	G		Boonyhill, James	B

Bow Leg, John	E		Catcher, Harjo chee	F
Bow Legs, John	E		Catcherhargo,	H,B
Bradly, Samuel	M		Cath lo na,	E
Brady, Samuel	M		Cawpitsaw fircico,	B
Brane, Samuel I			Ceasor,	L
Brewner, Alexander	G		Cezar,	L
Brewner, Joshua	G		Ch thla na,	E
Brewner, Louis	L		Cha cho char,	C
Brewner, Samuel	G		Cha pa na chully,	A
Bring, Samuel	M		Cha thla ne,	E
Brown, Daniel	F		Chac hee,	C
Brown, David	A		Chak kah,	C
Brown, Robert	E		Chan, Sang	E
Brown, Thomas	B		Chandler, S. E.	E
Bruner, Alex	G		Chanothlonnay,	E
Bruner, Jack	I		Chaplin, Thomas	H
Bruner, Josh	G		Char kar,	H
Bruner, Louis	L		Char lo, Fixico	A
Bruner, Samuel	I		Char luck ke,	H
Buck, John	E		Char thlen ney,	E
Burgess, Bean	C		Char was ti ee,	B
Burgess, Ben	I		Char woe ley,	M
Burgess, Benjamin	B		Char, Kah	H
Burgess, Jefferson	M,I		Charchoche,	C
Burgess, John	D		Charleesta,	D
Burgess, William	H,D		Charley,	A
Busheyhead, Samuel	E		Charley,	C
Bushyhead, John	E		Charley,	E
Buster, John	C		Charley,	F
Ca Co fan na,	E		Charley,	H
Ca co fun na,	E		Charlie,	C
Ca to,	A		Charlon, Fixico	K,A
Ca yo,	I		Charls e ca,	D
Cabbage, James	F		Charluster,	D
Caesar,	L		Charpitcher chully,	F
Cah tah que in na,	E		Charwax, C. Harjo	B
Cahpo yar thla na,	E		Chaw othan nay,	E
Capick cher, Harjo	G		Che lake ko chee,	F
Car pitcher, Hargo	G		Che loke kee,	F
Car thon na,	E		Che mar ley,	L
Catchar, Harjo	H,B		Che pa na chully,	C
Catcher, Fixico	D		Che pa na,	A

Che pa nah chully,	A	Childers, Robert	D
Che pa nah,	A	Chine be, Thomas	L
Che pa nah, C.	C	Chinnohe, Moses	I
Che pah nah,	C,D	Chishm, John	B
Che pan hut, Kee	C	Chishom, John	B
Che par ne chap co,	M	Chisom, Denis	G
Che par nee,	H,D	Cho cot te, Micco	H
Che par ney,	F	Cho cotte yahola,	M
Che par ney,	H,C	Cho cotte yoholo,	M
Che par ney,	K	Cho la chop co,	A
Che pon chep co,	I	Cho la chupco,	A
Che pon le be to,	M	Cho lah, Fixico	B
Che pon ne chopco,	I	Cho ne ker,	F
Che pon thlacco,	B,I	Cho was ti ee,	B
Che pun chupco,	F	Cho was ti ye,	A
Che pun Hut kee,	C	Cho was ti ye,	B
Che pune,	G,D	Cho wastae,	A
Che tulo che,	M	Cho, Harjo	E
Che yellee,	K	Choatka,	K
Chennebe, Thomas	L	Cholley,	I
Chep an thloe co,	B,I	Chona,	C
Chepan utche,	F	Choney,	C
Chepan, Chop ko	F	Chopco cho masta...,	A
Chepane,	C,D	Chopco, Chular	A
Chepar no chee,	F	Chopco, Samme	A
Cheparney, Gobson	A	Chrat ka,	M
Chepon, Chopco	I	Chu cot yar ho lar,	M
Chepon, Taylor	C	Chu kah,	B
Chepon, Thlocco	B,I	Chu lar, Chupco	A
Cherokee,		Chu lupe, Horchu	G
Chi ke,	G	Chuck, Chartee	K
Chi kee,	C	Chuk char te,	C
Chi she nay,	E	Chular, Chopco	A
Chikey,	G	Chular, Yarhola	B
Childers, C. James	D	Chular, Yoholar	B
Childers, Daniel	D	Chulle,	M
Childers, James C.	D	Chullukee,	D
Childers, James	D	Chullukkee,	D
Childers, Lewis	D	Chumpar, Charley	G
Childers, Lunday	D	Chumper, Charley	G
Childers, Pole	D	Chupitcher, Fixico	B
Childers, Reuben	H,D	Chupko, Huitchey	C

Chupko, John	C		Co tulke, Harjo	E
Chupko, Noherthlocko	C		Co u co tah la nay,	E
			Co w cha,	E
Chuslah, Yoholah	B		Co wak ke, Yarhola	H
Chut ke,	M		Co was, Sarte	A
Chuy, Aloku	D		Co we thla la,	E
Clos sa chu,	B		Co Yah,	C
Co ack cut che,	K		Co yo che,	E
Co al la,	E		Co yo co ton na,	E
Co Alley,	E		Co yo thla ne,	E
Co Ally,	E		Cochuckney, Sam	K
Co chas ye O Holo,	F		Cochus, Micco	F
Co chi e,	A		Coffee, John	F
Co chock nar, Harjo	G		Cohars se, Emarther	F
Co chock ne, Hargo	G		Cohars, Emarthlar	F
Co Chokney, Harjo	G		Cok ko,	C
Co co thle la na,	E		Con car kin ney,	E
Co co thle ne nay,	E		Con char to chee,	B
Co con thla ha na,	E		Con chato chee,	B
Co e thla la,	E		Con co qua na,	E
Co fan nay,	E		Con tul, Harjo	B
Co la ah co ta na,	E		Con tulle, Harjo	G
Co la ha co ta ney,	E		Con tully hargo,	M
Co la Sin nay,	E		Conip, Harjo	B
Co li coo ti nay,	E		Conip, Yoholah	B
Co lumee, Hargo	G		Conippe, Moses	I
Co nip, Yaholo	B		Cono chupco,	H
Co nip, Yar hola	B		Cono na,	E
Co nippo,	M		Cony, James	B
Co no chop ko,	H		Coo ck cutche,	K
Co no Fixeco,	M		Coody, Dempsey	H
Co no Fixico,	B		Coole coo qua nay,	E
Co no Fixico,	M		Cooney, Tim	K
Co que fon,	E		Cooper, John	E
Co so e far,	E		Coryah,	C
Co te ha,	E		Cot cher yaholo,	F
Co te na,	E		Cot cher, Harjo chee	I
Co te se,	E		Cot chus yar holar,	F
Co te sen na,	E		Cot chus, Mikko	C
Co to na,	E		Cotch ar, Harjo	B
Co to see,	E		Cotch key,	I
Co ton na,	E		Cotcha hargo chee,	I

Cotchar ho mahte,	L		Demilker, Brown	F	
Cotchar, Fircico	D		Demilker, Larney	F	
Cotchar, Fixico	H		Denton, John	H	
Cote ho se,	E		Denton, Randolph	H	
Covey, Harjo	K		Derrisaw, Chepany	C	
Covey, John	H,D		Dick,	C	
Cow ah pe,	C		Dick,	L	
Cow ch arty,	B		Dick, Taylor	L	
Cow etah, Micco	F		Dickey,	A	
Cowak ko che,	H		Dickson, John	E	
Cowars, Sarte	A		Dickson, Wiley	H,D	
Cowe Haj-chee,	F		Dicky,	A	
Cowe, John	H,D		Dimbo,	E	
Cowe, John	H,D		Dock,	E	
Crowell, John	C		Dodge, Sango	L	
Cud jo,	M		Dorsey,	F	
Cumpsey,	FHM		Doyle, Archibald	H,I	
Cumsey,	FHM		Dragon,	L	
Cun tul, Harjo	B		E tu nay,	E	
Cuntul, Fixico	B		Eat ka,	A	
Cupitchee, Harjo	B		Echee e mar thlar,	I	
Cupitcher, Fixico	B		Echo, Emarthla	I	
Cupitcher, Harjo	B		Echo, Emathla	I	
Cuppo, Yathlan na	E		Echo, Fixico	B	
Cusetah yoholah,	B		Echo, Fixico	K	
Cusse ta yaholo,	B		Echo, Harjo	L	
Cusseh ta yarholo,	B		Echuemar thler,	M	
Daniel,	M		Eco e, Marthla	I	
Dapey,	L		Econ nay,	E	
Davey,	A		Edward,	H	
Davey,	F		Elleck,	G	
Davey,	K		Ellick,	K	
David,	C		Elliott, Arch	B	
David,	G		Em oth lo che,	G	
David,	I		Emarthla,	M	
David,	K		Emarthler,		
David,	M		Ekerthlocko	C	
Davie, Wesley	B		Emarthler, Koher	C	
Davis, Thomas	H		Emarthler, Tomme	C	
Davis, Tommey	B		Emerthlo che,	G	
Davisher,	A		Enester,	D	
Daviskar,	A		Enthlac marlikey,	F	

Es Ko cho che,	H	Frank,	M
Es temi yeh pe,	H,D	Frank, Major	I
Esa pah,	C	Frank, Thomas	I
Esaper,	C	Frank, William	I
Eschulley,	L	Frank, William	M
Eserper,	C	Fucetustunnugge,	H
Eskah cho che,	H	Fus cos he,	M
Esten i yeh pe,	H,D	Fus Hajo,	B
Esternes, Yehee	H,D	Fus Hajo,	F
Etar co way,	E	Fus Har hola,	B,K
Etar co we,	E	Fus Harjo,	B
Eton, Harjo	B,I	Fus lar ho Car,	I
Fa lin ha,	C	Fus yo ho la,	B,K
Fa lin nah,	C	Fus yoholar,	B,K
Fa lin nee,	C	Fushutch chee Harjo,	F
Factor, Samuel	C	Fushutchee Fixico,	B
Feepkar,	K	Fuster nug ke,	A
Fife, Askellon	L	Fustus tar nuggy,	H
Fife, Jack	C	Fustus tu nuggee,	H
Fife, Jeffrey	L	Fuswar,	G
Fisher, Elijah	G	Futchullas,	C
Fixico Arholuk,	A	Gah ta na,	E
Fixico Echo,	C	Gah tah to ualana,	E
Fixico Hargo,	F	Gah thlo na,	E
Fixico Harjo,	B	Gaines, Doc	C
Fixico Harjo,	F	Garrett, John H.	B
Fixico Ictar Yarche,	C	George,	E
Fixico Nehematter,	C	George,	H
Fixico Nocosse,	C	George,	K
Fixico Thockosko,	C	George,	M
Fixico Tulse,	B	George, (Big)	M
Fixico Watko,	C	Gibson,	A
Fixico ya ho la,	A	Gibson,	I
Fixico Yarher,	C	Gibson, John	H
Flanly, Thomas	H	Gihu thla na,	E
Fletcher, John	M	Giu thlan ney,	E
Foreman, Arch	H	Goliath,	E
Fox, Jack	C,D	Good, Benjamin	H
Fox, Tomas	B	Goody, John	G
Francis,	I	Gordan, William R.	E
Francis, William	B	Gorden, W.R.	E
Frank Cheponne,	M	Grace, John	H

Grace, John	K		Harjo, Cupitcher	C	
Grason, Colbert	G		Harjo, Echo cha	C	
Grason, James	G		Harjo, Felterteek	C	
Grason, Tapes	G		Harjo, Huttip	C	
Gray, Noonan	M		Harjo, Kesarchee	C	
Grayson, Eli	M		Harjo, Kochucner	C	
Grayson, Jim	K		Harjo, Kono	C	
Grayson, Johnson	G		Harjo, Micco	C	
Greason, Buck	E		Harjo, Nuthcup	C	
Gregory, David	B		Harjo, Ochee	C	
Gregory, David	H		Harjo, Ochulloc	C	
Gregory, Edward	B		Harjo, Thlartac	C	
Grenpon, Johnson	G		Harjo, Thlockusko	C	
Griffeth, David	K		Harjo, Tomme	C	
Griffith, David	K		Harjo, Tulwer	C	
Grinpon, Johnson	G		Harjo, Waxey	C	
Gut thlar ne,	E		Harjo, Yarhollo	C	
Ha chu ta loa,	A		Harley,	F	
Ha fup of Harchu,	G		Harry,	F	
Ha gee,	E		Harry,	H	
Ha ke, E			Harry,	L	
Ha ya Kee,	C		Harthlon, Harjo	G	
Ha yo kee,	C		Harthlon, Harjo	G	
Hachu, Echn	A		Harvey, James	L	
Hachu, Echu	A		Hater,	B	
Hachu, Halputles	A		Hathlan, Hargo	G	
Hachu, Nocusse	A		Haynes, John	B	
Hachuche, Echu	A		He chittee, Joe	C	
Hailey,	F		He ne ha fir ci co,	B	
Hains, John	M		He tah con we,	E	
Haley,			Hector,	G	
Halputter, Emerthla	K		Hemster,	D	
Hana,	K		Herm echer,	F	
Hanes, John	M		Herod, John	C	
Haney,	C		Hi yo ke,	C	
Haney, John	C		Hi yo ke,	C	
Har far pof, Harjo	G		Hilaby,	F	
Har fup of, Harjo	G		Hillaby,	F	
Har lar tee,	A		Hilleby,	F	
Har yoh che,	H		Hillup pee,	F	
Hardage, Warier	B		Hinne har Fixico,	B	
Hardrage, Warrior	B		Hinne har, Fixico	B	

Hinne ho chee,	B		Ingrum, John	G
Hinne ho chee,	B		Is her lar tee,	F
Hitchity, Joe	C		Is po Ko chee,	C
Hitchity, Joe	C		Is pok of, Harjo	B
Ho be la han,	E		Is sa logh to,	F
Ho be lah hen,	E		Is so lah tah,	F
Ho lah ter, Harjo	B,I		Is te me chu,	B
Ho lar ter, Harjo	B,I		Is timu Yepee,	D
Ho lo tto, Harjo	B,I		Is ya he ke,	C
Ho tul kee,	E		Isaac,	C
Ho tulco chee,	B		Isaac,	E
Hocos, Yarholah	A		Issa lohto,	F
Holah tar, Fixico	B		Ista hui e thle,	C
Holah tar, Harjo	B,I		Iste ma ya chee,	D
Hollastas, Fixico	B		Iste Mi Yochee,	B
Holottar, Fixico	B		Istemu chepauchee,	D
Homan, Levi	E		Istemuchewuchee,	D
Hoparye, Echo	C		Istim machi wi chi,	A
Hopiah, Harjo	B		Istim mi che wiche,	D
Hopohethle,	C		It chas Heneha,	F
Hopohethle, Arpeker	C		Itch hars Eneher,	F
Hoponey, Robert	I,M		Itch hars, Fixseco	F
Hos per,	F		Itch hars, Fixseco	F
Hosse,	M,I		Its hars he ne har,	F
Hotalky, Harjo	E		Its hars wer,	K
Hoththe Toyer, Hajo	F		Its hurswer,	K
Hotulke, Harjo	F		Jack,	C
Hotulke, Yar hola	B		Jackley,	K
Hotulkee, Fixico	B		Jackson,	K
Hotulkee, Yoholah	B		Jacob,	A
Houge, Alvin	H		Jacob,	C
Houston,	H		Jacob,	E
Hul but ta, Hartjo	I		Jacob,	F
Hul but ter, Harjo	I		Jacob,	K
Hulputtar, Chupco	K		Jacob, Eli	A
Hulputtar, Emarthler	K		Jacobs,	A
Hulputter,	C,A		Jacobs, George	M
Hulwe,	G		Jake, -	G
Hus thun, Hargo	G		Jake, -	K
Ille, Echo	C		James,	K
In chee,	F		Je mar har,	D
Ingrum, David	G		Jemu hee,	D

Jemuhu,	D		Josey,	D
Jerry,	E		Kana,	K
Jess,	G		Kanard, Andrew	C
Jesse,	E		Kanard, Jack	C
Jessee,	G		Kapetsaw,	F
Jike,	C		Kapitsaw,	F
Jim,	2 I		Kar hik char chulee,	F
Jim, Mu	C		Kar Larney,	K
Jimme,	A		Kar tar kin na,	E
Jimme, Chee	K		Kar tin na,	E
Jimmoche,	K		Kar wappe key,	L
Jimmy,	B		Kar wappi key,	L
Jimochee,	F		Karchee,	F
Jo cah,	M		Karlarney, Daniel	K
Joe,	C		Karmar,	L
Joesey,	D		Karpitcher,	F
Johkar,	C		Karwappeke,	D
John,	C		Kasahcoyunta,	E
John,	E		Kasarcoco, Conthay	E
John,	H		Ke chart te,	G
John,	K		Ke co fan nay,	E
John,	M		Ke Ke chartee,	G
John, esse	M		Ke o mulka,	G
Johney, Micco	K		Ke sa chee,	C
Johnney,	A		Ke sa Kee,	C
Johnny,	E		Ke thlon nay,	E
Johnochee,	2 D		Keemarme, Harjo	B
Johnochee,	F		Kelley, Marshell	L
Johnson,	C		Kelley, Tobe	L
Johnson,	F		Kelly, Marshall	L
Johnson, James	E		Kelly, Tobe	L
Johnson, Thomas	H		Kenissee,	K
Jokah,	G		Ketto,	F
Joke, kar	G		Key sa co con ta,	E
Joke, ker	G		Ki chee,	C
Joker,	C		Ki yoker, Harjo	K
Jonas,	C		Kiemar, Harjo	B
Jones,	M		Killany, Daniel	F
Jones, Abram	H		Killarney, Daniel	F
Jones, Samuel	I		Kin kor til in	A, E
Jonney,	A		Kis ha tin han,	E
Joseph,	M		Kis sar tin ha,	E

Kittoe,	F		Lowe, Colbert	I
Ko ithe Cur la,	E		Lowrie, Walter	H
Ko kin thlin, A.	E		Lukuba, Jimme	I
Ko ko in fon,	E		Lumba, Jimmy	I
Koh tar ray,	E		Luny, Jimmey	G
Konco con nay,	E		Luppi chee chee,	C
Kotsky,	I		Luppie chi chee,	C
Kupitcher,	C		Ma hat che,	I
Larne, Jimme	M		Ma hit chee,	B
Larputker,	K		Ma wo ly,	M
Lasley,	L		Mackey, Abraham	H
Lasley, Sam	G		Madderson,	G
Latiffe,	A		Maddison,	G
Le tahne co har,	E		Madison,	G
Le wih chee,	F		Major See,	K
Leacher,	C		Major,	E
Lee,	G		Manack, Walles	I
Lin toh che,	A		Manack, Wollace	I
Lin tui che,	A		Manichka,	C
Litteef, Harjo	B		Mar na chi chi,	A
Littiffee,	A		Mar nih che,	G
Littiffey,	A		Mar wo che,	M
Little, John	I		March, Samuel	I
Lo car,	K		Marche,	C
Lobey,	B		Marchee,	F
Logan, James	C		Marchee,	K
Logan, Jimmie	C		Mark lah,	C
Loka,	M		Marklar,	C
Lokoh,	A		Marshall, John	G
Loler,	F		Martee,	K
Long, Fish	F		Martin, Harry	A
Looney, Walter	H		Martin, Henry	A
Lot, William	B		Martul, Ceh che	K
Lott, Thomas	G		Master, Pander	C
Louis,	C		McCombs, Daniel	D
Louis,	L		McCombs, James	H
Lovett, Filly	F		McComes, Daniel	D
Lovett, Phillip	F		McComes, James	H
Low wal con,	C		McComs, James	H
Low war lo,	C		McHodge, David	H
Low, Culbert	I		McIntosh, John	C
Lowar, C.	C		McIntosh, Thomas	F

McIntosh, William	C		Miste pointer,	C
McKellop, Robert	H		Misto poon ter, -	C
McKenzie,	B		Mitchell, -	C
McKillop, David	H		Mitchell, Levi	G
McKillop, Robert	H		Mitchell, Levi	H
Me lah we,	H		Mitchell, Love	I
Me leh chee,	F		Mon Ka,	E
Mea lah,	A		Mon tol Ca,	E
Meh lar,	H		Monday,	K
Meluwee,	D		Monkey,	D
Mer he chi ke,	F		Monkey, -	E
Meste sely,	H		Monkey,	F
Meste, Hailey	H		Monky,	E
Meste, Haily	H		Montul., C.	E
Meste, Haley	H		Morrison, John	H
Met kah,	A		Moses,	B,I
Meth cuppo far,	L		Moses,	M
Mi ni che ka,	C		Moses, Conippe	I
Mi nich Ka,	C		Mu ni ho che,	M
Micco,	A		Muk lah, -	C
Micco, -	B		Muk laoh,	C
Micco,	M		Munkey,	F
Micco, Harjo	M		Muth cup po far, -	L
Micco, Hatky	H		Muttul ichee,	K
Micco, Nubba	B		Muttul ih chee,	K
Micco, Nuppar	K		Na pui chee,	C
Micco, Nupper	K		Naipey,	A
Micco, Tusekiah	C		Namey,	F
Micco, Yahola	G		Nar har key,	F
Micco, Yar holar	G		Nar hay,	E
Micco, Yarhola	G		Narmey,	F
Micco, Yarholer	G		Ne ar Thlock ko,	G
Mikko,	A		Ne ha Thlocco,	G
Milford, Louis	H		Ne har thlocco che	G
Millah,	A		Ne har yar ho la,	A
Miller,	K		Ne har, Micco	B
Miller, David	F		Ne har, Micco	K
Miller, Jefferson	C		Ne har, Thlacco	F
Miller, Major	F		Ne her, Fixseco	F
Miller, Persimmon	A		Ne her, Thark Ko	F
Milliah,	A		Ne hi yar holar,	B
Minhonthla,	E		Ne hi yo ho la,	B

Ne hor Yoholah,	B	Nige,	E
Ne te cot chee,	I	Niger,	E
Nebey,	A	Nih che,	L
Neha Tlokko,	F	Nit tar po ke,	A
Nehar hargo,	F	Niter cah che,	M
Nehar thlocco che,	C	Niter par ker,	F
Nehar thlocco che,	H	No co cey,	G
Nehar thlocco,		No cos Harjo,	B
Chupeo	K	No cos o chee,	K
Nehar thlocco, Harjo	B	No cos see,	G
Nehar thloe,		No cos so che,	G
Emerthla	H	No cos, Hargo	A
Nehar, Harjo	F	No cos, Hargo	B
Nehar, Thlokke	F	No cos, Hargo	B
Neharthlocci		No cos, Silly	B
chukney,	K	No cus to tum ko,	B
Neharthlocco,		No cus, Sche	A
Kochuckney	K	No cus, Silly	B
Neharthloe		No cusse,	C
coyar hola,	B	No pui chee,	C
Neharthloeco,		Noah,	I
Yoholah	B	Noakey,	F
Neharthloeco,		Noco se kar,	H
Yoholar	B	Nocos, Ekar	K
Nehathlocco,		Nocos, Harjo	A
Emoethlee	H	Nocos, Harjo	B
Neher chis koche,	C	Nocose Yo, Hola	
Neher thloc kochee,	C	Nocus, Harjo	A
Nehu Thlooche,		Nocus, Harjo	B
Emethle	D	Nocusee chupeo,	E
Nehuthloccochu,		Noki cher,	C
Emuthlo	D	Noley,	M
Nehuthloco chee,		Nontul li key,	E
Emuthla	D	Nublar, Micco	B
Nekey,	F	Nuff kee,	C
Net tar cah che,	M	Nufky,	C
Net tar po ke,	A	Nul cup, Harjo	H
Netee,	I	Nuth cup Harjo,	H
Netey,	I	Nuth kup hergo,	H
Nickey,	M	Nuth kup Hujo,	H
Nickochee,	C	Oak Sam kar,	H
Nicky,	M	Oak Sumkar,	H

Name	Col
Ochchum puller,	G
Oche Lar sekney,	K
Oche se,	M
Ochee chup co,	F
Ochee Hargo,	M
Ochee Larsickney,	K
Ochee, John	C
Ock choat ker,	F
Ock chum puler,	G
Ock fuskee,	C
Ock Sumker,	F
Octeryer che Harjo,	B
Ok chim nar,	C
Ok chum pollar,	G
Ok chunwa,	C
Ok foce kee,	C
Oke chum pollar,	G
Oke chun war,	C
Oke fus ke,	C
Osar Harjo,	B
Osee,	E
Osochee,	K
Pah hos Harjo,	B
Pah hos ho pi ee che,	G
Pah ner,	K
Pah ney,	B
Pah suck Harjo,	B
Palmer,	F
Pamer,	F
Pane, Heaster	H
Par he cher,	E
Par hee,	F
Par hos ho pio che,	G
Par hos hopi yo che,	G
Par hose Tus ta nuggey,	I
Par hosse tus tar nuggy,	H
Par le cher,	F
Parche ko,	C
Parhos Hargo,	A
Parner,	F
Parney,	F
Parney, Harka	K
Pars co far,	K
Pars co fer,	K
Partarke, John	C
Parter, Steel	I
Parvney,	I
Pas ta lah,	C
Patton, John	G
Pattren, John	G
Pe bis eo,	F
Pe ne che,	K
Pennech che,	K
Pero, Thomas	G
Perow, Tecumseh	H
Perow, Thomas	G
Perrow, Tom	G
Perryman, David	H
Perryman, Harry	H
Perryman, Henry	H
Perryman, James	H
Perryman, John	M
Perryman, Joseph	H
Perryman, Josiah	H
Perryman, Louis	2 C
Perryman, Louis	F
Perryman, Louis	H
Perryman, Possonar	H
Perryman, Sanford	H
Perryman, Thomas	G
Perryman, Thomas	G
Perryman, Wesley	H
Peter, -	2 C
Peter, -	2 C
Peter, -	F
Peter, -	G
Peter, Jesse	L
Peth e nay,	E
Pethle Nay,	E
Phipps, William	M
Pich ke, -	2C
Pidgeon, Thomas	KG

Pigeon, Joseph	K		Raiford, H. Philip	C
Pigeon, Thomas	K		Redmouth, John	G
Piggeon, Thomas	K		Ri ke ly,	I
Pikee, -	2C		Richards, John A.	D
Pikey, -	1		Richirds, A. John	D
Pikey, -	2I		Richmond,	G
Pikity, -	2I		Ridgeway, Josiah	G
Pillar, -	F		Robberts, David	F
Piller, -	F		Robert,	K
Pillow, -	F		Roberts, David	F
Pilth nin a, -	E		Rogers, James	F
Pin e cher, -	K		Rogers, Jim	F
Pin har kee, -	2 I		Rogers, Robert	H
Pin har key, -	2 I		Rogers, William H.	H
Pinehill, Abner	L		Ross, John	C
Pinehill, Sandy	L		Rowland, Goliah	E
Platt, Ebenezer	F		Rowlin, Goliath	E
Plethle Ne,	E		Sa chik larf ka,	A
Plett, Ebenezer	F		Sa chum kah, -	A
Po na e co, -	A		Sa cot che, -	M
Po nar e co, -	A		Sa fun nah, -	A
Po nar ze ko, -	A		Sa hm thle, -	A
Poilth, Harjo	K		S lut ke, -	2 C
Pomar ye ko, -	A		Sa ma, -	C
Porter, John	H		Sa Mille, -	A
Porter, Peter	E		Sa pin cully, -	A
Powell, Jim	M		Sa port ta ke, -	A
Powell, John	M		Sa thlar ka, -	2 C
Prochee, -	B		Sachoo thla nay,	E
Puchee, -	B		Sah con thla na, -	E
Pulhumme, -	K		Sah con thlon nay, -	E
Pully, John	2C		Sah con we na, -	E
Pus suck ke, -	M		Sah cowin nay, -	E
Puske, -	M		Sah hin thli chee, -	2 C
Puslah, -	A		Sah hin thlo chee, -	2 C
Puslar, -	A		Sah ka to, -	E
Pusloh, -	A		Samee, -	2 C
Putty, John	2C		Samme, Chopco	A
Qin hay, -	E		Samme, Chupco	A
Quarsard, Fexico	B		Samp sey, -	F
Quarsard, Harjo	B		Sampson, -	A
Quarsord, Harjo	B		Sampson, -	B

Samson, -	2 I		Sarthay, -	E
Samson, -	A		Sarwoh ley, -	M
Samson, -	M		Saryee, -	C
Sandy No. 1,	A		Sathlakah, -	2 C
Sandy No. 2,	A		Sathle, -	2 I
Sandy,	F		Sathlu ku, -	2 C
Sapa lutke, -	A		Sato co thlo, -	B
Sar co co nay, -	E		Scott, Billy	2 D
Sar con ton na, -	E		Scott, Thomas	A
Sar fi ye, -	L		Scott, Wesley	C
Sar har fixico, -	B		Se chille, -	B
Sar he pah ke, -	K		Se ke ke,	M
Sar he park her, -	K		Se ki kee,	M
Sar he poh ke, -	K		Se mar te, -	F
Sar ka te ho, -	E		Se muppy, -	A
Sar ket ho, -	E		Se se pin che, -	2 C
Sar kin tar ha, -	E		Se wi ke, -	A
Sar la ho, -	H		Se wih ke, -	A
Sar lah ke, -	L		Se yert toh,	2 C
Sar lar ho, -	H		Sechilly, -	B
Sar lar hoh, -	H		See muppe,	A
Sar lar key, -	L		Selete ker,	F
Sar lar ti ke, -	L		Semissy, -	F
Sar loh ke, -	L		Seney, William	G
Sar loley, -	M		Senuppe, -	K
Sar pi yeh, -	L		Ser ki che chee,	F
Sar put toh ke, -	A		Sesa pochee, -	2 C
Sar thle, -	H		Seto no. 1, -	A
Sar to co thle, -	B		Seto no. 2, -	A
Sar to co thlo, -	B		Seto, -	K
Sar yum ka, -	2 C		Settler, Jack	K
Sar yum kah, -	2 C		Sewa nokee, -	2 D
Sar yum kala, -	2 C		Sewu nokee, -	D
Sarfulley, -	K		Sha con ta na, -	E
Sarfunnah, -	A		Shar campun nay,	E
Sark yar kah pe, -	H		Shar ko ko kinlin	A, E
Sarpartah ke, -	A		Sheep, William	B
Sarpettar, -	K		Shirley, William	F
Sarpincal lee, -	K		Short, Tom	E
Sarput tah ke, -	A		Sim jot kee,	2 C
Sarput tok ke, -	A		Sim meh se,	F
Sartee, -	M		Sime cy,	2 C

Name	Col
Simeyar, Chee	F
Simkar, -	K
Simkay, -	E
Simmon, Peter	H
Simmons, John	G
Simmuttulkee,	K
Simon, -	B
Simon, Peter	H
Simon, Peter	H
Sims, Mark	E
Simtul, Harjo	B
Sin car ne he,	M
Sin choatke,	2 C
Sin joker,	2 C
Sin na tar,	F
Sin nah,	A
Sinkar wahsee,	L
Sinnata, -	F
Sinne,	A
Sino mah kee,	K
Sio thi chee,	K
Sio thle chee,	K
Sippe, -	H
Sippie, -	H
Smith, John	B I
Smith, Shelton	G
So wi kar,	F
Sofah,	A
Soh lar ti ke,	L
Soh yar kay pe,	A
Soh yarkahpee,	A
Sok kos key,	F
Soney,	F
Sonney,	F
Sons, George	2 B
Sowa nokee, -	2 D
Soward, W.P.	1 E
Sowarky, Thomas	A
Sowika,	F
Soy ka,	F
Soyee,	1 C
Spanard, David	2 C
Spanard, George	2 C
Spaniard, George	2 C
Spaniard, Jackson	H
Stake, David	C
Stake, David	M
Star, Jim	G,C
Star, Tom	C
Starr, James	G,C
Steel, Parter	I
Steel, Peter	I
Stidham, John	B
Stidham, Johnson	B
Sto mit chey,	I
Suck kos kee,	F
Sugar, John	B
Sugar, Thomas	I
Sugar, Wesley	I
Sugars, John	B
Sugars, Thomas	H
Sugars, Thomas	I
Sun thappee,	K
Sun thla pe,	K
Sun thlappee,	K
Sunney,	F
Sunney,	M
Suntul Hairjo,	B
Suppetar,	K
Suppi chee chee,	C
Suppulper,	K
Sut chek lar kar,	A
Ta hok not chee,	C
Ta huk ni che,	C
Ta lum poo,	A
Ta na shay,	E
Ta we i thle,	C
Ta Yar tah nay,	E
Ta Yoh ta nay,	E
Tager, Daniel	H
Tager, Jefferson	H
Tah co fah na,	E
Tah co Kah na,	E
Tah hi ah,	E

Tah ke,	A	Te sa chee,	C
Tah ta ga,	E	Te sah we,	E
Tah ya ton na,	E	Te sah we,	E
Taik ke,	A	Te tah co we,	E
Talwar Fixico,	L	Te tar co har,	E
Tante,	A	Tecumseh unah,	A
Tar co fun na,	E	Tecumsey,	M
Tar har Yar,	E	Teyah ton na,	E
Tar hok ni che,	M	Th la fer chee,	K
Tar ko har,	E	Thah Yogh,	D
Tar le chee,	I	Ther tho chuper,	F
Tar loaf Harjo,	H	Thla con cha na,	E
Tar Nupse,	L	Thla yagh,	D
Tar Sey,	F	Thlah Yagh,	D
Tar ta ka,	E	Thlar chlo yahola,	C
Tar tar ka,	E	Thlar con cha ne,	E
Tar Wee,	H	Thlar con shun ney,	E
Tar weh,	H	Thlar feche,	K
Tars hoh che,	H	Thlar fichee,	K
Tarskee,	C	Thlar kin shin a,	E
Tarskey,	C	Thlar sah ye,	M
Tas keek Mikko,	C	Thlar si ye,	I
Tasho chee,	D	Thlar thlo Fixico,	G
Tate, David	M	Thlars le ti ke,	M
Tay ol see,	D	Thlars le ti key,	I
Tay olsey,	D	Thlars tuneke,	K
Taylor,	C	Thlars tunka,	K
Taylor,	C	Thlars yumkey,	K
Taylor,	I	Thlasle te kee,	I
Taylor,	M	Thle mar heh che,	H
Taylor, Dick	L	Thle muhe chee,	D
Taylor, John	D,H	Thle seh me,	K
Te co cha nay,	E	Thle wa ley,	A,D
Te co fon ne,	E	Thle wah le,	G
Te co funnay,	E	Thle wahley,	A,D
Te coo sah,	D	Thle wuley,	A,D
Te cum see,	G	Thlemn he chee,	D
Te Eksar,	H,D	Thlin e Hargo,	G
Te ho Sar,	H,D	Thlomar he che,	D
Te ho Yah nee,	K	Thlor Toy harjo,	I
Te ho Yah ney,	K	Thlos tum kee,	B
Te mo car le,	M	Thlum Hechee,	D

Thof ka, Jimmy	G		Tobey,	C
Thomas,	A		Tocharwer,	C
Thomas,	C		Toh co ca ne,	E
Thomas,	C,D		Toh cul kay,	E
Thomas, H.	D		Toh kal ke,	E
Thompson,	A		Toh kulke,	E
Thornberry, Mark	B		Toh ta go,	E
Thornburs, Mark	B		Toh tul li key,	H
Thornbury, Mark	B		Tom co chut nee,	B
Ti co Kan nay,	E		Tom,	C
Ti co kan ney,	E		Tomassee,	B
Ti coo ka nay,	E		Tomey chupco,	K
Tigar, Thomas	D		Tomme cho no ke,	A
Tigar, Wiley	D		Tomme hujo,	D
Tiger,	E		Tomme Sane,	F
Tiger, Daniel	H		Tomme,	M
Tiger, David	H		Tommey,	A
Tiger, George	A		Tommie,	C
Tiger, Jefferson	H		Tommoche,	M
Tiger, Thomas	D		Tommy cho no ke,	A
Tiger, Wilson	A		Tommy Harjo,	H,D
Tiger, Woley	D		Tommy Harjo,	K
Tilow,	A		Tommy Larney,	F
Tim o se li kee,	I		Tommy,	A
Tim o se li key,	I		Tommy,	C
Timme chi che,	C		Tommy,	H
Timmo Soliky,	I		Tomy,	C
Timmoche,	M		Ton tah co ka nay,	E
Tin char na,	E		Ton tar co ka na,	E
Tin shun na,	E		Tor kin a,	E
Tin shunnay,	E		Tos hoh che,	D
Tis e poh che,	G		Tubby, John	M
To clee,	C		Tuck a batchee	
To co co we,	E		Harjo,	B
To Co fon nay,	E		Tulhar,	K
To gah ga,	E		Tuliver,	F
To go not chee,	M		Tully, John	M
To ney,	A		Tulma chussey,	F
To path lar,	E		Tulmar Emerthla,	B
To tah co ka na,	E		Tulmars Emorthla,	B
Tobe,	E		Tulmars Fixico,	B
Tobee,	C		Tulmars see,	F

Name	Col
Tulmo chus Fixico,	B
Tulmo chussee,	F
Tulmus Hargo,	G
Tulse Hajo,	F
Tulsee Fixeco,	F
Tulwa Harjo,	G
Tulwar Fixico,	A
Tulwar Fixico,	L
Tulwar Harjo,	G
Tumme hugo,	D
Tur Kov ner Harjo,	K
Turskey,	C
Tus tun ok o che,	A
Tus ya holo,	I
Tuskeek Micco,	C
Tuskey,	B
Tussekiah Harjo,	H
Tussekiahhatke,	G
Tustenekenathlar,	A
Tusternug co che,	H
Tusternugke,	A
Tusternuyemerthla,	A
Tustonogogy,	H
Tustonugge,	C
U co nay,	E
U on tah,	E
U pe chee,	E
U pich chee,	E
U un tah,	E
Uche, Sandy	E
Uchee, John	E
Ufala,	A
Uly cully, Gray	M
Un thar pee,	F
Unah, John	A
Uner, John	A
Unusey,	C
Upah tar,	K
Upatter,	K
Upeh che,	E
Usley,	C
Usly,	C
Utche, John	E
Vann, David	D
Vann, John	D
Vann, Josh	D
Vann, William	D
Vann, Yahtunnu	D
Verdegris, Peter	C
Wa na ki, -	A
Wa nah ke, -	A
Wa sas sey, -	2 I
Wah nar,	K
Wah ner,	K
Waisarsimmer,	K
Waistunna,	C
Walker, John	2C
Walker, William	G
Wallesee, -	H
Wallesey,	H
Wallicee,	H
War sar sey, -	2 I
War thlocco, -	F
Warford, William	2C
Warsarsimer, -	K
Warsarsimner, -	K
Warsaw, Ben	G
Warthark, -	F
Wasey, -	1C
Washington, -	M
Washington, Lowike	F
Wath cokko, -	F
Wattey, -	1C
Watty, -	G
Waxcey, Hargo	A
Waxcey, Hargo	A
Waxcy, Hargo	B
Waxcy, Yarholar	F
Waxy, O. Holo	F
We lar kepe, -	K M
We lar keppee, -	K M
We thlocco, -	1F
Wellie, -	1C
Wema ke, -	2C

Wenukee, -	2C	Yah pun na,	E
Wenukey, -	2C	Yah tah co wa ne,	E
Whitekiller, Stevey	G	Yah tol la we,	E
Wildcat,	E	Yahar fircico,	B
Wiley,	E	Yar che co,	G
Wiley,	G	Yar che ko,	G
Wiley,	K	Yar har, Fixico	G
Wiley, C.	C	Yar hi co che,	H
William,	A	Yar hi coe che,	H
William,	C	Yar ho la,	A
William,	G	Yar holar, Fixico	F
William,	G	Yar holar, Fixico	G
William,	H	Yar kar pee,	I
Willingham, Moses	G	Yar kin kar,	F
Wilo chee,	K	Yar kin ker,	F
Wilson,		Yar teh ke, Harjo	L
Wilson,	H	Yar teh ker, Harjo	K
Wilson, Hugh	A	Yar thlin, A.	E
Win ar kee,		Yar tol oc wee,	E
Wohley,	E	Yarche che,	G
Wohly,	E	Yardee, Joseph	H
Wolf,	E	Yarge,	K
Wolfe,	E	Yargie,	K
Wooh ley,	E	Yarhar, Emarthlar	B
Wot chut he,	M,I	Yarhar, Emarthlee	B
Wot ko yar hola,	B	Yarhar, Emerthla	B
Wotkar, Yoholar	B	Yarhar, Fixeco	G
Wouton,	C	Yarhar, Fixico	B
Wox e yar holer,	F	Yarhar, Harjo	F
Woxcey, Hargo	A	Yarhollar, Cotcher	C
Woxcey, Harjo	A	Yarhollar, Itchhas	C
Woxcy, Harjo	B	Yarhollar, Waxey	C
Wuskey,	C	Yarholloche,	C
Ya chus, David	C	Yarjie,	K
Ya ha cui che,	A	Yarteehkar, Harjo	K
Ya ho la ne haw,	A	Yate ka, Hargo	L
Ya ho la, Ispokoke	A	Ye ki che,	E
Ya hola, Thlarthlo	C	Yelke, Harjo	K
Ya kin ka,	F	Yern ster,	C
Ya ma har ke,	C	Yhahketah,	A
Ya pe kah,	B	Yo fa lar,	A
Yah po na,	E	Yo fala,	A

Yo part tar,	K	Youngar,	A
Yoh pone,	E	Younger,	A
Yoh tul lo we,	E	Za cup pi chee,	G
Yol le car le,	M	Za hah, Fixico	G
Yope, Kar	B	Zar ti ki, Horgo	G
Yoster,	A	Zarte ker,	G

1st Creek Mounted Rifles

This is only a partial listing of this unit.

Che ko te, Samuel.	B	Lieutenant.Colonel
Brewner, Luney	L	Captain
Callahan, S.B.	K	Captain
Cully, Micco.	C	Captain
Ah far le, Hargo	A	First Lieutenant
Brown, John	D	First Lieutenant
Burgess, Jackson	B	First Lieutenant
Chustullee Co.	F	First Lieutenant
Adkins, Thomas	C	Second Lieutenant.
Anderson, Robert	L	Second Lieutenant.
Auster, ---	C	Second Lieutenant.
Bare Arm	E	Second Lieutenant.
Berrihill, Pleasant	C	Second Lieutenant.
Berryhill, Jim	F	Second Lieutenant.
Brewner, William	G	Second Lieutenant.
Brown, Samuel	E	Second Lieutenant.
Burgess, Toney.	B	Second Lieutenant.
Carr, Harry	K	Second Lieutenant.
Che ho Jim	H	Second Lieutenant.
Che par ney.	E	Second Lieutenant
Cowas sart Hachu	G	Second Lieutenant.
Co wak co chee	C	Junior Second Lieutenant.
Brown, Thomas	E	Lieutenant
Alexander, Geore A.	G	First Sergeant
Berryhill, Mark	F	First Sergeant
Burgess, John	B,I	First Sergeant
Carr, Richard W.	K	First Sergeant
Charlo Harjo	H	First Sergeant
Clark, William	K	First Sergeant
Clinton, William M.	E	First Sergeant
Ah har lock co Chee	B	Sergeant
Ah lock fixico	B	Sergeant.
Barnett, Chilly	M	Sergeant
Barnett, Toney	E	Sergeant
Brewner, Louis	G	Sergeant
Broun, Charley.	E	Sergeant

Burgess, Edward.	C, H	Sergeant
Burgess, Joseph 2nd Co.	C,.H	Sergeant
Carr, Washington.	K	Sergeant
Catcher Harjo.	D	Sergeant
Chark le chumper	A	Sergeant
Che navey	A	Sergeant
Che pa noh.	A	Sergeant
Chipley Carr	K	Sergeant
Cho ko te yoho lar	K	Sergeant
Chu lah	C	Sergeant
Co tch ar Harjo.	H	Sergeant
Co we Mathla	G	Sergeant
Conchartee tustenuggee.	B	Sergeant
Cos is tee Co.	F	Sergeant
Cot cher har chutche	F	Sergeant
Cuzzens, Pamy Co.	F	Sergeant
Allen, W.H.		Ordinance.Sgt.
Abraham, ---	G	Corporal
Arfa le Haehn	A	Corporal
Artus, Micco.	B	Corporal
Beaver, John	B,I	Corporal
Brewner, Jack	G	Corporal
Brown, Che par ney	F	Corporal
Bruner, George	G	Corporal
Burgess, Billy	F	Corporal
Burgess, Caesar	B, I	Corporal
Burgess, Peter	G	Corporal
Burgess, Zizer	I	Corporal
Captain, John	E	Corporal
Cart cher Hajo chee	F	Corporal
Cart chur Homahtee	K	Corporal
Cates, Jefferson	H	Corporal
Char lo tus tar Nuggy	H	Corporal
Chis soe	F	Corporal.
Chissey Harjo	A	Corporal
Cho cot tol Sam H,	D	Corporal.
Chular Fixico	B,E	Corporal
Chulmer	K	Corporal
Co li ke	C	Corporal
Conip Harjo chee	B	Corporal
Cosar Harjo	M	Corporal
Cow ock co chee	B	Corporal

Cowe harjo	C	Corporal
Cram, ---	E	Corporal
Ar har loc Harjo che	M	Music
Arparark, Harjo	K	Music
Barnett, Watty	M	Music
Burgess, Tyler.	B,.I	Music.
Chullar harjo	C	Music.
Coat ho hay.	E	Music.
Charley, ---	F	Bugler
Clinton, Chorley	E	Bugler

Privates

A har lock	F		Ar har luck Harjo	B
Abram, ---	M		Ar her lark Fixseco	F
Acly, Sandy	E		Ar her lark Yarholer	F
Adam, ---	H		Ar ho vin na	E
Adam, ---	M		Ar le char	G
Ah co nin nay	E		Ar le chi che	A
Ah Co Stun nay	E		Ar par lar Harjo	K
Ah lock Harjo	B		Ar pek kar	L
Ah mo li chu	B		Ar quina	E
Ah po lah le nay	E		Ar ye mah har	
Ah quan na	E		Ar yi chi chee	C
Ah tel ay	E		Ar yo che	H
Ah thle	M		Archey, ---	C
Al lut ter Harjo	B		Archi, ---	A
Alexander, ---	A		Arharloc Harjo	K
Alexander, ---	H		Arher lark o chee	F
Alge chi chee	C		Arke thli ye	F
Allickee, ---	G		Ars sey	H
An thlah pe	F		Artus hopi ye	L
Anderson, David	L		Aspberry, Daniel	B
Appolla, ---	A		Baker, Henry	F
Ar be ker Fixico	G		Bamnett, Dick	A
Ar che yar ho lar	M		Barnes, L.B.	G
Ar co qua	E		Barnes, Lenard	G
Ar cos ton nay	E		Barnett, Beaty	M
Ar har lock Fixico	K		Barnett, Charle	E
Ar har lock Yoholar	K		Barnett, Timothy	E
Ar har luck Fixico	B		Barnett, William	E

Bartlett, John	K		Brown, Robert	E
Battel, Jim	C		Brown, Thomas	B
Beaufort, Lewis	M		Bruner, Jack	I
Beaver, Alexander	M		Bruner, Samuel	I
Beaver, David	A		Buck, John	E
Beaver, Jack	M		Burgess, Bean	C
Bell, George	K		Burgess, Ben	I
Bellow, Joseph	F		Burgess, Benjamin	B
Beney, ---	M		Burgess, Jefferson	M, I
Benney, ---	A		Burgess, John	D
Benney, ---	B		Burgess, William	H, D
Benney, ---	C		Busheyhead, Samuel	E
Berrihill, Robert	C		Bushyhead, John	E
Berryhill, James	B		Buster, John	C
Berryhill, James	F		Ca co fun na	E
Berryhill, William	F		Ca to	A
Big Tim	E		Ca yo	I
Biggs, Pompey	L		Cabbage, James	F
Billey, ---	C		Caesar	L
Billey, ---	L		Cah po yar thla na	E
Billoche, ---	G		Cah tah que in na	E
Billy Harjo	B		Car pek char Harjo	G
Billy, ---	A		Car thon na	E
Billy, ---	B		Carbitschee, ---	
Billy, ---	E		Carpit chee Fixseco	F
Billy, ---	H		Carpit cher Yoholer	I
Billy, ---	K		Carpitcher Fixico	K
Blaylock, Henry	D		Carr, Thomas	A
Boatswin, John	M		Cart cher Harjo	K
Bolin, Goliah	E		Cartch chee yar holer	F
Boney, ---	M		Cas eta Yohola	B
Boonyhill, James	B		Casey, James	H
Bow Legs, John	E		Cat chee Micco	E
Bradly, Samuel	M		Cat ta ar	E
Brane, Samuel	I		Catchar Harjo	H,B
Brewner, Alexander	G		Catcher Fixico	D
Brewner, Joshua	G		Catcher Harjo chee	F
Brewner, Louis	L		Cath lo na	E
Brewner, Samuel	G		Cawpit Saw fircico	B
Bring, Lamuel	M		Ch thla na	E
Brown, Daniel	F		Cha cho char	C
Brown, David	A		Chac hee	C

Chak kah	C		Che pun Hut kee	C
Chan Sang	E		Che thlo che	M
Chandler, S.E.	E		Che yellee	K
Chaplin, Thomas	H		Chennebe, Thomas	L
Char kar	H		Chep an thloc	B, I
Char lo Fixico	A		Chepan utche	F
Char luck ke	H		Chepar no chee	F
Char ne way			Cheparney Gibson	A
noh wily	B		Cherokee	
Char th len ney	E		Chi ke	G
Char was ti ee	B		Chi kee	C
Char wax le Harjo	B		Chi she nay	E
Char woe ley	M		Childers, Daniel	D
Charchoche	C		Childers, James	D
Charleesta	D		Childers, James C.	D
Charley	A		Childers, Lewis	D
Charley	C		Childers, Lunday	D
Charley	E		Childers, Pole	D
Charley, ---	F		Childers, Reuben	H, D
Charley, ---	H		Childers, Robert	D
Charlie	C		Chishom, John	B
Charlon Fixico	K,A		Chisom, Denis	G
Charls e ca	D		Cho cot te Micco	H
Charpitcher chully	F		Cho cotte yoholo	M
Che lake ko chee	F		Cho Harjo	E
Che lo ke kee	F		Cho la chop co	A
Che mar ley	L		Cho lah Fixico	B
Che pa na	A		Cho ne ker	F
Che pa na chully	C		Cho was ti ee	B
Che pa nah	A		Cho was ti ye.	A
Che pa nah chully	A		Choatka	K
Che pa nah le	C		Cholley	I
Che pah nah	C,D		Chona, ---	C
Che par ne chap co	M		Choney, ---	C
Che par ney	F		Chop co cho wastae	A
Che par ney	H, D		Chopeo Samme	A
Che par ney	K		Chrat ka	M
Che pon chep co	I		Chu ekah	B
Che pon le be to	M		Chu lar Chupeo	A
Che pon Taylor	C		Chu lupe Horchu	G
Che pun chupeo	F		Chuck Chartee	K
Che pun e	G, D		Chucotyar ho lar	M

Chuk char te	C		Co was Sarte	A
Chular Yarhola	B		Co we thla la	E
Chular Yoholar	B		Co Yah 2nd	C
Chulle	M		Co yo che	E
Chullukee	D		Co yo co ton na	E
Chumpar, Charley	G		Co yo thla ne	E
Chupko Hintchey	C		Cochuckney, Sam	K
Chupko John	C		Cochus Micco	F
Chupko Neherthlocko	C		Coffee, John	F
Chut ke	M		Cok ko	C
Chuy aloku	D		Columee Hargo	G
Clo sa chu	B		Con car kin ney	E
Co alley	E		Con char to chee	B
Co chi e	A		Con co qua na	E
Co Chok ney Harjo	G		Con tul Harjo	B
Co co e far	E		Con tulle Harjo	G
Co co thle ne nay	E		Con tully hargo	M
Co e thla la	E		Conip Harjo	B
Co fan nay	E		Conippe Moses	I
Co hars se Emarther	F		Cono na	E
Co la ah co ta na	E		Cony, James	B
Co la Sin nay	E		Coock cutche	K
Co li coo ti nay	E		Coody, Dempsey	H
Co nip yar hola	B		Coole coo qua nay	E
Co nippo	M		Cooney, Tim	K
Co no chop ko	H		Cooper, John	E
Co no Fixico	B		Coryah	C
Co no Fixico	M		Cot cher Harjo chee	I
Co que fon	E		Cot chus yar holar	F
Co t chus Mikko	C		Cote ho se	E
Co tch ar Harjo	B		Covey Harjo	K
Co tch key	I		Cow ah pe	C
Co tchar Fixico	H		Cow ch arty	B
Co tchar ho mahte	L		Cow etah Micco	F
Co te ha	E		Cowak ko che	H
Co te sen na	E		Cowe Hajo chee	F
Co ton na	E		Cowe, John	H, D
Co tulke Harjo	E		Coyl, William	K
Co u co tah la nay	E		Crowell, John	C
Co w cha	E		Cud jo	M
Co wak ke yarhola	H		Cumpsey, ---	F,H,M
			Cun tul Harjo	B

Cuntul Fixico	B		Cuppo yathlan na	E
Cupitcher	B		Cusseh ta yarholo	B
Cupitcher Fixico	B			

2nd Regiment, Creek Mounted Volunteers, Special Services

McIntosh, Chilly	F&S	Colonel
Barnett, Timothy	F&S	Major
Hawkins, Pink		Lieutenant Colonel
Naroome,		Major
Sanger, E.E.		Captain/Acting Commissary of Subsistence
Sanger, F. M.		Captain/Acting Quartermaster
Ceasar, Augustus	I	Captain
Emarthle, Miche		Captain
Emarthlochee, Fushntchee	C	Captain
Hargo, Larcosar	A	Captain
Herrod, Goliah	L	Captain
Herrod, Goliath	L	Captain
Micco, Lotti	H	Captain
Tustunuggee Yarhar,	B	Captain
Yargee, David	F	Captain
Yarholar, Nehar	E	Captain
Emarthlar, No cas	B	First Lieutenant
English, William	K	First Lieutenant
Farley, Benjamin F.	C	First Lieutenant
Fife, John	F	First Lieutenant
Fisher, Richard	I	First Lieutenant
Fixico Talue,	D	First Lieutenant
Goodin, George W.	E	First Lieutenant
Gorden, George W.	E	First Lieutenant
Hargo, Micco	A	First Lieutenant
Harjo, Itschos	H	First Lieutenant
Harrison, William	G	First Lieutenant
Emarthlar, Chu	G	Brevet Second Lieutenant
Haynes, Lasley	B	Brevet Second Lieutenant
Yargee, John	E	Brevet Second Lieutenant

Hamilton, Samuel S.	F	Second Lieutenant Adjutant
Atkins, J.G.	F	Second Lieutenant
Atkins, James	F	Second Lieutenant
Barnett, Daniel	D	Second Lieutenant
Coachanny, Ward	E	Second Lieutenant
Coachman, Ward	E	Second Lieutenant
Danley, E.J.	H	Second Lieutenant
Emarthlar, Ock Choye	I	Second Lieutenant
Enehar, Tuske	K	Second Lieutenant
Eufaula, William	G	Second Lieutenant
Fixico Henihan,	H	Second Lieutenant
Harjo, Emar	D	Second Lieutenant
Harjo, Nalcup	B	Second Lieutenant
Ker, Tulchis	C	Second Lieutenant
Parseofer,	I	Second Lieutenant
Porter, Pleasant	A	Second Lieutenant
Simmons, John	C	Second Lieutenant
Tulmochussee,	A	Second Lieutenant
Wright, Edward	I	Second Lieutenant
Harjo, Harthlun	E	First Sergeant
Rogers, W.B.		Ordnance Sergeant
Sanger, Stephen S.		Quartermaster Sergeant
Yargee, Jefferson	E	Sergeant
Yarholar, Artus	E	Sergeant
Chufulloap, Harjo	E	Corporal
Yarholar,	E	Corporal
Yarholar, Harjo	E	Corporal
Hillis, Fixico	E	Corporal
Harp, Tommie		Chief Bugler

Privates

Arparle, Harjo	E		Chowastiye, Emarthler	E
Artus, Fixico	E		Chuckenl be ye,	E
Artus, Micco chee	E		Coatchus, Harjo	E
Bailey, Benjamin H.	A		Coatchus, Yarholar	E
Casar, Fixico	E		Conchart, Yarholar	E
Chi see, Larne	E		Coneas, Harjo	E
Chitto, Harjo	E		Cotcher, Emarthler	E
Choak ker,	E		Cotcher, Fixico	E
Chowaslarye, Harjo	E			

Culley,	E		Micco, Yarholar	E
Echo, Harjo	E		Mok ey lus tusker,	E
Echuilla, Harjo	E		Nehar, Harjo	
Emarthler,				E
Cochoconee	E		Neher thlocco, Harjo	E
Fulgham, Elias M.	F		Nocas, Harjo	E
Fus, Harjo	E		Nocasilla, Harjo	E
Fushutchee Fixico,	E		Oak chun, Harjo	E
Fushutchee Harjo,	E		Oettargar che,	
Gracen, Buck	E		Yoholar	E
Heneher, Fixico	E		Peter, Coachman	E
Hillerbbee, Harjo	E		Sarnutter, Fixico	E
Holartar, Emarthler	E		Sototeunne,	
Hotulga, Fixico	E		Emasthley	E
Hotulga, Harjo	E		Spokoak Yarholar,	E
Hotulga, Yarholar	E		Thlarthle, Harjo	E
Hulputter, Harjo	E		Tommy Yaholar,	E
Isparne, Harjo	E		Tulloaf Harjo,	E
Isparne, Yarholar	E		Tulwar Yarholar,	E
Ispokoak, Harjo	E		Tuskeheneher,	E
Ispokoaky,	E		Tusse Kiah Harjo,	E
Istinhe chee,	E		Tustumugga chee,	E
John, Randol	E		Tustunug, Chupco	E
Kee, Chi	E		Ufaula Fixico,	E
Lit te chi chee,	E		Woatco, Micco	E
Locher, Yoholar	E		Woxie, Harjo	E
Lottar, Yohola	E		Yarholar, Harjo	E
Lottar,	E		Yarholo chee,	E
Micco, Harjo	E		Yoholar, Yarteakkar	E

1st Creek Regiment Company H

McHenry, James	Major
Kanard, Washington	Captain
Kanard, William.	First Lieutenant
Perryman, J.M.	First Lieutenant
Winslett, David.	Second Lieutenant
Perryman Riley.	Second Lieutenant
Tuscooner	Second Lieutenant
Che ho Jim.	Second Lieutenant
Che par ney	Second Lieutenant
Perryman, Riley	Second Lieutenant/Ensign
So ual Joshua	Second Lieutenant
Tuso coner	Second Lieutenant
Winslett, David	Second Lieutenant
Perryman, Joseph M.	Lieutenant
Burgess, Joseph	Sergeant
Charlo, Harjo	Sergeant
Che ho, James	Sergeant
Echo, Harjo	Sergeant
Kanard, Harrison	Sergeant
Chaplin, Thomas	Corporal
Char lo Tus Tar Nuggy	Corporal
Cho cot to, Sam	Corporal
Haynes, Lasley	Corporal
McKellup, John	Corporal
No cos elle	Corporal
Phillip	Corporal
Somme chi che	Corporal
Tus ke he ne har	Corporal
Perryman, Josiah	Musician
Perryman, Legus	Musician
Perryman, John W.	Musician
McCombs, William	Musician
Johnson, Thomas	Musician
Spunk	Bugler

Privates

Adam　　　　　　　　　　　Alexander

Ar se sey
Ar ye mah har
Ar yo che
Are Sey
Billey
Burgess, William
Casey, James
Catchar, Harjo
Cates, Jefferson
Char Kah or Kar
Char luck ke
Charley
Childers, Reuben
Cho cot te Micco
Co no chop ko
Co tchar Fixico
Co wak ke yarhola
Coody, Dempsey
Cotchar Harjo
Cowak ko che
Cowe, John
Cumpsey
Davis, Thomas
Denton, John
Denton, Randolph
Dickson, Wiley
Doyle, Archibald
Edward
Es temi yeh pe
Eskah cho che
Flanly, Thomas
Foreman, Arche
George
Gibson, John
Good, Benjamin
Grace, John
Har yoh che
Hodge, Alvin
Hodge, David Mc.
Houston
John
Jones, Abram

Lowrie, Walter
Mackey, Abraham
McComes, James
McKillop, David
McKillop, Robert
Me lah we
Meste Hailey
Meste sely
Micco Hatky
Milford, Louis
Mitchell, Levi
Morrison, John
Ne har thloc Emerthla
Ne har thlocco che
No co se kar
Nuth cup Harjo
Oak, Sumkar
Pane, Heaster
Par hos se tus tar nuggy
Perow, Tecumseh
Perryman, David
Perryman, Harry
Perryman, Henry
Perryman, James
Perryman, Joseph
Perryman, Louis
Perryman, Possonar
Perryman, Sandford
Perryman, Thomas
Perryman, Wesley
Porter
Rogers, William H.
Sar lar ho
Sar thle
Sark yar kah pe
Simon, Peter
Sippe
Spaniard, Jackson
Sugars, Thomas
Ta ho sa
Tar loaf Harjo
Tar weh

Tars hon che
Taylor, John
Thlar con shun ney
Thle mar heh che
Tiger, Daniel
Tiger, David
Tiger, Jefferson
Toh tul li key
Tommy

Tommy Harjo
Tus se kiah Harjo
Tuster nug co che
Wallee sey
William
Wilson
Yar hi coe che
Yardy, Joseph

2nd Regiment Creek Cavalry Volunteers

This is only a partial roll

McIntosh, Chilly	F&S	Colonel
Hawkins, Pink	F&S	Lt. Colonel
Timothy Barnett	F&S	Major
Narcome	F&S	Major
Sanger, E. E. Sanger,	F&S	Captain/Assistant Chief Of Staff
Rogers, W. B.	F&S	Ordinance Sergeant
Harp, Tommy	F&S	Chief Bugler
Emarthlar, Miche	F	Captain
Harholar, Nehar	E	Captain
Harjo, Tulloaf	G	Captain
Harjo, Tulmachus	K	Captain
Harjo, Tusyannck	D.	Captain
Herrod, Goliah	L	Captain
Larcosar, Hargo	A	Captain
Micco, Lotti	H	Captain
Tustunugee, Yarner	B	Captain
Emarthlar, Noses (?Moses)	B	First Lieutenant
English, William	K	First Lieutenant
Fife John	F	First Lieutenant
Fixico Talue	D	First Lieutenant
Gordon George W.	E	First Lieutenant
Hargo, Micco	A	First Lieutenant
Harjo, Itschoo	H	First Lieutenant
Harrison William	G	First Lieutenant
Emarthlar, Chu	G	Brevet Second Lieutenant
Yargee, John	E	Brevet Second Lieutenant
Atkins, James	F	Second Lieutenant
Barnett, Daniel;	D	Second Lieutenant
Coachman, Ward	E	Second Lieutenant
Denley; E. J.	H	Second Lieutenant
Enehar Tuske	K	Second Lieutenant
Eufaula, William	G	Second Lieutenant
Fixico Henihan	H	Second Lieutenant

Harjo Nulcup	B	Second Lieutenant
Harjo, Emar	D	Second Lieutenant
Porter, Pleasant	A	Second Lieutenant
Tulmochussee	A	Second Lieutenant
Hillis Fixico	E	Corporal
Yarholer	E	Corporal
Yarholer, Harjo	E	Corporal
Hamilton Samuel S.,	F	Adjutant

Privates

Aparle, Harjo	E		Istinhe, Chee	E
Artus, Fixico	E		Lit te chi chee	E
Artus, Miccochee	E		Lotcher, Yoholat	E
Bailey, Benjamin	B		Lottar, --------	E
Casar, Fixico	E		Lottar, Yohola	E
Chi, Kee	E		Micco, Yohalar	E
Chitto, Harjo	E		Mokey lus tuskar	E
Chowastiye, Emarthar	E		Nehar, Harjo	E
Chufulloap, Harjo	E		Neherthlocco, Harjo	E
Chukenb be ye	E		Nocas, Harjo	E
Coatchus, Harjo	E		Nocasilla, Harjo	E
Conchart, Yarholar	E		Oak Chunn, Harjo	E
Cotcher, Emarthalar	E		Oettargarche,	
Culley, --------	E		Yoholar	E
Echo, Harjo	E		Peter, Coachman	E
Echulla, Harjo	E		Randol, John	E
Emarthler, Cochconee	E		Sarnutter, Fixico	E
Fulgham, Elias M.	F		Satoteunne,	
Fus, Harjo	E		Emarthlar	E
Fushutchee, Fixico	E		Spokoak, Yaholar	E
Fushutchee, Harjo	E		Thlarthle, Harjo	E
Gracen, Burk	E		Tommy, Yoholar	E
Halputter, Harjo	E		Tulloaf, Harjo	E
Harjo, Micco	D		Tulware, Yarholar	E
Hencher, Fixico	E		Tustumugga, Chee	E
Hillerbee, Harjo	E		Tustunug, Chupco	E
Holartar, Emathler	E		Ufaula, Fixico	E
Hotulga, Fixico	E		Woatco, Micco	E
Hotulga, Yarholer	E		Woxie, Harjo	E
Isopoak, Harjo	E		Yagee, David	E
Isopoaky, --------	E		Yargee, David	F
Isparne, Harjo	E		Yarholar, Chee	E

Yoholar, Yarteakker   E

Small Miscellaneous Confederate Units
30 members and less

Captain Asapah/Eso Habbe
Comanche
Washington's Squadron

Major George Washington
Caddo
Washington's Squadron

Captain Black Dog,
Osage
1st Osage Battalion

1st Battalion, Chickasaw Cavalry

Gardner, Geo. E.	E	First Sergeant
McKinney, William	E	Private

1st Battalion, Choctaw Cavalry, (McCurtain's)
No enlisted men were found for this unit.

Field and Staff

McCurtain, J.	F&S	Lieutenant Colonel
Page, John	F&S	Major

Officers

Portlock, E.E.		Colonel
Battice, Franceway		Lieutenant Colonel
Holtston, S.	B	Captain
Nanamontubbee,	D	Captain
Serton, Thompson	C	Captain
Willkins, J.	A	Captain
Colwell, R. J.		Acting Ordnance Officer

3rd Regiment Choctaw Cavalry

McCurtain, Jackson		Colonel
Mullatubbee, John	A	Lieutenant

1st OSAGE BATTALION
No Enlisted men found for this unit.

Louis Pharamond Chouteau	F&S	Captain/Adjutant/Osage Interpreter
Broke Arm, an Osage Indian.	F&S	Major

Black Dog,	B	Captain
Captans, A.	A	Captain
Wahti in joh,	C	Captain
Ne cah yar hre,	B	First Lieutenant
No pa walla,	A	First Lieutenant
None cher she,	C	First Lieutenant
Lewis, F. A.	C	Second Lieutenant
Sta hack Caton,	A	Second Lieutenant
Wah Kah chili,	A	Second Lieutenant
Wah skon mon ne,	C	Second Lieutenant
Wahshabenatmego,	B	Second Lieutenant
Woh-cho a moshe,	B	Second Lieutenant

2nd Regiment, Choctaw Cavalry

King, Asa	K	Captain

Privates

Brown, Carion	G,M
Brown, Karrew	G,M
Durant, Hicks	M,E
Duvant, Hicks	F,B
Folsom, Simpson	N.
Gracem, B.	C
Hague, Erastus S.	F
Hicks, Durant	MEF
Hoag, Erastus	F

Cherokee Regiment, Volunteer Cavalry

No others found for this unit

Thompson, S.J.	Private

Choctaw Infantry

Pickens, Edmund	Captain

284

Alexander, James	Sergeant
Hollins, William	Sergeant
Carney, William	Corporal
Henry, Matthew	Musician
Scanlan, Edward	Acting Quartermaster

Privates

Adam, John	Harlin, Lewis
Ahpo to bubbee,	Hays, Wesley
Alomolubbee,	Hecks, Lyon
Browning, William	Hocubbee,
Cherokee,	Hullotubbee,
Choate, Thomas	Humbee,
Clay, Henry	Hunter, James
Colbert, Jamerson	Hunter, Jim
Colbert, Thomas	Hush co char,
Colbert, Wallis	Ionubbee,
Coleman, Joseph	Ish to chubbee,
Compillubbee,	Ish to nubbee,
Criklin, Jesse	

Cooper's Battalion, 1st Indian Brigade (Miscellaneous)

Cooper, James W.	Major

Privates

Charles, John M.	Graham, Joel B

Washington's Squadron
Reserve Squadron of Cavalry

To act as Spies and for Protection of Wichita Agency. (Wichita Agency Papers)

Officers:

Jones, H. P.	Lieutenant General
George Washington (Caddo)	Major
Asapah,	Captain
McClusky, P.	First Lieutenant
Washington, Johnson	First Lieutenant
Williams,	First Lieutenant
Boo-ewa-sis-ka,	Second Lieutenant
Caw-wee-wah-now,	Second Lieutenant
Ese tu et,	Second Lieutenant
Pinahontsama	Sergeant
Pive-ahope	Corporal

Privates:

A-ri-ka-pap	Cur-su-ah
Ath-pah	Na-na-quathteh
Boo-y-wy-sis-ka	Pe-ah-ko-roh
Ca-na-with	Pe-ba-rah
Chickapoo, Jim	Pith-pa-wah
Chick-a-poo	Somo
Cow-ah-dan	To-no-kah
Cu-be-ra-wipo	

Union Troops

US Flag, 34 stars

Billy Bow Legs
Creek

Black Beaver
Delaware

Col. Lewis Downing
Cherokee

Union Introduction

Most of the teamsters of the First Indian Regiment were citizen employees, and were residents of Coffey County, Kansas. During the campaign in the Indian Territory, the summer of 1862, over one-half of the soldiers of the First Indian Regiment deserted and returned to Leroy, Kansas, due to the lack of military discipline. In November of that year Lieutenant Samuel S. Prouty was ordered by General Blunt, commanding the army of the frontier operating in northwestern Arkansas, to go to Coffey County and make an effort to induce the deserters to return to their command.

The Lieutenant, accompanied by a Sergeant Puffer and a couple of Indian soldiers, proceeded to Burlington, and there established his headquarters. A supply train filled with commissary stores and clothing, followed him from Fort Scott. By good tact and management on the part of Lieutenant Prouty and his assistants, all of the deserters were soon in camp in Burlington and over a hundred new men enlisted.

About six hundred Indian soldiers were encamped at Burlington, with only one white officer to command them. The Lieutenant divided his command into four companies, over which he placed an Indian commissioned officer, supplied his men with clothing, arms and rations, marched his men a distance of two hundred and fifty miles, and delivered them to the regiment at Rhea's Mill, Arkansas, without the desertion of a man.

As the war approached its end, anarchy prevailed throughout most of Indian Territory. Union and Confederate "deserters," Indians and non-Indians alike, formed outlaw gangs and roamed the countryside, indiscriminately killing, burning, and looting. In the last months of the war, some of the high-ranking Union officers joined in the lawlessness, stealing over three hundred thousand head of Indian-owned cattle and driving them to Kansas.

The Civil War in Indian Territory ended on July 14, 1865, when the Chickasaw and the Caddo surrendered. The war had been fought at an incredible cost. Estimates of those who were killed or died of war-related causes range as high as 25 percent for the Creeks, Seminoles, and Cherokees. Other estimates show that out of a total population in excess of sixty thousand for the Five Civilized Tribes, over six thousand and possibly as many as ten thousand died. The economy of Indian Territory was totally destroyed; almost every house, barn, store, and public building had been burned. The vast majority of Indian families had been reduced to impoverished, homeless refugees. Nevertheless, there was one more blow yet to fall. Even though as many members of the Five Civilized Tribes had served in the Union Army as had served in the Confederate Army, the federal government declared its treaties with the tribes to be void and forced the tribes to negotiate new treaties that ceded the western part of Indian Territory to the United States.

1st Regiment Indian Home Guards
Kansas Infantry

The First Indian Home Guard Regiment was a tri-racial Union regiment first organized in Leroy, Kansas, May 22, 1862, and attached to 3rd Brigade, Dept. of Kansas. The regiment was made up of Creek and Seminole Indians, African Creeks and African Seminoles with white officers commanding the unit. Though their numbers were few, the Blacks in the unit played a key role in the regiment. Because most of the Indians did not speak English, the bilingual Blacks served as interpreters and provided a cultural bridge between the white officers and the Indian soldiers.

The unit had its origins among those in the Creek and Seminole nations who opposed the signing of treaties with the Confederacy and followed the Creek chief Opothlayahola on his exodus from the Indian Territory to Kansas in November-December 1861. Along the way they fought the first three battles of the Civil War in the Indian Territory. The African Creeks and African Seminoles who joined the exodus were the first Black men in America to raise arms against the Confederacy. With the official organization and mustering of the First Indian in May 1862 the African Creeks and African Seminoles became the first Blacks to be mustered into the Union Army.

During the Indian Expedition into the Indian Territory in the summer of 1862 they became the first Blacks to participate in combat. At the Battle of Prairie Grove, Arkansas on December 7, 1862 they were the first Black soldiers to participate in a major battle. The First Indian Home Guards saw action on the battlefields of Missouri, Arkansas and the Indian Territory and was mustered out in May 1862.

Furness, Robert W.	F&S	Colonel
Wattles, Stephen H.	F&S	Colonel
Dole, George	F&S	Lieutenant Colonel
Ellathorp, E.C.	F&S	Major
Ellithorp, Albert C.	F&S	Major
Ellithorpe, Albert C.	F&S	Major
Phillips, James A.	F&S	Major
Phillips, William A.	F&S	Major
Chess, John	F&S	First Lieutenant/Adjutant
Gillpatrick, J. Howard	F&S	First Lieutenant/Adjutant

Coffin, O.S.	F&S	Regimental Quartermaster
Cox, J.T.	F&S	Regimental Quartermaster
Prouty, Samuel S.	F&S	First Lieutenant/ Regimental Quartermaster
Salisbury, Marquis D.	F&S	First Lieutenant/ Regimental Quartermaster
Proutz, Samuel S.	F&S	First Lieutenant Quartermaster
Rix, Charles N.	F&S	First Lieutenant
Perryman, Legus C.	F&S	Sergeant Major
Holladay, A.S.	F&S	Surgeon
Holleday, A.S.	F&S	Surgeon
Holliday, A.S.	F&S	Surgeon
Patee, Eliphalet L.	F&S	Surgeon
Jones, Eran	F&S	Chaplain
A k ti ya h gi ya ho la,	H	Captain
Ah ha la tus ta nuk ...,	B	Captain
Carts che her mick po,	E	Captain
Corto che her mic ko,	E	Captain
John-neh,	K	Captain
Jon-neh,	K	Captain
No co se lo ches,	G	Captain
No-ko-se-lo-chee,	G	Captain
So mik-mix-ko,	F	Captain
Ta-me-tus-te-muk-kee,	D	Captain
Ta-wa-tus-ta-muk-ka,	D	Captain
To ma tus ta mik ka,	D	Captain
Tuc ka bat chee har jo,	C	Captain
Tul se fix se ko,	I	Captain
Tul so fix se ko,	I	Captain
Tus te nup chup ko,	A	Captain
Willett, Oliver P.	H	Captain
Ayers, Benjamin F.	G	First Lieutenant
Bicking, A.F.	A	First Lieutenant
Burlingame, M.J.	H	First Lieutenant
Cook, Thomas F.	K	First Lieutenant
Crafts, Frederick	I	First Lieutenant

Dobler, George W.	G	First Lieutenant
Fat-ne-sha,	K	First Lieutenant
Flanders, Albert	F	First Lieutenant
Fox, Francis J.	E,K	First Lieutenant
Hall, Solomon C.	F	First Lieutenant
Ho-pi-ye-mar-lar,	E	First Lieutenant
Jacobs, Ferdinand R.	B	First Lieutenant
Kanel, Absolom	I	First Lieutenant
Ko-nos-sot-teh,	D	First Lieutenant
Ko-nots-sat-teh,	D	First Lieutenant
Konel, Absolem	I	First Lieutenant
Kowos sot teh,	D	First Lieutenant
Lowe, Eli C.	K	First Lieutenant
Nuk-ke-pa-kee,	B	First Lieutenant
Ok-gan-ya-ho-la,	H	First Lieutenant
Pas-ko-va,	F	First Lieutenant
Saxey, Alfred	H	First Lieutenant
Suk-ko-r-rah,	K	First Lieutenant
Tae-na-sha,	K	First Lieutenant
Tas-ne-sha,	K	First Lieutenant
Thompson, Robert J.	C	First Lieutenant
Tusta nuk e ma reh,	G	First Lieutenant
Tusta nuk ke ma rah,	G	First Lieutenant
Tuste nuk ke,	G	First Lieutenant
Watts, Caswell B.	D	First Lieutenant
Wright, E.M.	B	First Lieutenant
Yah hol la dy,	C	First Lieutenant
Yar hol lau duy,	C	First Lieutenant
A tam meh,	I	Second Lieutenant
A tam murch,	I	Second Lieutenant
A tem meh,	I	Second Lieutenant
Cat so gee,	G	Second Lieutenant
Caxot, Julien C.	F,L	Second Lieutenant
Clot-lo-fix-se-ho,	C	Second Lieutenant
Cot so gee,	G	Second Lieutenant
Hillis-yaw-hollar,	E	Second Lieutenant
Hotal-keah,	H	Second Lieutenant
Kaf-fes-seh,	K	Second Lieutenant
Kat-so-ge,	G	Second Lieutenant
Kof-fis-sah,	K	Second Lieutenant
Kot se ko keh,	G	Second Lieutenant
Kot so ge,	G	Second Lieutenant

Lat ca hat jo,	D	Second Lieutenant
Lats ku ha jo,	D	Second Lieutenant
Lus te nuk ko chu,	B	Second Lieutenant
Overton, Thompson	B	Second Lieutenant
Pa hare mah lah,	A	Second Lieutenant
Pa-ho-se-maht-loh,	A	Second Lieutenant
Roberts, William	C	Second Lieutenant
Tats-ca-ha-jo,	D	Second Lieutenant
Tus te nuk ko chee,	B	Second Lieutenant
Yah ha lo chee,	C	Second Lieutenant
Yar hol lan chay,	C	Second Lieutenant
Young, John D.	K,B	Second Lieutenant
Jo fo lup ha jo,	F	Lieutenant
Jo-ho-lup-ha-jo,	F	Lieutenant
Jo-lo hup-ha Jo,	F	Lieutenant
Manning, Edwin C.	C	Lieutenant
Brown, Charles	K	First Sergeant
Cho-cot ha jo,	B	First Sergeant
Isaac,	K	First Sergeant
Kag-ga-he-mat-leh,	A	First Sergeant
Kag-ga-he-mat-teh,	A	First Sergeant
Kay-ga-he-mot-teh,	A	First Sergeant
Long, John	F	First Sergeant
Meigs, John	E	First Sergeant
ne chup e ha jo,	E	First Sergeant
Perriman, Richard	C	First Sergeant
Perryman, Richard	C	First Sergeant
Sofley, George	D	First Sergeant
Sugar, George	H	First Sergeant
Yuk ah de ah ho la,	G	First Sergeant
He-tah-con-wa,	K	Third Sergeant
Jacob,	E	First Duty Sergeant
Ne ha luc que shee,	E	Second Duty Sergeant
Tus ha jo,	F	Second Duty Sergeant
Ne ha lok o chok ne,	E	Third Duty Sergeant
Pous ha jo,	F	Duty Sergeant
A ha hik ha jo,	G	Sergeant
A taes hom moppe,	H	Sergeant
A tas hom mop pen na,	H	Sergeant
Ah ha jo,	B	Sergeant
Ah har la ge mart le,	C	Sergeant
Ah luk fix se Ko,	G	Sergeant

Ar har lesc yar hol lar,	E	Sergeant
Billy, Hagen	F	Sergeant
Brown, Samuel	K	Sergeant
Car tch che huepog or,	C	Sergeant
Cart che hart le boyer,	C	Sergeant
Caynew, Jack	F	Sergeant
Che ne che pe,	K	Sergeant
Che-was-ti-a-clock-ko,	B	Sergeant
Cho was ta ye tlok lo,	B	Sergeant
Clinton, Charles	K	Sergeant
Co ah co che ha jo,	B	Sergeant
Co che tus te muh ko chee,	B	Sergeant
Co wa co che ha jo,	B	Sergeant
Co we ha goh,	H	Sergeant
Co wok ko che ha jo,	B	Sergeant
Colonel, Jack	C	Sergeant
Cot cha tue te muk ke ge,	B	Sergeant
Cow e ta ha jo,	C	Sergeant
Da tho fa ha goh,	A	Sergeant
Day, Warren	C,E	Sergeant
Echo e la fix se ko,	G	Sergeant
Echo-e-la-fix-e-ko,	G	Sergeant
Echo-ella-fix se ka,	G	Sergeant
Et kat ha ke,	D	Sergeant
Et kat-ha-ko,	D	Sergeant
Et kut ha jo,	D	Sergeant
Et-kat-ha-jo,	D	Sergeant
Et-kut-ha-ko,	D	Sergeant
Ets-geh,	I	Sergeant
Ets-get,	I	Sergeant
Ets-ha-fix-no-ko,	I	Sergeant
Ets-ha-fix-se-ko,	I	Sergeant
Ets-ha-fix-so-ko,	I	Sergeant
Fa-ya-ho-llah,	A	Sergeant
Fos-ha-go,	H	Sergeant
Francis, John	G	Sergeant
Fus ha jo,	F	Sergeant
Gal-leh,	H	Sergeant
Gallah,	H	Sergeant
Ge-lea-teh,	H	Sergeant
Geo-pa-geh,	H	Sergeant
Go-e-leh,	H	Sergeant

Gump, Benjamin E.	E	Sergeant
Hagan, Billy	F	Sergeant
Hele-shots-goh,	I	Sergeant
Henne-ha-cop-Ko,	G	Sergeant
Hes-se-kiah-hut-keh,	A	Sergeant
Hol-lap-to-me-mar-rah,	D	Sergeant
Hum-mets-geh,	I	Sergeant
Jack, Colonel	C	Sergeant
Johnson, Peter	C	Sergeant
Jup-pop-fush-huts-goh,	I	Sergeant
Kat-caf-fal-la-rah,	D	Sergeant
Kat-coffoe-la-rah,	D	Sergeant
Kat-so,	F	Sergeant
Kay-ga-fix-se-koh,	A	Sergeant
Kay-ya-fess-e-koh,	A	Sergeant
Ken-no-geh,	H	Sergeant
Ko wa ko chee ho jo,	B	Sergeant
Ko-mi-pi-yu-ho-lu,	A	Sergeant
Ko-na-kots-ka,	G	Sergeant
Ko-ne-pe-ho-la,	A	Sergeant
Ko-ne-pi-jo-ho-la,	A	Sergeant
Ko-nes-ha-joh,	H	Sergeant
Kog-ga-fix-se-koh,	A	Sergeant
Kot caf fa la rah,	D	Sergeant
Kot ge fix se koh,	A	Sergeant
Kowok ko che ha jo,	B	Sergeant
Koy ga fix se koh,	A	Sergeant
La la the ha goh,	A	Sergeant
La th la ha goh,	A	Sergeant
La the f ha goh,	A	Sergeant
La thi ha goh,	A	Sergeant
La-fa-ha-goh,	A	Sergeant
Let tif kah,	E	Sergeant
Not ke-put-ke,	B	Sergeant
Nulka-puk-kee,	B	Sergeant
Nulke-puk-he,	B	Sergeant
O-tul-ke-ye-o-hola,	I	Sergeant
Ochee-har-cho,	I	Sergeant
Oe-gus-ha-jo,	G	Sergeant
Oh-e-gus-ha-jo,	G	Sergeant
Ok John-E Mat la,	G	Sergeant
Ok la bis ye ha jo,	D	Sergeant

Os sa hen lah,	D	Sergeant
Os sa hen ne ha,	D	Sergeant
Pa hos fix se ko,	F	Sergeant
Pa hos ha ja,	F	Sergeant
Po has fix se Ko,	F	Sergeant
Sims, Mark	K	Sergeant
Sox see,	B	Sergeant
Spa he cha,	E	Sergeant
Ta-ka-ta-na,	K	Sergeant
Tah-co-to-ne,	K	Sergeant
Tah-ka-ta-na,	K	Sergeant
Tah-ko-ta-na,	K	Sergeant
Tah-ko-te-na,	K	Sergeant
Tem-meh,	K	Sergeant
Tol-y-tus-ta-me-ge,	I	Sergeant
Toby-tus-ta-nug-ge,	I	Sergeant
Tol-y-tus-ta-nag-ge,	I	Sergeant
Tol-y-tus-ta-nug-ge,	I	Sergeant
Tul man see,	C	Sergeant
Tul y tus ta nug ze,	I	Sergeant
Tus ta nuk hut ka,	F	Sergeant
Tus ta nuk hut ke,	F	Sergeant
Tus ta nuk hut ko,	F	Sergeant
Tus ta nuk ko zo one,	F	Sergeant
Tus ta nup hut ga,	F	Sergeant
Tus ta nup hut ka,	F	Sergeant
Tus ta nup ko cho kne,	F	Sergeant
Tus ta nup ko zo ne,	F	Sergeant
Tus ta nut hut ke,	F	Sergeant
Tus ta nut ko zo ne,	F	Sergeant
Tus te nuk ko chuk one,	F	Sergeant
Tus tu nuk ko chok one,	F	Sergeant
Tus tu nup ka cho kne,	F	Sergeant
Tusta nuk ko chok me,	F	Sergeant
Tusta nuk ko zo ko ne,	F	Sergeant
Wat-K-Ko-fix-se-Koh,	A	Sergeant
Wax-se-ho-la,	F	Sergeant
Wot-Ko-fix-e-Koh,	A	Sergeant
Ya ha lo ge,	G	Sergeant
Ya ho la seh,	G	Sergeant
Ya ho lah seh,	G	Sergeant
Ya ho lo ge,	G	Sergeant

Ya te ka ha goh,	H	Sergeant
Ya te ka ha joh,	H	Sergeant
Ya teh ka ha ha goh,	H	Sergeant
Ya-ha-lo-chee,	G	Sergeant
Ya-te-ya-hol-lah,	H	Sergeant
Yah teh kah ha ha goh,	H	Sergeant
Pah-say,	K	First Corporal
Pas-sa,	K	First Corporal
Pas-sah,	K	First Corporal
Baby,	E	Second Corporal
Co ka sa,	K	Second Corporal
Lo ah co,	F	Third Corporal
Lo-ah-lo,	F	Third Corporal
Brown, Robert	K	Fourth Corporal
Po se ah ho la,	F	Fourth Corporal
Pa-char-na,	K	Seventh Corporal
A fes ko geh,	H	Corporal
A pee ko geh,	H	Corporal
Ah ha lok fix se ko,	B	Corporal
Ah ha luke ho la,	G	Corporal
Ah than ha jo,	B	Corporal
Ah tlan ha jo,	B	Corporal
Al but ta ha jo,	B	Corporal
Anderson, David	A	Corporal
Ase hom mat te la go,	H	Corporal
Atkins, Sam	E	Corporal
Berry, Charley	D	Corporal
Berryhill, Simon	H	Corporal
Big, Jim	C	Corporal
Bil leh,	B	Corporal
Chas ... lee hee,	C	Corporal
Che`ho`yo`ho`lah,	D	Corporal
Chis-ki-li-ka,	C	Corporal
Cho cat ha jo,	B	Corporal
Cho-la-ha-jo,	E	Corporal
Cho-lo-yah-ho-la,	D	Corporal
Co cha ho ma ta,	E	Corporal
Co ho co chee,	E	Corporal
Co so fix e ko,	C	Corporal
Dennis,	C	Corporal
E-ma-sah,	H	Corporal
E-ma-soh,	H	Corporal

E-mar-rah,	A	Corporal
E-ne-ha-fix-e-co,	C	Corporal
Emar tlo tsi,	I	Corporal
Emar-lah,	H	Corporal
Ene ha fix e ko,	C	Corporal
Fa-lau-keh,	H	Corporal
Fi-e-mal-lah,	A	Corporal
Fi-he-mal-lah,	A	Corporal
Fo-lup-hi-ha-jo,	G	Corporal
Fo-lup-pi-ha-jo,	G	Corporal
Fos-hots-se-ya-ho-la,	G	Corporal
Fus-huch-chee,	B	Corporal
Ga-gee,	K	Corporal
Ga-ger,	K	Corporal
Go-gee,	K	Corporal
Go-he-mar-rah,	A	Corporal
Go-he-mol-lah,	A	Corporal
Go-ho-po-yah,	A	Corporal
Go-ho-ppa-yeh,	A	Corporal
Grace, John	I	Corporal
Grayson, Walter	G	Corporal
He lis-ha-jo,	G,H	Corporal
Hella-pe-ha-jo,	G,H	Corporal
Hil-lis-ha-jo,	G,H	Corporal
Ho-tol-ke-za-so-le,	E,I	Corporal
Ja-cop-pee,	B	Corporal
Jemboy, Love	E	Corporal
Jim,	C	Corporal
Jimboy, Love	E	Corporal
Jo-la-fix-se-ko,	F	Corporal
Ko-ar-sot-fix-e-ko,	G	Corporal
Ko-no-ha-jo,	G	Corporal
Ko-or-sart-fix-e-ko,	G	Corporal
Ko-or-sot-fix-se-ko,	G	Corporal
Ko-os-sot-fix-se-ko,	G	Corporal
Kol-lhe-ho-go,	I	Corporal
Kol-me-ha-go,	I	Corporal
Kol-me-ha-jo,	I	Corporal
Kol-ne-ha-jo,	I	Corporal
Lat a ha coh,	D	Corporal
Lee-nah,	K,F	Corporal
Leo-mat-te-ha goh,	H	Corporal

Lewis, John	D	Corporal
Lewis, Seaborn	I	Corporal
Love, Jimboy	E	Corporal
Lu tu ha cah,	D	Corporal
Luh-tam-mic-cor-chi,	I	Corporal
Lup tu ha cah,	D	Corporal
Lup-tu-ha-jo,	D	Corporal
Mack,	K	Corporal
Manuell,	F	Corporal
Me kul lah,	H	Corporal
Me kul leh,	H	Corporal
Me-gul-lah,	H	Corporal
Me-hel-let,	H	Corporal
Me-kul-la,	H	Corporal
Mik ko nup-pe,	G	Corporal
Mik ko up pa,	G	Corporal
Mik o nup pa,	G	Corporal
Mil ka,	E	Corporal
Na ha keeh,	I	Corporal
Na ko se mat to tse,	F	Corporal
Nar koh me koh,	A	Corporal
Nevins, Abb	D	Corporal
No cos fix e co,	E	Corporal
No kas fix se ko,	D	Corporal
No-ko-se-mat-lo-tse,	F	Corporal
No-kos-ha-jo,	B	Corporal
Nok kas fix se ko,	D	Corporal
Nos-fix-se-ko,	E	Corporal
Nul-kah-me-koh,	A	Corporal
O-k-gan-ho-pa-ya-geh,	A	Corporal
Ok-ga-u-ya-hol-loh,	A	Corporal
Ok-ti-a-chee-mek-ko,	C	Corporal
Ossog ffex se koh,	A	Corporal
Otul ke ya so le,	E,I	Corporal
Pa mos e ka,	C	Corporal
Pa se ah ho la,	F	Corporal
Pa-llat-koh,	A	Corporal
Pah ho se,	C	Corporal
Pas-cof-ha-jo,	G	Corporal
Peal-har-jo,	C	Corporal
Penn hatz jo,	E	Corporal
Perry, Charley	D	Corporal

Pet-tah,	I	Corporal
Petti ha jo,	C	Corporal
Pholop pa ha jo,	G	Corporal
Pillat Keh,	A	Corporal
Pith ha jo,	C	Corporal
Pul ha jo,	C	Corporal
Res fro ka ha goh,	H	Corporal
Sem-ma-po-na-geh,	H	Corporal
Sie mah,	A	Corporal
Ta -ko-se-ha-jo,	H	Corporal
Tal-mo-gu-ha-goh,	A	Corporal
Tan-me-ha-goh,	H	Corporal
Tas-co-nah,	D	Corporal
Te-mah,	A	Corporal
Tef-feh,	I	Corporal
Tes se ke ya hot kee,	A	Corporal
Thal la ya ho la,	D	Corporal
The-ha-jo,	F	Corporal
Thla-la-yo-ho-la,	D	Corporal
Thlo-kus-ha-jo,	G	Corporal
Ti-mah,	A	Corporal
Timmy,	K	Corporal
To to k-ka-kel,	G	Corporal
To-to-k-ka-keh,	G	Corporal
Toe mo gis ha goh,	A	Corporal
Tol no gee hu goh,	A	Corporal
Tom,	E	Corporal
Tu ke ba che ha jo,	D	Corporal
Tuc ke la che ha jo,	D	Corporal
Tue ke ba che ha jo,	D	Corporal
Tuk ke bac he ha jo,	D	Corporal
Wax-se-ha-jo,	G	Corporal
Wot-K-Ko-fix-se-Ko,	G	Corporal
Wox-see-hojo,	G	Corporal
Ya fix se ko,	G	Corporal
Ya ho fix e ko,	G	Corporal
Ya tah on na,	K	Corporal
Ya-ha-fix-se-ko,	G	Corporal
Yah tah hon na,	K	Corporal
Yah nar k kop me koh,	A	Corporal
Barnett, Harriet		Matron
Miller, Anna		Matron

Pearson, Nancy			Matron	
Pearson, Amelia			Nurse	
Onar Su gar,		K	Musician	
Onar se ga,		K	Musician	
Sah co fa na,		K	Bugler	

Privates

A Kel te fe ya hola,	G		Ac ti ar chee,	E
A gas ha jo,	G		Adams, Cully	G
A ge geh,	A		Adams, John	E
A ge lleh,	A		Add, Robert	F
A ha lak ya holo,	H		Af fee ya ho la,	H
A ha llk fix se ko,	A		Affa cla keh,	A
A ha lue Ko tse,	G		Affo llo keh,	A
A ha luk Ke Zone,	G		Ah Ro Stee na,	K
A ha luk ga,	G		Ah al luck fis seh,	I
A ha tle Ma rah,	H		Ah be Co chee,	H
A hah tak fix e ko,	E		Ah bi ak ha jo,	F
A hal li matha,	G		Ah bi yah hajo,	B
A hat luck har jo,	C		Ah chu le,	D
A ho si geh,	H		Ah cloule,	D
A hol lah ha cob cep,	D		Ah ge ya ho lah,	H
A hol luk ge ho lah,	D		Ah ha la kee grip ko,	B
A hos tom kee,	E		Ah ha lak homa tu,	B
A hos tun Kee,	E		Ah ha lla k if fose koh,	A
A la lla k ya ho la,	G		Ah ha loc a ho la,	A
A lle p pa tla ha jo,	G		Ah ha luk e mart la,	G
A lok ya ho lah,	D		Ah ha luk e mat la,	G
A luk e ma ta,	F		Ah ha luk fix e ko,	G
A luk e mat la,	F		Ah ha luk fix se vo,	G
A luk fix e Ko,	F		Ah ha luk ga,	K
A luke hola,	F		Ah ha luk ha jo,	B
A p pek kor ner,	K		Ah ha luk ke,	CKF
A pe ok jo,	E		Ah ha luk ke,	F
A swe ley,	E		Ah ha luk lah hol,	G
A ta yah ce mar rah,	D		Ah hah to ha jo,	B
A taes he ne ha,	H		Ah hea la jo,	CLF
A tas ha goh,	A		Ah ho we ah chee,	F
A ts ko lla ha jo,	G			
A tus fix se Ko,	H			

Ah ke ko ge mek koh,	H		Ar shun har jo,	C
Ah l hon nah,	K		Ar te har jo,	B,H
Ah la co ven ha,	K		Ar tes ne ho mar tes,	C
Ah la cocon tha na,	K		Ar tis har go,	E
Ah lac ha jo che,	D		Ar tis ho muty,	C
Ah lac hache jo,	D		Ar tis ho pi yee,	E
Ah luk har cho,	I		Ar tus ne ho mar to,	C
Ah pe ka ge mek ko,	H		Ar tus se ma lar,	E
Ah pe kar fix se ko,	I		Ar ward licher,	C
Ah pe ke mek ko,	H		Ar ward ti cher,	C
Ah pol te ha joh,	H		Arch a ho la,	A
Ah so nep ha jo,	A		Are you a hola,	A
Ah taes se mar lah,	H		Ark fus e Ka,	C
Ah te ha jo,	B		Armstrong,	A
Ah thlan ha jo,	B		Artus se mat an,	E
Ah tl yah ge ho jo,	H		As O luk ha jo,	G
Ah tus o nub be,	H		As s e ya ho la,	G
Ah wat te lega,	C		As san ha jo,	F
Air seh keh,	K		As san wa,	F
Ak te ya che			As tah,	D
har cho,	I		As tol,	D
Ak ti yah gi			At bert e fix se Ko,	D
ya ho la,	H		At tas ya ho la,	D
Ak tla ya le			At tay ya hol lah,	D
mc me ra,	G		Att tas mik Ko,	D
Al but ta ha jo,	A		Attas fix se Ko,	D
Al lek, Keh	H		Attas fix se Ko,	D
Al pat ta ha jo,	D		Balone, Louis	A
Al pot ta ha cha,	D		Bap ti yah,	H
Albert, A ha jo	F		Barnard, Dick	C
Alberta ha jo,	G		Barnard, Tom	D
Aleck,	I		Barnet, Sam	H
Alek, Kas mo nat	K		Barnet, Tom	D
Alick me nack,	H		Barnett, Dick	C
Alick mi neck,	H		Barnett, Jack	K
Anderson, James	K		Barnett, James	C
Ap eh ka ge me ko,	H		Barnett, Joseph	C
Ar che a ho la,	A		Barnett, Mot a le gee	
Ar che yallar,	E		Barnett, Timothy	K
Ar ge a ho la,	A		Barnett, Timothy	K
Ar had ho man lar,	C		Barnett, William	K
			Barney,	C

Barnwell, David	C	Ca `ka na,	K
Baronet mat a le gee,	E	Ca co ha goh,	A
Bear, Thomas	E	Ca`Cep,	D
Beaver, Joe	C	Ca`n`gua`na,	K
Beb-de-ah,	H	Caffa`nah,	D
Ben hog meat,	C	Cah cah ran fah,	K
Ben neh,	B	Cah ka na,	K
Big, Billy	C	Cah pe co na,	K
Big, Tom	K	Cah u guan na,	K
Bill, David	C	Can sot ha goh,	A
Billey,	A	Cap pe tan ne,	D
Billey,	C	Cap pista tus ta nuk kotse	F
Billie-umke,	B	Cap tah ka na,	K
Billy,	F	Cap`pe`la`ne,	D
Billy,	H	Captain, John	K
Billy,	H	Car chil lee,	K,C
Billy,	K	Car scat ter yar holler,	C
Billy Big,	C	Car se ti yar ho la,	C
Billy-mem-ka,	B	Car`him `me `ha `jo,	C
Bilo, David	C	Carr, Seman	D
Bob,	D	Carter, William	E,D
Bob de ah,	H	Cat lo ha jo,	F
Bole,	D	Cat ses se ma la,	D
Bollona, Dours	A	Cat shar jo,	
Book,	C	Cat so ha ja se,	F
Bor de zah,	H	Cat so har jo,	H
Bradly, Sam	B	Catch Killer,	E,D
Brady, Docks	E	Ce bah,	I
Brinton, Samuel	C	Ce ce pu che,	F
Broadenax, Alex	D	Ce co lis ho fro,	
Brodnax, Alex	D	Ce co pev cho,	
Brown, Simon	H	Ce gup pe,	F
Brown, Tom	K	Ce la lelot ha ha,	
Browner, Peter	D	Ce mut tok hoky,	E
Bruner, Peter	D	Ce pul lah,	K
Buck, John	K	Cha `ta `ya`ho`la,	B
Bunney, David	E	Cha bik ki ke,	B
Burney, David	E	Cha co wa,	
Burney, Dick	E	Cha gi,	D
Busset, Sim	D	Cha ya fix se ko,	G
Butter, Edmund	I		
By `haes `gah `ko,	H		

Chan cart tee hai jo,	C		Childress, Daniel	F
Chap`pe `tau`ne,	D		Childress, Napoleon	F
Char cah pan na,	K		Childress, Reuben	F
Char co co we,	K		Chimkee,	C
Char co con ta na,	K		Chip-la,	C
Char co te ten na,	K		Chis or wik kee,	G
Char lar ha jo,	C		Chis se mik ko,	D
Char leh,	H		Chis-ki-li-ka,	E
Char ta ta,	K		Chit oh fix se ko,	F
Charles,	D		Chit ta ho ja,	B
Charley,	D		Chit ta ya ho la,	B
Charley,	F		Chit to ha ja,	F
Charley,	F		Cho che ma ta,	A
Charley,	K		Cho-e-la,	A
Chart ta fix se ko,	E		Cho-fallop ha-jo,	E
Che fa ne,	E		Cho-fi-mik-ko,	D
Che fuk e neh,	B		Cho-fik-sek-kut,	D
Che hep lot,	K,C		Cho-fix-e ko,	B
Che jou ne,	C		Cho-fix-e ko,	B
Che l see,	C		Cho-fix-se ko,	H
Che le ta,	H		Cho-fo-lo-fix-se-ko,	B
Che lo ke hat jo,	G		Cho-fuk-ne,	B
Che mat la,	F		Cho-ho-lep har-jo,	E
Che pa che,	K		Cho-jo-fix-se-ko,	G
Che pa ne,	B		Cho-juk-ne,	B
Che pah na,	K		Cho-ki-gae,	E
Che pan nah,	B		Cho-la-ya-ho-la,	E
Che par ne,	B		Cho-te-ka,	E
Che-to-ma-ah-ha,	F		Choak, Charley	D
Che-to-ne,			Chock le,	D
Che-tum-ha,	F		Chole-o-kay-	
Che-tum-ho,	F		yar-hollie,	C
Che-wa-ka,	K		Chos-ha-j0,	C
Che-za-ho-la,	D		Chu-ko-lis-ha-jo,	C
Che-zap-kah,	F		Chuc-i-ga,	C
Che-zarp-kah,	F		Chuck-Chaxt-en-har,	C
Chelo`ke`yar`ho`ler,	C		Chuck-cur-yar-holler,	C
Chet-oh-fix-i-ko,	F		Chuck-lis-har-jo,	C
Chi-Re-le-Ro,	E		Chuk-so-liken-	
Chi-e-sa,	C		hop-ko,	E
Chi-key,	E		Chullar-yar-holler,	E
Chicki-lik-ka,	E		Cla-cla-ya-ho-la,	E

Cla-la-ha-jo,	D		Co sha wa,	K
Cla-lo-e-ah-ho-la,	G		Co sog gie,	A
Cle-seh-me,	E		Co toe ah,	K
Cleol lar-har-jo,	C		Co toe hay,	K
Clis-or-wi-ki,	G		Co toe hay,	K
Clock no, David	G		Co toe na,	K
Clot-le-ha-goh,	A		Co toe see,	K
Clot-lo-e-ho-lah,	A		Co u hay,	K
Co ac co che,	A		Co u ko tah la na,	K
Co ahteu shaw,	K		Co u pah pah na,	K
Co ar sart fix e ko,	C		Co ur sot fix eko,	B
Co as sat fix e ko,	B		Co wa ka,	K
Co as sot fix cha,	B		Co was to yeh,	D
Co ca ha goh,	A		Co wat co je ha jo,	D,C
Co cah thla na,	K		Co we ha jo,	C,I
Co ce ah cep,			Co we ha jo,	H
Co cep,	D		Cof fak nah,	D
Co cha fix e ko,	E		Cof fik sik kut,	D
Co char,	K		Cof fuk`nah,	D
Co chsa,	K		Coffe muk koh,	D
Co chus fix e ko,	C		Coffex sek poh,	D
Co chus har jo,	C		Coh fallop ha jo,	E
Co ci hi cep,	D		Coh le co na,	K
Co co we,	K		Cois the har jo,	C
Co e ka ha jo,	C		Col fios see,	E
Co ell fix se ko,	G		Col froup see,	E
Co fa na,	K		Col leh,	I
Co fuel leh,	K		Col umn me har jo,	C
Co har se mast ler,	C		Collins, Peter	I
Co hash e ma la,	A		Colonel, Redman	I
Co hop frah yeh,	D		Colonel, William	I
Co is te hav jo,	E		Con ar sart fix seho,	C
Co je ha jo,	C,J		Con cah cah na,	K
Co ke thes na,	K		Con char che	
Co nip pe ma la,	A		ya ho ler,	C
Co no ha goh,	A		Con char d dy,	C
Co no ha jo,	C		Con char te,	C
Co non che,	D		Con chart,	E
Co pi yie,	E		Con chart a fix e ko,	E
Co qua na,	K		Con contollar,	E
Co sa ha jo,	C,G		Con nipple mar lar,	E
Co sar fix se ko,	C		Con pah pah na,	K

Name	Code	Name	Code
Con pe thla na,	K	Dickey,	A
Con sot ha goh,	A	Dirk,	C
Con thut har jo,	E	Dixon,	C
Con we,	K	Do o ce,	I
Con y ka,	K	Doyle, Jackson	K
Conara, Jackson	F	Dyer, John	E,D
Conchard, Emarlar	E	E fee har jo,	C
Controllar,	E	E marthla,	B
Cooney, Timothy	E	E mee-tlak,	B
Cor cah pa na,	K	E ne ha,	C
Cor we so jo ha jo,	D,C	E pat goh,	I
Coro Charta,	C	E-chew-pin-cher,	C
Cot se har jo,	H	E-chu pi-e-ka,	C
Cot so ha jo se,	F	E-chu-pi-e-ko,	C
Cot tro chee,	B	E-chur-pi e ka,	C
Cousins, John	E	E-fo-la,	B
Cousins, Tom	I	E-fo-le,	B
Cow bith che ha jo,	C	E-lup-pi-ha-jo,	G
Cow pe thla na,	K	E-ma-tlak,	B
Crazy Tiger,	D	E-mal-rah,	A
Cre ah tu shun,	K	E-mal-seh,	A
Croslin, Edmon	E	E-man-laha jo,	C
Cum nip fix se ko,	C	E-man-tlak,	B
Cum seh,	C	E-mar-tlak,	B
Cun Nippe Mar lar,	E	E-mart-la-ha-jo,	C
Cun dar la ha jo,	C	E-mart-ler,	B
Cun nih fix e ko,	C	E-mart-lo-chee,	C
Cut sis se ma la,	D	E-mart-lo-e-chee,	C
Daniel,	E	E-marth-ler,	B
Daniel,	E	E-mat-la-gup-ko,	G
Darce,	I	E-mat-lo.chee,	C
David, James	F	E-mortler,	B
David,	C	E-na-hin-E-ha,	I
David,	F	E-tun-na,	K
David Bill,	C	Echew piches,	C
Davis, James	F	Echin-pi e ka,	C
Davis, John	K	Ee Markaa,	
De che char na,	K	Efa-ha-jo,	C
De co char na,	K	Efer-har-jo,	E
De co we na,	K	Ek-hort-tav-ver,	K
Deerhead, John	K	Ek-hort-too ver,	K
Dick,	E	Eli,	D

Elther-nis-har-jo,	E	Es-cho-not-le,	A
Em a-thlah,	B	Es-fa-na-hop-pa-yeh,	D
Em-mar-roth-geh,	I	Es-fa-ne-fix-a-kou,	A
Em-mar-roth-get,	I	Es-fan-me-fix-se-Ke,	D
Ema ha-jo,	D	Es-fan-na-hu-cah,	D
Eman loa hay,	C	Es-far-na-ha-cah,	D
Eman-lar-har-jo,	C	Es-ffa-ne-ffix-se-ko,	A
Emar-la-ha-jo,	C	Es-ffa-ne-fif-e-koh,	A
Emat-la-ha-jo,	G	Es-ffa-ne-fix-e-ko,	A
Emat-la-ho-jo,	G	Es-ffa-ne-fix-se koh,	A
Emat-lo-ha-jo,	G	Es-for-na-ha-cah,	D
Emot la ha jo,	G	Es-for-na-ha-jo,	D
Emot-la-gup-ko,	G	Es-fun ne-hah-poi-yeh,	D
Emot-la-ka-jo,	G	Es-fun-ne-ha-foi-yeh,	D
En na hen-ne hah,	D	Es-fun-ne-ha-poi-yeh,	D
En no hem no kah,	D	Es-fun-ne-hop-poi-yeh,	D
En-cah-Keh,	D	Es-hit-eo-geh,	E
En-coh-Keh,	D	Es-hok-ko-ja,	E
En-na hem ne Kah,	D	Es-huh-fix-se-ko,	I
En-na-hen ne ho,	D	Es-kip-es-geh,	E
En-war-dis-lik-hir,	C	Es-kit-es-geh,	E
Ena-hen-ne-hah,	D	Es-meh-fix-se-ko,	I
Ene har fix e Ko,	C,B	Es-mi-la,	E
Ene har water le hen,	C	Es-mi-le,	E
Ene hi-fix-e-ko,	C,B	Es-muh-fix-se-ko,	I
Ene-ha-ha-jo,	C	Es-pan-ner,	K
Ene-hi-fix-se-Ko,	C,B	Es-pon-nen,	K
Ene-hi-fx-eko,	C,B	Es-pot-goh,	I
Ene-ho-fix-so-Ko,	C,B	Es-pot-got,	I
Ene-mart-lo-chee,	C	Es-seh-lah,	K
English, George	F	Es-sel-leh,	K
English, William	F	Es-tal-leff-goh,	I
Enia La jo,	D	Es-te-ma-pa,	I
Enne hen ne ha,	D	Es-teep-bee,	A
Eo-pok-ko-ja,	E	Es-tepp-be,	A
Ep-pi-k-keh,	G	Es-tepp-he,	A
Es Rep es cha,	E	Es-to-ma-pa,	I
Es che nol le,	A	Es-tol-lepp-goh,	I
Es fan ne fix se ko,	D	Es-tot-leff-goh,	I
Es fan ne ha ko,	D	Espoh-Kojo,	E
Es fan ne hop pa ye,	D	Et-hav-per,	K
Es-chepp-be,	A	Et-hov-per,	K

Et-how-per,	K	Fex-se-ka-ha-go,	H
Et-thun-is-har-jo,	E	Fi-he-mat-leh,	A
Et-yoo-ver,	K	Fi-ne-mal-lah,	A
Et-you-ver,	K	Fick-se-ka-ha-go,	H
Etther-mis-har-jo,	E	Fik se ho goh,	A
Etum-na,	K	Fik-se-koh-ha-goh,	H
Euner-mo-har-jo,	E	Fin-ne-mal-ram,	A
F-kes-so-m-mek-ah,	G	Fin-se-ya-ho-la,	G
Fa ha-jo,	A	Fish,	H
Fa-ha-jo,	A	Fisher, George W.	E
Fa-hash-e-ma-la,	A	Fix se mik chee,	G
Fa-lin-ne,	F	Fix-se-ya-ho-la,	G
Facter, Johnston	D	Fo-che-ba-ka,	F
Factor, Johnson	D	Fo-che-tu-ka,	F
Fah-ha-jo,	A	Fo-ke-lo-ke,	I
Fah-yah-ne-ho-la,	A	Fo-lo-dy,	H
Fah-yah-ne-ho-lah,	A	Fo-mah,	D
Fal-lah-leh-tan-neh,	H	Fo-shut-go-ruk-koh,	I
Fal-lat-teh-no-has-mar-lah,	H	Foe-O-lor-teh,	I
		Fol-lat-teh,	H
Fan brok ke,	B	Fol-lot-teh (no-has-ma-ah),	H
Fan-na-ka,	B	Fom-ma-ha-Joh,	H
Fan-neh-ke,	B	Fon-mah-kee,	B
Fan-nok-ke,	B	Fon-nok-ke,	B
Farmer,	E,D	For-lup-pi-ha-jo,	G
Farnar,	E,D	Foreman, John	F
Fas-ha-go,	A	Form-hollar,	E
Fas-ha-ts-se-yo-ha-la,	G	Forman, John	F
Fas-hash-e-ma-la,	A	Formun, John	F
Fas-hat-ce-ha-cah,	D	Forn-hollar,	E
Fas-hock-e-ma-la,	A	Fos-ha-ge-ho-ga,	H
Fas-huts-ce-ha-jo,	D	Fos-ha-goh,	H
Fat-ker-har-see,	C	Fos-ha-jo,	A
Fat-ker-horse,	C	Fos-ha-jo,	G
Fe-al-pe-ka-ha-goh,	H	Fos-ha-jo,	H
Fe-mah,	D	Fos-hat-se-fis-se-ko,	G
Fe-so-ha-coh,	A	Fos-hut-se-fix-e-ko,	C
Feak-ha-jo,	C	Fos-ko-chuk-o-ne,	H
Felah-Kah,	H	Fos-koch e-ma-la,	A
Fens-hallar,	E	Fos-sa-ya-ho-lah,	H
Fens-hollar,	E	Fosh-hutche-ho-la,	G

Fosh-much-e-ho-la,	G
Fow-nok-ke,	B
Fox, Humphrey	D
Fox,	K,C
Fox-sa-gol-loh,	H
Frank,	G
Frater, Calvin	E
Frazer, Calvin	E
Fu-he-mat-lah,	A
Fus-ha-jo,	B
Fus-ha-jo,	B
Fus-ha-jo,	B
Fus-ha-jo,	B
Fus-hut-se-mah-lah,	K
Fus-so-key,	K,F
Fush ha Jo,	F
Fush huch e fix se ko,	G
Fush-E-ho-la,	E
Fush-ha-jo,	G
Fush-ha-jo-gee,	G
Fush-hutch-cho-fix se ko,	G
Fush-hutch-e-ho-la,	G
Fush-hutch-e-ho-la,	G
Fush-mutch-e-fix-e-ko,	G
Fush-ut-chay-horlar,	E
Fush-ut-chey-fix-se-ko,	E
Fut-hut-se-mah-leh,	K
Fy-yee,	E
G-was-ta-ye-ha-goh,	H
Ga-ne-llas-th,	A
Ga-ne-llos-th,	A
Gab boy,	A
Gan-ne-pa-tha-keh,	A
Gaw lo ha jo	D
Gaw lo har jo,	D
Ge, Barney	F
Ge-be-ke-k-ke-ya-holla,	A
Ge-kah-pee,	B
Ge-ke-pee,	B
Ge-ko-ke-pe-poh,	A
Ge-ko-p-peh,	A
Ge-ko-peh,	A
Ge-le-ke-ya-ho-lah,	A
Ge-le-ki-ya-ho-lah,	A
Ge-lo-ke-ya-ho-la,	A
Ge-me-meh,	H
Ge-ya-ho-la,	A
Gee, Bennett	I
Gel-lok-ka-ha-go,	H
Gem me lar neh,	H
Gem ne lau neh,	H
Gem-meh,	H
Geo-K-Kah,	G
George,	B
George,	C
George,	D
George,	I
Ges-pa-geh,	H
Gho e ker ha jo,	C
Go e leh,	H
Go fal lo fik se koh,	H
Go mek kel peh,	H
Go-e-Ker-ha-jo,	H
Go-e-ka-ha-jo,	H
Go-e-ker-ha-goh,	H
Go-ek-ka-ha-goh,	H
Go-el-le-ha-goh,	H
Go-el-le-ha-jo,	H
Go-fal-lop-fik-se-koh,	H
Go-fal-lop-fix-se-co.,	H
Go-fe-k-se-koh,	A
Go-fix-se-koh,	A
Go-fol-lop-fok-se-toh,	H
Go-k-g-got-ha-goh,	A
Go-lla-fix-se-ko,	G

Go-mas-ta-ye-mo-koh,	H	Hal-but-e-ha-jo,	E
Go-nas-te-ye-ha-go,	H	Hal-lo-top-ceh,	D
Go-ne-tha-fe,	G	Hal-luc-tic-mar-neh,	D
Go-was-ti-ye-mek-koh,	H	Hap'poor'har'cah,	D
		Har'ne'Ho'geh,	A
Go-was-to-ya-hol-loh,	H	Har-e-po-yoh,	A
		Har-roo-seh,	K
Go-ye-ho-la,	A	Harley, John	F
Gof-fer-se-ko,	H	Harod, Hardy	E
Gok-kot-pa-gon,	A	Hassod, Hardy	E
Goke-got-ha-goh,	A	Hat'tul'ka'fix'se'ko,	D
Gon la go qua na,	K	Hat-tal-ka-ye-hal-loh,	D
Gon-e-lles-th,	A	Hawkins, Alexander	C
Gon-na-pa-tha-kan,	A	Hawkins, Dickson	D
Gon-ne-pa-tha-keh,	A	Hawkins, George	C
Gooner, Perryman	E	Hawkins, Jack	G
Grason, Bob	D	Hawkins, Joseph	E
Grayson, Albert	A	Hawkins, Morris	E
Grayson, Bob	D	Hawkins, Thomas	E
Grayson, Charles	E	Hawkins, William	E
Grayson, Daniel	I	Hay-Key,	E
Grayson, Elijah	E	He-lis-fix-e-koh,	A
Grayson, George	D	He-ly-out-tah,	K
Grayson, Henderson	D	He-sah-lah,	K
Grayson, Henry	G	He-se-his-hajo,	D
Grayson, Henry	I	Hear, Howlar	E
Grayson, Isum	D	Heard, Dennis	H
Grayson, James	G	Hee-pah-keh,	I
Grayson, Josiah	D	Heela'p'pa'ho'jo,	GH
Grayson, William	G	Hel'lis'fix'se'ko,	D
Grooner, Perryman	E	Hel-ler-fix-se-Ko,	D
Gut-tah-la,	K	Hel-lis-ha-jo,	G
Gut-teh-lah,	K	Hel-lot-pe-neh-neh-ha...-rako,	D
Gut-teh-leh,	K		
Ha-haes-gop-koh,	H	Hell-ubee-marlar-har-jo,	C
Ha-tul-ke-mal-loh,	A		
Hah'hau'gop'ko,	H	Hen'ne'ha'jo,	G
Hak'ke'les'sah,	D	Hen-ar-ene-har,	E
Hal'lat'fre'ne' ha'auk'ko,	D	Hen-ne-ha-ma-rah,	A
		Hen-ten-na,	K
Hal'lep'te'me'mar'reh,	D	Henne'ha'jo,	G
		Henneck,	D

Hennuch,	D
Henry,	B
Herod, Dennis	H
Herrod, Dennis	H
Herrod, Hardy	E
Hil'la'be'mar'lah,	E
Hilbul-E-Har-jo,	E
Hilla he-E-mar-lar,	E
Hille'be'martla'ha'jo,	C
Hillis-fix-e-Ko,	C
Hillis-ha-jo,	G
Hin-e-ha-o-wol-e-li-ga,	C
Hin-ne-ho-chee 2nd,	G
Hin-ne-ho-glup-kor,	G
Hin-nee-ho-chee 1st,	G
Hioshebe, John	E,D
Ho ke-les-sah,	D
Ho lah te mot to chee,	B
Ho peltch-hin-ne-ho-chee,	G
Ho'poh'e'hely,	E
Ho'the'mak'tu,	F
Ho'tul'te'fix'se'ko,	F
Ho-doe-ye-let,	E
Ho-la-ta-fix-si-to,	B
Ho-la-ta-gup-ko,	B
Ho-la-tat-se,	G
Ho-lar-toh,	E
Ho-lok-to-che,	G
Ho-luc-to-chee,	G
Ho-meh,	H
Ho-nuk-ha-jo,	B
Ho-pa-ya-ho-la,	A
Ho-pa-yo-geh,	A
Ho-tal-ke-fix-se-ko,	G
Ho-tal-ke-ga-ho-koh,	A
Ho-tal-te-fix-de-ko,	F
Ho-tl...-mak-te,	F
Ho-tla-el-k-ya-ho-la,	G
Ho-tle-po-yah,	B
Ho-tul-ge-en-o-hue-co,	C
Ho-tul-ke-fix-e-koh,	A
Ho-tul-ke-fix-e-koh,	A
Ho-tul-kee,	I
Ho-tul-te-e-mar-tle,	I
Ho-tul-to-fix-e-ko,	G
Ho-tul-to-fix-e-koh,	G
Ho-tul-to-fix-se-ho,	I
Hok-ke-lis-hop-poe-her-neh,	D
Hol'lok'tol'che,	D
Hol-lis-ha-jo,	G
Hol-lot-pe-ne-ha-rah-kah,	D
Hol-lot-tos-gel,	I
Hol-met-tol-tun,	I
Holt-le-lo-yoh,	A
Holts-le-boy-yah,	A
Homer, Alexander	C
Hop'poor'ha'jo,	D
Hop-ga-z-ho-loh,	A
Hop-pets-tav-ver,	K
Hop-poor'ha'jo,	D
Hop-poor-har-cob,	D
Hop-poor-he-ne-hah,	D
Hopoh-e-mal-a,	E
Hor-epo-geh,	A
Hor-ne-ho-geh,	A
Hot'ne'ka'won 'ha'le'ko,	C
Hot-sat-tye-ho-la,	I
Hot-tol-ke-fix-se-ko,	D
Hot-tuk-le-chut-goh,	I
Hoth-la-po-yoh,	B
Hots-co-n-na-p-pa-p,	G
Hull-butter,	C
Hull-butter-hor-jo,	C
Hup'pets'har'er'ver,	K
Hy'haes'gop'ko,	H
I-to-ka-jo,	E
Ich-har-se-yar-ho-ler,	C

Il-far-ne-mik-ko,	D	Jah-con-thla,	K
Ima-me,	B	Jah-hap-par-ser,	K
In claw nis ha jo,	E	Jak-cep,	D
In le ti ke,	B	Jak-ka,	K,C
In-pso-gho-geh,	G	Jak-ke,	K,C
Insley, John	C	Jak-kee,	I
Insty, John	C	Jak-kik-o-men,	K
Io-lup-hi-hajo,	G	Jak-ko-k-heh,	K
Io-pi-kee,	B	Jak-kol-ran-ver,	K
Iow-neh,		Jak-kup-pav-ver,	K
Is pa co har jo,	C	James,	E
Is-fa-ne-ho-clok-he,	H	Jameson, Harry	E
Is-nuh-fix-se-ko,	I	Jamieson, Harry	E
Is-pi-kee,	B	Jammerson, Harry	E
Is-tar-tis-che,	D	Jap-ful-leh,	K
Isaac,	I	Jap-keh,	E
Ish-poh-koh,	H	Jar-gup-koh,	I
Ispa-o-yar-holla,	C	Jas-seh,	I
Iteh-ka-ha-jo,	E	Jas-sin-yah,	I
Its has-wah,	H	Je-puts-jeh,	K
Its-chas-na,	B	Je-yol-seh,	K
Its-has-ya-hol-lah,	H	Je-yot-geh,	K
J,cha,e la a che,	A	Jefferson,	C
J.cho.e.la-cho-gee,	A	Jefferson,	C
Ja-ka-pe,	F	Jek-ko-er-er,	K
Ja-ke,	C	Jek-ko-reh,	K
Ja-kes-tus-two- vok-ker,	K	Jek-koh-reh,	K
Ja-pe-la-co-fee-na,	K	Jek-kol-ren-ver,	K
Ja-tah-na-thla-na,	K	Jek-kup-pa-ver,	K
Jacha-ne-lac-co-che,	A	Jem-mah,	K
Jack, Cup	D	Jem-meh,	I
Jack,	C	Jer-cep-per,	K
Jack,	E,D	Jerry,	C
Jacka-ne-lo-co-che,	A	Jessy,	K
Jackey,	E	Jho-e-ka-ha-jo,	G,C
Jacksay,	A	Jil-kar-har-jo,	G,C
Jackson, Doyle	K	Jim,	B
Jackson,	I	Jim,	D
Jacob,	C	Jim,	H
Jacob,	F	Jim,	H
Jacop-pie,	B	Jim,	I
		Jim hia to,	C

313

Jim-kah,	I		JoK, Kee	I
Jim-koh,	I		Jobee,	B
Jim-meh,	H		Jocksay,	A
Jim-much-chee,	E		Joe,	C
Jo Ka-pe,	F		Joh bee,	B
Jo la-fix-se-ko,	I		Joh nee,	B
Jo na ta ye mar tla,	I		John, Harley	F
Jo was te ya-hol lah,	G		John, Yadger	C
Jo-Kay,	B		John,	B
Jo-cah-sun ga pa,	K		John,	C
Jo-cha,	B		John,	D
Jo-coh-san-yoh fah,	K		John,	E
Jo-coh-smo-go pa,	K		John gup ko,	F
Jo-cop-pee,	B		John gup to,	F
Jo-coppee,	B		John ne,	B
Jo-cup-pee,	B		John nee,	B
Jo-e-dah,	G		John neh,	D
Jo-e-ka-ha-jo,	G,C		John neh,	D
Jo-e-kah,	G		John ny,	E
Jo-e-kah,	G		John ny she ah,	K
Jo-e-mos-tu-get,	I		John-e-chup-	
Jo-fix-e-ko,	A		co-chee,	C,K
Jo-fix-se-ko,	G		John-kut-yo,	F
Jo-fix-si-ko,	B		John-ne-ha,	G
Jo-ha Jo,	B		John-neh,	H
Jo-ha-jo,	G		John-s-got-goh,	I
Jo-ko-de,	F		Johnes, Samuel	E
Jo-ko-te-yah-ho-la,	B		Johnny,	D
Jo-la fix e ko,	G		Johnson, James	K
Jo-la-fix-e-ko,	G		Johnson, Lewis	D
Jo-lo-hots jo,	E		Johnson, Robert	F
Jo-me-ko,	G		Johnson, Wiley	D
Jo-mot-whe-ge,	F		Johnson,	G
Jo-nos-ta-ye-ma-lat,	I		Jok kot rah,	K
Jo-pe-luk-kop-			Jon-ne-she-ah,	K
ful-leh,	K		Jon-nee,	B
Jo-was-taw-ye-			Jon-neh,	F
ha-jo,	E		Jon-neh,	H
Jo-was-ti-yah,	I		Jones, Samuel	E
Jo-was-ti-ye-ma-loh,	B		Jonny, Chup co chee	C,K
Jo-was-tie,	F		Jonny,	D
Jo-was-tow-ye,	E		Jop-ful-leh,	K

Jos sin yah,	I
Jos-sin-yot,	I
Jos-was-to-a-mort-ler,	B
Joseph,	F
Jousey,	A
Ju kes-tus-two-rok koh,	K
Ju-hut-koh,	K
Ju-la-fix-se-ko,	D
Jua-ran-ver,	K
Juk kik-koe-mer,	K
Juk-hot-tel-har-ver,	K
Jul-leth,	I
Jun-ha-jo,	C
Jur-gup-koh,	I
Jura-ran-over,	K
Jus-par-ver,	K
Jus-se-meh,	K
Jus-see-meh,	K
Jut hol ten over,	K
K-kus-ha-jo,	D
Ka-ba-ya-ho-lah,	A
Ka-be-ya-ho-lah,	A
Ka-g-ge-me-koh,	A
Ka-ga-ya-ho-lah,	H
Ka-ge-fik-se-koh,	H
Ka-ge-ya-hol-lah,	H
Ka-ge-ya-hol-lah,	H
Ka-gi-fik-se-koh,	H
Ka-gi-fix-se-koh,	H
Ka-gi-ya-hol-la,	H
Ka-gi-ya-hol-lah,	H
Ka-gi-yoh-hol-lah,	H
Ka-ha-la-fix-se-co,	C
Ka-p-pts-ka-ya-ho-la,	G
Ka-pe-chee,	E
Ka-pet-ge-mar-lah,	H
Ka-pit-say-ga-hola,	F
Ka-pits-sah,	E
Ka-pous,	E,D
Ka-put-gi-ma-loh,	H
Ka-put-so-fix-se-ko,	F
Ka-puts-se-ya-hola,	F
Ka-sak-co-ta-ne,	K
Ka-seinst-to-fix-se-ko,	G
Ka-ss-tha-fix-se-ko,	G
Ka-ts-ka-fix-se-ko,	G
Ka-wa-kats-kah,	G
Ka-yok-lee,	B
Kag-ga-fix-se-koh,	A
Kag-gee-me-koh,	A
Kah-gi-feh-se-koh,	H
Kah-kia-van-ner,	K
Kal-pur-seh,	E
Kal-pus-sch,	E
Kals-tse-mat-la,	E
Kan-at-ha-gohe,	H
Kan-at-ha-joh,	H
Kan-ca-te-man-neh,	D
Kan-gah-ha-go,	H
Kan-gat-ha-gohe,	H
Kan-gut-ha-goh,	H
Kan-kat-te-marrah,	D
Kan-nah,	H
Kan-neh,	H
Kan-net-teh-tat-seh,	H
Kan-tel-la-ha-goh,	H
Kan-thla-wa-thla,	K
Kap-e-ge-go-geh,	A
Kap-pats-ca-fix-se-ko,	D
Kap-pe-cha-ha-jo,	F
Kap-pe-che-mar-lah,	H
Kap-pe-go-geh,	A
Kap-pe-k-ge-ma-rah,	H
Kap-pe-mek-koh,	H
Kap-peh-ga-he-goh,	H
Kap-peh-ya-ha-goh,	H
Kap-pet-ge-ha-goh,	H
Kap-pet-ge-mar-lah,	H
Kap-pets-co-fix-se-co,	D

Kaps-e-g-go-geh,	A	Ke-tsah-tee,	B
Kas sah,	I	Ke-we-ha-jo,	F
Kas-suk-ket-her-ver,	K	Ke-yok-la,	B
Kat-ce-ha-cots-ceh,	D	Kee-yah-pe-nah-na,	K
Kat-cus-ha-cah,	D	Kee-yar-sax-pe-na-va,	K
Kat-le-mat-la,	G	Keh-sat-ye-a-lisla,	I
Kat-ne-mat-la,	G	Kei-be-ya-ho-lah,	A
Kat-se-fix-e-ko,	G	Kel-veh,	K
Kat-se-ha-jo-che,	D	Keler-ver,	K
Kat-se-ma-la,	G	Kelley, Marshall	D
Kat-se-te,	K,C	Kelly, Marshall	D
Kat-so-bar-ne,	F	Kelly, Tom	I
Kat-so-fix-se-ko,	G	Kelly, Watson	D
Kat-so-fix-se-ko,	G	Kels-veh,	K
Kat-so-fix-se-ko,	K,B	Kemp, Robert	D
Kat-so-fix-se-ko,	I	Ken-ah-ha-goh,	H
Kat-so-fix-se-ko,	G	Kep-har-ver,	K
Kat-so-ha-jo,	F	Ker-suk-kot-t-he-ne,	K
Kat-so-ha-jo,	G	Kernel, James	E
Kat-so-la-ne,	F	Kes-cha,	E
Kat-so-lar-ne,	F	Kes-suk-hot-t-he-ner,	K
Kat-so-mat-la,	G	Kes-suk-kot-te-he-noh,	K
Kats-co-n-na-p-pa-h,	G	Ket-tuk-ki-veh,	K
Kats-se-mat-lah,	G	Kettah,	H
Kats-tre-mat-la,	E	Kez-cha,	E
Kay-ga-ya-holloh,	A	Kill, Him	D
Kay-gee-ne-koh,	A	Kin-ne-ho-ma-ta,	F
Ke-be-yo-ho-lah,	A	Kios-seh-leh,	K
Ke-el-te,	E	Kla-lo-ha-jo,	F
Ke-gis-l-mar-lah,	H	Kla-lo-hi-e-ke,	F
Ke-kas-ha-coh,	D	Kla-thlo-ha-jo,	F
Ke-llah,	A	Klah-la-fix-se-ke,	K,C
Ke-mar-har-ko,	D	Klah-lo-fix-se-ko,	K,C
Ke-na-ha-jo,	D	Klah-lo-hi-ke,	F
Ke-na-hah-coh,	D	Klar-lor-fix-e-ko,	K,C
Ke-na-han-cah,	D	Klo-we-ley,	E
Ke-na-hut-cah,	D	Kloh-la-fix-se-ko,	K,C
Ke-nulth-ha-jo	D	Klor-lor-fix-e-co,	K,C
Ke-ot-see,	F	Klos-le-ti-ga,	E
Ke-tash-tee,	B		
Ke-tsah-chee,	B		

Klos-swe-ley,	E	Ko-nip-ha-jo,	E
Ko ceh,	D	Ko-nip-hatz-zo,	I
Ko luk te not		Ko-no-fix-e-ko,	E
co chee,	B	Ko-no-fix-se-ko,	G
Ko nee ha jo,	G	Ko-no-ha-jo,	D
Ko nip e ah ho la,	E	Ko-no-ha-jo,	G
Ko nup ha jo,	E	Ko-no-ya-ho-la,	I
Ko to ah,	K	Ko-noh-ke,	K
Ko wa ko chee,	B	Ko-nos-satt-	
Ko we ha jo,	G	fix-se-ko,	G
Ko wok ko chee,	B	Ko-nots-sut-teh,	D
Ko yok la,	B	Ko-now-wa-ha-jo,	D
Ko-ak-ko-gee,	G	Ko-nuk-ha-jo,	B
Ko-as-sot-fix-se-ko,	G	Ko-nup ha jo,	D
Ko-auk-ko-geh,	A	Ko-nup-ha-jo,	F
Ko-auk-kor-goah,	A	Ko-ok-a-ge,	G
Ko-ge-ya-hol-loh,	H	Ko-ok-ko-ge,	G
Ko-gis-the-ha-jo,	C	Ko-ok-o-ge,	G
Ko-ha-cup,	G	Ko-os-sot-fix-se-ko,	G
Ko-ha-se-mar-tla,	I	Ko-ot-see,	F
Ko-ha-se-mat-la,	I	Ko-pet-cho-sha-go,	A
Ko-ha-se-mot-la,	I	Ko-pit-cha-ha-goh,	A
Ko-har-teh,	K	Ko-pit-cha-ha-jo,	A
Ko-jok-lee,	B	Ko-pit-cha-he-jo,	A
Ko-kia-van-ner,	K	Ko-pit-so-fix-se-ko,	F
Ko-lame-ha-jo,	C	Ko-sa-har-jo,	B
Ko-lo-te-jup-ko,	B	Ko-sah-ko-po-let-la,	D
Ko-lum e ha jo,	C	Ko-se-ha-jo,	B
Ko-me-ha-goh,	A	Ko-se-ha-jo,	C,G
Ko-miss-hatz-yo,	I	Ko-sis-the-ha-jo,	C
Ko-na-ha-goh,	A	Ko-so-fix-e-ko,	G
Ko-nar-kah,	K	Ko-so-fix-se-ko,	G
Ko-ne-ha-jo,	F	Ko-so-fix-se-ko,	G
Ko-ne-pa-a-ho-la,	A	Ko-so-ha-jo,	C,G
Ko-neh,	H	Ko-swit-to-fix-	
Ko-nep-ha-goh,	A	se-ko,	G
Ko-nep-ha-jo,	F	Ko-was-satt-	
Ko-nes-ha-goh,	A	fix-se-ko,	G
Ko-nes-ha-goh,	H	Ko-we-ha-goh,	H
Ko-nik-hor-jo,	B	Koe-mer,	K
Ko-nip-eh-ha-la,	E	Koh-e-les-hop-	
Ko-nip-ha-goh,	A	poe-her-reh,	D

Koh-ker-ner,	K		Kot ne ma la,	G
Koh-pe-go-geh,	A		Kot ne mart la,	G
Koh-sah,	I		Kot ne mat la,	G
Kok-hoe-mer,	K		Kot op hi ke,	B
Kok-kea-nan-ner,	K		Kot op hi-hee,	B
Kok-kes-sa,	K		Kot sah ha jo,	B
Kok-kia-ran-ner,	K		Kot sat tye a ho la,	I
Kok-kia-van-ner,	K		Kot so fix e ko,	G
Kok-koe-mer,	K		Kot so fix se ko,	G
Kol-heh,	K		Kot so fix se ko,	K,B
Kol-meh-tav-ver,	K		Kot so fix se ko,	G
Kol-mek-tor-veh,	K		Kot so fix se ko,	I
Kol-muher,	K		Kot so lar ne,	F
Kol-muk-ker,	K		Kot so ma la,	A
Kon-dah-le-ma-tha,	F		Kot so mart la,	G
Kon-gats-tro-geh,	E		Kot so mat la,	G
Kon-gatz-tro-geh,	E		Kot so mo lo,	A
Kon-gots-tso-geh,	E		Kot sto ma la,	A
Kop-fits-co-fix-se-ko,	D		Kot swit to fix se ko,	G
Kop-pe-go-geh,	A		Kot tuk he v ver,	K
Kop-per-cor-ver,	K		Kot up ho ho,	B
Kop-per-cw-ver,	K		Kot-cus-ha-coh,	D
Kop-per-rov-ver,	K		Kot-cus-ha-jo,	D
Kop-pets-co-fix-se-ko,	D		Kot-gee-me-koh,	A
Kor-kuk-ku-v-ver,	K		Kot-gis-se-mar-lah,	H
Kor-kus-ha-cah,	D		Kot-kus-ha-coh,	D
Kor-kus-ha-jo,	D		Kot-so-ha-jo,	G
Kor-se-to,	K,C		Kot-so-har-jo,	B
Kor-ste,	K,C		Kot-tro-chee,	B
Kos-gu-hat-s-goh,	I		Kots geh,	I
Kos-kus-ha-cah,	D		Kots ka fix se ko,	G
Kos-kus-ha-coh,	D		Kots se fin e co,	D
Kos-mar,	K		Kots se ha jo,	G
Kos-op-o-gee,	B		Koy-ge-me-koh,	A
Kos-su-hat-s-goh,	I		Kuk ker ner,	K
Kos-su-hut-s-goh,	I		Kul met tah,	I
Kot ash te,	B		Kum sar tee,	I
Kot ga se ma cah,	H		Kun de la ma tha,	F
Kot ga se mar lah,	H		Kun-ca-te-mar-reh,	D
Kot ges se mar lah,	H		Kun-ce-te-mar-leh,	D
			Kun-sar-tee,	I
			Kup ha cha ha jo,	F

Kup pa che ha jo,	F		Las-fi-ni-kee,	B
Kup pe cha ha jo,	F		Lau-eh,	H
Kup per rov-ver,	K		Lauf-feh,	A
Kup te,	D		Le hoh mok ta	
Kup ya per ver,	K		har cho,	I
Kup-rov-ver,	K		Le kum e fix e co,	C
Kur ca te mar reh,	D		Le this ha jo,	G
Kus-tor-ser,	K		Le tt f fix se ko,	G
Kut-ce-ha-cats-ceh,	D		Le tte fa goh,	A
Kuts se fix se ko,	D		Le war lar,	E
Kwo-cus ha jo,	D		Le-bler-ha-goh,	H
L ha wa ha go,	A		Le-chum-e-fix-ki,	C
L la tha ha go,	A		Le-cum-a-fix-e-ko,	C
L tra-foa-ha-goh,	A		Le-har-jo,	E
La bis chee,	B		Le-na,	K,F
La chip,	E		Leat-tet,	H
La ha wa ha goh,	A		Leck um fix si loo,	C
La meh,	I		Lee, Bennett	I
La ta ma ti gee,	B		Lee mah,	K,F
La tah ye ho lah,	H		Lee war cla,	E
La ti ya hol lah,	H		Leh se me,	B
La-fu-ni-kee,	B		Lep pu mort ler,	B
La-har-la,	K		Les san ten ner,	K
Lac-meh,	I		Les ser ten ner,	K
Lae meh,	I		Les-leh,	H
Lae-ne-sha,	K		Lester,	A
Laf-fi-chee,	B		Letlip-har-jo,	G
Lah ta fix e ko,	B		Leuf-eveh,	A
Lah ta yah he lah,	H		Lincoln,	K
Lah tam mik Pah,	I		Lis leh,	H
Lah tla fix se ko,	G		Lit te fix se ko,	G
Landrum, Daniel	I		Lit tif ha jo,	G
Lap ro lo,	K		Little Alexander,	C
Lap ta fix se ko,	D		Little Bear,	D
Lar bith chee,	B		Lo Ella fix see ko,	G
Lar bith chee,	C		Lo cha ha jo,	E
Lar peck chay,	C		Lo che fix se ko,	G
Lar te fix eko,	B		Lo he nok tse,	A
Lar-bick-chee,	C		Lo kes ha goh,	A
Lar-bis-chee,	B		Lo so fix se ko,	D
Lar-pee,	F		Lo so ha jo,	D
Las fa ni ke,	B		Lo t kers ha goh,	A

Lo tsa fix se ho,	G	Ma fus ge,	K,F
Lo war la gah,	C	Ma he si ke,	F
Lo was se mau lar,	C	Ma ho si ke,	F
Lo-e-nat-se,	A	Ma hu no ha,	G
Lo-hah,	D	Ma ll ss eh,	A
Lo-he-nut-seh,	A	Ma ll ss seh,	A
Lo-wee,	B	Ma llas seh,	A
Lobbay,	A	Ma llis eh,	A
Loc che fix se ko,	G	Ma po hai geh,	A
Loc mok ta ho la,	G	Ma-git-ha-jo,	B
Loc ta fix se ko,	G	Ma-git-ho-he,	B
Loc-nok-to-ho-la,	G	Ma-ha-ke-keh,	I
Loch-ti-ya-ho-la,	D	Ma-her,	K
Loe mok to ho la,	G	Ma-ho-se-ke,	F
Lof-fi-chee,	B	Ma-lles-Steh,	A
Loh-hoh,	D	Ma-pe-he,	F
Long, Jim	H	Ma-pi-he,	F
Long, Sam	D	Ma-ta-na-ha-coh,	D
Looney, James	E	Mackintosh, Morris	I
Los-fa-ni-ko,	B	Magelbra, Dan	D
Lot tah hes rah,	K	Magelbra, Greene	D
Lot te ma to gee,	B	Magelbra, Jack	D
Lots e ha jo,	E	Magelbra, York	D
Lou-ffeh,	A	Magilbra, Dan	D
Lou-ie,	H	Magilbra, Greene	D
Lou-weh,	H	Magilbra, Jack	D
Lou-wet,	E	Magilbra, York	D
Louie,	F	Magrilba, Greene	D
Louis,	B	Magrilba, Jack	D
Low weh,	E	Mah hah ke,	K,F
Lowe,	B	Mah hap ke,	K,F
Lowe-wie,	D	Mah hep ka,	K,F
Lozeman, David	I	Mah-bo-hep-teh,	A
Lub-tam-mek-kah,	I	Major,	K
Luc-a-loc-ta,	E	Mals-seh,	K
Luc-to-fix-se-ko,	G	Man-le-see,	C
Luh tam mek keh,	I	Mapiloa, Jack	D
Luk tam mek kah,	I	Mar, Shee	K
Lup-pe-ma-la,	B	Mar thla-na ke,	F
Lup-tu-fin-e-co,	D	Mar-leh,	K
M-ma-r-rah-gup-ge-go,	G	Mar-see,	E
		Mar-thla-no-ke,	F

March,	B	Me quah ho la,	A
Marshall, Bill	D	Me-chep huts goh,	I
Marshall, George	E	Me-chis-ko-chee,	C
Marshall, John	K	Me-cho-wek-keh,	H
Marshall, Marshy	K	Me-chop-huts-goh,	I
Marshall, William	E	Me-chup-huts-goh,	I
Marshey, Marshall	K	Me-ga-leh,	H
Marthal, Make	F	Me-gis-co-ha-jo,	G
Martial, George	E	Me-gis-ka-ha-jo,	E
Martial, William	E	Me-ha-k-keh,	A
Mat teh loh keh,	H	Me-ha-keh,	A
Mathy,	E	Me-hit-ces-ka-ha-coh,	D
McCleesh, Quash	H		
McCles, Quash	H	Me-hur-mik-hol-fix-se-ko,	I
McGilbi, Lipscone	G		
McGilbra, Daniel	D	Me-ka-keh,	A
McGilbra, Greene	D	Me-ko-ha-jo,	A
McGilbra, York	D	Me-kup-kes-seh-hol,	I
McGilby, Lipsone	G	Me-lah,	E
McIntosh, Harry	E	Mech is co chay,	C
McKinney, Steward	E	Meck-ko mots cos sap,	D
McLeesh, Quash	H		
McNelly, Newton	D	Meh-its-ah,	A
McQueen, David	H	Meh-ka-ho-jo,	A
McQuen, David	G	Mek ka ha yoh,	A
McQuene, David	H	Mek ke ha goh,	A
McQuin, David	G	Mek kew mat loh,	G
McVay, James H.	B	Mek ko gat teh,	H
Mch-ke-ha-goh,	A	Mek ko hut ka,	H
Me Sel by Lips con,	G	Mek ko hut kee,	H
Me chis co chee,	C	Mek ko ya ha lah,	D
Me gis ko ha jo,	G	Mek-ko-fix-e-koh,	H
Me ha-ka-heh,	A	Mek-ko-gap-koh,	H
Me hur ruk kol fir se ko,	I	Mek-ko-got-toh,	H
		Mek-ko-meh-cas-sep,	D
Me jis co ha jo,	G		
Me k kem ma ra,	G	Mek-ko-mets-cos-sop,	D
Me ka ha jo,	B		
Me kal ler na goh,	H	Mek-ko-ye-hol-lah,	D
Me kes k ka ha jo,	G	Mel-Kah,	E
Me ko hu goh,	A	Mel-lah,	H
Me law ee,	I	Messigee,	B

Met ga ye kee,	H		More, Lemuel	D
Met ga yi kee,	H		Mornieux, Peter	I
Met gi ye kee,	H		Mornioux, Peter	I
Met ko hut kee,	H		Morrioux, Peter	I
Met tah lo keh,	H		Moses,	E
Met-ge-wi-kee,	H		Mosey,	E
Met-toh,	H		Mosey,	E
Mettah,	H		Mu ker chee,	G
Mi Reh,	A		Muc Ker chee,	G
Mi kie,	A		Much-so-chee,	C
Mi ko hu goh,	A		Muk er che,	G
Mi-eh-pa,	F		Muller, Elijah	E
Mi-ets-ah,	A		Mun nat ta,	C
Mi-its-ah,	A		Mun nat tee,	C
Mici noj har jo,	E		Munak, John	I
Mick ko ha jo,	E		Mundy, Durant	C
Mik E ma la,	G		Muney, Durant	C
Mik E mat la,	G		Munnak, John	I
Mik Que ah ho la,	F		N ha ya ho la,	G
Mik e mat la,	G		Na bie cha ha jo,	G
Mik e mot la,	G		Na brie che ha jo,	G
Mik ke mat la,	G		Na ha fix se ko,	I
Mik l ma la,	G		Na ha ha jo,	G
Mik-ko-ge-hal-lah,	D		Na ko se fix se ko,	F
Mik-ko-ha-jo,	E		Na kos ko zo ne,	F
Mik-ko-mat-la,	G		Na lo,	F
Mik-ko-ye-hal-lah,	D		Na poh ge feh se koh,	H
Mik-que-ah-ho-la,	D		Na poh ge fik se koh,	H
Mikeh,	A			
Mikke Mart len,	C		Na pots ce ha jo,	G
Mil li ka,	E		Na pus ge,	F
Mil-la-ka,	C		Na ta geh,	H
Miller, Daniel	I		Nak fa ha jo,	F
Miller, Elijah	E		Nak kas hoto ceh,	D
Mis-te-lee,	E		Nar har j fur a ho ja,	K
Mis-to-lee,	E		Nar man,	C
Missigee,	B		Nar put che,	I
Mo see,	B		Nath kup ha jo,	
Mon-i-ho-chee,	B		Ne bah,	D
Mondy, Durant	C		Ne ha ha goh,	H
Moore, Lem	D		Ne ha ha jo,	D
Mor shee,	K			

Ne ha ha jo,	G	No kas ha che,	G
Ne ha hago geh,	H	No kas ko zo ne,	F
Ne ha lack hots se,	E	No kas mik koh,	D
Ne ha lok ko,	E	No kas se ho lah,	A
Ne ha mik ko,	E	No kas se ma rah,	A
Ne ha ya ho la,	A	No kas se mal lah,	A
Ne ha ya ho la,	D	No kas sel leah,	G
Ne hai ar har jo,	C	No kas ya hola,	G
Ne hal ar har jo,	C	No ke sho la tah,	A
Ne hal ar har jo,	C	No ker hatz goh,	E
Ne har co chuc ne,	C	No-k-kos-ffix-e-koh,	A
Ne has fix se ko,	H	No-ko-se-ah-ho-la,	F
Ne he ha go gee,	I	No-ko-se-fix-se-ko,	F
Ne hur ruk kol		No-ko-se-ho-lah,	A
fix se ko,	I	No-ko-se-le,	F
Ne nits gap ya		No-ko-se-lee,	A
bats gat,	E	No-ko-se-ma-lah,	H
Ne or ha goh,	H	No-ko-se-mat-la,	F
Ne ya ha jo,	I	No-ko-se-o-ho-la,	I
Nek ka uch,	A	No-ko-se-se-la,	G
Nero, John	E	No-ko-se-ya-ho-la,	C
Nero, Samuel	D	No-ko-se-ye-ho-la,	G
Nero,	D	No-kor-ha-goh,	A
Net ge gi me keh,	H	No-kor-ho-pop-	
Nha ha jo,	G	e-reh,	A
Nhe he ha jo,	G	No-kos-fe-ke,	B
Nic cli gha,	G	No-kos-fix-e-koh,	A
Nik cli leh,	G	No-kos-fix-se-ko,	B
Nin		No-kos-fix-se-ko,	G
Nin ne ho math ta,	F	No-kos-fix-se-ko,	G
Nis cos yar lar,	E	No-kos-ha-jo,	B
Nix si ri leh,	G	No-kos-ha-jo,	G,E
Nka ne,	B	No-kos-ko-	
No co se ma la,	H	chuck-nee,	B
No cos ha jo,	G,E	No-kos-ko-zo-ne,	F
No juk ke,	B	No-kos-mik-ko,	G
No k kas ffix e koh,	A	No-kos-sch-lch,	G
No ka se ho lah,	A	No-kos-se-mar-reh,	D
No ka se mar la,	H	No-kosh-e-lo-geh,	H
No kas fix e koh,	A	No-kot-se-be,	F
No kas fix se ko,	G	No-kox-tol-lou-koh,	H
No kas fix se kokt,	G	No-kus-fe-ke,	B

No-kus-fix-e-ko,	G	O such har jo,	G
No-kus-fix-e-tokt,	G	O we no ka,	C
No-kus-fix-se-ko,	G	O-Kee-la-suh,	I
No-kus-hutch-see,	G	O-ches-hu-jo,	G
No-kus-me-ko,	G	O-e-gus-ha-jo,	G
No-kus-ye-ho-la,	G	O-gis-ha-jo,	G
No-los-se-ma-wah,	A	O-kos-ho-jo,	G
No-noo-nuk-ko,	G	O-rah-k-kah,	G
No-pai-hai-got,	A	O-sa-ya-ho-lah,	A
No-pas-ge,	F	O-sats-ya-hol-lah,	D
No-pay-hai-geh,	A	O-vali-k-kah,	G
Nok fa ya ho la,	B	O-we-wo-ka,	C
Nok fa ya tus ta		OK gon ha goh,	A
mik ke,	B	OK san wa,	F
Nok kas mek koh,	D	OK-ha-ye-fix-se-ko,	G
Nok kos nots cep,	D	Oak chi e fixe ko,	C
Nok-kas-se-mar-reh,	D	Oak er lisser,	C
Nok-kas-sots-cep,	D	Oak ta ha jo go,	C
Nok-kos-stos-ceh,	D	Oak-chaw-ho-lu-ta,	C
Nok-na,	B	Oak-chi, E-Mart-ler	C
Nok-sok-ha-jo,	B	Oak-chun, E. Marlor	E
Nok-we,	B	Oak-fos-ka,	C,K
Nolt-leh-boy-yah,	A	Obe ah hat ke,	F
Nor-Kai-ho-he-leh,	A	Obi a huh ke,	F
Nor-kai-ha-yah,	A	Obok ko ko,	G
Nor-man,	C	Oc John ha Jo,	F
Nor-mar,	C	Oc ta oh ses sep ko,	D
Norf-olk,	C	Oc te a h se fix so ko,	F
Nost-co-fix-e-co,	A	Oc ti ah chee,	I
Nuk-fa-ha-jo,	F	Oc tis ya h ge	
Nuk-fa-ya-ho-la,	B	chep ko,	F
Nuk-fa-ye-tus-		Oc-che-har-jo,	E
te-nuk-ke,	B	Oc-cla-cle,	K,F
Nuk-ke-pa-he,	B	Oc-kas-ha-jo,	G
Nuk-ko-put-ko,	B	Oc-san-wah,	F
Nus-cos-yar-lar,	E	Oc-ta ha cho che,	F
Nuth-kup-ha-jo,	F	Och-mat-la,	G
O chu see,	E	Ocla clee,	K,F
O ge see,	H	Octi-ah-se-fix-se-ko,	F
O ges ha go,	H	Odell-ca-ha-jo,	D
O ne wo ka,	C	Odull ca ha jo,	D
O sat se,	F	Oe Kus ha Jo,	F

Oe sa lup pe,	G		Ok-ti-ah-se-mat-la,	G
Oe yoke kiya ho la,	G		Ok-tis-ya-ge-	
Oe-has-ha-jo,	G		chop-ko,	F
Oe-jo-ke-ki-ga-ho-la,	G		Ok-ye-te-chee,	E
Oejo kegh ho la,	G		Oke chun wa,	B
Oety arch che cliy,	C		Oks tran ha jo,	B
Og ha goh,	A		Ol les ha jo,	G
Oge gup ko,	B		Ola ta ha jo,	B
Oge ha, Jo	F		Omer ha goh,	H
Oge ko guk ne,	B		On woh k koh,	G
Oge mar rah,	G		Ona tar sar te,	K
Oge mat lah,	G		One dar sar te,	K
Oge ya ho la,	B		One no kee,	C
Ogon ha goh,	A		Ones-ha-goh,	H
Oh la ya ge ha jo,	G		Or-tar-se,	I
Oh lee,	K		Os e chay ar hollar,	C
Oh te ya ge ha jo,	G		Os fa ni ko,	B
Oh tul ke har cho,	I		Os la ti ke,	B
Ok ar lissar,	C		Os sots hat shut go,	I
Ok ca ye mar rah,	D		Os stos ya ha lah,	D
Ok ca ye ne			Os tos fix se ko,	D
hor rak ko,	D		Os-ha-jo,	C
Ok can fix se ko,	G		Os-sots fix se ko,	D
Ok cha-ne-mat-lah,	G		Osa ha jo,	B
Ok chi uppe,	G		Osa-ha-jo,	D
Ok fus-ke,	C,K		Osah fix e ko,	D
Ok ko lus fiv e koh,	A		Ose-ah-ho-la,	G
Ok san mat la,	G		Osee chee marlar,	E
Ok sau-fix se ko,	G		Ossa ha coh,	D
Ok ta chee mat la,	G		Ossa-fix-se-ko,	D
Ok-chan-e-ma-la,	E		Ot s ceh ha go,	I
Ok-che-see,	E		Otce-at-se-ha-jo,	E
Ok-er-lis-ser,	C		Otch chee fix se ko,	C
Ok-for-ka,	C,K		Ote ah se fix seko,	F
Ok-ja-ya-peh,	G		Ote ko e ho la,	G
Ok-ka-ni-ma-ra,	G		Ote ko e ho la,	G
Ok-la-le,	K,F		Ote ko fix e ko,	G
Ok-la-pe-sa-ha-go,	A		Ote sa tup pe,	G
Ok-sa-ya-ph,	G		Otece at se pa jo,	E
Ok-si-ye-fix-se-ko,	G		Oti ah che chap ko,	F
Ok-ta-ha-Jo-chee,	C		Otu-ke-ho-la,	B
Ok-ta-ha-jo,	C		Otul ke ha jo,	B

Pa ha ha goh,	A		Pai hos ha jo,	A
Pa ha le,	B		Pai-you-meh,	A
Pa ha lla theh,	A		Painter, Joseph	I
Pa har sem mar nah,	H		Pal-ham-me,	E
Pa has ha jo,	G		Pap-ti-yah,	H
Pa has ko cah,	G		Papp-nah,	G
Pa has na gah, 2,	H		Par ho shimeha,	B,C
Pa has se ah ho la,	H		Par hosay,	C
Pa ho se, 1,	F		Par-lo,	I
Pa ho see, 1,	B		Pas co fo chee,	F
Pa ho-se, 2,	F		Pas sa ga,	F
Pa ho-se-mat-to-se,	F		Pas-ko-fo-ge,	F
Pa hos fix-se-koh,	H		Pawn, Nero	D
Pa hos ha go,	B		Pe a net,	C
Pa hos ha goh,	H		Pe-me-mah-rah,	A
Pa hos ha jo,	F		Pea-neh,	C
Pa hos hin ne ha,	B,C		Peeryman, Gooner	E
Pa hose ha jo,	A		Pei har jo,	B
Pa hu hu goh,	A		Pen no ts eh,	G
Pa me ha goh,	A		Pen-ha-goh,	A
Pa nas ke,	CKF		Pen-ha-jo,	A
Pa nuk ko ge,	F		Pen-hats jo, 2,	E
Pa nuk-ke,	CKF		Pen-neh,	I
Pa os ha jo,	B		Perryman, Gooner	E
Pa os ha jo,	G		Perryman, Henry	I
Pa-as-ha-jo,	G		Perryman, Isaac	I
Pa-con-thla,	K		Perryman, Jacob	C
Pa-he-hag-goh,	A		Perryman, Jim	C
Pa-ho-se-mar-reh,	D		Perryman, John W.	I
Pa-hoce-fix-se-ko,	I		Perryman, Joseph K.	I
Pa-la-ge-ha-goh,	A		Perryman, Josiah	I
Pa-lee,	B		Perryman, Pompey	I
Pa-los-har-jo,	B		Perryman, S.W.	I
Pa-rosa-har-jo-chay,	C		Perryman, Thomas	I
Pacon-thla-na,	K		Perryman, 2, John	I
Paf na,	G		Pet ta ten,	H
Pah co ka na,	K		Pet-tah,	K
Pah ho-see, 1,	B		Petah, 1,	H
Pah ho-see, 2,	B		Petah, 2,	H
Pah-ha-gho-goh,	H		Peter,	B
Pah-la,	B		Peter, 1,	F
Pah-lee,	B		Peter, 2,	F

Pi gee,	B	Re ha se mat lee,	I
Pi ha jo,	B	Rec ca me ha cah,	D
Pi o ha jo,	B	Reed, Joseph	H
Pi sho le toh,	A	Ren mo geh,	H
Pi-coth-ley,	G	Res ba ne har ak koh,	H
Picath lez,	G	Res fa ne ha gohs,	H
Picket,	B	Res froh ka ha goh,	H
Pie ha jo,	B	Res so fix e ko,	I
Pihk Kost leh,	G	Ret tah,	H
Pin e mart len,	C	Rey op pe ma lee,	K
Pin ne mat la,	G	Rin har jo,	E
Pin no chee,	G	Ris fa ne ha go,	H
Pin wa,	B	Ris fa ne ha joh,	H
Pine mart lar,	C	Ro no ja ho la,	I
Pirser,	K	Robinson, Johnson	D
Piss-ser,	K	Robison, Johnson	D
Po con thla,	K	Roe ma per,	K
Po con thle na,	K	Rok kas ha jo,	G
Po ha se ma lotsu,	F	Rok kas k ke ma ra,	G
Po has se mar rah,	D	Rok p pa lle ech,	G
Po no che,	D	Roland, Goliah	K
Po nos Ka,	CKF	Rul met tah,	I
Po nuk Ko ge,	F	Rut tuk e v veh,	K
Porter, Peter	K	S-ya-tlah,	G
Pos moo ver,	K	Sa tah pe mo koh,	H
Pos-mav-ver,	K	Sa wan nah kep,	D
Pot gat se mar lah,	H	Sa-le-chee,	B
Pous ha jo,	G	Sa-lo-hi-ke,	F
Prince,	K	Sa-read-n-noh-ha-jo,	G
Pum ffi Koh,	A	Sa-yot-ton-neh,	K
Pum ffix e Koh,	A	Saf-fer-neh,	K
Pun ffe res se Koh,	A	Saffo-lis-chu,	B
Pus hin ne ha,	B,C	Sah ko te na,	K
Pus se Kah,	F	Sah no che,	F
Que Kos fix e Ko,	C	Sah qua na,	K
Que Kos hin e ha,	C	Sah yah hi kee,	B
Que us fix e Ko,	C	Sak ko ta,	K
Que-has-hin-e-ha,	C	Sak koe mer,	K
Ra ba ya ho loh,	A	Sak of fer ver,	K
Ra gi ya hol lah,	H	Sak-co-foh-na,	K
Ra no her cah,	D	Sak-quan-na,	K
Rar no ha coh,	D	Sal-le-chee,	B

Sal-ya-ho-ke,	B	Seds-sum-hah,	E
Sale-yah-hi-ker,	B	Seh-pah,	D
Sam,	E	Sek-ka-weh,	A
Sam Me, (1),	F	Sem meh,	H
Sam Me, (2),	F	Semah,	G
Sam Sen, 2,	H	Sha-qua-na,	K
Sam Sin,	H	Shan fah,	K
Sam meh,	G	Shar na kee,	K
Sam meh,	H	Shawnee,	A
Sam meh,	I	Shuk-chel-ho-e,	H
Sam-in-mak-ha-jo,	G	Siets-sum-koh,	E
Sam-ke,	K	Silas,	D
Sam-mi-yeh,	H	Sim ma he,	F
Sam-nekah,	H	Sim me hark te,	K
Samokee, Isaac	I	Sim-ah-la-che,	G
Sampson,	D	Sim-gin-ge,	I
Sampson,	F	Sim-i-na-chee,	B
Sampson, 1,	A	Sim-seh,	I
Sampson, 2,	A	Sin cla pe,	E
Samuel, Brinton	C	Sin li te ke,	F
San ne kah,	H	Sin-neh,	H
San-tan-nah,	H	Sis seh,	D
Sap-hi-ki,	A	Sizemon, David	I
Sar whe ts geh,	I	Sla lo e ho la,	A
Sar-che-a-ho-la,	C	Slof ke,	G
Sar-lul-loh,	I	Smith, Caesar	D
Sark-harlotty,	E	Smith, Jeff	D
Sarmokkee, Isaac	I	So cat e man leh,	D
Sat Kah,	K	So fah la,	K
Scott, John	E	So fix se ko, 1,	F
Scott, Thomas	D	So fix se ko, 2,	F
Se burn,	D	So ha jo,	F
Se lih cha,	B	So ha jo chee, 2,	F
Se nup pe,	D	So ha yo chee,	F
Se teh he geh,	H	So hat jo,	F
Se-ha-lack-kots-se,	E	So hat zo,	F
Se-he-ha-go-gee,	I	So hat zo see, 1,	F
Se-hok-mok-ta-har-cho,	I	So kat-hat go,	F
		So kot se fix se ko,	E
Se-nets-gah-ya-hatz-goh,	E	So la fix se ko,	I
		So-ha-jo,	F
Se-pah,	I	So-ha-jo-ze,	F

So-hat-go-see,	F		Spawne,	K,C
So-ko-se loh get,	H		Spe ko ke e mar-thla,	H
So-ko-se-ya ho la,	E		Spon na,	K
So-let-kah,	A		Stake, David	H
So-me chee,	B		Stake, Jonas	H
So-me-chee,	B		Stake ya to chee,	H
So-mi chee,	B		Steadham, John	C
So-mi-chee,	B		Steadman, Hardy	G
So-mis-Chee,	B		Stedam, Hardy	G
So-mis-chee,	B		Steel, Louis	H
So-mix-see,	B		Steel,	E
So-pah-ne,	E		Step-ne,	E
So-philip ha jo,	F		Step-ush,	C
So-pho-ne,	E		Stephen,	E
So-poh-ne,	E		Stephen,	E
So-pok-at-ko,	E		Stephen,	E
So-te-chee,	B		Stephendy,	E
So-toh,	H		Stidam, Hardy	G
So-whe-ley,	E		Stik of fo nee,	I
So-ya-ho-la,	F		Stin-ha loc ta,	G
Soc-see,	B		Stuart,	F
Sof-fer-neh,	K		Stun hi e jut se,	C
Soffe na,	K		Su-see,	K
Sofo-le-chee,	B		Suc-ha-loc-ta,	E
Sol-lek-koh-het,	I		Suf-fer-neh,	K
Sol-sa ha jo,	B		Suf-fo-lis chee,	B
Sol-ya-che-ke,	B		Suf-fus-ser,	K
Solet-keh,	A		Sugar, Joseph	C
Son-me-yah,	H		Suh-tam-mek-	
Sop hi ki,	A		ko che,	E
Sop-see,	G		Suk op fev-ver,	K
Sore arl let cho,	E		Suk-kik-kok-her,	K
Sore art let cho,	E		Suk-ko-r reh,	K
Sot kes ha goh,	A		Suk-kov-ver,	K
Sou in noke ha jo,	G		Sul-le-la,	B
Spa hi ga,	D		Sul-lek-koh-het,	I
Span neah buck ko,	H		Sulivan, Samuel	C
Span-ne-ma-la,	E		Sullivan, Saml	C
Spar he che,	E		Sum-po,	C
Spar-ne-ha-jo, 1st,	C		Sumps-ke,	K
Spar-ne-har-jo,	C		Sun-O-Kee-chee,	I
Spar-ne-mar-lar,	C		Sun-nah-keigh-tae,	H

Sun-not-gots-geh,	I	Tah-ko-sa-ha-jo,	D
Sup-pits geh-geh,	I	Tah-pan-lo-we,	K
Sur-ruk-ka,	K	Tah-sa-we,	K
Sus-sot-hav-er,	K	Tah-sak-ta-na,	K
Sut-taps-he-o-veh,	K	Tah-see,	B
Sut-to,	K	Tah-sok-ta-na,	K
Ta-bee,	D	Tah-wa-thla-na,	K
Ta-bi-co-lis-chee,	C	Tah-ya-ta-na,	K
Ta-bic-se,	G	Tah-yah-ta-na,	K
Ta-co-hah,	K	Tahok-pohnechee,	E
Ta-fits-kah,	G	Tail-seh,	E
Ta-hos-ha-jo,	F	Tak-kas-sa-ha-coh,	D
Ta-ko-se-fix-se-ko,	F	Tak-ko-bi-he,	C
Ta-ko-so-fix-se-ko,	F	Tak-ko-k-keh,	K
Ta-ko-so-ha-jo,	D	Tak-ko-sa-ha-goh,	H
Ta-ko-twa,	K	Tak-ko-se-ha-goh,	H
Ta-lle-ma-ya-ho-la,	G	Tak-sok-ta-na,	K
Ta-lle-maga-ho-llak,	G	Tal-a-poo-sa,	C
Ta-ma-lan-ne,	D	Tal-buts-th-heh,	I
Ta-ma-lu-na,	D	Tal-e-mas-fix-eko,	C
Ta-ma-luc-na,	D	Tal-e-mas-ha-jo,	G
Ta-man-xeh,	D	Tal-e-mas-hin-ne-ha,	G
Ta-mar-xeh,	D	Tal-e-mat-ha-jo,	G
Ta-mas-sah,	D	Tal-ges-kam-me-koh,	H
Ta-mat-le-ya-hol-ler,	C	Tal-ges-kam-mek-ko,	H
Ta-me-ha-gah,	A	Tal-ges-kam-mek-koh,	H
Ta-me-la-ha-ho-la,	H	Tal-ges-som-ma-ko,	H
Ta-mo-koh,	A	Tal-ha-sa-ha-goh,	H
Ta-ne-har-rah-kah,	D	Tal-has-sa-ha-goh,	H
Ta-pau-lo-we,	K	Tal-has-se-ha-jo,	H
Ta-se-ha-ya-ha-jo,	H	Tal-k-kes-ha-jo,	G
Ta-se-ka-al-ha-goh,	H	Tal-leh-che,	I
Ta-se-ka-ya-ha-go,	H	Tal-ma-fix-se-co,	G
Ta-se-ka-ya-ha-goh,	H	Tal-mar-se-ne-ha,	H
Ta-tegth-che,	I	Tal-mar-seh,	H
Ta-yah-to-ma,	K	Tal-mar-sen,	H
Ta-yoh-ta-na,	K	Tal-mar-sin-ne-ha,	H
Tae-na-sha,	K	Tal-mas-fix-e-ko,	C
Taf-utch-ka,	G		
Tah-co-hah,	K		
Tah-co-on-na,	K		
Tah-con-thla,	K		

Tal-mas-he-ne-ha,	H	Te cumseh,	E
Tal-mo-tus-fix-e-ko,	I	Te se Ho gah,	A
Tal-ne-fix-se-ko,	G	Te wal tis chee,	E
Tal-ne-gas-mek-ko,	D	Te war lah,	E
Tal-no-tus-fix-se-ko,	I	Te was e mar ler,	C
Tal-se-ye-ya-ha-hah,	A	Te weh,	H
Tal-seh,	E	Te-al-pa-tah-ha-goh,	H
Tal-sey,	E	Te-al-par-ta-ha-goh,	H
Tal-sy-fix-se-ko,	C	Te-cum-seh,	A
Tal-we-ne-ha-xuk-kap,	D	Te-ha-lla-ttch,	A
		Te-la,	G
Talley,	C	Te-wah,	A
Tally,	C	Te-wee,	E
Tam-mah-te,	C	Tee me ha goh,	A
Tam-me-ga-che,	A	Tee-mor-neh,	D
Tam-me-ha-goh,	H	Tee-nee,	H
Tam-me-ha-goh, 2,	H	Tee-teghth-che,	I
Tam-me-ha-goh, 3,	H	Tee-wee,	H
Tam-me-ha-joh, 1,	H	Tee-wee,	I
Tam-me-ya-ho-lah,	H	Teen n seh,	A
Tam-me-ya-ho-loh,	H	Tef-fah, 2,	I
Tam-ss-ch,	A	Tef-feh, 2,	I
Tan-la-bus-teh,	A	Tef-fet,	I
Tan-mah-lee,	C	Teh ko seh,	K
Tan-me-ha-goh, 2,	H	Teh-pah,	D
Tan-ne-ha-goh,	H	Teh-so-ha-goh,	A
Tan-tah-la-co-ka-na,	K	Tek koh reh,	K
Tap-pets-ceh,	G	Tek kol mer ver,	K
Tap-pts-eeh,	G	Tek se ka goh,	H
Tar-bic-see,	G	Tek-hol-mer-ver,	K
Tar-see,	B	Tel-lah,	G
Tark-hoe-reh,	I	Tem mi ye,	I
Tas-co-nap,	D	Tem mo ye,	I
Tas-ha-jo,	F	Ten-ffo-llot Keh,	A
Tas-ke-hen-ne-hah,	D	Tep-pah,	D
Tas-ke-hen-ne-pah,	D	Tes-ke-hot-ka,	A
Tas-ko-nah,	D	Tet So ha go,	A
Tat-ko-bi-he,	C	Tew-ee,	I
Tawee,	I	Than bus har jo,	C
Taylor,	C	Thar bus har jo,	C
Te al pa ta ha goh,	H	Thars-ka-yar-Hollar,	C
Te cum seah,	A	Thlo-pa-lic-cha,	G

Thloe pa lic che,	G		To wee,	I
Thoc-ya-lic-cha,	G		To wul li ge,	C
Thoe ya lic chee,	G		To-bee,	G
Thomas, B.	B		To-bi-ah,	F
Thomas,	I		To-ffa-lla-fix-e-koh,	A
Thul-la-har-go,	C		To-ke-se-not-lo-tse,	K
Thus-i-hiar-ho-jo,	C		To-ko-put-seh,	I
Thus-i-ker-ha-ja,	C		To-ko-put-si,	I
Thus-ie-i-a-ha-la,	C		To-ko-put-tsi,	I
Thusic i a hajo,	C		To-mar-reh,	D
Ti-bi-ya,	F		To-se-ah ho la,	F
Tick ta net tse,	A		To-see,	G
Tick-la-nut-tse,	A		To-shut-gor-suk-hoh,	I
Tick-ta-mit-see,	A		To-was-e-mar-lar,	C
Tie-dar-kee,	I		To-wul-li je,	C
Tie-dar-tee,	I		To-wul-li-ge,	C
Tif-fit,	H		Tobe,	K
Tiger,	K		Toc co longe,	B
Tim y,	K		Toe-O-lor-tee,	I
Tim-is-che-chee,	C		Toe-o-lar-tee,	I
Tim-mah-te,	C		Toh-sak-ta-na,	K
Tim-me,	F		Toh-wa-thla-na,	K
Tim-my,	F		Tok kas se hu cah,	D
Tim-nie-ma-to-chee,	G		Tok ker-vev-ver,	K
Tin-me-chit-chee,	C		Tok-kes-ha-gah, 2,	A
Tis ik ur har jo,	C		Tok-kes-ha-goh, 1,	A
Tiur-me-e-chit-chee,	C		Tok-kor-vev-ver,	K
To be,	C		Tol a pa sa,	C
To be ya,	F		Tol se ya ya ho keh,	A
To bi co lis chee,	C		Tol-but-th heh,	I
To che ba ka,	F		Tol-mo-tus-fix-se-ko,	I
To che ba kah,	F		Tol-no-tus-fix-se-ko,	I
To he e mun nets cha,	D		Tol-wah-fix-se-ko,	K
			Toll-mar-fix-e-co,	C
To hi e man nets cho,	D		Tolly,	C
To ke se not lo che,	K		Tom,	B
To ko se fix se ko,	F		Tom,	I
To la,	G		Tom gup to,	F
To neh,	H		Tom ma ha jo,	H
To nul li gi,	C		Tom ma ha jo, 2,	H
To ulli gi,	C		Tom me,	B
			Tom me ha goh, 2,	H

Tom-e-ya-ho-loh,	E		Tu ket tus vok	
Tom-ma-ha-jo,	C,E		gup kot,	K
Tom-ma-ha-joh, 1,	H		Tuc O lor tec,	I
Tom-ma-ya-hol-loh,	H		Tuck a longa,	B
Tom-me-ha-goh, 1,	H		Tucker,	I
Tom-me-ya-ha-loh,	H		Tuco longe,	B
Tom-me-ya-hol-la,	H		Tuk hoe reh,	I
Tom-me-ya-hol-loh,	H		Tuk hor reh,	I
Tom-me-yah-hol-lah,	H		Tuk hut mer,	K
Tom-meh,	I		Tuk ko er er,	K
Tom-my,	C		Tuk ko ev er,	K
Tom-se-kok,	H		Tuk ko k ket,	K
Tomy,	I		Tuk ko rah,	K
Ton neh,	H		Tuk kor sev ver,	K
Ton tah la ko ka,	K		Tuk kot ter veh,	K
Ton tal la Co ka na,	K		Tuk kot ter ver,	K
Ton tel la ko kan na,	K		Tuk kut mar,	K
Ton tella co qua-na,	K		Tuk s se hut goh,	I
Ton tolla con na,	K		Tul ke ya ha lloh,	A
Ton-ney,	B		Tul m seh,	I
Toney-tephsey,	E		Tul mo seh,	I
Tonny,	I		Tul ne gus mik ko,	D
Tony,	I		Tul no tus fix se ko,	I
Tora tal la co quana,	K		Tul s se hut goh,	I
Tos-ke-ne ho-chee,	I		Tul se ha jo,	B
Tos-see,	G		Tul se ye ya ha loh,	A
Tot co hi he,	C		Tul sy ya ho la,	I
Tot kes ha ge,	A		Tul wa fix e ko,	K
Tot ks ha goh,	A		Tul wa fix i ko,	K
Tot la ha goh,	A		Tul wa fix se ko,	K
Tot-her-ars-se,	C		Tul we fix e ko,	K
Tot-ka-ha se,	F		Tul wu ne ruk ko,	D
Tox-sa-ge-ho-la,	H		Tully,	C
Troy,	D		Tulmusseh,	I
Trusty, John	C		Tulse fix e co, 2,	C
Tu ha e man tlo che,	D		Tulsy har cho,	I
Tu hut koh,	K		Tulsy hor cho,	I
Tu hut kot,	K		Tulsy ya ha la,	I
Tu ket tus tav			Tum marl gar hellar,	C
voh he,	K		Tum me ma lo chee,	G
Tu ket tus tov			Tum mi s seh,	I
vok koh,	K		Tum ne mat lo chee,	G

Tun ne ma to che,	G	Uc fus Kee,	F,K
Tun ne mar to che,	G	Up pen ne,	G
Tun ne mat to chee,	G	Up pi uk ke,	B
Tup pat loe mer,	K	Wa ta geh,	H
Tup put loe mer,	K	Wa-gin-nah,	K,C
Tur coon ner,	E	Wa-k-se-ho-la-toh,	A
Tus coon ner,	E	Wa-le-ah,	K,F
Tus ge ga har jo,	B	Wa-nee,	A
Tus ha jo,	F	Wa-nett-kee,	G
Tus he ne ho chee,	I	Wa-seu-tah,	H
Tus ic i a ha jo,	B	Wa-tel-lah,	H
Tus ic i a ho ler,	C	Wah-ne,	E
Tus ka a ha goh,	B	Wah-tel-lah,	H
Tus ke ha jo,	A	Wak-se-ho-la-to-ch,	A
Tus ke ne ho chee,	I	Wak-se-mie-co-chi,	I
Tus ke ya ha jo,	B	Wak-se-no-la-teh,	A
Tus ke yar ho jo,	B	Wak-so-chee,	I
Tus par ver,	K	Walker, John	I
Tus per ver,	K	Walker, William	I
Tus se ka ya,	F	Wan-ut-key-chop-ho,	E
Tus se ka ya ha jo,	F	Warford, William	F
Tus se ka ya ho jo,	F	Wark-se-har-jo,	E
Tus se ki ya,	F	Warrior,	E
Tus se ki ya ha jo,	F	Wart-ta-War-ha-jo,	E
Tus see meh,	K	Was-ser-tah,	I
Tus ta nuc ha jo,	F	Washington,	I
Tus ta nuk ha jo,	F	Wat-Ka-ya-ho-la,	G
Tus ta vak gup koh,	K	Wat-Ke ah ho-la,	K,F
Tus te nuk ho gee,	B	Wat-Ke-ah-ho-tah,	K
Tus to nuk ke mort tro che,	B	Wat-Ke-fix-se-Ko,	K
Tus tuo vak gup hoh,	K	Wat-Ke-goh,	A
		Wat-Ko-fix-se-Ko,	C
Tus tuo vak gup kot,	K	Wat-Koo,	C
		Wat-see,	G
Tusic ia hajo,	C	Wat-so-fix-e-Ko,	G
Tusko nah,	D	Watley, James	E
Tut hut mar,	K	Watley, James	H
Twa ran ver,	K	Watly,	
Twa san ver,	K	Watly,	I
Twa ser ver,	K	Watson, Daley	D
Ty yee,	E	Watson, Josiah	D
		Wau-K-Ko-ge-goh,	A

Wau-Kee,	G	Wo ke se ho la teh,	A
Wax-se-ha-go,	I	Wo-t-Ke-Koh,	A
Wax-se-ha-jo,	F	Wock-se-ha-jo,	B
Wax-se-ha-jo-che,	F	Woh-let-loh,	H
Wax-se-har-jo-mi-jara,	B	Wok-se-he-la-to-geh,	A
		Wok-so-ho-la-teh,	A
Wax-se-ho-le-te-goh,	A	Wolf, Simon	D
		Won-Ka,	G
Wax-see-ha-go-gee,	B	Woolf,	F
Wax-see-ha-jo,	B	Wot ke ah ho la,	K,F
Wax-so-ha-jo,	F	Wot-K-Ko-ya-ho-la,	G
Waxe-ha-go,	E	Wot-Ka,	C
Way-se-ha-go-chee,	B	Wot-Ke-ap-ho-la,	K
We le ah,	K,F	Wot-ka-fix-e-ko,	C
We wa ki e ho lah,	G	Wot-ka-ho-jo,	C
We-con-nis-que-en-chao-ar,	C	Wox-fa-ya-tu-ta-mick-ke,	B
Wesley, John	D	Ya cho lie cha,	G
Wesley,	D	Ya fix se ko,	F
West, Charley	D	Ya fix so ko,	F
Westley,	B	Ya ha e mar rah,	A
What-sear-te-fix-se-ko,	E	Ya ha e mas set ceh,	D
		Ya ha eek mar rah,	A
What-teh,	I	Ya ha ha cah,	G
Whet-yot-hoe,	K	Ya ha ha ceh,	G
White, John	I	Ya ha ha jo,	B
Wic us fix se ko,	C	Ya ha ha jo,	G
Wick ko nup pah,	G	Ya ha la ha gah,	A
Wild Cat,	E	Ya ha lah,	H
Wild Cat,	K	Ya ha tas tan mik,	A
Wiley,	F	Ya ha tas tan nee keh,	A
Wiley,	K		
Willey,	A	Ya ha tos to nuc keh,	A
Willey,	G		
Willey,	I	Ya ha tus tee mic keh,	A
William,	B		
William,	K,F	Ya ha yup ko,	G
William,	E	Ya hats jol,	E
Willis,	D	Ya he e man nets cho,	D
Willis,	E		
Willy,	B	Ya he la ha goh,	A
Wilsey,	A	Ya hi e mal lah,	A

Ya hi ga,	G	Ya tus ta mic keh,	A
Ya hi gee,	G	Ya-eat,	H
Ya hi k keh,	G	Ya-fala-fix se ko,	D
Ya ho chee,	F	Ya-hartz-jo,	E
Ya ho chu,	F	Ya-hats-joh,	E
Ya ho hee,	CFK	Ya-her,	K
Ya ho ker,	K	Ya-hol-lah-gap-yoh,	H
Ya ho la ha goh,	A	Ya-k-kap-po-keh,	G
Ya ho lah,	H	Ya-la-kan,	K
Ya hol la gap koh,	H	Ya-tte-ke-ka-ha-goh,	A
Ya hol la ha joh,	H	Ya-tte-ko-ha-goh,	A
Ya hol lah,	H	Yach neh,	H
Ya hol tah,	H	Yachey,	A
Ya hol tah ha go,	H	Yadger, John	C
Ya hol zee,	F	Yah ha fix e ko,	C
Ya hots goh,	D	Yah hol lah,	H
Ya ka fix se ko,		Yah hol lah,	H
Ya ka lic che,	G	Yah hol lah gap koh,	H
Ya ka zup ka,	G	Yah hol lah ha goh,	H
Ya ker,	K	Yah keh ka,	E
Ya ko se fix se ko,	D	Yah lah kan,	K
Ya ko zup ko,	G	Yah po soc so,	F
Ya koh,	K	Yah ta wa ha goh,	H
Ya kot,	K	Yah ta war har jo,	E
Ya la co qua na,	K	Yah tah ya hol lah,	H
Ya no Uu ha gon,	A	Yah tee chee,	H
Ya no ken,	A	Yah-hah,	K
Ya pe zuc zo,	F	Yah-la-coquan-na,	K
Ya pe zup zo,	F	Yak har fix e ko,	C
Ya se cah ha jo,	A	Yak ker,	K
Ya ta ma ha go,	I	Yal lek ko ver,	K
Ya ta ma ha jo,	I	Yal lek kon,	K
Ya ta na ha goh,	H	Yal luk koe,	K
Ya ta tas ta me keh,	A	Yal luk koh,	K
Ya ta y ha jo,	D	Yal ta ya hot lah,	H
Ya ta ya ho Jo,	F	Yal-leh,	H
Ya to lit to be,	G	Yal-luk koe he,	K
Ya to ma ha jo,	I	Yan la bas lef,	A
Ya toe ke ka ha goh,	A	Yan meh yoch neh,	H
		Yan-meh,	H
Ya tuk ho koe mer ner,	K	Yan-neh,	H
		Yap-po-soc-so,	F

Yar dicher har jo,	E	Yo far le martla,	I
Yar ho lar,	E	Yo ffa lla fix e koh,	A
Yart to war har jo,	E	Yo ko lit to be,	G
Yat tae mar goh,	I	Yock neh,	H
Yat toe mar goh,	I	Yof-kee,	E
Yat-tee,	G	Yoh la co quan na,	K
Ye at,	H	Yok ko yop pa,	G
Ye-ko-lit-te-be,	G	Yon gup to,	F
Yec chee,	E	Yot tol mar goh,	I
Yef kee,	E	Yu hi e ma rah,	A
Yis ta gum ah,	E	Yut tee,	G
Yo fa le mar tha,	I	Yut tuk ko	
Yo fa le mar tla,	I	ko mer ner,	K
Yo fa le mot ba,	I		

2nd Regiment, Indian Home Guards, Kansas Infantry

The 2nd Regiment, Indian Home Guards was organized on Big Creek and at Five-Mile Creek, Kansas, June 22 to July 18, 1862, and attached to the 1st Brigade, Dept. of Kansas to August, 1862. This unit consisted of Cherokee, Osage, Delaware, Quapaw and Shawnee that had gone north with O-Pothle-Yahola.

Name	Company	Rank
Corwin, David B.	F&S	Lieutenant Colonel
Schaurte, Fred W.	F&S	Lieutenant Colonel
Wright, Moses B.C.	F&S	Major
Dole, George	F&S	First Lieutenant/Adjutant
Robinson, Ezra W.	F&S	First Lieutenant/Adjutant
Howard, Charles A.	F&S	Sergeant Major
Huey, Samuel E.	F&S	Quartermaster Sergeant
Bowers, Lewis	F&S	Sergeant
Baldridge, Edward	F&S	Corporal
Ritchie, Andrew J.	F&S	Surgeon
Campdoras, M.A.	F&S	Assistant Surgeon
Campdoris, Marie Antonin	F&S	Assistant Surgeon
Hitchcock, D.D.	F&S	Assistant Surgeon
Crane, Frank L.	F&S	Hospital Steward
Kenney, Charles	F&S	Hospital Steward
Jones, John B.	F&S	Chaplain
Ritchie, John		Colonel
Ah lee cher,	F	Captain
Belne, John	G	Captain
Besaillion, Joe	C	Captain
Bruce, J.H.	C	Captain
Chetopa,	E	Captain
Cochran, John	B	Captain
Dirt Throw Tiger,	H,I	Captain
Fall, Leaf	D	Captain
Gritts, Budd	G	Captain
Jim, Ned	C	Captain
Lombard, Robert P.	B	Captain
McDaniel, James	A	Captain
Moody, Joel	I	Captain
Price, Moses	D,B	Captain

Prior, William	F	Captain
Pryor, William	F	Captain
Rogers, Jackson	C	Captain
Scraper, Archibald	D	Captain
Scraper, George	I,H	Captain
Spring Frog,	K	Captain
Stand, Whirlwind	I,H	Captain
Tadpole, Eli	C	Captain
Whirlwind, Stand	I,H	Captain
Cox, John T.	A	First Lieutenant
Gillpaterick, E.P.	G	First Lieutenant
Gillpatric, E.P.	G	First Lieutenant
Gillpatrick, E.P.	G	First Lieutenant
Gilpatrick, Ernestus P.	G	First Lieutenant
Hunter, John Na	B	First Lieutenant
Hunter, Silas	H,I	First Lieutenant
Kendall, William H.	E	First Lieutenant
Lenhart, Charles	B	First Lieutenant
McClain, Theophilus	A	First Lieutenant
McHenry, James	B	First Lieutenant
McLain, Theophilus	A	First Lieutenant
Metchoshiuka,	E	First Lieutenant
Mithoshinka,	E	First Lieutenant
Moffitt, John	F	First Lieutenant
Moses, John	D	First Lieutenant
O'Connor, Timothy	C	First Lieutenant
Painter, David A.	K	First Lieutenant
Palmer, John C.	D	First Lieutenant
Scott, John S.	E	First Lieutenant
Stop, Watt	A	First Lieutenant
Wa ne saw ke,	F	First Lieutenant
Waterhouse, Andrew J.	H	First Lieutenant
Huston, George W.		First Lieutenant/ Regimental Quartermaster
Chewick, Joseph	D	Second Lieutenant
Chuwee, Joseph	D	Second Lieutenant
Comin Ole me,	D	Second Lieutenant
Chuwik, Joseph	D	Second Lieutenant
Downing, Samuel H.	G	Second Lieutenant
Hawk, Alexander	K,B	Second Lieutenant
Henry, Jesse	H,I	Second Lieutenant

Name	Company	Rank
Jacob,	F	Second Lieutenant
Lewis, John	B	Second Lieutenant
McCoy,	A	Second Lieutenant
Ole-me-Comin,	D	Second Lieutenant
Rabbitt, Andrew	F	Second Lieutenant
Rice, Luther	I,H	Second Lieutenant
Scraper, William	G,A	Second Lieutenant
Spears, Eli	C	Second Lieutenant
Tyger, Wheeler	B	Second Lieutenant
Wa row nin ka,	G	Second Lieutenant
Wa-taw-Nin-Ka,	G	Second Lieutenant
Wickliff, Charles	K	Second Lieutenant
Wickliffe, Charles	K	Second Lieutenant
Wood, Alvin	E	Lieutenant
Armstrong, Samuel D.	G	First Sergeant
Brittain, John W.	B	First Sergeant
Britton, John W.	B	First Sergeant
California, Wm. Mills	A	First Sergeant
Chauteau, Peter	E	First Sergeant
Choteau, Peter	E	First Sergeant
Cochran, Jesse	B	First Sergeant
Crittenten, Samuel	C	First Sergeant
Daniel, Will	B	First Sergeant
De ne no le,	K	First Sergeant
Der ne no le,	K	First Sergeant
Der ne no leque che,	K	First Sergeant
Downing, Robert	H	First Sergeant
Hicks, Daniel R.	E	First Sergeant
Jackson, General	D	First Sergeant
McCoy, Thomas	C	First Sergeant
Mills, William	A	First Sergeant
Ross, Robert	E	First Sergeant
Rusel, Wat	H,I	First Sergeant
Russel, Watt	H,I	First Sergeant
Scraper, George W.	D	First Sergeant
Springston, Isaac	H	First Sergeant
Sundow,	F	First Sergeant
Wa-caw-wa-rhe,	G	First Lieutenant
White-Water,	G	First Sergeant
Yok ah de ah ho la,	G	First Sergeant
Ga nee ge,	H,I	Second Sergeant
Watts, Peach	C	Second Sergeant

Ar tar nee sar le ge ge,	H,I	Third Sergeant
Delaware six killer,	D	Third Sergeant
John, Little	C	Third Sergeant
Sau-ne-coo-ya,	B	Third Sergeant
Schneider, Listen	E	Third Sergeant
Schnider, Listen	E	Third Sergeant
Starr, Deerwater	G	Third Sergeant
Arche Sar le yo go,	H,I	Fourth Sergeant
Brown, Dick	D	Fourth Sergeant
Scraper, Henry H.	D	Fourth Sergeant
Boggs, Richard	G	Fifth Sergeant
Jones,	D	Fifth Sergeant
Adain, Ross	E	Sergeant
Adair, Ross	E	Sergeant
Ahda taske lah lahghe,	I,H	Sergeant
Baldridge, David	D	Sergeant
Bigmouth, Littlehair	C	Sergeant
Blackfox, Ezekiel	I	Sergeant
Bolin, James	F	Sergeant
Bottome, Polet	B	Sergeant
Carter, Asa	H	Sergeant
Chasteen, L.M.	E	Sergeant
Chastine, L.M.	E	Sergeant
Che Co hee,	C	Sergeant
Chee Co hee,	C	Sergeant
Christa, Wat	K	Sergeant
Christie, Watt	K	Sergeant
Christy, Jack	B	Sergeant
Christy, Watt	K	Sergeant
Chu-he-tla (Iowa),	B	Sergeant
Cochran, Will	I	Sergeant
Cristy, Watt	K	Sergeant
Daugherty, David	G	Sergeant
Do de cah ne Ka ah dah he,	I,H	Sergeant
Doo le ste,	I,H	Sergeant
Duck, Watt	A	Sergeant
Enoleg,	C	Sergeant
Fleetwood, Charles	H	Sergeant
Ga-nu-ge,	I	Sergeant
Ganuga,	I	Sergeant
Golargar,	F	Sergeant
Hammer, John	A	Sergeant

Name	Company	Rank
Hare, Elk	D	Sergeant
Hicks, John	E	Sergeant
Holt, Soldier	A,F	Sergeant
Ja-gee-se-me-salah-gee-squa,	I,H	Sergeant
Jack, Red Bird	D	Sergeant
Jackel, Yellow	C	Sergeant
Jug, White Path	A	Sergeant
Ka-sa-ka-re,	E	Sergeant
Ke-co-pe-she,	G	Sergeant
Ke-ke-or-po-she,	G	Sergeant
Lacy,	D	Sergeant
Lasley, George	F	Sergeant
Little Hair Big Mouth,	C	Sergeant
Loocking, James	H	Sergeant
Looking, James	H	Sergeant
Lovett, George	F	Sergeant
Lovitt, George	F	Sergeant
Ma ska gla sa,	B	Sergeant
McNair, Louis	A	Sergeant
Me Ros pe da,	B	Sergeant
Me-cos-pe-da,	B	Sergeant
Merrell, William	E	Sergeant
Merrill, William	E	Sergeant
Miller, Willson	C	Sergeant
Mills, James	A	Sergeant
Mouse, Adam	K	Sergeant
Muskrat, James	H	Sergeant
Nata ton ga wa ku,	E	Sergeant
Naw caw to ho,	F	Sergeant
Ne cha o le biah,	F	Sergeant
O Sah, Josiah	K	Sergeant
O Sar, Josiah	K	Sergeant
O Yu Sar Dar,	K	Sergeant
Ohlaner,	F	Sergeant
Ohlanew,	F	Sergeant
Oo you sut tah,	K	Sergeant
Oohlanee,	F	Sergeant
Oohlarnee,	F	Sergeant
Oolane,	F	Sergeant
Orh larnee,	F	Sergeant
Packingham,	C	Sergeant

Parkingham,	C	Sergeant
Peacheater, Stephen	G	Sergeant
Peachwater, Stephen	G	Sergeant
Po-haw-nan-she,	F	Sergeant
Proctor, Adam	I	Sergeant
Proctor, Arch	I	Sergeant
Red Bird,	F	Sergeant
Robin, Johnson	G	Sergeant
Robbins, Johnson	G	Sergeant
Rodger, F.A. Henry	C	Sergeant
Rogers, Henry F.A.	C	Sergeant
Russell, Adam	H	Sergeant
Scraper, Lewis	I,H	Sergeant
Se qua ya,	K	Sergeant
Se-ge-le,	H	Sergeant
Skou-na-ta-he,	B	Sergeant
Skskenney,	F	Sergeant
Sundown,	F	Sergeant
Te ca na cha ske,	B	Sergeant
Thornton, Lewis	E	Sergeant
Ti lar gah, Clark	F	Sergeant
Toney, George	C	Sergeant
Tucker, William	B	Sergeant
Twist, Beaver	G	Sergeant
Wa sha pa wa ta inka,	E	Sergeant
Wah Yah Ne De,	K	Sergeant
Watts, Jolly	C	Sergeant
Waw-shaw-ocaw-shaw,	G	Sergeant
West, James	E	Sergeant
Wickliff, John	K	Sergeant
Wickliffe, John	K	Sergeant
Wo ya ne da,	K	Sergeant
Wo yah ne De,	K	Sergeant
Wo yah ne dah,	K	Sergeant
Wo-yer-ne-der,	K	Sergeant
Wo-yoh-ne-da,	K	Sergeant
Wofford, J.D.	B	Sergeant
Young, William	G	Sergeant
Chu wa no ski,	G	First Corporal
Elic, E	H,I	First Corporal
Jackson, Jack	H	First Corporal
Adair, Benjamin	E	Second Corporal

Jack, Moses	G	Second Corporal
Metan ne tu cah,	F	Second Corporal
O tah da ge ske,	H,I	Second Corporal
Wicked, Ned	C	Second Corporal
Wickeds, Ned	C	Second Corporal
Wicket, Ned	C	Second Corporal
Bear Paw,	D	Third Corporal
Christy, Walter	G	Third Corporal
Iseral, David	D	Third Corporal
Israel, David	D	Third Corporal
Isreal, David	D	Third Corporal
McCoy,	C	Third Corporal
Odar ne yer der,	I,H	Third Corporal
Me lo tah me ne,	F	Fourth Corporal
Oo gar si no ti, William	G	Fifth Corporal
Walker, Edward	D	Fifth Corporal
Good, Money	G	Sixth Corporal
Stand ar ga lo gar,	I,H	Sixth Corporal
Whailer,	D	Sixth Corporal
Whaler,	D	Sixth Corporal
Allen de see ne ...,	H,I	Seventh Corporal
Albones, Edward	H	Corporal
Aneke, Joseph	I	Corporal
Ar Dar Chu Le,	K	Corporal
Ar da chu le,	K	Corporal
Ar du chula,	K	Corporal
Arda Chertle,	K	Corporal
Arder Chu Cle,	K	Corporal
Ardse Chule,	K	Corporal
As i ki,	B	Corporal
Augur, Wat	F	Corporal
Bark, Prince	C	Corporal
Beamer, George	I	Corporal
Beamer, Sam	H	Corporal
Beemer, Sam	H	Corporal
Bigmoney, William	H	Corporal
Bird Chopper,	G	Corporal
Buck,	A	Corporal
Bullfrog, Isaac	I	Corporal
Cah meh chee,	F	Corporal
Cah nu chee,	F	Corporal
Catcher, Colahtse	I	Corporal

Catcher, Man Killer	C	Corporal
Catcher, Moses	C	Corporal
Cha na nu ski,	G	Corporal
Chu-wa-ya-ga-le,	B	Corporal
Chu-wer-yu-ga-tle,	B	Corporal
Chu-wo-ya-ga-le,	B	Corporal
Chu-wo-ya-ga-te,	B	Corporal
Chu-wo-yah-ga-tle,	B	Corporal
Chu-wor-ya-ga-te,	B	Corporal
Chu-wor-ya-ga-tle,	B	Corporal
Chu-wow-yah-a-tle,	B	Corporal
Cohone, George	C	Corporal
Coldwater, Jack	D	Corporal
Coldweather, Jack	D	Corporal
Coldwether, Jack	D	Corporal
Colster, Bat	I	Corporal
Cuming,	C	Corporal
Cutter Head,	G	Corporal
Da gah gee de squa de ski,	I,H	Corporal
Da me (O. ste),	B	Corporal
Da ne le wah yah,	B	Corporal
Da we (oo s te ka),	B	Corporal
Dah ge nah ya,	H	Corporal
Dah ge ye yoh yah,	H	Corporal
Dah gee yah noh yah,	H	Corporal
Dah ye yah hoh yah,	I,H	Corporal
Dane le ga loo ya,	B	Corporal
Daniel, Ross	G	Corporal
Davis, John	K	Corporal
Deer in the Water,	D	Corporal
Der ner E,	K	Corporal
Diamond, Jacob	A	Corporal
Dick, Isaac	K	Corporal
Dlar mo har,	H,I	Corporal
Dlo yar gar,	H,I	Corporal
Do yee ne see,	K	Corporal
Do you ne see,	K	Corporal
Downing, Hyden	D	Corporal
Downing, Moses	A	Corporal
Downing, Walter	B	Corporal
Feeling, Walt	K	Corporal
Felen, Walt	K	Corporal

Feneer, Richard	H	Corporal
Fields, Johnson	H	Corporal
Fields, Thomas	A	Corporal
Get up,	D	Corporal
Girl Catcher, James	B	Corporal
Girlkatcher, James	B	Corporal
Glory, Mose	A	Corporal
Gourd, Walter	G	Corporal
Harrey,	F	Corporal
Harry, John	K	Corporal
Harry, John ter we	K	Corporal
Harry,	F	Corporal
Haw-ka-wa-la,	F	Corporal
He wa ha cah,	F	Corporal
He-chaw-Kaw-he,	G	Corporal
Heavy,	H	Corporal
Hendrix, David	E	Corporal
Hu law-wa-shin-Ka,	G	Corporal
Hu-chaw-Kaw-he,	G	Corporal
Hyder, Daniel	C	Corporal
Ja-Je-oo-Ke-soo-gee-ske,	I,H	Corporal
Ja-ne-se-ga-lo-noo-hes-Ke,	B	Corporal
Jim, Bob	C	Corporal
John, Raincrow	D	Corporal
Ju-ne-ha-gu-klaw-kace,	I,H	Corporal
Keener, Joseph	C	Corporal
Keener, Ned	I	Corporal
Kenee, Ned	I	Corporal
Kenner, Ned	I	Corporal
Kickapoo, Billy	D	Corporal
Kickapoo, Parks	D	Corporal
Lands, James	C	Corporal
Long Horn,	C	Corporal
Love, Alexander	I	Corporal
Love, George	E	Corporal
Meke, Joseph A.	I	Corporal
Mixed, Water	H	Corporal
Movingstar, George	H	Corporal
Movingstars, George	H	Corporal
Muskrat, Jackson	H	Corporal
Muskrat, Johnson	H,I	Corporal
Musrat, Johnson	H,I	Corporal

Name	Company	Rank
Ne Ga Wee,	K	Corporal
Ne ke de Su co ske,	I,H	Corporal
Ned, Wicked	C	Corporal
Nom pa pe,	E	Corporal
Nom pa wa re,	E	Corporal
Nov ts a wi,	D	Corporal
Nov-ta-ha-wi,	D	Corporal
OKi stau tsha wrigh ta,	B	Corporal
Oldfield, Dick	I	Corporal
Ole sha ma he,	E	Corporal
Oler no te ske,	K	Corporal
Onno da nah, Jack	K	Corporal
Oo gee jah tah gee nah de de,	G,H	Corporal
Oo li stoo,	G	Corporal
Oo saw we,	B	Corporal
Oo-na-gur-sur,	G	Corporal
Oolstoo,	G	Corporal
Paine, Thomas	E	Corporal
Parchmeal, William	C	Corporal
Payne, Thomas	E	Corporal
Peacheater, John	F	Corporal
Pearchmeal, William	C	Corporal
Potatoes, Thomas	A	Corporal
Potatoes, William	A	Corporal
Prince, Bark	C	Corporal
Qua-qua Ja-se,	I,H	Corporal
Rabbitt, James	F	Corporal
Red Bird,	I	Corporal
Rider, Wilson	D	Corporal
Rodgers, Charles	G	Corporal
Rogers, Charles	G	Corporal
Rooster, Thomas	F	Corporal
Runion, Joseph	E	Corporal
Scott, Eli	D	Corporal
Scraper, David	I,H	Corporal
Scraper, Nicholas	H	Corporal
Sixkiller, Peacheater	D	Corporal
Soo wa kee,	D	Corporal
Sparks, Jacob	D	Corporal
Spoon, Lewis	F	Corporal
Squah Da Leche,	K	Corporal

Squah De Leche,	K	Corporal
Stay at Home,	D	Corporal
Still, Jack	I	Corporal
Su wa he,	D	Corporal
Su wa hi,	D	Corporal
Sweet Killer, Alek	F	Corporal
Ta noo we,	B	Corporal
Tallow, James	A	Corporal
Tallowe, James	A	Corporal
Tanner, Aaron	I	Corporal
Tarpenhead, Jack	F	Corporal
Tarpin head, Jack	F	Corporal
Tarpon head,	F	Corporal
Terpin head,	F	Corporal
Thirsty Tiger,	I	Corporal
Thompson, Jack	A	Corporal
Thompson na,	B	Corporal
Tollow, James	A	Corporal
Tucker, Daniel	B	Corporal
Tucker, Samuel	C	Corporal
Tuff,	C	Corporal
Wa ke wa shee,	E	Corporal
Wa pe son sa,	E	Corporal
Wa sha pa sha,	E	Corporal
Wa-chu-shin-ka,	E	Corporal
We le ah da la qua,	I,H	Corporal
Wolf, Young P.	H	Corporal
Wolf pea, Young	H	Corporal
Wolfe, P. Young	H	Corporal
Writer,	F	Corporal
Ce ghe le se gah we,	I,H	Teamster
Keyes, George	K	Teamster
Keys, George	K	Teamster
Ar le te ske,	H,I	Musician
Ar tar wee de nar la nester,	H,I	Musician
E goo we wah yah,	I,H	Musician
La ce Sa le ce,	I,H	Musician
Lace ha le ce,	I,H	Musician

Privates

A Kikto,	C	Ah ya ah ta ke,	B
A Se ge,	H,I	Ah ye yhe Gah h	
A ka ka,	C	noo le ske,	I,H
A to la he (Big),	B	Ah yeyhe Gah	
A to la he (Little),	B	noo leske,	I,H
A to la he (oo ste),	B	Ahchilla,	F
Aaron Sker lor lee,	A	Ahdah lia loo ski,	D
Accident,	H	Ahdah we ah dah,	I,H
Adair, Poker	G	Ahdahgohagee	
Adam,	F	vo gahlak,	I,H
Adohequalungsah		Ahe le ste,	G
yohhoh,	I,H	Ahgeyahghede eah	
Ah Kotha,	D	do yah ske,	I,H
Ah We,	D	Ahgua tai Ki, John	G
Ah cum no was,	D	Ahnahsoo ye os	
Ah h sti,	G	stah le,	I,H
Ah he sah dah she		Ahnedungos ne	
tor wa gee,	I,H	loh woh	I,H
Ah his tu chee,	F	Ahnucher,	F
Ah ka she nin kah,	F	Ale tah,	C
Ah le jah Degung		Alex,	F
gee ske,	I,H	Alexander,	A
Ah le te she yung		Alltime, William	D
ove seedung,	I,H	An ke taw chin ...,	G
Ah le te ske dah		An ke taw gooh,	G
le ma cine,	I,H	Anucha,	F
Ah lei tia,	G	Aquaha,	C
Ah ma ye yah daw		Ar gar le gar,	K
cha joh me ne,	I,H	Ar le char,	H,I
Ah mah sov ye ah		Ar le char gar ner	
nah yah day he,	I,H	tah la ge,	H,I
Ah mah ya do he		Ar le char see	
ah ce ne,	I,H	dar le do,	H,I
Ah nelageyego lah hah,	I,H	Ar mar cher nar,	K
Ah sol le cle ski,	G	Ar mar chur nar,	K
Ah sol le de ski,	C	Ar mar de sge,	H,I
Ah squa lah dege		Ar mer cher nar,	K
de le ste,	I,H	Ar nar dar ne ski,	K
Ah ta yoh hi,	B	Ar nar tah ne ske,	K
Ah ulah Dagahna Kah,	I,H	Ar ne yar ne sge,	H,I

Ar ye Ge,	K		Bear Skin,	D
Arch, Ga le Peter	K		Bearpaw,	H
Arch, Ga li Clay	K		Beaver, John	I
Arch, Young Chicken	G		Beaver,	F
Arch Bear Paw,	C		Beaver,	G
Arch che lar degrdeske,	H,I		Beck, James	G
Arch go kah nee,	H,I		Beloit, Wilson	C
Archilla, Raincoon	D		Beloxt, Jim	C
Are de dle,	H,I		Bendabout, Moses	F
Aro ho ka da,	C		Benge, James	C
Arrow Keeper,	I		Benjamin,	D
Artice, Archilla	I		Berryman, Joseph	D
Ashhopper, George	F		Besayan, Joseph	C
Askwater,	I		Bick, James	G
Au caw haw mah ne,	F		Big, Beaver	D
Austin, Simlen	F		Big, Drum	D
Auye,	B		Big, Feather	D
Aw le,	B		Big, Field	D
Aw se,	B		Big, Lewis	K
Awe do les kie,	C		Big, Mocasin	D
Awe do us kie,	C		Big, Track	B
Awee,	F		Big Feather, Wn'ter	A
Back water,	A		Bigheart, James	B
Bah se mo ne,	F		Bill, Bird Chopper	D
Bailey,	D		Billy, Jim Ned	C
Baldridge, Andrew	A		Bird, Turner	I
Baldridge, John	G		Bird,	B
Baldridge, John	H		Birdchop, Walter	H
Ballew, David	A		Black,	D
Ballors, David	A		Black Fox, Henry	B
Ban Char kar,	H,I		Black Fox,	K
Barber, William	C		Black Haw,	K
Bark, David	I		Black Hawk,	B
Bark,	G		Black Horse,	D
Barridge, John	F		Black Stump	D
Bartholimew, Lewis	B		Black Wing,	D
Batie, Robert	E		Blackburn, Jumper	G
Beamer, West	A		Blackfeather, John	C
Bean, John	G		Blackfeather,	C
Bear, George	G		Blackfoot,	C
Bear, Sweat Bee	I		Blackfox, David	I
Bear Paw,	D		Blackfox,	I

Blacksmith,	I	Cah na noo li ski,	G
Blair, Esquire	H	Cah nah noo li ski,	G
Blair, Harry	G	Cah ne,	B
Bloodhead, George	D	Cah ne noo li ski,	G
Board,	B	Cah nee doo,	F
Bob,	F	Cah no he gah tah,	B
Boles, James	A	Cah no no,	B
Bowles, James	A	Cah noo he yah toh,	B
Brady, Samuel	A	Cah nor h yah tah,	B
Broken Knife,	D	Cah nor he ya tah,	B
Brown, Hunter	C	Cah nor he yah tah,	B
Brown, Jones	G	Cah nor hi yah tah,	B
Brown, Jones	G	Cah sa wa hi lo,	G
Brown, Moses	B	Cah sah dah,	F
Brush,	I	Cah wah yehe saw	
Buckfly,	H	ske seque ne day,	I,H
Buffalo,	A	Cah yo lee,	F
Buffalo Bill,	D	Cahna ne li ski,	G
Buffalow,	A	Calf,	B
Bull Frog,	G	Camanchee,	D
Bullfrog, David	I	Camanshee,	D
Bumster, Daniel	F	Campbell, Ed	F
Bushy Head,	C	Campdoras,	H
Bushyhead, Jacob	E	Candle,	B
Buster,	C	Candy, Webster	H
Butler, Thomas	D	Canoe, Arch	F
Buzzard, Nelson	H	Captain, Joe	C
Ca na noo li ski,	G	Catchee,	B
Ca na wa sa ski,	G	Catcher, Charles	C
Ca na wa so ski,	G	Catcher, Ke	C
Ca she caw ma un ka,	G	Catcher, Samuel	C
Ca she caw wa		Catcher, Seed	C
taw nin ka,	G	Catcher, William	C
Cado, Tom	C	Catcher,	A
Cah Ha Sah,	B	Catcher,	B
Cah La wi hi lo,	G	Cavison, John	C
Cah Neh,	B	Caw ha no pa,	G
Cah ha sa,	B	Caw he ka tla jah,	F
Cah lo nar has key,	F	Caw he ki wa cha he,	G
Cah lo ne has key,	F	Caw ra he la,	A
Cah lo ne has ky,	F	Caw sa he la,	G
Cah lo nes has key,	F	Caw taw maw ne,	F

352

Caw wa tong gah,	F	Charley,	A
Ce gah le se gahwe,	I,H	Charley,	F
Ce nah ne yo ghi jah,	I,H	Charley,	F
Ce quah ne ya hah dah yo ski,	I,H	Charley (Boots),	A
		Che Ca sha,	E
Ceghele Se gah we,	I,H	Che Muck que,	D
Cegie me yo hah dah yes he,	I,H	Che Nuc We,	D
		Che Nuck yue,	D
Cehone, George	C	Che cha nah tah,	E
Ces a mone,	E	Che ke le,	D
Ces a monne,	E	Che le dar da ge,	H,I
Cha ha ba,	C	Che le dar da ge,	H,I
Cha ha wa gra Toho,	E	Che maw caw,	G
Cha kah sa cle,	C	Che mek que,	D
Cha kah sa de,	C	Che nack quah,	D
Cha la ga te he,	B	Che nack que,	D
Cha la ge te he,	B	Che nak que,	D
Cha la te he,	B	Che nar star lar,	H,I
Cha le te he,	B	Che ne quah,	E
Cha na no li ski,	G	Che no be yah ho lah,	C
Cha na noo le ski,	G	Che nuck que,	D
Cha na noo li ski,	G	Che nuck qush,	D
Cha na noo ski,	G	Che sa tong,	E
Cha pa chin ka,	E	Che sha hon gru,	E
Cha pa ka ha,	E	Che sha wa cot tah,	B
Cha po in ka,	E	Che sho hon gue,	E
Cha sin sa,	E	Che squa ga loo yeh,	B
Cha ta Cow Shin Caw,	G	Che squa ga too ya,	B
Cha we nooli ski,	G	Che squah ga loo ya,	B
Chac ta mo nu ga hah,	H	Che-Squah-Sa-large-sqush,	H,I
Chak ke ar ish,	C		
Chanle te he,	B	Che-squah-ga-loo-zah,	B
Char tah go char ya,	H,I	Che-squah-ya-looya,	B
Charle te he,	B	Che-squah-ya-looyeh,	B
Charle to he,	B	Cheater,	C
Charles, Big Drum	G	Chee nar no der sge,	H,I
Charles,	B	Chee nar no dr sge,	H,I
Charles,	F	Chee ste quah te,	H,I
Charles,	F	Cheetah yu lah tah,	F
Charles,	H	Cheeter,	I
Charles Johnstoote,	H	Cher nar star lar,	H,I
Charley, Stimpson	A	Ches a ton ga,	E

Ches sin che na pe,	F	Chu-he-clah,	C
Ches-sin-no-pe,	F	Chu-he-sa-tah,	C
Chi-no-bie-yah-ho-leh,	C	Chu-he-sah-toh,	A
Chickasaw, Captain	C	Chu-mie-kwa, Charles	H
Chicken, John Y.	G	Chu-ne-loss-ky,	F
Chief, Ioni	C	Chu-noo-la-ha-ski,	B
Chillie,	F	Chu-nu-lis-ki,	B
Chin-E-quah,	E	Chu-nu-lus-ke,	B
Chinobe-ya-ho-lah,	C	Chu-nu-lus-ki,	B
Chinobee, McCoy	C	Chu-sa-le-ta,	D
Chis-E-waw-taw-		Chu-sa-le-tah,	D
ne-Caw,	F	Chu-saw-law-ta,	B
Cho-wa-na-ski,	G	Chu-ta-ya-la-tah,	F
Chocke, Benjamin	I	Chu-wa-na-ski,	G
Choh-lah-ke-te-he,	B	Chu-wa-ya-ga-tle,	B
Choo-we, Isaac	G	Chu-wo-ya-ga-tle,	B
Christie, Arch	G	Chuckaluck,	H
Christie, James	G	Chucker, Benjamin	I
Christie, William	G	Chue-sa-leh-tah,	D
Christy, Arch	G	Chue-tah-yer la tah,	F
Christy, James	G	Chuesuegahlee,	F
Christy, William	G	Chuetahyerlahtah,	F
Chu Wee,	K	Chumastoole, James	H
Chu da ya la ta,	F	Chun-un-lus-ke,	B
Chu go ner Der, Isaac	K	Chupa-ha-ku,	E
Chu he sah tah,	A	Chute-zoo,	F
Chu he soh toh,	A	Chuwaluki, David	I
Chu no nae ti ski,	G	Clahmaha, Sammmo	B
Chu saw lun ta,	B	Clay, Wash	H
Chu saw lun to,	B	Clerk,	F
Chu squa ga too ya,	B	Co-che-to-ba,	B
Chu squa ya too ya,	B	Co-rhe che-gra,	G
Chu squah ya loo yah,	B	Co-rhe-wa-cha,	G
Chu-cah-nah-tak,	E	Co-ri-he,	G
Chu-cha-noh-tah,	E	Co-she-ju-ne-ka,	G
Chu-che saw tah,	A	Cobfish, Edward	A
Chu-chu,	E	Cochran, Wind	I
Chu-co-nea-dar,	F	Codrey, David	E
Chu-co-nea-dar,	F	Coffee,	D
Chu-co-nun-ter,	E	Coh nor hi yoh tah,	B
Chu-dah-cah-hah, Isaac	H	Coh-no-no, (Bull Frog)	B
Chu-he-Lah-tah,	C	Colston, Alex	C

Com-lile mar-she,	F	Cul sa we,	B
Come-saw-she-la,	F	Da char ker,	B
Come-shaw-she-la,	F	Da de sta ski,	F
Comin Lew nine,	D	Da ga no he le,	K
Comingdeer, Joseph	H	Da ga ya da,	C
Con sa na tah ne ka,	F	Da gar na me,	K
Con-flow-now-she,	G	Da gar no se ne,	K
Conah-deah-ghejah,	I,H	Da law un ce de	
Coo-lahstee,	F	ske ah de laqua,	I,H
Coo-saw-maw-ne,	G	Da me,	B
Cooking, Potatoes	H	Da ne chee	
Cordry, Andrew	E	na lee ke,	H,I
Cordry, David	E	Da ne der ne no le,	H,I
Corn Stalk,	C	Da ne nah yar	
Corn Tassle,	K	go lee ne,	H,I
Cornpuller, Archilla	I	Da ne se,	
Cornsilk, Joseph	A		H
Cornsilk, Thomas	F	Da ne se ne,	H,I
Cow ha ce,	G	Da wah wah loh gee,	I,H
Cow he ka sta jah,	F	Da yune ye oo joh de,	I,H
Cow tow mow ne,	F	Dah ee le ce	
Cow wa ta in ka,	E	blimg dahgee,	I,H
Cow wartun gah,	F	Dah gah no ha land,	
Crane, Jim	C	Dah gah we smoke,	H
Crawfish,	F	Dah guh woh ah si,	B
Crawford, Press	G	Dah jime lime ske	
Crawler,	D	yah we jah,	I,H
Crawler,	D	Dah june si ne ske	
Crawling		yah we gah,	I,H
Hummingbird,	I	Dah me ce ne Da	
Creek, Tom	F	la ghe squa,	I,H
Crehfield, Edward	A	Dah ya wa,	B
Crichfield, Edward	A	Dah yak yah,	H
Cristy, Arch	G	Daniel,	K
Cristy, William	G	Daniel,	G
Crittendon, Dick	D	Daniel Big Head,	C
Crittenten, De yul ce ne	C	Dar gar no he ler,	K
Crittenten, Joseph	C	Dar lar lar,	K
Cro wa ta in ka,	E	Dar nar e,	K
Crossland, Samuel	E	Dar noo me,	B
Crutchfield, Edward	A	Dar su wa ha lah,	C
Crying Buck,	G	Dar yah sche sta che,	H,I

Dar yee no yer le,	H,I		Deer, Standing	A
Dark Hogshooter,	I		Dega le sar der ske,	H,I
Darkurstoskee,	F		Degah noo ta you	
Daugherty, Charles	G		he oo de dome,	I,H
Daugherty, George	D		Degeny John,	H
David,	K		Delaware, Bob	C
Davidson,	I		Delaware, John	D
Davis, David	K		Delaware, Thomas	C
Davis, Joseph	K		Dew Sure Bear,	B
Day oo ye chan ne,	B		Di su wo lar tah,	K
Daylight, Tom	G		Di su wo lar toh,	K
De Gar che ne ster,	K		Dick, Charles	D
De San da Sge,	H,I		Dick, John	H,I
De Su yoh Kie,	C		Dick, Leach	H
De ce no ske de			Dick, Little	A
loh ske ske,	I,H		Dick, Richard	E
De ge le yoh ske,	H,I		Didappel, Taylor	H
De gee ne Gee			Didapper, Taylor	H
Sta gee,	I,H		Didapple, Edward	H
De gee ne ah			Dirt Eater,	D
yung Ene,	I,H		Dirt Pot Dick,	A
De he a tah,	F		Dirt Pot Robin,	A
De la de ski,	C		Ditapple, Edward	H
De la ske ski Di			Dlar na mar,	K
re ne ski,	H		Dlar na nar,	K
De sah ne he			Dlar no nah,	K
Charles,	H		Do char Ker,	B
De see yo se,	K		Do chee nah,	H,I
De so yo he,	K		Do sar wo le dar,	K
De squah ne,	C		Do you nisi,	F
De su ne ne he			Dogwood, Jesse	F
Jah le,	I,H		Dohirty, John	C
De tah sah,	B		Dohorty, George	D
De we Joh le,	I,H		Dohyahwoh,	B
De yah gle ske soo			Dollar,	C
we gah loh,	I,H		Doo cha lah,	C
Dear, Bob	C		Doo nah he sah	
Dee yoh ne se to			de jah,	I,H
ya neesy,	F		Doocharkee,	B
Deer, Bob	C		Doublehead, Eli	H
Deer, Daniel Y.	G		Dougherty, David	G
Deer, George	G		Dougherty, George	D

Downing, Daniel	I		Eli,	G
Downing, Henry	C		Elic gan ne sene,	H,I
Downing, James	C		Elijah,	B
Downing, John	H		Elleten no kem a,	D
Downing, Locust	A		Enchee,	C
Downing, Robert	I		Enoley,	C
Drag, Alexander	I		Epe sow sa,	E
Dre we kah no			Ephraim,	G
no nee,	H,I		Esi,	G
Drum, George	G		Eston, Elijah	G
Drum, Wilson	B		Eucha ta wa ta in ka,	E
Dry Hunter,	C		Eucha ta wa ta in ka,	E
Dry Hunter,	H		Eucher,	C
Dry Squirrel,	D		Falling, Buzzard	H
Dry Water,	G		Falling, John	I
Du sa wo lar tah,	K		Falling, John	I
Du yah ni si,	F		Falling, Leaf	A
Duck, Richard	A		Falling, Pot	C
Dunback, Lewis	E		Falling, Water	C
Duncan, Edmond	B		Farmer,	B
Dunkin, Edmond	B		Feeling, Robert	I
Durneenolee,	F		Felin, Walt	K
Dutch Canoe,	F		Fence, Maker	A
E goo da,	B		Field, Squirrel	A
E-he-sow-cha,	G		Fields, Elijah	B
E-ka-li-ka,	F		File, Benjamin	D
E-no-le,	H,I		Finger,	B
Ea ta gue, Star Bird	G		Fish, Hawk	D
Eagle, War	E		Fish, Houk	D
Eagle,	B		Fish, John	H
Eaten, Elijah	G		Fish, Kickapoa	C
Eaton, Elijah	G		Fish, Levi	A
Eba-da-kah,	B		Fisher,	D
Ebes-cah,	B		Flat Foot	C
Edok go ski,	G		Flea,	D
Edwards,	G		Fly, John	C
Ego-de,	B		Fly, Wilson	A
Egoowa, Wolf	H		Flying, Squirrel	H
Ela, we	K		Flying,	D
Elah we lah le			Fog,	I
joo skaw,	I,H		Foreman, Tyler	E
Elar, Wee	K		Foster, Benjamin	E

Foster, James	E		Gales,	A
Foster, John	E		Gall Catcher, Thomas	A
Foster, Lyon	H		Galomookeskee, Lacy	I
Four Mile,	D		Gals,	A
Fox, Mouse	K		Gaps, Moses	H
Fox,	A		Gar Kar nee, Daniel	I
Fox,	D		Gar dar gee ske,	K
Fox,	G		Gar do lah stah,	H,I
Foxet, Jack	A		Gar lar no ha	
Fruit, Picker	H		ske, Adam	K
Furgerson, John	E		Gar le sto ske,	K
Furgeson, John	E		Gar ne chee, nah yur,	H
Fuzzy, Thomas	A		Gar ne le sar,	K
Ga de ga, Joseph	H		Gar no ske ske,	K
Ga lar che,	K		Gar,lar,ste,horske,	K
Ga na le ser,	K		Gar,le,no,he sge,	I
Ga no he lo ske,	K		Gar-no-he-lo-ske,	K
Ga no ske ske,	K		Garlarche,	K
Ga,la,na,sar,	K		Gass, Moses	H
Ga,le,sto,ske,	K		Gau,we,chu,yoo,la,	B
Ga,lo,no,ha,ske, Adam	K		Gaw,we,chu,yoo,la,	B
Ga,we,che,yoe,la,	B		Ge ne Ga naronoSote,	K
Ga-lo-no,he,ske,	H,I		Ge-do-nar-ge,	H,I
Ga-lo-no,ho,ske, Adam	K		Ge-lo-ste-gar,	H,I
Ga-na,le-car,	K		Ge-nar-de-he,	K
Ga-wo-he lo,ske,	K		Ge-ne-Ga-naronesote,	K
Ga-ye-go-ge,	H,I		Geirity, Studd	C
Gage, G.W.	E		Geirity, Willson	C
Gah ga we, Dick	C		George, Bear Paw	C
Gah gah we jah le,	I,		George, Billey	C
Gah gah we smoke,	H		George, E.	F
Gah we,cher,you,la,	B		George, Welene E.	I
Gah,la,no,ha,ske, Lacy	I		George,	B
Gah,lah,ner ter,	C		George,	C
Gah,lah,stoo,hung,ske,ge,			George gala,	F
Soo,gah,nah,	I,		Georgey, E.	F
Gah,we,che,yoo-la,	B		Georgey,	F
Gah,we,chu,yoo-la,	B		Gerity, Studd	C
Gahlarmoheske, Lacy	I		Get-on get-la-ba,	B
Gahleska,we-do-			Get-on get-ta-ba,	B
way-yah-lan,	I,H		Gierity, Snake	C
Gal Catcher, Thomas	A		Gierity, Studd	C

358

Gierity, Wilson	C		Goo-sah-de-he-le-goo-ge	I,H
Gilbert,	B		Goo-sah-de-he-sele-go-gee,	I
Girt, Walter	I		Goo-tam-te-ske,	B
Girth, Walter	I		Goo-taw-te-ske,	B
Glar na nar,	K		Goo-tom-te-ski,	B
Glass, Judge	F		Goo-tow-te-ske,	B
Glass,	A		Goring, Snake	F
Glo-lah-stoo-ah-me-do-navah,	I		Goss, Moses	H
Glo-yah-gah-ah-me-do-na-ah,	I,H		Gow-me-che-you-la,	B
Glory, Richard	A		Gow-we-che-you-la,	B
Go da qua ski,	B		Gra-taw-maw-ne,	G
Go dle ner ske,	H		Gra-tow-maw-ne,	G
Go-back,	G		Grapes,	A
Go-back,	H		Grass,	B
Go-char-Ge-ske,	K		Greece,	D
Go-da-qua ske,	B		Green, William	E
Go-dler ner ske,	H,I		Grimet, Harry	G
Go-la-Quah, Johnson	K		Grimett,	F
Go-larquah, Johnson	K		Grimitt,	F
Go-lo-no-ha-ske, Adam	K		Grimmett, Harry	G
Go-lo-no-he-ske, Lacy	I		Grimmett,	F
Go-na-qua-she,	B		Grimmit, Harry	G
Go-ne-chu-squah-le,	K		Grimmit,	F
Go-ne-ske-ske,	K		Grinnett,	F
Go-no-le-sar,	K		Grinty, Stud	C
Go-no-lo-ha-ske, Lacy	I		Grinty, William	C
Go-no-ske-ske,	K		Grise, Gola	F
God-a-qua ska,	B		Grits, William	D
Goe back,	G		Gritts, William	D
Goh-le-ska-we-doo-way-yah-law,	I		Grog,	D
Goin Water	H		Ground, Squirrell	F
Going Snake	D		Ground Hog,	F
Going Snake	F		Grow-wa-taw-ne-ka,	G
Going Water	H		Gu-lah-soh,	F
Going to Mill,	D		Gu-lah-stah,	F
Goingsnake, Clark	I		Gu-lah-ster,	F
Gola, Grise	F		Gu-loh-stah,	F
Gone, Water	H		Gu-loh-sti,	F
Gone to Sleep,	H		Gua-la-ta,	B
			Gue-le-ke,	B

Guess, Moses	H		Washington	G
Ha kon koh,	B		Hendricks, William	C
Ha maw se,	G		Henry, John	I
Ha-con-te-no-she,	B		Henry, William	C
Ha-ha-ma-ae,	E		Hes caw-mo-ne,	F
Ha-ha-ma-he,	E		Hes ka moe,	E
Ha-ko-ta-no-she,	B		Hes-cah-mo-ne,	F
Ha-tat-se-kah,	B		Hi-us-te be, John	B
Hah, George E.	D		Hicks, Charles	E
Hah-koh-koh,	B		Hicks, Jay	C
Hain, James	E		Hicks, John J.	C
Haines, Stephen	C		Hicks, Louis	E
Hains, Stephen	C		Hicks, Taylor	I,D
Hair, James	E		High,	C
Hall, George	A		Hight, James	C
Hamer, James	C		Hilderbrand, Nelson	D
Hamilton, David	B		Hill, Delaware	D
Hammer, James	C		Hill, Jake	D
Han-naw-pa-so,	G		Hill,	D
Hanes, Stephen	C		Hin-ka-he-a,	E
Harris, David	C		Hin-ka-he-la,	E
Harris, William	E		Hitcher,	G
Hary, John	K		Hitcher,	I
Hatchet, Dixon	B		Ho, Sae	D
Haw-Kaw-na-la,	G		Ho-taw-nao-ne,	F
Haw-ka-ma-la,	G		Hog, Shorter	A
Haw-ka-wa-la-she-cah,	F		Hog, Shorter	H
			Hog, Wily	G
Haw-sha-she,	F		Hog Shooter, Se quoy yab	A
Hawk, Isaac	K		Hoister,	G
Hawk, William	H		Hooper,	D
He Ka ka,	E		Horn, Thomas	C
He dat sah,	B		Horsefly, Walter	H
He ha caw,	F		Horsfly, Walter	H
He-dat-Sa-war-lat-he,	B		Hosfly, Walter	H
He-dat-se-kah,	B		Hoskins, John	I,H
He-dat-tah,	B		Hothouse,	H
He-naw-co-law,	G		How-sha-na-la,	G
Heath, Adoniron J.	D		Howk, Isaac	K
Height, James	C		Howling, Wolf	I
Height, Hendricks,	C		Hu bra pa sa,	G

360

Hu law gra sha,	G	Jesse yar E yar,	H,I
Hue lah wa shoska,	F	Jeus, Harp	D
Hue-law-shin-jah,	F	Jim, Big	H
Hue-saw-rah-shin-ka,	F	Jim, Creek	E
Huh tah tuh sah,	B	Jin-kin-ne,	B
Hum-pa-wa-Kun-rah,	B	Jo, Spanard	F
Hum-pa-wa-wah-Kon ta	B	Jo-gan-cey,	F
		Jo-see-sah-de-yah,	I,H
Hungry,	A	Joh ne goo da gua ske,	H
Hunter, Jack	C	John, Big Leg	C
Hunter, William	A	John, Bill	D
Huston,	C	John, Blackfeather	C
Hyder, Andy	C	John, Bull	C
Hyder,	D	John, Cup	A
In scaw,	F	John, Desah-da-ske	I
In scraw,	F	John, Horseskin	I,H
Ioni, Tom	C	John, Raincrow	D
Isaac,	G	John, Watsata	A
Ja-gee-oo-yah-sah-de,	I,H	John,	A
Ja-ha-ne,	F	John,	D
Ja-ne-ceah-da-lar-ceh-na-wechi,	I,H	John (Chick),	B
		John (Watase-ta),	A
Jack, No ye	H,I	John na le se,	H,I
Jack, Snake	K	Johnny cake, Benjam	D
Jack,	B	Johnsa,	H
Jackson, Chickasaw	B	Johnson, Christy	H,I
Jackson, Lacy	H	Johnson, Creek	D
Jackson, Levi	F	Johnson, Dew	F
Jackson,	B	Johnson, Field	H
Jacob, John	C	Johnson, Go la quah	K
Jah ne ga soo go ske,	I,H	Johnson, John	E
Jah-ne-ga-goo-tah-gee-ske,	I,H	Johnson, Little	C
		Johnson, Tobacco	H
Jah-squa-ne-dun-ce-oo-sah-we,	I,H	Johnson, We	B
		Johnson,	D
James, Beck	G	Johnson,	F
James,	G	Johnson,	K
Je-ne-o-dune-no-de,	I,H	Johnston,	F
Jefferson,	G	Johnstoote, Osahwe	I,H
Jeffry, Isaac	H	Johnstoote, William	H
Jen-wah-ah-we-da-yae,	I,H	Jones, Bird	K
Jesse,	F	Jones, Brown	G

Jones, Jerry	K	Kah-se-loh-wi,	D
Jones, Pig	H	Kah-sku-nah-he,	A
Joo-naw-stoo-te-jah-le,	I,H	Kah-su-he-le,	A
		Kah-wah-he-law-ska,	A
Joolar-gah,	F	Kah-woh-he-law-skeh,	A
Josaye,	B	Kahlungkahlooplie,	I,H
Joseph, Kabert	D	Kalarhae,	K
Joseph,	A	Kar-lar-stvo-hu-ske,	K
Josey,	C	Kar-lee-quah-duge,	H,I
Jug, Levi	A	Kar-ler-sar-yar-har,	H
Jumper, Jack	C	Kar-tu-ki-ski,	K
Jumper, Jack	C	Kartar, Peter C.	F
Jumper, Stealer	C	Karter, William	B
Jumper,	B	Kaw-Kaw-we, William	I
Jus-ki-yo-gee,	F	Kaw-ay-nus-te,	B
Justice, Adam	A	Kaw-haw-we, Daniel	I
Justice, John	A	Kaw-he-ha-ko-lah,	G
Justice, John	F	Kaw-he-hu-shin-ka,	G
Jusugala,	F	Kaw-he-ka-ko-lah,	G
Ka na le ser,	K	Kaw-kaw-we, Arch	I
Ka-ha-sa-o-ha,	E	Kawkawwe, Nicholas	I
Ka-ha-we, Arch	I	Ke-ko-s-a,	F
Ka-ka-we, David	I	Ke-paw-law-he,	F
Ka-man-o-chee,	C	Ke-wa-re-she,	E
Ka-man-o-shee,	C	Kelly, John	C
Ka-na-no,	C	Kelly, Thomas	C
Ka-sku-na-he,	A	Kerwanaste,	B
Ka-skuh-nah-he,	A	Kes-ko-kow-wha,	D
Ka-skuh-nah-heh,	A	Ket-ke-lon-jo,	D
Ka-un-cush,	C	Key, Daugherty	F
Kabert, Joseph	D	Kickapooshe,	C
Kado, George	C	Killeneger,	F
Kado-A-ha-he,	C	Killenegre,	F
Kado-a-kahho,	C	Killenegro,	F
Kah-he-kah-wah-he-peshe,	F	Killer, Creek	H
		Killerleenegee,	F
Kah-koh-we, Arah	I	Killerniger,	F
Kah-koh-wee, Daniel	I	Killinniger,	F
Kah-lah-che, Nicholas	I	Kis-ki-kaw-wah,	D
Kah-lah-tse, Nicholas	I	Kit-ke-longa,	D
Kah-ne-she-kah,	B	Kitch-Kah,	C
Kah-se-la-we,	D	Ko-lar-har,	K

Kodaske,	H		Lee, Edward	G
Kodaske,	K		Lee,en,yih,tshoe,te,	
Koh-he-koh-washe			qua,nah,tli,ki,	B
-pea-she,	F		Left Hand,	A
Koh-sa-he-la,	A		Len yih tshoe tle	
Koh-sa-he-le,	A		quah nah tle ki,	B
Koh-se-lah-we,	D		Len yih tshoo quah	
Koh-she-kah,	B		nah tle ki,	B
Koh-so-he-le,	A		Leu-yih gah loo	
Koh-so-he-le,	A		wihe ske,	B
Koh-soh-he-le,	A		Leurey, Ei	F
Kohlaste, Nicholas	I		Levi,	A
Kohsohela,	A		Lewis, Big	D
Kolahste, Nicholas	I		Lewis, Josiah	H
Koolahste, Nicholas	I		Lewis, Old	B
Koolatse, Nicholas	I		Lewis, Old	B
hap			Lewis,	F
Kow-a-hot-sa,	E		Liar,	I
Kow-o-hot-sare,	E		Lim-yeh-gah-lor-	
Kow-wo hot sure,	E		nahes-ke,	B
Kow-wo-hot-sa,	E		Linyihgahlor-	
La me,	F		noo-has-ke,	B
La see Ia gee ce ne,	I,H		Linyihtshactle-	
La-yah-ste-ske,	B		quahnootleki,	B
Lacry de ge,	H,I		Little Dog,	I
Lacy, Bird	I		Little Moses,	D
Lacy, Wilson	D		Little Osage,	C
Lacy,	G		Little Rider,	B
Lacy,	K		Little Snake,	B
Lacy du ge,	H,I		Little Taripen,	D
Lacy-gah-lo-no-ho-sou,	I		Little Tarpin,	D
Lamey,	F		Little Tarrapin,	D
Lami,	F		Little Terapin,	D
Lanee,	F		Little Tom,	C
Langley, Martin	A		Little Tom,	C
Lar nah ne,	H,I		Liver,	D
Lar woh ne,	H,I		Lo-chu-wa-she,	E
Law ha ne ka,	G		Lo-ha-wah-tah-ne-hah,	F
Leach, Rice	I		Long Jack,	C
Leach, Richard	H		Long Starr,	G
Leach, Ridge	I		Loo gah,	B
Leaves on a tree,	D		Loo-na,	B

Loo-ye-Io-sah-yi,	I,H	Mathew,	F
Looyah,	B	Matoy, Robbin	A
Louis, Dew	F	Maw he caw ha,	G
Louis, Josiah	H	Maw he ha,	G
Louis,	F	Maw ne caw maw ne,	G
Love, Johnson	C	Maw shaw Ocaw shaw,	G
Lowery, Bob	F	Maw shaw cash shaw,	F
Lowery, Eli	F	Maw shaw ka,	G
Lowrie, Bob	F	Maw shaw ke taw,	G
Lowrie, Eli	F	Maxfield, Olmstead	E
Lowry, Bob	F	Maxwell, Olmstead	E
Lowry, Ely	F	Mayfield, Ed	F
Lowy, Bob	F	Mayfield, Huston	F
Lu-yih-gah-law-		Maysfield, Huston	F
no-he-ske,	B	McCay, William	E
Lun-yih-gah-law-		McCollough, George	D
no-ha-ske,	B	McCollough, Richard	E
Lurise, Felise		McCoy, Chinobe	C
Lying down,	H	McCoy, Edward	E
Ma ha ka ha,	E	McCoy, James	C
Ma ha no pa,	G	McCoy, William	E
Ma he caw ha,	G	McCullar, Richard	E
Ma hu ka ha,	E	McElmore,	D
Ma ka ha she she,	E	McElroy, John	M
Ma ka saw bru,	G	McIntosh, John	A
Ma pe ma ne,	E	McKey, Moses	G
Ma pe mure,	E	McKinsey, David	A
Ma sha ke ta,	E	McKinsey, Jack	A
Ma shaw shin kee,	F	McKinzie, David	A
Ma shaw sink er,	F	McKinzie, Jack	A
Ma she ta mae,	E	McLimore,	D
Ma shu etsa mar,	E	Me caw natah me cap,	F
Ma shu ta mae,	E	Me caw shin caw,	F
Ma shuta ha mane,	E	Me cow na toh ne cop,	F
Ma ska she kah,	B	Me cow shin kah,	F
Madison, John	B	Me ha cha ee,	F
Mah-teh,	A	Me ho chee me,	G
Major,	A	Me ho ka,	F
Major Robinson,	D	Me ka ha she she,	E
Maners, William	D	Me ka no tah,	B
Manus, William	D	Me ka wa ta in ka,	E
Marion, Thomas	D	Me kow wa ta in ka,	E

Name	Col
Me kow wo she,	E
Me la toh me ne,	F
Me le ba shin goh,	F
Me le lan shin gah,	F
Me quet sua,	E
Me wa caw taw,	G
Me wa con low,	G
Me-quet sea,	E
Me-quet sea,	E
Mean man,	C
Mean man,	C
Measure,	A
Meches kah,	G
Meckko, William	C
Megg, E.	K
Megge,	K
Meggs, E.	K
Mellton, Clinton	C
Melton, Clinton	C
Merrell, James	E
Merrill, James	E
Merry, Ea	D
Mery, Ea	D
Messenger,	G
Mighs, John	I
Might, Nelson	I
Mike,	G
Miller, Cabin	G
Miller, David	C
Miller, David	D
Miller Bug,	G
Mills, George	A
Mills, Jumper	A
Mills, Moses	D
Millton, Clinton	C
Mitchel, Johnson	B
Mitchel, Levi	B
Mo sah poo way,	B
Mo say ko nah,	B
Mo shaw ke taw,	F
Mo shoa to pa,	E
Mo shon tom pa,	E
Mo tah te kah,	B
Mo tah tea ning,	B
Mo tah-Konah,	B
Mo-sa-poo-wa,	B
Moble tah neh,	B
Mocking, Bird	D
Monas, William	D
Money, Hunter	C
Moon, Shine	D
Mose, Little	D
Moseh-con-neh,	B
Moses, Little	D
Mouse, De giny	H
Mouse, De grene	H
Mouse, De-ge-ny	H
Mouse, Degene	H
Mouse, Digeny	H
Mouse, Tincup	H
Mouse,	F
Much a lo ha ba,	B
Muk ko la ha tah,	B
Mumaw, Abrm R.	G
Murphy, Cummins	A
Muskrat, James	I
Muskrat, Thompson	H
Musrat, James	I
Na da ce ne soo le,	I,H
Na da soo lah hah,	I,H
Nadsan,	F
Nah tu wa gah,	A
Nan she che leh,	F
Naw haw caw she,	F
Ne caw caw he,	G
Ne caw co lah,	G
Ne caw ha ha,	G
Ne caw o hah che,	G
Ne caw un paw,	G
Ne caw wa she ton caw,	G
Ne caw wa she von caw,	G
Ne de ce ne de yah gna ne,	I,H

Ne do da eo na,	C	O Ke-na-she,	G
Ne ge a do he,	I	O Ko Ko,	K
Ne ge a do he,	H	O Sah we, Bark	H,I
Ne ge go lar che,	H,I	O Sar we,	I,H
Ne haw O kah che,	G	O har na,	C
Ne ka na sa,	E	O her che mon ne,	F
Ne kah no tah,	B	O ho Ka sah,	F
Ne ne hi ja gna Jov gah dun a gah,	I	O how Ka show,	F
		O no la,	H,I
Ne no he ja qua Jov gahsah te,	H	O paw haw me ne,	F
		O pesh ta pa she,	F
Ne soo ye de Iah dah we,	I,H	O saw we bark,	I,H
		O sawe Bark,	I,H
Ne tah gur gah,	I	O taw saw ne ka,	G
Ne wa kue,	E	O yah skar no de,	K
Necktie,	H	O yo dle a,	K
Ned, Jim	C	O-Ka-Kotck,	C
Nee caw numb bah,	F	O-pin-a-ta-gish,	C
Nee ta gah gah,	D	Oak, Ball	D
Nelson,	F	Oakball, Beaver	D
Nen ka wa le,	E	Oakball, Edward	D
Ni hy ta ya gah,	B	Ocaw-shaw-maw-ne,	G
Ni ki,	B	Ochar lu de,	K
Nin-go-me-ning,	D	Ocher a he,	H,I
Ninj go me ninj,	D	Odar ne yer Der,	K
No Be tha,	D	Oganiah, Peter	A
No Har nah,	C	Oganiah, Weleny	A
No ho lar,	K	Ogartree,	F
No ye, Jack	H	Ogeniah, Peter	A
Noah, James	I	Ogeniah, Weleneh	A
Non ka na waw che,	G	Oha Ra Tah,	C
Non sa in Ka,	E	Oha ha mae,	E
Non son tah she,	F	Oke pa la,	E
Non-son-taw-ha,	G	Oke sha,	E
Noo we Dah hoo we,	I,H	Ola Sa der, David	K
Nose, Tea	D	Ola So der, Davis	K
Now son tan she,	F	Ola nah de,	H,I
Now sow tow she,	G	Ola pa she,	E
Now-ka-wa-waw-he,	G	Ola sa der, Joseph	K
Nu cher wi,	G	Ola ser der, Davis	K
O Jine a ta gish,	C	Old, Bill	D
O Kah Ra Dar,	C	Old Eagle,	B

Ole La go ge der,	H,I	Otshuhtoh,	B
Ole sher ne ka ne to,	K	Owa tar sar te,	K
Ole skar ne,	K	Owa wa Kue,	E
Oler-ner-nah,	H,I	Pa Me Ma texse,	D
Olin can nah she,	F	Pa-caw-haw-she,	F
On Ge Holland,	D	Pa-cho-hau-ka,	
Oo Gartree,	F	Pa-ha pe,	E
Oo Jarlarnerhee,	F	Pa-ma-Pum,	D
Oo ca too tla a, James	G	Pah-se-ma-ne,	G
Oo cah yah dunce		Par nee,	F
cah no le cahe,	I,H	Paris, Johnson	D
Oo cha loo te,	B	Parris, Henry	E
Oo de sa ne dah		Parris, Johnson	D
a le ske,	I,H	Path, Killer	A
Oo ga sa tis ski,	G	Path, September	H
Oo gar si sa ti sti,	G	Patterson, John	B
Oo lar naw stie sky,	F	Pau-chu-maw-ne,	F
Oo le say go ge ta,	B	Paulston, Joseph	E
Oo lo na sti ski,	G	Paw-caw-wa-taw-no-ka,	G
Oo lup Ko Kitch,	B	Paw-cha-o-lah-ha,	F
Oo na cho la,	G	Paw-haw-he,	G
Oo na tlo sur,	G	Paw-taw-he-scho-la,	F
Oo sah E dunce		Paxton, John D.	D
Desau yaw he,	I,H	Pay-no-pa-wa-hu,	G
Oo wah-wah suh,	A	Pe-saw-lah-psha,	F
Oo-da-wa-sa-a,	B	Peacemaker,	H
Oo-ga-da-ga-tle,	B	Peacheater,	G
Oo-gung-squdunce-		Peale, Robert	A
oo- yah-dunce-yah,	I,H	Peck, James	A
Oo-lay-Watter,	B	Peeke, James	A
Oo-na-ga,	B	Peel, Robert	A
Oo-na-ka,	B	Pelecan, Leaf	H
Oo-tah-le-dah,		Pelican,	D
Oo-wo ha-say-he,	B	Peligan, Leaf	H
Ooggadatte,	B	Pelligan, Leaf	H
Ootaheder,	F	Perry, Oliver	H
Ooyertree,		Pettet, Charles	E
Opa ton Ka,	E	Pettit, Charles	E
Ore, Thomas	G	Pheasant,	F
Osi,	G	Phillips,	F
Ostlee ge,	H,I	Picker, Picker	H
Ots-puh-tah,	B	Pidgeon, Jack	I

Pidgeon,	H	Red, Blanket	C
Pig,	G	Red Bird, Tiger	
Pole cat,	F	Red Bird,	
Polk, James K.	K	Red Bird,	A
Pot, Richard	A	Red Bird, 2,	D
Potatoe, John	A	Red Black Fox,	B
Potts, Thomas	I	Red River, Ezekiel	A
Poulston, Joseph	E	Redbird, Jess	D
Powers, Sam	D	Redwing, Ezekiel	A
Prichett, Charles	D	Rice, Leach	I
Prince, Jackson	C	Richard,	F
Prince, Taylor	C	Rider-grass,	B
Prince, Walker	H	Ridge, Leach	I
Pritchet, George	H	Ridges,	D
Pritchett, Charles	D	Riley, John M.	E
Pritchett, Montgomery	D	Riley, Samuel	E
Proctor, John	G	Robert,	B
Prophet, James	C	Robertson, Richard	E
Prophet, Samuel	C	Robertson, Watie	E
Proud,	C	Robinson, Jefferson	E
Pumkin, Jesse	I	Robinson, Richard	E
Pumpkin, Jesse	I	Robinson, Watie	E
Pumpkin, Tom	C	Robison, Jefferson	E
Quar-quah,	H,I	Robison, Richard	E
Quawpaw, Jack	B	Rock, William	G
Quawpaw, Jackson	B	Rockey, Mountain	A
Que like,	B	Rogers, John	A
Queen,	D	Rogers, John	B
Quo Nah,	C	Rolinson,	E
Rain Crow, Washington	D	Rooster, Jefferson	I
Ratingoard, Richard	E	Root,	G
Rattinggourd, Rider	I	Ross, John	G
Rattingoard, Ellis	E	Rotten,	G
Rattingoard, James	E	Rotton,	G
Rattingoard, Sooney	E	Rough & Ready,	C
Rattingourd, Ellis	E	Runabout,	B
Rattingourd, James	E	Runabout,	I
Rattingourd, Looney	E	Runabout,	D
Rattingourd, Richard	E	Runnabout,	D
Raymer,	B	Runnabout,	I
Raymor,	B	Runner, Parchmial	
Reader,	I	Runner,	D

Runner,	I		Scatter, Albones	H
Sa Sae mae,	E		Scatter, Coldwater	H
Sa-ne-gah-goo-nah-lah,	I,H		Scott, Archy	I
			Scott, George	D
Sa-wa-noi,	B		Scott, Green	G
Saddle Blanket,	F		Scott,	F
Sah dah gah, Jose	H		Screamer,	C
Sah-de-yah-Jose,	H		Scullole, Alexander	A
Sah-mi-chah-ma-ha,	B		Scullole, Thomas	A
Sahnee,	F		Scullole, William	A
Salt, Adam	C		Scullule, Thomas	A
Salt, Toby	C		Se gnah we,	A
Sam-se-Wah-te,	K		Se que yah, Duck	I
Samgater,	F		Se-con-wi,	D
Samson, David	C		Se-da-sa-ho-sa,	F
Samuel,	B		Se-gnah ya, John	C
Samuel,	D		Seabolt, Charles	F
San-wa-noi,	B		Seabolt, John	G
Sand,	D		Searcher,	D
Sanders, Eli	E		Sebold, John	G
Sanders, James	C		Seer Ke,	K
Sanders, Jesse	E		Segnah ya, Thomas	C
Sanders, Nicholas B.	E		September Path,	H
Sanders, Samuel	E		Ser Kee,	K
Sanders, Thomas	D		Ser chu ke-lah,	I
Sanecooyoh (Bird),	B		Serthloo, Killah	I
Sangader,	F		Serthu-keelah,	I
Santon, John D.	D		Severe, Joseph	E
Sapsucker, Joseph	H		Sha Ka le he,	F
Sar-lo-le-he-ne-le,	H,I		Sha-te-cha-wa-she-pe-she,	F
Sar-o-ge-see-gee-she,	H,I			
Sarcoxie, Wilson	D		Shade,	A
Saunders, Bird	C		Shanghai, Little	D
Saunders, George	C		Sharp, Sam	K
Saunders, James	C		Shaw-ba-che-gra,	F
Saunders, Thomas	D		Shawnee, Sam	C
Savage, E. George	H		Shawnee,	D
Saw-go-dar,	F		She Kille,	D
Sawny Sucker,	I		She Killer,	D
Scah-ha-Joh,	A		She Paw,	D
Scah-ya-do-gah,	A		She She,	D
Scarret, William	C		Shen wa kan tah,	B

Shepherk, Washington	F		Soldier, Mistletoe	I
Shin-ka-ka-he-ka,	G		Soldier,	D
Shin-kah-ki-he-ka,	F		Solin,	F
Sho Ku hah,	F		Something, John	A
Sho-cha-be-he,	G		Son sa mae,	E
Sho-me-caw se,	F		Soo-Wa-ner,	D
Shon kat sea,	E		Soowa-gee, Egah-gee	H
Shon-ka-he-ka,	E		Soowage, E.George	H
Shooter,	C		Soowage, James	H
Short Arrow,	B		Sow, Wanner	D
Shos-cah,	F		Sow, Warner	D
Shotpouch, Jack	H		Sow, Wumer	D
Shy Buck,	C		Sow, Wunner	D
Sicoxie, Wilson	D		Spa day,	B
Silversmith, Johnson	H		Spanard, Jo	F
Silversmith, Wilson	H		Spears, Arch	B
Simbling,	F		Spears, John	C
Simmons, Lacy	H		Spellen, John	
Simmons, William	C		Spen wa con tah,	B
Simon,	A		Spirit, Beamer	H
Six, Downing	C		Spotted Eagle,	B
Ska-Quah,	K		Springston, Johnson	H
Skah yah do gat,	A		Squah da leeche,	F
Skah-gin-ne,	I		Squahda lieche,	F
Ske-no-yer,	F		Squahtalecha,	F
Skeleate, John	D		Soil, George	
Sker loo lee, Bill	A		Squash,	B
Sker loo lee, Tom	A		Squataleche,	F
Skileate, John	D		Squhtaleche,	F
Sky,	B		Squirrel, Samuel	I
Sky,	C		Squirrel, Star	C
Small Dirt Pot,	A		Squirrel, Ta-na-wa	G
Smiling,	F		Squirrel, Wat	I
Smith, James	C		Squirrel,	B
Smith, James	I		Squirrell,	F
Smith, Samuel	I		Stagger,	A
Smoke, David	H		Stand, George	I
Smoke, Samuel	G		Standing, Swallow	H
Smoke path,	H		Standing, Water	H
Snake, Jim	D		Standingdeer, Joseph	I
Snell, John	H		Star, George	K
Sneyader,	FC		Star, Tom	G

Star,	C		Sullivan, Young	C
Starr,	G		Sullivan, Young	C
Stars,	G		Sunday, John	H
Ste gah wi,	D		Sundy, John	H
Ste he geh,	D		Sunke,	G
Ste ne se nah te,	H,I		Sunkey,	G
Ste ne white killer,	H,I		Sunki,	G
Ste we,	B		Sutles, George W.	E
Ste-gah-we,	D		Sutlis, George W.	E
Stealer,	C		Suwago, George E.	H
Steaphen,	D		Suwago, James	H
Steeny soo water,	H,I		Swallow, Tanner	I
Steme,	B		Sweet Water,	A
Stene so wa te,	H,I		Swimmer, Degene	H
Stenesoowate,	H,I		Swimmer, Degeny	H
Steny se wate,	H,I		Swimmer, Deginy	H
Stephen, Olesto	D		Swimmer, Walkingstick	A
Stephen, Oolsto	D		Swimmer,	I
Stephen,	C		Swimmer, 2nd,	A
Stephen,	I		Ta ha ma ne,	E
Stephen,	D		Ta ha wa,	E
Still, John	I		Ta she kah,	B
Stiphen-oo-wa-etha,	D		Ta shin ka,	E
Sto-not-to ba,	B		Ta ter ghe sah,	A
Stock,	I		Ta ton ga shin ka,	E
Stone Thrower,	C		Ta-co-te-ske,	B
Stooty, William John	H		Ta-ha-lo-sah,	D
Stop, Adam	I		Ta-kon-tah,	B
Stop, Moses	C		Tah che se,	H,I
Stop, Scondy	A		Tah lo see,	F
Storekeeper, Stop	A		Tah no we, Squirrel	G
Stork,	I		Tah yer ser ne le,	H,I
Strong Man, Joe	C		Tah yo ha na,	G
Studd,	C		Tah-lo-sah,	D
Stuge,	F		Tahyolarneer,	F
Su wa ke, James	H		Tail,	G
Su yoh sti,	F		Talker,	G
Su yoh stoh,	F		Tap, Moses	F
Su-Wache,	K		Tar hah shin kav,	F
Sue-ya-der,	F		Tar wa ha ry, John	K
Suk thu ke lar,	I		Tar wee, John	K
Sulevan, Young	C		Tar-ne-mo-le,	K

Tats-kar-obha,	C	Ti-es-ka, George	E
Taw ha maw he,	G	Tiblo, Sion	C
Taw he ho cha,	G	Tigar, Wheeler	B
Taw mah,	G	Tiger, John	H,I
Taw na le he,	F	Tiger,	G
Taw tah ka shin ka,	F	Tigro, John	H
Taw waw caw ha,	G	Tincup, James	H
Taylor, James	C	Tire, John	B
Taylor, Moses	F	Tlar gar,	H,I
Taylor, Thomas	F	Tlo yar gar,	H,I
Taylor, Yankee	C	To cos que ken pi,	D
Tayolaner,	F	To wa tom pa,	E
Te ca ne eske,	B	To war no she,	B
Te ga na skie,	C	To-ga-ha-na,	G
Te she war how tah,	B	To-no-whai-la-ni,	G
Te su yo gah,	A	Tobacco, James	I
Te tun nus ke,	B	Tobacco, Johnson	H
Te yoh sti ski,	B	Toh che gee suo,	A
Te-coo-te-ske,	B	Tole se ge,	H,I
Te-no-she-Kah,	B	Tom-ha-mone,	E
Tecahlogeskie,	F	Tommyhawk, John	C
Tecumseh, John	C	Ton no she kah,	B
Tee-gah-lo-ge-sky,	F	Ton-ni,	G
Teesoweskie,	F	Ton-tai-to-nic,	G
Teeyastaskee,	F	Too nah e,	G
Ter ne no he,	K	Too-ni,	G
Ter-we-honey, John	K	Too-qua-tah,	D
Ter-wee, John	K	Tos se haw,	F
Teyasteskie,	F	Toxe, Tube	D
Thomas, Bear Paw	C	Toyanney,	F
Thomas, Isaac	H	Track, Charles	A
Thomas, John	D	Track, Stinson	A
Thompson, Jesse	A	Trotting Wolf,	A
Thompson, John	D	Ts ho wah nor ah ski,	B
Thompson, Muskrat	H	Tsane coo yah, Bird	B
Thompson, Richard	E	Tsha goh no tah,	D
Thompson, William	G	Tsha laugh, John	B
Thompson,	F	Tshimitshestalsty, Pochi	B
Thomson,	F	Tshlo sah,	D
Thornton, Amos	E	Tshu ti or wa,	B
Thornton, William	E	Tsu-ga-no-tah,	D
Three Killer,	D		

Tu Tu-ition,	G		Wa Stee,	K
Tu quah tah,	D		Wa ba que,	E
Tu-no-who-lo-ni,	G		Wa ba sha kah,	B
Tu-tai-tioni,	G		Wa he sah,	B
Tucah lo ges kie,	F		Wa ho pa shin ka, 1,	E
Tucker, John	C		Wa ho pa shin ka, 2,	E
Tucker, Young	C		Wa hon ka shee,	E
Tuition,	G		Wa hon ke shu,	E
Tun-tah-ton-mia,	G		Wa how raw ne,	G
Tunatai toni,	G		Wa ka at sea,	E
Tuni,	G		Wa kan se la,	E
Tur na tai ta mi,	G		Wa ke re she,	E
Tur no whai la ni,	G		Wa kon se a,	E
Tur-na-e,	G		Wa kon ta she kah,	B
Tur-no-whiee-lue,	G		Wa le glaw ne ka,	G
Turick, Felix	E		Wa le gra ne ka,	G
Turix, Felix	E		Wa le saw kaw she,	G
Turtle,	C		Wa leh grah nin ka,	F
Twist, John	G		Wa ma ha,	G
Twister,	H		Wa ma wa she,	G
Tyer, Mouse	I		Wa na hu,	G
U co be ta ba,	B		Wa no pa she,	F
U-co-be-ta-be,	B		Wa nom pa she,	E
Uh tah yole,	A		Wa pa ka lah she,	G
Uh-tah-yo-lah, Robin	A		Wa pa sae,	E
Uh-tah-yo-lah,	A		Wa quatshee,	C
Uhnahgay, Black Bat	B		Wa raw caw,	G
Uhnohgoy, Black Bat	B		Wa sa to shin ka,	E
Umphrey, Richard	G		Wa sar tar we,	K
Umphries, Richard	G		Wa saw ba shin cah,	F
Utaw, Arch	B		Wa saw bra she caw,	G
Vann, Hector	G		Wa saw bru she caw,	G
Vann, Henry	F		Wa sha sha	
Vann, James	G		wa ta inka,	E
Vann, Jeff	G		Wa she cah se wa la,	F
Vann, Moses	F		Wa she ha,	E
Vann, Reed	G		Wa she ho cha,	F
Vicery, Wilburn	E		Wa she ka sa pa,	E
Vickeory, Wilburn	E		Wa she nin ka,	G
W Skay ale-los ke,	B		Wa she on car,	B
W-cha-no-ske-ske,	B		Wa she saw pe,	F
W-ske-le-los-ke,	B		Wa shee pa shee,	E

Wa shin caw la gra,	G	Wa-qua-tse,	C
Wa shin caw la gre,	G	Wa-quah-chee,	C
Wa shin caw saw bra,	G	Wa-she-Hoo-tah,	B
Wa shin ka,	F	Wa-ta-she-Kak,	B
Wa shin ka sa pa,	E	Wa-ta-she-ka,	B
Wa shin pe she,	G	Wa-taw-che-Kah,	G
Wa sho na gra,	G	Wa-te-Koon-tah,	B
Wa sho sha,	E	Wa-te-hoon-Kah,	B
Wa sho she,	E	Wa-te-quee-nee,	B
Wa ta in Ka,	E	Wa-tee,	B
Wa ta sah,	B	Wa-tu-Wa-Con-tah,	B
Wa-bau-cu-a,	F	Wa-tu-seh,	B
Wa-bosh-kah,	F	Wa-who-wha,	G,F
Wa-caw-taw-ko-law,	G	Wa-who-who,	G,F
Wa-cha-she-caw,	G	Wa-ya,	B
Wa-cha-tong-gah,	F	Wa-ya-goo-loo-ne,	B
Wa-cha-wa-he-she-ka,	G	Wadego, John	H
Wa-che-ne-caw,	G	Wadegoo, John	H
Wa-con-raw-ko-law,	G	Wadgoo, John	H
Wa-con-ta-she-ka,	B	Waggon,	D
Wa-con-te-no-sha,	B	Wah de Jesqua	
Wa-con-te-no-she,	B	gah loo yah,	I,H
Wa-cun-tah-e-		Wah de de ah mah gah,	I,H
paw-honi-pe,	F	Wah nah de dunc	
Wa-gla-na-she,	B	yaw noo wah sce ah,	I,H
Wa-glen-o-sha,	B	Wah nah de dunce	
Wa-ha-che,	G	you now wah chee,	I,H
Wa-ha-ha,	G,F	Wah te,	B
Wa-ha-nin-ka,	G	Wah yah en dunce	
Wa-ha-tia,	E	so cling dah tah,	I,H
Wa-ha-tie,	E	Wah-de-dah-mah-gah,	I,H
Wa-haw-kah,	F	Wah-ho-ho,	K
Wa-haw-ke-she,	G	Wah-tee,	B
Wa-haw-taw-ne,	G	Wah-tok-she-kah,	B
Wa-he-gah-ha,	F	Wahdegoo, John	H
Wa-he-ha,	E	Wak-to-che-kah,	G
Wa-he-sa,	B	Walasa-ta, John	A
Wa-hon-gea,	E	Walker, John	E
Wa-hon-grea,	E	Walker, Nicholas	I
Wa-le-che-lin-ka,	F	Walker, Samuel	D
Wa-po-se,	G	Walker, Stean	H
Wa-pu-sa,	E	Walker, William	E

Walkingstick, Jackson	A
Walkingstick, Swimmer	A
War Eagle,	E
War Ho Ho,	K
War-she-on-gar,	B
War-ta-war-kon-tah,	B
Was ko moe,	E
Was kot sea,	E
Was kut sae,	E
Washington, George	C
Washington, George	F
Washington, Shepherd	F
Watasata, John	A
Wate-Sa-lo le,	H,I
Water Falling	C
Water, Gone	H
Water, Hunter	F
Water, Standing	H
Watshe,	C
Watt, George	H
Watt,	D
Watt Ge-dle-ga-no-ske,	K
Watt-Ge-dle-ga-No-ske,	K
Watt-Ge-dle-gar-No-ske,	K
Watt-ner-dar-Wee,	K
Watt-sar-lo-le,	H,I
Watte Wat, Big Head	B
Watte de squah,	H,I
Watte-de-squah dar-no-ste,	H,I
Watts, Johnson	C
Watts, William	C
Watts,	D
Waw me paw kewha,	D
Waw-haw-nin-Ka,	G
We le, Pigeon	K
We le Jo nah stoo de,	I,H
We le La wah de,	I,H
We le ce ne Ja ne de yah,	I,H
We le cene ah dah lume cah na we ske,	I,H
We le gar Kar Mar,	H,I
We le ne,	H,I
We le ne E, George	I
We le se ne,	B
We so E pa ho,	D
Wee-le, Charley	K
Wee-le,	K
Welch, John	I
Welch, William	C
Welsh, William	C
Wesley, John	D
West, Beamer	A
West, Rufus	E
Wett,	I
Wh-Nah-Gay, Black Batt	B
Wh-wah-gay, Black Fox	B
Whe la he,	E
Whe o Ka shal,	E
Whipperwill,	D
Whippoor-Will,	A
White, Jim	D
White Path, Lewis	D
White Path,	D
Whitepot,	H
Wild Cat,	C
Wildcat-yo-ha-lah,	C
Will, Pidgeon	
Willey,	F
William, Bob	C
William, Pidgeon	
Williams, George	C
Williams, John	D
Willie, Charley	K
Willis,	B
Willson,	F
Willy, Charley	K

Willy,	F	Woodward, Jack	E
Wilson, Andrew	H	Wool, Moses	G
Wilson, Bull	C	Worcester,	D
Wilson, Chap	I	Wright, Benjamin	D
Wilson, Drum	B	Wright, James	K
Wilson, Ezekiel	H	Wright, John	H
Wilson, Fly	A	Wright, Nelson	H
Wilson, Hunter	A	Writer,	D
Wilson, Joseph	A	Writer,	G
Wilson, Lacy	D	Y-see-que-yar-	
Wilson, Silversmith	H	kar-no-nee,	H,I
Wilson, Terge-ske	K	Y-skar-che,	H,I
Wilson,	F	Ya Se, John	K
Wilson Tar ge ske,	K	Ya-ka-ta-ha,	C
Wilson gar le yah,	H,I	Yah we ar te dle,	K
Wilson ner dar Wee,	K	Yar-gan-cy,	F
Wilson tar ye ske,	K	Yellow Jacket,	C
Wily, Hoy	G	Yellow Jacket,	F
Wirrah,	C	Yellow Leaf,	D
Wo hung Ka shaw,	F	Yer-we-ar-de-dle,	K
Wo-yer-Ger-ge-ske,	H,I	Yo nah,	H,I
Wo-yoh,	B	Yo-le-Sar-che,	H,I
Wofford, Lewis	B	Yo-noo-wah-ye-oh-	
Wofford, William S.	B	gah-yah-gah-to-yoh,	I,H
Woh yoh goo loo ne,	B	Yoholah, Thomas	C
Wolf, Billy	C	Yoo-che-de-he,	C
Wolf, David	C	Young, Bob	C
Wolf, Egoowa	H	Young, Ketchem	C
Wolf, P. Yaung	H	Young, Sulevan	C
Wolf, Yaung	H	Young, Wolf	K
Wolf,	A	Young, Woolf	K
Wolf,	D	Young Beaver,	A
Wolftrack, David	I	Young Beaver,	K
Wolt Ge Dle Ga		Young Beaver,	D
No Ske,	K	Young Beaver,	G
Wood, Adam	H	Young Bird,	H
Wood, Burner	F	Young Chicken,	B
Wood, Samuel	G	Young Crow,	B
Woodard, Jack	E	Young Deer,	B
Woodbounter, Daniel	F	Young Deer,	K
Woodbumter, Daniel	F	Young Deer,	C
Woodbunter, Daniel	F	Young Duck, Joseph	K

Young Duck,	K	Young war we ar de dle,	K
Young Elk,	B	Youngbird, Isaac	I
Young Nar War de dle,	K	Z-se-que-yarkor-nonee,	H,I
Young Pig,	A	Z-skar-che,	H,I
Young Possum,	C	Zeck,	F
Young Raccoon,	D	Zo-le-sur-che,	H
Young Squirrel,	A	Zo-noo-woh-ye-oh-	
Young Squirrel,	C	yah-gah-te-yah,	H
Young War de dle,	K	Zonah,	
Young Wolf,	H	Zone hut sa in ka,	E
Young Wott-ko-lar-har,	K	Zone ka co lo,	E

3rd Regiment, Indian Home Guards, Kansas Infantry

The 3rd Regiment, Indian Home Guards was organized at Carthage, Mo., September 16, 1862 and attached to the 1st Brigade, Dept. of Kansas. This regiment, consisting of Cherokees, was formed after the battle at Locust Grove.

Phillips, William A.	F&S	Colonel
Downing, Lewis	F&S	Lieutenant Colonel
Foreman, John	F&S	Major
Gallagher, William	F&S	Adjutant
Gallaher, William	F&S	Adjutant
Largelere, Alfred	F&S	Regimental Quartermaster
Larzalaer, Alfred	F&S	Regimental Quartermaster
Larzelere, Alfred	F&S	Regimental Quartermaster
Walgamott, George W.	F&S	Surgeon
Wolgamott, George W.	F&S	Surgeon
Wolgomott, George	F&S	Surgeon
Kenney, Charles	F&S	Assistant Surgeon
Kinney, Charus	F&S	Assistant Surgeon
Tuttle, Henry D.	F&S	Assistant Surgeon
Shannon, John L.	F&S	Regimental Commissary of Subsistance
Walker, T.H.B.	F&S	Sergeant Major
Landers, John	F&S	Commissary Sergeant
Landice, John	F&S	Commissary Sergeant
Landis, John	F&S	Commissary Sergeant
Laundis, John	F&S	Commissary Sergeant
Anderson, Henry S.	G,M	Captain
Catcher, White	I	Captain
Christie, Smith	A	Captain
Christy, Smith	A	Captain
Downing, Huckleberry	F	Captain
Feelings,	B	Captain
Fish, Nathan	C	Captain
Grasshopper, Daniel	M	Captain

Kaufman, Solomon	L	Captain
Pegg, Thomas	E	Captain
Phillips, Maxwell	A,G	Captain
Shell, John	L	Captain
Shell, Simon	H	Captain
Smith, Eli	G	Captain
Snell, Simon	H	Captain
Spilman, Alexander C.	B	Captain
Tahlala,	D	Captain
Talalah,	D	Captain
Tar lar la,	D	Captain
Vann, James	K	Captain
Webber, William	E	Captain
White, Chatcher	I	Captain
Benge, Huston	A	First Lieutenant
Blunt, John E.	D	First Lieutenant
Brown, Charles	I	First Lieutenant
Crafts, William G.	M	First Lieutenant
Ely, Eugene H.	G	First Lieutenant
Hanway, John S.	E	First Lieutenant
Harway, John S.	E	First Lieutenant
Howard, Charles A.	I	First Lieutenant
Parsons, Luke F.	C	First Lieutenant
Redbird, Sixkiller	L	First Lieutenant
Robb, Andrew	F	First Lieutenant
Scott, Herman	H	First Lieutenant
Turner, Isaac	B	First Lieutenant
Whitlow, Benjamin	K	First Lieutenant
Bear, Brown	E	Second Lieutenant
Butler, John	M	Second Lieutenant
Carsalawi,	G	Second Lieutenant
Carselain, Proctor	G	Second Lieutenant
Cayot, Julian C.	F,L	Second Lieutenant
Dick, Juniper	F	Second Lieutenant
Downing, Jack	D	Second Lieutenant
Duck, Juniper	F	Second Lieutenant
Foxskin, Flute	C	Second Lieutenant
McCrea, Basil G.	H	Second Lieutenant
McCulloch, William	K	Second Lieutenant
McRea, Basil G.	H	Second Lieutenant
Proctor, Carsubawi	G	Second Lieutenant
Stephens, Spencer S.	G,A	Second Lieutenant

Sunday, William	B	Second Lieutenant
Tanner, Jack	H	Second Lieutenant
Timpson, James	I	Second Lieutenant
Turner, Josh	H	Second Lieutenant
Walkingstick, Fenni	K	Second Lieutenant
Bushyhead, Jesse	L	Sergeant Major
Bainstick, Samuel	F	First Sergeant
Beanstick, Samuel	F	First Sergeant
Beck, John M.	K	First Sergeant
Catching Sunday,	M	First Sergeant
Crimpet, William	M	First Sergeant
Criplet, William	M	First Sergeant
Hanway, Samuel B.	H,F	First Sergeant
Hayway, S.B.	H	First Sergeant
Hendricks, William	L	First Sergeant
Hendrix, William	L	First Sergeant
Hunway, Samuel B.	H	First Sergeant
Jeramiah, Theodore	D	First Sergeant
Jeremiah, Thadeus	D	First Sergeant
Jerimiah, Theodore	D	First Sergeant
Jermiah, Theodore	D	First Sergeant
McPhail, John	G	First Sergeant
Meggs, John	E	First Sergeant
Ross, George W.	I	First Sergeant
Ross, John	K,M	First Sergeant
Service, Peter	D	First Sergeant
Stahl, Elias	A	First Sergeant
Thornton, William R.	L	First Sergeant
Tick Eater,	B	First Sergeant
Heffleman, Tobias Aug	L	Second Sergeant
Martin, Alecha	M	Second Sergeant
Samuel, Creek	E	Second Sergeant
Chambers, James	L	Third Sergeant
Balard, Thomas	E	Fourth Sergeant
Ballard, Thomas	E	Fourth Sergeant
Bollard, Thos	E	Fourth Sergeant
Hendricks, John	L	Fourth Sergeant
Hendrix, John	L	Fourth Sergeant
Archa, Levi	K	Sergeant
Balon, Jeff	D	Sergeant
Balovo, Jeff	D	Sergeant
Bann, Arch	A	Sergeant

Bann, Joseph	A	Sergeant
Bear, John	B	Sergeant
Beavertail, James	M	Sergeant
Bell, Jack	K	Sergeant
Ben, Josiah	A	Sergeant
Benge, Anderson	I	Sergeant
Benge, Harrison	F	Sergeant
Bevertail, James	M	Sergeant
Big, Falker	D	Sergeant
Bird, Jackson	H	Sergeant
Blue Bat,	H	Sergeant
Bowlin, William	G	Sergeant
Burgess, George W.	G	Sergeant
Butler, Joseph	C	Sergeant
Butter, Joseph	C	Sergeant
Canee, Jack	F	Sergeant
Canew, Jack	F	Sergeant
Cano, Jack	F	Sergeant
Canoe, Jack	F	Sergeant
Catcher, Ben	D	Sergeant
Christie, Jake	G	Sergeant
Clay, Henry	F	Sergeant
Crafard, Robert	E	Sergeant
Crawford, Robert	E	Sergeant
Crawler, Charles	E	Sergeant
Creek, Samuel	E	Sergeant
Crier Money,	A	Sergeant
Crofford, Robert	E	Sergeant
Cryer, Maney	A	Sergeant
Daniels, Oseola P.	I	Sergeant
Dobletooth, Jack	K	Sergeant
Downing, George	D	Sergeant
Drapper,	H	Sergeant
Droper,	H	Sergeant
Dropper,	H	Sergeant
Duck, John	F	Sergeant
Elliott, George W.	B	Sergeant
Flute, John	M	Sergeant
Fowler, Oscar	I	Sergeant
Go Back,	C	Sergeant
Goard, Charles R.	F	Sergeant
Goingwolf, Aaron	L	Sergeant

Gompiss, Edward	F	Sergeant
Gord, Charles R.	F	Sergeant
Gourd, Charles R.	F	Sergeant
Gowrd, Charles R.	F	Sergeant
Gritts, Franklin	G	Sergeant
Gritts, Wesley F.	G	Sergeant
Gumpie, Edward	F	Sergeant
Gunpile, Edward	F	Sergeant
Gurmpile, Edward	F	Sergeant
Hair, Wilson	C	Sergeant
Harlin, Ellis	K	Sergeant
Harling, Ellis	K	Sergeant
Hawk, Fishing	F	Sergeant
Hilderbrand, George	H	Sergeant
Hook, Fishing	F	Sergeant
Horn, David	D	Sergeant
Horsefly, James	H	Sergeant
Justice, Sidney	E	Sergeant
Killer, Stephen	A	Sergeant
Kingfisher, John	H	Sergeant
Lasly, George	F	Sergeant
Lastly, Jess	E	Sergeant
Little Bird,	I	Sergeant
McTeer, William	E	Sergeant
Mortar, Van	F	Sergeant
Nowife, Andrew	C	Sergeant
Passen, Peter	M	Sergeant
Passon, Peter	M	Sergeant
Pea Pile, George	D	Sergeant
Pile, George P.	D	Sergeant
Procter, Ezekiel	L	Sergeant
Procter, Johnson	L	Sergeant
Procter, Runabout	H	Sergeant
Proctor, Ezekiel	L	Sergeant
Proctor, John	G	Sergeant
Proctor, Johnson	L	Sergeant
Proctor, Runabout	H	Sergeant
Ridge, John	B	Sergeant
Roberson,	E	Sergeant
Row, Franch	K	Sergeant
Roe, French	K	Sergeant
Roe, Levi	K	Sergeant

Rope, Jack	B	Sergeant
Ross, Silas D.	I	Sergeant
Row, Levi	K	Sergeant
Runabout, Procter	H	Sergeant
Scott, Thomas	I	Sergeant
Scrug Bark,	E	Sergeant
Seabolt, Richard	A	Sergeant
Sixkiller, Kunnic	K	Sergeant
Snail, Blackfox	H	Sergeant
Snail, Jackson	H	Sergeant
Snale, Blackfox	H	Sergeant
Snale, Young Bird	H	Sergeant
Snell, Benjamin	H	Sergeant
Snell, Blackfox	H	Sergeant
Snell, Jackson	H	Sergeant
Snell, Young Bird	H	Sergeant
Snelle, Benjamin	H	Sergeant
Snelle, Jackson	H	Sergeant
Spike, Alick	B	Sergeant
Spikes, Thomas	M	Sergeant
Squirrel, Isaac	G	Sergeant
Star, Joseph	A	Sergeant
Trotting Wolf,	A	Sergeant
Tulsey, John	K	Sergeant
Tulsy, John	K	Sergeant
Vann, Arch	A	Sergeant
Vann, Joseph	A	Sergeant
Vann, Josiah	A	Sergeant
Vann, Morter	F	Sergeant
Waker, Charles	I	Sergeant
Walker, Charles	I	Sergeant
Walkingstick, Levi	G	Sergeant
Welch, John	H	Sergeant
Welsh, John	H	Sergeant
Young Duck,	B	Sergeant
Young Rouch,	E	Sergeant
Young Wolf,	C	Sergeant
Deecke, Lewis	B	Quartermaster Sergeant
Ice, John	M	Second Corporal
Bird, Humming	A	Third Corporal
Humming, Bird	A	Third Corporal
Duvall, Dave	M	Fourth Corporal

Williams, Mitchel	M	Sixth Corporal
Haw, Black	D	Eighth Corporal
Aaron, Little	A	Corporal
Acorn, Ned	K	Corporal
Adam, Little	A	Corporal
Arch, Daniel	K	Corporal
Baylock, William	G	Corporal
Bear Paw, Richard	B	Corporal
Bearpaw, Charles	A	Corporal
Beaver, Lewis	G	Corporal
Bendabout,	E	Corporal
Benge, Riddle	A	Corporal
Bigfeather, Tyres	F	Corporal
Bird Bunches,	K	Corporal
Blackbird,	M	Corporal
Bowlin, Johnson	G	Corporal
Broom,	H	Corporal
Brown,	H	Corporal
Brush, George	F	Corporal
Buckhorn, Ned	B	Corporal
Cequoyah,	C	Corporal
Cequoyer,	C	Corporal
Channlicksie,	F	Corporal
Cher ner que,	D	Corporal
Chicken, Christie	G	Corporal
Chickuly,	F	Corporal
Chulicklie,	F	Corporal
Chulicksie,	F	Corporal
Chuliscia,	F	Corporal
Chuliscis,	F	Corporal
Cloud, Samuel	I	Corporal
Cochran, Elisha	D	Corporal
Cockrum, Elisha	D	Corporal
Coleman, John	F	Corporal
Colston, Samuel	I	Corporal
Colston, William	E	Corporal
Columbus,	A	Corporal
Conseen, David	K	Corporal
Cornelius,	F	Corporal
Cornelius,	G	Corporal
Crawler,	M	Corporal
Crittenden, Andrew	I	Corporal

Crying Bear,	A	Corporal
David, Stephen	C	Corporal
Daylight,	M	Corporal
Deer, Coming	C	Corporal
Deerhead, Walker	G	Corporal
Dirt Allgone,	M	Corporal
Dollar, Arch	B	Corporal
Doublehead luladulthe,	F	Corporal
Downing, Abbot	L	Corporal
Downing, Johnson	D	Corporal
Dry, Peter	B	Corporal
Ellis, Red	B	Corporal
Field, Willey	H	Corporal
Fields, Wiley	H	Corporal
Fisher, Johnson	D	Corporal
Flute, William	M	Corporal
Fodder, Chi-War sky	D	Corporal
Foreman, Rider	H	Corporal
Forman, Rider	H	Corporal
Foster, Daniel	F	Corporal
French,	C	Corporal
Frog, Decaske	K	Corporal
Frog, Sixkiller	L	Corporal
Gess, Bob	H	Corporal
Glass, Thomas	E	Corporal
Goard, John R.	I	Corporal
Gourd, John R.	I	Corporal
Grape Soup,	B	Corporal
Grease,	I	Corporal
Greece, Ned	C	Corporal
Green, Ned	C	Corporal
Grimett, William	G	Corporal
Grinnett, Little	G	Corporal
Grubbs, Wilson	I	Corporal
Guess, Bob	H	Corporal
Guess, William	I	Corporal
Guliskey,	F	Corporal
Gulisky,	F	Corporal
Guss, Bob	H	Corporal
Hair, Nicholas	I	Corporal
Hawk, Lewis	C	Corporal
Hawkins, Leslie	F	Corporal

Head, Naked	K	Corporal
Hendricks, Thomas	L	Corporal
Hendricks, Willis	L	Corporal
Henry, Young Bird	L	Corporal
Hildebrand, Michael	I	Corporal
Hog, George	D	Corporal
Housebug, Jackson	K	Corporal
Hummingbird, William	L	Corporal
Ingland, Joseph	B	Corporal
Johnson, Ellis	C	Corporal
Johnston, Ellis	C	Corporal
Ka-lo-ge-ta,	M	Corporal
Keener, Arch	D	Corporal
Keener, Joe W.	D	Corporal
Kener, Arch	D	Corporal
Kener, Joe W.	D	Corporal
Killerwith, Sam	A	Corporal
Killewith, Samuel	A	Corporal
Kinner, Joe W.	D	Corporal
Kolo-ge-ta,	M	Corporal
Laslie, Hawkins	F	Corporal
Lessy, Hawkins	F	Corporal
Lifter,	E	Corporal
Martin,	B	Corporal
McDaniels, Walter	I	Corporal
McLane, Luna	C	Corporal
Middlestriker, Lowly	A	Corporal
Mike Pig,	H	Corporal
Mole, Ned	A	Corporal
Mose, Stephen	K	Corporal
Mosely,	H	Corporal
Mosley,	H	Corporal
Murphy, Saturday	C	Corporal
Museler,	E	Corporal
Mussels,	E	Corporal
Nickojack, Daniel	C	Corporal
Pass,	G	Corporal
Passen, John	M	Corporal
Passon, John	M	Corporal
Pathkiller, John	A	Corporal
Peter, Proctor	F	Corporal
Pig, Mike	H	Corporal

Pigeon, Drywater	B	Corporal
Powel,	B	Corporal
Procter, Elegant	H	Corporal
Procter, Peter	F	Corporal
Proctor, Eligat	H	Corporal
Proctor, Peter	F	Corporal
Prote, Peter	F	Corporal
Proter, Petter	F	Corporal
Puff, Runabout	B	Corporal
Pumpkin, Pile	D	Corporal
Pumpkin Pilee,	D	Corporal
Punkin, Pile	D	Corporal
Punking, Pile	D	Corporal
Rabbit,	F	Corporal
Rabbit Bunch,	K	Corporal
Rabbit Bunches,	K	Corporal
Red,	A	Corporal
Redbird, Daniel	I	Corporal
Ridge, John L.	D	Corporal
Ridge, Jonah	E	Corporal
Ridge, Sweetwater	E	Corporal
Runabout, Puff	B	Corporal
Sapsucker, Snail	B	Corporal
Saunders, Johnson	F	Corporal
Saunders, Joseph	I	Corporal
Scott, John	H	Corporal
Sequo yah,	C	Corporal
Sitawaca,	E	Corporal
Sixkiller, Moses	H	Corporal
Sixkiller, Samuel	L	Corporal
Sixkiller, Soldier	L	Corporal
Sixkiller, Tyler	L	Corporal
Skift-tah-teer-sky,	F	Corporal
Skitt, Hulsey	G	Corporal
Soap, George	D	Corporal
Soldier, Sixkiller	L	Corporal
Spring,	E	Corporal
Springfrog, Sawnee	E	Corporal
Springston, John	I	Corporal
Squirel, Walter	I	Corporal
Squirrel, Walter	I	Corporal
Squirril, Walter	I	Corporal

Stand,	G	Corporal
Star, Edward	A	Corporal
Stealer, Josiah	E	Corporal
Stela, Josiah	E	Corporal
Steler, Josiah	E	Corporal
Stellor, Josiah	E	Corporal
1818Stock, Wasody	H	Corporal
Stop, Wasseckey	H	Corporal
Sunday, John	F	Corporal
Sunday, Young Duck	L	Corporal
Swimer, George	D	Corporal
Swimmer, Rider	A	Corporal
Tadpole, John	C	Corporal
Taner, S.	H	Corporal
Tanner, Sequayah	H	Corporal
Tener, Arch	D	Corporal
Tener, Joe W.	D	Corporal
Terapin, Nelson	I	Corporal
Terrapin, Nelson	I	Corporal
Thompson, Charles	H	Corporal
Thomson, Charles	H	Corporal
Turner, S.	H	Corporal
Tutt, John	C	Corporal
Uprim,	K	Corporal
Uprom,	K	Corporal
Vann, Abe	F	Corporal
Walker, Eli	E	Corporal
Walker, John	E	Corporal
Walker, Nick	B	Corporal
Walker,	H	Corporal
Walkingstick, Charles	G	Corporal
Walkingstick, Drinker	F	Corporal
Water, Elijah	F	Corporal
Water, George	K	Corporal
Waterbrook, Daniel	F	Corporal
Waters, Elijah	F	Corporal
Waters, Mike	A	Corporal
Watters, Elijah	F	Corporal
Whetter,	G	Corporal
Wilson, Turnover	H	Corporal
Wolf, Alex	K	Corporal
Woodall, Oceotla	D	Corporal

Young Bird Killer,	L	Corporal
Young Turkey Belt,	B	Corporal
Baker, Addison	D,C	Regimental Quartermaster
Buffington, Dorcas		Matron
Chandler, Daniel L.	G	Hospital Steward

Privates:

Aaron, Long	A		Arron,	G
Aaron,	F		Artsey, Nedson	C
Ackibald, Hardshell	F		Artsey, Wilson	C
Acorn, Rider	L		Artsy, Nedson	C
Acorn, Writer	L		Atolahee, Oldcorn	C
Adam, Doublehead	K		Atollahee, Oldcorn	C
Adam, George	C		Au m cah lee,	F
Adam, William	G		Ave Liver,	K
Adam,	F		Awa, July	K
Addam, George	C		Away, July	K
Ah m tsa,	G		B Poor Wolf,	A
Ah ne tsa,	G		Babing, Haming	E
Alexander,	A		Back, Heavy	H
All gone,	G		Bailey, John	L
Anderson, James	M		Bainstick, James	F
Andrew, George	C		Baldridge, Benjamin	G
Ar na yes ka,	E		Baldridge, Columbus	C
Ar ne zes kee,	E		Baldridge, James	A
Arch, Alexander	A		Baldridge, James	I
Arch, Beamor	H		Baldridge, Jesse	C
Arch, Cloud	M		Baldridge, Samuel	A
Arch, Little	M		Baldridge, Thicket	F
Arch, Looker	F		Baldridge, Wheat	F
Arch Silk,	A		Baldridge, William	I
Arch Waw sau te,	B		Baldridge, Wilson	I
Archbold, Hardshell	F		Baldrige, Benjamin	G
Archibald, Hardshell	G		Baldrige, Bird	M
Archilla,	E		Baldrige, William	I
Archilla,	H		Baldrige, Wilson	I
Archlla,	E		Baldwine, James	A
Archubald, Hardshell	F		Ballard, Thomas	I
Arnold, Jesse	I		Bamstick, James	F
Aron,	G		Banjo, Ned	M

Banon, Jack	M		Benge, Obediah	A
Bare Poor Charley,	K		Benge, Richard	A
Bark, Nugin	I		Benge, Robert	A
Bark,	H		Benge, William	A
Bark,	I		Benjamin,	A
Barrow, Jack	M		Big, Bullet	G
Basket,	A		Big, Feather	B
Batt sah doo lah,	F		Big, Robbin	B
Beamer, John	B		Bigfeather, Ellis	K
Beamor, George	H		Bigfether, Cloud	K
Beamor, Johnson	H		Bigfoot, Arch	F
Bean, Charley	M		Bigmush, Henry	I
Bean, Hail	H		Bigside, John	D
Bean, Thompson	C		Bill, Ketcher	C
Bean, William	M		Bill Chew new	
Beane, Thompson	C		law husky,	K
Beans,	E		Bird, Beldrage	M
Beanstick, Alex	K		Bird, Chopping	D
Beanstick, James	F		Bird, Humming	A
Beanstick, John	K		Bird, Humming	D
Bear, Hail	H		Bird Bill,	C
Bear Paw,	M		Black Bird,	A
Bearmeat, John	A		Black Bird,	D
Bearpaw, Isaac	G		Black Fox,	K
Bearpaw, John	G		Blackbird, David	K
Beaver, George	G		Blackbird, Tobaccowell	A
Beaver, Hickory	G		Blackbird, William	A
Beaver, John	B		Blackfoot, George	M
Beaver, Johnson	H		Blackwood, Lewis	L
Beaver, Silk	A		Blair, Charles	A
Beaver Toter, Lacy	B		Blair, Lewis	G
Beavertoter, Benjamin	H		Blair, Thomas	A
Beavertoter, Jesse	H		Blanket, Falden	D
Beenstick, Alex	K		Blanket, George	D
Beerpaw, Isaac	G		Blossom,	F
Bemer, George	H		Blue,	B
Bemor, Johnson	H		Blue Bird, Stephen	B
Ben, Blackfoot	M		Blue Wolf,	B
Bendabout, John	H		Blythe, John	M
Benge, George	A		Boiles, John G.	M
Benge, George	M		Boldridge, Thicket	F
Benge, McElmore	A		Boldridge, Wheat	F

Bolin, Edward	I		Bulpag, Jackson	E
Bolin, Haman	E		Bulpaz, Jackson	E
Boling, Haming	E		Bump, William	A
Bolling, Haming	E		Bunches Hammer,	K
Bone Eater,	F		Burk, Spike	D
Boorke, Spike	D		Burke, Spike	D
Bottle Hogshooter,	L		Burns, James	I
Bout, Turning	G		Burnt,	A
Bowlin, John	G		Bush, George	F
Bowling, Haming	E		Bush, Samuel	F
Boyle, J.G.	M		Bush, William	F
Boylsom, Joseph	H		Bushyhead, Henry	L
Brad, Seneca	L		Bushyhead, Joseph	F
Brady, Bucks	D		Bushyhead Buck,	B
Brewer, Jackson	K		Buster, Thomas	I
Brewner, Isac	D		Buterfly,	E
Broad, Seneca	L		Butler, Joseph	C
Broken Feather,	I		Butterfly,	E
Brown, Henry	H		Buttler, Judge	C
Brown, Nelson	M		Ca se la wa,	M
Brown, William	M		Cabbage Head,	M
Bruner, Isaac	D		Cacher Goll,	D
Brunner, Isaac	D		Cade, William	E
Brushes,	H		Cah lau noo	
Bryant, Jo	M		hasky Blue,	C
Buck, Eli	C		Cah le sca wei, Joseph	C
Buffalo Tom,	K		Calling,	D
Buffalo Walkabout,	K		Camp, Samuel	A
Buffington, Harry	K		Camp Chicken,	F
Buffington, Henry	D		Camp Chickens,	F
Buffington, Henry	K		Campbell, Rope	G
Bufington, Henry	D		Cane, Levi	M
Bug, Culy	K		Car law noo	
Bug, Joshua	M		kasky Blue,	C
Buley, Charles	M		Car le sca we, Joseph	C
Bull, Tom	M		Carey, Michael	I
Bull Frog,	C		Carlaw noo hasky Blue,	C
Bull Frog,	D		Carlaweskee,	C
Bullfrog, Jackson	E		Carlescawe, Moses	C
Bullfrog, Ned	L		Carmy, Jack	D
Bullfrog, Wilson	L		Carson, Dave	M
Bullfrog Coming,	K		Carver, Jarrell	M

Casha too tee, Jess	F		Chickille,	F
Catcher, Gall	D		Chicklle,	F
Catcher, Moses	D		Chist, John	L
Catcher, Running	G		Christie, Henry	G
Catfish, Jack	C		Christie, Jesse	G
Cauling,	D		Christie, Jim	M
Caulling,	D		Christie, Measley	G
Ceasar,	F		Christie, Richard	G
Ceaseer,	F		Christie, Thomas	G
Ceaser,	F		Christie, William	G
Ceteyah, Iuecnna	C		Christy, Eater	H
Chah wanee,	F		Christy, Swimmer	H
Chah wanner,	F		Chu-wa-loo-ky,	C
Chah wee skah,	C		Chucalata, Benjamin	F
Chah wun ee,	F		Chucalata, Richard	F
Chah wunnee,	F		Chucalati, Benjamin	F
Chambers, Anderson	F		Chucalati, Richard	F
Chambers, James	I		Chucalita, Benjamin	F
Chamberson, Anderson	F		Chucalita, Richard	F
Chananna,	F		Chucker, Joe	D
Chanonee,	F		Chuculati, Benjamin	F
Char no que,	D		Chuculati, Richard	F
Char war ne,	F		Cla sta ma,	D
Char wee skah,	C		Clah ster mer,	D
Char wes cah,	C		Clah-star-mer,	D
Charles,	B		Clark, George	E
Charlesenco,	E		Claus tar mer,	D
Chau naw nee,	F		Clay, Washington	F
Chawanee,	F		Claymore,	A
Che no que,	M		Cloud, John	C
Cheawame,	F		Cloud, John	K
Cherwarnee,	F		Cloud,	M
Chest, John	L		Cloude, John	K
Chew-new-la-husty, Bill	K		Cloy yeh cah,	D
			Cloyer cah,	D
Chi-ne-que,	M		Cloyercha,	D
Chickelle,	F		Cochram, Elisha	D
Chicken, Albert	M		Cochran, Avery	I
Chicken, Ned	K		Cochran, Price	I
Chickenroost,	K		Cochran, Walker	I
Chickens, Camp	F		Cockcome, Watt	K
Chickill,	F		Cockrem, James	K

Cockrem, Watt	K		Crawler,	E
Cockrom, George	K		Creek, James	A
Cockrom, James	K		Creek, John	I
Cockrom, Watt	K		Creek, Thomas	A
Cockrum, George	K		Creek, William	I
Cockrum, James	K		Cristie, Jim	M
Cockrum, Watt	K		Critendon, James	D
Cockum, George	K		Crittenden, Aaron	L
Cold Weather,	B		Crittenden, Berry	I
Cole, Cooley	K		Crittenden, Jack	I
Columbus,	M		Crittenden, James	D
Comeing, Edward	G		Crittenden, Michil	I
Coming, Bulfrog	K		Crittenden, Nick	I
Coming, Bullfrog	K		Crope, Lewis	F
Coming, Company	G		Crossing, Tadpole	C
Coming, Deer	A		Crossland, Andy	F
Coming, Edward	G		Crying Bear,	B
Coming, Wilson	I		Crying Bear,	D
Coming Company,	G		Crying Bird,	D
Comingdeer, Peter	A		Crying Wolf,	H
Comings, Edward	G		Cuh la we sky Tobacco,	C
Conner, Jim	C		Culy Bug,	K
Conseen, Frank	K		Cumming, Edward	G
Consene, Frank	K		Cummings, Ned	L
Coo-we-scoo-nee-geo,	C		Cummins, Ned	L
Cooly, Bug	K		Cut Law,	E
Corn Silk,	L		Cutter, Harry	B
Cornelius,	B		Dab, Eunice	G
Corner, Jack	D		Dab, John	G
Cornsilk Cutter,	I		Dah ner ser ni,	D
Cornstalk Cutter,	I		Daller, Charles	F
Counting, Jim	M		Dallohia, John	H
Counting Man,	M		Daniel, Abe	F
Courting, Jim	M		Daniel, James	B
Courting Man,	M		Daniel, Phillips	K
Couson, Dave	M		Daniel, Richard	F
Crane Eater Turtle,	C		Daniel,	E
Crape, Lewis	F		Darley, Josiah	H
Crapo, Issac	E		Darley, Josiah	H
Crapo, Lewis	G		David, Canen	F
Crawfish, Stand	I		Davidson,	I
Crawler, Proctor	A		Davis, Alexander	D

Davis, Jesse	E		Downing, Dragon	D
Davis, Jesserson	M		Downing, Flea	H
Davis, Little	B		Downing, George	I
De ca nee,	E		Downing, Jack	I,D
Deer, Coming	A		Downing, James	L
Deer, In the water	A		Downing, Joe	D
Deer, Little	A		Downing, Joshua	M
Deer, Watering	K		Downing, Lewis	M
Deercoming, Peter	A		Downing, Sam	K
Deerhead, James	G		Downing, Wolf	H
Deerhead, John	G		Dragger, Osa	L
Delohe, John	H		Dragging, Canol Foder	I
Denton, John	M		Dragging, George	C
Despiser,	G		Drapee, Duck	K
Dick, Bill	M		Drunkard,	M
Dick, Henry	C		Dry,	I
Dick, Hungry	C		Dry Jumping,	I
Dick, Johnson	B		Dry water, John	B
Dick, Matien	F		Duck, Edward	F
Dipper, Thompson	E		Duck, Levi	B
Dirt, Seller	F		Dyer, Bill	M
Dirt, Seller	M		Eagle, John	E
Dirt, Thrower	A		Eagle,	I
Dirt, William	A		Ear, Ike	M
Dirt Eater,	D		Eatin,	G
Dirt Seller,	G		Eli, Pot	A
Dirteater, Bigmush	B		Elias, Samuel	A
Disappointed,	M		Eligah,	H
Diver, Harris	F		Elijah,	H
Dixon, Henry	L		Elijah,	I
Dixon, John	M		Elis, C.	H
Dixon, William	M		Elis, James	H
Doctor,	G		Elis, Nathaniel	F
Dolohu, John	H		Ellis, C.	H
Double, Jack	D		Ellis, James	H
Douning, Mink	A		Ellis, Nathaniel	F
Down, Water	G		Ellis, Samuel	A
Downing, Aaron	D		Emery, Peter	E
Downing, Aleck	D		England, Jackson	L
Downing, Charles	H		England, Lincoln	L
Downing, Dall	D		Falling, Pot	B
Downing, David	G		Faster, Solomon	A

Fawn, Killer	G	
Fawnkiller, Peter	C	
Fawnkiller, Robert	E	
Fealding,	H	
Fealing,	H	
Feather, Jess	K	
Feather, Johnson	F	
Feeling, Adam	B	
Feeling,	H	
Fence, George	A	
Field, Lawyer	L	
Field, Thomas	K	
Fields, George	G	
Fields, Jim	M	
Fields, Lawyer	L	
Fire, Back	G	
Fire, Sitting	G	
Firethrower, Henderson	K	
Fish, Wade B.	F	
Fish, Watt	K	
Fisher, Isaac	M	
Fishinghawk, Charles	F	
Fixing, Felix	L	
Flower Killer, Ned	M	
Flute, Joe Rice	B	
Flying, Bird	F	
Fodder, Runabout	D	
Fomy, Jim	M	
Fonkiller, Robert	E	
Foreman, Jack	B	
Foreman, Jesse	I	
Foreman, Nelson	L	
Forman, Jack	B	
Forman, Jesse	I	
Forman, Nelson	L	
Foster, Archilla	F	
Fourkiller, Hawk	G	
Fourkiller, Larkin	L	
French, Feather	K	
French,	A	
Frisley, David	C	
Frog, Spring	G	
Frog,	A	
Ge squa i gee,	C	
Geeskey, Johnson	H	
George, Arch	M	
George, Goo-ne-sho-we	C	
George, Henry	A	
George, John	C	
George, Six killer	L	
George,	B	
Geskey, Johnson	H	
Get up,	C	
Gettingen,	A	
Gettingni,	A	
Glaa staak noh,	F	
Glaspie, Joe	H	
Glaspin, Joe	H	
Glass, Isaac	F	
Glass, James	A	
Glass, Jesse	F	
Glass, Josiah	F	
Glass, Panther	F	
Glass, Robbert	F	
Glass, Samuel	F	
Glass, Tully	F	
Glass,	A	
Gliss, Panther	F	
Go Round,	G	
Goard, Charles R.	I	
Goard, Daniel R.	I	
Going Backwards,	M	
Goingman, Tom	B	
Goingsnake, Hooper	M	
Goingwolf, Johnson	L	
Goo-wee-sko-we, George	C	
Gooddollar, Young Bird	B	
Goodmoney, Eli	B	
Goodmoney, John Rogers	B	
Goodmoney, Johnson	B	
Goosley, Joseph	I	

Grass, Jessee	F		Hawkins,	M
Grass,	B		Haynie, Benjamin K.	L
Grasshopper, Driver	I		Head, Guiney	F
Grasshopper, Jack	H		Head, Poke	K
Grasshopper, Jack	H		Heavy, Back	H
Greece, David	C		Heder,	H
Greece, George	C		Heel, John	B
Grimett, Robert	G		Heider, Catcher	L
Grinnett, Robert	G		Hendricks, James R.	L
Grinsmith, William	M		Hendricks, Joseph	L
Guess, Looney	I		Hendrix, Joseph	L
Guhlawiski, Pathkiller	L		Henry, Bushyhead	L
Guskey, Johnson	H		Henry, George	A
Gutter,	H		Henry, Samuel	D
Gutter,	M		Henson, Grubb	I
Hail Bear,	H		Henson, Jacob	I
Hainie, Benjamin K.	L		Henson, John	I
Hair, John	D		Henson, Washington	I
Hair, Throwing	G		Hickory,	A
Halcum, Samuel	F		Hicks, Crawler	F
Halfbreed, Johnson	I		Hicks, George	K
Hammar, Tassle	I		Hicks, Samuel	M
Hammer, Bunch	K		Hider, Catcher	L
Hammer, Tom	C		Hider, Youngwolf	L
Hammer,	A		Hider,	H
Hammond, Thomas	D		Hight, John	D
Hamond, Thomas	D		Hildebrand, Joe	B
Hana,	E		Hilderand, Joe	B
Hanna,	E		Hilderbrand, Joe	B
Harjo, Charles	E		Hillcum, Samuel	F
Harris, Diver	F		Hockory, Beaver	G
Hatchet, Fisher	M		Hogany, Ellis	K
Hatchet, John	F		Hogg, Different	L
Hatchet, Thomas	F		Hoggany, Ellis	K
Hauk, Wolf	G		Hogner, Ellis	L
Haw, Black	D		Hogshooter, Bird	B
Haw, James B.	D		Hogshooter, Bird	B
Hawk, Adam	L		Hogshooter, Bottle	L
Hawk, Elisha	D		Hogshooter, WarKiller	B
Hawk, John	A		Hogshooter,	H
Hawk, Little	G		Hogskin, James	I
Hawk, Wolfe	G		Hogtoter, George	F

Holcum, Samuel	F		Jesse, Washington	L
Hood, Borrow	A		Jesse,	M
Hood, Richard	F		Jey-che-chy,	E
Hooper, Joseph	G		Jim, George	M
Hoopin, Seecahwe	F		Jim, Johnson	M
Hoopin,	F		Jo-hoo-ster,	
Horn, Thompson	F		Deer in water	C
How, James B.	D		Jo-hoo-ster,	C
Howard, Nicholas	M		Jock, Wait	D
Hoyt, George W.	H		Joe hoo stah,	
Hoyt, Hinman B.	H		Deer on the Water	C
Hulcum, Samuel	F		John, Tutt	C
Huming, Bird	D		John, Wright	D
Humming-bird,	A		John,	D
Hungry, Jesse	H		John,	E
Husky, Chilluly	K		Johnson, Duck	K
Ice, Jack	G		Johnson, Hughs	E
Ice, William	M		Johnson, Jack	F
Ike, Ere	M		Johnson, Jug	B
In the Water,	L		Johnson, Ola he at er	C
Ingles, John F.	D		Johnson, Ola he	
Israel, Phillip	M		yar tar	C
Isreal, Phillip	M		Johnson,	M
Iye che chy,	E		Johoostah,	
Jack, Catfish	C		Deer in water	C
Jack, Watt	D		Jones, Charles	D
Jack,	E		Jones, Tom	M
Jackin,	A		Jones,	B
Jackisa,	A		Jonson,	
Jackson, Dave	M		Oo la-he-ya-tah	C
Jackson, Duck	K		Joseph,	A
Jackson,	D		Josiah,	B
Jackson,	E		Ju wa lu key, Old	H
James, Charles	D		Ju wa lus key,	H
James, Nick	K		Ju wa luskey, Old	H
James, Swimmer			Ju-wa-lu-key, Davis	H
James,	E		Judge, Otter	G
Jar-ne-na-ner,	E		Judge,	M
Jar-ne-wa-ner,	E		July, John	K
Jaybird, Raf...	C		Jumper,	A
Jehola, James	E		Jumper,	F
Jess, Washington	L		Jumper,	E

Jumper,	B		Killer,	D
Justice, Richard	G		Killey,	D
Juwaluker, Old	H		Killy,	D
Jye-che-chy,	E		Kingfisher, Arch	C
Ka do jo lot se,	M		Kingfisher, Jim	B
Ka-du-yo-lot-se,	M		Kingfisher, John	B
Kah mi gi,	D		Kingfisher, Old	H
Kah-nu-gi,	D		Kingfisher,	B
Kah-yer-sco-ni-he,	D		Knab,	A
Kah-yer-skon-he,	D		Knight, George	C
Kak yer sco ni he,	D		Knight, John	D
Kalmige, Keener	D		Knight, Samuel	D
Kar-yer-sco-mi-hi,	D		Knobb,	A
Keath, George	I		Kobley,	D
Kebler, Ned	D		Koh-nu-gi,	D
Keener, Daniel	I		Kohmigi, Kener	D
Keer, Frank	E		Koon, Richard	I
Keet-lee-chee-lee,	I		Lacy, William	C
Keith, George	I		Landhunter,	E
Keith,	F		Large,	D
Keitlee, Che-ley	I		Lasley, Charles	L
Keller, John	M		Lasley, Leach	L
Kelly, John	M		Laslie, Charles	L
Kener, Fox	G		Lassley, Charles	L
Kener, Kak-mur-ge	D		Lassley, Leach	L
Kener-koh-mi-gi,	D		Latamore, Ezekel	A
Kenner, Fox	G		Latamore, Sam	A
Kerr, Frank	E		Law-cut,	E
Kesterson, George M.	L		Lawlee,	E
Ketcher, Bill	C		Lawnah,	M
Keys, Fish	B		Lawyer,	C
Keys,	E		Leach, George	C
Kilinigi,	D		Leach, John	M
Kill, Chicksaw	H		Leach, Wick	C
Killakee,	F		Leacy, William	C
Killar, Ned	D		Leaf, Carrier	L
Killer, Chicksaw	D		Leaf,	H
Killer, Jackson	K		Learge,	D
Killer, John	M		Lee, Alex	K
Killer, Knight	F		Lee, James	A
Killer, Lally	K		Lee, John	A
Killer, Ned	D		Lee, John	K

Lee, Johnson	K		Martere, Bill	M
Lee, Sam	K		Marteri, Bill	M
Leftar,	D		Martese, Bill	M
Legg, James	K		Martier, William	M
Leslie, James	M		Martin, Bill	M
Leslie, Lacy	F		Martin, Jackson	M
Lewis, Parchmeal	I		Martin, Tawchulonar	C
Lias, Pigeon	B		Mathew,	A
Lie,	K		Matie, Bill	M
Lief,	H		Matoye, Jim	C
Lifter,	D		Mattoy, Jim	C
Lightening bug,	M		Mawhee, John	C
Lincoln, Abraham	G		Mayes, Tallow	C
Little Girl,	A		McClelland, Jacob C.	G
Liver,	A		McCloud,	E
Livingston, Ned	H		McCoy, John	I
Livingstones, Ned	H		McCoy,	M
Lizard, James	E		McDonald, Archibald	M
Logan,	M		McDonel, Samuel	L
Long, Charley	H		McElery, John	M
Long, Eli	L		McEllmore, Franch	K
Long, Jess	E		McHeanson, Bob	M
Long, William	I		McIntosh, John	A
Looker, Arch	F		McIntush, John	A
Looney, Louis	H		McLettan, Jacob C.	G
Louney, Louis	H		McPherson, Bob	M
Lovit, William	M		McRemore, French	K
Luney, Louis	H		Measurer,	E
Lunny, Louis	H		Merideth, George	I
Luny, Tom	H		Messenger,	G
Lying Water,	B		Middlestrikes, Dragon	A
Mackey, George	M		Mike,	B
Maise, Tarlow	C		Miller Green,	M
Man Counting,	M		Mistake, Louis	H
Mann, Ice	F		Mistela,	E
Mann, P.S.	F		Mixed Water,	A
Mannan, James	G		Mixedwater, Alexander	L
Manstealer, Standing	G		Mixwater, Alexander	L
March, William	D		Molten, Lack	M
Marchall, Jack	F		Monkey Water,	A
Marshall, Jack	F		Monkey Waters,	A
Marten, William	M		Morgan, Henry	I

Morten, Lock	M		Noysey,	E
Morten, William	M		Nuggin, Bark	I
Morton, William	M		Nugin, Bark	I
Mose, George	K		Nusky, Eli-reta	K
Mose, Toeneate	K		Nusky, Sanee reta	K
Moten, Lack	M		O-war-las-ky,	D
Moten, William	M		Ochescawle, Ned	C
Moton, William	M		Old,	I
Mouse,	C		Old John,	D
Musgrove, George	M		Old Looney,	H
Mush, Zeke	B		Old Luney,	H
Mushmelon,	B		Old Lunney,	H
Musk, Lewis	F		Oo cha looda, Jesse	F
Muskrat, Daniel	I,H		Oo choloo a, Jess	F
Muskrat, Darley	H		Oo-cha-loo-or, Jessy	F
Muskrat, David	K		Oo-ge-lul-e,	B
Muskrat, William	K		Oo-le-shum-e,	B
Muskroe, George	M		Oo-le-skun-ee,	B
Must, Lewis	F		Oo-squa-too-cha,	F
Naches, Ezekiel	E		Oo-squh-too-cha,	F
Nachies, James	E		Oo-sul a te na tue,	C
Nail, Tassil	D		Oo-sul-ta-na-tur,	C
Nake, Tassale	D		Oo-tahl-tki,	M
Nale, Tassel	D		Oo-tald-tki,	M
Nar too wr yar,	C		Oo-to-la-ta-na,	EMC
Natches, James	E		Oo-to-leah-nan,	E
Natchez, Ezekiel	E		Oo-wa-le-tee, Sam	C
Natt, Spade	K		Oo-wau-sawty,	C
Nave, Henry	E		Ook-to-blow ah,	C
Ned, Lookingoat	L		Ook-too-claw-wah,	C
Ned, Prince	C		Opossum, Six Killer	L
Ned,	D		Or-gah-tak-ca,	F
Ned Fal las see,	E		Osage, Jackson	I
Ned-bal-low-see,	E		Osage, Samuel	I
Nelson, Ben	D		Osage,	C
Nettletoler, Ned	F		Ostile, Joseph	A
Nettletoter, Hock	F		Ostile,	A
Nick, Tar che che	K		Otter, Charles	F
Nickey,	E		Otter, Lifter	B
Niggar, Jack	B		Otter, Scraper	L
Noisey,	E		Otter,	B
Nole, Tassel	D		Otterlifter, Dave	K

Our-war-lon sky,	D		Pile, Moses P.	D
Owaltar, Sam	C		Polone, Soldier	
Owawsoty,	C		Poor Bear,	M
Palone, Andrew	C		Poor Boy,	L
Palore, Andrew	C		Poor Wolf,	A
Pan tola lah,	D		Poorboy, Eli	I
Panther,	E		Poorboy, Jackson	L
Parchmeal, Lewis	I		Poorboy, Samuel	I
Paris, Jesse	M		Pot, Eli	A
Parris, Jessy	M		Pot, Falling	B
Partridge,	G		Potato,	A
Passon, Stephen	M		Pott, George	E
Paten, J.O.	L		Pott, Isaac	C
Pathkiller, Guhlawiski	L		Potts, George	E
Patridge,	G		Pouch, Charles	D
Paunch,	M		Price, Ansil D.	L
Payton, J.O.	L		Price, Joseph	I
Peacheater, George	K		Prince, Ned	C
Peter, Fawnkiller	C		Prisby, James	A
Peter, John	A		Pristy, James	A
Peter,	G		Pritchett, Jack	G
Petit, Curry	I		Pritchett, John	G
Petitt, Charles	E		Pritchett, Mike	G
Pett, Charles	E		Pritchett, Sieska	G
Pettit, Curry	I		Procter, Aleck	H
Peyton, John Oliver	L		Proctor, Alexander	G
Pheasant,	C		Proctor, Alick	H
Pheasant,	I		Proctor, Crawler	A
Phillipp, Pipe	B		Proctor, Drinker	A
Pichard, Thomas	E		Proctor, George	M
Pickup, John	D		Proctor, James	I
Pidgeon, Josiah	G		Proctor, Joseph	G
Pidgeon, Young	I		Puller, Dave	M
Pigeon, John	C		Pumkin, Charles	D
Pigeon, Josiah	G		Pumpkin, Charles	D
Pigeon, Let	L		Punkin, Charles	D
Pigeon, Lias	B		Puppy, Young	C
Pigeon, Lit	L		Queenceteyar,	C
Pigeon, Turner	M		Quinton, Daniel	K
Pigeon,	H		Quinton, Louis	K
Pigeon,	M		Rabbat, John	B
Pike, John	M		Rabbit, Jack	B

Rabbit,	D		Rodgers, John	G
Rail, Jackson	C		Rodgers, John	M
Raper, Richard	I		Rodgers, Joseph	I
Ratliff, John	C		Rodgers, Moncelles	I
Ratling,	G		Rogers, Blossom	F
Ratling Gourd, Toney	M		Rogers, John	F
Ratling Gourd, Turtle	M		Rogers, John	G
Ratlingoard, Daniel	I		Rogers, John	M
Ratt, John	L		Rogers, Joseph	I
Rattling,	G		Rogers, Monceles	I
Rattling Gourd Turtle,	M		Roggers, Blossom	F
Rattlingguard, Daniel	I		Roggers, John	F
Ravin, Bony	H		Rooster, George	F
Reader, Beaver	L		Rope,	G
Rebner, Charles D.	B		Rosin,	E
Red Skynick,	M		Ross, Allen	I
Redbird, Miles	L		Ross, David	A
Redbird, Minnie	I		Ross, George	G
Redbird, Tarlouse	I		Ross, James	D
Reeder, Beaver	L		Ross, John	L
Rester, George	F		Ross, Thomas	A
Richard, Round	F		Roster, George	F
Richard, Thomas	E		Round,	G
Riddle,	G		Runabout, James	H
Rider,	M		Runabout, Rider	H
Ridge, George	B		Runabout,	A
Ridge, Johnson	B		Runabout,	E
Ridge,	A		Runabout Bear,	B
Ridge,	D		Running Bear,	A
Riley, John	C		Runningabout,	A
Roach, James	M		Ruster, George	F
Road, Aleck	H		Sah te zah,	E
Roastter, George	F		Salt,	E
Robber, Cole	K		Samcey,	E
Robbert, Heavy	F		Samsy,	E
Robbin, Davesy	C		Samuel, Spirit	D
Robert, (Creek)	I		San we kie, Young Bird	B
Robert, Heavy	F		Sanders, Aaron	G
Robin, Davey	C		Sanders, Archibold	L
Roche, James	M		Sanders, Benjamin	G
Rock, Jackson	L		Sanders, Bird	D
Rodgers, Izaah	M		Sanders, David	C

Sanders, George	C		Shade, Johnson	G
Sanders, John	C		Shade, Joseph	C
Sanders, John	F		Shade, Killer	H
Sanders, Jolly	G		Shade, Samuel	G
Sanders, Joseph	G		Shade, Tom	C
Sanders, Joseph	I		Shade,	H
Sanders, Osey	G		Shaking Bush,	G
Sanders, Thomas	F		Shakumbush, Tontaska	K
Sanders, Thomas	M		Sharp, John	B
Sanders, Watson	D		Sharp,	B
Sanders,	D		Shaunee, Teekner	F
Sandy, Archilla	E		Shavehead, James	A
Sash Taker,	K		Shawnee, Tekmee	F
Saunders, Aaron	G		Shawnee,	A
Saunders, Asi	G		Shell, Jesse	L
Saunders, Benjamin	G		Shell, Toss	M
Saunders, David	C		Shelton, James	I
Saunders, George	C		Shin, John	M
Saunders, John	C		Shin, Nelson	F
Saunders, Jolly	G		Shoe Boots,	C
Saunders, Joseph	G		Shooter, Teskaha	K
Saunders, Thomas	M		Shooter Hog,	H
Saw Taker,	K		Shoulder, Charles	H
Scarcewater, Alexander	A		Si-da-wa-gi,	D
Scarcewater, Charley	M		Sicahwe, Isreal	F
Scatter,	A		Sicahwee, Hoopin	F
Scontihee, Moses	C		Sick Warrior,	D
Scontohee, Suttoleah	C		Sick a yah wee,	C
Scott, Bajo	K		Sickey, John	E
Scott, Ball	M		Silk, Charles	F
Scowser, Call	K		Silk, George	A
Scowtohe, Lewis	C		Silk, Samuel	A
Scrimcha, Joseph	D		Silkcorn,	
Se-te-yuh, Queen	C		Simco, Cephas	A
Seabolt, Henry	A		Sinking Water,	E
Seckiner, Shawn	F		Sit a waca, James	E
See Ben,	K		Sitar, John	B
Seen, George	E		Sittawagi, Johnson	F
Seminole, John	A		Six, James	H
Sequaya,	A		Six, Runabout	H
Setting Bear,	G		Sixkiller, Abraham	L
Seven, George	B		Sixkiller, Jacob	L

Sixkiller, John	G		Spear, Bird	F
Sixkiller,	G		Spears, Joseph	I
Ska bor-la, James	I		Spears, Stephen	I
Skit-hu chu wi,	G		Spike, Buck Thomas	B
Skuntia, Dryhead	K		Spirit, James	A
Smell, Jack	H		Spirit, Samuel	D
Smith, George	G		Spoon, John	L
Smith, Jack	K		Springfrog, Jim	D
Smith, John	E		Springfrog, Road	L
Smith, John	I		Springwater,	A
Smith, Teacker	E		Squall, Lee	K
Smoke, Jesse	D		Squirl, Lowry	F
Smoke, Nelson	I		Squirrel, Bill	K
Smoke,	H		Squirrel, Seneca	L
Smoker, John	I		Squirrel, Young	B
Smoker,	B		Squirrel, Young	F
Smoky,	A		Squirrel, Young	G
Snake, Wolf	B		Squirrel,	F
Snake carrier,	L		Stainer,	H
Snell, George	H		Stall, John R.	I
Snell, Jack	H		Stand, Crawfish	I
Snell, Walker	H		Stand, Fourkiller	A
Snelle, George	H		Stand, Grape	A
Snelle, Walker	H		Stand, Muskmelon	A
Snipe,	H		Stand, Thomas	A
Soap, John	D		Standing, Door	H
Soap, Thomas	L		Standing, Manstealer	G
Soap, William	L		Standing, Water	L
Sold,	G		Star, John	B
Soowakee, Thomas	L		Star, Thomas	A
Soowaky, Thomas	L		Starr, Thomas	H
Sorrel, George	C		Stebela,	E
Sort, Every	A		Steel,	G
Soup,	B		Stena,	E
Sourjohn, William	D		Stener,	E
Sowell, George	C		Step, Stop	L
Spade,	C		Step, Stwist	L
Sparrow, Weaver	C		Stephen,	H
Sparrowhach, Jo	H		Still, Cook	G
Sparrowhawk, Joe	H		Still, George	D
Sparrowhead, Joe	H		Still, George	L
Sparrowhock, Joe	H		Still, James	L

Still, Samuel	L		Swinger, Moses	I
Stinging Dollar,	L		Ta chulanah,	F
Stoal,	A		Ta ga hu ges ka,	M
Stop, Johnston	H		Ta ka nes ke, Shawnee	F
Stop, Step	L		Ta le sky, Daniel	C
Stop, Wittey	H		Tadpole, Crossing	C
Store Keepr,	M		Tadpole, David	D
Strike Shin Shooter,	K		Tadpole, John	D
Striker, Hammer	K		Tah cha cho a noah,	F
Su wa kee, Tom	C		Tah hu les ku,	B
Su wae ke, Jackson	B		Tahlawsah, Joe	C
Sucker, Joseph	A		Tahwanee, Sallateeska	F
Sueteescah, Tahnoowe	F		Tail Winner,	B
Sulah-teas-kie,	F		Tailor, Mose	M
Sun scoo yah,	C		Talalah, Pan	D
Sunday, Arch	M		Talaski, Shine	K
Sunday, Archilla	E		Talaskia, Swimmer	K
Sunday, Tom	B		Talasky, Shine	K
Sunday,	C		Talesky, Shine	K
Sutton, William	M		Tan wau lu ka,	I
Sweecalla, Hindman	F		Tanah,	M
Sweecaller, Hindman	F		Tanapin, Joshua	M
Sweecaular, Hindman	F		Taner, Phesant	H
Sweetcaller, James	F		Tanner, Pheasant	H
Swimer, Alex	K		Tar a fren,	C
Swimer, Jess	K		Tar lar lar, Pan	D
Swimer, John	F		Tar lar lar,	I
Swimer, John	K		Tar law sha, Joseph	C
Swimer, Joseph	K		Tar lee ske,	C
Swimer, Tom	M		Tar noo we, Robin	C
Swimer, 2, Joseph	K		Tar ye ske, John	C
Swimmer, Alex	K		Tarapin, Little	D
Swimmer, Blossom	I		Tarlouse,	I
Swimmer, Jack	B		Tarpin, Johnson	K
Swimmer, James	A		Tarpin, Joshua	M
Swimmer, James	M		Tarpin, Little	A
Swimmer, Jesse	K		Tarpin,	C
Swimmer, John	F		Tarrapen,	C
Swimmer, John	K		Tas star noa,	F
Swimmer, Joseph	K		Tater, Daniel	B
Swimmer, Tom	M		Tau chu la wa, Nicholas	F
Swimmer, 2, Joseph	K		Tau u nee see,	B

Name	Col
Taw che la nah, Above	C
Taw che la nah, Martin	C
Tawchulanah, Nicholas	F
Tayler, Mose	M
Taylor, Bushyhead	L
Taylor, Ike	M
Taylor, Mose	M
Te Ka Ko yon gek,	M
Teacher, Little	E
Teacher,	G
Tearpin, Head	A
Tee Kin nee, Shawnee	F
Tee gah Kle,	F
Tee yoh hlee,	F
Teecellsky,	F
Teeolle,	F
Teeyehle,	F
Terapin, Joshua	M
Terapin, Little	A
Terapin,	I
Terapin head,	A
Terrapin, Charles	B
Terrapin, Joshua	M
Terrapin,	C
Terrapin,	I
Terripin, Johnson	K
Thicket, Baldridge	F
Thomas, Cockran	F
Thomas, John	L
Thompson, John	B
Thompson, Like	M
Thompson, Steen	M
Thomson, Stem	M
Thorn, Gay	A
Thorn, Silas	A
Thornton, John	L
Thornton, Stephen	L
Throw, Chickasaw	K
Thrower, Hammer	L
Ti e skee,	B
Ti ee skee, David	B
Ti ye sky, John	C

Name	Col
Tic a nee skee,	B
Tic a nee sky, Jefferson	L
Tic a nee sky, John	L
Tica neesky, Richard	L
Tick Eater, George	B
Tick a nee sky, Jefferson	L
Tick a nee sky, John	L
Tick a nee sky, Richard	L
Tilla, Jeff	M
Timberlake, Charles	F
Timpson, Ned	I
Tlaws tah nah,	F
Tlus tuh noh,	F
Tobacco, Cah la we sky	C
Tobacco, Car la we ski	C
Tolan, Soldier	G
Tom,	D
Tomas, Dick	M
Tona, James	M
Toney,	D
Toni, Jim	M
Tontee, Feather	K
Tony,	D
Toslie, James	M
Toss Shell,	M
Townsend, Looney	L
Townsend, Solomon	L
Track, Wolf	L
Trampabout, Leasu	D
Trompabout, Lusee	D
Tryeskee, John	C
Tsu wae lo kee,	I
Tsult clareh,	C
Tu cla ri,	C
Tucker, Charles	L
Tucker, David	I
Tucker, Dick	D
Tucker, Eli	H
Tucker, Jake	D
Tucker, Mulberry	H
Tucker, Samuel	H

Tucker, William	I		Walker, James	C	
Tuh chu la ua, Nicholas			Walker, John	C	
Tulonesky, Eli	K		Walker, John	L	
Turkey, Joseph	M		Walker, Snell	H	
Turky, Joseph	M		Walkingbout, Henry	M	
Turnabout, Lown	D		Walkingstick, James	L	
Turner, Charles	A		Walkingstick, John	G	
Turner, Davis	B		Walkingstick, Samuel	I	
Turner, Ike	M		Walkingstick, Thomas	L	
Turner, James	F		Wallaskasky,	F	
Turner, Peter	D		Wallaskey,	F	
Turner,	D		Walleska,	F	
Turtle, Charles	H		Walter, Ben	K	
Turtle, Crane-eater	C		Walter,	G	
Turtle, Joe	H		Wan haw chir,	F	
Turtle,			Wan san te, Son wake	B	
Tutonesky, Sanee	K		Wan san to Arch,	B	
Twist,	F		Waner, John	G	
Umphris, Ephrim	K		Wanner, John	G	
Van, Cornelius	D		War Club,	E	
Van, Jesse	G		Warclub, Wilson	I	
Vann, Alexander	A		Warkiller, Hogshooter	B	
Vann, Cornelius	D		Warrion, Sexit	D	
Vann, George	B		Warrior, Sick	D	
Vann, George	F		Wash,	F	
Vann, James	H		Washburn,	M	
Vann, Jesse	G		Washington, James	I	
Vann, John	A		Washington,	D	
Vann, Joseph	F		Washington,	M	
Vann, Moses	A		Waster,	F	
Vann, Saturday	H		Water, Ben	K	
Vann, Tanner	K		Water, Bird	D	
Wah laskie,	F		Water, Bottom	G	
Wahawchee,	F		Water, Hunter	B	
Waheuche,	F		Water, Killer	G	
Wainscott, Cash	L		Water, Lying	B	
Waker, John	H		Water, Sinking	I	
Waleska,	F		Watermix, Alexander	L	
Waleskie,	F		Waters, Dick	A	
Walkabout, Buffalo	K		Waters, George	E	
Walkabout, Henry	M		Waters, Monkey	A	
Walker, George	E		Watie,	A	

Watt, Barney	H		Wolf, Hawk	G
Watt, Ellis	D		Wolf, John	K
Watt, James	E		Wolf, Nelson	H
Watt, Joe	L		Wolf,	A
Watt,	E		Wolfe, Harrison	A
Watters, George	E		Wood, Nathaniel B.	E
Wau hau chee,	F		Woodall, Andrew	L
Weattia,	F		Woodall, Robert	D
Weaver, George	C		Woodall, William	D
Weaver, Sparrow	C		Woodpecker, Joe	B
Webber, John	M		Woods, Nicholas B.	E
Webber, Walter	M		Woodward, Leuch	F
Webber Jr., William	E		Woosqualeke,	F
Webe, Walter	M		Wooster,	F
Weber, William	E		Worm,	I
Webster, Daniel	L		Woster,	F
Wesley,	C		Writer, Kulsatchee	I
West, Robert	C		Yahola, Jack	E
Whinery, William	M		Yahola, James	E
Whiney, William	M		Yahola, Sampson	E
Whiparwill,	D		Ye-ho-la, Jack	E
White, John	M		Yellowhummer, Waker	L
Wich, Jesse	B		Yo-ho-la, Jack	E
Wick, Leach	C		Young, John	E
Wildcat, Will	C		Young, John D.	M
Wilden, John Jackson	L		Young, Joseph	E
Wilder, John Jackson	L		Young, Padgoon	I
Wiley,	D		Young, Thomas	E
Wilhain, Long	I		Young Beaver,	B
Willey,	D		Young Bird,	A
William,	E		Young Bird,	G
Williams, John	D		Young Chicken,	M
Wilson, Artsey			Young Dog,	H
Wilson, Bird	A		Young Puppy,	C
Wilson, Thomas	I		Young Squirrel,	B
Wilson,	A		Young Turkey,	M
Wind, Davie	C		Young Wolf, Sixkiller	H
Wind,	I		Young bird,	F
Witch, Jessee	B		Young bird,	M
Wochatooder, Jessy	F		Youngbird, Isaac	L
Wofford, Samuel	I		Youngbird, Johnson	A
Wolf, Harrison	A		Youngduck, Robin	L

Indian Home Guard Discharges

Cherokee Advocate
Tahlequah, Cherokee Nation, Indian Territory
January 14, 1871

List of Discharges now in the possession of Messrs. Webster and Foster at Pension Agency, Fort Gibson, C. N., upon which, except those of the officers, original Bounty and additional Bounty appears to have been paid by the U. S., to someone; whether to the rightful claiments or not, is the question to be settled by the persons named, or those entitled on their account, appearing at the Penison Agency and furnishing proof:

Name	Rank	Co. Commander	Co.	Regiment
Aaron	Pvt.	Capt. H. Downing	F	3d IHG
Aaron, ??le	Cpl.	Capt. Smith Christy	A	3d IHG
Ah-dah-ha-loos-ke	Pvt.	Capt. Arch Scraper	D	2d IHG
A-luk-e-ho-la	Pvt.	Lt. Albert Flanders	F	1s IHG
Archilla, Comprilla	Pvt.	Lt. Jesse Henry	I	2d IHG
Away, July	Pvt.	Capt. Jas. Vann	K	3d IHG
Bean, John	Pvt.	Capt. Budd Gritts	G	2d IHG
Beane, Thompson	Pvt.	Capt. Nathaniel Fish	C	3d IHG
Bear Paw, Richard	Pvt.	Capt. Alex C. Spilman	B	3d IHG
Bearmeat, John	Pvt.	Capt. Smith Christy	A	2d IHG
Beaver Toter, Lacy	Pvt.	Capt. Alex C. Spilman	B	3d IHG
Beaver, James	Pvt.	Capt. Budd Gritts	G	2d IHG
Beaver, Joe	Pvt.	Capt. Tuc-a-bache-Hajo	C	1s IHG
Beaver, Reader	Pvt.	Capt. Soloman Kaufman	L	3d IHG
Beinstick, James	Pvt.	Capt. H. Downing	F	3d IHG
Big Billy	Pvt.	Capt. Tuc-a-bache-Hajo	C	1s IHG
Big Mush, Henry	Pvt.	Capt. White Catcher	I	3d IHG
Big Mush, Little Hair	Sgt.	Capt. James H. Bruce	C	2d IHG
Black Fox, Henry	Pvt.	Capt. Moses Price	B	2d IHG
Blackbird, David	Pvt.	Capt. James Vann	K	3d IHG
Blackburn, Jumper	Pvt.	Capt. Budd Gritts	G	2d IHG

Blackwood, Lewis	Pvt.	Capt. Soloman Kaufman	L	3d IHG
Blair, Thomas	Pvt.	Capt. Smith Christy	A	2d IHG
Bullfrog	Pvt.	Capt. Budd Gritts	G	2d IHG
Bullfrog	Pvt.	Capt. Nathaniel Fish	C	3d IHG
Bullfrog, Isaac	Cpl.	Lt. Jesse Henry	I	2d IHG
C?-wor-yah-gale	Cpl.	Lt. Moses Price	B	2d IHG
Cah-nor-he-yah-tah	Pvt.	Lt. Moses Price	B	2d IHG
Cha-ka-sa-cle	Pvt.	Lt. James H. Bruce	C	2d IHG
Charles 1st.	Pvt.	Lt. Ah-lee-cher	F	2d IHG
Charlie, Long	Pvt.	Lt. Simon Snell	G	3d IHG
Che-hes-lat	Pvt.	Capt. Jonneh	K	1s IHG
Cho-fo-la-la-fix-e-co	Pvt.	Lt.Ah-ha-la-tus-ta-nek-ke	B	1s IHG
Christie, Henry	Cpl.	Lt. Maxwell Phillips	G	3d IHG
Chu-he-ca (Iowa)	Sgt.	Lt. Moses Price	B	2d IHG
Chu-wee, Joseph	Pvt.	Lt. Arch Scraper	D	2d IHG
Coleman, John	Cpl.	Lt. H. Downing	F	3d IHG
Collins, Peter	Pvt	Lt. Fred Craft	I	1s IHG
Coming Deer, Peter	Pvt.	Lt. Smith Christy	A	3d IHG
Crawford, Robert	Cpl.	Lt. Thos. Regg	E	3d IHG
Crittenden, Aaron	Cpl.	Lt. Sol Kaufman	L	3d IHG
Crittendon, Samuel	1st Sgt.	Lt. James H. Bruce	C	2d IHG
Cutter, Harry	Cpl.	Lt. Alex C. Spillman	B	3d IHG
Dah-ner-sa-ne	Pvt.	Capt. Ta-la-lah	F	3d IHG
Dah-yah-wah-ah-si	Pvt.	Capt. Moses Price	B	3d IHG
Dick, Isaac	Cpl.	Capt. Spring Frog	K	2d IHG
Dick, Richard	Pvt.	----- -- ---- --------	?	2d IHG
Dickey	Pvt.	Lt. M. F. Bicking	A	1s IHG
Dirt Seller	?	Capt. Max Phillips	G	3d IHG
Dirt, William	Pvt.	Lt. Smith Christy	A	3d IHG
Downing, Dragen	?	Capt. Ta-la-lah	D	3d IHG
Downing, H.	Capt.	Capt. Ta-la-lah	F	3d IHG
Downing, James	Pvt.	Capt. Sol Kaufman	L	3d IHG
Downing, Joseph	Pvt.	Capt. Ta-la-lah	F	3d IHG
Drum, George	Pvt.	Capt. Budd Gritts	G	2d IHG
Dry, Peter	Cpl.	Capt. Alex C. Spilman	B	3d IHG
Duval, Dave	Cpl.	Capt. Henry S. Anderson	M	3d IHG
Dyer, John	Pvt.	Lt. Chas. N. Rix	A	3d IHG
E-lar-we	Pvt.	Capt. Spring Frog	K	3d IHG

Elijah	Pvt.	Capt. White Catcher	I	3d IHG
Feeling, Adam	Pvt.	Capt. Alex C. Spilman	B	3d IHG
Fish	Pvt.	Lt. Cot-so-gee	H	1s IHG
Fisher, Isaac	Pvt.	Capt. Henry S. Anderson	M	3d IHG
Fodder, Runabout	Pvt.	Capt. Ta-la-lah	D	3d IHG
Foreman, Rider	Cpl.	Capt. Simon Snell	H	3d IHG
Gah-ga-wee, Dick	Pvt.	Capt. Jas. H. Bruce	C	2d IHG
Gaw-wah-chee-ya-la	Pvt.	Capt. Moses Price	B	2d IHG
George	Pvt.	Capt. Jas. H. Bruce	C	2d IHG
George	Pvt.	Capt. Alex C. Spilman	B	3d IHG
Getting Inn	Pvt.	Capt. Smith Christy	A	3d IHG
Gierity, Wilson	Pvt.	Capt. Jas. H. Bruce	C	2d IHG
Glass, Joseph T.	Pvt.	Capt. H. Downing	F	3d IHG
Go-Back	Sgt.	Capt. Nathaniel Fish	C	3d IHG
Go-e-ker-ha-go	Pvt.	Lt. Cot-so-gee	H	1s IHG
Goo-we-skoo-wi, George,	Pvt.	Capt. Nathaniel Fish	C	3d IHG
Grass Hopper, Diver	Pvt.	Capt. White Catcher	I	3d IHG
Grass, Jessie	Pvt.	Capt. H. Downing	F	3d IHG
Grayson, Henderson	Pvt.	Lt. Chas. N. Nix	D	1s IHG
Grayson, Walter	Cpl.	Capt. No-co-se-lo-clee	G	1s IHG
Guess, Moses	Pvt.	Lt. A. J. Waterhouse	H	2d IHG
Gu-lah-stah	Pvt.	Capt. Ah-le-chee	F	2d IHG
Gutter	Pvt.	Capt. H. S. Anderson	M	3d IHG
Hair, Wilson	Sgt.	Capt. Nathaniel Fish	C	3d IHG
Hammer Thrower	Pvt.	Lt. Francis J. Fox	K	1s IHG
Harley	Pvt.	Lt. Albert Flanders	F	1s IHG
Haskins, John	Pvt.	Capt. A. J. Waterhouse	H	2d IHG
Hawkins, Lacey	Pvt.	Capt. H. Downing	F	3d IHG
Hicks, Taylor	Pvt.	Capt. Jesse Henry	I	2d IHG
Hildebrand, Joe	Pvt.	Capt. James Vann	K	3d IHG
Hitcher	Pvt.	Lt. Albert F. Bicking	A	1s IHG
Ho-lar-tah	Pvt	Capt. Ah-ha-la-tus-ta-nuck-ke	B	1s IHG
Horn, David	Pvt.	Capt. Ta-la-lah	D	3d IHG
Horsefly, Walter	Pvt.	Capt. A. J. Waterhouse	H	2d IHG

Ho-tul-ya-ho-lah	Pvt.	Capt. Nathaniel Fish	C	3d IHG
Housebug, Jackson	Cpl.	Capt. Sol Kaufman	L	3d IHG
Huibutter	Pvt.	Capt. Tuc-a-bache-ha-jo	C	1s IHG
Hungary Dick	Pvt.	Capt. Alex. C. Spilman	B	3d IHG
Jah-kay	Pvt.	Capt. No-co-so-lo-chee	G	1s IHG
Jim-kah	Pvt.	Lt. Fred Craft	I	1s IHG
Joe-dah	Pvt.	Capt. Smith Christy	A	3d IHG
Joe-kah	Pvt.	Capt. No-co-so-lo-chee	G	1s IHG
Johnson, Dick	Pvt.	Capt. Alex C. Spilman	B	3d IHG
Johnson, Ellis	Cpl.	Capt. Nathaniel Fish	C	3d IHG
Johnson, Jack	Pvt.	Capt. H. Downing	F	3d IHG
Johnson, Jug	Pvt.	Capt. Alex C. Spilman	B	3d IHG
Jumper	Pvt.	Capt. H. Downing	F	3d IHG
Kelly, Marshal	Pvt.	Lt. Chas. N. Nix	D	1s IHG
Kerr, Frank	Pvt.	Capt. Thos. Pegg	E	3d IHG
Kerr, Kanerque	Pvt.	Capt. Ta-la-lah	D	3d IHG
Ketcher, Bill	Pvt.	Capt. Nathaniel Fish	C	3d IHG
Knight, Samuel	Pvt.	Capt. Ta-la-lah	D	3d IHG
Ko-no-wa-ha-jo	Pvt.	Lt. Chas. N. Nix	D	1s IHG
Kossah	Pvt.	Lt. Fred Craft	I	1s IHG
Kun-ca-te-mar-reh	Pvt.	Lt. Chas. N. Nix	D	1s IHG
Latimore, Samuel	Pvt.	Capt. Smith Christie	A	3d IHG
Le-wa-te, Sam	Pvt.	Capt. Spring Frog	K	2d IHG
Lewis, John	Cpl.	Lt. Chas. N. Nix	D	3d IHG
Lief	Pvt.	Capt. Simon Snell	H	3d IHG
Little Bird	Sgt.	Capt. White Catcher	I	3d IHG
Loo-nok-tu-ho-la	Pvt.	Capt. Ne-co-se-lo-chee	G	1s IHG
Man Killer Catcher	Cpl.	Capt. Jas. H. Bruce	C	2d IHG
Ma-thla-na-ke	Pvt.	Lt. A. Flanders	F	1s IHG
Mayfield, Ed	Pvt.	Capt. Ah-ler-cher	F	2d IHG
McIntosh, John	Pvt.	Capt. Smith Christie	A	3d IHG
McLane, Luna	Cpl.	Capt. Nathaniel Fish	C	3d IHG
Mole, Edward	Cpl.	Capt. Smith Christie	A	3d IHG
Muskrat, Daniel	Pvt.	Lt. A. J. Waterhouse	H	2d IHG
Ne-ha-fix-e-co	Pvt.	Lt. Cot-so-gee	H	1s IHG

Name	Rank	Officer	Co.	Regt.
Ne-he-me-ka	Pvt.	Lt. Francis J. Fox	E	1s IHG
Nerve, Henry	Pvt.	Capt. Thos. Pegg	E	3d IHG
No-kus-fix-se-ko	Pvt.	Capt. No-co-se-lo-chee	G	1s IHG
No-wife, Andrew	Sgt.	Capt. Nathaniel Fish	C	3d IHG
Oak-chi-e-fix-e-ko	Pvt.	Capt. Pue-a-bach-e-ha-jo	C	1s IHG
Old Corn, Attolahie	Pvt.	Capt. Nathaniel Fish	C	1s IHG
Oo-nar-gur-sah	Cpl.	Capt. Budd Gritts	G	2d IHG
Ossa-ha-jo	Pvt.	Lt. Chas. N. Nix	D	1s IHG
Ote-ko-e-ho-la	Pvt.	Capt. No-co-se-lo-che	G	1s IHG
O-war-las-ky	Pvt.	Capt. Ta-la-lah	D	1s IHG
O-ya-ska-noo-de	Pvt.	Capt. Spring Frog	K	2 IHG
Pa-nuk-lo-ge	Pvt.	Lt. A. Flander	F	1s IHG
Par-lo	Pvt.	Lt. Fred Craft	I	1s IHG
Parris, Jesse	Pvt.	Capt. H. S. Anderson	M	3d IHG
Passon, John	Pvt.	Capt. H. S. Anderson	M	3d IHG
Pen-la-jo	Cpl.	Lt. Francis J. Nix	E	1s IHG
Pidgeon, Josiah	Pvt.	--- ----- Phillips	G	3d IHG
Pimkin, Charles	Pvt.	--- --------------	D	3d IHG
Price, Jackson	Pvt.	--- --------------	C	--- ------
Prince, Taylor	Pvt.	--- --------------	?	--- ------
Pritchet, Tieski	Pvt.	--- ------ Philliips	G	3d IHG
Proctor, Johnson	Pvt.	Capt. Sol Kaufman	L	3d IHG
Pumpkin, Jesse	Pvt.	Lt. Jesse Henry	I	2d IHG
Rabbit, Jack	Pvt.	Capt. Alex Spilman	B	3d IHG
Rag, Jones	Pvt.	Lt. A. J. Waterhouse	H	2d IHG
Ridge, George	Pvt.	Capt. Alex Spilman	B	3d IHG
Ridge, Johnson	Pvt.	Capt. Alex Spilman	B	3d IHG
Ridge, Josiah	Cpl.	Capt. Thos. Pegg	E	3d IHG
Riley, John R.	Pvt.	Capt. Nathaniel Fish	C	3d IHG
Rocky Mountain	Pvt.	Lt. T. McClain	A	2d IHG
Ross, David	Pvt.	Capt. S. Christy	A	3d IHG
Sammeh	Pvt.	Lt. Fred Craft	I	1s IHG
Sammeh	Pvt.	Lt. Cot-so-gee	H	1s IHG
Sand	Pvt.	Capt. Arch Scraper	D	2d IHG
Saunders	Pvt.	Capt. Ta-la-lah	D	3d IHG
Scontihee, Lewis	Pvt.	Capt. Nathaniel Fish	C	3d IHG
Scraper, Henry	Sgt.	Capt. Arch Scraper	D	2d IHG
Seabolt, Henry	Pvt.	Capt. Smith Christy	A	2d IHG
Sea-Kee	Pvt.	Capt. Smith Christy	A	2d IHG

Name	Rank	Captain	Co.	Regiment
Seneca Squirrel	Pvt.	Capt. Sol Kaufman	L	3d IHG
Seven, George	Pvt.	Capt. Alex C. Spilman	B	3d IHG
Sharp	Pvt.	Capt. Alex C. Spilman	B	3d IHG
Sharp, John	Pvt.	Capt. A. C. Spilman	B	2d IHG
Shoe Boots	Pvt.	Capt. Nathaniel Fish	C	3d IHG
Silk, Beaver	Pvt.	Capt. Smith Christy	A	2d IHG
Six Killer, Young Wolf	Pvt.	Capt. Simon Snell	H	3d IHG
Sixkiller, Moses	Cpl.	Capt. Simon Snell	H	3d IHG
Smith, James	Pvt.	Lt. Jesse Henry		I2d IHG
Smith, John	Pvt.	Capt. White Catcher	I	3d IHG
Smoke, Jesse	Pvt.	Capt. Ta-la-lah	D	3d IHG
Smoker	Pvt.	Capt. Alex C. Spilman	B	3d IHG
Soap, George	Cpl.	Capt. Ta-la-lah	D	3d IHG
Soap, Thomas	Pvt.	Capt. Sol Kaufman	L	3d IHG
Sold	Pvt.	Capt. Max Phillips	G	3d IHG
Sol-ya-che-ka	Pvt.	Capt. Ah-ha-la-tus-ta-nuk-ke	B	1s IHG
Span-ne-ma-le	Pvt.	Capt Francis J. Fox	C	1s IHG
Spirit, Samuel	Pvt.	Capt. Ta-la-lah	D	3d IHG
Spring Frog	Capt.	Capt. ------ -----	K	2d IHG
Squirrel, Walter	Cpl.	Capt. White Catcher	I	3d IHG
Standing Deer, Joseph	Pvt.	Lt. Jesse Henry	I	2d IHG
Starr, John	Pvt.	Capt. Alex C. Spilman	B	3d IHG
Starr, Thomas	Pvt.	Capt. Simon Snell	H	3d IHG
Steele	Pvt.	Capt. Max Phillips	G	3d IHG
Sue-ya-der	Pvt.	Capt. Ah-lee-cher	F	2d IHG
Su-lah-tus-skie	Pvt.	Capt. H. Downing	F	3d IHG
Sullivan, Samuel	Pvt.	Capt. Tuc-a-bac-e-ha-jo	C	1s IHG
Sunday, Tom	Pvt.	Capt. Alex C. Spilman	B	3d IHG
Sunday, William	2d Lt.	Capt. A. C. Spilman	B	2d IHG
Swimmer, Dekeny	Pvt.	Lt. A. J. Waterhouse	H	2d IHG
Swollow Standing	Pvt	Lt. A. J. Waterhouse	H	2d IHG
Tadpole, John	Pvt.	Capt. Ta-la-lah	D	3d IHG
Ta-la-lah	Capt.	Capt. ------ --------	D	3d IHG
Tanner, Pheasant	Pvt.	Capt. Simon Snell	H	3d IHG

Tarlow-Maise	Pvt.	Capt. Nathaniel Fish C	3d IHG
Taylor, James	Pvt.	Capt. Jas. H. Bruce C	2d IHG
Taylor, Moses	Pvt.	Capt. H. S. Anderson M	3d IHG
Ter-ne-no-le	Pvt.	Capt. Spring Frog K	2d IHG
Te-suh-yah-yah	Pvt.	Lt. T. McClain A	2d IHG
Te-ya-ste-ke	Pvt.	Capt. Ah-lee-cher F	2d IHG
Thompsonna	Cpl.	Capt. Moses Price B	2d IHG
Tick-eater	Sgt.	Capt. Alex C. Spilman B	3d IHG
Too-quah-tah	Pvt.	Capt. Arch Scraper D	2d IHG
Tsho-wah-nor-ah-ski	Pvt.	Capt. Moses Price B	2d IHG
Tucker, Daniel	Pvt.	Capt. Moses Price B	2d IHG
Tuff	Pvt.	Capt. Jas. H. Bruce C	2d IHG
Tulsy-ya-hola	Pvt.	Lt. Fred Craft I	1s IHG
Twist	Pvt.	Capt. H. Downing F	3d IHG
Umpries, Ephraim	Pvt.	Capt. Jas. Vann K	3d IHG
Vann, James	Capt.	Capt. ----- ---- K	2d IHG
Vann, James	Pvt.	Capt. Budd Gritts G	2d IHG
Walking-stick, Charles	Cpl.	Capt. Max Phillips G	3d IHG
Walking-stick, John	Pvt.	Capt. Max Phillips G	3d IHG
Water, Asa	Pvt.	Lt. Jesse Henry G	2d IHG
Wax-se-ha-jo-ne-joo-a	Pvt.	Capt. Ah-ha-la-tus-ta-nuck-ke B	------
Webber, William	Pvt.	Capt. Thomas Pegg E	3d IHG
We-le-et	Pvt.	Capt. Jonneh K	1s IHG
Weleny, Oganiah	Pvt.	Lt. T. McClain A	2d IHG
Westley	Pvt.	Capt. Ah-ha-la-tus-ta-nuck-ke B	--------
Wetka	Pvt.	Capt. Tac-a-bache-ha-jo C-	----------
White, John	Pvt.	Lt. Fred Craft I	1s IHG
Wick, Jesse	Pvt.	Capt. Alex Spilman B	3d IHG
Wiley	Pvt.	Capt. Ta-la-lah D	3d IHG
Wind	Pvt.	Capt. White Catcher I	3d IHG
Wolfe	Pvt.	Capt. Smith Christie H	3d IHG
Wright, John	Sgt.	Lt. A. J. Waterhouse H	2d IHG
Writer, Kul-su-tchee	Pvt.	Capt. White Catcher I	3d IHG
Ya-hol-da-ha-job	Pvt.	Lt. Cot-so-gee H	1s IHG
Ya-hol-loh	Pvt.	Lt. Cot-so-gee H	1s IHG
Yarapen	Pvt.	Capt. Nathaniel Fish C	3d IHG
Young Bird	Pvt.	Capt. H. S. Anderson M	3d IHG
Young Deer	Pvt.	Capt. James H. Bruce C	2d IHG

Young, P. Wolfe   Cpl.   Lt. A. J. Waterhouse H   2d IHG

Indian Home Guards Pensions Applications

Cherokee Advocate
Tahlequah, Cherokee Nation, Indian Territory
January 14, 1871

The Pensioners named below are desired to appear at the Pension Agency at Fort Gibson with witnesses, so that their papers may be made out in Proper Form.

Name	Rank	Company	Regiments.
---- Lasse-See	Pvt	G	1s IHG
Acorn, Writer	Pvt	L	3d IHG
Ah-ha-loc-a-ho-la	?	A	1s IHG
Asike	Pvt	F	1s IHG
Baldridge, Thicket	Pvt	E	3d IHG
Barnett, Jack	Pvt	K	1s IHG
Batt,	-------	??	---------
Beamer, Vest	?	A	2d IHG
Big Talker	Sgt	D	3d IHG
Bird, Jackson	Pvt	H	3d IHG
Bird, Turner	Pvt	I	2d IHG
Black Fox	Pvt	I	2d IHG
Blacksmith	Pvt	I	2d IHG
Borrow, Jack	Pvt	M	3d IHG
Brown, Isaac	Sgt	K	1s IHG
Brown, Thomas	Pvt	K	---------
Brush, George	Pvt	F	3d IHG
Bump, William	?	A	3d IHG
Bunches Hammer	Pvt	K	3d IHG
Butler, Joseph	?	?	---------
Can-tel-ha-yo	Pvt	E	1s IHG
Carts-che-her-mek-ko	Capt	E	1s IHG
Catching, Sunday	Sgt	M	3d IHG
Cau-con-pa-na	Pvt	K	1s IHG
Ce-say-gil	Pvt	A	1s IHG
Char-co-co-wee	Pvt	K	1s IHG
Char-lah-kee-tee-hee	Pvt	B	2d IHG
Charlie	Pvt	F	1s IHG
Che-pa-na	Pvt	K	1s IHG
Chickasaw Throw	Pvt	K	3d IHG

Name	Rank	Co.	Regt.
Cho-che-ma-ta	Pvt	A	1s IHG
Cho-e-la	Pvt	A	1s IHG
Cla-cla-ya-hala	?	E	1s IHG
Cole, Curley	Pvt	K	3d IHG
Co-mal-co-ye-ha-jo	Pvt	D	1s IHG
Conseene, David	Cpl.	B	3d IHG
Crawler	Pvt	M	1s IHG
Crawler	Pvt	D	2d IHG
Davidson	Pvt	I	2d IHG
Davis, Jesse	Pvt	E	3d IHG
Double Jack	Pvt	D	3d IHG
Downing, Alex	Pvt	D	3d IHG
Downing, George	Pvt	I	3d IHG
Downing, Walter	Cpl.	B	2d IHG
Dragger, Ose	?	L	3d IHG
Duck, John	Pvt	F	3d IHG
Elias, Samuel	Pvt	A	3d IHG
Ellis, Edward	Pvt	A	3d IHG
Ellis, Red	Cpl.	B	3d IHG
Ellis, Samuel	Pvt	A	3d IHG
E-mart-la-hajo	Pvt	C	1s IHG
E-mart-lo-cha	Pvt	I	1s IHG
English, George	Pvt	F	1s IHG
Falling, John	Pvt	I	2d IHG
Far-yah-ne-ho-lah	Pvt	A	1s IHG
Feeling	Capt.	B	3d IHG
Fielding, Robert	Pvt	I	2d IHG
Flying Squirrel	Pvt	H	2d IHG
Ga-na-ga	Sgt	I	2d IHG
Goard, John R	Pvt	I	3dIHG
Go-fol-lup-fix-e-co	Pvt	H	1s IHG
Going To Mill	Pvt	D	2d IHG
Go-lah-ke-hagoh	Pvt	H	1s IHG
Go-ne-chu-squah-le	Pvt	K	2d IHG
Good Money, Eli	?	?	2d IHG
Grayson, Robert	Pvt	D	1s IHG
Green, John W.	Pvt	?	---------
Hair, Nickolas	Pvt	I	3d IHG
Hammer, Tom	Pvt	C	3d IHG
Hammond, Thos.	Pvt	D	3d IHG
Harling, Ellis	Sgt	K	3d IHG
Hawk, Four Killer	Pvt	G	3d IHG

Name	Rank	Co.	Unit
Hee-Kee	Pvt	E	1s IHG
Height, James	Pvt	C	3d IHG
Hel-lis-fix-se-co	Pvt	D	1s IHG
Hendricks, David	Cpl	E	2d IHG
Hicks, Sam	Pvt	M	3d IHG
Hilderbrand, George	Pvt	H	3d IHG
Hin-ne-pi-march	Pvt	A	1s IHG
Hog, George	Pvt	D	3d IHG
Ho-tul-ke-fix-e-kok	Pvt	A	1s IHG
Ho-tul-ke-mal-lak	Pvt	A	1s IHG
Howling Wolf	Pvt	I	2d IHG
Hummingbird, Wm	Cpl	L	3d IHG
Jay Bird, Raft	Pvt	C	3d IHG
Jim-me-lor-me	Pvt	?	----------
Jimmy	Pvt	F	1s IHG
Jo-ha-jo	?	G	1s IHG
Johnson, Jas.	Pvt	K	1s IHG
Jo-lo-hap-hago	Lt	F	1s IHG
Jo-lo-hap-jajo	2d Lt.	F	1s IHG
Kah-sah-heli	Pvt	D	2d IHG
Kennard, Jackson	Pvt	F	1s IHG
Ko-ha-se-mart-la	Pvt	I	1s IHG
Kome-hago	Pvt	A	1s IHG
Ko-mep-hajo	Pvt	D	1s IHG
Ko-so-fix-e-co	Pvt	G	1s IHG
Kot-cus-ha-coh	Pvt	D	1s IHG
La-me-ht-geh	Pvt	?	----------
Leach, Mick	Pvt	?	----------
Le-he-lea-theh	Pvt	A	1s IHG
Little, Grimit	Cpl	G	----------
Liver, Ave	Pvt	?	----------
Long, Eli	Pvt	L	----------
Lookingout, Ned	Pvt	?	----------
Lovitt	Pvt	F	----------
Ne-or-ha-got	?	H	1s IHG
Night Killer	Pvt	F	3d IHG
Ok-cha-ne-ma-la	Pvt	E	1s IHG
Ola-he-ater	Pvt	C	3d IHG
Oo-wan-soaty	Pvt	C	3d IHG
Opossum, Sixkiller	Pvt	L	3d IHG
Pa-com-thla	Pvt	K	1s IHG
Pa-lage-hagoh	Pvt	A	1s IHG

Peach-eater, George	Pvt	K	3d IHG
Pigeon	Pvt	M	3d IHG
Poor Boy	Pvt	L	3d IHG
Price, Joseph	Pvt	I	3d IHG
Puppy, Young	Pvt	C	3d IHG
Rail, Jackson	Pvt	C	3d IHG
Re-ca-ne-ha-coh	Pvt	D	1s IHG
Reese, F. Joe	Pvt	B	3d IHG
Riley, John	Pvt	E	2d IHG
Rooster, George	Pvt	F	3d IHG
Ross, Daniel	Pvt	G	2d IHG
Schneider, Lester	Pvt	E	2d IHG
Shave Head, James	Pvt	A	3d IHG
Sid-a-wa-gy	Pvt	D	3d IHG
Ske-no-yah	Pvt	K	2d IHG
Smith, Samuel	Pvt	I	2d IHG
So-fix-se-ho	Sgt	F	1s IHG
So-ha-jo	Pvt	F	1s IHG
So-kat-ha-yo	Pvt	F	1s IHG
Sour John, Wm	Pvt	D	3d IHG
Stand	Pvt	G	3d IHG
Steeler, Josiah	Pvt	E	3d IHG
Steny, White Killer	Pvt	I	2d IHG
Stewart	Pvt	F	1s IHG
Stop, Wasody	Pvt	H	3d IHG
Sumpka	Pvt	K	1s IHG
Su-wa-ke, Tom	Pvt	C	3d IHG
Swinger, Moses	Pvt	I	3d IHG
Ta-ca-ne-e-ski-ooste	Pvt	B	2d IHG
Tadpole, Crossing	Pvt	C	3d IHG
Ta-mat-le-ge-ho-la	Pvt	C	1s IHG
Tem-meh	Pvt	I	1s IHG
Toney	Pvt	D	3d IHG
Trotting Wolf	Sgt	A	3d IHG
Tu-sie-la-hago	Pvt	C	1s IHG
Tute-ka-ho-see	Pvt	F	1s IHG
Vann, Ave	Cpl	F	3d IHG
Vann, Moses	Pvt	A	3d IHG
Wah-yoh-goo-loo-nr	Pvt	B	2d IHG
Wak-se-ha-go	Pvt	I	1s IHG
Walker, John	Cpl	D	2d IHG
Walker, Nicholas	Pvt	I	2d IHG

Walkingstick, Drinker	Pvt	F	3d IHG
Walkingstick, Samuel	Pvt	I	3d IHG
Watt	Pvt	D	2d IHG
Weaver, George	Pvt	C	3d IHG
White Path, Jug	Sgt	A	2d IHG
Wicked, Ned	Cpl	C	2d IHG
Wild Cat	Pvt	E	1s IHG
Wilson, Joseph	Pvt	A	2d IHG
Wilson, Lacy	Pvt	D	2d IHG
Woodall, Andrew	Pvt	L	3d IHG
Woodward, Jack	Pvt	E	2d IHG
Ya-ha-lo-chee	Lt	C	1s IHG
Young Deer	Pvt	G	2d IHG
Yo-ho-lo, Jim	Pvt	E	3d IHG

Indian Home Guard Pensions

Cherokee Advocate
Tahlequah, Cherokee Nation, Indian Territory
January 14, 1871

List of claimants for Pension, whose applications have been filed in the Pension Office at Washington, and which will be examined by Messrs. Foster and Webster, U. S. Special Agents, at Pension Office, Fort Gibson. The persons named are desired to appear at this Agency, with their witnesses:

Name	Rank	Co.	Regiment
Adair, Polk	Pvt.	G	2d IHG
Adams, George	Pvt	C	3d IHG
Ah-ha-Jo	Pvt.	B	1s IHG
Ah-ha-le-ma-lah	Pvt.	H	1s IHG
Ah-nu-chee	Pvt.	F	2d IHG
A-hol-lok-ya-hol-lah	Pvt.	D	1s IHG
Ah-pe-ker-fix-e-ko	Pvt.	I	1s IHG
Ah-wa-tul-e-co	Pvt.	C	1s IHG
Ak-ta-yoh-ce-mar-reh	Pvt	D	1s IHG
Allercher	Cpl.	F	2d IHG
Al-pust-e-fix-e-ko	Pvt	D	1s IHG
Archy	Pvt.	F	2d IHG
Arnold, Jesse	Pvt.	I	3d IHG
Ato-la-he, Osti	Pvt	B	2d IHG
At-ta-ga-hol-lah	Pvt.	D	lst. IHG
Baldridge, John	Pvt.	F	2d IHG
Baldridge, Samuel	Pvt.	A	3d IHG
Blackbird,,William	Pvt.	A	3d IHG
Barnett, Young	Pvt.	K	1st IHG
Batt, War-le-ksi	Pvt.	F	3d IHG
Beans	Pvt.	E	3d IHG
Bear Paw, Charles	Pvt.	A	3d IHG
Bear, John	Pvt	B	3d IHG
Beaver Tail, Jas.	Pvt.	M	3d IHG
Bee, Bearsweat	Pvt	I	2d IHG
Bendabout	Pvt.	I	2d IHG
Big Drum, Charles	Pvt.	G	2d IHG
Big Tom	Pvt.	F	2d IHG

Big Tom	Pvt.	K	1s IHG
Bird, Jackson	Pvt.	H	3d IHG
Black Haw	Pvt.	D	3d IHG
Boulin, Edmund	Pvt.	I	3d IHG
Bowlegs, March	Pvt.	B	1s IHG
Bowlin, James	Pvt.	F	2d Ihg
Broome, Horace	Pvt.	G	3d IHG
Buck, Eli	Pvt.	C	3d IHG
Bushy Head, Henry	Pvt.		3d IHG
Butler, John	Pvt.	M	3d IHG
Cade, William	Pvt.	C	3d IHG
Cah-nah-o-sa-ski	Pvt.	G	2d IHG
Cah-pit-sah-tus-cum-nuck-ke	Pvt.	F	1s IHG
Cak-ka-na	Pvt.	K	1s IHG
Canaquauua	Pvt.	K	2d IHG
Ca-na-wa-sa-ski	Pvt.	G	2d IHG
Canoe, Arch	Pvt.	F	2d IHG
Cas-se-la-we	Pvt.	M	3d IHG
Cat	Pvt.	A	2d IHG
Catcher	Pvt.	L	3d IHG
Catcher, Runner	Pvt.	G	3d IHG
Charlie	Pvt.	M	3d IHG
Chee-ne-sa-ta	Pvt.	C	2d IHG
Cho-co-ah-hajo	Pvt.	F	1s IHG
Christie, Richard	Pvt.	G	3d IHG
Chu-sa-lun-tas	Pvt.	B	2d IHG
Clinton, W. M.	Pvt.	K	1s IHG
Cockram, Wind	Pvt.	I	2d IHG
Cockrum, Watt	Pvt.	K	3d IHG
Colston,	Pvt.	I	3d IHG
Cone-ah-hajo	Pvt.	C	1s IHG
Con-e-ta-hajo	Pvt.	C	1s IHG
Cornsilk, Tom	Pvt.	F	2d IHG
Cot-sar-hajo	Pvt.	I	1s IHG
Cot-se-hajo	Pvt.	H	1s IHG
Co-we-na	Pvt.	K	1s IHG
Co-wit-che	Pvt.	F	1s IHG
Crittenden, Dick	Pvt.	D	2d IHG
Daniel, Arch	Pvt.	K	3d IHG
Dave	Pvt.	F	3d IHG
Davis, John	Pvt.	K	3d IHG

Name	Rank	Co.	Unit
Daylight	Pvt.	M	2d IHG
Deer In The Water	Pvt.	K	3d IHG
Deer, Henry	Pvt.	I	83 Col.
Deer, Young	Pvt.	K	2d IHG
Dick, Little	Pvt.	A	2d IHG
Dirt Seller, Adam	Pvt.	G	2d IHG
Doctor	Pvt.	G	3d IHG
Downing, Abot	Cpl.	L	3d IHG
Downing, Dull	Pvt.	D	3d IHG
Drum, Wilson	Pvt.	B	2d IHG
Drummer, Wilson	Pvt.	B	2d IHG
Dry Water	Pvt.	G	2d IHG
Dry, Jumper	Pvt.	L	3d IHG
Dryhead, Scunti	Pvt.	K	3d IHG
Duck, John	Pvt.	F	3d IHG
Duck, Young	Pvt.	K	2d IHG
Eagle War	Pvt.	E	2d IHG
E-cho-e-fix-e-co	Sgt.	G	1s IHG
Elijah	Pvt.	H	3d IHG
Ellis, Nathaniel	Pvt.	F	3d IHG
E-lou-we	Pvt.	C	2d IHG
Emory, Peter	Pvt.	E	3d IHG
Es-fa-na-hop-pa-ya	Pvt.	D	1s IHG
Fas-lah-goh	Pvt.	A	1s IHG
Field, Lawyer	Pvt.	L	3d IHG
Fish, John	Pvt.	H	2d IHG
Fish, Watt	Pvt.	K	3d IHG
Foster, Daniel	Pvt.	F	3d IHG
Foster, John	Pvt.	D	2d IHG
Gah-sai-hee-ley (Raincrow)	Pvt.	D	2d IHG
Ge-lok-ka-ha-goh	Pvt.	H	1s IHG
George, Creek	Pvt.	D	2d IHG
George, E.	?	F	2d IHG
Glass, Judge	Pvt.	F	2d IHG
Go Back	Pvt.	G	2d IHG
Gooseby, Joseph	Pvt.	I	3d IHG
Go-tu-la-sta, Harry	Pvt.	I	2d IHG
Gourd, Daniel R.	?	I	3d IHG
Go-was-ta-ye-meh-co	Pvt.	H	1s IHG
Grass	Pvt.	A	3d IHG
Greece	Pvt.	I	3d IHG

Gutter	Pvt.	H	3d IHG
Hair, Jim	Pvt.	E	2d IHG
Hajo, Ka-peh-ge	Pvt.	H	1s IHG
Hal-lok-to-me-mar-reh	Sgt.	D	1s IHG
Hammer	Pvt.	A	3d IHG
Harjo, Charles	Pvt.	E	2d IHG
Harris, James	Pvt.	F	3d IHG
Hawk, Isaac	Pvt.	D	2d IHG
Hawkins, Charles	Pvt.	D	1s IHG
Hawkins, Jack	Pvt.	G	1s IHG
He-le-on-to	Pvt.	K	1s IHG
Henry, Samuel	Pvt.	D	3d IHG
Henson, Washington	Pvt.	I	3d IHG
Hickory	Pvt.	A	3d IHG
Hider	Pvt.	D	2d IHG
Hin-ne-ho-guh-ko	Sgt.	G	1s IHG
Hog Shooter	?	H	2d IHG
Hog Shooter	Pvt.	L	3d IHG
Hok-ke-les-hop-ha-he-she	Pvt.	D	1s IHG
Ho-kus-ya-ho-lo	Pvt.	G	1s IHG
Ho-lock-e-ho-lo	Sgt.	E	1s IHG
Homes, David	Pvt.	F	2d IGH
Hungary	Pvt.	A	2d IHG
Hunter	Pvt.	D	3d IHG
Hunter, Sam	Pvt.	H	3d IHG
Hunter, Water	Pvt.	F	2d IHG
In-dio-i s-har-jo	Pvt.	E	1s IHG
James	Pvt.	E	3d IHG
Janes-a-nega-a-lou-no-his-ki	Cpl.	B	2d IHG
Jim-meh (Jummcy)	Pvt.	C	2d IHG
Johnson	Pvt.	F	2d IHG
Johnson, James	Pvt.	K	1s IHG
Jo-la-fix-e-co	Pvt	I	1s IHG
Jonneh	Pvt.	D	1s IHG
Jumper	Pvt.	E	3d IHG
Justice, Sidney	Sgt.	E	3d IHG
Ju-was-to-yu-hol-lah	Pvt.	G	1s IHG
Kah-hah-hms-	Pvt.	A	Paw. Scouts
Kan-tella-hogoh Kee-you-hah	Pvt.	H	1s IHG

(Ground Squirrel)	Pvt.	F	2d IHG
Kew-tsa-fix-e-ko	Pvt.	E	1s IHG
Killer, Lawly	Pvt.	K	3d IHG
Killernick	Pvt.	F	3d IHG
Killerwith, Samuel	Pvt.	A	3d IHG
Knob	Pvt.	A	3d IHG
Ko-ai-fix-e-co	Pvt.	C	1s IHG
Ko-ha-se-martler	Pvt.	I	1s IHG
Ko-nulth-hajo	Pvt.	D	1s IHG
Kupte	Pvt.	D	1s IHG
Kus-ka-las-ky	Pvt.	H	3d IHG
Landrum, Thomas	Pvt.	M	3d IHG
Lasley, Ned	Pvt.	L	3d IHG
Leach, Beaver	Pvt.	I	2d IHG
Leach, Dick	Pvt.	H	2d IHG
Leak, Ned	Pvt.	G	2d IHG
Lee, Edward	Pvt.	G	2d IHG
Legg, John	Pvt.	K	3d IHG
Le-hom-mot-to-hajoh	Cpl.	H	1s IHG
Lester	Pvt	A	1s IHG
Limber-leg, Charles	Pvt.	F	3d IHG
Looney	Pvt.	G	2d IHG
Lowery, Eli	Pvt.	F	2d IHG
Lowery, Squirl	Pvt.	F	3d IHG
Mah-les-neh	Pvt.	A	1s IHG
Mankiller, Scott	Pvt.	F	2d IHG
Marshall, Lester	Pvt.	A	1s IHG
McCoy, Thos.	Sgt.	C	2d IHG
Me-het-ces-ka-ha-coh	Pvt.	D	1s IHG
Middlestriker, Lowly	Pvt.	A	3d IHG
Misteala	Pvt.	E	3d IHG
Morgan, Henry	Pvt.	I	3d IHG
Moses	Pvt.	H	2d IHG
Muffee, Iste	Pvt.	I	1s IHG
Nah-mah-co-cee	Pvt.	C	1s IHG
Nelson	Pvt.	F	2d IHG
Nelson, Len	Pvt.	A	3d IHG
Nicholson, Scraper	Cpl.	H	2d IHG
No-co-se-yo-ho-le	Pvt.	F	1s IHG
No-ha-lar	Pvt.	K	2d IHG
No-ke-se-lee	Pvt.	A	1s IHG
Nok-kas-hats-leah	Pvt.	D	1s IHG

Ochee-sha-go	Sgt.	G	1s IHG
Ok-cage-ne-ha-rak-ko	Pvt.	D	1s IHG
O-la-yo-a	Pvt.	B	3d IHG
Olor-no-to-ski	Pvt.	K	2d IHG
Oo-chur-lude	Pvt.	B	2d IHG
Oo-gu-da-gathe	Pvt.	B	2d IHG
Ool-stoo, Stephen	Pvt.	D	2d IHG
Oo-sar-lah-ner-hee	Pvt.	F	2d IHG
Oo-sow-wee	Pvt.	H	2d IHG
Oo-sqaw-(Bolly)	Pvt.	M	3d IHG
Oo-stur-la-tah	Pvt.	F	3d IHG
Oo-wa-ha-saki	Pvt.	B	2d IHG
Oo-wah-ho-saki-	Pvt	B	2d IHG
Oo-wa-soty	Cpl	H	3d IHG
Otter-lifter	Pvt.	B	3d IHG
Ow-wit-toost	Pvt.	I	3d IHG
Ow-wit-toost	Pvt	A	Paw. Scouts
O-yo-dle-a	Pvt.	K	2d IHG
Pah-co-ca	Pvt	K	1s IHG
Pas-lof-hazo	Cpl.	G	1s IHG
Passon, Stephen	Pvt.	M	3d IHG
Pelican	Pvt	D	2d IHG
Pellican, Leaf	Pvt.	H	2d IHG
Pickup, John	Pvt.	D	3d IHG
Pig, Mike	Pvt.	H	3d IHG
Pike	Pvt.	M	3d IHG
Pisser	Pvt	K	1s IHG
Plow	Pvt.	F	2d IHG
Poorboy	Pvt.	L	3d IHG
Poorboy, Samuel	Pvt.	I	3d IHG
Potato	Pvt	A	3d IHG
Potato, Tom	Cpl.	A	2d IHG
Proctor, Alex	Pvt.	G	3d IHG
Puller, David	Pvt.	M	3d IHG
Ridge	Pvt	A	3d IHG
Robertson, Water	Pvt.	E	2d IHG
Rock-kos-ko-ne-rah	Pvt	G	1s IHG
Rogers, Marcellus	Pvt.	I	3d IHG
Sak-co-teu-na	Pvt	K	1s IHG
Sanders, Arch	Pvt.	L	3d IHG
Sanders, Ben	Pvt	G	3d IHG

Sanders, Samuel	Pvt	E	2d IHG
San-yah-pah-ka	Pvt	K	1s IHG
Sash-ko-hon-quet	Pvt	K	1s IHG
Scraper, George	Pvt	H	2d IHG
Se-kee-kee, John	Pvt	H	2d IHG
Seller, Dirt	Pvt.	F	3d IHG
Sem-me-po-wa-ge	Cpl.	H	1s IHG
Sequoyah	Pvt	K	2d IHG
Shade	Pvt	A	2d IHG
Shade, Johnson	Pvt	G	3d IHG
Sharp, Samuel	Pvt.	K	2d IHG
Si-cou-wi	Pvt	D	2d IHG
Simmons, Lacy	Pvt	H	2d IHG
Sit-cawne	Pvt	F	1s IHG
Sit-ta-waga, Johnson	Pvt	F	3d IHG
Sit-u-wake	Pvt	G	2d IHG
Sixkiller, Delaware	Pvt	D	2d IHG
Ska-oua	Pvt	K	2d IHG
Smith, John	Pvt	I	3d IHG
Smoker, John	Pvt	I	3d IHG
Snake, Going	Pvt.	D	2d IHG
Sort, Every	Pvt.	A	3d IHG
Spade, Watt	Pvt	K	2d IHG
Spikebuck, Thomas	Pvt	B	3d IHG
Spirit	Pvt	F	2d IHG
Spoona	Pvt	K	1s IHG
Starr, Squirrel	Pvt	C	2d IHG
Stean, Walker	Pvt.	H	2d IHG
Stooty, John	Pvt.	H	2d IHG
Stop, Walter	Lt	A	2d IHG
String, Fick	Pvt	B	2d IHG
Sunday	Pvt	E	3d IHG
Sunshine	Pvt	K	3d IHG
Swimmer	Pvt	A	2d IHG
Swimmer, Joseph	Pvt	A	2d IHG
Tadpole, Eli	Pvt	C	2d IHG
Tah-la-sar, Creek	Pvt	F	2d IHG
Te-char-go	Pvt	K	1s IHG
The Kee, Charles	Pvt	A	3d IHG
Thornton, William	Sgt	L	3d IHG
Tie-ska, George	Pvt	E	2d IHG
Tiger, Red Bird	Pvt	B	2d IHG

Name	Rank	Co.	Unit
Tiger, Wheeler	Lt	B	2d IHG
Timmy	Pvt	K	1s IHG
Tobacco, James	Pvt	I	2d IHG
Tsa-ga-wo-ra-	Pvt	D	2d IHG
Tuc-a-bach-a-hojo	Capt	C	1s IHG
Tuck-co-ser-hage	Pvt	H	1s IHG
Tucker, William	Pvt	B	2d IHG
Tuck-oo-wa-te-roo	Sgt	A	Paw. Scouts
Tul-se-fix-e-co	Capt	I	1s IHG
Tun-ne-lo-lee	Pvt	A	2d IHG
Turner, Josh	Lt	H	3d IHG
Turning, About	Pvt	G	3d IHG
Tus-cum-mich-co-chee	Pvt	B	2d IHG
Tus-hut-chee-hajo	Pvt	H	1s IHG
Van, Henry	Pvt	F	2d IHG
Wa-ha-chi	Pvt	F	3d IHG
Wa-hoo-hoo	Pvt	K	2d IHG
Wah-we-see	Pvt	A	2d IHG
Walkabout, Buffalo	Pvt	K	3d IHG
Walker, Edward	Pvt	D	2d IHG
Walker, Edward	Pvt	D	2d IHG
Walter	Pvt	D	2d IHG
Walter, Boltem	Pvt	G	3d IHG
Waner, Jarne	Pvt	E	3d IHG
Washington	Pvt	I	1s IHG
Wastee	Pvt	K	2d IHG
Water Hunter	Cpl	B	3d IHG
Watt	Pvt	I	2d IHG
Wax-se-harjo	Pvt	I	1s IHG
Webber, Wm	Capt	E	2d IHG
Welch, John	Pvt	I	2d IHG
Whaler	Pvt	D	2d IHG
White Killer, Starr	Pvt	G	2d IHG
Wolf Crying	Pvt	H	3d IHG
Wolf, Ta-qua-yh	Pvt	H	2d IHG
Wox-se-harjo	Pvt	F	1s IHG
Yso-ful-lup-har	Pvt	E	1s IHG
Ze-coo-te-ske	Pvt	B	2d IHG

Widows' Pension Checks
Indian Home Guards

TO:
Capt. F. A. Field
U. S. Ind. Agent
Creek Agency

A July 1870 list of 46 pension checks sent to widows and mothers of Seminole and Creek Indian soldiers in compliance with your verbal request of the 30 ultimo that the names of certain deceased members of the 1st Regt. Ind. Home Guards might be furnished you by this office, in order that the claimants of the checks sent you the 19th of May last can be more clearly identified. I send you a list showing the number of check, name of the payee or claimant, and the relation of such claimant to the deceased soldier as appears from the records of this office.

No. of check	Name of Payee	Name of Soldier	Company
24608	Winna, mother of	Charles Clinton	K
24610	Eliza, widow of	Jo la fix se ko	I
24614	Cat se ah Yo ho lo, father of	Homeh	H
24616	Ko ko thlo na, widow of	Kel ver	K
24620	Keen sah, widow of	Ne or ha goh	H
24622	Louisa, widow of	Koneh	H
24624	Heah, widow of	Ge lsh ka ha jah?	H
24626	Co tow she, widow of	Go fol lop fix e co	H
24628	Sally, widow of	A lok yah ho lah	C
24630	Wah te thla, mother of	Ka sak co la na	K
24632	Sa con we, father of	Co ke thla na	K
24634	Nen sen nee, widow of	Ap peh ker ver	
24636	Martha Rogers, widow of	Jackson Conrad	F

24638	Te th lic ke, widow of	Ko ot see	F
24640	Roady McIntosh, mother of	Harry McIntosh	E
24642	Tuck wee hick chee, widow of	Och ees hargo	H
24646	Pittee, widow of	Lit tif ha jo	G
24648	Pokoflash Sponna, widow of	Sponna	K
24650	I ya be, widow of	Tusci cia hajo	C
24652	Rachel Yarcher, mother of	Jack	C
24654	Pa ne, mother of	Ya ha e mas set ceh	D
24656	Sampson Steadhim, father of	John Steadhim	C
24658	Tiffy, widow of	Me hit ces ka hu coh	D
24660	Low we sa, widow of	Hok e co hop poe per she	D
24662	Ann Brown, widow of	Isaac, o-d Sergt.	K
24664	Molly, widow of	Wild Cat	E
24666	Li mar ta, mother of	Ar tus se mar ler	E
24668	Fow we che, widow of	Sem me co na yeh	H
24670	Mis teh a kee, widow of	No kos ya ho la	G
24672	Ish chim bah, widow of	Ka keh ge he goh	H
24792	Nancy Marshall, widow of	Lester	A
24794	Nanny, widow of	Cottroche	B
24802	Le wah hok te, widow of	Te ha lla theh?	A
24812	Lup ho kee, widow of	Fas ha goh	A
24814	Sally, widow of	Ma lles sseh	A
24820	Char cher mek ko, father of	A ha llak if fose koh	A
25907	Tilda, widow of	Ar lar luc yar hollar	E
26273	John Sheah, guardian minor child of	Car cah pa na	K
26302	John Harrison,		

guardian minor child of	Emarlo hajo	C
28135 Cinta, widow of	Fah yah ne ho la	A
28145 Pinsa, mother of	John Walker	
28149 Tick lum mi gee, widow of	Kan tella ha goh	H
28151 Yah nee, widow of	Ko nup ha jo	D
28153 Pa con thla, widow of	James Johnson	K
28155 Lizzie, widow of	Jack Hawkins	G
28157 Lucinda Grayson, widow of	Robert Grayson	D

Very Respectfully
Your Obt. Servt.
W. F. Cady
Actg. Commissioner

THE CEASE FIRE TREATY.

Treaty stipulations made and entered into this 23rd day of June 1865 near Doaksville, Choctaw Nation, between Sent. Colonel A. C. Mathews and W. H. Vance U. S. V., commissioners appointed by Major General Herron U. S. A., on part of the military authorities of the United States and Brig. General Stand Watie, Governor and Principal Chief of that part of the Cherokee Nation lately allied with Confederate States in acts of hostilities against the Government of the United States as follows to wit:

ARTICLE 1. All acts of hostilities on the part of both armies having ceased by virtue of a convention entered into on the 26th day of May 1865 between Major General E. R. S. Gantry, United States Army, Commanding, TransMissississippi Department.

The Indians of the Cherokee Nation here represented, lately allied with the Confederate States in acts of hostilities against the Government of the United States, do agree at once to return to their respective homes and there remain at peace with United States, and offer no indignities, whatever, against the whites or Indians of the various tribes who have been friendly to or engaged in the service of the United States during the war.

ARTICLE II. It is stipulated by the undersigned commissioners on part of the United States, that so long as the Indians aforesaid observe the provisions of article first of this agreement, they shall be protected by the United States authorities in their person and property, not only from encroachment on the part of the whites, but also from the Indians who have been engaged in the service of the United States.

"ARTICLE III. The above articles of agreement to remain and be in force and effect until the meeting of the Grand Council to meet at Armstrong Academy, Choctaw Nation, on the 1st day of September, A. D. 1865, and until such time as the proceedings of said Grand Council shall be ratified by the proper authorities both of the Cherokee Nation and the United States. In testimony, whereof the said Lieut. Col. A. C. Mathews and Adjutant W. H. Vance, commissioners on part of the United States and Brig. General Stand Watie Governor and Principal Chief of the Cherokee Nation, have hereunto set their hands and seals.

Signed.A. C. Mathews, Sent. Col.
W. H. Vance, Adjt.
Commissioners.

Stand Watie, Brig. Genl. Governor and Principal Chief Cherokee Nation,

Sale of Arkansas Cherokee Nation Land

Less than a year after the Cease Fire that was signed by General Watie, the Federal Cherokee delegates sold the old agency site of the Arkansas Cherokees: Transfer of 3400 acres of land, more or less. Situated in Township 7 Range 21, State of Arkansas. Said land being the former agency and residue of the tract disposed of by Cherokees by treaty of 1828. This effectively moved the Cherokee out of the state of Arkansas, at least on paper. Many Cherokee did not acknowledge this and stayed behind, since many of their ancestors had moved to the Missouri and Arkansas area before the end of the 1700's. The sale document states:

"Know all men by these presents, that whereas the Cherokee Nation owns a tract of land in the state of Arkansas, known as the Cherokee reservation lying in township No. 7, range 21, west of the Fifth Principal Meridian, and containing three thousand four hundred (3400) acres more or less, and all which is occupied or claimed by squatters and others claiming title adverse to the said Nation, under color of various titles. And whereas it is provided by the 4th Article of the treaty between the United States and the Cherokee Nation, of May 6th 1838, said tract shall be sold under the direction of the agent of the Cherokee Nation. And whereas the Cherokee Nation by its delegation hereto duly authorized, have sold said lands to John Brown Wright, of the city of Washington, and have received in payment therefore, the sum of five thousand dollars which they agree shall be applied by the Nation to the use named in said treaty and amendments thereto. Said sale having been made by direction and with the approval of Justin Harlin, the agent appointed by the United States for the Cherokee Nation. Now therefore, the said Cherokee Nation by its delegation hereto fully authorized to do, hereby request the Secretary of the Interior to cause a patent to be issued for the said John Brown Wright for the said land and do release the United States from all liability for said land or its proceed.

Witness our hands this, 10th day of May A. D. 1866.

Daniel H. Ross
White Catcher
I. H. Benge
James McDaniel
Smith Christie
J. B. Jones

City of Washington, District of Columbia.

I, Justin Harlan agent of the United States for the Cherokee Nation, do hereby approve of and consent to the above sale, which was made by my direction this tenth day of May.

J. Harlan, U. S. Indian Agent."

August 11, 1866 Treaty, United States and Cherokee Nation, Southern Cherokee

The United States Government knew the fighting between Cherokee factions in Indian Territory would certainly leave hard feelings and scars for many years to come. They needed to resettle Stand Watie's Southern Cherokees, their associated freed persons and former slaves and assure their civil rights and ability to govern themselves. Without looking to Ross Party Cherokees for justice and to avoid possible discrimination, this 1866 treaty established the Canadian district (and elsewhere if necessary) as their place of settlement. It also establishes seats or seats on the Cherokee National council for their representatives. The Dawes Commission enrollment procedures and lack of council representation after the turn of the century were injurious, unjust, and discriminatory towards Southern Cherokee. They were discouraged from settling in their rightful and promised lands in Indian Territory because of the defacto policies of the ruling Ross Party.

The Ross action leadership, later ratified by Congress - the Law of the Land, agreed to this treaty. One note, treaties *supersede* even the Constitution of the United States. The same signatures on this treaty are the ones who signed the previous document, selling the agency lands in Arkansas.

{July 19, 1866 | 14 Stat., 799 | Ratified July 27, 1866 | Proclaimed August 11, 1866}

Preamble

Treaty of February 18, 1863 between the Cherokees and the United States is declared void. A mutual amnesty is declared by both the Cherokee Nation and the United States, Confiscation laws are repealed, property sales which occurred under such laws are declared null and void, former ownership restored, purchasers repaid, etc.

The Canadian district established as a place of settlement for Southern Cherokees, freedmen and their former slaves.

Articles of agreement and convention at the city of Washington, on the nineteenth day of July, in the year of our lord One Thousand Eight Hundred and Sixty-six, between the United States represented by Dennis N. Cooley, Commissioner of Indian Affairs, Elijah Sells superintendent of Indian Affairs for the southern superintendency, and the Cherokee Nation of Indian, represented by its delegates, James McDaniel, Smith Christie, White Catcher, S. H. Benge, J. B. Jones and Daniel H. Ross, principal chief of the Cherokees, being too unwell to join in these negotiation.

WHEREAS the existing treaties between the United States and the Cherokee Nation are deemed to be insufficient, the said contracting parties as follows, viz:

ARTICLE 1: The pretended treaties between the United States and the Cherokee Nation on the seventh day of October, eighteen hundred and sixty-one, and repudiated by the national council of the Cherokee Nation on the eighteenth of February, eighteen hundred and sixty-three is hereby declared to be void.

ARTICLE 2: Amnesty is hereby declared by the United States and the Cherokee Nation for all crimes and misdemeanors committed by one Cherokee on the person or property of another Cherokee or a citizen of the United States, prior to the fourth of July, eighteen hundred and sixty-six; and no right of action arising out of wrongs committed in aid or in the suppression of the rebellion shall be prosecuted or maintained in the courts of the United States or in the courts of the Cherokee Nation. But the Cherokee Nation stipulate and agree to deliver up to the United States, or their duly authorized agent, any or all public property, particularly ordnance stores, arms of all kinds, and quartermaster's stores, in their possession or control, which belonged to the so-called confederate States, without any reservation.

ARTICLE 3: The confiscation laws of the Cherokee Nation shall be repealed, and the same, and all sales of farms and improvements on real estate, made or pretended to be made in pursuance thereof, are hereby agreed and declared, to be null and void, and the former owners of such property, their heirs and assigns, shall have the right to peaceably reoccupy their homes and the purchaser under the confiscation laws, or his heirs and assigns, shall be repaid by the treasurer of the Cherokee Nation from the national funds, the money paid for such property and the cost of permanent improvements on such real estate, made thereon by since the confiscation sale; the cost of such improvements to be fixed by a commission , to be composed by one person assigned by the Secretary of the Interior and one by the principal chief of the Nation, which two may appoint a third in cases of disagreement, which cost so fixed shall be refunded to the national treasurer by the returning Cherokees within three years of the ratification thereof.

ARTICLE 4: All of the Cherokees and freed persons who were formerly slaves to any Cherokee and all free Negroes not having been such slaves, who resided in the Cherokee Nation, prior to June first, eighteen hundred and sixty-one, who may reside northeast of the Arkansas River and Southeast of the Grand River, shall have the right to settle in and occupy the Canadian district southwest of the Arkansas River, and also all of that tract of country lying northwest of Grand River, and bounded on the southeast by Grand River and west by the Creek reservation to the northeast corner thereof; from thence west on the north line of the creek reservation to the ninety-sixth degree of west longitude; thence north on said line of longitude so far that a line due east to Grand River will include a quality of land equal to one hundred and sixty acres for each person who may so elect to reside in the territory above -described in this article; Provided, that said part of said district north of the Arkansas River shall not be set apart until it shall be found the Canadian district is not sufficiently large to allow one hundred and sixty acres to each person desiring to obtain settlement under the provisions of this article.

ARTICLE 5: The inhabitants electing to reside in the district described in the preceding article shall have the right to elect all their local officers and judges, and the number of delegates to which their numbers may be entitled in any general council to be established in the Indian Territory under provisions of this treaty as stated in Article 12, and to control all their local affairs, and to establish all necessary police regulations and rules for the administration of justice in said district, not inconsistent with the constitution of the Cherokee Nation or the laws of the United States; Provided, the Cherokees residing in said district shall enjoy all the rights and privileges of other Cherokee who may elect to settle in said district under the provisions of this treaty; Provided also, That if any such police regulations or rules be adopted which in the opinion of the President, bear oppressively on any citizen of the nation, he may suspend the same. And all rules and regulations in said district, or in any other district of the nation, discriminating against citizens of other districts, are prohibited, and shall be void.

ARTICLE 6: The inhabitants of the said district hereinbefore described shall be entitled to representation according to numbers in the national council, and all laws of the Cherokee Nation shall be uniform throughout said nation. And should any law, either in its provisions or in the manner of its enforcement, in the opinion of the President of the United States, operate unjustly or injuriously in said district, he is hereby authorized and empowered to correct such evil, and to adopt the means necessary to secure the impartial administration of justice, as well as fair and equitable application and expenditure of national funds as between the people of this and every other district in said nation.

ARTICLE 7: The United States court to be created in the Indian Territory; and until such court is created therein, the United States district court, the nearest to the Cherokee Nation, shall have exclusive original jurisdiction of all causes, civil and criminal, wherein an inhabitant of the district hereinbefore described shall be a party, and where an inhabitant outside of said district, in the Cherokee nation, shall be he other party, as plaintiff or defendant in a civil case, or shall be defendant or prosecutor in a criminal case, and all process issued in said district by any officer of the Cherokee Nation, to be executed on an inhabitant residing outside of said district. And all process issued by any officer of the Cherokee Nation outside of said district, to be executed on an inhabitant residing in said district, shall be to all intents and purposes null and void, unless endorsed by the district judge for the district where such process is to be served, and said person, so arrested, shall be held in custody by the officer so arresting him, until he shall be delivered over to the United States marshal, or by consent to be tried by the Cherokee court;

Provided, That any or all provisions of this treaty, which make any distinction in rights and remedies between the citizens of any district and the citizens of the rest of the nation, shall be abrogated whenever the President shall have ascertained, by an election duly ordered by him, that a majority of the voters of such district desire them to be abrogated, and he shall have declared such abrogation: And provided further that no law or regulation, to be hereafter enacted within said district thereof, prescribing a penalty for its violation, shall take effect or be enforced until ninety days from the date of its promulgation, either by publication in one or more newspapers of general circulation in said Cherokee Nation, or by posting up copies thereof in the Cherokee and English languages in each district where the same is to take effect, at the usual place of holding district courts.

ARTICLE 8: No license to trade in goods, wares, or merchandise shall be ranted by the United States to trade in the Cherokee Nation, unless approved by the Cherokee council except in the Canadian district, and such other district north of the Arkansas River and west of the Grand River occupied by the so-called Southern Cherokee, as provided in Article 4 of this treaty.

These articles pertain to Stand Watie's Southern Cherokee, showing them to be an "exception to the rule," and upholding their status as a separate government entity. Though Watie lobbied for a separate Nation for his Southern Cherokee, the government refused recognition and insisted on a single Nation.

Annie Abel defined the reconstruction period in Indian Territory as "political re-adjustment." The treaties of 1866 re-established relations between the Five Nations and the United States.

The United States government abandoned the Indians of Indian Territory in 1861 when it re-assigned troops to other areas and virtually invited the Confederacy to take over. After the Tribes had signed treaties with the Confederate Government, the United States failed to care for and help the Indian refugees that had fled to Kansas. Federal civilian and military officers joined in the theft of thousands of head of Indian owned livestock, magnifying the difficulty of post war economic recovery. U. S. Senator James Lane and Congressman S. C. Pomeroy, both from Kansas, pushed legislation in Congress to invalidate all previous treaties that defined and protected the land rights of the five tribes and authorize the removal of other Indian people from Kansas into Indian Territory. Iowa Senator James Harlan prepared legislation that would formally make Indian Territory a federal territory, complete with a governor and legislature, in effect denying the Nations Sovereignty status.

Combined, these measures made up a massive campaign to strip the nations of Indian Territory of their political independence, their land, and natural resources. When coupled with the further requirements to free their slaves and admit Freedmen to full equality, reduced their citizens to poverty and dependence.

The negotiations of the 1866 Reconstruction Treaties, orchestrated by a trio of greedy anti-Indian legislators, former Iowa Senator, now Secretary of State, James Harlan, Commissioner Indian Affairs Dennis N. Cooley, and head of the Southern Superintendency, Eligah Sells, (also Iowans) reflected the principles of the Lane-Pomeroy legislation. The Harlan bill went beyond the grants of land for railroad construction through Indian lands. The negotiations rested on a single policy of expansion and development at the expense of the Indians. These treaties forced the Southern Nations to grant railroads rights of ways. This was the beginning of the land hungry whites to challenge Indian sovereignty.

OFFICIAL RECORDS: Series 4, vol 1, Part 1
Pages 669-687
Confederate States of America - Cherokee

A TREATY of friendship and alliance made and concluded at Tahlequah, in the Cherokee Nation, on the seventh day of October, A. D. one thousand eight hundred and sixty-one, between the Confederate States of America, by Albert Pike, commissioner with plenary powers, of the Confederate States, of the one part, and the Cherokee Nation of Indians, by John Ross, the principal chief, Joseph Verner, assistant principal chief, James Brown, John Drew, and William P. Ross, executive councilors, constituting, with the principal and assistant principal chiefs, the executive council of the nation, and authorized to enter into this treaty by a general convention of the Cherokee people, held at Tahlequah, the seat of government of the Cherokee Nation, on the twenty-first day of August, A. D. one thousand eight hundred and sixty-one; together with Lewis Ross, Thomas Pegg, and Richard Fields, commissioners selected and appointed by the principal chief with the advice and consent of the executive council to assist in negotiating the same, of the other part.

The Congress of the Confederate State of America, having by an "Act for the protection of certain Indian tribes," approved the twenty-first day of May, A. D. one thousand eighth hundred and sixty-one, offered to assume and accept the protectorate of the several nations and tribes of Indians occupying the country west of Arkansas and Missouri, and to recognize them as their wards, subject to all the rights, privileges and immunities, titles and guaranties with each of said nations and tribes under treaties made with them by the United States of America; and the Cherokee Nation of Indians having assented thereto upon certain terms and conditions:

Now, therefore the said Confederate States of America, by Albert Pike, their commissioner, constituted by the President, under authority of the act of Congress in that behalf, with plenary powers for these purposes, and the Cherokee Nation, by the principal chief, executive council, and commissioners aforesaid, has agreed to the following articles, that is to say:

ARTICLE I. There shall be perpetual peace and friendship, and an alliance, offensive and defensive, between the Confederate States of America and all of their States and people, and the Cherokee Nation and all the people thereof.

ART. II. The Cherokee Nation of Indians acknowledges itself to be under the protection of the Confederate States of America, and of no other power or sovereign whatever; and does hereby stipulate and agree with them that it will not hereafter contract any alliance, or enter into any compact, treaty, or agreement with any individual, State, or with a foreign power; and the said Confederate States do hereby assume and accept the said protectorate, and recognize the said Cherokee Nation as their ward; and by the consent of the said nation now here freely given, the country whereof it is proprietor in fee, as the same is hereafter described, is annexed to then Confederate States in the same manner and to the same extent as it was annexed to the United States of America before that Government was dissolved, with such modifications, however, of the terms of annexation, and upon such conditions as are herein in addition to all the rights, privileges, immunities, titles, and guaranties with or in favor of the said nation, under treaties made with it, and under the statutes of the United States of America. And in consequence of the obligations imposed on the Cherokee people by this article, it is agreed on the part of the Confederate States that they will not at any time enter into any compact, treaty, or agreement with any individuals or party in the Cherokee Nation, but only with the constitutional authorities of the same, that will in any way interfere with or affect any of their national rights of the Cherokee people.

ART. II. The Confederate States of America, having accepted the said protectorate, hereby solemnly promise the said Cherokee Nation never to desert or to abandon it, and that under no circumstances will they permit the Northern States or any other enemy to overcome them and sever the Cherokees from the Confederacy; but that they will, at any cost and all hazards, protect and defend them and maintain unbroken the ties created by identity of interests and institutions, and strengthened and made perpetual by this treaty.

ART. IV. The boundaries of the Cherokee country shall forever continue and remain the same as they are defined by letters patent thereof given by the United States to the Cherokee Nation on the thirty-first day of December, A. D. one thousand eight hundred and thirty-eight, which boundaries are therein defined as follows:

Beginning at a mound of rocks four feet square at base, and four and a half feet high, from which another mound of rocks bears south one chain, and another mound of rocks bears west one chain, on what has been denominated the old western territorial line of Arkansas Territory, twenty-five miles north of Arkansas River; thence south twenty-one miles and twenty-eight chains to a post on the northeast bank of the Verdigris River, from which a hackberry, fifteen inches diameter, bears south sixty-one degrees thirty-one minutes east, forty-three links, marked C. H. L., and a cottonwood, forty-two inches diameter, bears south twenty-one degrees fifteen minutes east, fifty links, marked C. R. R. L. ; thence down the Verdigris River, on the northeast bank, with its meanders to the junction of Verdigris and Arkansas Rivers; thence from the lower bank of Verdigris

River, on the north bank of Arkansas River, south forty-four degrees thirteen minutes east, fifty-seven chains, to a post on the south bank of Arkansas, opposite the eastern bank of Neosho River, at its junction with Arkansas, from which a red oak, thirty-six inches diameter, bears south seventy-five degrees forty-five minutes west, twenty-four links, and a hickory, twenty-four inches diameter, bears south eighty-nine degrees east, four links; thence south fifty-three degrees west, one miles, to a post from which a rock bears north fifty-three degrees east, fifty links, and a rock bears south eighteen degrees eighteen minutes west, fifty-links; thence south eighteen degrees eighteen minutes west, thirty-three miles, twenty-eight chains and eighty links, to a rock, from which another rock bears north eighteen degrees eighteen minutes east, fifty-links, and another rock bears south fifty links; thence south four miles to a spot on the lower bank of the North Fork of Canadian River at its junction with Canadian River, from which a cottonwood, twenty-four inches diameter, bears north eighteen degrees east, forty links, and a cottonwood, fifteen inches diameter, bears south nine degrees east, fourteen links; thence down the Canadian River on its north bank to its junction with Arkansas River; thence down the main channel of Arkansas River to the western boundary of the States of Arkansas at the northern extremity of the eastern boundary of the lands of the Choctaws, on the south bank of Arkansas River, four chains and fifty-four links east of Fort Smith; thence north degrees twenty-five minutes west with the western boundary of the State of Arkansas, seventy-six miles sixty-four chains and fifty-links, to the southeast corner of the State of Missouri; thence north on the western boundary of the State of Missouri eight miles forty-nine chains and fifty links to the north bank of Cowskin or Seneca River, at a mound six feet square at base and five feet high, in which is a post marked on the south side Cor. Ch. Ld. ; thence west on the northern boundary of the lands of the Senecas, eleven miles and forty chains, to a post on the east bank of Neosho River, from which a maple, eighteen inches diameter, bears south thirty-one degrees east, seventy-two links; thence up Neosho River, with its meanders, on the east bank to the southern boundary of Osage lands, Thirty-six chains and fifty links, west of the southeast corner of the lands of the Osages, witnessed by a mound of rocks on the west bank of Neosho River; thence west on the southern boundary of the Osage lands to the line diving the territory of the United States from that of Mexico, two hundred and eighty-eight miles thirteen chains and sixty-six links, to a mound of earth six feet square at base and five and a half feet high, in which is deposited a cylinder of charcoal twelve inches long and four inches diameter; thence south along the line of the territory of the United States and of Mexico, sixty-miles and twelve chains, to a mound of earth six feet square at base and five and a half high, in which is deposited a cylinder of charcoal eighteen inches long and three inches diameter; thence east along the northern boundary of Creek lands, two hundred and seventy-three miles fifty-five chains and sixty-six links, to the beginning, containing within the survey 13,547,135. 14 acres.

ART. V. The Cherokee Nation hereby gives its full, free, and unqualified assent to those provisions of the act of Congress of the Confederate States of America entitled "An act for the protection of certain Indian tribes," approved the twenty-fourth day of May, A. D. one thousand eight hundred and sixty-one, whereby it was declared that all reversionary and other interest, right, title, and proprietorship of the United States in, unto, and over the Indian country, in which that of the said Cherokee Nation is included, should pass to and vest in the Confederate States; and whereby the President of the Confederate States was authorized to take military possession and occupation of all said country; and whereby all the laws of the United States, with the exception thereinafter made, applicable to and in force in said country, and not inconsistent with the letter or spirit of any treaty stipulations entered into with the Cherokee Nation, were enacted, continued in force, and declared to be in force in said country as laws and statutes of the Confederate States: Provided, however, And it is hereby agreed between the said parties that whatever in the said laws of the United States contained is or may be contrary to or inconsistent with any article or provision of this treaty is to be of none effect henceforward, and shall, upon the ratification hereof, be deemed and taken to have been repealed and annulled as of the present date, and this assent, as thus qualified and conditioned, shall relate to and be taken to have been given upon the said day of the approval of the said act of Congress.

ART. VI. The Confederate States of America do hereby solemnly guarantee to the Cherokee Nation, to be held by it to its own use and behalf in fee simple forever, the lands included within the boundaries defined in Article IV of this treaty; to be held by the people of the Cherokee Nation in common as they have heretofore been held, if the said nation shall so please, but with power of making partition thereof and dispositions of parcels of the same by virtue of laws of said nation duly enacted, and approved by a majority of the Cherokee people in general convention assembled; by which partition or sale title if fee simple absolute shall vest in parleyers and purchasers whenever it shall please said nation, will and accord and without solicitation from any quarter, to do so; which solicitation the Confederate States hereby solemnly agree never to use; and the title and tenure hereby guaranteed to the said nation is and shall be subject to no other restrictions, reservations, or conditions whatever than such as are hereinafter specially expressed.

ART. VII. None of the lands hereby guaranteed to the Cherokee Nation shall be sold, ceded, or otherwise disposed of to any foreign nation or to any State or government whatever; and in case any such sale, cession, or disposition should be made without the consent of the Confederate States, all the said lands shall thereupon revert to the Confederate States.

ART. VIII. The Confederate States of America do hereby solemnly agree and bind themselves that no State or Territory shall ever pass laws for the government of the Cherokee Nation; and that no portion of the lands guaranteed to it shall ever be embraced or included within or annexed to any Territory or province; nor shall any attempt ever be made, except upon the free, voluntary, and unsolicited application of said nation, to erect its said country, by itself or within any other, into a State or any other territorial or political organization, or to incorporate it into any State previously created.

ART. IX. All navigable streams of the Confederate States and of the Indian country shall be free to the people of the Cherokee Nation, who shall pay no higher toll or tonnage duty or other duty than the citizens of the Confederate States; and the citizens of that nation living upon the Arkansas River shall have, possess, and enjoy upon that river the same ferry privileges, to the same extent in all respects, as citizens of the Confederate States on the opposite side thereof, subject to on other or a different tax or charge than they.

ART. X. The Cherokee Nation may by act of its legislative authorities receive and incorporate in the nation thereof, or permit to reside and settle upon the national lands, such Indians of any other nation or tribe as to it may seem good; and may sell them portions of its land, and receive to its own use the consideration therefor; and the nation alone shall determine who are members and citizens of the nation entitled to vote at elections and share in annuities: Provided, That when person of another Indian nation or tribe shall once have been received as members of the nation, they shall not be disfranchised or subjected to any other restrictions upon the right of voting than such as shall apply to the Cherokees themselves. But no Indians not settled in the Cherokee country shall be permitted to come therein to reside without the consent and permission of the legislative authority of the nation.

ART. XI. So far as may be compatible with the Constitution of the Confederate States and with the laws made, enacted, or adopted in conformity thereto, regulating trade and intercourse with the Indian tribes, as the same are modified by this treaty, the Cherokee Nation shall possess the otherwise unrestricted right of self-government and full jurisdiction, judicial and otherwise, over persons and property within its limits, excepting only such white persons as are not by birth, adoption, or otherwise members of the Cherokee Nation; and that there may be no doubt as to the meaning of this exception, it is hereby declared that every white person who, having married a Cherokee woman, resides in said Cherokee country, or who, without intermarrying, is permanently domiciled therein with the consent of the authorities of the nation, and votes at elections, is to be deemed and taken to be a member of the said nation within the true intent and meaning of this article; and that the exception contained in the laws for the punishment of offenses committed in the Indian country, to the effect that they shall not extend or apply to offenses committed by one Indian against the person or property of another Indian, shall be so extended and enlarged by virtue of this article, when ratified and apply to any offense committed by any Indian, or negro, or mulatto, or by any white person, so by birth, adoption, or otherwise a member of the Cherokee Nation, against the person or property of any Indian, negro, or mulatto, or any such white person, when the same shall be committed within the limits of the said Cherokee Nation as hereinbefore defined; but all such persons shall be subject to the laws of the Cherokee Nation, and to prosecution and trial before its tribunals, and punishment according to such laws, in all respects like native members of the said nation.

ART. XII. All persons not members of the Cherokee Nation, as such membership is hereinbefore defined, who may be found in the Cherokee country, shall be considered as intruders, and be removed and kept out of the same either by the civil officers of the nation under the direction of the Executive or Legislature or by the agent of the Confederate States for the nation, who shall be authorized to demand, if necessary, the aid of the military for that purpose; with the following exceptions only, that to say: Such individuals with their families as may be in the employment of the Government of the Confederate States; all persons peaceably traveling, or temporarily sojourning in the country, or trading therein under license from the proper authority, and such persons as may be permitted by the legislative authority of the Cherokee Nation to reside within its limits without becoming members of the said nation
.

ART. XIII. A tract of two sections of land in the said nation, to be selected by the President of the Confederate States, or such officer or person as he may appoint, in conjunction with the authorities of the Cherokee Nation, at such a point as they may deem most proper, is hereby ceded to the Confederate States, for the purpose of an agency; and when selected shall be within their sole and exclusive jurisdiction, expected as to offenses committed therein by one member of the Cherokee Nation against the person or property of another member of the same: Provided, That whenever the agency shall be discontinued, the tract so selected therein shall revert to the said nation, with all the buildings that may be thereupon: And provided also, That the President, conjointly with the authorities of the nation, may at any time select, in lieu of said reserve, any unoccupied tract of and in the nation, and in any other part thereof, not greater in extent than two sections, as a site for the agency of the nation, which shall in such case constitute the reserve, and that first selected shall thereupon revert to the Cherokee Nation.

ART. XIV. The Confederate States have the right to built, establish, and maintain such forts and military posts, temporary or permanent, and such military and post roads as the President may deem necessary in the Cherokee country; and the quantity of one mile square of land, including each fort or post, shall thereby vest as by cession in the Confederate States and be within their sole and exclusive jurisdiction, except as to offenses committed therein by members of the Cherokee Nation against the persons or property of other members of the same, so long as such fort or post is occupied; but no greater quantity of land beyond one mile square shall be used or occupied, nor any greater quantity of timber felled than of each is actually requisite; and if in the establishment of such fort, post, or road, or of the agency, the property of any individual member of the Choctaw [Cherokee] Nation, other than land, timber, stone, and earth, be taken, destroyed, or impaired, just and adequate compensation shall be made by the Confederate States

ART. XV. No persons shall settle or raise stock within the limits of any post or fort or of the agency reserve, except such as are or may be in the employment of the Confederate States in some civil or military capacity, or much as, being subject to the jurisdiction and laws of the Cherokee Nation, are permitted by the commanding officer of the fort or post to do so thereat, or by the agent to do so upon the agency reserve.

ART. XVI. An agent of the Confederate States for the Cherokee Nation and an interpreter shall continue to be appointed, both of whom shall reside at the agency. And whenever a vacancy shall occur in either of the said offices the authorities of the nation shall be consulted as to the person to be appointed to fill the same, and no one shall be appointed against whom they in good faith protest, and the agent may be removed on petition and formal charges preferred by the constituted authorities of the nation, the President, upon full investigation, that there is sufficient cause for such removal.

ART. XVII. The Confederate States shall protect the Cherokees from hostile invasion and from aggression by other Indians and white persons not subject to the laws and jurisdiction of the Cherokee Nation; and for all injuries resulting from such invasion or aggression full indemnity is hereby guaranteed to the party or parties injured, out of the Treasury of the Confederate States, upon the same principle and according to the same rules upon which white persons are entitled to indemnity for injures or aggressions upon them committed by Indians.

ART. XVIII. It is further agreed between the parties that the agent of the Confederate States, upon the application of the authorities of the Cherokee Nation, will not only resort to every proper legal remedy, at the expense of the Confederate States, to prevent intrusion upon the lands of the Cherokees and to remove dangerous or improper persons, but he shall call upon the military power of necessary; and to that end all commanders of military posts in the said country shall be required and directed to afford him, upon his requisition, whatever aid may be necessary to effect the purposes of this article.

ART. XIX. If any property of any Cherokees be taken by citizens of the Confederate States by stealth or force, the agent, on compliant made to him in due form by affidavit, shall use all proper legal means and remedies in any State where the offender may be found to regain the property or compel a just remuneration, and on failure to procure redress payment shall be made for the loss sustained by the Confederate States upon the report of the agent, who shall have power to take testimony and examine witnesses in regard to the wrong done and the extent of the injury.

ART. XX. No person shall be licensed to trade with the Cherokees except by the agent and with the advice and consent of the National Council. Every such trader shall execute bond to the Confederate States in such form and manner as was required by the United States, or as may be required by the Bureau of Indian Affairs. The authorities of the Cherokee Nation may, by a general law, duly enacted, levy and collected on all licensed traders in the nation a tax of not more than one-half of 1 per cent. on all goods wares, and merchandise brought by the into the Cherokee country for sale, to be collected whenever such goods, wares, and merchandise are introduced, and estimated upon the first cost of the same at the place of purchase, as the same shall be shown by the copies of the invoices filed with the agent. No appeal shall hereafter lie from the decision of the agent or council refusing a license to the Commissioner of Indian Affairs, or elsewhere, except only to the superintendent in case of a refusal by the agent. And no license shall be required to authorize any member of the Cherokee Nation to trade in the Cherokee country, nor to authorize any person to sell flour, meats, fruits, and other provisions, or stock, wagons, agricultural implements, or arms brought from any of the Confederate States into the country, nor shall any tax be levied upon such articles or the proceeds of the sale thereof. And all other goods, wares, and merchandise exposed to sale by a person not qualified, without a license, shall be forfeited and be delivered and given to the authorities of the nation, as also shall all wines and liquors illegally introduced.

ART. XXI. All restrictions contained in any treaty made with the United States, or created by any law or regulation of the United States, upon the limited right of any member of the Cherokee Nation to sell and dispose of, to any person whatever, any chattel or other article of personal property, are hereby removed; and no such restrictions shall hereafter be imposed, except by their own legislation.

ART. XXII. It is hereby further agreed by the Confederate States that all the members of the Cherokee Nation, as hereinafter defined, shall be henceforward competent to take, hold, and pass, by purchased or descent, lands in any of the Confederate States, heretofore or hereafter acquired by them.

ART. XXIII. In order to secure the due enforcement of so much of the laws of the Confederate States in regard to criminal offenses and misdemeanors as is or may be in force in the said Cherokee country, and to prevent the Cherokees from being further harassed by judicial proceedings had in foreign courts and before juries not of the vicinage, the said country is hereby erected into and constituted a judicial district, to be called the Chalahki district, for the special purposes and jurisdiction hereinafter provided; and there shall be created and semi-annually held, within such district as Tahlequah, or in case of the removal of the seat of government of the nation, then at such place as may become the seat of government, a district court of the Confederate States, with the powers of a circuit court, so far as the same shall be necessary to carry out the provisions of this treaty, and with jurisdiction co-extensive with the limits of such district, in such matters, civil and criminal, to such extent and between such parties as may be prescribed by law, and in conformity to the terms of this treaty.

ART. XXIV. In addition to so much and such parts of the acts of Congress of the United States enacted to regulate trade and intercourse with the Indian tribes, and to preserve peace on the frontiers as have been re-enacted and continued if force by the Confederate States, and as are not inconsistent with the provisions of this treaty, so much of the laws of the Confederate States as provides for the punishment of crimes amounting to felony at common law or by statute, against the laws, authority, or treaties of the Confederate States, and over which the courts of the Confederate States have jurisdiction, including the counterfeiting the coin of the United States or of the Confederate States, or the securities of the Confederate States, and so much of the said laws as provides for punishing violators of the neutrality laws and resistance to the process of the Confederate States, and all the acts of the Provisional Congress providing for the common defense and welfare, so far as the same are not locally inapplicable, shall hereafter be in force in the Cherokee country, and the said distinct court shall have exclusively jurisdiction to try, condemn, and punish offenders against any such laws, to adjudge and pronounce sentence, and cause execution thereof to be done in the same manner as in done in any other district court of the Confederate States.

ART. XXV. The said district court of the Confederate States of America for the district of Chalahki shall also have the same admiralty jurisdiction as other district courts, of the Confederate courts against any person or persons residing or found within the district, and in all civil suits at law or in equity when the matter in controversy is of greater value then $500, between a citizen of citizens of any State or States of the Confederate

States or any Territory of the same, or an alien or aliens and a citizen or citizens of the said district, or person or persons residing therein; and the Confederate States will, by suitable enactments, provide for the appointment of a judge and other proper officers of the said court, the clerk and marshal being members of the Cherokee Nation, and make all necessary enactments for the complete establishment and organization of the same, and to give full effect to its proceedings and jurisdiction.

ART. XXVI. The said district court shall have no jurisdiction to try and punish any person for any offense committed prior to the day of the singing of this treaty; nor shall any action in law or equity be maintained therein, except by the Confederate States or one of them, when the cause of action shall have accrued before the same day of the signing hereof.

ART. XXVII. If any citizen of the Confederate States or any other person, not being permitted to do so by the authorities of said nation or authorized by the terms of this treaty, shall attempt to settle upon any lands of the Cherokee Nation, he shall forfeit the protection of the Confederate States, and such punishment may be inflicted upon him, no being cruel, unusual, or excessive, as may have been previously prescribed by law of the nation.

ART. XXVIII. No citizens or inhabitant of the Confederate States shall pasture stock on the lands of the Cherokee Nation, under the penalty of $1 per head for all so pastured, to be collected by the authorities of the nation; but their citizens shall be at liberty at all times, and whether for business or pleasure, peaceably to travel the Cherokee country, and to drive their stock to market or otherwise through the same, and to halt such reasonable time on the way as may be necessary to recruit their stock, such delay being in good faith for that purpose.

ART. XXIX. It is also further agreed that the members of the Cherokee Nation shall have the same right of traveling, driving stock, and halting to recruit the same in any of the Confederate States as is given citizens of the Confederate States by the preceding article.

ART. XXX. If any person hired or employed by the agent or by any other person whatever, within the agency reserve, or any post or fort, shall violate the laws of the nation in such manner as to become an unfit person to continue in the Cherokee country be removed by the superintendent upon the application of the Executive of the nation, the superintendent being satisfied of the truth and sufficiency of the charges preferred.

ART. XXXI. Any person duly charged with a criminal offense against the laws of either the Creek, Seminole, Choctaw, or Chickasaw

Nations, and escaping into the jurisdiction of the Cherokee Nation, shall be promptly surrendered upon the demand of the proper authority of the nation within whose jurisdiction the offense shall be alleged to have been committed; and in like manner any person duly charged with a criminal offense against the laws of the Cherokee Nation, and escaping into the jurisdiction of either of the said nations, shall be promptly surrendered upon the demand of the proper authority of the Cherokee Nation.

ART. XXXII. The Cherokee Nation shall promptly apprehended and deliver up all persons duly charged with any crime against the laws of the Confederate States, or of any State thereof who may be found within its limits, on demand of any proper officer of the State or of the Confederate States; and in like manner any person duly charged with a criminal offense against the laws of the Cherokee Nation, and escaping into the jurisdiction of a State, shall be promptly surrendered, on demand of the Executive of the nation.

ART. XXXIII. Whenever any person who is a member of the Cherokee Nation shall be indicted for any offense in any court of the Confederate States, or of a State, he shall be entitled, as of common right, to subpoena, and, if necessary, to compulsory process for all such witnesses in his behalf as his counsel may think necessary for his defense; and the cost of process for such witnesses and of service thereof; and the fees and mileage of such witnesses shall be paid by the Confederate States, being afterward made, if practicable, in case of conviction, of the property of the accused. And whenever the accused is not able to employ counsel the court shall assign him one experienced counsel for his defense, who shall be paid by the Confederate States a reasonable compensation for his services, to be fixed by the court, and paid upon the certificate of the judge.

ART. XXXIV. The provisions of all such acts of the Congress of the Confederate States as may now be in force, or as may hereafter be enacted, for the purpose of carrying into effect the provisions of the Constitution in regard to the redelivery or return of fugitive slaves, or fugitives from labor and service, shall extend to and be in full force within the said Cherokee Nation; and shall also apply to all cases of escape of fugitive slaves from the said Cherokee Nation into any other Indian nation, or into one of the Confederate States; the obligation upon each such nation or State to redeliver such slaves being in every case as complete as if their had escaped from another State and the mode of procedure the same.

XXXV. All persons who are members of the Cherokee Nation shall hereafter be competent as witnesses in all case, civil and criminal, in the courts of the Confederate States, unless rendered incompetent from some other cause than their Indian blood or descent.

ART. XXXVI. The official acts of all judicial officers in the said nation shall have the same effect and be entitled to the like faith and credit everywhere as the like acts of judicial officers of the same grade and jurisdiction in any of the Confederate States; and the proceedings of the court and tribunals of the said nation and copies of the laws and judicial and other records of the said nation shall be authenticated like similar proceedings of the courts of the Confederate States, and the laws and office records of the same, and be entitled to like faith and credit.

ART. XXXVII. It is hereby declared and agreed that the institution of slavery in the said nation is legal and has existed from time immemorial; that slaves are taken and esteemed to be personal property; that the title to slaves and other property having its origin in the said nation shall be determined by the laws and customs thereof, and that the slaves and other personal property of every person domiciled in said nation shall pass and be distributed at his or her death in accordance with the laws, usages, and customs of the said nation, which may be proved like foreign laws, usages, and customs, and shall every where be held binding within the scope of their operations.

ART. XXXVIII. No ex post facto law, or law impairing the obligation of contracts, shall ever be enacted by the legislative authority of the Cherokee Nation; nor shall any citizen of the Confederate States, or member of any other Indian [nation], or tribe, be disseized of his property or deprived or restrained of his liberty, or fine, penalty, or forfeiture be imposed on him in the said country, except by the law of the land, nor without due process of law; nor shall any such citizen be in any way deprived of any of the guaranteed to all citizens by the Constitution of the Confederate States.

ART. XXXIX. It is further agreed that the Congress of the Confederate States shall establish and maintain post-offices at the most important places in the Cherokee Nation, and cause the mails to be regularly carried, at reasonable intervals, to and from the same, at the same rates of postage and in the same manner as in the Confederate States; and the postmasters shall be appointed from among the citizens of the Cherokee Nation.

ART. XL. In consideration of the common interest of the Cherokee Nation and the Confederate States, and of the protection and rights guaranteed to the said nation by this treaty, the Cherokee Nation hereby agrees that it will raise and furnish a regiment of ten companies of mounted men, with two reserve companies, if allowed, to serve on the armies of the Confederate States for twelve months; the men shall be armed by the Confederate States, received the same pay and allowances as other mounted troops in the service, and not be moved beyond the limits of the Indian country west of Arkansas without their consent.

ART. XLI. The Cherokee Nation hereby agrees to raise and furnish, at any future time, upon the requisition of the President, such number of troops for the defense of the Indian country, and of the frontier of the Confederate States, as he may fix, not out of fair proportion to the number of its population, to be employed for such terms of service as the President may determine; and such troops shall receive the same pay and allowances as other troops of the same class in the service of the Confederate States.

ART. XLII. It is further agreed by the said Confederate States, that the said Cherokee Nation shall never be required or called upon to pay, in land or otherwise, any part of the expenses of the present war, or of any war waged by or against the Confederate States.

ART. XLIII. It is further agreed that after the restoration of peace the Government of the Confederate States will defend the frontiers of the Indian country, of which the Cherokee country is a part, and hold the forts and posts therein, with native troops, recruited among the several Indian nations herein, under the command of officers of the Confederate States, in preference to other troops.

ART. XLIV. In order to enable the Cherokee Nation to claim its rights and secure its interests without the intervention of counsel or agents, it shall be entitled to a Delegate to the House of Representatives of the Confederate State of America, who shall serve for the term of two years, and be a native-born citizen of the Cherokee Nation, over twenty-one years of age, and laboring under no legal disability by the law of the said nation; and each Delegate shall be entitled to the same rights and privileges as may be enjoyed by Delegates from any Territories of the Confederate States to the said House of Representatives. Each shall receive such pay and mileage as shall be fixed by the Congress of the Confederate States. The first election for Delegate shall be held at such time and places, and shall be conducted in such manner as shall be prescribed by the principal chief of the Cherokee Nation, to whom returns of such election shall be made, and who shall declare the person having the greatest number of votes to be duly elected, and give him a certificate of election accordingly, which shall entitle him to his seat. For all subsequent elections, the time, places, and manner of holding them, and ascertaining and certifying the result, shall be prescribed by the Confederate States.

ART. XLV. It is hereby ascertained and agreed between the parties to this treaty, that the United States of America, of which the Confederate States of America were heretofore a part, were, before the separation, indebted, and still continue to be indebted, to the Cherokee Nation, and bound to the punctual payment to them of the following sums annually on the first day of --- in each year, that is to say: It was agreed by the tenth article of the treaty of the twenty-ninth day of December, A. D. one thousand eight hundred and thirty-five, that the sum of $200,000 should be invested by the President of the United States, in some safe and most productive public stocks of the country, for the benefit of the whole Cherokee Nation, in addition to the annuities of the nation theretofore payable, to constitute a permanent general fund, and that net income of the same should be paid over by the President annually to such person or persons as should be authorized or appointed by the Cherokee Nation to receive the same, whose receipt should be a full discharge for the amount paid to them, the same interest to be applied annually by the council of the nation to such purposes as they might deem best for the general interests of their people; and it was agreed by the eleventh article of the same treaty that the permanent annuity of $10,000 of the Cherokee Nation should be commuted for the sum of $214,000, and that the same should be invested by the President of the United States as a part of the said general fund of the nation, which thus became $414,000. And it was agreed by the tenth article of the same treaty that the President of the United States should invest in some safe and most productive public stocks of the country the further sum of $50,000, to constitute a permanent orphan's fund; and that he should pay over the net income of the same annually to such person or persons as should be authorized or appointed by the Cherokee Nation to receive the same, whose receipt should be a full discharge for the amount paid to them; which net annual income should be expended toward the support and education of such orphan children of the Cherokees as might be destitute of the means of subsistence. And it was agreed by the tenth article of the same treaty that the further sum of $150,000 should be invested by the President of the United States in some safe and most productive public stocks of the country for the benefit of the whole Cherokee Nation, which should constitute, in addition to the existing school fund of the nation, a permanent School fund, the net income whereof the President should pay over annually to such person or persons as should be authorized or appointed by the Cherokee Nation to receive the same, whose receipt should be a full discharge for the amount paid to them; and that the interest should be applied annually by the council of the nation for the support of common schools and such a literary institution of a higher order as might be established in the Cherokee country; and it was estimated by the eleventh article of the same treaty that the then existing school of the nation amounted to about $50,000, which, it was thereby agreed, should constitute a part of the permanent school fund aforesaid. And it is also further greed between the said parties to this treaty that the United States of America, while the said Confederate States were States of the said United States, did invest the whole of the said several principal sums of money, except the sum of $5,000, in stocks of the States hereinafter named, and of the United States, to the amount hereinafter named in each, that is to say:

THE PERMANENT GENERAL FUND OF THE NATION.

In 7 per cent. stock of the State of Florida, $7,000;
In 6 per cent. stock of the State of Georgia, $1,500;
In 5 per cent. stock of the State of Kentucky, $94,000;
In 6 per cent. stock of the State of Louisiana, $7,000;
In 6 per cent. stock of the State of Maryland, $761. 39;
In 6 per cent. stock of the State of Missouri, $50,000;
In 6 per cent. stock of the State of North Carolina, $20,000;
In 6 per cent. stock of the State of South Carolina, $117,000;
In 5 per cent. stock of the State of Tennessee, $125,000;
In 6 per cent. stock of the State of Tennessee, $5,000, and
In 6 per cent. stock of the State of Virginia, $90,000.
Making the whole capital so invested $517,261. 39, the net annual income whereof was and is $28,914. 91.

THE PERMANENT ORPHAN FUND.

In 6 per cent. stock of the State of Virginia, $45,000. The net annual income whereof was and is $2,700, leaving the sum of $5,000 uninvested, and which still so remains.

THE PERMANENT SCHOOL FUND.

In 7 per cent. stock of the State of Florida, $7,000;
In 6 per cent. stock of the State of Louisiana, $ 2,000;
In 5 ½ per cent. of the State of Missouri, $10,000;
In 6 per cent. stock of the State of Missouri, $5,000;
In 6 per cent. stock of the State of North Carolina, $21,000;
In 5 per cent. stock of the State of Pennsylvania, $4,000;
In 6 per cent. stock of the State of South Carolina, $1,000;
In 6 per cent. stock of the State of Tennessee, $7,000;
In the United States 6 per cent. loan of 1847, $5,800, and
In 6 per cent. stock of the State of Virginia, $135,000.
Making the whole capital so invested, of the said permanent school fund, $197,000, the net annual income whereof was and is $11,848.

All of which stocks the said United States now and do still continue to hold, or ought to have, in their hands.

And it is also hereby ascertained and agreed between the parties to this treaty that there will be due to the Cherokee Nation on the first day of

January, A. D. one thousand eight hundred and sixty-two, fore and on account of the said annually accruing interest on the said principal sums, and of arrearage thereof, the sum of $65,644. 36, as follows, that is to say:

For the installments of interest on the permanent general fund, as invested, for July, 1860, and January and July, 1861, $43,372. 36;

For the installments of interest on the permanent orphan fund, as invested and uninvested, for July, 1860, and January and July, 1861, $4,500;

For the installments of interest on the permanent school fund, as invested, for July, 1860, and January and July, 1861, $17,772.

And it not being desired by the Confederate States that the Cherokee Nation should continue to receive these annual sums of interest or the said arrearage from the Government of the United States, or otherwise have any further connection with that Government; therefore the said Confederate States of America do hereby assume the payment for the future of the annual interest on the said sum of $5,000, part of the permanent orphan fund, which was never invested, and on so much and such parts of said principal sums as, having once been invested, may now be in the hands of the United States uninvested; and also of the annual interest on so much and such parts of the said several principal sums as have been invested in stocks of the United States or in the bonds or stocks of any of the States other than the said Confederate States; and do agree and bind themselves regularly and punctually hereafter, on the first day of July in each and every year, to pay the same; and they do also agree and bind themselves to pay to the treasurer of the Cherokee Nation, immediately upon the complete ratification of this treaty, the said sum of $65,644. 26 for such interest and arrearage now due and which will be due on the first day of January, A. D. one thousand eight hundred and sixty-two, as are above stated.

And the said Confederate States of America do hereby assume the duty and obligation of collecting and paying over as trustees to the said Cherokee Nation all sums of money not hereby agreed to be assumed and paid by them, accruing whether from interest or capital of the bonds of the several States of the Confederacy now held by the Government of the United States as trustee for the Cherokee Nation, and the said interest and capital, as collected, shall be paid over to the said Cherokee Nation.

And the said Confederate States will request the several States of the Confederacy whose bonds are so held to provide by legislation or otherwise that the capital and interest of such bonds shall not be paid to the Government of the United States, but to the Government of the Confederate States in trust for the said Cherokee Nation.

And the said Confederate States of America do hereby guarantee to the said Cherokee Nation the final settlement and full payment upon and after the restoration of peace and recognition of their independence as of debts in good faith and conscience, as well as in law, due and owing on good and valuable consideration, by the said Confederate States and other of the United States jointly before the secession of any of the States, of any and all parts of the said several principal sums of money which may have remained uninvested in the hands of the United States, or which may have been again received by them after investment and may now be held by them; and do also guarantee to the said Cherokee Nation the final settlement and full payment, at the same period, of the capital of any and all bonds or stocks of any State not a member of the Confederate and of any and all stocks of the United States in which any of the Cherokee funds may have been invested.

ART. XLVI. All the said annual payments of interest and the arrearage shall be applied under the exclusive direction of the legislative authority of the Cherokee Nation, to the support of their Government, to the purposes of education, to the maintenance of orphans, and to such other objects for the promotion and advancement of the improvement, welfare, and happiness of the Cherokee people and their descendants as shall to the Legislature seem good, the same being in accordance with treaty stipulations and maintaining unimpaired the good faith of the Cherokee Nation to those persons and in regard to those objects for whom and which it has become trustee. And the capital sums aforesaid shall be invested or reinvested with any other moneys hereby guaranteed, after the restoration of peace, in stocks of the States of the Confederate, at their market price, and in such as bear the highest rate of interest, or shall be paid over to the Cherokee Nation after reasonable notice, to be invested by its authorities as its legislature may request. And no department or officer of the Government of the Confederate States shall hereafter have power to impose any conditions, limitations, or restrictions on the payment to the said nation of any [of] said annual sums of interest, or of any arrearage, or in any wise to control or direct the mode in which such moneys when received by the authorities of the nation shall be disposed of or expended.

ART. XLVII. Whereas, by the treaty of the twenty-ninth day of December, A. D. one thousand eight hundred and thirty-five, the United States of America in consideration of the sum of $500,000, part of the sum of $5,000,000 agreed by that treaty to be paid to the Cherokee Nation for the cession of all their lands and possessions east of the Mississippi River, did covenant and agree to convey to the Cherokees and their descendants by patent in fee simple the certain tract of land between the State of Missouri and the Osage reservation, the boundary line whereof it was provided should begin at the southeast corner of the said Osage Reservation and run north along the east line of the Osage lands fifty miles to the northeast corner thereof; thence east to the west line of the State of Missouri; thence with that line south fifty miles, and thence west to the place of beginning, which tract of country was estimated to contain 800,000 acres of land; and Whereas, the same has been seized and settled upon by lawless intruders from the Northern States, and may become totally lost to the Cherokees: Now, therefore, it is further hereby agreed between the parties to this treaty that in case the said tract of country should be ultimately lost to the Cherokees by the chances of war, or terms of a treaty of peace or otherwise, the Confederate States of America do assure and guarantee to the Cherokee Nation the payment therefor of the said sum of $500,000, with interest thereon at the rate of 5 per cent. per annum from the said twenty-ninth day of December, A. D. one thousand eight hundred and thirty-five, and will either procure the payment of the same by the United States or pay the same out of their own Treasury after restoration of peace.

ART. XLVIII. At the request of the authorities of the Cherokee Nation, and in consideration of the unanimity and promptness of their people in responding to the call of the Confederate States for troops, and of their want of means to engage in any works of public utility and general benefit, or to maintain in successful operation their made and female seminaries of learning, the Confederate States do hereby agree to advance to the said Cherokee Nation immediately after the ratification of this treaty on account of the said sum to be paid for the said lands mentioned in the preceding article the sum of $15,000, to be paid to the treasurer of the nation and appropriated in such manner as the Legislature may direct; and to hold in their hands as invested for the benefit of the said nation the further sum of $50,000, and to pay to the treasurer of said nation interest thereon annually on the 1st day of July in each year, at the rate of 6 per cent. per annum, which shall be sacredly devoted to the support of the said two seminaries of learning, and to no other purpose whatever.

ART. XLIX. It is further ascertained and agreed by and between the Confederate States and the Cherokee Nation that the treaty of the sixth day of August, A. D. one thousand eight hundred and forty-six, was negotiated and concluded with the United States by three several parties; that is to say, the Cherokee Nation by delegates appointed by its constituted authorities, that portion of the nation known as "the treaty party," being those who made and those who agreed to the treaty of the year one thousand eight hundred and thirty-five, and "the Western Cherokees" or "Old Settlers," being those who had removed west prior to that date of that treaty and were then residing there; that the said three parties, by their delegates, after the making of the said treaty of the year one thousand eight hundred and forty-six borrowed from Corcoran & Riggs, bankers in the city of Washington, the sum of $60,000 upon agreement indorsed by the Secretary of War, by which the same was to the repaid with interest when the moneys payable under said treaty should be appropriated, as follows, that is to say: $25,000 by the treaty party, $20,000 by the Western Cherokees or Old Settler party, and $15,000 by the Cherokee Nation; that at the session of Congress next after the making of that treaty the sum of $27,000 for the Cherokee Nation was appropriated under the eighth article of the same, and the sum of $100,000 under the sixth article for the treaty party; but no appropriation was made for the Western Cherokees or Old Settler part under the fourth article (whereunder only any moneys were payable to them), the amount due them, and which was to be wholly paid per capita under that article, not having as yet been ascertained; that consequently the sum borrowed as aforesaid, with the accrued interest, was repaid out of the two appropriations aforesaid, one-half of the principal and interest which should have been paid by the Western Cherokees or Old Settler party being deducted from and paid out of the appropriation made for each of the others; and there being thus paid out of the moneys so appropriated under the eighth article for various purposes for the whole nation over and above its proportion the sum of $10,300, and out of the moneys appropriated under the sixth article for those of the treaty party who had sustained losses and damage in consequence of the treaty of the year one thousand eight hundred and thirty-five, over and above the proportion of that party, a like sum of $10,300; that when afterward the amount ascertained to be due to the Western Cherokees or Old Settlers, under the fourth article, was appropriated, the whole amount was paid to and distributed among them per capita, and no part of the sum so advanced for them out of the other and previous appropriations was reserved, nor has any part thereof whatever hitherto been reimbursed to those entitled to receive the same by the Western Cherokees or by the United States, or otherwise howsoever -

Therefore, it is further hereby agreed that the Confederate States will pay, upon the ratification of this treaty, to the Cherokee Nation this sum of $10,300; and will also appropriate and place in the hands of the agent for the Cherokees the further sum of $10,300, to be distributed among the claimants of the treaty party, provided for by the sixth article of the said treaty, or their representatives under the laws of the nation, in such proportions as it shall be certified to him by Stand Watie, the only surviving member of the committee of five appointed under that article to audit such claims, that it ought, in accordance with the allowances made by the committee, to be distributed among them.

And it was agreed by the said eighth article of the said treaty of the year one thousand eight hundred and forty-six that of the sum of $27,000, provided thereby to be paid to the Cherokee Nation, the sum of $5,000 should be equally divided among all those whose arms were taken from them previous to their removal west, by order of an officer of the United

States, and of that sum of $5,000, $3,000 was applied to the payment in part of the proportion of the money borrowed as aforesaid, due by the Western Cherokees or Old Settler party; and as the authorities of the nation declined to receive the residue of said sum of $5,000, it being but $1,700, and that residue never was paid by the United States, and still remains due by them -

Therefore, it is hereby further agreed that the Confederate States will also pay, upon the ratification of this treaty, to the treasurer of the Cherokee Nation, the further sum of $1,700, making, with the said sum of $10,300, the sum of $12,000; and that out of the same the sum of $5,000 shall, by the authorities of the action, be distributed among those persons and their legal representatives whose arms were taken from them as aforesaid; and that any part of that sum finally remaining undistributed, together with the residue of $7,000, shall be used and appropriated in such manner as the national council shall direct.

ART. L. It is hereby further agreed that all claims and demands against the Government of the United States in favor of the Cherokee Nation or any part thereof, or of any individuals thereof, and which have not been satisfied, released, or relinquished, arising or accruing under former treaties, shall be investigated upon the restoration of peace, and be paid by the Confederate States, which do hereby take the place of the United States and assume their obligations in that regard.

ART. LI. It is further agreed between the parties that all provisions of the treaties of the Cherokee Nation with the United States, which secure or guarantee to the Cherokee Nation or individuals thereof any rights or privileges whatever, and the place whereof is not supplied by, and which are not contrary to, the provisions of this treaty, and so far as the same are not obsolete or unnecessary, or repealed, annulled, changed, or modified by subsequent treaties or laws, or by this treaty, are and shall be continued in force, as if made with the Confederate States.

ART. LII. In further evidence of the desire of the Confederate States to advance the individual interests of the Cherokee people, it is further agreed that the Delegate in Congress from the Cherokee Nation may, with the approbation of the President, annually select one youth, a native of the nation, who shall be appointed to be educated at any military school that may be established by the Confederate States, upon the same terms as other cadets may be appointed. And the Confederate States also agree that the same privilege shall be exercised by the Delegate from the Choctaw and Chickasaw Nations and the Creek and Seminole Nations, respectively.

ART. LILI. A general amnesty of all past offenses against the laws of the United States, and of the Confederate States, committed in the Indian country before the signing of this treaty, by any member of the Cherokee Nation, as such membership is defined by this treaty, is hereby declared; and all such persons, if any, whether convinced or not, imprisoned or at large, charged with any such offense, shall receive from the President full and free pardon, and be discharged.

ART. LIVE. A general amnesty is hereby declared in the Cherokee Nation; and all offenses and crimes committed by a member or members of the Cherokee Nation against the nation, or against an individual or individuals, are hereby pardoned, and this pardon and amnesty shall extend as well to members of the nation now beyond its limits as to those now resident therein.

ART. LV. This treaty shall take effect and be obligatory upon the contracting parties from the seventh day of October, A. D. one thousand eight hundred and sixty-one, whenever it shall be ratified by the general council of the Cherokee Nation and by the Provisional President and Congress, or the President and Senate of the Confederate States; and no amendment shall be made thereto by either, but it shall be wholly ratified or wholly rejected.

In perpetual testimony whereof the said Albert Pike, as commissioner with plenary powers, on the part of the Confederate States, doth now hereunto set his hand and affix the seal of his arms, and the said principal and assistant principal chiefs, executive councilors and special commissioners, on the part of the Cherokee Nation, do hereunto set their hands and affix their seals.

Thus done and interchanged in duplicate, at the place, in the year, and on the day in the beginning hereof mentioned.

[SEAL.]

ALBERT PIKE,

Commissioner of the Confederate States to the Indian Nations West of Arkansas.

Jno.. Ross, principal chief
J. Vann, assistant chief
James Brown, executive councilor
John Drew, executive councilor
Will. P. Ross, executive councilor
Lewis Ross, commissioner Cherokee Nation
Thomas Pegg, commissioner Cherokee Nation

Richard Fields, commissioner Cherokee Nation

Signed, sealed, and delivered in presence of us.

W. E. Quesenbury, secretary to the commissioner
E. Rector, Superintendent IndianAffairs, Confederate States
W. Warren Johnson
Geo. M. Murrell.

RATIFICATION.

Resolved (two-thirds of the Confederate concurring), That the Congress of the Confederate States of America do advise and consent to the ratification of the articles of a treaty made by Albert Pike, commissioner of Confederate States to the Indian nations west of Arkansas, in behalf of the Confederate States, of the one part, and the Cherokee nation of Indians, by its principal and assistant principal chiefs, executive councilors and commissioners, for that purpose only, authorized and powered, of the other part, concluded at Tahlequah, in the Cherokee Nation, on the seventh day of October, A. D. one thousand eight hundred and sixty-one, with the following amendments:

I. Add at the end of the Article XXXV the following words, "and the Confederate States will request the several States of the Confederacy to adopt and enact the provisions of this article in respect to suits and proceedings in their respective courts. "

II. Strike out from Article XLIV the following words, "the same rights and privileges as may be enjoyed by Delegates from any Territories of the Confederate States to the said House of Representatives," and insert in lieu thereof the following words, "a seat in the hall of the House of Representatives, to propose and introduce measures for the benefit of the said nation, and to be hear in regard thereto, and no other questions in which the nation is particularly interested, with such other rights and privileges as may be determined by the House of Representatives. "

III. Strike out from Article XXXIII the following words, "or of a State," and insert in lieu thereof the following words, "or of a State, subject to the laws of the State. "

NOTE. - The foregoing amendments were subsequently concurred in and adopted by the Cherokee Nation.

OFFICIAL RECORDS: Series 4, vol 1, Part 1
Pages 445-466
Confederate States of America - Choctaw-Chickasaw

A TREATY of friendship and alliance, made and concluded at the North Fork Village, on the North Fork of the Canadian River, in the Creek Nation, west of Arkansas, on the twelfth day of July, A. D. one thousand eight hundred and sixty-one, between the Confederate States of America, by Albert Pike, commissioner with plenary powers, of the Confederate States, of the one part, and the Choctaw Nation of Indians, by Robert M. Jones, Sampson Folsom, Forbis Leflore, George W. Harkins, Jr., Allen Wright, Alfred Wade, Coleman Cole, James Riley, Rufus Folsom, William B. Pitchlynn, McKee King, William King, John P. Turnbull, and William Bryant, commissioners appointed by the principal chief of the said Choctaw Nation, in pursuance of an act of the Legislature thereof, and the Chickasaw Nation of Indians, by Edmund Pickens, Holmes Colbert, James Gamble, Joel Kemp, William Kemp, Winchester Colbert, Henry C. Colbert, James N. McLish, Martin W. Allen, John M. Johnson, Samuel Colbert, Archibald Alexander, Wilson Frazier, Christopher Columbus, A-sha-lah Tobbe, and John E. Anderson, commissioners elected by the Legislature of the said Chickasaw Nation, of the other part.

The Congress of the Confederate States of America having, by "An act for the protection of certain Indian tribes,: " approved the twenty-first day of May, A. D. one thousand eight hundred and sixty-one, offered to assume and accept the protectorate of the several nations and tribes of Indians occupying the country west of Arkansas and Missouri, and to recognize them as their wards, subject to all the rights, privileges, and immunities, titles, and guarantees with each of said nations and tribes under treaties made with them by the United States of America; and the Choctaw and Chickasaw Nations of Indians having each assented thereto, upon certain terms and conditions:

Now, therefore, the said Confederate States of America, by Albert Pike, their commissioner, constituted by the President, under authority of the act of Congress in their behalf, with plenary powers for these purposes, and the Choctaw and Chickasaw Nations, by their respective commissioners aforenamed, have agreed to the following articles, that is to say:

ARTICLE 1. There shall be perpetual peace and friendship and an alliance, offensive and defensive, between the Confederate States of

America and all of their States and people and the Choctaw and Chickasaw Nations and all the people thereof.

ART. II. The Choctaw and Chickasaw Nations of Indians acknowledge themselves to be under the protection of the Confederate States of America, and of no other power or sovereign whatever; and do hereby stipulate and agree with them that they will not hereafter, nor shall any one of their people, contract any alliance, or enter into any compact, treaty, or agreement with any individual State or with a foreign power; and the said Confederate States do hereby assume and accept the said protectorate, and recognize the said Choctaw and Chickasaw Nations, now here freely given, the country whereof they are proprietors in fee, as the same is hereinafter described, is annexed to the Confederate States in the same manner and to the same extent as it was annexed to the United States of America before the Government was dissolved, with such modifications, however, of the terms of annexation, and upon us are hereinafter expressed, in addition to all the rights, privileges, immunities, titles, and guarantees with or in favor of the said nations, under treaties made with them, and under the statutes of the United States of America.

ART. III. The Confederate States of America having accepted the said protectorate, hereby solemnly promise the said Choctaw and Chickasaw Nations never to desert or abandon them, and that under no circumstances will they permit the Northern States or any other enemy to overcome them and sever the Choctaws and Chickasaws from the Confederacy; but that they will, at any cost and all hazards, protect and defend them and maintain unbroken the ties created by identity of interests and institutions, and strengthened and made perpetual by this treaty.

ART. IV. The following shall constitute and remain the boundaries of the Choctaw and Chickasaw country, that is to say: Beginning at a point on the Arkansas River 100 paces east of old Fort Smith, where the western boundary line of the State of Arkansas crosses that river, and running thence to Red River by the line between the State of Arkansas and the Choctaw and Chickasaw country, as the same was resurveyed and marked under the authority of the United States, A. D. one thousand eight hundred and fifty-five; thence up Red River to the point where the meridian of 100 degrees west longitude crosses the same; thence north along said meridian to the main Canadian River; thence down said river to its junction with the Arkansas River; thence down said river to the place of beginning. The boundaries of the said country, on the north and on the south, between the said east and west lines being the same in all respects, with all riparian and other rights and privileges, as they were fixed, created, and continued by the treaties of the eighteenth day of October, A. D. one thousand eight hundred and twenty, and of the twenty-seventh day of September, A. D. one thousand eight hundred and thirty.

ART. V. It is hereby agreed by and between the Choctaw and Chickasaw Nations that the boundaries of the Chickasaw country shall hereafter continue to be as follows, that is to say: Beginning on the north bank of Red River, at the mouth of Island Bayou, where it empties into Red River, about twenty-six miles on a straight line, below the mouth of False Washita; thence running a northwesterly course along the main channel of said bayou to the junction of the three prongs of said bayou nearest the dividing ridge between the Washita and Low Blue Rivers, as laid down on Captain R. L. Hunter's map; thence northerly along the eastern prong of Island Bayou to its source; thence due north to the Canadian River; thence west along the main Canadian to the ninety-eighth degree of west longitude; thence south to Red River, and thence down Red River to the beginning: Provided, however, If the line running due north from the eastern source of Island Bayou to the main Canadian shall not include Allen's or Wa-pa-nacka Academy within the Chickasaw district, then on offset shall be made from same line so as to leave said academy two miles within the Chickasaw district, north, west, and south from the lines of boundary.

ART. VI. The remainder of the country held in common by the Choctaw and Chickasaw, including the leased district, shall constitute the Choctaw district, and their officers and people shall at all times have the right of safe conduct and free passage through the Chickasaw district.

ART. VII. The Choctaw and Chickasaw Nations hereby give their full, free, and unqualified assent to those provisions of the act of Congress of the Confederate States of America entitled "An act for the protection of certain Indian tribes," approved the twenty-first day of May, A. D. one thousand eight hundred and sixty-one, whereby it was declared that all reversionary and other interest, right, title, and proprietorship of the United States in, unto, and over the Indian county in which that of the said nations is included, should pass to and vest in the Confederate States; and whereby the President of the Confederate States was authorized to take military possession and occupation of all said country; and whereby all the laws of the United States, with the exception thereinafter made, applicable to and in force in said country, and not inconsistent with the letter or spirit of any treaty stipulations entered into with the Choctaw and Chickasaw Nations, in force in said country, and not inconsistent with the letter or spirit of any treaty among others were re-enacted, continued in force, and declared to be in force in said country, as laws and statutes of the said Confederate States: Provided, however, And it is hereby agreed between the said is or may be contrary to or inconsistent with any article or provision of this treaty is to be of none effect henceforward, and shall, upon the annulled as of the present date, and this assent, as thus qualified and conditioned, shall relate to and be taken to have been given upon the said day of the approval of the said act of Congress.

ART. VIII. The Confederate States of America do hereby solemnly guarantee to the Choctaw and Chickasaw Nations, to be held by them to their own use and behalf in fee simple forever, the lands included within the boundaries defined in Article IV of this treaty; to be held by the people of both the said nations in common, as they have heretofore been held, so long as grass shall grow and water run, if the said nations shall so please, but with power to survey the same, and divide it into sections and other legal subdivisions when it shall be so voted by a majority of the legal voters of each nation, respectively; and of making partition thereof and disposition of parcels of the same by virtue of the laws of both said nations, duly enacted; by which partition or sale title in fee simple absolute shall vest in parceners and purchasers whenever it shall please both nations of their own free will and accord and without solicitation from any quarter to do so; which solicitation the Confederate States hereby solemnly agree never to use; and the title and tenure hereby guaranteed to the said nations is and shall be subject to no other conditions, reservations, or restrictions whatever than such as are hereinafter specially expressed.

ART. IX. None of the lands hereby guaranteed to the Choctaw and Chickasaw Nations shall be sold, ceded, or otherwise disposed of to any foreign nation or to any State or government whatever; and in case any on, or disposition should be made without the consent of the Confederate States, all the said lands shall thereupon revert to the Confederate States.

ART. X. The Confederate States of America do hereby solemnly agree and bind themselves that no State or Territory shall ever pass laws for the government of the Choctaw and Chickasaw Nations, and that no portion of the country guaranteed to them shall ever be embraced or included within or annexed to any territory or province; nor shall any attempt ever be made, except upon the free, voluntary, and unsolicited application of both said nations, to erect their said country, by itself or with any other, into a State or any other territorial or political organization, or to incorporate it into any State previously created.

ART. XI. The lease made to the United States by the treaty of the twenty-second day of June, A. D. one thousand eight hundred and fifty-five, by the Choctaw and Chickasaw Nations of all that portion of their common territory which lies west of the ninety-eighth parallel of west longitude is hereby renewed to the Confederate States, but for the term of ninety-nine years only from the date of this treaty; and it is agreed that the Confederate States may settle and maintain therein, upon reserves with definite limits, but of sufficient extent, all the bands of the Wichitas or Fa-wai-hash, Huecos, Caddos, Fa-hue-cu-ros, Ana-dash-cos, Kichais, Ton-ca-wes, Ionais, Cumanches, Delawares, Kickapoos, and Shawnees, and any other bands whose permanent ranges are south of the Canadian, or between it and the Arkansas, and which are now therein or that they may desire hereafter to place therein, but no including any of the Indians in New Mexico and description, without the consent of both the Choctaw and Chickasaw Nations: Provided, And it is hereby further agreed that whenever the said Choctaw and Chickasaw Nations become a State the reserves so apportioned to the said several bands shall belong to them in fee, not exceeding, however, for each band the same quantity of good land as would belong, upon a partition of the lands of the two nations, to an equal number of Choctaws and Chickasaw in the whole country; and when the said bands consent to a partition among themselves each individual shall have and receive in fee within the said leased country as large a quantity of good land as shall or would be apportioned to each Choctaw or Chickasaw in partition of all the national lands, with the right, however, now and in all future time, to the said several bands so settled or to be settled in said leased district to hunt upon all the vacant and unoccupied parts' of the same without let or molestation.

ART. XII. It is hereby further agreed between the parties to this treaty that the Indians so settled upon reserves in the county so leased shall be, until they are capable of self-government, or until they shall be, with their own consent, incorporated among the Choctaws and Chickasaws, subject to the laws of the Confederate States and to their exclusive control, under such rules and regulations, not inconsistent with the rights and interests of the Choctaws and Chickasaws, or with the Constitution and laws of the Confederate States, as may from time to time be prescribed by the President for their government: Provided, however, That the county so leased shall continue open to settlement by the Choctaws or Chickasaws as heretofore; and all members of each nation settled therein shall be subject to the jurisdiction and laws of the Choctaw Nation, except as hereinafter provided; for which purpose the said leased district may be a district of that nation; but no interference with or trespass upon the settlements or improvements of the reserve Indians shall be permitted under any pretext whatever; nor shall any of the laws of either the Choctaw or Chickasaw Nations be in force in said leased country, except so far as those of the Choctaw Nation can without infraction of this treaty, apply to the members of either nation residing in the district in question.

ART. XIII. All navigable streams of the Confederate States and of the Indian country shall be free to the people of the Choctaw and Chickasaw Nations, who shall pay no higher toll or tonnage duty or other duty than the citizens of the Confederate States; and the citizens of those nations living upon Red River shall have, possess, and enjoy upon that river the same ferry privileges, to the same extent, in all respects, as citizens of the Confederate States on the opposite side thereof, subject to no other or a different tax or charge than they

ART XIV. so far as may be compatible with the Constitution of the

Confederate States and with the laws made, enacted, or adopted in conformity thereto regulating trade and intercourse with the Indian tribes, as the same are limited by this treaty, the Choctaw and Chickasaw nations shall possess the otherwise unrestricted right of self-government and full jurisdiction, judicial and otherwise, over persons and property within their respective limits, excepting only such white persons as are not, by birth, adoption, or otherwise, members of either the Choctaw or Chickasaw Nation; and that there may be no doubt as to the meaning of this exception it is hereby declared that every white person who, having married a Choctaw or Chickasaw woman, resides in the said Choctaw or Chickasaw country, or whom, without intermarrying, is permanently domiciled therein with the consent of the authorities of the nation, and votes at elections, is to be deemed and taken to be a member of the said nation within the true intent and meaning of this article; and that the exception contained in the laws for the punishment of offenses committed in the Indian country, to the effect that they shall not extend or apply to offenses committed by one Indian against the person or property of article when ratified, and without further legislation, as that none of said laws shall extend and apply to any offense committed by any Indian, or negro, or mulatto, or by any white person so by birth, adoption, or otherwise a member of such Choctaw or Chickasaw Nation against the person or property of any Indian, negro, mulatto, or any such white person, when the same shall be committed within the limits of the said Choctaw or Chickasaw Nation as hereinbefore defined; but all such persons shall be subject to the laws of the Choctaw and Chickasaw Nations, respectively, and to prosecution and trial before their tribunals, and to punishment according to such laws, in all respects like native members of the said nations, respectively.

ART. XV. All persons not members of the Choctaw or Chickasaw Nation who may be found in the Choctaw and Chickasaw country as hereinbefore limited shall be considered as intruders, and be removed and kept out of the same, either by the civil officers of the nation, under the direction of the Executive or Legislature, or by the agent of theirs for the nation, who shall be authorized to demand, if necessary, the aid of the military for that purpose, with the following exceptions only, that is to say: Such individuals, with their families, as may be in the employment of the Government of the Confederate States; all persons peaceably traveling or temporarily sojourning in the country, or trading therein under license from the proper authority; and such persons as may be permitted by the Choctaws or Chickasaws, with the assent of the agent of the Confederate States, to reside within their respective limits without becoming members of either of said nations.

ART. XVI. A tract of two sections of land in each of said nations, to be selected by the President of the Confederate States, at such points as he may deem most proper, ceded to the Confederate States; and when selected shall be within their sole and exclusive jurisdiction: Provided, That whenever the agency for either nation shall be discontinued the tract so selected therein shall revert to the said Choctaw and Chickasaw Nations, with all the buildings that may then be thereon: And provided also, That the President may at any time, in his discretion, select in lieu of either said reserves any unoccupied tract of land in the same nation, and in any other part thereof, not greater in extent than two sections, as a site for the agency for such nation, which shall in such case constitute the reserve, and that first selected shall thereupon revert to the Choctaw and Chickasaw Nations.

ART. XVII. The Confederate States shall have the right to build, establish, and maintain such forts and military posts, temporary or deem necessary within the Choctaw and Chickasaw country; and the quantity of one mile square of land, including each for or post, shall be reserved to the Confederate States, and within their sole and exclusive jurisdiction, so long as such fort or post is occupied; but no greater quantity of mile square shall be used or occupied, nor any greater quantity of timber felled than of each is actually requisite; and if, in the establishment of such fort, post, or road, or of the agency, the property of any individual member of the Choctaw or Chickasaw Nation, or any property of either nation, other than land, timber, stone, and earth, be taken, destroyed, or injured, just and adequate compensation shall be made by the Confederate States.

ART. XVIII. The Confederate States, or any company incorporated by them, or any one of them, shall have the right of way for railroads or telegraph lines through the Choctaw and Chickasaw country; but in the case of any incorporated company, it shall have such right of way only upon such terms and payment of such amount to the Choctaw and Chickasaw Nations as may be agreed on between it and the National Councils thereof; or, in case of disagreement, by making full compensation not only to individual parties injured, but also to the nation for the right of way; all damage and injury done to be ascertained and determined in such manner as the President of the Confederate States shall direct. And the right of way granted by said nations for any railroad shall be perpetual, or for such shorter term as the same may be granted, in the same manner as if no reversion of their lands to the Confederate States were provided for in case of abandonment by them or extinction of their nation.

ART. XIX. No person shall settle, farm, or raise stock within the limits of any post or fort, or of either agency, except such as are or may be in the employment of the Confederate States in some civil or military capacity; or such as, being subject to the jurisdiction and laws of the Choctaw or Chickasaw Nation, are permitted by the commanding officer of the fort or post do so thereat, or by the agent to do so upon the agency reserve.

ART. XX. An agent of the Confederate States for the Choctaw and Chickasaw an interpreter for each shall continue to be appointed. The interpreters shall reside at their respective agencies, and the agent at one of them, or alternately at each. And whenever a vacancy shall occur in either of the said offices the authorities of the nation shall be consulted as to the person to be appointed to fill the same, and no one shall be appointed against whom they protest; and the agent may be removed on petition and formal charges preferred by the constituted authorities of the nation, the President being satisfied, upon full investigation, that there is sufficient cause for such removal.

ART. XXI. The Confederate States shall protect the Choctaws and Chickasaws from domestic strife, from hostile invasion, and from aggression by other Indians and white persons not subject to the jurisdiction and laws of the Choctaw or Chickasaw Nation; and for all injuries resulting from such invasion or aggression full indemnity is hereby guaranteed to the party or parties injured, out of the Treasury of the Confederate States, upon the same principle and according to the same rules upon which white persons are entitled to indemnity for injuries or aggressions upon them committed by Indians.

ART. XXII. It is further agreed between the parties that the agent of the Confederate States upon the application of the authorities of the Choctaw and Chickasaw Nations will not only resort to every proper legal remedy, at the expense of the Confederate States, to prevent intrusion upon the lands of the Choctaws and Chickasaws, and to remove dangerous or improper persons, but he shall call upon the military power, if necessary; and to that end all commanders of military posts in the said country shall be required and directed to afford him, upon his requisition, whatever aid may be necessary to effect the purposes of this article.

ART. XXIII. If any property of any Choctaws or Chickasaws be taken by citizens of the Confederate States by stealth or force, the agent, on complaint made to him affidavit, shall use all proper legal means and remedies, in any State where the offender may be found, to regain the property or compel a just remuneration, and on failure to procure redress payment shall be made for the loss sustained, by the Confederate States, upon the report of the agent, who shall have power to take testimony and examine witnesses in regard to the wrong done and the extent of the injury.

ART. XXIV. No person shall be licensed to trade with the Choctaws and Chickasaws except by the agent, and with the advice and consent of the National Council. Every such trader shall execute bond to the Confederate States in such form and manner as was required by the United States, or as may be required by the Bureau of Indian Affairs. The authorities of the Choctaw and Chickasaw Nations may, by a general law, duly enacted, levy and collect on all licensed traders in the nation a tax of not more than one-half of one per cent. on all goods, wares, and merchandise brought by them into the Choctaw and Chickasaw country for sale, to be collected whenever such goods, wares, and merchandise are introduced, and estimated upon the first cost of the same at the place of purchase, as the same shall be shown by the copies of the invoices filed with the agent: Provided, That no higher tax shall be levied and collected than is actually levied and collected in the same year of native traders in the nation; nor shall one be taxed at all unless the others are. No appeal shall hereafter lie from the decision of the agent or council refusing a license to the Commissioner of Indian Affairs or elsewhere, except only to the superintendent, in case of refusal by the agent. And no license shall be required to authorize any member of the Choctaw or Chickasaw Nation, who is by birth and blood an Indian, to trade in the Choctaw and Chickasaw country; nor to authorize any person to sell flour, meat, fruits, and other provisions, or stock, wagons, agricultural implements, or arms brought from any of the Confederate States into the country; nor shall any tax be levied upon such articles or the proceeds of sale thereof. And all other goods, wares, and merchandise exposed to sale by a person not qualified, without a license, shall be forfeited and be delivered and given to the authorities of the nation, as also shall all wines and liquors illegally introduced.

ART. XXV. All restrictions contained in any treaty made with the United States, or created by any law or regulation of the United States, upon the unlimited right of any member of the Choctaw or Chickasaw Nation to sell and dispose of, to any person whatever, any chattel or other article of personal property are hereby removed, and no such restrictions shall hereafter be imposed except by their own legislation.

ART. XXVI. It is hereby further agreed by the Confederate States that all the members of the Choctaw Nations as hereinbefore defined shall be henceforward competent to take, hold, and pass, by purchase or descent, lands in any of the Confederate States heretofore or hereafter acquired by them.

ART. XXVII. In order to enable the Choctaw and Chickasaw Nations to claim their rights and secure their interests without intervention of agents or counsel, and as they are now entitled to reside in the country of each other, they shall be jointly entitled to a Delegate to the House of Representatives of the Confederate States of America, who shall serve for the term of two years and be a member, by birth or blood, on either the father's or mother's side, of one of said nations, over twenty-one years of age, and laboring under no legal disability by the laws of either nation; and such Delegate shall be entitled to the same rights and privileges as may be enjoyed by Delegate from any Territory of the Confederate States. The first election for Delegate shall be held at such time and places and be conducted in such manner as shall be prescribed by the agent of the Confederate States, to whom returns of such election shall be made; and he shall declare the person having the greatest number of votes to be duly elected, and give him a certificate of election accordingly, which shall entitle him to his seat. For all subsequent elections the times, places, and manner of holding them, ascertaining and certifying the result, shall be prescribed by law of the Confederate States. The Delegates shall be elected alternately from each nation, the first being a Choctaw, by blood, on either the father's or mother's side, and resident in the Choctaw country, and the second a Chickasaw, by blood, on either the father's or mother's side, and resident in the Chickasaw country, and so on alternately. At the respective elections such persons only as fulfill the foregoing requisites shall be eligible, and when one is elected to fill a vacancy and serve out an unexpired term he must belong to and be a resident in the same nation as the person whose vacancy he fills.

ART. XXVIII. In consideration of the uniform loyalty and good faith and the tried friendship for the people of the Confederate States of the Choctaw and Chickasaw people, and of their fitness and capacity for self-government, proven by the establishment and successful maintenance by each of a regularly organized republican government, with all the forms and safeguards to which the people of the Confederate States are accustomed, it is hereby agreed by the Confederate States that whenever and so soon as the people of each of said nations shall, by ordinance of a convention of delegates, duly elected by majorities of the legal voters, at an election regularly held after due and ample notice, in pursuance of an act of the Legislature of each, respectively, declare its desire to become a State of the Confederacy, the whole Choctaw and Chickasaw country as above defined shall be received and admitted into the Confederacy as one of the Confederate States, on equal terms in all respects with the original States, without regard to population; and all the members of the Choctaw and Chickasaw Nations shall thereby become citizens of the Confederate States, not including, however, among such members the individuals of the bands settled in the leased district aforesaid: Provided, That as a condition precedent to such admission the said nations shall provide for the survey of their lands, the holding in severalty of parts thereof by their people, the dedication of at least one section in every thirty-six to purposes of education, and the sale of such portions as are not reserved for these or other special purposes to citizens of the Confederate States alone, on such terms as the said nation shall see fit to fix, not intended or calculated to prevent the sale thereof.

ART. XXIX. The proceeds of such sales shall belong entirely to members of the Choctaw and Chickasaw Nations, and be distributed among them or invested for them in proportion to the whole population of each in such manner as the Legislatures of said nations shall provide; nor shall any other persons ever have any interest in the annuities or funds of either the

Choctaw or Chickasaw people, nor any power to legislate in regard thereto.

ART. XXX. Whenever the desire of the Creek and Seminole people and the Cherokees to become a part of the said State shall be expressed, in the same manner and with the same formalities as is above provided for in the case of the Choctaw and Chickasaw people, the country of the Creeks and Seminoles and that of the Cherokees, respectively, or either by itself, may be annexed to and become an integral part of said State upon the same conditions and terms and with the same rights to the people of each in regard to citizenship and the proceeds of their lands.

ART. XXXI. The Choctaw and Chickasaw Nations may, by joint act of their legislative authorities, receive and incorporate in either nation as members thereof, or permit to settle and reside upon the national lands, such Indians of any other nation or tribe as to them may seem good; and each nation alone shall determine who are members and citizens of the nation entitled to vote at elections and share in annuities: Provided, That when persons of another nation or tribe shall once have been received as members of either nation they shall not be disfranchised or subjected to any other restrictions upon the right of voting than such as shall apply to the Choctaws or Chickasaws themselves. But no Indians, other than Choctaws and Chickasaws, not Choctaw and Chickasaw country shall be permitted to come therein to reside without the consent and permission of the legislative authority of each nation

ART. XXXII. If any citizen of the Confederate States or any other person, not being permitted to do so by the authorities of either of said nations or authorized by the terms of this treaty, shall attempt to settle upon any lands of said nation, he shall forfeit the protection of the Confederate States, and such punishment may be inflicted upon him, not being cruel, unusual, or excessive, as may have been previously prescribed by the law of said nation.

ART. XXXIII. No citizen or inhabitant of the Confederate States shall pasture stock on the lands of the Choctaw or Chickasaw Nation; but their citizens shall be at liberty at all times, and whether for business or pleasure, peaceably to travel the Choctaw and Chickasaw country, to drive their stock through the same, and to halt such reasonable time on the way as may be necessary to recruit their stock, such delay being in good faith for that purpose and for no other; and members of the Choctaw and Chickasaw Nations shall have the same rights and privileges under the same and no other restrictions and limitations in each of the Confederate States.

ART. XXXIV. If any person hired or employed by the agent, or by any other person whatever, within the agency reserve, or any post or fort, shall violate the laws of the nation in such manner as to become an unfit person to continue in the Choctaw or Chickasaw country, he or she shall be removed by the superintendent upon the application of the Executive of the nation in which such person is, the superintendent being satisfied of the truth and sufficiency of the charges preferred.

ART. XXXV. The officers and people of the Choctaw and Chickasaw Nations, respectively, shall at all times have the right of safe conduct and free passage through the lands of each other; and the members of each nation shall have the right freely, and without seeking license or permission, to settle within the country of the other, and shall thereupon be entitled to all the rights, privileges, and immunities of members thereof, including the right of voting at all elections and of being deemed qualified to hold all offices whatever, except that no Choctaw shall be eligible in the Chickasaw Nation to the office of Chief Executive or to the Legislature: And provided also, That no member of either nation shall be entitled to participate in any funds belonging to the other. Members of each nation shall have the right to institute and prosecute suits in the courts of the regulations as may from time to time be prescribed by their respective Legislatures.

ART. XXXVI. Any person duly charged with a criminal offense against the laws of either the Choctaw or Chickasaw Nation, and escaping into the jurisdiction of the other, shall be promptly surrendered upon the demand of the proper authority of the nation within whose jurisdiction the offense shall be alleged to have been committed.

ART. XXXVII. The Choctaw and Chickasaw Nations shall promptly deliver up all persons accused of any crime against the laws of the Confederate States, or any State thereof, who may be found within their limits, on the demand or requisition of the Executive of a State, or the Executive or other proper officer of the Confederate States; and each of the Confederate States shall, on the like demand or requisition of the Executive of the Choctaw and Chickasaw Nation, promptly deliver up all persons accused of any crime against the laws of such nation who may be found within their limits.

ART. XXXVIII. In order to secure the due enforcement of so much of the laws of the Confederate States in regard to criminal offenses and misdemeanors as is or may be in force in the said Choctaw and Chickasaw country, and to prevent the Choctaws and Chickasaws from being further harassed by judicial proceedings had in foreign courts and before juries not of the vicinage, the said country is hereby erected into and constituted a judicial district of the Confederate States to be called the Tush-ca-hom-ma district, for the special purposes and jurisdiction hereinafter provided; and there shall be created and semiannually held, within such district, at Boggy Depot, a district court of the Confederate States, with the powers of a circuit court so far as the same shall be necessary to carry out the provisions of this treaty, and with jurisdiction coextensive with the limits of such district in such matters, civil and criminal, to such extent and between such parties as may be prescribed by law and in conformity to the terms of this treaty.

ART. XXXIX. In addition to so much and such parts of the acts of Congress of the United States enacted to regulate trade and intercourse with Indian tribes, and to preserve peace on the frontiers, as have been re-enacted and continued in force by the Confederate States, and as are not inconsistent with the provisions of this treaty, so much of the laws of the Confederate States as provides for the punishment of crimes amounting to felony at common law or by statute against the laws, authority, or treaties of the Confederate States, and over which the courts of the Confederate States have jurisdiction, including the counterfeiting the coin of the United States or of the Confederate States, or the securities of the Confederate States, and so much of said laws as provides for punishing violators of the neutrality laws, and resistance to the process of the Confederate States, and all the acts of the Provisional Congress providing for the common defense and welfare, so far as the same are not locally inapplicable, shall hereafter be in force in the Choctaw and Chickasaw country; and the said district court shall have exclusive jurisdiction to try, condemn, and punish offenders against any such laws, to adjudge and pronounce sentence, and cause execution thereof to be done in the same manner as is done in any other district courts of the Confederate States.

ART. XL. The said district court of the Confederate States of America for the district of Tush-ca-hom-ma shall also have the same admiralty jurisdiction as other district courts of the Confederate States; and jurisdiction in all civil suits for fines, penalties, and forfeitures of the Confederate States against any person or persons whatever residing or found within the district; and in all civil suits at law or in equity, when the matter in controversy is of greater value than $ 500, between a citizen or citizens of any State or States of the Confederate States, or any Territory of the same, or an alien or aliens and a citizen or citizens of the said district, or person or persons, residing therein; and the Confederate States will, by suitable enactments, provide for the appointment of a judge and other proper officers of the said court, and make all necessary enactments and regulations for the complete establishment and organization of the same and to give full effect to its proceedings and jurisdiction.

ART. XLI. The trial of all offenses, amounting to felony at common law or by statute, committed by an Indian of any one of the tribes or bands settled in the leased district aforesaid against the person or property of a member of the Choctaw or Chickasaw Nation, or by one of the latter against the person or property of one of the former, shall be had in the district court of the Confederate States hereby provided for; and until such court is established, in the district court of the Confederate States for the district, or for the western district of Arkansas.

ART. XLII. The district court shall have no jurisdiction to try and punish any person for any offense committed prior to the day of the signing of this treaty; nor shall any action in law or equity be maintained therein except by the Confederate States or one of them, where the cause of action shall have accrued more than three years before the same day of the signing hereof, or before the bringing of the suit.

ART. XLIII. All persons who are members of the Choctaw or Chickasaw Nation, and are not otherwise disqualified or disabled, shall hereafter be competent witnesses in all civil and criminal suits and proceedings in any court in the Confederate States, or any one of the States, any law to the contrary notwithstanding.

ART. XLIV. Whenever any person, who is a member of the Choctaw or Chickasaw Nation, shall be indicted for any offense in any court of the Confederate States, including the district court of the Tush-hom-ma district, or in a State court, he shall be entitled, as of common right, to subpoena and, if necessary, compulsory process for all such witnesses in his behalf as his counsel may think material for his defense; and the costs of process for such witnesses, and of service thereof, and the fees and mileage of such witnesses, shall be paid by the Confederate States, being afterward made, if practicable, in case of conviction, out of the property of the accused. And whenever the accused is not able to employ counsel, the court shall assign him one experienced counsel for h is defense, who shall be paid by the Confederate States a reasonable compensation for his services, to be fixed by the court and paid upon the certificate of the judge.

ART. XLV. The provisions of all such acts of Congress of the Confederate States as may now be in force or as may hereafter be enacted, for the purpose of carrying into effect the provision of the Constitution in regard to the redelivery or return of fugitive slaves or fugitives from labor and service, shall extend to and be in full force within the said Choctaw and Chickasaw Nations; and shall also apply to all cases of escape of fugitive slaves from the Choctaw and Chickasaw Nations into any other Indian nation, or into one of the Confederate States, the obligation upon each such nation or State to redeliver such slaves being in every case as complete as if they had escaped from another State, and the mode of procedure the same.

ART. XLVI. The official acts of all judicial officers in the said nations shall have the same effect and be entitled to like faith and credit everywhere, as like acts of judicial officers of the same grade and jurisdiction in any one of the Confederate States; and the proceedings of the courts and tribunals of the said nations, and the copies of the laws and judicial and other records of the said nations, shall be authenticated like similar proceedings of the courts of the Confederate States, and the laws and office records of them entitled to the like faith and credit.

ART. XLVII. It is hereby declared and agreed that the institution of slavery in the said nations is legal, and has existed from time immemorial; that slaves are taken and deemed to be personal property; that the title to slaves and other property having its origin in the said nations shall be determined by the laws and customs thereof; and that the slaves and other personal property of every person domiciled in said nations shall pass and be distributed at his or her death in accordance with the laws, usages, and customs of the said nations, which may be proved like foreign laws, usages, and customs, and shall everywhere be held valid and binding within the scope of their operation.

ART. XLVIII. It is further agreed that the Congress of the Confederate States shall establish and maintain post-offices at the most important places in the Choctaw and Chickasaw Nations, and cause the mails to be regularly carried, at reasonable intervals, to and from the same, at the same rate of postage, and in the same manner as in the Confederate States.

ART. XLIX. In consideration of the common interests of the Choctaw and Chickasaw Nations and the Confederate States, and of the protection and rights guaranteed to the said nations by this treaty, the said nations hereby agree that they will raise and furnish a regiment of ten companies of mounted men to serve in the armies of the Confederate States for twelve months. The company officers of the regiment shall be elected by the members of each company respectively; the colonel shall be appointed by the President and the lieutenant-colonel and major be elected by the members of the regiment. The men shall be armed by the Confederate States, receive the same pay and allowances as other mounted troops in the service, and not be marched beyond the limits of the Indian country west of Arkansas against their consent.

ART. L. It is further agreed by the Confederate States that neither the Choctaw nor Chickasaw Nation shall ever be called on or required to pay, in land or otherwise, any part of the expenses of the present war, or of any war waged by or against the Confederate States.

ART. LI. The Choctaw and Chickasaw Nations hereby agree and bind themselves at any future time to raise and furnish, upon the requisition of the President, such number of troops for the defense of the Indian country and of the frontier of the Confederate States as he may fix, not out of fair proportion to the number of their inhabitants, to be employed for such terms of service as the President may fix; and such troops shall always receive the same pay and allowances as other troops of the same class in the service of the Confederate States.

ART. LII. It is further agreed that after the restoration of peace the Government of the Confederate States will defend the frontiers of the Indian country of which the Choctaw and Chickasaw country is a part, and hold the forts and posts therein with native troops, recruited among the several Indian nations included, under the command of officers of the Army of the Confederate States, in preference to other troops.

ART. LIII. It is hereby ascertained and agreed by and between the Confederate States and the Choctaw Nation that the United States of America, of which the Confederate States were heretofore a part, were, before the separation, indebted, and still continue to be indebted, to the Choctaw Nation, and bound to the punctual payment thereof, in the following sums annually, on the first day of July of each year; that is to say:

Perpetual annuities amounting to $ 9,000, under the second article on the sixteenth day of November, A. D. one thousand eight hundred and five, and the second article of the treaty of the twentieth day of January, A. D. one thousand eight hundred and twenty-five.

The sum of $ 600 per annum for the support of light horsemen, under the thirteenth article of the treaty of the eighteenth day of October, A. D. one thousand eight hundred and twenty

.

The sum of $ 600 per annum, in lieu of the permanent provision for the support of a blacksmith, and the sum of $ 320, in lieu of permanent provision for iron and steel, under the sixth article of the said treaty of the eighteenth day of October, A. D. one thousand eight hundred and twenty, and the ninth article of the said treaty of the twentieth day of January, A. D. one thousand eight hundred and twenty-five.

The annual interest on the sum of $ 500,000, held in trust for the Choctaw Nation by the United States, under the thirteenth article of the treaty of the twenty-second day of June, A. D. one thousand eight hundred and fifty-five, which by that article was to be held in trust for the said nation and to constitute part of a general Choctaw fund, yielding an annual interest of not less than 5 per cent. per annum; and no part thereof has been invested in stocks or bonds of any kind, but remains in the hands of the United States.

And it is hereby ascertained and agreed between the said Confederate States and the Choctaw Nation that there was due to the said nation on the first day of July, A. D. one thousand eight hundred and sixty-one, for and on account of these annuities, annual payments, and interests, the sum of $ 35,520; that is to say:

For the permanent annuities and other annual payments and allowances then due, $10,520.

For interest on the said sum of $ 500,000 for the year which ended on the thirtieth day of June, A. D. one thousand eight hundred and sixty-one, $ 25,000.

And it not being desired by the Confederate States that the Choctaw Nation should continue to receive these annual sums from the Government of the United States, or otherwise have any further connection or communication with that Government and its superintendent and agents, therefore the Confederate States of America do hereby assume the payment for the future of all the above-recited annuities, annual payments, and interest, and do agree and bind themselves regularly and punctually to pay the same to the treasurer of the said nation, or to such other person or persons as shall be appointed by the general council of the Choctaw Nation to receive the same; and they do also agree and bind themselves to pay to the treasurer of the said nation, immediately upon the ratification by all parties of this treaty, the said sum of $ 35,520, due on the first day of July of the present year, as aforesaid.

ART. LIV. And it is further ascertained and agreed between the Confederate States and the Choctaw Nation that the United States of America, while the said several Confederate States were included in the said Union, held, and do continue to hold, in their hands the sum of $ 500,000, paid by the Chickasaw Nation to the United States for the Choctaw Nation under the treaty of the seventeenth day of January, A. D. one thousand eight hundred and thirty-seven, and which it was agreed by that treaty should be invested in some safe and secure stocks, under the direction of the Government of the United States, redeemable within a period of not less than twenty years, and the interest thereon be annually paid to the Choctaw Nation and be subject to the entire control of the general council; and which sum having been invested in bonds or stocks of certain States, part or all whereof are now members of the Confederate States, it was agreed by the United States, by the thirteenth article of the treaty of the twenty-second day of June, A. D. one thousand eight hundred and fifty-five, that the same should continue to be held in trust by the United States and constitute, with certain other sums, a general Choctaw fund, yielding an annual interest of not less than 5 per cent

And it being further agreed that, in addition to the sums of money above mentioned, other moneys were justly due and owing from the United States of America when the Confederate States were parts thereof, and still continue due and owing and unpaid to the said Choctaw Nation, in part appropriated and in part unappropriated, by the Congress of the United States under existing treaties:

Therefore, the Confederate States do hereby assume the duty and obligation of collecting and paying over as trustees to the said Choctaw Nation all sums of money accruing, whether from interest or capital of the bonds of the several States of the Confederacy, or of any bonds or stocks guaranteed by either of them, now held by the Government of the United States in trust for the Choctaw Nation, and will pay over to the said nation the said interest and capital as the same shall be collected. And the said Confederate States will request the several States of the Confederacy whose bonds or stocks, or any bonds or stocks guaranteed by them, are so held to provide, by legislation or otherwise, that the capital and interest of such bonds or stocks shall not be paid to the Government of the United States, but to the Government of the Confederate States in trust for the Choctaw Nation.

And the said Confederate States do hereby guarantee to the Choctaw Nation the final settlement and full payment upon and after the restoration of peace and the establishment and recognition of their independence, as of debts in good faith and conscience, as well as in law, due and owing, on good and valuable consideration, by the said Confederate States and the other of the United States jointly before the secession of any of the States, of all sums of money that are so as aforesaid justly due and owing by the late United States under existing Choctaw Nation or people, for itself or in trust for individuals, and of any sums received by that Government and now held by it by way of interest on or as part of the capital of any of the bonds or stocks of any of the States wherein any funds of the Choctaws had been invested; and do also guarantee to it the final settlement and full payment at the same period of the capital and interest of all bonds or stocks of any of the Northern States in which any of the said Choctaw funds may have been invested.

ART. LV. All the said annuities, annual payments, and interest and the arrearages thereof shall be applied, under the exclusive direction of the general council of the Choctaw Nation, to the support of their government, to the purposes of education, and to such other objects, for the promotion and advancement of the improvement, welfare, and happiness of the Choctaw people and their descendants, as shall to the general council seem good; and the capital sums of $ 500,000 each shall be invested or reinvested, after the restoration of peace, in stocks of the States, at their market price, and in such as bear the highest rate of interest, or be paid over to the Choctaw Nation, to be invested by its authorities or otherwise used, applied, and appropriated, as its Legislature may direct; and the other moneys due and owing to the said nation, and payment whereof is hereby guaranteed, shall be used, applied, and appropriated by the Choctaw Nation in accordance with treaty stipulations, and so as to maintain unimpaired the good faith of the Choctaw Nation to those for whom it will thus become trustee. And no department or office of the Government of the Confederate

States shall have power to impose any conditions, limitations, or restrictions on the payment to the said nation of any of said annual sums or arrearages of the said capital sums of $ 500,000 each, or in any wise to control or direct the mode in which such moneys, when received by of the nation, shall be disposed of or expended. Nor shall any appeal lie to any department, bureau, or officer of the Confederate States from the decision of the general council of the Choctaw Nation, or of any committee, court, or tribunal to which it may commit the adjudication, by any person or persons from any decision that may be rendered under the twelfth article of the treaty of the twenty-second day of June, A. D. one thousand eight hundred and fifty-five, adverse to the justice and equity of any claim presented as one of those which, under that article, the Choctaw Nation became liable and bound to pay; but the adjudication and decision of the Legislature, or of any committee, court, or tribunal to which it may intrust the investigation or decision, against any such claim shall be absolutely final.

ART. LVI. It is hereby ascertained and agreed by and between the Confederate States and the Chickasaw Nation, that the United States of America, of which the Confederate States were heretofore a part, were, before the separation, indebted, and still continue to be indebted, to the Chickasaw Nation, and bound to the punctual payment thereof, in the following amounts annually, on the first day of July in each year; that is to say:

Permanent annuity of $ 3,000 under the act of Congress of the United States, approved on the -- day of ----, A. D. one thousand seven hundred and ninety.

The annual interest at 6 per cent. on the sum of $ 276,781. 57, the amount of so much of the United States 6 per cent. loans in which the funds of the Chickasaw Nation were invested, under the third and eleventh articles of the treaty of the twenty-fourth day of May, A. D. one thousand eight hundred and thirty-four.

And the annual interest at 6 per cent. on the further sum of $ 100,000, the principal of that amount of Ohio 6 per cent. stock, in which part of the Chickasaw fund had been invested under the same articles of the same treaties, and which was paid into the Treasury of the United States on the ninth day of January, A. D. one thousand eight hundred and fifty-seven, to the credit of the Treasurer of the United States, and having been duly covered into the Treasury on fourteenth day of January in that year, there still remains.

And it is also hereby ascertained and agreed between the said Confederate States and the Chickasaw Nation that there was due to the said nation on the first day of July, one thousand eight hundred and sixty-one, for and on account of the said annuity and interest, the sum of $ 25,606. 89.

And it not being desired by the Confederate States that the Chickasaw Nation should continue to receive these annual sums from the Government of the United States, or otherwise have any communication or connection with that Government, its superintendent, and agents, therefore the Confederate States of America do hereby assume the payment for the future of the above-recited annuity and interest, and do agree and bind themselves regularly and punctually to pay the same to the treasurer of the said nation, or to such other person or persons as shall be appointed by the Legislature of the Chickasaw Nation to receive the same; and they do also agree and bind themselves to pay to the treasurer of the said nation, immediately upon ratification by all parties of this treaty, the sum of $ 25,606. 89, due on the first day of July of the present year, as aforesaid.

ART. LVII. Whereas, it was agreed between the United States and the Chickasaw Nation, by the third article of the treaty made between them on the twentieth day of October, A. D. one thousand eight hundred and thirty-two, that as a full compensation to the Chickasaw Nation for the country ceded to the United States by that treaty the United States would pay over to the said nation all the moneys arising from the sales of lands so ceded after deducting therefrom the whole cost and expenses of surveying and selling the lands, including every expense attending the same;

And whereas, by the eleventh article of the treaty of the twenty-fourth day of May, A. D. one thousand eight hundred and thirty-four, between the United States and the Chickasaw Nation, it was agreed that all funds resulting from all entries and sales of such lands after deduction of the expenses of surveying and selling, and other advances made by the United States, should, from time to time, be invested in some secure stocks, redeemable within a period of not more than twenty years, the interest whereon the United States should cause to be annually paid to the Chickasaws;

And whereas, by the fifth article of the treaty of the twenty-second day of June, A. D. one thousand eight hundred and fifty-two, it was agreed between the United States and the Chickasaw Nation that the United States should continue to hold in trust the national fund of the Chickasaws and constantly keep the sum invested in safe and profitable stocks, the interest of which should be annually paid to the Chickasaw Nation;

And whereas, it is now, by the Confederate States and the Chickasaw Nation, ascertained and agreed that the following sums, part of the said fund of the Chickasaws, arising from the sales of their lands, were invested by the United States, while the Confederate States were part thereof, in bonds and stocks of certain of the States, in manner following, that is to say:

In the 5 per cent. stock of the State of Indiana, $ 210,000;
In 6 per cent. stock of the State of Maryland, $ 14,499. 75;
In 6 per cent. stock of the State of Tennessee, $ 170,666. 66;
In 6 per cent. stock of the State of Arkansas, $ 90,000, on which no interest has been paid since the 1st day of July, A. D. 1842;
In 6 per cent. stock of the State of Illinois, $ 17,000;
In 6 per cent. stock of the Richmond and Danville Railroad, guaranteed by the State of Virginia, $ 100,000;
And in 6 per cent. stock of the Nashville and Chattanooga Railroad, guaranteed by the State of Tennessee, $ 512,000;

And it being claimed by the Chickasaws that all the moneys received by the United States from the sales of their lands, after deduction of proper disbursements out thereof, have not been invested, that they have been charged with losses and expenses which should properly have been borne by the United States, and that in many cases moneys held in trust by the United States for the benefit of the orphan and incompetent Chickasaws had been wrongfully paid out to persons having no right to receive the same; in consequence of which complaints, then as now made, it was agreed by the fourth article of the treaty between the same parties, of the twenty-second day of June, A. D. one thousand eight hundred and fifty-two, that an account should be stated as soon thereafter as practicable, under the direction of the Secretary of the Interior, exhibiting in detail all the moneys that had from time to time been placed in the Treasury to the credit of the Chickasaw Nation, resulting from the said treaties of the years 1832 and 1834, and all the disbursements made therefrom; and that to the account so stated the Chickasaws should be entitled to take exceptions, which should be referred to the Secretary of the Interior, who should adjudicate the same according to the principles of law and equity, and his decision should be final; and it was also, by the same article, agreed that the cases of wrongfully made payments should be investigated by the Congress of the United States, under the direction of the Secretary of the Interior, and if any person had been defrauded by such payments, the United States should account for the amounts so misapplied as if no such payment had been made:

Therefore, the Confederate States do hereby assume the duty and obligation of collecting and paying over as trustees to the said Chickasaw Nation, at par, and dollar for dollar, all sums of money accruing, whether from interest or capital of the said bonds or stocks of the said States of the Confederacy, or of stocks guaranteed by them, so held by the Government of the United States in trust for the Chickasaw Nation, and will pay over to the said nation the said interest and capital as the same shall be collected. And the said Confederate States shall request those States to provide, by legislation or otherwise, that the capital and interest of such bonds or stocks shall not be paid to the Government of the United States, but to the Government of the Confederate States in trust for the Chickasaw Nation.

And the said Confederate States do hereby guarantee to the said Chickasaw Nation the final settlement and full payment, upon and after the restoration of peace and the establishment of independence, as of debts of good faith and conscience, as in law due and owing, on good and valuable consideration, by the said Confederate States and the other of the United States jointly before the secession of any of the States, of all sums of money received by that Government from the sales of the Chickasaw lands or otherwise however, in trust for the Chickasaw nation or individuals thereof, and which remain uninvested, or which it expended in unwarranted disbursements or in the payment of charges or expenses not properly chargeable to the Chickasaws; for the ascertainment whereof such account shall be taken, after the restoration of peace, by or under the direction of the Commissioner of Indian Affairs, as was directed by the fourth article of the treaty of the twenty-second day of June, A. D. one thousand eight hundred and fifty-two, and in accordance with the legal rules of stating accounts of trust funds and investments.

And the Confederate States also hereby guarantee to the Chickasaw Nation the final settlement and full payment, at the same period, of all moneys belonging to orphans or incompetent persons, or to other Chickasaws, and wrongfully paid by the United States to persons unauthorized to receive them, and for that reason, or for any other, not yet paid to the proper persons, under the same fourth article of the treaty last mentioned, as qualified and limited by the proviso added thereto by way of amendment, or under Article X of the said treaty; which cases shall be investigated by the Commissioner of Indian Affairs or by the agent under his direction.

And they also guarantee to it the final settlement and full payment, after the same period, of the said sums invested in U. S. stocks, and the said sum of $ 100,000, so covered into the Treasury on the fourteenth day of January, A. D. one thousand eight hundred and fifty-seven, and of any other sums received by that Government and now held by it by way of interest on or as part of the capital of any of the bonds or stocks of any of the States wherein any funds of the Chickasaws had been invested; and they do also guarantee to it the final settlement and full payment, at the same period, of the capital and interest of all bonds or stocks of any of the Northern States in which any of said Chickasaw funds have been invested

.

ART. LVIII. It is further hereby agreed that the said annuity, interest, and arrearages hereby assumed and agreed to be paid by the Confederate States shall be applied, under the exclusive direction of the

Legislature of the Chickasaw Nation, to the support of their government, to purposes of education, and to such other objects for the promotion and advancement of the improvement, welfare, and happiness of the Chickasaw people and their descendants as shall to the Legislature seem good; and the capital in full of all the said bonds and stocks of States, corporations, and the principal of moneys due by the United States shall be invested or reinvested, after the restoration of peace, in stocks of the States, at their market price, and in such as bear the highest rate of interest, or be paid over to the Chickasaw Nation to be invested by its authorities, or otherwise used, applied, and appropriated as its Legislature may direct, without any control or interference on the part of any department, bureau, or officer of the Confederate States.

ART. LIX. It is hereby further agreed that no claim or account shall hereafter be paid by the Government of the Confederate States out of the Chickasaw funds, unless the same shall have first been considered and allowed by the Chickasaw Legislature

ART. LX. Whereas, by the first article of the treaty between the United States of America and the Choctaw and Chickasaw Nations, on the twenty-second day of June, A. D. one thousand eight hundred and fifty-five, it was provided that the boundary of the Choctaw and Chickasaw country should begin "at a point on the Arkansas River 100 paces east of old Fort Smith, where the western boundary of the State of Arkansas crosses the said river," and run thence "due south to Red River," which also was the line of boundary fixed by the treaties of the twentieth day of January, A. D. one thousand eight hundred and twenty-five, and the twenty-seventh day of September, A. D. one thousand eight hundred and thirty;

And whereas, when the said line was originally run between the State of Arkansas and the Choctaw Nation it was erroneously run to the westward of a due south line from that point of beginning on the Arkansas River;

And whereas, when the said line was again run by the United States, after the making of the said treaty of the twenty-second day of June, A. D. one thousand eight hundred and fifty-five, it was arbitrarily ordered by the Secretary of the Interior, in violation of the said treaties, that the said line should not be run due south in accordance therewith, but that the old erroneous lines should in lieu thereof be retraced, and the same was accordingly done, thus leaving within the limits of the State of Arkansas a strip of country belonging to the Choctaw and Chickasaw Nations in the shape of a triangle, having Red River for its base;

And whereas, all the lands contained therein that are of any value were sold or granted by the United States, and are chiefly held and have been improved by private individuals: It is therefore agreed by the Confederate States and the said Choctaw and Chickasaw Nations that the said line so run and retraced shall be perpetuated as the line between the Choctaw and Chickasaw country and the State of Arkansas, and that the said triangular tract of land shall belong to and continue to form an integral part of that State; and all titles to lands therein from and under the United States be confirmed; and it is further agreed that in consideration therefor the said Choctaw and Chickasaw Nations shall, upon the restoration of peace and the establishment and recognition of the independence of the Confederate States, be paid by them the fair value of the lands included in said tract, in their natural state and condition and unimproved, and of all the salt springs therein at the date of the said treaty, A. D. one thousand eight hundred and fifty-five, and without interest; which fair actual value shall be ascertained by a commission of four persons, two of whom shall be appointed by the President of the Confederate States, one by the Choctaw Legislature, and one by the Chickasaw Legislature, and the expenses of which commission shall be borne by the Confederate States.

ART. LXI. It is further agreed that if the present war continues the Confederate States will, upon the request of the Executive of the Choctaw and Chickasaw Nations, respectively, advance to the Choctaw Nation the sum of $ 50,000 and to the Chickasaw Nation $ 2,000, in discharge of so much of the moneys due to each, respectively, by the United States, and will invest each sum in the purchase for each nation, respectively, of such arms and ammunition as shall be specified by the Executive
.

ART LXII. All provisions of the treaties made by the Choctaws and Chickasaws, or either, with the United States, under which any rights or privileges were secured or guaranteed to the Choctaw or Chickasaw Nation, or to individuals of either, and the place whereof is not supplied by any provision of this treaty, and the same not being obsolete or no longer necessary, and so far as they are not repealed, annulled, changed, or modified by subsequent treaties or statutes, or by this treaty, are continued in force as if the same had been made with the Confederate States.

ART. LXIII. It is further agreed that the sum of $ 2,000 shall be appropriated and paid by the Confederate States, immediately upon the ratification of this treaty, to defray the expenses of the delegations of Choctaws and Chickasaws by whom this treaty has been negotiated, and that the same shall be paid over to R. M. Jones and by him equally divided among the members of the said delegations.

ART. LXIV. A general amnesty of all past offenses against the laws of the United States or of the Confederate States, committed before the signing of this treaty, by any member of the Choctaw or Chickasaw Nation, as such members in this treaty, is hereby declared; and all such persons, if any, charged with any such offense shall receive from the President full and free pardon, and if imprisoned or held to bail, before or after conviction, be discharged; and the Confederate States will especially request the States of Arkansas and Texas to grant the like amnesty as to all offenses committed by Choctaw or Chickasaw against the laws of those States, respectively, and the Governor of each to reprieve or pardon the same if necessary.

In perpetual testimony whereof the said Albert Pike, as commissioner with plenary powers, on the part of the Confederate States, doth now hereunto set his hand and affix the seal of his arms, and the undersigned commissioners, with full powers of the Choctaw and Chickasaw Nations, do hereunto set their hands and affix their seals.

Done in triplicate at the place and upon the day in the year first aforesaid.

[SEAL.]

ALBERT PIKE,

Commissioner of the Confederate States.

R. M. JONES,
JAMES RILEY,
SAMPSON FOLSOM,
RUFUS FOLSOM,
FORBIS LEFLORE,
WM. B. PITCHLYNN, GEO. W. HARKINS, Jr.
MCKEE KING,
ALLEN WRIGHT,
WILLIAM KING,
ALFRED WADE,
JOHN P. TURNBULL,
COLEMAN COLE,
WILLIAM BRYANT,
Commissioners of the Choctaw Nation.

EDMUND PICKENS,
MARTIN W. ALLEN,
HOLMES COLBERT,
JOHN M. JOHNSON,
JAMES GAMBLE,
SAMUEL COLBERT,
JOEL KEMP,
A. ALEXANDER,
WILLIAM KEMP,

WILSON FRAZIER,
WINCHESTER COLBERT,
C. COLUMBUS,
HENRY C. COLBERT,
A-SHA-LAH TOBBE,
JAMES N. MCLISH,
JOHN E. ANDERSON,
Commissioners of the Chickasaw Nation.

Signed, sealed, and copies exchanged in our presence, July 12, 1861.

WM. QUESENBURY,
Secretary of the Commissioner.

W. WARREN JOHNSON.
W. L. PIKE.
WM. H. FAULKNER.

RATIFICATION.

Resolved (two-thirds of the Congress concurring), That the Congress of the Confederate States of America do advise and consent to the ratification of the articles of a treaty made by Albert Pike, commissioner of the Confederate States to the Indian nations west of Arkansas, in behalf of the Confederate States, of the one part, and by the Choctaw and Chickasaw Nations of Indians, by their respective commissioners thereunto appointed and elected, of the other part, concluded at the North Fork Village, on the North Fork of the Canadian River, in the Creek Nation, on the twelfth day of July, A. D. one thousand eight hundred and sixty-one, with the following amendments:

I. Strike out from Article XXVII the words, "to the same rights and privileges as may be enjoyed by delegates from any Territory of the Confederate States," and insert in lieu thereof the following words, "to a seat in the hall of the House of Representatives, to propose and introduce measures for the benefit of said nations, and to be heard in regard thereto, and on other questions in which either of said nations is particularly interested, with such other rights and privileges as may be determined by the House of Representatives. "

II. Strike out from Article XXVIII the following words, "the whole Choctaw and Chickasaw country, as above defined, shall be received and admitted into the Confederacy as one of the Confederate States, on equal terms in all respects with the original States, without regard to population, and," and insert in lieu thereof the following words, "the application of the said nations to be admitted as a State into the Confederacy, on equal terms in all respects with the original States, shall be referred to and considered by the Congress of the Confederate States, by whose act alone, under the Constitution, new States can be admitted and whose consent it is not in the power of the President of the present Congress to guarantee in advance, and if the Congress shall assent to such admission, the whole Choctaw and Chickasaw country, as above herein defined, shall constitute the State so admitted, and in case of such admission. "

III. Strike out from Article XLIII the following words, " or of any one of the States," and add at the end of this article the following words," and the Confederate States will request the several States of the Confederacy to adopt and enact the provisions of this article in respect to suits and proceedings in their several courts. "

IV. Strike out from Article XLIV the following words, "or in a State court," and insert in lieu thereof the following words, "or in a State court subject to the laws of the State. "

V. Strike out from the fourth paragraph of Article LVII, in the phrase "two hundred and ten thousand dollars," the word "ten," and insert in lieu thereof the word "two. "

NOTE. - The foregoing treaty, together with the amendments, was duly ratified by the Choctaw and Chickasaw Nations, respectively.

OFFICIAL RECORDS: Series 4, vol 1, Part 1
Pages 426-443
Confederate States of America - Creek

A TREATY of friendship and alliance made and concluded at the North Fork Village, on the North Fork of the Canadian River, in the Creek Nation, west of Arkansas, on the tenth day of July, A. D. one thousand eight hundred and sixty-one, between the Confederate States of America, by Albert Pike, commissioner, with plenary powers, of the Confederate States, of the one part, and the Creek Nation of Indians, by its chiefs, headmen, and warriors in general council assembled, of the other part.

The Congress of the Confederate States of America having, by "An act for the protection of certain Indian tribes," approved the twenty-first day of May, A. D. one thousand eight hundred and sixty-one offered to assume and accept the protectorate of the several nations and tribes of Indians occupying the country west of Arkansas and Missouri, and to recognize them as their wards, subject to all the rights, privileges and immunities, titles and guaranties, with each of said nations and tribes under treaties made with them by the United States of America; and the Creek Nation of Indians having assented thereto upon certain terms and conditions:

Now, therefore, the said Confederate States, by Albert Pike, their commissioner, constituted by the President under authority of the act of Congress in their behalf, with plenary powers for these purposes, and the Creek Nation, in general council assembled, have agreed to the following articles, that is to say:

ARTICLE I. There shall be perpetual peace and friendship, and an alliance, offensive and defensive, between the Confederate States of America, and all of their States and people, and the Creek Nation of Indians, and all its towns and individuals.

ART. II. The Creek Nation of Indians acknowledges itself to be under the protection of the Confederate States of America, and of no other power or sovereign whatever; and doth hereby stipulate and agree with them that it will not hereafter, nor shall any of its towns or individuals, contract any alliance or enter into any compact, treaty, or agreement with any individual State or with a foreign power: Provided, That it may make such compacts and agreements with neighboring nations and tribes of Indians for their mutual welfare and the prevention of difficulties as may not be contrary to this treaty, or inconsistent with its obligations to the Confederate States; and the said Confederate States do hereby assume and accept the said protectorate, and recognize the said Creek Nation as their ward; and by the consent of the said Creek Nation, now here freely given, the country whereof it is proprietor in fee, as the same is hereinafter defines, is annexed to the Confederate States, in the same manner and to the same extent as it was annexed to the United States of America before that Government was dissolved, with such modifications as are hereinafter expressed, in addition to all the rights, privileges, under treaties made with it, and under the statutes of the United States of America.

ART. III. The following shall constitute and remain the boundaries of the Creek country, viz: Beginning at the mouth of the North Fork of the Canadian River and running northerly four miles; thence running a straight line so as to meet a line drawn from the south bank of the Arkansas River, opposite the east or lower bank of Grand River, at its junction with the Arkansas, and which runs a course south 44 degrees west, one mile, to a post placed in the ground; thence along said line to the Arkansas and up the same to the Verdigris River, to where the old Territorial line crosses it; thence along said line north to a point twenty-five miles from the Arkansas River, where the old Territorial line crosses the same; thence running west with the southern line of the Cherokee country to the North Fork of the Canadian River, where the boundary of the cession to the Seminole Nation defined in the first article of the treaty between the United States of America and the Creek and Seminole Nations, of August seventh, A. D. one thousand eight hundred and fifty-six, fist strikes said Cherokee line; thence down said North Fork to where the eastern boundary line of the said cession to the Seminole Nation strikes the same; thence with that line due south to the Canadian River, at the mouth of the Ok-hai-ap-po, or Pond Creek, and thence down said Canadian River to the place of beginning.

ART. IV. The Creek Nation hereby gives its full, free, and unqualified assent to those provisions of the act of Congress of the Confederate States of America entitled "An act for the protection of certain Indian tribes," approved the twenty-first day of May, A. D. one thousand eight hundred and sixty-one, whereby it was declared that all reversionary and other interest, right, title, and proprietorship of the United States in, unto, and over the Indian country in which that of said nations is included should pass to and vest in the Confederate States; and whereby the President of the Confederate States was authorized to take military possession of all said country; and whereby all the laws of the United States, with the exception hereinafter made, applicable to and in force in said country, and not inconsistent with the letter or spirit of any treaty stipulations entered into with the Creek Nation among others were re-enacted, continued in force, and declared to be in force in said county as laws and statutes of the Confederate States: Provided, however, And it is hereby agreed between the said parties that whatever in the said laws of the United States contained is or may be contrary to or inconsistent with any article or provision of this treaty is to be of none effect henceforward, and shall, upon the ratification hereof, be deemed and taken to have been repealed and annulled as of the present date; and this assent, as thus qualified and conditioned, shall relate to and be taken to have been given upon the said day of the approval of the said act of Congress

ART. V. The Confederate States of America do hereby guarantee to the Creek Nation, to be held by it to its own use and behalf in fee simple forever, the lands included within the boundaries defined in the preceding article of this treaty; to be held by the people of the Creek Nation to be held by the people of the said nation in common, as they have heretofore been held, so long as grass shall grow and water run, if the said nation shall so please, but with power of making partition thereof and disposition of parcels of the same by virtue of laws of the nation duly enacted; by which partition or sale title in fee simple absolute shall vest in parceners and purchasers, whenever it shall please the nation of its own free will and accord and without solicitation from any quarter to do so; which and the title and tenure hereby guaranteed to the said nation is and shall be subject to no other conditions, reservations, or restrictions whatever than such as are hereinafter specially expressed.

ART. VI. None of the said lands hereby guaranteed to the Creek Nation shall be sold, ceded, or otherwise disposed of to any foreign nation or to any State or Government whatever; and in case any such sale, cession, or disposition should be made without the consent of the Confederate States all the said lands shall thereupon revert to the Confederate States.

ART. VII. The Confederate States hereby agree and bind themselves that in guaranteeing to the Seminole Nation of Indians the country granted, ceded, and conveyed to it by the Creek Nation by the treaty of the seventh day of August, A. D. one thousand eight hundred and fifty-six, it shall be provided, as it was in that treaty, that no part thereof shall every be sold or otherwise disposed of by the said Seminole Nation without the consent of the Creek Nation formally and explicitly given.

ART. VIII. The Confederate States of America do hereby solemnly agree and bind themselves that no State or Territory shall every pass laws for the government of the Creek Nation, and that no portion of the country hereby guaranteed to it shall ever be embraced or included within or annexed to any Territory or province; nor shall any attempt ever be made, except upon the free, voluntary, and unsolicited application of the said nation, to erect the said country, by itself or with any other, into a State, or any other Territorial or political organization, or to incorporate it into any State previously created

ART. IX. So far as may be compatible with the Constitution of the Confederate States and with the laws made, enacted, or adopted in conformity thereto, regulating trade and intercourse with the Indian tribes, as the same are limited and modified by this treaty, the Creek Nation shall possess the otherwise unrestricted right of self-government, and full jurisdiction, judicial and otherwise, over persons as are not, by birth, adoption, or otherwise, members of either the Creek or Seminole Nation; and that there may be no doubt as to the meaning of this exception, it is hereby declared that every white person who, having married a Creek or Seminole woman, resides in the said Creek country, or who, without intermarrying, is permanently domiciled therein with the consent of the authorities of the nation, and votes at elections, is to be deemed and taken to a member of the said nation within the true intent and meaning of this article; and that the exception contained in the laws for the punishment of offenses committed in the Indian country, to the effect that they shall not extend or apply to offenses committed by one Indian against the person or property of another Indian, shall be so extended and enlarged by virtue of this article when ratified, and without further legislation, as that none of said laws shall extend or apply to any offense committed by any Indian, or negro, or mulatto, or by any such white person, so by birth, adoption, or otherwise a member of such Creek or Seminole Nation, against the person or property of any Indian, negro, mulatto, or any such white person, when the same shall be committed within the limits of the said Creek Nation as hereinbefore defined; but all such persons shall be subject to the laws of the Creek Nation, and to prosecution and trial before its tribunals, and to punishment according to such laws, in all respects like native members of the said Creek Nation.

ART. X. All persons who are not members of either the Creek or Seminole Nation found in the Creek country, as hereinbefore limited, shall be considered as intruders, and be removed and kept out of the same, either by the civil officers of the nation under the direction of the executive or the general council, or by the agent of the Confederate States for the nation, who shall be authorized to demand, if necessary, the aid of the military for that purpose, with the following exceptions only, that is to say: Such individuals with their families as may be in the employment of the Government of the Confederate States; all persons peaceably traveling or temporarily sojourning in authority; and such persons permitted by the Creeks or Seminoles, with the assent of the agent of the Confederate States, to reside within their respective limits without becoming members of either of said tribes.

ART. XI. The tract of two sections of land, selected by the President of the United States, under the treaty with the Creek Nation concluded on the twenty-fourth day of January, A. D. one thousand eight hundred and twenty-six, at which the Creek Agency is now maintained, and whereon the public buildings of that agency have been erected, is hereby reserved to the Confederate States in the same manner as the same was by that treaty reserved to the United States, and is not included in the guarantee of lands aforesaid, but shall be within the sole and exclusive jurisdiction of the Confederate States, except as to members of the Creek or Seminole Nation as above defined; all offenses committed by whom thereon shall be punished by the laws and courts of the said nation whenever they would be so punished if committed elsewhere in the nation: Provided, That whenever the agency for the said nation shall be discontinued by the Confederate States, and an agent no longer appointed, the said tract of two sections of land shall pass to and vest absolutely in the Creek Nation in the same manner as its other lands with all the buildings that may be thereupon.

ART. XII. The Confederate States shall have the right to build, establish, and maintain such forts and military posts, temporary or permanent, and to make and maintain such military and post roads as the President may deem necessary within the Creek country; and the quantity of one mile square of land, including each fort or post, shall be reserved to the Confederate States, and within their sole and exclusive jurisdiction, so long as such fort or post is occupied; but no greater quantity of land beyond one mile square shall be used or occupied, nor any greater quantity of timber felled than of each is actually requisite; and if in the establishment of such fort, post, or roads, or of the agency, the property of any individual member of the Creek Nation, or any property of the nation itself, other than land, timber, stone, and earth, be taken, destroyed, or injured, just and adequate compensation shall be made by the Confederate States.

ART. XIII. The Confederate States or any company incorporated by them, or any one of them right of way for railroads or telegraph lines through the Creek country; but in case of any incorporated company, it shall have such right of way only upon such terms and payment of such amount to the Creek Nation as may be agreed upon between it and the national council thereof; or, in case of disagreement, by making full compensation, not only to individual parties injured, but also to the nation for the right of way; all damage and injury done to be ascertained and determined in such manner as the President of the Confederate States shall direct. And the right of way granted by said nation for any railroad shall be perpetual, or for such shorter term as the same may be granted, in the same manner as if no reversion of their lands to the Confederate States were provided for, in case of abandonment by them or of extinction of their tribe.

ART. XIV. No person shall settle, farm, or raise stock within the limits of any post or fort, or of the agency, except such as are or may be [in] the employment of the Confederate States in some civil or military capacity, or such as, being subject to the jurisdiction and laws of the Creek Nation, are permitted by the commanding officer of the fort or post to do so thereat, or by the agent to do so upon the agency reserve.

ART. XV. The Confederate States shall protect the Creeks from domestic strife, from hostile invasion, and from aggression by other Indians and white persons not subject to the jurisdiction and laws of the Creek Nation; and for all injuries resulting from such invasion or aggression full indemnity is hereby guaranteed to the party or parties injured, out of the Treasury of the Confederate States, upon the same principle and according to the same rules upon which white persons are entitled to indemnity for injuries or aggression upon them committed by Indians.

ART. XVI. No person shall hereafter be licensed to trade with the Creeks, except by the agent, and with only the exceptions hereinafter mentioned, with the advice and consent of the National Council. Every such trader shall execute bond to the Confederate States in such form and manner as was required by the United States, or as may be required by the Bureau of Indian Affairs; and hereafter it shall be in the power of the general council of the Creek Nation to levy and collect of all licensed traders a tax not exceeding 1 1/4 per cent. on the first cost of all goods, wares, and merchandise hereafter brought by them into the nation for sale; which first cost shall, in all cases, be ascertained from the invoices, copies whereof are required to be furnished to the agent. Such tax shall be payable immediately upon and after the importation into the nation for sale; which first cost shall, in all cases, be ascertained from the invoices, copies whereof are required to be furnished to the agent. Such tax shall be payable immediately upon and after the importation into the nation of each stock of goods, but shall in no case be levied twice on the same stock or party of the same: Provided, That no tax shall be levied for the present year upon the stocks of goods now held by licensed traders, but only upon such as they shall hereafter receive, and upon so much of their present stock as shall remain on hand on the 1st day of January next. No appeal shall hereafter lie to any officer whatever from the decision of the agent refusing to license any applicant.

ART. XVII. Immediately upon the signing of this treaty the agent of the Confederate States shall notify each licensed trader in the Creek Nation that he is required to apply for a license under the laws of the Confederate States within thirty days after the date os such notice; and any one failing to do so shall be considered as an intruder and be immediately removed from the country. Upon each such application the agent shall decide and grant or refuse the same at his discretion, as heretofore, and his decision shall be final. every license so granted by him shall be for the term of twelve months exception to be unexpired portion of the year 1861; and if, at the expiration of the year 1862, a renewal of license should not be granted to any such trader he shall, nevertheless, be entitled to remain in the country such reasonable length of time as may, in the opinion of the agent, be necessary, under the protection of the laws of the Confederate States, as a person peaceably sojourning therein, for the purpose of collecting such debts as may be due him: Provided, That no such license shall be granted by the agent unless the party applying shall have paid the whole amount of compensation for land and timber assessed for the year 1861 by the council with the assent of the agent; and that any license hereafter granted shall be revoked on failure or refusal to pay in due time the tax that may be legally assessed in any year. when a second license is applied for by any such party, or hereafter when any new party applies for license, it shall be granted with the advice and consent of the National Council: And provided also, That if the general council has any well-founded objection to the present renewal of any license to any person now licensed as a trader, for which such renewal ought not, under the law, to be granted, it may present such objection to the agent, who shall refuse to renew the license in that case if he finds such objection to be well founded and sufficient; and if he do not so refuse the general council may carry the matter before the superintendent, whose decision shall be final.

ART. XVIII. All restrictions and limitations heretofore imposed or existing by treaty, law, or regulation upon the right of any member of the Creek Nation freely to sell and dispose of to any person whatever any chattel or article of personal property whatever are hereby removed and annulled, except such as the laws of the nation itself may have created.

ART. XIX. An agent of the Confederate States and an interpreter shall be continued to be appointed for the Creek Nation, both of whom shall reside at the agency; and whenever a vacancy shall occur in either of the said offices the authorities of the nation shall be consulted as to the person to be appointed to fill the same, and no one shall be appointed against whom they in good faith protest; and the agent may be removed on petition and formal charges preferred by the constituted authorities of the nation, the President being satisfied, upon full investigation, that there is sufficient cause shown for such removal.

ART. XX. The Creek Nation may, by act of its legislative authorities, receive and incorporate in itself as members of the nation, or permit to settle and reside upon the national lands, such Indians of any other tribe as to it may seem good; and may sell such Indians portions of land, in fee or by less estate, or lease them portions thereof for years or otherwise, and receive to its own use the price of such sales or leases; and it alone shall determine who are members and citizens of the nation entitled to vote at elections, hold office, or share in the common lands: Provided, That when persons of another tribe shall once have been received as members of the Creek Nation they shall not be disfranchised or subjected to any other restrictions upon the right of voting than such as shall apply to the Creeks themselves. But no Indians other than Creeks and Seminoles not now settled in the Creek country shall be permitted to come therein to reside without the consent and permission of the legislative authority of the nation.

ART. XXI. If any citizen of the Confederate States or any other person, not being permitted to do so by the authorities of said nation or authorized by the terms of this treaty, shall attempt to settle upon any lands of the Creek Nation, he shall forfeit the protection of the Confederate States, and such punishment may be inflicted upon him, not being cruel, unusual, or excessive, as may have been previously prescribed by law of the nation.

ART. XXII. No citizen or inhabitant of the Confederate States shall pasture stock on the lands of the Creek Nation, under the penalty of $1 per head for all so pastured, to be collected by the authorities of the nation; but their citizen shall be at liberty at all times, and whether for business or pleasure, peaceably to travel the Creek country, and to drive their stock to market or otherwise through the same, and to halt such reasonable time on the way as may be necessary to recruit their stock, such delay being in good faith for that purpose.

ART. XXIII. It is also further agreed that the members of the Creek Nation shall have the same right of traveling, driving stock, and halting to recruit the same in any of the Confederate States as is given citizens of the Confederate States by the preceding article.

ART. XXIV. The officers and people of the Creek and Seminole Nations, respectively, shall at all times have the right of safe conduct and free passage through the lands of each other; and the members of each nation shall have the right freely, and without seeking license to settle within the country of the other, and shall thereupon be entitled to all the rights, privileges, and immunities of members thereof, including the right of voting at elections and of being deemed qualified to hold office, and excepting only that no member of either nation shall be entitled to participate in any funds belonging to the other nation. Members of each nation shall have the right to institute and prosecute suits in the courts of the other, under such regulations as may from time to time be prescribed by their respective Legislature.

ART. XXV. Any person duly charged with a criminal offense against the laws of either the Creek or Seminole Nation, and escaping into the jurisdiction of the other, shall be promptly surrendered upon the demand of the proper authority of the nation within whose jurisdiction the offense shall be alleged to have been committed.

ART. XXVI. The Creek Nation shall promptly apprehend and deliver up all persons accused of any crime against the laws of the Confederate States or any State thereof, who may be found within its limits, on demand of any proper officer of a State or the Confederate States.

ART. XXVII. In addition to so much and such parts of the act of Congress of the United States enacted to regulate trade and intercourse with

Indian tribes and to preserve peace on the frontiers as have been re-enacted and continued in force by the Confederate States, and as are not inconsistent with the provisions of this treaty, so much of the laws of the Confederate States as provides for the punishment of crimes amounting to felony at common law or by statute against the laws, authority, or treaties of the Confederate States, and over which the courts of the Confederate States have jurisdiction, including the counterfeiting the coin or securities of the Confederate States or uttering counterfeit coin or securities, and so much of such laws as provides for punishing violators of the neutrality laws, and resistance to the progress of the Confederate States, and all the acts of the Provisional Congress providing for the common defense and welfare, so far as the same are not locally inapplicable, shall hereafter be in force in the Creek country.

ART. XXVIII. Whenever any persons who is a member of the Creek Nation shall be indicted for any offense in any court of the Confederate States or in a State court he shall be entitled as of common right to subpoena and, if necessary, compulsory process for all such witnesses in his behalf as his counsel may think necessary for his defense; and the costs of process for such witnesses, and of service thereof, and the fees and mileage of such witnesses shall be paid by the Confederate States, being afterward made, if practicable, in case of conviction, of the property of the accused. And whenever the accused is not able to employ counsel the court shall assign him one experienced counsel for his defense, who shall be paid by the Confederate States a reasonable compensation for his services, to be fixed by the court and paid upon the certificate of the judge.

ART. XXIX. The provisions of all such acts of Congress of the Confederate States as may now be in force, or may hereafter be enacted, for the purpose of carrying into effect the provision of the Constitution in regard to the redelivery or return of fugitive slaves, or fugitives from labor and service, shall be in full force within the said Creek Nation, and shall also apply to all cases of escape of fugitive slaves from the said Creek Nation into any other Indian nation or into one of the Confederate States, the obligation upon each such nation or State to redeliver such slaves being in every case as complete as if they had escaped from another State, and the mode of procedure the same.

ART. XXX. Persons belonging to the Creek Nation shall hereafter be competent as witnesses in all cases, civil and criminal, in the courts of the Confederate States, unless rendered incompetent from some other cause than their Indian blood or descent.

ART. XXXI. The official acts of all judicial officers in the said nation shall have the same effect and be entitled to the like faith and credit everywhere as the like acts of judicial officers of the same grade and jurisdiction in any of the Confederate States; and the proceedings of the courts and tribunals of the said nation and copies of the laws and judicial and other records of the said nation shall be authenticated like similar proceedings of the courts of the Confederate States and the laws and office records of the same, and be entitled to like faith and credit.

ART. XXXII. It is hereby declared and agreed that the institution of slavery in the said nation is legal and has existed from time immemorial; that slaves are taken and deemed to be personal property; that the title to slaves and other property having its origin in the said nation shall be determined by the laws and customs thereof; and that the slaves and other personal property of every person domiciled in said nation shall pass and be distributed at his or her death in accordance with the laws, usages, and customs of the said nation, which may be proved like foreign laws, usages, and customs, and shall everywhere be held valid and binding within the scope of their operation.

ART. XXXIII. No ex post facto law or law impairing the obligation of contracts shall ever be enacted by the legislative authority of the Creek Nation to affect any other persons than its own people; nor shall any citizen of the Confederate States or member of any other Indian nation or tribe be deprived of his property or deprived or restrained of his liberty, or fine, penalty, or forfeiture be imposed on him in the said country, except by the law of the land, nor without due process of law; nor shall any such citizen be in any way deprived of any of the rights guaranteed to all citizens by the Constitution of the Confederate States; and it shall be within the province of the agent to prevent any infringement of such rights and of this article, if it should in any case be necessary.

ART. XXXIV. That the Congress of the Confederate States shall establish and maintain post-offices at the most important places in the Creek Nation, and cause the mails to be regularly carried at reasonable intervals to and from the same, at the same rates of

ART. XXXV. Whenever any stream, over which it may be desirable to establish ferries, forms the boundary of the Creek country, members of the Creek Nation shall have the right of ferriage from their own land to the opposite shore; and no more onerous terms shall be imposed by the State or nation opposite than such as it imposes upon its own citizens having ferries on the same stream.

ART. XXXVI. In consideration of the common interests of the Creek Nation and the Confederate States, and of the protection and rights guaranteed to the said nation by this treaty, the Creek Nation hereby agrees that it will, either by itself or in conjunction with the Seminole Nation, raise and furnish a regiment of ten companies of mounted men to serve in the armies of the Confederate States for twelve months, the company officers whereof shall be elected by the members of the company, and the field officers by a majority of the votes of the members of the regiment. The men shall be armed by the Confederate States, receive the same pay and allowances as other mounted troops in the service, and not be moved beyond the limits of the Indian country west of Arkansas without their consent.

ART. XXXVII. The Creek Nation hereby agrees and binds itself at any future time to raise and furnish, upon the requisition of the President, such number of troops for the defense of the Indian country and of the frontier of the Confederate States as he may fix, not out of fair proportion to the number of its population, to be employed for such terms of service as the President may fix; and such troops shall always receive the same pay and allowances as other troops of the same class in the service of the Confederate States.

ART XXXVIII. It is further agreed by the said Confederate States that the said Creek Nation shall never be required or called upon to pay, in land or otherwise, any part of the expenses of the present war, or of any war waged by or against the Confederate States.

ART. XXIX. It is further agreed that, after the restoration of peace, the Government of the Confederate States will defend the frontiers of the Indian country, of which the Creek country is a part, and hold the forts and posts therein with native troops recruited among the several Indian nations included therein, under the command of officers of the Army of the Confederate States, in preference to another troops.

ART. XL. In order to enable the Creek and Seminole Nations to claim their rights and secure their interests without the intervention of counsel or agents, and as they were originally one and the same people and are now entitled to reside in the country of each other, they shall be jointly entitled to a Delegate to the House of Representatives of the Confederate States of America, who shall serve for the term of two years, and be a member of one of the said nations, over twenty-one years of age, and laboring under no legal disability by the law of either nation; and each Delegate shall be entitled to the same rights and privileges as may be enjoyed by Delegates from any Territories of the Confederate States to the said House of Representatives. Each shall receive such pay and mileage as shall be fixed by the Congress of the Confederate States. The first election for Delegate shall be held at such time and places, and be conducted in such manner as returns of such election shall be made, and he shall declare the person having the greatest number of votes to be duly elected, and give him a certificate of election accordingly, which shall entitle him to his seat. For all subsequent elections, the times, places, and manner of holding them and ascertaining and certifying the result shall be prescribed by law of the Confederate States.

ART. XLI. It is further ascertained and agreed between the parties to this treaty that the United States of America, of which the Confederate States of America were heretofore a part, were before the separation indebted, and still continue to be indebted, to the Creek Nation, and bound to the punctual payment to them of the following sums annually, on the first day of July of each year, that is to say:

Perpetual annuities, amounting in the aggregate to $24,500, under the fourth article of the treaty of the seventh day of August, A. D. one thousand seven hundred and ninety; the second article of the treaty of the sixteenth day of June, A. D. one thousand eight hundred and two; and the fourth article of the treaty of the twenty-fourth day of January, A. D. one thousand eight hundred and twenty-six.

Interest at the rate of 5 per cent. per annum on $200,000, which, by the sixth article of the treaty of the seventh day of August, A. D. one thousand eight hundred and forty [fifty]-six, the United states interest, and to pay the interest regularly and faithfully, to be applied to purposes of education among the Creeks, but which they never invested; being $10,000 per annum or more, payable perpetually.

The sum of $1,710 perpetually, the agreed cost of the wheelwright, blacksmith, and assistant blacksmith, shop and tools, and iron and steel, annually, under the eighth article of the treaty of the twenty-fourth day of January, A. D. one thousand eight hundred and twenty-six.

The sum of $8,220, payable annually, until and upon and ending upon the first day of July, A. D. one thousand eight hundred and sixty-four, being for the sums of $6,000 per annum, for education for seven years from and after the fiscal year ending thirtieth of June, A. D. one thousand eight hundred and fifty-seven, under the fourth article of the treaty of the fourth day of January, A. D. one thousand eight hundred and forty-five, as the same is recited in the fifth article of the treaty of the seventh day of August, A. D. one thousand eight hundred and fifty-six; and of $2,220, being the estimated annual cost of the provision for two blacksmiths and assistants, shops and tools, iron and steel, under the thirteenth article of the treaty made the twenty-fourth day of March, A. D. one thousand eight hundred and thirty-two, and which was continued for seven years from and after that fiscal year by the treaty of the seventh day of August, A. D. one thousand eight hundred and fifty-six.

The sum of $4,710, which was payable during the pleasure of the President of the United States, as follows, to wit: $2,000 per annum for assistance in agricultural operations, under the eighth article of the treaty of the twenty-fourth day of January, A. D. one thousand eight hundred and twenty-six; $1,000 per annum for education, under the fifth article of the treaty of the fourteenth day of February, A. D. one thousand eight hundred and thirty-three; and $1,710 per annum, the estimated annual cost of the wagon-maker, blacksmith, and assistant, shop and tools, iron and steel, under the same fifth article of the same treaty last aforesaid; indefinite continuance of the payment of which three sums was provided for by the treaty of the seventh day of August, A. D. one thousand eight hundred and fifty-six.

And it is also hereby ascertained and agreed between the parties to this treaty that there was due to the Creek Nation on the first day of July, A. D. one thousand eight hundred and sixty-one, for and on account of these annuities, interest, and annual installments, and of arrearages thereof, the sum of $71,960, as follows, that is to say:

For the perpetual annuities then due, $24,500.

For interest and arrearages on the said sum of $200,000, provided to be invested for purposes of education by the sixth article of the treaty of the seventh day of August, A. D. one thousand eight hundred and fifty-six, which has never been invested, and the five installments of interest whereon, at the rate of 5 per cent. per annum, due up to and upon the first day of July, A. D. one thousand eight hundred and sixty-one, amount to the sum of $50,000, whereof $21,000 only has been paid, the sum of $29,000.

For the two sums aforesaid due for educational purposes, $7,000.

For sums due for wagon-makers, blacksmiths, shops, iron and steel, and agricultural purposes, $7,640, and for arrearages of same, being one-half of the annual sum due on the first day of July, A. D. one thousand eight hundred and sixty, and unpaid, $3,820, or together, $11,460. And it not being desired by the Confederate States that the Creek Nation should continue to receive these annual sums from the Government of the United States, or otherwise have any further connection or communication with that Government and its superintendents and agents, therefore the said Confederate States of America do hereby assume the payment for the future of all the above-recited annuities and annual payments, and agree and bind themselves regularly and punctually to pay the same; and do also agree and bind themselves to pay immediately upon the complete ratification of this treaty the said sum of $71,960 for such annuities and annual payments due on the first day of July, A. D. one thousand eight hundred and sixty-one, and for arrearages as above stated.

ART. XLII. It is also further agreed between the said parties to this treaty that the United States of America, while the said several Confederate States were States of the said United States, held, and do still continue to hold, in their hands, invested in bonds and stocks of certain States, part of all of which are now members of the said Confederacy of States, the sum of $200,742. 60, bearing an annual interest of $11,694. 54, and also arrearages of interest on the same in money, which amounted on the first day of July, A. D. one thousand eight hundred and sixty-one, to so much as to make, with the principal, the sum of $249,937. 14, in bonds, stocks, and money, in the hands of the United States, and belonging to those persons surviving, and the legal representatives of those persons deceased, who were orphan children of the Creeks on the twenty-fourth day of March, A. D. one thousand eight hundred and thirty-two, the same being the proceeds of the twenty sections of land selected under the direction of the President of the United States for such orphan children of the Creeks under and by virtue of the second article of the treaty of that date, and which were sold and the proceeds invested in such stock as aforesaid, under the direction of the President of the United States, in conformity to the provision of that article that said twenty sections should be divided and retained or sold for the benefit of such children as the President might direct.

And it is further agreed that in addition to this sum and to the sum of $200,000, which should have been invested under the sixth article of the treaty of the seventh day of August, A. D. one thousand eight hundred and fifty-six, there has also long been and still is due and owing from the said United States to certain individuals in the Creek Nation, from claims allowed by William Armstrong as commissioner, in their favor, on account of depredations by the Osages, as provided by treaty, the sum of $9,757. 70, to pay which and other like claims there has long remained in the Treasury of the United States the sum of $16,000, remainder of the sum of $30,000 allowed by treaty with the Osages, made the eleventh day of January, A. D. one thousand eight hundred and thirty-nine, for the purpose of paying what should be adjudged for such depredations; and the said Confederate States of America do hereby assume the duty and obligation of collecting and paying over as trustees to the said Creek Nation, for the said orphans and legal representatives of orphan children of the Creeks, all sums of money accruing, whether from interest or capital of the bonds of the several States of the Confederacy now held by the Government of the United States as trustee for the said orphans and legal representatives of orphan children of the Creeks or for the Creek Nation; and the said interest and capital as collected shall be paid over to the said orphans or legal representatives of orphans of the Creeks or to the Creek Nation for them. And the said

Confederate States will request the several States whose bonds are so held to provide, by legislation or otherwise, that the capital and interest of such bonds shall not be paid to the Government of the United States, but to the Government of the Confederate States, in trust for the said orphans and legal representatives or orphans. And the said Confederate States hereby guarantee to the said Creek Nation the final settlement and full payment, upon and after the restoration of peace and the establishment and recognition of their independence, as of debts in good faith and conscience, as well as in law due and owing, on good and valuable consideration, by the said Confederate States and other of the United States, jointly, before the secession of any of the States, of all the said sums of money so due and owing by the late United States and of any sums received by that Government and now held by it by way of interest on a capital of said bonds of the States; and do also guarantee to it the full and final settlement and payment, at the same period, of the capital and interest of any and all bonds or stocks of any Northern States in which any of the Creek funds may have been invested.

ART. XLIII. Ir agreed that whatever sums of money are by this treaty provided to be settled and paid by the Confederate States to the Creek Nation, for itself, upon the restoration of peace, not including those belonging to the said orphans, shall be paid over to the authorities of the nation, to be held by them invested in stocks, or shall be by the Government of the Confederate States so invested, in stocks bearing the best rate of interest, and at the market rate of such stocks, as the authorities of the nation may require, so that the nation may in either mode have all the advantages of the investment; and that, if paid over to the authorities of the nation, the Government of the Confederate States shall have no further control over the same in any wise nor be in any wise responsible for its proper investment or disposition.

ART. XLIV. It is further agreed between the parties that all provisions of the treaties of the Creek Nation with the United States which secure or guarantee to the Creek Nation, or individuals thereof, any rights or privileges whatever, and the place whereof is not supplied by, and which are not contrary to, the provisions of this treaty, and so far as the same are not obsolete and unnecessary, or repealed, annulled, changed, or modified by subsequent treaties or laws or by this treaty, are and shall be continued in force as if made with the Confederate States.

ART. XLV. It is hereby further agreed by the Confederate States that all the members of the Creek Nation as hereinbefore defined shall be henceforward competent to take, hold, and pass by purchase or descent, lands in any of the Confederate States heretofore or hereafter acquired by them, and to sue and implead in any of the courts of each of the States in the same manner and as fully, and under the same terms and restrictions and the same condition only, as citizens of another of the Confederate States can do.

ART. XLVI. A general amnesty of all past offenses against the laws of the United States and of the Confederate States in the Indian country before the signing of this treaty by any member of the Creek Nation as such membership is defined by this treaty is hereby declared, and all such persons, if any, whether convicted or not, imprisoned or at large, charged with any such offense shall receive from the President full and free pardon and be discharged.

ART. XLVII. It is also further agreed that the sum of $750 shall be appropriated, upon the ratification of this treaty, by the Congress of the Confederate States to pay the expenses of the commissioners of the Creek Nation who have negotiated the same, and that the same shall be paid to the principal chief, Motey Kinnaird, who shall distribute the same among the commissioners as they shall agree and direct.

ART. XLVIII. This treaty shall take effect and be obligatory upon the contracting parties from the tenth day of July, A. D. one thousand eight hundred and sixty-one, whenever it shall be ratified by the general council of the Creek Nation, and by the Provisional President and Congress, or the President and Senate of the Confederate States.

In perpetual testimony whereof the said Albert Pike, as commissioner with plenary powers, on the part of the Confederate States, doth now hereunto set his hand and affix the seal of his arms, and the undersigned, the commissioners appointed in this behalf by the general council of the Creek Nation, do hereunto set their hands and affix their seals.

Done in duplicate, at the place, and upon the day, in the year aforesaid.

[SEAL.]

ALBERT PIKE,

Commissioner of the Confederate States to the Indians West of Arkansas.

MOTEY KINNAIRD,
Principal Chief.

ICHO HACHO,
Principal Chief Upper Creeks.

CHILLY McINTOSH.
LOUIS McINTOSH.
JAMES M. C. SMITH.
G. W. STIDHAM.
THOS. C. CARR.
JOHN L. SMITH.
TIM. BARNETT.
W. F. McINTOSH.
GEO. W. BRINTON.
OK-CHUN HACHO.
CO-AS-SAT-TI FIX-I-CO.
JOSEPH CORNELLS.
GEO. W. WALKER.
SAMUEL CHECOTE.

Signed in duplicate in our presence.

W. H. GARRETT, C. S. Agent.
G. W. STIDHAM, C. S. Interpreter.
W. WARREN JOHNSON.
WM. QUESENBURY, Secretary to Commissioner.
H. S. BUCKNER.
W. L. PIKE.

Whereas, a treaty of alliance and friendship was made and concluded, subject to the ratification of the general council of the Creek Nation, on the tenth day of July, A. D. one thousand eight hundred and sixty-one, by and between Albert Pike, commissioner with plenary powers, of the Confederate States of America, on the part and behalf of the Confederate States, and Motey Kinnaird, principal chief; Icho Hacho, first chief of the Upper Creeks; Chilly McIntosh, Louis McIntosh, James M. C. Smith, George W. Stidham, Thomas C. Carr, John L. Smith, Timothy Barnett, William F. McIntosh, George W. Brinton, Ok-Chun Hacho, Co-as-sat-ti Fix-I-co, Joseph Cornells, George W. Walker, Samuel Checote, and Daniel N. McIntosh, a committee appointed by the general council of Musko-ki Nation, at the North Fork Village, on the North Fork of the Canadian River, in the said Creek Nation; and whereas, by the forty-ninth [forty-eighth] article thereof it is provided in these words, that "This treaty shall take effect and be obligatory upon the contracting parties from the tenth day of July, A. D. one thousand eight hundred and sixty-one, whenever it shall be ratified by the general council of the Creek Nation, and by the Provisional President and Congress, or the President and Senate of the Confederate States:"

Now, therefore, be it known that the Creek or Mus-ko-ki Nation, in general council assembled, on this the twentieth day of July, A. D. one thousand eight hundred and sixty-one, at the council ground of the said nation, having maturely considered the said treaty, and every article and clause thereof, and being satisfied therewith, doth, upon ts part, assent to, ratify, and confirm the same as its solemn act and compact, as is therein stipulated, and doth direct that a copy of this ratification, signed by the principal chief and national clerk, be annexed to each part of the said treaty for authentication thereof.

Thus done and approved the day and year aforesaid.

A true copy of the original act of ratification as adopted by the general council.

MOTEY KINNAIRD, Principal Chief.

Attest.

D. N. McINTOSH, National Clerk.

Signed and attested in our presence.

W. H. GARRETT, C. S. Agent for the Creeks.
G. W. STIDHAM, C. S. Interpreter for the Creeks.

Names of the chiefs who signed the treaty concluded on the tenth day of July, one thousand eight hundred and sixty-one, and approved by the general council of the Creek Nation on the twentieth July, one thousand eight hundred and sixty-one, between the Confederate States of America and the Creek Nation of Indians:

Echur Harjo.
Cowassart Harjo.
Nocus Emathla.
Us-so-na Harjo.
In-suk-ko.
Tustunnuk Kee.
Ar-chu-le Harjo.
Oh-sa Ya-ho-LA.
He-ne-matheo-che.
Tullissee Fixico.
Tallor Harjo.
No-cus-illy.
Cha-low Harjo.

Ok-ta-ha-hasee Harjo.
Ho-siche Boatswain.
Thear-ke-ta.
Ya-ha Harjo.
Fixico Harjo.
Ok-chun Harjo.
Ne-ha Ya-ho-LA.
Tallise Fixico.
Jimmy Larney.
Halputter Mikko.
Samuel Lasley.
Ya-ha Tustunnukke.
Ne-ha Ya-hola.
Co-we Harjo.
Wm. Bruner.
Jacob Derrysaw.
E-ne-ha.
Car-pit-char Ya-ho-LA.
It-chin Ya-ho-LA.
Nocus Fixico.
Mikko Hutke.
Napoche Fixico.
Cotchar Fixico.
James McHenry.
Cully Mikko.
Pow-has-e Marthla.
Ok-cus-ca Fixico.
Ar-hul Le-mathla.
Tul-wa Mikko.
Ar-ha-luk Fixico.
Lou-cher Harjo.
Carpechar Fixico.

Attest.
--- ---,

National Clerk.

ARTICLE SUPPLEMENTARY to the treaty concluded between the Confederate States of America and the Creek Nation of Indians, at the North Fork Village, in the Creek Nation, on the tenth day of July, A. D. one thousand eight hundred and sixty-one.

ARTICLE. The survivors, now residing in the Creek Nation, of the Apalachicola band of Indians have earnestly represented to the commissioner of the Confederate States the facts following, that is to say:

That the Apalachicola band of Indians, being by origin a part of the Creek Nation, long resided on the Apalachicola River, in what is now the State of Florida, and were parties to the treaty concluded at Camp Moultrie, with the Florida tribes of Indians, on the eighteenth day of September, A. D. one thousand eight hundred and twenty-three.

That by two treaties made and concluded with the United States on the eighteenth day of June, A. D. one thousand eight hundred and twenty-three, by different portions of the said Apalachicola band, the chiefs and warriors of that band relinquished all the privileges to which they were entitled as parties to the treaty aforesaid, concluded at Camp Moultrie, and all their right and title to certain reservations by it secured to them; and in consideration of that cession the United States agreed to grant and to convey within three years, by patent to certain named chiefs for the benefit of themselves and of the sub-chiefs and warriors of the said Apalachicola band, the quantity, in all, of six sections of land, to to be laid off under the direction of the President after the lands should have been surveyed

That it was provided by the same two treaties that the said six sections of land might be disposed of by the chiefs with the consent and advice of the Governor of Florida, at any time before the expiration of said term of three years, and that the said band might thereupon migrate to a county of their choice. And it was further thereby provided that if, at any future time, the chiefs and warriors of the Apalachicola band should feel disposed to migrate from Florida to the Creek and Seminole country west, they might either sell the grants of land made by those treaties, and in that case must themselves bear the whole expense of their migrations, subsistence, &c., or they might surrender to the United States all the rights and privileges acquired under said two treaties, in which case they should become parties to the obligations, provisions, and stipulations of the treaty of Payne's Landing, made with the Seminoles on the ninth day of May, A. D. one thousand eight hundred and thirty-two, as a constituent part of that tribe, and reunite with that tribe in their abode west, in which case the United states would pay $6,000 for the reservations in that case relinquished by the first article of the said two treaties.

That in the hostilities that afterward took place between the Creeks and Seminoles and the United States the said Apalachicola band remained loyal to the United States, and maintained their peace and friendship unbroken; but in the year 1837 they were induced, by the urgent solicitation of the emigrating agent of the United States, to remove from the country occupied by them in Florida to the Indian country west of Arkansas, leaving the lands so granted them as aforesaid, and a large number of horses, mules, cattle, hogs, wagons, and other articles which they could not collect together and carry with them, and which the said emigrating agent persuaded them to leave in his charge, on his promise that the owners should be paid the value of all such their property in money by the agent of the United States on their arrival in the country provided for them on the west side of the Mississippi; a schedule* of all of which property so abandoned, and of its value, and of the improvements on lands abandoned by them, and the value of each is annexed to this article and forms a part of it.

That by the treaty of Payne's Landing, made on the ninth day of May, A. D. one thousand eight hundred and thirty-two, the United States agreed to pay the Seminole Indians, in full compensation for all

----

*Omitted.

their claim to lands in the Territory of Florida, and for all improvements on the lands so ceded, the sum of $15,400, to be divided among the chiefs and warriors of the several towns in a ration proportioned to their population; and they further agreed to take the cattle belonging to the Seminoles at the valuation of some person to be appointed by the President, and to pay the valuation in money to the respective owners or give them other cattle; and the expenses of removal were to be paid by the United States and subsistence for twelve months to all emigrants furnished by them;

And that no compensation has ever been made any of the said Apalachicola band for the lands or improvements so abandoned by them, or for the horses, mules, cattle, and other property abandoned by them; nor have they ever received any part of the annuities paid the Seminole or Creek Nation since their removal west, or been recognized as an integral part of the Seminole Nation, as it was provided they should be;

And inasmuch as the forced emigration of the said band, and their surrender and abandonment of their lands, improvements, horses, cattle, and other property in consequence thereof, was equivalent, as against the United States, to an election by them to surrender the rights and privileges secured by the treaties of the eighteenth of June, one thousand eight hundred and thirty-three, and to claim the rights and privileges thereby vesting in them, as parties to the treaty of Payne's Landing, of the ninth of May, one thousand eight hundred and thirty-two:

Therefore, it is hereby agreed by the Confederate States of America, by Albert Pike, its commissioner with full powers, with the members and survivors of the Apalachicola band of Florida Indians, that upon and after the restoration of peace the said claims of the members of that band to compensation for the loss of the lands, improvements, horses, cattle, mules, and other property shall be fairly investigated, in a generous and liberal spirit, by an officer or commissioners, to whom that duty shall be assigned by the Confederate States; and that whatever shall appear upon such investigation to be justly or equitably owing to members of the said band on account of such losses as aforesaid shall be paid to the persons originally entitled to the same, or to the legal representatives of such of them as may be deceased.

And it is also further agreed that the foregoing provisions of this article shall extend to and include the claims for losses of the same kind by members of Black Dirt's band of friendly Seminoles, who lost property in like manner in consequence of their hurried removal west, as the same is contained in the schedule thereof, marked B,* annexed to this article.

And it is also agreed that the claims to money, in lieu of bounty-land warrants, of the persons whose names and those of their heirs are contained in the schedule marked C,* annexed to this article, shall, in like manner and at the same period, be investigated, and so far as they shall be found to be well founded shall be paid by the Confederate States.

In perpetual testimony whereof the said Albert Pike, commissioner with full powers of the Confederate States of America, doth hereunto set his hand and affix the seal of his arms.

----

*Omitted.

Thus done, signed, and sealed, at the North Fork Village, on the North Fork of the Canadian River, this tenth day of July, A. D. one thousand eight hundred and sixty-one.

[SEAL.]

ALBERT PIKE,

Commissioner of the Confederate States to the Indian Nations West of Arkansas.

RATIFICATION by the Congress.

Resolved (two-thirds of the Congress concurring), That the Congress of the Confederate States of America do advise and consent to the ratification of the articles of treaty, including the secret article and supplementary article, made by Albert Pike, commissioner of the Confederate States to the Indian nations west of Arkansas, in behalf of the Confederate States of the one part and the Creek council assembled, of the other part, concluded at the North Fork Village, on the North Fork of the Canadian River, in the Creek Nation, on the tenth day of July, A. D. one thousand eight hundred and sixty-one, with the following amendments:

1. Strike out from Article XXVIII the following words, "and the State court," and insert in lieu thereof the following words, "or in a State court, subject to the laws of the State. "

2. Add at the end of Article XXX the following words, "and the Confederate States will request the several States of the Confederacy to adopt and enact the provisions of this article in respect to suits and proceedings in their respective courts. "

3. Strike out from Article XI the following words, "the same rights and privileges as may be enjoyed by Delegates from any Territories of the Confederate States in the said House of Representatives," and insert in lieu thereof the following words, "a seat in the hall of the House of Representatives, to propose and introduce measures for the benefit of said nations, and to be heard in regard thereto, and on other questions in which either of said nations is particularly interested, with such other rights and privileges as may be determined by the House of Representatives. "

NOTE. - The foregoing amendments were subsequently ratified by general council of the Creek Nation.

OFFICIAL RECORDS: Series 4, vol 1, Part 1
Pages 513-527
Confederate States of America - Seminole

A TREATY of friendship made and concluded at the Seminole council-house, in the Seminole Nation, west of Arkansas, on the first day of August, A. D. one thousand eight hundred and sixty-one, between the Confederate States of America, by Albert Pike, commissioner with plenary powers of the Confederate States, of the one part, and the Seminole Nation of red men, by its chiefs, headmen, and warriors in general council assembled, of the other part.

The Congress of the Confederate States of America having, by "An act for the protection of certain Indian tribes," approved the twenty-first day of May, A. D. one thousand eight hundred and sixty-one, offered to assume and accept the protectorate of the several nations and tribes of Indians occupying the country west of Arkansas and Missouri, and to recognize them as their wards, subject to all the rights, privileges, and immunities, titles, and guarantees with each of the said nations and tribes under treaties made with them by the United States of America; and the Seminole Nation of red men having assented thereto upon certain terms and conditions:

Now, therefore, the said Confederate States of America, by Albert Pike, their commissioner, appointed by the President, under authority of the act of Congress in their behalf, with plenary powers for these purposes, and the Seminole Nation, in general council assembled, have agreed to the following articles, that is to say:

ARTICLE I. There shall be perpetual peace and friendship between the Confederate States of America and all of their States and people and the Seminole Nation of red men and all its towns and individuals.

ART II. The Seminole Nation of red men acknowledges itself to be under the protection of the Confederate States of America, and of no other power or sovereign whatever, and doth hereby stipulate and agree with them that it will not hereafter, nor shall any of its towns or individuals, contract any alliance or enter into any compact, treaty, or agreement with any individual State or with a foreign power: Provided, That it may make such compacts and agreements with neighboring nations and tribes of Indians for their mutual welfare and the prevention of difficulties as may not be contrary to this treaty or inconsistent with its obligations to the Confederate States; and the said Confederate States do hereby assume and accept the said protectorate, and recognize the said Seminole Nation as their ward; and by the consent of the said Seminole Nation, now here freely given, the country whereof it is proprietor in fee, as the same is hereinafter defined, is annexed to the Confederate States, in the same manner and to as it was annexed to the United States of America before that Government was dissolved, with such modifications, however, of the terms of annexation and upon such conditions as are hereinafter expressed, in addition to al the rights, privileges, immunities, titles, and guarantees with or in favor of the said nation under treaties made with it and under statutes of the United States of America.

ART. III. The following shall constitute and remain the boundaries of the Seminole country, viz: Beginning on the Canadian River a few miles east of the ninety-seventh parallel of west longitude, where Ok-hai-ap-po, or Pond Creek, empties into the same; thence due north to the North Fork of the Canadian; thence up the said North Fork of the Canadian to the southern line of the Cherokee country; thence with that line west to the one-hundredth parallel of west longitude; thence south along said parallel of longitude to the Canadian River, and thence down and with that river to the place of beginning.

ART. IV. The Seminole Nation hereby gives its full, free, and unqualified assent to those provisions of the act of Congress of the Confederate States of America entitled "An act for t he protection Confederate States of America entitled "An act for the protection of certain Indian tribes," approved the twenty-first day of May, A. D. one thousand eight hundred and sixty-one, whereby it was declared that all the reversionary and other interest, right, title, and proprietorship of the United States in, unto, and over the Indian country in which that of the said nation is included should pass to and vest in the Confederate States; and whereby the President of the Confederate States was authorized to make military possession of all said country; and whereby all the laws of the United States, with the exception thereinafter made, applicable to and in force in said country and not inconsistent with the letter or spirit of any treaty stipulations entered into with the Seminole Nation, among others were re-enacted, continued in force, and declared to be in force in said country as law and statutes of the said Confederate States contained is or may be is to be of none effect henceforward, and shall upon the ratification hereof be deemed and taken to have been repealed and annulled as of relate to and be taken to have been given upon the said day of the approval of the said act of Congress.

ART V. The Confederate States of America do hereby solemnly guarantee to the Seminole Nation, to be held by it to its own use and behold in fee simple forever, the lands included within the boundaries defined in the preceding article of this treaty, to be held by the people of the said nation in common, as they have heretofore been held, so long as grass shall grow and water run, if the said nation shall so please, but with power of making partition thereof and disposition of the same by laws of the nation duly enacted; by which partition or sale title in fee simple absolute shall vest in parcener and purchasers whenever it shall please the nation, of its own free will and accord and without solicitation from any quarter, to dos o; which solicitation the Confederate States hereby solemnly agree never to use; and the title and tenure hereby guaranteed to the said nation is and shall be subject o no other conditions, reservations, or restrictions whatever than such as are hereinafter specially expressed.

ART. VI. None of the said lands hereby guaranteed to the Seminole Nation shall be sold, ceded, or otherwise disposed of to any foreign power, or to any state or government whatever; and in as any such sale, cession, or disposition should be made without the consent of the Confederate States, all the said lands shall thereupon revert to the Confederate States.

ART. VII. It is further hereby agreed and stipulated that no part of the tract of country hereinbefore guaranteed to the Seminole Nation, being the same that was ceded to it by the treaty of the seventh August, A. D. one thousand eight hundred and fifty-six, between the United States of America and the Creek and Seminole Nations of Indians, shall ever be sold or otherwise disposed of without the consent of both of said nations being legally given.

ART. VIII. The Confederate States of America do hereby solemnly agree and bind themselves that no State or Territory shall ever pass laws for the government of the Seminole Nation; and that no portion of the country hereby guaranteed to it shall ever be embraced or included within or annexed to any Territory or providence; nor shall any attempt ever be made, except upon the free, voluntary, and unsolicited application of the said nation, to erect the said country, by itself or with any other, into a State or any other territorial or political organization, or to incorporate it into any State previously created.

ART. IX. So far as may be compatible with the Constitution of the Confederate States, and with the laws made, enacted, or adopted in conformity thereto, regulating trade and intercourse with the Indian tribes as the same are limited and modified by this treaty, the Seminole Nation shall possess the otherwise unrestricted right of self-government and full jurisdiction, judicial and otherwise, over persons and property within its limits, excepting only white persons as are not, by birth, adoption or otherwise, members of either the Seminole or Creek Nation; and that there may be no doubt as to the meaning of this exception it is hereby declared that every white person who, having married a Seminole or Creek woman, resides in the said Seminole country, or who, without intermarrying, is permanently domiciled therein with the consent of the authorities of the nation and votes at elections, is to be deemed and taken as a member of the said nation within the true intent and meaning of this article; and that the exception contained in the laws for the punishment of offenses committed in the Indian country, to the effect that they shall not extend or apply to offenses committed by the Indian against the person and property of another Indian, shall be so extended and enlarged by virtue of this article when ratified, and without further legislation, as that none of said laws shall extend or apply to any offense committed by any Indian or negro or mulatto, or by any such white person, so by birth, adoption, or otherwise, a member of the Seminole or Creek Nation against the person or property of any Indian, negro, or mulatto, or any such white person, when the same shall be committed within the limits of the said Seminole Nation as hereinbefore defined; but all such persons shall be subject to the laws of the Seminole Nation and to prosecution and trial before its tribunals, and to punishment according to such laws in all respects like native members of the said nation.

ART. X. All persons who are not members of either the Seminole or Creek Nation found in the Seminole country as hereinbefore limited, shall be considered as intruders and be removed and kept out of the same, either by the civil officers of the nation, under the direction of the Executive, or the general council, or by the agent of the Confederate States for the nattion authorized to demand, if necessary, the aid of the military for that purpose, with the following exceptions only; that is to say, such individuals with their families as may be in the employment of the Government of the Confederate States; all persons peaceably traveling our temporarily sojourning in the country, or trading therein under license from the proper authority; and such persons as may be permitted by the Seminoles or Creeks, with the assent of the agent of the Confederate States, to reside within their respective limits without becoming members of either of said tribes.

ART. XI. A tract of two sections of land, to be laid off under the direction of the President of the Confederate States, and to include the site of the present Seminole agency, whereon the public buildings of that agency have been erected, is hereby reserved to the Confederate States and not included in the guarantee of lands aforesaid, but shall be within the sole and exclusive jurisdiction of the Confederate States, except as to members of the Seminole or Creek Nation as above defined, all offenses committed by whom thereon shall be punished by the laws and courts of the Seminole Nation whenever they would be so punished if committed elsewhere in the nation: Provided, That whenever the agency for the said nation shall be discontinued by the Confederate States, and an agent no longer appointed, the said tract of two sections of land shall pass to and vest absolutely in the Seminole Nation in the same manner as its other lands, with all the buildings that may be thereupon.

ART. XII. The Confederate States shall have the right to build, establish, and maintain such forts and military posts, temporary or permanent, and to make and maintain such military and post roads the quantity of one mile square of land, including each fort or post, shall be reserved to the Confederate States, and within their sole and exclusive jurisdiction, so long as such for or post is occupied; quantity of land beyond one mile square shall be used or occupied, nor any greater quantity of timber felled than of each is road, or of the agency, the property of any individual member of the Seminole Nation, or any property of the nation itself, other than land, timber, stone, and earth, be taken, destroyed, or injured, just and adequate compensation shall be made by the Confederate States.

ART. XIII. The Confederate States, or any company incorporated by them, or any one of them, shall have the right of way for railroads or telegraph lines through the Seminole country; but in the case of any incorporated company, it shall have such right of way only upon such terms and payment of such amount to the Seminole Nation as may be agreed upon between it and the National Council thereof; or, in case of disagreement, by making full compensation, not only to individual parties injured, but also to the nation for the right of way; all damage and injury done to be ascertained and determined in such manner as the President of the Confederate States shall direct. And the right of way granted by said nation for any railroad shall be perpetual, or for such shorter term as the same may be granted, in the same manner as if no reversion of their lands to the Confederate States were provided for, in case of abandonment by them or of extinction of their tribe.

ART. XIV. No person shall settle, farm, or raise stock within the limits of any post or fort, or of the agency, except such as are or may be in the employment of the Confederate States in some civil or military capacity, or such as, being subject to the jurisdiction and laws of the Seminole Nation, are permitted by the commanding officer of the post or fort or by the agent to do so upon the reserve.

ART. XV. The Confederate States shall protect the Seminoles from domestic strife, from hostile invasion, and from aggression by other Indians and white persons not subject to the jurisdiction and laws of thn; and from all injuries resulting from such invasion or aggression full indemnity is hereby guaranteed to the party or parties injured out of the Treasury of the Confederate States upon the same principle and according to the same rules upon which white persons are entitled to indemnify for injuries or aggressions committed upon them by Indians.

ART. XVI. No person shall hereafter be licensed to trade with the Seminoles except by the agent and with the advice and consent of the National Council, which advice and consent, however, shall not be necessary in the case of traders now trading under license until the expiration trader shall execute bond to the Confederate States in such form and manner as was required by the United States or as may be required by the Bureau of Indian Affairs; and no appeal shall hereafter lie to any officer whatever from the decision of the agent refusing license to any applicant.

ART. XVII. All persons licensed by the Confederate States to trade with the Seminoles shall be required to pay to the authorities of the Seminole Nation a moderate annual compensation for the land and timber used by them, the amount of such compensation in each case to be assessed by the proper authorities of the said Seminole Nation, subject to the approval of the Confederate States agent thereof.

ART. XVIII. It is further hereby agreed that no license shall hereafter be granted to any trader who is in arrear on account of any amount legally assessed to be paid by him as compensation for land revoked on failure or refusal to pay in due time the amount that may be thereof legally assessed in any years. And when a renewal of license is refused any trader he shall, nevertheless, be entitled, if he country such reasonable length of time as may, in the opinion of the agent, be necessary for the purpose of collecting such debts as may be due him, being during such time under the protection of the laws of the Confederate States as a person peaceably sojourning in the country.

ART. XIX. All restrictions or limitations heretofore imposed or existing by treaty, law, or regulation upon the right of any member of the Seminole Nation freely to sell and dispose of to any person whatever any chattel or article of personal property whatever are hereby removed and annulled, except such as the laws of the nation itself may have created.

ART. XX the Confederate States and an interpreter shall continue to be appointed for the Seminole Nation, both of whom shall reside at the agency; and whenever a vacancy shall occur in either of the said officers the authorities of the nation shall be consulted as to the person to be appointed to fill the same, and no one shall be appointed against whom they in good faith protest; and the agent may be removed on petition and formal charges preferred by the constituted authorities that there is sufficient cause for such removal.

ART. XXI. The Seminole Nation may, by act of its legislative authorities, receive and incorporate in itself as members of the nation or permit to settle and reside upon the national lands such Indians of any other tribe as to it may seem good, and may sell to such Indians portions of land, in free or by less estate, or lease them portions thereof for years or otherwise, and receive to its own the price of such sales or leases; and it alone shall determine who are members and citizens of the nation entitled to vote at elections, hold office, or share in annuities or in the common lands: Provided, That when persons of another tribe shall once have been received as members of the Seminole Nation they shall not be disfranchised or subjected to any other restrictions upon the right of voting than such as shall apply to the Seminoles themselves. But no Indians other than Seminoles and Creeks not now reside without the consent or permission of the legislative authority of the nation.

ART. XXII. If any citizen of the Confederate States or any other persons not being permitted to do so by the authorities of said nation any lands of the Seminole Nation he shall forfeit the protection upon him, not being cruel, unusual, or excessive, as may have been previously prescribed by law of the nation.

ART. XXIII. No citizen or inhabitant of the Confederate States shall pasture stock on the lands of the Seminole Nation under the penalty of $1 per head for all so pastured, to be collected by the authorities of the nation; but their citizens shall be at liberty at all times, and whether for business or pleasure, peaceably to travel the Seminole country and to drive their stock t market or otherwise through the same, and to halt such reasonable time on the way as may be necessary to recruit their stock, such delay being in good faith for that purpose. It is also further agreed that the members of the Seminole Nation shall have the same right of traveling, driving stock, and halting to recruit the same in any of the Confederate States.

ART. XXIV. The officers and people of the Seminole and Creek Nations, respectively, shall have at all times the right of safe conduct through the lands of each other; and the members or each nation shall have the right, freely and without seeking license or permission, to settle within the country of the other, and shall thereupon be entitled to all the rights, privileges, and imers thereof, including the right of voting at all elections and being deemed qualified to hold office, and excepting only that no member of either nation shall be entitled to participate in any funds belonging to the other nation. Members of either nation shall have the right to institute and prosecute suits in the courts of the other under such regulations as may from time to time be prescribed by their respective Legislatures.

ART. XXV. Any person duly charged with a criminal offense against the laws of either the Seminole or Creek Nation and escaping into the jurisdiction of the other shall be promptly surrendered upon the demand of the proper authority of the nation within whose jurisdiction the offense shall be alleged to have been committed.

ART. XXVI. The Seminole Nation shall promptly apprehend and deliver up all persons accused of any crime against the laws of the Confederate States or any State thereof who may be found within its limits, on demand of any proper officer of a State of the Confederate States; and the authorities of each of said States shall in like manner deliver up, on demand of the executive authority of the Seminole Nation, any person subject to the jurisdiction of the tribunals of such nation and accused of any crime against its laws.

ART. XXVII. In addition to so much and such parts of the acts of Congress of the United States enacted to regulate trade and intercourse with Indian tribes and to preserve peace on the frontiers as may have been re-enacted and continued in force by the Confederate States, and as are not inconsistent with the provisions of this treaty, so much of the laws of the Confederate States as provide for the punishment of crimes amounting to felony at common law or by statute against the laws, authority, or treaties of the Confederate States, and over which the courts of the Confederate States have jurisdiction, including the counterfeiting the coin of the Confederate States or of the United States, or the securities of the Confederate States, or in uttering counterfeit coin or securities, and so much of such laws as provides for the punishment of violators of neutrality laws and resistance to the process of the Confederate States and all the facts of the Provisional Congress providing for the common defense and welfare, so far as the same are not locally inapplicable, shall hereafter be in force in the Seminole country.

ART. XXVIII. Whenever any person who is a member of the Seminole Nation shall be indicted for any offense in any court in the Confederate States, or in a State court, he shall be entitled as of common right to subpoena, and, if necessary, compulsory process for all such witnesses in his behalf as his counsel may think material for his defense; and the costs of process for such witnesses and of service thereof, and the fees and mileage of such witnesses, shall be paid by the Confederate States, being afterward made, if practicable, in the case of conviction, of the property of the accused. And whenever the accused is not able to employ counsel, the court shall assign him one experienced counsel for his defense, who shall be paid by the Confederate States a reasonable compensation for his services, to be fixed by the court and paid upon the certificate of the judge.

ART. XXIX. The provisions of all such acts of the Congress of the Confederate States as may now be in force, or as may hereafter be enacted for the purpose of carrying into effect the provisions of the Constitution in regard to the fugitive slaves or fugitives from labor and service, shall extend to and be in full force within the said Seminole Nation, and shall also apply to all cases of escape of fugitive slaves from the said Seminole Nation into any other Indian nation or into one of the Confederate States, the obligation upon each such nation or State to redeliver such slaves being in every case as complete as if they had escaped form another State, and the mode of procedure the same.

ART. XXX. Persons belonging to the Seminole Nation shall hereafter be completed witnesses in all cases, civil and criminal, in the courts of the Confederate States, unless rendered incompetent from some other cause than their Indian blood or descent.

ART. XXXI. It is hereby further agreed by the Confederate States that all the members of the Seminole Nation, as hereinbefore defined, shall be henceforward competent to take, hold, and pass, by purchase or descent, lands in any of the Confederate States heretofore or hereafter acquired by them, and to sue and implead in any of the courts of each of the States in the same manner, and as fully and under the same terms and restrictions and on the same conditions only, as citizens of another of the Confederate States can do.

ART. XXXII. Whenever regular courts of justice shall be established in the Seminole Nation the official acts of all its judicial officers shall have the same effect, and be entitled to the like faith and credit everywhere, as the like acts of judicial officers of the same grade and everywhere, as the like acts of judicial officers of the same grade and jurisdiction in any one of the Confederate States; and the proceedings of the courts and tribunals of the said nation, and copies of its laws and judicial and other records, shall be authenticated like similar proceedings of the courts of the Confederate States and the laws and office records of the same, and be entitled to the like faith and credit.

ART. XXXIII. It is hereby declared the institution of slavery in the Seminole Nation is legal and has existed from time immemorial; that slaves are taken and deemed to be personal property; that the title to slaves and other property having its origin in the said nation shall be determined by the laws and customs thereof, and that the slaves and other personal property of every person domiciled in said nation shall pass and be distributed at his or her death in accordance with the laws, usages, and customs of the said nation, which may be proved like foreign laws, usages, and customs, and shall everywhere be held varied and binding within the scope of their operations.

ART. XXXIV. No ex post facto law or law impairing the obligation of contracts shall ever be enacted by the legislative authority of the Seminole Nation to affect any other persons that its own people; nor shall any citizen of the Confederate States or member of any other Indian nation or tribe be deprived of his property, or deprived or restrained of his liberty, or fine penalty, or forfeiture be imposed on him in the said country, except by the law of the land, nor without due process of the law; nor shall any such citizen by in any way deprived of any of the rights guaranteed to all citizens by the Constitution of the Confederate States; and it shall be within the province of the agent to prevent any infringement of such rights and of this article, if it should in any case be necessary.

ART. XXXV. It is hereby further agreed that the Congress of the Confederate States shall establish and maintain post-offices at the most important places in the Seminole Nation, and cause the mails to be regularly carried, at reasonable intervals, to and from the same, at the same rates of postage and in the same manner as in the Confederate States.

ART. XXXVI. It is further agreed by the said Confederate states that the said Seminole Nation shall never be required or called upon to pay, in land or otherwise, any part of the expenses of the present war, or of any war waged by or against the Confederate States.

ART. XXXVII. In order to enable the Creek and Seminole Nations to claim their rights and secure their interests without the intervention of counsel or agents, and as they were originally one and the same people and are now entitled to reside in the country of each other, they shall be jointly entitled to a Delegate to the House of Representatives of the Confederate States of America, who shall serve for the term of two years, and be a member of one of said nations, ever twenty-one years of age, and laboring under no legal disability by the law of either nation; and each Delegate shall be entitled to the same rights and privileges as may be enjoyed by the Delegate from any Territory of the Confederate States to the said House of Representatives. Each shall receive such pay and mileage as shall be fixed by gate shall be held at such time and places, and be conducted in such manner as shall be prescribed by the agent of the Confederate states for the Creeks, to whom returns of such election shall be made, and he shall declare the person having the greatest number of votes to be duly elected and give him a certificate of election accordingly, which shall entitle him to his seat. For all subsequent elections the times, and judicial and other records, shall be authenticated like similar proceedings of the courts of the Confederate States and the laws and office records of the same, and be entitled to the like faith and credit.

ART. XXXIII. It is hereby declared the institution of slavery in the Seminole Nation is legal and has existed from time immemorial; that slaves are taken and deemed to be personal property; that the title to slaves and other property having its origin in the said nation shall be determined by the laws and customs thereof, and that the slaves and other personal property of every person domiciled in said nation shall pass and be distributed at his or her death in accordance with the laws, usages, and customs of the said nation, which may be proved like foreign laws, usages, and customs, and shall everywhere be held varied and binding within the scope of their operations.

ART. XXXIV. No ex post facto law or law impairing the obligation of contracts shall ever be enacted by the legislative authority of the Seminole Nation to affect any other persons that its own people; nor shall any citizen of the Confederate States or member of any other Indian nation or tribe be deprived of his property, or deprived or restrained of his liberty, or fine penalty, or forfeiture be imposed on him in the said country, except by the law of the land, nor without due process of the law; nor shall any such citizen by in any way deprived of any of the rights guaranteed to all citizens by the Constitution of the Confederate States; and it shall be within the province of the agent to prevent any infringement of such rights and of this article, if it should in any case be necessary.

ART. XXXV. It is hereby further agreed that the Congress of the Confederate States shall establish and maintain post-offices at the most important places in the Seminole Nation, and cause the mails to be regularly carried, at reasonable intervals, to and from the same, at the same rates of postage and in the same manner as in the Confederate States.

ART. XXXVI. It is further agreed by the said Confederate states that the said Seminole Nation shall never be required or called upon to pay, in land or otherwise, any part of the expenses of the present war, or of any war waged by or against the Confederate States.

ART. XXXVII. In order to enable the Creek and Seminole Nations to claim their rights and secure their interests without the intervention of counsel or agents, and as they were originally one and the same people and are now entitled to reside in the country of each other, they shall be jointly entitled to a Delegate to the House of Representatives of the Confederate States of America, who shall serve for the term of two years, and be a member of one of said nations, ever twenty-one years of age, and laboring under no legal disability by the law of either nation; and each Delegate shall be entitled to the same rights and privileges as may be enjoyed by the Delegate from any Territory of the Confederate States to the said House of Representatives. Each shall receive such pay and mileage as shall be fixed by gate shall be held at such time and places, and be conducted in such manner as shall be prescribed by the agent of the Confederate states for the Creeks, to whom returns of such election shall be made, and he shall declare the person having the greatest number of votes to be duly elected and give him a certificate of election accordingly, which shall entitle him to his seat. For all subsequent elections the times, places, and manner of holding them and ascertaining and certifying the result shall be prescribed by law of the Confederate States.

ART. XXXVIII. It is hereby ascertained and agreed by and between the Confederate States and the Seminole Nation that the United States of

America, of which the Confederate States were heretofore a part, were, before the separation, indebted and still continue to be indebted to the Seminole Nation in the following sums annually, and bound to the punctual payment thereof to them, on the thirteenth [thirtieth] day of December in each year, that is to say:

Perpetual annuities, amounting to the sum of $25,000, being the annual interest at the rate of 5 per cent. per annum on the two sums of $250,000 each, which were, by the eighth article of the treaty of the seventh day of August, A. D. one thousand eight hundred and fifty-six, to be invested by the United States at that rate of interest, and the interest to be regularly paid over to the nation per capita as annuity, no part of which was ever invested. And the sums of $3,000 for the support of schools, $2,000 for agricultural assistance, and $2,200 for the support of smiths and smith shops among the Seminoles, which were by the same treaty to be paid annually for ten years from and after the making of the said treaty.

And it is hereby further ascertained and agreed that there was due to the Seminole Nation form the United States of America, on the thirtieth day of December, A. D. one thousand eight hundred and sixty, on account of said annual payments and the arrearage thereof, the sums following, that is to say:

For arrearage of the said sum of $3,000 annually for the support of schools, from the seventh day of August, A. D. one thousand eight hundred and fifty-six, until and including the payment for the thirtieth day of December, A. D. one thousand eight hundred and sixty, $13,000.

The sum of $2,000 for agricultural assistance and the sum of $2,200 for the support of smiths and smith shops, both payable on the day last mentioned.

And it not being desired by the Confederate States that the Seminole Nation should continue to receive these annual sums from the Government of the United States, or otherwise have any further connection or communication with that Government, and they being willing for the benefit and improvement of the seminole people to extend the time during which the said annual sums of $3,000 for the support of schools and of $2,200 for the support of smiths and smith shops shall be paid; therefore, the said Confederate States of America do hereby assume the payment for the future of the above-recited annuity and annual payments, and do agree and bind themselves regularly and punctually to pay the same in manner following, that is to say:

The said annuity or annual interest of $25,000 annually forever, commencing with the thirtieth day of December next, $5,000 thereof annually to the treasurer of the nation, to be used and disbursed as the general council shall direct for governmental and other purposes, and the residue of $20,000 annually per capita to all the individuals of the Seminole Nation, equally and share and share alike: Provided, That after the restoration of peace and the establishment and recognition of the independence of the Confederate States, and if it be required by the general council of the Seminole Nation, the capital sum of $500,000, on which the said annual interest is hereby provided to be paid, shall be invested by the President in safe stocks, at their market value, bearing an annual interest of at least 6 per cent., so that the most advantageous investment possible shall be made for the Seminole Nation; which stocks shall be thereon collected by the Confederate States and by them paid annually to the Seminoles, $5,000 in each year to the treasurer of the nation, to be applied to such governmental and other purposes as the general council shall direct, and the whole residue per capita to all the individuals of the nation. The said sum of $3,000 for the support of schools annually for twenty years from and after the making of this treaty, beginning with the present year of our Lord, one thousand eight hundred and sixty-one, and payable on the thirtieth day of December in each year, to be expended and applied under the direction of the President of the Confederate States by the agent of the Seminoles.

The said sum of $2,200 for the support of smiths and smith shops annually for ten years from and after the making of this treaty, beginning with the present year of our Lord, one thousand eight hundred and sixty-one, and payable on the thirtieth day of December in each year, to be expended and applied by or under the direction of the general council for the support of smiths and smith shops in the said nation

The said sum of $2,000 for agricultural assistance annually for five years from and after the making of this treaty, beginning with the present year of our Lord, one thousand eight hundred and sixty-one, and payable on the thirtieth day of December in each year, to be expended and applied, under the direction of the Confederate States for the said nation.

And the said Confederate States do also agree and bind themselves to appropriate and pay, immediately after the complete ratification of this treaty, time sum of $17,200, the aggregate of the sums which were so due and payable as aforesaid on the thirtieth day of December, A. D. one thousand eight hundred and sixty; the sums of $13,000 and $2,000, part thereof, to be expended and disbursed by the agent, under the direction of the President, the former for the support of schools and the latter in the way of agricultural assistance, and the sum of $2,200, the residue thereof, to be paid to the treasurer of the nation and applied by the general council to the support of smiths and smith shops: *Provided*, That the President shall not be required to extend the whole of said sum of $13,000 at once, but shall apply the same judiciously from time to time and at such times and in such sums as shall seem to him best calculated to diffuse the benefits of education and knowledge among the children of the Seminoles. And it is further agreed by the Confederate States that they will also add to the aid sum the further sum of $1,000, to be applied by the agent to the erection of two additional school-houses at suitable points in the Seminole country.

ART. XXXIX. It being alleged by the Seminole people that certain persons among them are entitled to compensation for the loss sustained by them by being dispossessed of a large number of slaves about the year one thousand eight hundred and forty-seven by an illegal order of General Thomas S. Jesup, and which were protected against the claims of the owners by order of that general, at Fort Gibson or elsewhere, for a long time, and until they were delivered up to the United States sub-agent for the Seminoles about the first of January, A. D. one thousand eight hundred and forty-nine, by virtue of an order from the President, promulgated by the Secretary of War in an order dated fifth of August, one thousand eight hundred and forty-eight, to be by the sub-agent delivered to the chiefs of the Seminoles, who were to decide the right of property in and to said slaves; and that this was done by a decree of the general council of the fifteenth day of May, one thousand eight hundred and forty-nine, by which decree all the slaves and their increase, having formerly belonged to King Payne, were decided to belong to and to be under the control of Micco Nut-cha-sa or Jem Jumper, the principal chief of the nation;

And it being also alleged by the Seminoles that the claims of the various owners of said slaves, so dispossessed of their property and deprived of the use of the same for three years or more, were made out before and filed with Marcellus Du Val, the sub-agent for the Seminoles, prior to the fifth of September, one thousand eight hundred and fifty-four;

And it being alleged by them that fifty of said negroes belonged to Car-pit-cha Micco, now deceased; seven to Chilto, forty to Nelly Factor, and thirty to Eliza Chopco, daughter of Billy Bowlegs;

And it being also alleged by the Seminoles that they could never obtain any consideration or hearing of or for these claims from the Government of the United States, not even at the time of making the treaty of the year of our Lord one thousand eight hundred and fifty-six, on account of the determination of Northern members of the Cabinet and of Congress not to admit any right of property in slaves or pay any claim on account of the seizure or detention of slaves, even to foreign governments;

And the said negroes being alleged to have been illegally seized and detained without warrant of law of law of color of right, of war, or otherwise:

Therefore, it is hereby further agreed by and on the part of the Confederate States that the said claims shall, at the earliest convenient season, be examined and investigated by the Commissioner of Indian Affairs, who shall do so under the direction of the Secretary of War, and subject to an appeal to him, and from him to the President, in such manner as shall be just and liberal under the circumstances and after such lapse of time, and shall adjudicate the same upon such principles as shall be just and equitable; and if it be upon such investigation ascertained and determined that the slaves in question were illegally detained, then the Confederate States will pay to the several or their heirs within a reasonable time such amounts of money as shall be determined to have been justly and equitably due to the said several owners for the loss of service of said slaves during such times as they shall be found to have been so detained, according to the current value of such service in the Seminole country at the time.

ART. XL. Whereas, during the war between the United States and the Seminoles, in Florida, in the years from one thousand eight hundred and forty-six to one thousand eight hundred and forty----, inclusive, the United States military authorities in Florida compelled July and Murray, two slaves of Sally Factor, now deceased, to serve as interpreters, and retained them in such service and had them in possession for the space of nearly or quite four years until both of them were killed-one by a soldier of the United States and the other by the hostile Seminoles-whereby the owner lost both and their services for four years; but her claim for compensation could never obtain a hearing or consideration at the hands of the United States, because to pay it would have been to admit the legality of property in slaves, and therefore even an examination of it was refused at the making of the treaty of the year one thousand eight hundred and fifty-six: Therefore, the Confederate States do hereby agree to pay to the heirs of the said Sally Factor, deceased, in full satisfaction for said claim, the sum of $5,000 immediately after the ratification of this treaty.

ART. XLI. It being urged, with much reason, by the authorities of the Seminole Nation that the delegates, forty in number, who went with the Superintendent of Indian Affairs to Florida in one thousand eight hundred and fifty-seven to bring about the removal of the hostile Seminoles, received but an insufficient compensation of the sum of $200 each for four months' absence from their homes; and the said Confederate States being desirous to leave no just and fair claim of the Seminoles or any of them unadjusted, or any of their friends among the red men justly dissatisfied, it is therefore hereby agreed on the part of the Confederate States that they will pay, upon the ratification of this treaty, to the principal chief, John Jumper, or Hin-I-ha Micco, for his services at that time and in consideration of his loyalty at the present time, the sum of $500 for himself and the sum of $1,250 to be equally divided by him among five of the principal men among the said delegates, and will also pay to him for each of the other thirty-four delegates the sum of $100 in full of all their claims and in view of their present loyalty and good faith.

ART. XLII. It is hereby further agreed by the Confederate States that they will pay, upon the complete ratifications of this treaty, to the principal chief of the Seminole Nation, to be equally divided by him among the commissioners appointed by the general council and who have negotiated this treaty, the sum of $500 by way of compensation for their time and services therein.

ART. XLVIII. To give the Seminoles full and entire assurance of the completeness of their title to their lands, the Confederate States hereby agree that there shall be executed and delivered to the Seminole Nation letters patent of conveyance and assurance of the same, whereby the same shall be guaranteed to them in fee simple forever, with power of disposition, in the language of Article IV of this treaty, under the great seal of the Confederate States, and signed by the President, upon parchment, so that it may not decay or its letters fade.

ART. XLIV. A general amnesty of all past offenses against the laws of the United States and of the Confederate States, committed in the Indian country before the signing of this treaty by any member of the Seminole Nation, as such membership is defined in this treaty, is hereby declared, and all such persons, if any, whether convicted or not, imprisoned or at large, charged with any such offense, shall receive from the President full and free pardon and be discharged.

ART. XLV. It is further agreed between the parties that all provisions of the treaties of the Seminole Nation with the Union States which secure a guarantee to the Seminole Nation, or individuals thereof, any rights or privileges whatever, and the place whereof is not supplies by and which are not contrary to the provisions of this treaty, and so far as the same are not obsolete or unnecessary, or repealed, annulled, changed, or modified by subsequent treatie this treaty, are and shall be continued in force as if made with the Confederate States.

ART. XLVI. This treaty shall take effect and be obligatory upon the contracting parties from the first of August, A. D. one thousand eight hundred and sixty-one, whenever it shall be ratified by the Provisional President and Congress, or the President and Senate of the Confederate

States.

In perpetual testimony whereof the said Albert Pike, as commissioner with plenary powers, on the part of the Confederate States, doth now hereunto set his hand and affix the seal of his arms, and the undersigned chiefs, headmen, and warriors of the Seminole Nation, do hereunto powers thereof, on hereunto set their hands and affix their seals.

Done in duplicate at the place and upon the day in the year first aforesaid.

[SEAL.]

ALBERT PIKE,

Commissioner of the Confederate States of America to the Indian Nations West of Arkansas.

John Jumper, principal chief of the Seminole Nation;
Pas-co-fa, town chief;
George Cloud, town chief;
Foshut-chi Tus-ti-nik-ki, town chief;
Fos-hut-chi Ha-chochi, town chief;
O-chi-si Cho-of-to-a, town chief;
Tus-ti-nuk Co-cho-top Hacho, town chief;
Su-nuk Micco, town chief;
Ta-co-sa Fic-si-sa Fic-si-co, town chief;
Hal-pa-ta, town chief;
I-ma-thla, town chief.

Signed, sealed and mutually delivered in our presence.

Wm Quesenbury, secretary to the commissioner;
E. Rector, superintendent of Indian affairs for the Western Superintendency;
Samuel M. Rutherford, agent of the Confederate States for the Seminoles;
James M. C. Smith,
Charles B. Johnson,
W. Warren Johnson,
W. L. Pike,
W. H. Faulkner.

(To the Indian names are subjoined marks.)

A CONVENTION supplementary to the treaty of friendship this day made and concluded at the council-house of the Seminole Nation, on the first day of August, A. D. one thousand eight hundred and sixty-one, between the Confederate States of America, by Albert Pike, their commissioner, with full powers, of the one part, and the Seminole Nation of red men, by their chiefs, headmen, and warriors in general council assembled, of the other part.

In addition to the said treaty, and by way of separate convention and agreement, it is hereby agreed between the said parties that in consideration of the common interests of the Confederate States and the Seminole Nation, and of the protection and rights secured and guaranteed to the latter by said treaty, the said Seminole Nation will raise and furnish, and the Confederate States will receive into their service, not less than two nor more than five companies of mounted men, to serve in the armies of the Confederate States for twelve months. Each company shall be composed of not less than 64 nor more than 100 men in all. The company officers shall be elected by he members of the company, and the major commanding by a majority of the votes of all the members of the battalion. The men shall be armed by the Confederate States, receive the same pay and allowances as other mounted troops in the service, and not be moved beyond the limits of the Indian country west of Arkansas, without their consent.

In testimony whereof the said Albert Pike, as such commissioner of the Confederate States, doth hereunto set his hand and affix the seal of his arms, and Hin-I-ha Micco or John Jumper, principal chief of the Seminole Nation, Pas-co-fa, George Cloud, Fos-hut-chi Tus-ti-nuk-ki, Ta-co-sa Fic-si-co, Hal-pa-ta, I-ma-thla, Fos-hut-chi Ha-chochi, Sa-to-a Hacho, O-chi-si Cho-of-to-a, Cho-of-top Hacho, Su-nuk plenary powers thereof, on the part of the Seminole Nation, do hereby unto set their hands and affix their seals.

Done in duplicate at the Seminole Agency, in the Seminole Nation, do hereby set their hands and affix their seals.

Done in duplicate at the Seminole Agency, in the Seminole Nation, on the second day of August, in the year first aforesaid.

[SEAL.] ALBERT PIKE,

Commissioner of the Confederate States of America to the Indian Nations West of Arkansas.

John Jumper, principal chief of the Seminole Nation;
Pas-co-fa, town chief;
George Cloud, town chief;
Fos-hut-chi Tus-ti-nuk-ki, town chief;
Fos-hut-chi Ha-cho-chi, town chief;
O-chi-si Cho-of-to-a, town chief;

Tus-ti-nuk Co-cho-co-ni, town chief;
Sa-to-a Hacho, town chief;
Cho-of-top Hacho, town chief;
Su-nuk Micco, town chief;
Ta-co-sa Fic-si-co, town chief;
Hal-pa-ta, town chief;
I-ma-thla, town chief.

Signed, sealed, and mutually delivered in our presence.

Wm. Quesenbury, secretary to the commissioner;
E. Rector, superintendent of Indian affairs for the Western Superintendency;
Samuel M. Rutherford, agent of the Confederate States for the Seminoles;
James M. C. Smith, special interpreter;
Charles B. Johnson,
W. Warren Johnson,
W. L. Pike,
W. H. Faulkn er.

(To the Indian names are subjoined marks.)

RATIFICATION.

Resolved (two-thirds of the Congress concurring), That the Congress of the Confederate States of America do advise and consent to the ratification of the articles of a treaty made by Albert Pike, commissioner of the Confederate States to the Indian nations west of Arkansas, in behalf of the Confederate States, of the one part, and by the Seminole Nation of Indians, by its chiefs, headmen, and warriors in general council assembled, of the part, concluded at the Seminole council-house, in the Seminole Nation, on the first day of August, A. D. one thousand eight hundred and sixty-one, with the following amendments:

I. Add at the end of Article XXX the following words, "and the Confederate States will request the several States of the Confederacy to adopt and enact the provisions of this article in respect to suits and proceedings in their respective courts. "

II. Strike out from Article XXXVII the following words, "the same rights and privileges as may be enjoyed by the Delegates from any Territory of the Confederate States to the said House of Representatives," and insert in lieu thereof the following words, "a seat in the Hall of the House of Representatives, to propose and introduce measures for the benefit of said nations and to be heard in regard thereto and on other questions in which either of said nations is particularly interested, with such other rights and privileges as may be determined by the House of Representatives. "

III. Strike out from Article XXXVIII the following words, "or in a State court," and insert in lieu thereof the following words," or in a State court," and insert in lieu thereof the following words, "or in a State court, subject to the laws of the State. "

Resolved further (two-thirds of the Congress concurring), That the Congress do also advise and consent to the ratifications of the convention, supplementary to the aforesaid treaty with the Seminoles, made by the same parties of each part and concluded at the same time and place with the same.

NOTE. -The foregoing treaty, together with the amendments, was duly ratified by the Seminole Nation.

OFFICIAL RECORDS: Series 4, vol 1, Part 1
Pages 636 - 646
Confederate States of America - Great Osage

ARTICLES OF A CONVENTION entered into and concluded at Park Hill, in the Cherokee Nation, on the second day of October, A. D. one thousand eight hundred and sixty-one, between the Confederate States of America, by Albert Pike, their commissioner, with full powers, appointed by the President, by virtue of an act of the Congress in that behalf, of the one part, and the Great Osage tribe of Indians, by its chiefs and headmen, who have signed these articles, of the other part.

ARTICLE I. The Great Osage tribe of Indians and all the persons thereof do hereby place themselves under the laws and protection of the Confederate States of America, in peace and war, forever, and agree to be true and loyal to them under all circumstances.

ART. II. The Confederate States of America do hereby promise and firmly engage themselves to be, during all time, the friends and protectors of the Great Osage tribe of Indians, and to defend and secure them in the enjoyment of all their rights; and that they will not allow them henceforward to be in any wise troubled or molested by any power or people, State or person whatever.

ART. III. The Confederate States of America do hereby assure and guarantee to the Great and Little Osage tribes of Indians the exclusive and undisturbed possession, use, and occupancy during all time, as long as grass shall grow and water run, of the country heretofore secured to them by treaty with the United States of America, and which is described in the treaty of the second day of June, A. D. one thousand eight hundred and twenty-five, as being thus bounded, that is to say: Beginning at a point dues east of White Hair's village, and twenty-five miles west of the western boundary-line of the State of Missouri, fronting on a north and south line, so as to leave ten miles north and forty miles south of the point of said beginning, and extending west, with the width of fifty miles, to the western boundary of the lands ceded and relinquished by said nations by that treaty, which lands shall not be sold or ceded by the said tribes, nor shall any part thereof, to any nation or people, except to the Confederate States, or to any individuals whatever; and the same shall vest in the Confederate States in case the said tribes become extinct or abandon the same.

ART. IV. The right is hereby reserved to the Confederate States to select, in any unoccupied part of said country, a tract of two sections of land, as a reserve and site for an agency for the said tribes, which shall revert to the said tribes whenever it shall cease to be occupied for an agency.

ART. V. The Confederate States shall have the right to establish in the said country such forts and military posts as they may deem necessary, and shall have the right to select for each such fort or post a tract of land one mile square, on which such fort or post shall be established: Provided, That if any person or persons have any improvements on any tract so selected, the value of such improvements shall be paid by the Government to the owner thereof.

ART. VI. No person whatever shall be permitted to settle or reside upon the agency reserve when it shall have been selected, except by the permission of the agent; nor upon any reserve for a fort or military post, except by the permission of the commanding officer; and every such reserve, for the agency or the forts or military posts, shall be within the sole and exclusive jurisdiction of the Confederate States.

ART. VII. The Confederate States shall forever have the right of free navigation of all navigable streams and water-courses within or running through the country hereby assured and guaranteed to said tribes.

ART. VIII. The Confederate States hereby guarantee that the country hereby secured to said Great and Little Osage tribes shall never be included within the bounds of any State or Territory, nor shall any of the laws of any State or Territory every be extended over or put in force within any part of the said country; and the President of the Confederate States will cause the said tribes to be protected against all molestation or disturbance at the hands of any other tribe or nation of Indians, or of any other person whatever; and he shall have the same care and superintendence over them as was heretofore had by the President of the United States.

ART. IX. The members of the said Great and Little Osage tribes of Indians shall have the right henceforward of hunting and killing game in all the unoccupied country west of the possessions of the Cherokees, Seminoles, Choctaws, and Chickasaws, without molestation from any quarters, being, while so engaged therein, under the protection of the Confederate States

ART. X. There shall be perpetual peace and brotherhood between the Great and Little Osage tribes of Indians and the Cherokees, Musko-kis, Seminoles, Choctaws, and Chickasaws, and the bands of Wichitas, Cado-Ha-da-chaos, Hue-cos, Ta-hua-ca-ros, A-na-dagh-cos, Ton-ca-wes, Ki-chais, Ai-o-nais, Shawnees, and Delawares living in the country leased from the Choctaws and Chickasaws, and the Pen-e-tegh-ca, No-co-ni, Ta-ne-I-weh, Ya-pa-rih-ca, and Co-cho-tih-ca bands of the Ne-um or Comanches;

and every injury or act of hostility which either has heretofore sustained or met with at the hands of the other shall be forgiven and forgotten.

ART. XI. The Great and Little Osage tribes of Indians and the said several other nations, tribes, and bands shall henceforth be good neighbors to each others, and there shall be a free and friendly intercourse among them. And it is hereby agreed by the said Great Osage tribe, as has already been agreed by all the others except the Little Osage tribe, that the horses, cattle, and other stock and property of each nation, tribe, or band, and of every person of each, is his or its own; and that no person belonging to the Great Osage tribe shall, or will hereafter, kill, take away, or injure any such property of another tribe or band, or of any member of any other tribe or band, or in any other way do them any harm

ART. XII. Especially there shall be perpetual peace and friendship between said Great Osage tribe and the Cherokees, Mus-ko-kis, Seminoles, Choctaws, and Chickasaws, and the chiefs and headmen of the said Great Osage tribe shall do all in their power to take and restore any negroes, horses, or other property stolen from white men, or from persons belonging to either of said five nations, and to catch and give up any person among them who may kill or steal, or do any other evil act.

ART. XIII. In order that the friendship now established between the said Great Osage tribe of Indians and the Confederate States and the other Indian nations, tribes, and bands aforesaid, may not be interrupted by the misconduct of individuals, or bands of individuals, it is hereby agreed that for injuries done by individuals, no private revenge or retaliation shall taken place, but instead thereof complaint shall be made by the said Great Osage tribe of Indians, when any individual thereof is injured, to the agent of the Confederate States for the Osages and other tribes, who shall investigate the complaint, and, if he finds it well founded, shall report the same to the superintendent, who will cause the wrong to be redressed, and the person or persons doing the wrong to be arrested, whether he be a white man or an Indian; and he or they shall be tried for the same agreeably to the laws of the Confederate States or of the State or Territory against which he may have offended, and be punished in the same manner and with the same severity as if the injury had been done to a white man. And it is also agreed that if any member of the Great Osage tribe shall do any injury to the person or property of any white man or of a member of any other Indian nation or tribe under the protection of the Confederate States, the offender shall be given up to the agent, upon complaint made to him and on his demand, the wrong shall be redressed by him, and the offender be tried for the offense agreeably to the laws of the Confederate States, or of the State, Territory, or nation against which he may have offended: Provided, That he shall be punished in nor with any great severity than a citizen of the Confederate

States, or of such State, Territory, or nation would be, if he had committed the same offense.

ART. XIV. It is hereby further agreed that the chiefs of the Great Osage tribe shall use every exertion in their power to recover any horses or other property that may be stolen from any citizen of the Confederate States or from any member of any other Indian tribe under the protection of the Confederate States by any person or persons whatever, and found within the limits of their country; and the property so recovered shall be forthwith delivered to the owner or to the agent to be restored to him. If in any case the right to the property claimed is contested by the person in possession, the agent shall summarily investigate the case, and upon hearing the testimony of witnesses, shall decide the right to the property, and order it to be retained or delivered up accordingly. Either party may appeal from his decision to the superintendent, whose decision shall be final in all cases, the property, in the meantime, remaining in the custody of the agent. If in any case the exertions of the chiefs to cause the restoration of stolen property prove ineffectual, and the agent is satisfied from the testimony that it was actually stolen, or received with knowledge of its being stolen, by any person belonging to the Great Osage tribe, he shall so report to the superintendent, with a copy of the testimony; which shall for that purpose be always reduced to writing; and the superintendent shall, if satisfied from the testimony, deduct from the annuity of the tribe a sum equal to the value of the property stolen.

ART. XV. The Confederate States hereby guarantee full and fair payment to the owner of the actual and full value of all horse and other property stolen from any person or persons belonging to the Great Osage tribe, by any citizen of the Confederate States, or by any Indian of any other under their protection, in case the same control be recovered and restored, and upon sufficient proof being made before the superintendent or any agent of the Confederate States for any of such nations or tribes that such property was actually stolen by a citizen or citizens of the Confederate States, or by an Indian or Indians of any nation or tribe under their protection.

ART. XVI. An agent for the Great and Little Osage tribes, the Quapaws, Senecas, and Senecas and Shawnees shall be appointed by the President, and an interpreter for the Great and Little tribes of Osages, for their protection and that their complaints may be heard by and their wants made known to the President. The agent shall reside continually in the country of one or the other of said tribes or bands, and the interpreter shall reside among either the Great or Little Osage; and neither of them shall ever be absent from their posts, except by the permission of the superintendent.

ART. XVII. None of the braves of the Great Osage tribe shall go upon the warpath, against any enemy whatever, except with the consent of the agent, or unless it be to pursue hostile bands of white men or Indians entering their country and committing murder, robbery, or other outrage when immediate pursuit is necessary; nor shall hold any talks or councils with any white men or Indians without his knowledge and consent. And they especially agree to attend no councils or talks in the country of any people, or with the officers or agents of any people, with whom the Confederate States are at war; and in case they do so, all the benefits secured to them by this treaty shall immediately and forever cease.

ART. XVIII. The Confederate States will not permit any improper persons to reside or be in the Great or Little Osage country, but only such persons as are employed by them, their officers or agents, and traders licensed by them, who shall sell to the Osages and buy from them, at fair prices, under such regulations as the President shall make from time to time.

ART. XIX. To steal a horse or any other article of property from a white man or an Indian not at war with the Confederate States shall always be regarded as disgraceful, and the chiefs of the Osages will discountenance and prevent it by every means in their power. For if they should not there never could be peace.

ART. XX. The Confederate States with the Osage to settle upon and cultivate their land, build houses, and dig wells, and by industry become enabled to support themselves; and in order to encourage and assist them, and because of the chattels and articles promised to the Great Osage and Little Osage by the treaty of the eleventh day of January, A. D. one thousand eight hundred and thirty-nine, a considerable portion never was furnished them, to wit, 1,200 hogs, 700 plows, 700 sets of horse gear, 800 axes, and 800 hoes, the Confederate States agree to give them 1,200 breeding hogs, 50 yoke of oxen with ox wagons, horse gear, plows, yokes, axes, spades and hoes, and other useful implements, to the value of $15,000, at the first cost in the place in the Confederate States where the same shall be purchased; of which stock 900 hogs, 40 yoke of oxen, and such implements as aforesaid to the value of $11,000 shall be given to the Great Osages, and the residue to the Little Osages if they unite in this treaty. But such stock and implements shall only be issued from time to time, and to such persons as shall be reported by the agent to the superintendent to be engaged or ready to engage in farming, and who will take care of and profitably use the same, and be benefitted by them, and not sell, waste, or destroy the same; upon which reports and so only, the superintendent shall cause the issue to such persons only of so much of said stock and so many of said implements as he would be entitled to upon a distribution of all per capita; and it shall be the duty of the chiefs and of the agent to see that what is so issued is not destroyed or wasted; and if waste or destruction can in no otherwise be prevented, to reclaim the same and issue them elsewhere.

ART. XXI. The Confederate States also agree to build and put in running order a grist and saw mill, at some suitable point in Osage country, and to employ a miller for each mill for the term of nine years from the date of this treaty, and an assistant to each for the same time; the latter to be selected from the Osage Nation, and each of them to receive $225 per annum as his compensation; and each miller shall be furnished with a dwelling-house; this article being agreed to by the Confederate States because the mill erected by the United States, under the treaty of the year one thousand eight hundred and thirty-nine, was burned down after being in operation only six years.

ART. XXII. The Confederate States also agree that the agent for the Osages shall be authorized to employ, for and during the term of ten years from the day of the signing of this treaty, ten agricultural and other laborers, to assist the Great and Little Osages in opening and preparing for cultivation their fields, and building their houses, who shall be, at all times, under the control and direction of the agent.

ART. XXIII. For the same purpose, the Confederate States will also provide, furnish, and support for and during the term of twenty years from the date of this treaty, for the Great Osages upon and after the ratification of this treaty, and for the Little Osages when they shall become parties to this treaty, to each a blacksmith and an assistant, who shall be one of their own people, and for each, annually, a suffi- cient supply of coal, with 500 pounds of iron and 60 pounds of steel to the blacksmith for the Great Osages, and 250 pounds of iron and 25 pounds of steel to the blacksmith for the Little Osages, that their farming utensils, tools, and arms may be seasonably repaired; and also one wagon-maker for each; and will furnish each smith and wagon-maker with the necessary tools and with a shop and the wagon-maker with the necessary wood and other materials from time to time.

ART. XXIV. The Confederate States will also furnish, at proper places, the Great and Little Osages with such medicines as may be necessary, and will employ a physician for each, who shall reside among them during the pleasure of the President.

ART. XXV. The Confederate States also agree to furnish each warrior of said Great Osage tribe, who has not a gun, with a good rifle and a supply of powder and lead and percussion-caps or flints as soon as it may be found practicable. The arms and ammunition are never to be given away, sold, or exchanged, and the chiefs will punish any one who so disposes of either; and the Confederate States will severely punish any trader or other white man who may purchase either from them.

ART. XXVI. No State or Territory shall ever pass laws for the government of the Osage people; and except so far as the laws of the

Confederate States are in force in their country, they shall be left free to govern themselves, and to punish offenses committed by one of themselves against the person or property of another: Provided, That if one of them kills another without good cause or justification, he shall suffer death, but only by the sentence of the chiefs, and after a fair trial, all private revenge being strictly forbidden.

ART. XXVII. Every white man who marries a woman of the Osages, and resides in the Osage country, shall be deemed and taken, even after the death of his wife, to be an Osage and a member of the tribe in which he resides, so far as to be subject to the laws of the tribe in respect to all offenses committed in its country against the person or property of another member of the tribe, and as not to be considered a white man committing such offenses against the person or property of an Indian, within the meaning of the acts of the Congress of the Confederate States. And all negroes and mulattoes, bond or free, committing any such offense in said country shall, in like manner, be subject to the laws of the tribe.

ART. XXVIII. The Confederate States shall have the right to establish, open, and maintain such military and other roads through any part of the Osage country as the President may deem necessary, without making any compensation for the right of way, or for the land, timber, or stone used in constructing the same; but if any other property of the tribe, or any other property or the improvements of an individual, be used or injured therein, just and adequate compensation shall be made.

ART. XXIX. The Confederate States may grant the right of way for any railroad through any part of the said country; but the company to which any such right may be granted shall pay the tribe therefor such sum as shall, in the opinion of the President, be its fair value; and shall also pay to individuals all damages done by the building of said road to their improvements or other property to such amount in each case as commissioners appointed by the President shall determine.

ART. XXX. The agent of the Confederate States for the Osages and other bands shall prevent all intrusions by hunters and others upon the lands of the Osages, and permit no white men or other Indians to settle thereon, and shall remove all such persons, calling, if necessary, upon the military power for aid; and the commanders of military posts in that country shall be required to afford him such aid upon his requisition.

ART. XXXI. If any trader or other person should purchase from any Osage any of the cattle or other chattels or articles given him by the Confederate States, he shall be severely punished.

ART. XXXII. The Great and Little Osages may allow persons of any other tribe of Indians to settle among them, and may receive from them, for their own benefit, compensation for such lands as they may sell or assign to such persons.

ART. XXXIII. No citizen or inhabitant of the Confederate States or member of any friendly nation or tribe of Indians shall pasture stock on the lands of the Osages; but all such persons shall have full liberty, at all times, and whether for business or pleasure, peaceably to travel in their country, on the roads or elsewhere, to drive their stock through the same, and to halt such reasonable time on the way as may be necessary to recruit their stock, such delay being in good faith for the purpose and for no other.

ART. XXXIV. Any person duly charged with a criminal offense against the laws of the Confederate States, or of any State or Territory, or of any Indian nation or tribe under the protection of the Confederate States, escaping into the Osage country, shall be promptly taken and delivered up by the chiefs of the Osages on the demand of the proper authority of the Confederate States, or of the State, Territory, nation, or tribe within those jurisdiction the offense shall be alleged to have been committed.

ART. XXXV. In addition to the laws of the Confederate States expressly applying to the Indian country, so much of their laws as provides for the punishment of crimes amounting to felony at common law or by statute against them, or treaties, and over which the courts of the Confederate States have jurisdiction including the counterfeiting the coin of the United States or of the Confederate States, or any other current coin, or the securities of the Confederate States, or the uttering of such counterfeit coin or securities; and so much of said laws as provides for punishing violations of the neutrality laws, and resistance to the process of the Confederate States; and all the acts of the Provisional Congress providing for the common defense and welfare, so far as the same are not locally inapplicable; and the laws providing for the capture and delivery of fugitive slave shall be in force in the Osage country; and the district court for the Chalahki district, when established, shall have exclusive jurisdiction to try, condemn, and punish offenders against those laws, to adjudge and pronounce sentence, and cause execution thereof to be done.

ART. XXXVI. Whenever any person who is a member of the Great or Little Osage tribe shall be indicted for any offense in any court of the Confederate States, or in a State court, he shall be entitled as of common right to subpoena, and, if necessary, to compulsory process for all such witness in his behalf as his counsel may think material for his defense; and the costs of process for such witnesses, and of the service thereof, and fees and mileage of such witnesses shall be paid by the Confederate States; and whenever the accused is not able to employ counsel the court shall assign him one experiences counsel for his defense, who shall bee paid by the Confederate states a reason- able compensation for this services, to be fixed by the court and paid upon the certificate of the judge.

ART. XXXVII. It is hereby declared and agreed that the institution of slavery in the said Great and Little Osage tribes is legal, and has existed from time immemorial; that slaves are personal property; that the title to slaves and other property having its origin in the said tribes is to be determined by the laws and customs thereof; and that the slaves and personal property of every person domiciled in the country of the said tribes shall pass and be distributed at his or her death in accordance with the laws, usages, and customs of the said tribes, which may be proved by oral evidence, and shall everywhere be held valid and binding within the scope of their operations. And if any slaves escape from any of said tribes, the laws of the Confederate States for the capture and delivery of fugitive slave shall apply to such cases, whether they escape and delivery of fugitive slaves shall apply to such cases, whether they escape into a State or Territory or into any Indian nation or tribe under the protection of the Confederate States; the obligation upon each such State, Territory, nation, or tribe to deliver up the same being in every case as complete as if they had escaped from a State, and the mode of procedure the same.

ART. XXXVIII. The Great Osage tribe of Indians hereby makes itself a party to the existing war between the Confederate States and the United States of America as the ally and ward of the former; and, in consideration of the protection guaranteed by this treaty and of their common interests, hereby agrees to raise and furnish, whenever they shall be called on, a force of 500 men for the service of the Confederate States, or any less number, who shall receive the same pay and allowances as other troops of the same calls in that service, and remain in the service as long as the President shall require; a general or other commanding officer of the Confederate States in the Indian country, who shall receive such compensation as such officer shall fix.

ART. XXXIX. In consideration of the loyalty of the Great Osage tribe and of their readiness to place themselves under the protection of the Confederate States, and of their poverty, and of the great losses in horses and other property sustained by them at the hands of lawless persons for many years, the Confederate States do hereby agree to expend for the benefit of the Great and Little Osage tribes, for the full term of twenty years from the date of this treaty, the sum of $15,000 annually, of which sum $5,000 per annum shall be added to the interest on the school fund of the nation, hereinafter provided for, and $10,000 shall be divided fairly in each year, after the Little Osage tribe shall have united in this convention, between the two tribes in proportion to the number of souls in each; and the said sum of $10,000 shall be divided fairly in each year, after the Little Osage tribe shall have united in this convention, between the two tribes in proportion to the number of souls in each; and the said sum of $10,000 shall, in each year, be applied by the superintendent to the purchase of such articles of clothing, household utensils, blankets, and other articles as shall tend to the comfort of the Osages and encourage them in their endeavors to improve, and which articles the agent shall distribute among them in the same manner and nearly as possible as money would be distributed per capita: Provided, That in the distribution any person may be excluded by him if reported by the chiefs to be worthless, idle, or dissolute, or a bad and mischievous person, and that he may do the same upon his own knowledge, taking care, as far as may, be that only the good and worthy shall be the recipients of the bounty of the Government of the Confederate States.

ART. XL. It is hereby agreed and ascertained that by the sixth article of the treaty with the Great Osage, of the second day of June, A. D. one thousand eight hundred and twenty-five, it was agreed that from the lands ceded and relinquished by the Osages by that treaty a reservation should be made of fifty-four tracts of land of a mile square each, to be laid off under the direction of the President of the United States and sold for the purpose of raising a fund to be applied to the support of schools for the education of the Osage children, in such manner as the President might deem advisable for the attainment of that end; that fifty-four sections of land were accordingly selected and afterward sold, and the proceeds of the same amounted to $31,724. 02, which sum remains invested as follows, that is to say:

In 6 per cent. stock of the State of Missouri, $7,000;
In United States 6 per cent. loan of 1842, $24,679. 56;
And in United States 6 per cent. loan of 1847, $44. 46;

And as it will be useless for the Osages hereafter to expect anything from the justice of the United States, and the Confederate States do not desire that they should hereafter look to that quarter for any moneys, it is therefore further hereby agreed that the Confederate States will hereafter pay, annually, on the first day of January in each year, perpetually, commencing with the year one thousand eight hundred and sixty-two, for the benefit of the Great and Little Osage tribes, the sum of $1,903. 44, being the annual interest on said sums of money so as aforesaid in U. S. stocks and stocks of the State of Missouri, at the rate of 6 per cent. per annum, and will look to the State of Missouri for the payment of the principal and interest of said sum of $7,000, as invested in stocks of that State, to which sum shall be annually added, on the same day, commencing with the same year, the sum of $5,000, part of the annuity provided for in the thirty-ninth article of this treaty, and the whole shall be applied by the agent to the support and maintenance of the Osage manual-labor school, now in operation at the mission on the Neosho River, as the said interest has therefore been applied.

ART. XLI. A tract of land of the quantity of two sections, or two tracts of one section each, to be selected by the agent of the Confederate States for the Osages and other tribes, and in which or one of which the present site of the mission and its buildings is to be included, is hereby forever dedicated to the use of the Osage manual-labor school, to be under the exclusive control of those who have charge of that institution, and for its exclusive use; and not to be sold or disposed of, or applied to any other use or purpose whatsoever.

ART. XLII. All just claims and demands against the United States, of the Great Osage tribe, or of any individual or individuals thereof, not herein specified, arising or due under former treaties with the United States, are hereby assumed, and shall, after the restoration of peace, be investigated by the President, and, so far as they are found to be just, shall be paid in full by the Confederate States; and all provisions of the several treaties with the United States, made by the Osages, under which any rights or privileges were secured or guaranteed to the Great Osage tribe, or to any individual or individuals of the same, and the place whereof is not supplied by any provision of this treaty, and the same not being obsolete or no longer necessary, and so far as they are not annulled, repealed, changed, or modified by subsequent treaties or statutes, or are not so by this treaty, are hereby continued in force as if the same had been made with the Confederate States.

ART. XLIII. A general amnesty of all past offenses against the laws of the United States or of the Confederate States, committed before the signing of this treaty, by any member of the Great Osage tribe, as such membership is defined by this treaty, is hereby declared; and all such persons, if any, charged with any such offense shall receive from the President full and free pardon, and if imprisoned or held to bail, before or after conviction, shall be discharged.

ART. XLIV. The Confederate States of America hereby tender to the Little Osage tribe the same protection and guaranties as are hereby extended and given to the Great Osage tribe, and the other benefits offered them specifically by this treaty; and if the said Little Osage tribe shall give no aid to the Confederate States, and shall, within one year from the day of the signing of this treaty and accept and agree to all the terms and conditions of the same, then it shall, to all intents and purposes, be regarded as having been made with them originally, and they be deemed and taken to be parties thereto, as if they were now to sign the same.

ART. XLV. This convention shall be obligatory on the Great Osage tribe of Indians from the day of its date, and on the Confederate States from and after its ratification by the Senate or Provisional Congress.

In perpetual testimony whereof the said Albert Pike, as commissioner with plenary powers, on the part of the Confederate States, doth now hereunto set his hand and affix the seal of this arms; and the undersigned, chiefs and headmen of the Great Osage tribe of Indians, do hereunto set their hands and affix their seals.

This done in duplicate at the place and upon the day in the month and year first aforesaid.

[SEAL.]

ALBERT PIKE,

Commissioner of the Confederate States of the Indian Nations West of Arkansas.

Ka-hi-ke-tung-ka, chief of Clermont's band Great Osages
Pa-hiu-ska, chief of White Hair's band
Chi-sho-hung-ka, chief of Big Hill band
Shon-tas-sap-pe, or Black Dog, chief of Black Dog's band
Sha-pe-shing-ka, or Beaver, second chief of White Hair's band
Wash-ka-che, second chief of Clermont's band
Ta-wan-che-he, or Tall Chief, second chief of Big Hill band
Wa-ho Pe-eh, second chief of Black Dog's band
Wa-ta-en-ka, or Dry Feather, councilor of Clermont's band
Kan-se-ka-hri, councilor of Big Hill band
Ka-hi-ke Wa-ta-en-ka,
Ka-hi-ke Shing-ka,
Chi-sho-wa-ta-eng-ka,
E-e-shi-ka-hri,
Sho-meh-kas-si,
Ni-ih-ka-ki-pa-na,
Sa-peh-ky-yeh,
Wah-kan-ta-chi-leh,
Wa-sha-shi Wa-sha-on-chi,
O-shang-ke-tung-ka,
Wa-a-han-na,
Ha-ka-she,
Wa-no-pah-she,
Shing-kaka-hu-ke,
Wa-che-wa-he,

Na-hin-ta-pi,
Ah-kih-ta-tung-ka,
Ni-ka-ka-hri,
Sha-a Ke-to-pa,
To-ti-na-he,
O-lo-ing Ka-shi,
Ka-wa-si,
Wa-hu-nomp-I,
Wa-ak-an-chi-le,
? -ki-pa-hra,
Tre-nom-pa-shi,
A-ki-ki-sha,
Wa-to-ki-ka,
I-ka-sha-pe,
A-no-hra-pi,
Min-che-eh-na,
Wa-che-na-shiu,
Ma-hing-ka-he,
Tan-was-shing-ka,
Miink-shes-ka,
To-ta-na-she,
Ka-wa-ka-hii-ki,
Mu-ka-ke-shing-ka,
Gesso Choutau,
Augustus Captain,
Louis P. Chouteau,
Che-e-se-tung-ka,
Wa-ta-sho-we

Signed, sealed, and delivered in the presence of us.

Wm. Quesenbury, secretary to the commissioner;
E. Rector, Superintendent of Indian Affairs, Confederate States,
Andrew J. Dorn, agent for Osages and other tribes, Confederate States
Louis P. Chouteau, C. S. interpreter for Osages
John Drew,
George M. Murrell,
J. W. Washbourne,
W. Warren Johnson.

(To the Indian names are subjoined marks.)

RATIFICATION.

Resolved (two-thirds of the Congress concurring), That the Congress of the Confederate States of America do advise and consent to the ratification of the articles of a convention made by Albert Pike, commissioner of the Confederate States to the Indian nations west of Arkansas, in behalf of the Confederate States, of the one part, and the Great Osage tribe of Indians, by its chiefs and headmen, who signed the same articles, of the other part, concluded at Park Hill, in the Cherokee Nation, on the second day of October, A. D. one thousand eight hundred and sixty-one, with the following amendment:

In Article XXXVI, at the end of the words "or in a State court," insert the following words, 'subject to the laws of the State. "

OFFICIAL RECORDS: Series 4, vol 1, Part 1
Pages 659-666
Confederate States of America - Quapaw

ARTICLES OF A CONVENTION, entered into and concluded at Park Hill, in the Cherokee Nation, on the fourth day of October, A. D. one thousand eighth hundred and sixty-one, between the Confederate States of America, by Albert Pike, their commissaries, with full powers, appointed by the President, by virtue of an act of the Congress in that behalf, of the one part, and the Quapaw tribe of Indians, by its chiefs and warriors, who have signed these articles, of the other part.

ARTICLE I. The Quapaw tribe of Indians, and all the persons thereof, do hereby place themselves under the laws and protection of the Confederate States of America, in peace and in war, forever and agree to be true and loyal to them under all circumstances.

ART. II. The Confederate States of America do hereby promise and firmly engage themselves to be, during all time, the friends and protectors of the Quapaw tribe of Indians, and to defend and secure them in the enjoyment of all their rights; and that they will not allow them henceforward to be in any wise troubled or molested by any power or people, State, or person whatever.

ART. III. The Confederate States of America do hereby assure and guarantee to the Quapaw tribe of Indians the exclusive and undisputed possession, use, and occupancy, during all time, as long as grass shall grow and water run, of the country heretofore secured to them by treaty with the United States of America, and which is described in the treaty of the thirteenth day of May, A. D. one thousand eight hundred and thirty-three, as follows, that is to say: "One hundred and fifty sections of and, west of the State of Missouri, and between the lands of the Senecas and Shawnees, not heretofore assigned to any other tribe of Indians; " and as the same was afterward selected and assigned to said Quapaw tribe, and is now held and occupied by them, which lands shall not be sold or ceded by said tribe, nor shall any part thereof, to any nation or people, expect to the Confederate States, nor to any individuals whatever, except as hereinafter provided, and the same shall vest in the Confederate States in case the said tribe becomes extinct or abandons the same.

ART. IV. The right is hereby reserved to the Confederate States to select in any unoccupied part of said country, if they shall desire to do so, a tact of land one mile square, as a reserve and site for an agency for the said, tribe, which shall revert to the said tribe, with all the buildings thereon, whenever it shall cease to be occupied for an agency.

ART. V. The Confederate States shall have the right to establish in the said country such forts and military posts an they may deem necessary, and shall have the right to select for each such fort or post a tract of land one mile square, on which such fort or post shall be established: Provided, That if any person have any improvements on any tract so selected, the value of such improvements shall be paid by the Government to the owner thereof.

ART. VI. No person whatever shall be permitted to settle or reside upon the agency reserve, when it shall have been selected, expect by permission of the agent; nor upon any reserve for a fort or military post, expect by the permission of the commanding officer; and every such reserve for forts or military posts shall be within the sole and exclusive jurisdiction of the Confederate States.

ART. VII. The Confederate States hereby agree that the country hereby secured to the said tribe shall never be included within the bounds of any State or Territory, nor shall of any State of Territory ever be extended over, or put in force within, any part of the said country; and the President of the Confederate States will cause the said tribe to be protected against all molestation or disturbance at the hands of any other tribe or nation of Indians, or of any other person or persons whatever; and shall have the same care and superintendence over them as was heretofore had by the President of the United States.

ART. VIII. The members of the said Quapaw tribe of Indians shall have the right henceforward of hunting and killing game in all the unoccupied country west of the possessions of the Cherokees, Seminoles, Choctaws, and Chickasaws, without molestation from any quarter, being while so engaged therein, under the protection of the Confederate States.

ART. IX. There shall be perpetual peace and brotherhood between the Quapaw tribe of Indians and the Osages, Senecas, Senecas and Shawnees, Mus-ko-kis, Seminoles, Choctaws, and Chickasaws, and the Pen-e-tegh-ca, No-co-ni, Ta-ne-I-weh, Ya-pa-rih-ca, and Co-cho-tih-ca bands of the Ne-um or Comanches; and every injury or act of hostility which either has heretofore sustained or met with at the hands of the other shall be forgiven and forgotten.

ART. X. The Quapaw tribe of Indians and the said several other nations, tribes, and bands shall henceforth be good neighbors to each other, and there shall be a force and friendly intercourse among them. And it is hereby agreed by the said Quapaw tribe, as has already been agreed by all the others, that the horses, and other stock and property of each nation, tribe, or hand, and of every person of each, is his or its own; and that no person belonging to the Quapaw tribe shall or will hereafter kill, take away, or injure any such property of another tribe or hand, or of any member of any other tribe or band, or in any other way do them any harm.

ART. XI. Especially there shall be perpetual peace and friendship between said Quapaw tribe and the Osage, Senecas, Senecas and Shawnees, Cherokees, Mus-ko-kis, Seminoles, Choctaws, and Chickasaws; and the chiefs and headman of the said Quapaw tribe shall do all in their power to take and restore any negroes, horses, or other property stolen from white men or from persons belonging to either of said nations and tribes, and to catch and give up any persons among them who may kill or steal or do may other evil act.

Art. XII. In order that the friendship now established between the said Quapaw tribe of Indians and the Confederate States and the other Indian nations, tribes, and bands aforesaid may not be interrupted by the misconduct of individuals or bands of individuals, it is hereby agreed that for injures done by individuals no private revenge or retaliation shall take place, but instead thereof complaint shall be made by the said Quapaw tribe of Indians, when any individual thereof is injured, to the agent of the Confederate States for the Osages and other tribes, who shall investigate the compliant, and if he finds it well founded shall report the same to the superintendent, who shall cause the wrong to be redressed and the person doing [it] to be arrested, whether he be a white man of an Indian; and he or they shall be tried for the same agreeably to the laws of the Confederate States or of the State or Territory against which he may have offended, and be punished in the same manner and with the same severity as if the injury had been done to a white man. And it is also agreed that if any member of the Quapaw tribe shall do any injury to the person or properly of any white man, or of a member of any other nation or tribe under the protection of the Confederate States, the offender shall be given up to the agent upon compliant made to him, and on his demand the wrong shall be redressed by him, and the offered be tried for the offense agreeably to the laws of the Confederate States, or of the State, Territory, or nation against which he may [have] offended: Provided, That he shall be punishenner nor with any greater severity than a citizen of the Confederate States or of such State, Territory, or nation would be if he had committed the same offense.

ART. XIII. It is hereby further agreed that the chiefs of the Quapaw tribe shall use every exertion in their power to recover any horses or other property that may be stolen from any citizen of the Confederate States, or from any member of any other Indian nation or tribe under the protection of the Confederate States, by any person or persons whatever, and found within the limits of their country; and the property so recovered shall be forthwith delivered to the owner or to the agent to be restored to him. If any case the right to the property claimed is contested by the person in possession, the agent shall summarily investigate the case, and, upon hearing the testimony of witness, shall decide the right to the property, and order it to be detained or delivered up accordingly. Either party may appeal from his decision to the superintendent, whose decision shall be final in all cases, the property in the meantime remaining in the custody of the agent. If any case the exertions of the chiefs to cause the restoration of stolen property prove ineffectual, and the agent is satisfied from the testimony that it was actually stolen, or received with knowledge of its being stolen, by any person belonging to the Quapaw tribe, he shall so report to the superintendent, with a copy of the testimony, which shall, for that purpose, be always reduced to writing; and the superintendent shall, if satisfied from the testimony, deduct from the annuity of the tribe a sum equal to the value of the property stolen.

ART. XIV. The Confederate States hereby guarantee full and fair payment to the owner of the actual and full value of all horses and other property stolen from any person or persons belonging to the Quapaw tribe by any citizen of the Confederate States, or by any Indian of any Other nation or tribe under their protection, in case the same cad and restored, and upon sufficient proof being made before the superintendent, or any agent of the Confederate States for any such nations or tribes, that such property was actually stolen by a citizen or citizens of the Confederate States, or by an Indian or Indians of any nation or tribe under their protection. ,br> ART. XV. An agent for the Great and Little Osage tribes, the Quapaws, Senecas, and Senecas and Shawnees shall be appointed by the President, and an interpreter for the Quapaw tribe for their protection, and that their complaints may be heard by, and their wants made known to, the President. The agent shall reside continually in the country of one or the other of said tribes or hands, and the interpreter shall reside continually amongst the Quapaws, and neither of them shall ever be absent from their posts, except by permission of the superintendent.

ART. XVI. None of the braves of the Quapaw tribe shall go upon the warpath against any enemy whatever, except with the consent of the agent, or unless it be to pursue hostile bands of white men or Indians entering their country and committing murder, robbery, or other outrage, when immediate pursuit is necessary; nor shall hold any talks or councils with any white men or Indians without his knowledge and consent. And they especially agree to attend no councils or talks in the country of any people with whom the Confederate States are at war; and in case they do so, all the benefits secured to them by this treaty shall immediately and forever cease.

ART. XVII. The Confederate States will not permit any improper person to reside or be in the Quapaw country, but only such persons as are employed by them, their officers, or agents, and traders, licensed by them, who shall sell to the Quapaws and buy from them at fair prices, under such regulations as the President shall make from time to time.

ART. XVIII. No State or Territory shall ever pass laws for the government of the Quapaw people, and, except so far as the laws of the Confederate States are in force on their country, their shall be left free to governor themselves and to punish offenses committed by one of themselves against the person or property of another: Provided, That if one of them kills another without good cause or justification he shall suffer death, but only by the sentence of the chiefs, and after a fair trial, all private revenge being strictly forbidden.

ART. XIX. Every white man who marries a woman of the Quapaws and resides in the Quapaw country shall be deemed and taken, even after the death of his wife, to be a Quapaw and a member of the tribe so far as to be subject to its laws in respect to all offenses committed in its country against the person or property of another member of his tribe, and as not to be considered a white man committing such offense against the person or property of an Indian within the meaning of the acts of the Congress of the Confederate States; and all negroes or mulattoes, bond or free, committing any such offense in said country shall in like manner be subject to the laws of the tribe.

ART. XX. The Confederate States shall have the right to establish, open, and maintain such military and other roads through any part of the Quapaw country as the President may deem necessary without making any compensation for the right of way or for the land, timber, or stone used in constructing the same; but if any other property of the tribe or any other property or the improvements of an individual be used or injured therein, just and adequate compensation shall be made.

ART. XXI. The Confederate State my grant the right of way for any railroad through any part of the Quapaw country; but the company to which any such right may be granted shall pay to the tribe therefor such sum as shall, in the opinion of the President, be its fair value, and shall also pay to individual all damages done by the building of said road to their improvements or other property, to such amount in each case as commissioners appointed by the President shall determine.

ART. XXII. The agent of the Confederate States for the Osages and other tribes shall prevent all instructions by hunters and others upon the lands of the Quapaws, and permit no white men or other Indians to settle thereon, and shall remove all such persons, calling, if necessary, upon the military power for aid; and the commanders of military posts in that or the adjoining country shall be required to afford him such aid upon his requisition.

ART. XXIII. The Quapaws may allow person of any other tribe of Indians to settle among them, and may received from them, for their own benefit, compensation for such lands as they may sell or assign to such persons.

ART. XXIV. No citizens or inhabitant of the Confederate States or member of any friendly nation or tribe of Indians shall pasture stock on the lands of the Quapaws; but all such persons shall have full liberty at all times, and whether for business or pleasure, peaceably to travel in their country, on the roads or elsewhere, to drive their stock through to halt such reasonable time on the way as may be necessary to recruit their stock, such delay being in good faith for that purpose and no other.

ART. XXV. Any person duly charged with a criminal offense against the laws of the Confederate States, or of any States or Territory, or of any Indian nation or tribe under the protection of the Confederate States, escaping into the Quapaw country, shall be promptly taken and delivered up by the chiefs of the Quapaws, on the demand of the proper authority of the Confederate States, or of the State, Territory, nation, or tribe within whose jurisdiction the offense shall be alleged to have been committed.

ART. XXVI. In addition to the laws of the Confederate States expressly applying to the Indian country, so much of their laws as provides for the punishment of crimes amounting to felony at common law, or by statute against their laws, authority, or treaties, and over which the courts of the Confederate States have jurisdiction, including the counterfeiting the coin of the United States or of the Confederate States, or any other current coin, or the securities of the Confederate States, or the uttering os such counterfeit coin or securities; and so much of said laws as provides for punishing violations of the neutrality laws, and resistance to the process of the Confederate States; and all the acts of the Provisional Congress providing for the common defense and welfare, so far as the same are not locally inapplicable, and the laws providing for the capture and delivery of fugitive slaves, shall be in force in the Quapaw country; and the district court for Outcast district, when established, shall have exclusive jurisdiction to try, condemn, and punish offenders against those laws, to adjudge and pronounce sentence, and cause execution thereof to be one.

ART. XXVII. Whenever any person who is a member of the Quapaw tribe shall be indicted for any offense in any court of the Confederate States, or in a State court, he shall be entitled, as of csubpoena and, if necessary, to compulsory process for all such witness in his behalf as his counsel may think material for his defense; and the costs of process for such witnesses, and of the service thereof, and fees and mileage of such witnesses, shall be paid by the Confederate States; and whenever the accused is not able to employ counsel, the court shall assign him one experienced counsel for his defense, who shall be paid by the Confederate States a reasonable compensation for his service, to be fixed by the court and paid upon the certificate of the judge.

ART. XXVIII. It is hereby declared and agreed that the institution of slavery in the said Quapaw tribe is legal, and has existed from time immemorial; that slaves are personal property; that the little to slaves and other property having its origin in the said tribe is to be determined by the laws and customs thereof, and that the slaves and personal property of every person domiclined in the country of said tribe shall pass and be distributed at his or her death in accordance with the laws, usages, and customs of the said tribe, which may be proved by oral evidence, and shall everywhere be held valid and binding within the scope of their operation. And if any slave escape from said tribe, the laws of the Confederate States for the capture and delivery of fugitive slaves shall apply to such cases, whether they escape into a State or Territory or into any Indian nation or tribe under the protection of the Confederate States, the obligation upon each States, Territory, nation, or tribe to deliver up the same being in every case as complete as if they has escaped from a State, and the mode of procedure the same.

ART. XXIX. The Quapaw tribe of Indians hereby makes itself a party to the existing war between the Confederate States and the United States of America, as the ally and ward of the former; and, in consideration of the protection guaranteed by this treaty, and of their country hereby agrees to aid in defeating its country against any invasion thereof by the common enemy; and it is agreed that all warriors furnished by it for the service of the Confederate States, and which shall be mustered into that service, shall receive the same pay and allowances as other troops of the same class therein, and remain in the service as long as the President shall require.

ART. XXX. The Confederate States hereby agree to furnish each warrior of the Quapaw tribe, who has not a gun, with a good rifle, and also to furnish each warrior a sufficient supply of ammunition during the war.

ART. XXXI. The Confederate States will also furnish the Quapaws, at a proper place, with such medicines as may be necessary, and will employ a physician for them and for the Senecas, and Senecas and Shawnees, who shall reside at a convenient place in the country of one or the other tribe, during the pleasure of the President; and any physician employed shall be discharged by the superintendent, and another be employed in his place, in case of incompetency or inattention to his duties.

ART. XXXII. In consideration of the uniform loyalty and good conduct of the Quapaw tribe, and of their necessities, arising from the sale by them of their lands in Arkansas for a grossly inadequate price, by the treaty of the year one thousand eight hundred and twenty-four, the Confederate States hereby agree to expend for the benefit of the Quapaws, in each year, for and during the term of twenty years from the day of the signing of this treaty, commencing with the year one thousand eight hundred and sixty-two, the sum of $2,000, which shall be applied each year by the superintendent to the purchase of articles costing that sum at the place of purchase in the Confederate States, to consist of blankets, clothing, tobacco, household and kitchen furniture and utensils, and other articles of ease and comfort for the Quapaws, which shall be distributed among them by the agent, as equally as possible, regard being had in the distribution to the character for industry or idleness, and good or bad conduct, on the part of the recipient, as well as the necessities of each, so that the good and needy shall be preferred, and in determining which the agent shall pay due respect to the opinions and judgment of the chiefs.

ART. XXXIII. The Confederate States also agree to employ a blacksmith for the Quapaws for and during the term of twenty years from the date of this treaty, and an assistant, who shall be one of the Quapaw people, and receive a compensation of $250 per annum; and they will also furnish the blacksmith with a dwelling-house, shop, and tools, and supply the stop with coal and with 600 pounds of iron and 100 pounds of steel annually.

ART. XXXIV. The Confederate States will also employ one wagon-maker and wheelwright for the Quapaws for and during the term of twenty years from the date of this treaty, and furnish him with a dwelling-house, shops, tools, and the necessary materials.

ART. XXXV. The Confederate States hereby agreed to built and put un running order for the Quapaws, at some suitable point in their country, to be selected by the agent, a good grist and saw mill, and to deliver the same when completed to the Quapaw people, whose absolute property it shall at once become. And the Confederate States will also employ for the term of ten years an experienced miller for each mill, to be selected, if possible, from among the Quapaws, and if such millers, can be had at a compensation not exceeding $600 per annum for each.

ART. XXXVI. The Confederate States also further agreed to purchase for the Quapaws four good wagons and harness for four horses for each wagon, ten yoke oxen, and ten sets of horse gear complete, to be delivered to the chiefs, and used for the general benefit of their people.

ART. XXXVII. The Confederate States also further agree perpetually to pay regularly and annually hereafter the sum of $1,000 for education of their children, provided by the treaty of the thirteenth day of May, A. D. one thousand eight hundred and thirty-three, and also to add to that sum in each and every year the further sum of $1,500, which sums shall be payable on the first day of January in each year, commencing with the year one thousand eight hundred and sixty-two, and shall be applied by the agent to the education of Quapaw children and youths in the Osage manual-labor school, until an institution of learning can be, with the aid of this perpetual fund, established in the country of the Quapaws.

ART. XXXVIII. Inasmuch as the Quapaws have no fund out of which to pay the salaries of their chiefs, or the expenses of their government, the Confederate States further agree to pay to each of the present chiefs, Wat-to-shi-nek Kat-eh-de, the first chief, Ka-hi-keh-toh-te, the second chief, for each year, and during his natural life, an annuity of $100 in money per annum, payable on the first day of January in each year, commencing with the year one thousand eight hundred and sixty-two.

ART. XXXIX. If any trader or other person should purchase from any Quapaw any of the chattels or articles given him by the Confederate States, he shall be severely punished.

ART. XL. A general amnesty of all past offenses against the laws of the United States or of the Confederate States, committed before the singing of this treaty by any member of the Quapaw tribe, as such membership is definite in this treaty, is hereby declared; and all such person, if any, charged with such offense shall receive from the President full and free pardon, and if imprisoned or held to bail, before or after conviction, shall be discharged.

ART. XLI. This convention shall be obligatory on the Quapaw tribe of Indians from the day of its date, and on the Confederate States from and after its ratification by the Senate or Provisional Congress.

In perpetual testimony whereof the said Albert Pike, as commissioner with plenary powers, on the part of the Confederate States, doth now hereunto set his hand and affix the seal of his arms; and the undersigned, chiefs and headmen of the Quapaw tribe of Indians, do hereunto set their hands and affix their seals.

This done in duplicate at the place and upon the day in the year first aforesaid.

[SEAL.]

ALBERT PIKE,

Commissioner of the Confederate States to the Indian Nations West of Arkansas.

Wat-to-shi-nek Kat-eh-de, principal chief of the Quapaws
George Lane,
Elijah H Fields,
Not-tet-tu,
Ka-ni,
Mos-ka-zi-ka,
A-hi-sut-ta,
Nik-kat-toh,
Mo-zek-ka-ne,
S. G. Wallar,
R. P. Lombard.

Signed, sealed, and delivered in the presence of us.

Wm. Quesenbury, secretary to the commissioner
E. Rector, Superintendent Indian Affairs, Confederate States
Andrew J. Dorn, C. S. agent for the Quapaws, &c.
W. Warren Johnson,
R. H. Bean,
J. W. Washbourne.

(To the Indian names are subjoined marks.)

RATIFICATION.

Resolved (two thirds of the Congress concurring), That the Congress of the Confederate States of America do advise and consent to the ratification of the articles of a convention, made by Albert Pike, commissioner of the Confederate States to the Indian nations west of Arkansas, of the one part, and the Quapaw tribe of Indians, but its chiefs and warriors, who signed the same articles, of the other part, concluded at Park Hill, in the Cherokee Nation, on the fourth day of October, A. D. one thousand eight hundred and sixty-one, with the following amendment:

Strike out from Article XXVII the following words, "or in a State court," and insert in lieu thereof the following words, "or in s State court, subject to the laws of the State. "

NOTE. - The amendment was agreed to and ratified by the Quapaws as a part of the treaty.

OFFICIAL RECORDS: Series 4, vol 1, Part 1
Pages 647-658
Confederate States of America - Seneca, Shawnees

ARTICLES OF A CONVENTION entered into and concluded at Park Hill, in the Cherokee Nation, on the fourth day of October, A. D. one thousand eight hundred and sixty-one, between the Confederate States of America, by Albert Pike, their commissioner, with full powers, appointed by the President, by virtue of an act of Congress in that behalf, and the Seneca tribe of Indians, formerly known as the Senecas of Sandusky, formerly known as the Senecas and Shawnees of Lewistown, or the mixed bands of Senecas and Shawnees, each tribe for itself by its chiefs and warriors, who have signed these articles, of the other part.

ARTICLE I. The Seneca tribe of Indians, formerly known as the Senecas of Sandusky, and the Shawnees of the tribe or confederacy of Senecas and Shawnees, formerly known as the Senecas and |Shawnees of Lewiston, or the mixed bands of Senecas and Shawnees, and all the persons of each, do hereby place themselves under the laws and protection of the Confederate States of America, in peace and war forever, and agree to be true and loyal to them under all circumstances.

ART. II. The Confederate States of America do hereby promise and firmly engage themselves to be, during all time, the friends and protectors of the Seneca tribe of Indians, formerly known as the Senecas of Sandusky, and the Shawnees of the tribe or confederacy of Senecas and Shawnees, formerly known as the Senecas and Shawnees of Lewistown, or the mixed bands of Senecas and Shawnees, and to secure and defend them in the enjoyment of all their rights, possessions, and property; and that they will not allow them henceforward to be in any wise troubled or molested by any power or people, State, or person whatever.

ART. III. The Confederate States of America do hereby assure and guarantee to the Seneca tribe aforesaid, and to the Senecas and Shawnees, formerly known as the Senecas and Shawnees of Lewistown, or the mixed bands of Senecas and Shawnees of Lewistown, or the mixed bands of Senecas and Shawnees, in case the Senecas thereof should hereafter unite in this treaty, by a convention for that purpose made and concluded, or to the Shawnees thereof aforesaid alone, in case the Shawnees should refuse so to unite herein, to each tribe or band, respectively, the title in fee simple, as long as each, respectively, shall exist as a nation and remain thereon, and the exclusive possession and undisturbed use, occupancy, and enjoyment, as long as grass shall grow and water run, of the country heretofore secured to each, respectively, by treaties with and patents from the United States of

America, and which countries are thus described and ascertained, that is to say:

By the treaty with the Senecas of Sandusky made and concluded on the twenty-eighth day of February, A. D. one thousand eight hundred and thirty-one, a country was ceded and granted to that tribe, therein described as "a tract of land situate on and adjacent to the northern boundary of the lands heretofore grated to the Cherokee Nation of Indians, and adjoining the boundary of the State of Missouri, which tract shall extend fifteen miles from east to west, and seven miles from north to south, containing about 67,000 acres, be the same more or less. " By the treaty made and concluded with the mixed bands of Seneca and Shawnee Indians residing at and around Lewistown, on the twentieth day of July, in the same year, a country was ceded and granted to these bands therein described as "a tract of land to contain 60,000 acres, to be located under the direction of the President of the United States, contiguous to the lands grated to the Senecas of Sandusky by the treaty made with them at the city of Washington, on the twenty-eighth of February, one thousand eight hundred and thirty-one, and the Cherokee settlements; the east line of said tract shall be within two miles of the west lines of the lands granted to the Senecas of Sandusky, and the south line shall be within two miles of the north line of the lands held by the Cherokees; " and by the treaty made and concluded on the twenty-ninth day of December, A. D. one thousand eight hundred and thirty-two, with the united nation or tribe of Senecas and Shawnees, by which that united tribe ceded, relinquished, and quit claimed to the United States all their lands west of the Neosho or Grand River, the United States agreed to grant by patent, in the manner thereinafter mentioned, the country therein described as follows, that is to say: "The following tract of land lying on the east side of Neosho or Grand River, viz: Bounded on the east by the west line of the State of Missouri; south by the present established line of the Cherokee Indians; west by Neosho or Grand River, and north by a line running parallel with said south line, and extending so far from the present north line of the Seneca Indians from Sandusky as to contain 60,000 acres, exclusive of the land now owned by said Seneca Indians, which said boundaries included within said boundaries the United States thereby agreed to grant by two letters patent, the north half in quantity to the mixed bands of the Senecas and Shawnees of Ohio, or of Lewistown, and the south half to the Senecas from Sandusky, the whole to be occupied in common so long as the said tribes or bans should desire the same, and the grant to be in fee simple, but the lands not to be sold or ceded without the consent of the United States; which lands shall not be sold or ceded by the said tribes or bands, nor shall any part thereof, to any nation or people, except to the Confederate States, or to any individuals whatever, except as hereinafter provided; and the same shall vest in the Confederate States in case the said tribes or bands, respectively, become extinct or abandon the same.

ART. IV. The Seneca tribe of Indians aforesaid, and the Senecas and Shawnees alone, aforesaid, as the case may be, may respectively by a majority vote of the whole people of each, respectively, receive and incorporate, each in itself, as members of the tribe, or permit to settle and reside upon the lands of the tribe, such Shawnees of Kansas, or Indians of any other tribe, e Confederate States, as to it may seem good; and may sell such Indians portions of land, in fee or by less estate, or lease them portions thereof for years or otherwise, and receive to its own use the price and consideration of such sales or leases; and it alone shall determine who are citizens of the tribe entitled to vote at elections, hold office, or share the annuities or other moneys of the tribe or in the common lands: Provided, That when persons of another tribe shall once have been received as members of either of said tribes, they shall not be disfranchised or subjected to any other restrictions upon the right of voting than such as shall apply to the Senecas or Senecas and Shawnees, respectively, themselves. But no Indians of any other tribe or band them these shall be permitted to come within their country to reside without the consent and license of the people of each tribe respectively.

ART. V. The right is hereby reserved to the Confederate States to select in any unoccupied part of the country of either of said tribes or band, if they should desire to do so, a tract of land one mile square as a reserve and site for an agency, for the said tribes and for the Quapaws and Osages, which shall revert to the tribe in whose country it is selected, with the buildings thereon, whenever it shall cease to be occupied as an agency.

ART. VI. The Confederate States shall have the right to establish in the said country such forts and military posts as they may deem necessary, and shall have the right to select for each such fort or post a tract of land one mile square, on which such fort or post shall be established: Provided, That if any person have any improvements on any tract so selected, the value of such improvements shall be paid by the Government to the owner thereof.

ART. VII. No person whatever shall be permitted to settle or reside upon the agency reserve, when it shall have been selected, except by the permissionor upon any reserve for a fort or military post, except by the permission of the commanding officer; and every such reserve, for the agency, or for forts or military posts, shall be within the sole and exclusive jurisdiction of the Confederate States.

ART. VIII. The Confederate States hereby guarantee that the country hereby secured to the said Senecas and Senecas and Shawnees shall never be included within the bounds of any State or Territory, nor shall any of the laws of any State or Territory ever be extended over or put in force within any part of the said country; and the President of the Confederate States will cause the said tribes to be protected against all molestation or disturbance at the hands of any other tribe or nation of Indians, or of any other person or persons whatever; and he shall have the same care and superintendence over them as was heretofore had by the President of the United States.

ART. IX. The members of the said Seneca tribe and the said Seneca and Shawnee mixed bands shall have the right henceforward of hunting and killing game in all the unoccupied country west of the possessions of the Cherokees, Seminoles, Choctaws, and Chickasaws, without molestation from any quarter, being while so engaged therein under the protection of the Confederate States.

ART. X. There shall be perpetual peace and brotherhood between the Seneca tribe and the Shawnees aforesaid, and the Osages, Cherokees, Mus-ki-is, Seminoles, Choctaws, and Chickasaws, and the bands of the Wichitas, Cado-Ha-da-chos, Hue-cos, Ta-hua-ca-ros, A-na-dagh-cos, Ton-ca-wes, Ki-chais, Ai-o-nais, Shawnees, and Delewares living in the country leased from the Choctaws, and Chickasaws, and the Pen-e-tegh-ca, No-co-ni, Ta-ne-I-weh, Ya-pa-rih-ca, and Co-cho-tih-ca bands of the Ne-um or Comanches; and every injury or act of hostility which either has heretofore sustained or met with at the hands of the other shall be forgiven and forgotten.

ART. XI. The Seneca tribe and the Shawnees aforesaid and the said several other nations, tribes, and shall henceforth be good neighbors to each other, and there shall be a free and friendly intercourse among them. And it is hereby agreed by the said Seneca tribe and the said Shawnees, as has already been agreed by all the others, that the horses, cattle, and other stock and property of each nation, tribe, or band, and every person of each, is his or its own; and that no person belonging to the Senecas or Shawnees aforesaid shall or will hereafter kill, take away, or injure any such property of another tribe or band, or of any member of any other tribe or band, or in any other way do them any harm.

ART. XII. Especially there shall be perpetual peace and friendship between said Senecas and Shawnees aforesaid, and the Osages, Quapaws, Cherokees, Mus-ko-is, Seminoles, Choctaws, and Chickasaws; and the chiefs and headmen of the said Seneca tribe and Shawnees shall do all in their power to taken and restore any negroes, horses, or other property stolen from white men or from persons belonging to either of said five nations, and to catch and give up any person among them who may kill or steal or do any other civil act.

ART. XIII. In order that the friendship now established between the Seneca tribe and Shawnees, the Confederate States, and the other Indian nations, tribes, and bands aforesaid, may not be interrupted by the misconduct of individuals, or bands of individuals, it is hereby agreed that for injuries done by individuals no private revenge or retaliation shall take place, but instead thereof complaint shall be made by the said Seneca tribe and Shawnees, when any individual thereof is injured, to the agent of the Confederate States for the Osages and other tribes, who shall investigate the complaint, and if he finds it well founded shall report the same to the superintendent, who will cause the wrong to be redressed, and the person doing the wrong to be arrested, whether he be a white man or an Indian; and he or they shall be tried for the same agreeably to the laws of the Confederate States or of the State or Territory against which he may have offended, and be punished in the same manner and with the same severity as if the injury had been done to a white man. And it is also agreed that if any member of the Seneca tribe or any one of the Shawnees shall do any injury to the person or property of any white man or of a member of any other Indian nation or tribe under the protection of the Confederate States, the offender shall be given up to the agent upon complaint made to him, and on his demand, the wrong shall be redressed by him, and the offender be tried for the offense agreeably to the laws of the Confederate States or of the State, Territory, or nation against which he may have offended, and be punished in the same manner e severity as if the injury had been done to a white man. And it is also agreed that if any member of the Seneca tribe or any one of the Shawnees shall do any injury to the person or property of any white man or of a member of any other Indian nation or tribe under the protection of the Confederate States, the offender shall be given up to the agent upon complaint made to him, and on his demand, the wrong shall be redressed by him, and the offender be tried for the offense agreeably to the laws of the Confederate States or of the State, Territory, or nation against which he may have offended: Provided, That he shall be punished in no other manner nor with any greater severity than a citizen of the Confederate States or of such State, Territory, or nation would be if he had committed the same offense.

ART. XIV. It is hereby further agreed that the chiefs of the Senecas and of the Shawnees shall use every exertion in their power to recover any horses or other property that may be stolen from any citizen of the Confederate States or from any member of any other Indian nation or tribe under the protection of the Confederate States, by any person or persons whatever, and found within the limits of their country; and the property so recovered shall be forthwith delivered to the owner or to the agent to be restored to him. If in any case the right to the property claimed is contested by the person in possession, the agent shall summarily investigate the case, and upon hearing the testimony of witnesses, shall decide the right to the property and order it to be retained or delivered up accordingly. Either party may appeal from his decision to the superintendent, whose decision shall be final in all cases, the property in the meantime remaining in the custody of the agent. If, in any case, the exertions of the chiefs to cause the restoration of stolen property prove ineffectual and the agent is satisfied from the testimony that it was actually stolen, or received with knowledge of its being person belonging to the Seneca tribe or by any one of the Shawnees, he shall so report to the superintendent, with a copy of the testimony, which shall for that purpose be always reduced to writing; and the superintendent shall, if satisfied from the testimony, deduct from the annuity of the tribe a sum equal to the value of the property stolen.

ART. XV. The Confederate States hereby guarantee full and fair payment to the owner of the actual and full value of all horses and other property stolen from any person or persons belonging to the Seneca tribe, or being of the Shawnees aforesaid, by any citizen of the Confederate States or by any Indian of any other nation or tribe under their protection, in case the same cannot be recovered and restored, and upon sufficient proof being made before the superintendent, or any agent of the Confederate States for any such nations or tribes, that such property was actually stolen by a citizen or citizens of the Confederate States or by an Indian or Indians of any nation or tribe under their protection.

ART. XVI. An agent for the Great and Little Osage tribes, the Quapaws, Senecas, and Senecas and Shawnees shall be appointed by the President, and an interpreter for the Seneca tribe and one for the Shawnees for their protection, and that their complaints may be heard by, and their wants made known to, the President. The agent shall reside continually in the country of one or the other of said tribes or bands, and the interpreter shall reside continually among the people for whom he is employed, and neither of them shall ever be absent from their posts, except by the permission of the superintendent.

ART. XVII. The Senecas and the Senecas and Shawnees shall hold no talks or councils with any white men or Indians without the knowledge and consent of the agent of the Confederate States. And they especially agree to attend no councils or talks in the country of any people or with the officers or agent with whom the Confederate States are at war; and in case they do so, all the benefits secured to them by this treaty shall immediately and forever cease.

ART. XVIII. The Confederate States will not permit any improper persons to reside or to be in the country of the Senecas, or in that of the Senecas and Shawnees, but only such persons as are employed by them, their officers or agents, and trades licensed by them, who shall sell to the said Indians and buy from (them) at fair prices, under such regulations as the President shall make from time to time.

ART. XIX. No State or Territory shall ever pass laws for the government of the Seneca tribe or of the Seneca and Shawnee people; and except so far as the laws of the Confederate States are in force in their country, they shall be left free to govern themselves and to punish offenses committed by on themselves against the person or property of another: Provided, That if one of them kills another without good cause or justification he shall suffer death, but only by the sentence of the chiefs, and after a fair trial, all private revenge being strictly forbidden.

ART. XX. Every white man who marries or has married a woman of the Senecas or of the Shawnees and resides in the Seneca or Seneca and Shawnee country, respectively, shall be deemed and taken, even after the death of his wife, to be a member of the tribe in which he marries or has married, so far as to be subject to its laws in respect to all offenses committed in its country against the person or property of another member of the tribe and as not to be considered a white man committing such offense against the person or property of an Indian, within the meaning of the act of Congress of the Confederate States. And all negroes and mulattoes, bond or free, committing any such offense in said country shall, in like manner, be subject to the laws of the tribe.

ART. XXI. The Confederate States shall have the right to establish, open, and maintain such military and other roads through any part of the Seneca or Seneca and Shawnee country as the President may deem necessary, without making anor the right of way, or for the land, timber, or stone used in constructing the same; but if any other property of the tribe, or any other property or the improvements of an individual be used or injured therein, just and adequate compensation shall be made.

ART. XXII. The Confederate States my grant the right of way for any railroad through any part of the Seneca or Seneca and Shawnee country; but the company to which any such right of way may be granted shall pay the tribe thereof through whose country any part of the road runs sums as in the opinion of the President be its fair value; and shall also pay to individuals all damages done by the building of said road to their improvements or other property to such amount in each case as commissioners appointed by the President shall determine.

ART. XXIII. The agent of the Confederate States for the Osages and other tribes shall prevent all instructions by hunters and others upon the lands of the Senecas and of the Senecas and Shawnees, and permit no white men or other Indians to settle thereon, and shall remove all such persons, calling, of necessary, upon the military power for aid; and the commanders of military posts in that or the adjoining country shall be required to afford him such aid upon his requisition.

ART. XXIV. No citizen or inhabitant of the Confederate States or member of any friendly nation or tribe of Indians shall pasture stock on the lands of the Senecas or Senecas and Shawnees; but all such persons shall have full liberty, at all times, and whether for business or pleasure, peaceably to travel in their country, on the roads or elsewhere, to drive their stock through the same and to halt such reasonable time on the way as may be necessary to recruit their stock, such delay being in good faith for that purpose and for no other.

ART. XXV. Any person duly charged with a criminal offense against the laws of the Confederate States, or of any State or territory, or of any Indian nation or tribe, under the protection of the Confederate States, escaping into the Seneca or Seneca and Shawnee country, shall be promptly taken and delivered up by the chiefs of the Senecas or Senecas and Shawnees, on the demand of the proper authority of the Confederate State, or of the State, Territory, nation, or tribe within whose jurisdiction the offense shall be alleged to have been committed.

ART. XXVI. In addition to the laws of the Confederate States, expressly applying to the Indian country, so much of their laws as provides for the punishment of crimes amounting to felony at common law, or by statute against their laws, authority, or treaties, and over which the courts of the Confederate States have jurisdiction, including the counterfeiting the coin of the United States or of the Confederate States, or any other current coiniges of the Confederate States, or the uttering of such counterfeit coin or securities; and so much of said laws as provides for punishing violations of the neutrality law, and resistance to the process of the Confederate States; and all the acts of the Provisional Congress providing for the common defense and welfare, so far as the same are not locally inapplicable; and the laws providing for the capture and delivery of fugitive slaves, shall be in force in the Seneca and the Seneca and Shawnee country; and the district court for the Chalahki district, when established, shall have exclusive jurisdiction to try, condemn, and punish offenders, against those laws, to adjudge and pronounce sentence, and cause execution thereof to be done.

ART. XXVII. Whenever any person, who is a member of the Seneca or Seneca and Shawnee tribe, shall be indicted for any offense in any court of the Confederate States, or in a State court, he shall be entitled, as of common right, to subpoena, and if necessary, to compulsory process for all such witnesses in his behalf as his counsel may think material for his defense; and the costs of process for such witnesses and of the service thereof, and mileage of such witnesses shall be paid by the Confederate States; and whenever the accused is not able to employ counsel the court shall assign him one experienced counsel for his defense, who shall be paid by the Confederate States a reasonable compensation for his services, to be fixed by the court and paid upon the certificate of the judge.

ART. XXVIII. It is hereby declared and agreed that the institution of slavery in the said Seneca and Seneca and Shawnee tribes is legal, and has existed from time immemorial; that slaves are personal property; that the title to slaves and other property having its origin in either of the said tribes os to be determined by the laws and customs thereof; and that the slaves and personal property of every person domictry of either of said tribes shall pass and be distributed at his or her death on accordance with the laws, usages, and customs of the said tribes, which may be proved by oral evidence, and shall everywhere be held valid and binding within the scope of their operations. And if any slaves escape from either of the said tribes, the laws of the Confederate States for the capture and delivery of fugitive slaves shall apply to such cases, whether they escape into a State or territory, or into any Indian nation or tribe under the protection of the Confederate States; the obligation upon each such State, Territory, nation, or tribe to deliver up the same being, in every case, as complete as if they had escaped from a State, and the mode of procedure the same.

ART. XXIX. The Seneca tribe and the Shawnees of the Seneca and Shawnee tribe hereby make themselves parties to the existing war between the Confederate States and the United States of America, as the allies and wards of the former; and, in consideration of the protection guaranteed by this treaty, and of their common interests, hereby agree to aid in defending their country against any invasion thereof by the common enemy; and it is agreed that all warriors furnished by them for the service of the Confederate States, and which shall be mustered into that service, shall receive the same pay and allowances as other troops of the same class therein, and remain in the service as long as the President shall require.

ART. XXX. It is further agreed and ascertained, by and between the Confederate States and the said Seneca tribe of Indians, formerly known as the Senecas of Sandusky, that the United States of America were, while the several States of the Confederacy were members of the same, and still remain indebted to the said Seneca tribe, and had and still have in their hands moneys in trust for the said tribes, as follows, that is to say:

By the fourth article of the treaty made with the Wyandot, Seneca, and other tribes of Indians, on the twenty-ninth day of September, A. D. one thousand eight hundred and seventeen, the United States agreed and bound themselves to pay annually, forever, to the Seneca tribe, the sum of $500, in specie, at Lower Sandusky;

By the fourth article of the treaty made the seventeenth day of September, A. D. one thousand eight hundred and eighteen, with the Wyandot, Seneca, Shawnee, and Ottawa tribes of Indians, the United States agreed and bound themselves to pay to the Senecas of Sandusky and additional annuity of $500 forever;

By the eighth article of the treaty with the Seneca tribe of Sandusky, made on the twenty-eighth day of February, A. D. one thousand eight hundred and thirty-one, the United States agreed to sell the land thereby ceded to them by the said tribe, by that treaty; and it was that, after certain deductions therefrom to be made, as therein specified, any balance that might remain of the proceeds of sale of such lands should constitute a fund for the future exigencies of the tribe, on which the United States would pay to the chiefs of the tribe, for the use and general benefit of the tribe, annually, 5 per cent, as annuity, which sales being accordingly effected, the fund thus created amounted to $5,000, which was invested by the United States, and yet remains invested, in 5 per cent, stock of the State of Kentucky, now held by the United States.

It is further hereby agreed and ascertained, by and between, the Confederate States and the Shawnees, of the said Senecas and Shawnees of Lewistown, that the United States of America were, while the several States of the Confederacy were members of the same, and still remain, indebted to the mixed bands of Senecas and Shawnees, and had and still have in their hands moneys in trust for the said tribe, as follows, that is to say:

By the fourth article of the treaty made with the Wyandot, Seneca, Shawnee, and Ottawa tribes on the seventeenth day of September, A. D. one thousand eight hundred and eighteen, the United States agreed and bound themselves to pay "to the Shawnees and to the Senecas of Lewistown" an additional annuity of $1,000 forever;

By the eighth article of the treaty made with the mixed band of Seneca and Shawnee Indians residing at and around Lewistown, in the State of Ohio, on the twentieth day of July, A. D. one thousand eight hundred and thirty-one, the United States agreed to sell the lands ceded to them by the Senecas and Shawnees by that treaty; and it was also agreed that, after certain deductions, therein provided for, any balance of the proceeds of such lands that might remain should constitute a fund for the future necessities of the tribes, on which the United States would pay the chief, for the use and general benefit of the said tribes, annually, 5 per cent, as an annuity, which sales being accordingly effected, the fund thus created amounted to $16,466.10, which was invested by the United States, and yet remains invested, as follows, that is to say:

Six thousand dollars in 5 per cent, stock of the State of Kentucky; Seven thousand dollars in 5 1/2 per cent, stock of the State of Missouri; Three thousand dollars in 6 per cent. stock of the State of Missouri;

And $466. 10 in the United States 6 per cent. loan of the year 1847;

Which stocks are held by the United States, and the annual interest thereon amounted to the sum of $892. 96.

Therefore, and as the said Senecas and the Shawnees aforesaid are indigent, and have nothing to expect from the justice of the Northern States, and will be greatly distressed if the annual payments are not promptly made, and as the Confederate States do not wish them any longer to look to the Northern States or receive any moneys from them, and are willing to make the necessary advances for the States of Missouri and Kentucky:

Therefore, it is further agreed by the said Confederate States of America that they will pay annually forever, in each and every year after the day of the signing of this treaty, on the first day of January in each, year, commencing with the year one thousand eight hundred and sixty-two, in money:

To the Seneca tribe, formerly known as the Senecas of Sandusky, to the chiefs, for the use and general benefit of the people, $1,250;

And to the Shawnees, of the mixed bands of the Senecas and Shawnees, formerly of Lewistown, or to the Senecas and Shawnees together when the Senecas shall have united in this treaty, but until then to the Shawnees alone, to the chiefs, for the use and general benefit of the people, $1,892. 96.

And it is further agreed by the Confederate States that they will look to the States of Missouri and Kentucky for repayment of the principal and interest of the said sums so invested in their stocks.

ART. XXXI. Whereas, by the treaty made between the State of New York and the Cayuga tribe of Indians, in the month of June, A. D. one thousand eight hundred and fifty, it was agreed that the said State should pay annually thereafter forever, on the first day of June in each year, to that portion of the Cayuga tribe which resided West, the sum of $1,146, which was has been regularly paid until the present year, and the check of the treasure of the State of New York on the Commercial Bank of Albany, in that State, for the payment of the year one thousand eight hundred and sixty-one, in the hands of Andrew J. Dorn, the agent of the Osages and other tribes; and

Whereas, the Cayugas of the West, to whom the said annuity is payable, reside among and are fully accepted as members of the Seneca tribe aforesaid, with the exception of a few reside among the Senecas and Shawnees, and the said annuity has, therefore, been in each year, by the consent of all, distributed by the agent among all, the Senecas, formerly known as the Senecas of Sandusky, and such Cayugas as reside among the Senecas and Shawnees, and the Cayugas, as are willing it shall forever continue to be distributed; and

Whereas, by placing themselves under the protection of the Confederate States, the Senecas and Cayugas so entitled to said annuity will forfeit the same, and, in all probability, forever:

Therefore, it is hereby further agreed by the Confederate States that they will pay hereafter annually forever, on the first day of January in each year, commencing with the year one thousand eight hundred and sixty-two, to the said Seneca tribe of Indians, including the Cayugas, and to the Cayugas residing among the Senecas and Shawnees jointly, the said sum of $1,146, in money, and that if the said check should not be paid they will also pay the amount thereof, to be in line manner distributed on the first day of January, A. D. one thousand eight hundred and sixty-two: Provided, That if the State of New York should at any time hereafter resume the regular payment of the said annuity, then the Confederate States shall no longer, while it continues to do so, be bound to pay the same

ART. XXXII. Inasmuch as the Seneca tribe and the Senecas and Shawnees have received among them persons of the Wyandot tribe to the number of 113, and have given them land to live on without chargem and in consideration of the loyalty of the Seneca tribe, including the Cayugas and Mohawks, who are members of the tribe of the Senecas aforesaid, and of the Wyandots who reside among them, and of their great necessities, the Confederate States do hereby further agree that they will expend in each and every year hereafter, for the term of twenty years from the day of the singing of this treaty, commencing with the year one thousand eight hundred and sixty-two, and in the early part of each year, the sum of $2,400, for the benefit of the Seneca tribe, including the Cyaugas and Mohawks, who form part of the tribe of the Shawnees aforesaid, forming part of the mixed bands of Senecas and Shawnees, of the Wyandots residing among each, and of the Senecas of the said mixed bands, if they shall unite int his treaty, but not otherwise, which sum of money shall be annually expended in the purchase by the superintendent, at first cost at the place of purchase in the Confederate States, of such articles of clothing, blankets, utensils, and other useful articles as he shall, aided by the report and recommendation of the agent in each year, judge to be most desirable, and as will conduce to the health and comfort of the Indians; and which article shall be annually distributed by the agent as equally as possible among the persons composing the Seneca tribe as aforesaid, the Shawnees, and Wyandots aforesaid, and the Senecas of the said mixed bands of Senecas and Shawnees; in which distribution, however, regard may be had by the agent, by the advice of the chiefs, to the character and circumstances of the recipients, and the needy who are industrious and worthy be especially provided for, and the idle and dissolute not be encouraged.

ART. XXXIII. The Senecas and the Senecas and Shawnees not being able to maintain schools among them, and being anxious their children should not grow up in ignorance, the Confederate States hereby agree to built a comfortable school-house in each tribe, and that they will employ during the term of twenty years a competent male teacher and a competent female teacher, pay their salaries, and furnish the schools with the necessary stationery and such books as are needed for instruction in common schools. The repairs of school-houses shall be made and fuel furnished by the Senecas, the Senecas and Shawnees, and Wyandots themselves, and the schools shall be open to children of all alike.

ART. XXXIV. Whenever it shall be desired either by the Senecas or the Shawnees of the mixed bands after the said Senecas shall have united in this treaty, a division of their joint annuity of $1,892. 96 shall be made between them in the ration of their numbers, and each band shall thereafter receive to its sole use the share of said annuity belonging to it, as thus determined, whatever their respective numbers may afterward be.

ART. XXXV. The Confederate States will also furnish the Senecas, formerly of Sandusky, and the Shawnees aforesaid, and the Senecas of the mixed bands when they shall have united in this treaty, with such medicines as may be necessary, and will employ a physician for them and for the Quapaws, who shall reside at a convenient place in the country of one or the other tribe during the pleasure of the President; and any physician employed shall be discharged by the superintendent and another be employed in his place in case of incompetency or inattention to his duties.

ART. XXXVI. The Confederate States also agree to employ a blacksmith for the Senecas and one for the Senecas and Shawnees for and during the term of twenty years from the date of this treaty, and an assistant for each, who shall be one of the Seneca or Shawnee people, and received a compensation of $250 per annum; and they will also furnish each blacksmith a dwelling-house, shop, and tolls, and supply each shop with local and with 600 pounds of iron and 100 pounds of steel annually.

ART. XXXVII. The Confederate States will also employ one wagon-maker and wheelwright for the Senecas, and one for the Senecas and Shawnees, for and during the term of twenty years from the date of this treaty, and furnish each with a dwelling-house, shop, tools, and the necessary materials.

ART. XXXVIII. The Confederate States also hereby agree to built and put in running order for the Senecas and the Senecas and Shawnees, at some suitable point in their country, convenient to both, to be selected by the agent, a good grist and saw mill, and to deliver the same when completed to the Seneca and Seneca and Shawnee people, whose joint absolute property it shall at once become. And the Confederate States will also employ for the term of ten years an experienced miller for each mill, to be selected, if possible, from among the Senecas or Shawnees, and if such millers can be had at a compensation not exceeding $600 for each per annum.

ART. XXXIX. The Confederate States hereby agree to furnish each warrior of the Seneca tribe, and of the Shawnees aforesaid, and of the Senecas of the mixed bands aforesaid, when they shall have united in this treaty, who was not a gun, with a good rifle, and also to furnish each warrior of the same with a sufficient supply of ammunition during the war.

ART. XL. If any trader or other person should purchased from the Senecas or Shawnees, aforesaid, any of the articles given them by the Confederate States, he shall be severely punished.

ART. XLI. A general amnesty of all past offenses against the laws of the United States, or of the Confederate States, committed before the singing of this treaty, by any person of the Seneca tribe, or by any Shawnee of the mixed bands, is hereby declared; and all such persons, if any, charged with any such offense, shall receive from the President full and free pardon, and if imprisoned or held to bail, before of after conviction, shall be discharged.

ART. XLII. The Confederate States of America hereby tender to the Senecas, of the mixed bands of Senecas and Shawnees, the same protection and guarantees as are hereby extended and given to the Seneca tribe, and to the Shawnees aforesaid, and the other benefits offered to the said Senecas specifically by this treaty; annecas, of the mixed bands, shall give no aid to the enemies of the Confederate States, and shall, within one year from the day of the signing of this treaty, enter into a convention whereby they shall unite in this treaty, and shall accept and agree to all the terms and conditions of the same, then it shall, to all intents and purposes, be regarded as having been originally made with them also, and they be deemed and taken to be parties hereto as if they were now to sign the same.

ART. XLIII. This convention shall be obligatory on the Seneca tribe, and on the Shawnees, aforesaid, of the mixed bands, from the day of its date, and on the Confederate States from and after its ratification by the Senate of Provisional Congress.

In testimony whereof the said Albert Pike, as commissioner with plenary powers, on the part of the Confederate States, doth now hereunto set his hand and affix the seal of his arms; and the undersigned, chiefs and headmen of the Seneca tribe of Indians, and of the Shawnees of the mixed bands of Senecas and Shawnees, do hereunto set their hands and affix their seals.

This done in duplicate at the place and upon the day in the month and year first aforesaid.

[SEAL.]

ALBERT PIKE,

Commissioner of the Confederate States to the Indian Nations West of Arkansas.

Little Town Spicer, principal chief of Seneca tribe;
Small Cloud Spicer, second chief of Seneca tribe;
Moses Crow, councilor of Seneca tribe;
John Much, councilor of Seneca tribe;
George Spicer, councilor of Seneca tribe;
John Smith,
James King,
Isaac Warior,
Jim Big-Bone,
Buck Armstrong,
Jo Crow,
David Smith,
George Keron, C. S. interpretor for the Seneca tribe (warriors of the Seneca tribe);
Lewis Davis, principal chief of the Senecas and Shawnees;
Joseph Mohawk, second chief of the Shawnees;
John Tomahawk;
White Deer, councilor of the Shawnees;
Silas Dougherty, councilor of the Shawnees;
William Barbee, C. S. interpret for the Shawnees.

Signed, sealed, and delivered in presence of us.

Wm. Quesenbury, secretary to the commissioner;
E. Rector, Superintendent of Indian Affairs, Confederate States;
Andrew J. Dorn, C. S. agent for Osages, Senecas, &c. ;
W. Warren Johnson,
Luther H. Pike,

J. W. Washbourne.

(To the Indian names are subjoined marks.)

RATIFICATION.

Resolved (two thirds of Congress concuring), That the Congress of the Confederate States of America do advise and consent to the ratification of the articles of a convention made by Albert Pike, commissioner of the Confederate States to the Indian nations west of Arkansas, in behalf of the Confederate States of the one part, and the Seneca tribe of Indians, formerly known as the Senecas of Sandusky, and the Shawnees of the tribe or confederacy of Senecas and Shawnees, formerly known as the Senecas and Shawnees of Lewistown, or the mixed bands of Senecas and Shawnees, each tribe for itself, by the chiefs and warriors who signed the same articles, of the other part, concluded at Park Hill, in the Cherokee Nation, on the fourth day of October, A. D. one thousand eight hundred and sixty-one, with the following amendment:

In Article XXVII, at the end of the words "or in a State court," add the following words, 'subject to the laws of the State. "

NOTE. - The amendment was agreed to and ratified by the Senecas and Shawnees as a part of the treaty

OFFICIAL RECORDS: Series 4, vol 1, Part 1
Pages 548-554
Confederate States of America - Comanche

ARTICLES OF A CONVENTION entered into and concluded at the Wichita Agency, near the False Washita River, in the country leased from the Choctaws and Chickasaws, on the twelfth day of August, A. D. one thousand Albert Pike, their commissioner with full powers, is appointed by the President by virtue of an act of the Congress in that behalf, of the one part, and the No-co-ni, m Ta-ne-weh, Co-cho-tih-ca, and Ya-pa-rih-ca bands of the Ne-um or Comanches of the Prairies and Staked Plain, by their chiefs and headmen, who have signed these articles, on the other part.

ARTICLE I. The No-co-ni, Ta-ne-I-weh, Co-cho-tih-ca, and Ya-pa-rish-ca bands of the Ne-um, called by the white men the Comanches of the Prairies and the Staked Plain, do hereby make peace with the Confederate States of America, and do renew and continue the peace heretofore existing between them and the Cherokee, Mus-ko-ki, Seminole, Choctaw, and Chickasaw Nations of red men, and do hereby take each and all of them by the hand of friendship, having smoked with them the pipe of peace, and received the wampum of peace; and do hereby place themselves under the laws and protection of the Confederate States of America, and agree to be true and loyal to them in peace and in war forever, and to hold them by the hand, and have but one heart with them always.

ART. II. The Confederate State of America do hereby promise and engage themselves to be, during all time, the friends and protectors of the Non-co-ni, Ta-ne-I-weh, Ya-pa-rih-ca, and Co-cho-tih-ca bands of the Ne-um, and that they will not allow them to be molested by any power or people, State, or person whatever.

ART. III. The Non-co-ni, Ta-ne-I-weh, Ya-pa-rih-ca, and Co-cho-tih-ca bands of the Ne-um hereby agree that they will abandon their wandering mode of life and come in from the Prairies and Staked Plain, and settle upon reserves to be allotted to them in that country which lies north of the Red River and south of the Canadian, and between the ninety-eighth and one hundredth parallels of west longitude, and which has been leased for them and other tribes of red men by the Confederate States from the Choctaws and Chickasaws, and in which the Confederate States have offered all the Ne-um homes.

ART. IV. The No-co-ni, Ta-ne-I-weh, Ya-pa-rih-ca, and Co-cho-toh-ca bands of the Ne-um shall be allowed to choose their own homes in any unoccupied part of the said leased country on or near the Canadian or

False Washita Rivers, or near the Wichita Mountains, as may best suit them, with the concurrence and assent of the agent of the Confederate States for the reserve Indians. Each reserve shall be of sufficient extent of arable and grazing lands amply to supply their needs; and the bands may have one reserve together or four separate reserves, as they may choose. The reserve or reserves shall, as far as practicable, be defined by the natural boundaries that may be described, and so far as this is not practicable, by permanent monuments and definite courses and distances; and full and authentic descriptions of the reserves shall be made out and reserved by the Confederate States.

ART. V. The said No-co-ni, Ta-ne-I-weh, Ya-pa-rih-ca, and Co-cho-tih-ca bands of the Ne-um shall have the right to possess, occupy, and use the reserve or reserves allotted to them as long as grass shall grow or water run; and the reserves shall be their own property, like their horses and cattle.

ART. VI. The members of the said No-co-ni, Ta-ne-I-weh, Ya-pa-rih-ca, and Co-cho-tih-ca bands of the Ne-um shall have the right during all time to hunt and kill game in all the unoccupied part of said leased country without let or molestation from any quarter.

ART. VII. There shall be perpetual peace and brotherhood between the Non-co-ni, Ta-ne-I-weh, Ya-pa-rih-ca, and Co-cho-thi-can bands of the Ne-um, and between each of them and all the other tribes and bands of the Ne-um and of the Wichita, Cado-Ha-da-cho, Hue-co, A-na-dagh-co, Ki-chai, Ai-o-nai, Ta-hua-ca-ro, Ton-ca-we, Shawnee, and Delaware Indians occupying reserves in the said leased country, and any other bands of the Ne-um that may hereafter settle in said leased country; and every injury or act of hostility which either has heretofore sustained at the hands of the other shall be forgiven and forgotten forever.

ART. VIII. The said several tribes and bands of the Ne-um and the said other tribes and bands shall henceforth be good neighbors to each other, and there shall be free and friendly intercourse among them. And it is hereby agreed by the said four bands of the Ne-um that the horses, cattle, and other stock and property of every tribe or band and every person of each is his or its own, and that no one of said four tribes or bands, nor any person belonging to any one of them, shall or will hereafter kill, take away, or injure any such property of another tribe or band, or of any member of any other tribe or band, or in any other way do them any harm.

ART. IX. There shall be perpetual peace and brotherhood between each and all of the No-co-ni, Ta-ne-I-weh, Ya-pa-rih-ca, and Co-cho-tih-ca bands of the Ne-um and the Cherokee, Mus-ko-ki, Seminole, Choctaw, and

Chickasaw Nations; and the chiefs and headmen of each of the said bands shall do all in their power to take and return any negroes, horses, or other property stolen from white men or from persons belonging to the Cherokee, Mus-ko-ki, Seminole, Choctaw, or Chickasaw Nations, and to catch and give up any person among them who may kill or steal or do any other very bad thing.

ART. X. It is distinctly understood by the said four bands of the Ne-um that the State of Texas is one of the Confederate States and joins in this convention, and signs it when the commissioner signs it, and is bound by it; and that all hostilities and enmities between it and them are now ended and are to be forgotten and forgiven forever on both sides.

ART. XI. None of the braves of the said four bands of the Ne-um shall go upon the warpath after they are settled upon reserves against any enemy whatever, or as guides to any war party, except with the knowledge and consent of the agent, nor hold any councils or talks with any white men or other Indians without his knowledge and consent. And the Confederate States will not permit improper persons to live among them, but only such persons as are employed by the Confederate States and traders licensed by them, who President shall make.

ART. XII. To steal a horse or any other article of property from another Indian or white man shall hereafter be considered disgraceful, and the chiefs will discountenance it by every means in their power. For if they should not there never could be any permanent peace. ,br>
ART. XIII. If there should be among the No-co-nis, Ta-ne-I-wehs, Ya-pa-rih-cas, or Co-cho-tih-cas any white prisoner or prisoners it is agreed that they shall be delivered up when come in to settle; and that if they can peaceably procure possession of any that may be held by any other band of the Ne-um, or by the Cai-a-was or any other Prairie tribe, they will also bring them in to be restored to liberty. And the Confederate States agree that if any prisoners are so brought in and restored, suitable rewards shall be given the band that brings them in for doing so. But this article creates no obligation to deliver up Mexicans who may be prisoners.

ART. XIV. The Confederate States also agree that if there be any person or persons held as prisoners in Texas or any other of the Confederate States, or in the Cherokee, Mus-ko-ki, Seminole, Choctaw, or Chickasaw Nations, who are of the Ne-um or Comanches, that all such persons shall be set free and delivered up and restored to their band without charge or expense to the Ne-um.

ART. XV. The Confederate States ask nothing of the bands of the Ne-um, except that they will settle upon their reserves, become industrious, prepare to support themselves, and live in peace and quietness; and in order to encourage and assist them in their endeavors to become able to support themselves the Confederate States agree to furnish them rations of provisions in the same manner as they are now doing for the Wichitas and other tribes and bands settled upon reserves, to include also sugar and coffee, salt, soap, and vinegar, for such time as may be necessary to enable them to feed themselves. They agree to furnish each of the said bands of the Ne-um with twenty cows and calves for every fifty persons contained in the same, and one bull for every forty cows and calves; and also other stock, at the discretion of the superintendent, when they desire to have the same; all of which animals shall be distributed by the agent to such persons and families as shall, in his judgment, be most likely to take care of them. And they also agree to furnish for the use of the said bands of the Ne-um such number of draft oxen, wagons, carts, plows, shovels, hoes, pickaxes, spades, scythes, rakes, axes, and seeds as may be necessary to enable them to farm successfully. They also agree to furnish the said bands of the Ne-um annually with such quantities as the agent shall estimate for and the superintendent require of all such articles as are mentioned and constrained in schedule hereunto annexed, marked A,* to be issued and delivered to them by the agent.

ART. XVI. The Confederate States will maintain one agency for the tribes and bands now settled upon the reserves in the said leased country and for the said four bands and all the other bands of the Ne-um that may settle therein, which agency shall be kept either at the present agency house or some other convenient location, at which the agent shall continually reside; and they do promise the said four bands and all the other bands of the Ne-um that may settle in reserves that they shall never be abandoned by the agent and that he shall not be often nor for any long time away from his agency.

ART. XVII. The Confederate States will employ and pay one interpreter for all the bands of the Ne-um settled upon the reserves; and an additional blacksmith, another striker, and another striker, and another wagon-maker shall be employed for the bands of the Ne-um alone, when the said four bands of the Ne-um shall have come in and settle upon reserves. The interpreter, blacksmith, striker, and wagon-maker shall reside with some one of the bands. The Confederate States will also furnish, from time to time, such tools and such supplies of iron, steel, and wood as may be needed for the work of the said bands, and will also furnish them with medicines and medical advice at the agency, where a physician shall be employed to reside for their benefit exclusively. And they will also employ for five years, and as much longer as the President shall please, a farmer for each reserve, to instruct them in cultivating the soil, so that they may soon be able to feed themselves; and will erect such a number of horse-mills to grind their corn as the superintended shall consider to be necessary in order to accommodate all.

ART. XVIII. The Confederate States also agree to erect such buildings for the mills, and the blacksmith shops, and houses for the farmers, interpreters, and physicians as have been erected among the other Indian tribes, and also to assist the said Indian as in building houses for themselves, and in digging wells for water, and opening their lands.

ART. XIX. The said four bands agree to remain upon their reserves, when they shall have settled thereon, and not, at any time, to leave then in order to make crops elsewhere. And if they should leave them the Confederate States shall not be bound any longer to feed them or make them presents or give them any assistance.

ART. XX. The Confederate States also agree to furnish each warrior of the said four bands who has not a gun with a flint-lock rifle and ammunition, which he agrees never to sell or give away; and the Confederate States will punish any trader or other white man who may purchase one from them.

ART. XXI. The Confederate States will invite all the other bands of the Ne-um or Comanches to abandon their wandering life and settle within the leased country aforesaid; and do promise them, in that case, the same protection and care as is hereby promised to the tribes and bands now residing therein; and that there shall be allotted to them reserves of good land, of sufficient extent, to be held and owned by them forever; and that all the other promises made by these articles shall be considered as made to them also, as well as to the tribes and bands now residing on reserves; and that the same presents shall be made to them and assistance given them in all respects; and

----

*Omitted.

----

the same things, in all respects, are also hereby offered the Cai-a-was and agreed to be given them if they will settle in said country, atone for the murders and robberies they have lately committed, and show a resolution to lead an honest life; to which end the Confederate States send the Cai-a-was with this talk the wampum of peace and the bullet of war, for them to take their choice now and for all time to come.

ART. XXII. The Confederate States hereby guarantee to the members of the aforesaid four bands full indemnity for any horses or any other property that may be killed or stolen from them by any citizen of the Confederate States or by any other Indians: Provided, That the property, if stolen, cannot be recovered and restored, and that sufficient proof is produced to satisfy the agent that it was killed or stolen within the limits of the Confederate States.

ART. XXIII. The Seminoles having asked the Confederate States to pay them for certain horses stolen from them by some of the Ne-um two years ago, and which the United States were bound to pay for if they could not be recovered, the Confederate States have accordingly agreed to do so, at the time of making the treaty lately with the Seminoles; and they do hereby agree, in order that the Ne-um may not hereafter be troubles about the horses so taken, to pay for them the sums, and to the persons mentioned in the schedule thereof hereunto annexed, marked B; * but as the Seminoles allege that one or more of their horses is now here in the possession of some of the No-co-ni, Ta-ne-I-weh, Ya-pa-rih-ca, or Co-cho-tih-ca band of Ne-um, it is agreed that, if it be so, such horse or horses shall be given up and the person in possession shall be compensated for the loss of the same. To this end the chiefs will let the Seminoles see all their horses; and after this time it is distinctly understood that no one can get any right to property by stealing it, and that no compensation will ever again be made to any one who has given up stolen property. And the Confederate States to hereby agree with the several persons from whom horses were stolen, and the heirs of such of them as are deceased, and whose names are found in the said Schedule B,* hereunto annexed, that they will pay, immediately upon the ratification of this treaty, through the agent for the Seminoles, the amount of loss sustained by each respectively, accordingly to the said schedule, except for such horses as may be returned as above provided for and noted as returned on the said schedule.

ART. XXIV. If any difficulty should hereafter arise between any of the other tribes or bands settled on reserves, in consequence of the killing of any one, of the stealing or killing of horses, cattle, or other stock, or of injury in any other way to person or property, the same shall be submitted to the agent of the Confederate States, who shall settle and decide the same equitably and justly, to which settlement all parties agree to submit, and such atonement and satisfaction shall be made as he shall direct.

ART. XXV. In order that the friendship which now exists between the said several tribes country, and the Choctaws and Chickasaws and the people of the Confederate States, may not be interrupted by the conduct of individuals, it is hereby agreed that if any white man or any Choctaw or Chickasaw injures an Indian of any one of said tribes

----
*Omitted.

and bands, or if any one of them injures a white man or a Choctaw or Chickasaw no private revenge or retaliation shall take place, nor shall the Choctaws or Chickasaws try the person who does the wrong, and punish him in their courts, but he shall be tried and punished by the Confederate States; and the life of every person belonging to said tribes and bands shall be of the same value as the life of a white man; and any Indian or white man who kills one of them without cause shall be hung by the neck until he is dead.

ART. XXVI. In case either of the bands of the Ne-um, with whom this convention is made, should not consent to come in and settle, and should prefer to continue to live as they have heretofore, then there shall still be peace and friendship between them and the people of the Confederate States and the Cherokees, Mus-ko-kis, Seminoles, Choctaws, and Chickasaws, and all the tribes and bands settled upon reserves in the country aforesaid; and all of the same shall travel, without injury or molestation, thorough the hunting-grounds of the Ne-um, and shall be treated with kindness and friendship.

ART. XXVII. It is further hereby agreed by the Confederate States that all the Texan troops now within the limits of said leased country shall be withdrawn across Red River, and that no Texas troop shall hereafter be stationed in forts or garrisons in the said country, or be sent into the same, except in the service of the Confederate States and when on the warpath against the Cai-a-was or other hostile Indians.

ART. XXVIII. It is further agreed by the chiefs and headmen of the bands of the Ne-um who have signed this convention that upon their return to their bands they will take this talk and the wampum of peace from the Confederate States and from the Mus-ko-kis, Seminoles, Choctaws, and Chickasaws to the bands of the Ne-um, and tell them what they have seen and heard, and persuade them also, if they can, to come in and settle upon reserves in the leased country, and at any rate to make peace by the time when the leaves fall before the next snows.

ART. XXIX. It is agreed by the parties that the making of this convention shall in nowise interrupt the friendly relations between the Ne-um and the people of Mexico, and that the Confederate States desire that perfect peace should exist between the Ne-um and all the Mexicans.

ART. XXX. This convention shall be obligatory on the bands whose chiefs and headmen sign the same from the day of its date, and on the Confederate States from and after its ratification by the proper authority.

In perpetual testimony whereof the said Albert Pike, as commissioner with plenary powers of the Confederate States of America to the Indian nations and tribes west of Arkansas, for and on behalf of the said Confederate States, doth now hereunto set his hand and affix the seal of his arms; and Qui-na-hi-wi, or the Drinking Eagle, chief of the No-co-ni band of the Ne-um, and the undesigned headmen of the same, for and in behalf of that band; and the same Qui-na-hi-wi, chief of the No-co-nis, by special authorization and direction of Po-ho-wi-ti-quas-so, or Iron Shirt, the chief of the Ta-ne-I-weh band of the Ne-um, who has been present, but is now absent mourning for a relative deceased, with Ke-e-na-toh-pa, a headman of the Ta-ne-I-weh band, for and on behalf of the same; and Te-hi-a-quah, chief of the Ya-pa-rih-ca band of the Ne-um, with the undersigned headmen of the same, for and on behalf of the Ya-pa-rih-ca band; and Ma-a-we, chief of the Co-cho-tih-ca band of the Ne-um, with the undersigned headmen of the same, for and on behalf of the Co-cho-tih-ca band, do now hereunto respectively set their hands and affix their seals.

Done at the Wichita Agency aforesaid on the twelfth day of August, A. D. one thousand eight hundred and sixty-one.

[SEAL.]

ALBERT PIKE,

Commissioner of the Confederate States to the Indian Nations and Tribes West of Arkansas.

Qui-na-hi-wi, principal chief of the No-co-ni band
O-te, sub-chief of the No-co-nis
Ke-pa-he-wa, sub-chief of the No-co-nis
Cho-o-shi, retired chief of the No-co-nis
Po-ho-wi-ti-quas-so, principal chief of Ta-ne-I-weh band, by Qui-na-hi-wi, principal chief of the No-co-ni band
Ke-e-na-toh-pa, sub-chief of the Ta-ne-I-weh band
Te-hi-a-quah, chief of the Ya-pa-rih-ca band
Bis-te-Va. -na, principal chief of the Ya-pa-rih-ca band
Pe-hai-e-chi, chief of the Ya-pa-rih-ca band
Ma-a-we, principal chief of the Cho-co-thi-ca band
Cho-co-ra, chief of the Co-cho-tih-ca band
Te-co-wih-ap, chief of the Co-cho-tih-ca band.

Signed, sealed, and copies exchanged in presence of us.

Wm. Quesenbury, secretary to the commissioner
E. Rector, Superintendent of Indian Affairs for the Confederate States
M. Leeper, agent of the Wichita and affiliated bands of the Confederate States
Motey Kinnaird, principal chief of the Mus-ko-kis
John Jumper, principal chief of the Seminoles
Chilly McIntosh,
Israel G. Vore,
W. Warren Johnson
W. L. Pike,
Jesse Chisholm
H. P. Jones
Charles B. Johnson
J. J. Strum, Wm. Shirley,
Wm. H. Faulkner.

(To the Indian names are subjoined marks.)

RATIFICATION.

Resolved (two-thirds of the Congress concurring), That the Congress of the Confederate States of America do advise and consent to commissioner of the Confederate States to the Indian nations west of Arkansas, in behalf of the Confederate States, of and one part, and the No-co-ni, Ta-ne-I-weh, Co-cho-tih-ca, and Ya-pa-rih-ca bands of the Ne-um or Comanches of the Prairies and Staked Plain, by their chiefs and headmen, who signed the same articles, of the other part, concluded at the Wichita Agency, near the False Washita River, in the country leased from the Choctaws, on the twelfth day of August, A. D. one thousand eighth hundred and sixty-one, with the following amendments, to wit:

First. In the last paragraph of Article XIII, where occur the words, "but this article creates no obligation to deliver up Mexicans who may be prisoners," strike out all after the word "up" and insert in lieu thereof the following words, "other prisoners than inhabitants of the Confederate States of Territories thereof. "

Second. Strike out all of Article XX.

Third. Strike out all of Article XXVII.

OFFICIAL RECORDS: Series 4, vol 1, Part 1
Pages 542-548
Confederate States of America - Wichita, et. al.

ARTICLES OF A CONVENTION entered into and concluded at the Wichita Agency, near the False Washita River, in the country leased from the Choctaws and Chickasaws, on the twelfth day of August, D. C. one thousand eight hundred and sixty-one, between the Confederate States of America, by Albert Pike, their commissioner with full powers, appointed by the President by virtue of an act of the Congress in that behalf, of the one part, and the Pen-e-tegh-ca band of the Ne-um or Comanches, and the tribes and bands of Wichitas, Cado-Ha-da-chos, Hue-cos, Ta-hua-ca-ros, A-na-dagh-cos, Ton-ca-wes, Ai-o-nais, Ki-chais, Shawnees, and Delawares residing in the said leased country, by their respective chiefs and headmen, who have signed these articles, of the other part.

ARTICLE I. The Pen-e-tegh-ca band of the Ne-um or Comanches, and the tribes and bands of the Wichitas, Cado-Ha-da-chos, Hue-cos, Ta-hua-ca-ros, A-na-dagh-cos, Ton-ca-wes, Ai-o-nais, Ki-chais, Shawnees, and Delawares now residing within the country north of Red River and south of the Canadian, and between the ninety-eighth and one hundredth parallels of west longitude, leased for them and other tribes from the Choctaw and Chickasaw Nations, do hereby place themselves under the laws and protection of the Confederate States of America in peace and war forever.

ART. II. The Confederate States of America do hereby promise and engage themselves to be during all time the friends and protectors of the Pen-e-tegh-ca band of the Ne-um, and of the Wichitas, Cado-Ha-da-chos, Hue-cos, Ta-hua-ca-ros, A-na-dagh-cos, Ton-ca-wes, Ai-o-nais, Ki-chais, Shawnees, and Delawares residing, or that may hereafter come to reside, in the said leased country; and that they will not allow them henceforward to be in any wise troubled or molested by any power or people, State or person whatever.

ART. III. The reserves at present occupied by the said several tribes and bands may continue to be occupied by them if they are satisfied therewith; and if any of them are not the tribe or tribes, band or bands dissatisfied, may select other reserves instead of those now occupied by them, in the same leased country, with the concurrence and assent by the agent of the Confederate States for the reserve Indians, at any time within two years from the day of the signing of these articles.

ART. IV. Each reserve shall be of sufficient extent of good arable and grazing land amply to supply the needs of the tribe or band that is to occupy it; and each shall have a separate reserve, unless two or more elect to settle and reside together and hold their reserves in common. The reserves shall, as far as practicable, be defined by natural boundaries that may be described, and so far as this is not practicable, by permanent monuments and definite courses and distances; and full and authentic descriptions of the reserves shall be made out and preserved by the Confederate States.

ART. V. Each or band shall have the right to possess, occupy, and use the reserve allotted to it as long as grass shall grow and water run, and the reserves shall be their own property, like their horses and cattle.

ART. VI. The members of all the said several bands and tribes of Indians shall have the right, henceforward forever, to hunt and kill game in all the unoccupied part of the said leased country without let or molestation from any quarter.

ART. VII. There shall be perpetual peace and brotherhood between the Pen-e-tegh-ca band of the Ne-um or Comanches, and the tribes and bands of the Wichitas, Cado-Ha-da-chos, Hue-cos, Ta-hua-ca-ros, A-na-dagh-cos, Ton-ca-wes, Ai-o-nais, Ki-chais, Shawnees, and Delawares, between each of them and each and all of the others; and every injury or act of hostility which either has heretofore sustained at the hands of the other shall be forgiven and forgotten.

ART. VIII. The said several tribes and bands shall henceforth be good neighbors to each other, and there shall be a free and friendly intercourse among them. And it is hereby agreed by all that the horses, cattle, and other stock and property of each tribe or band and of every person of each, is his or its own, and that no tribe or band nor any person belonging to any tribe or band shall, or will hereafter, kill, take away, or injure any such property of another tribe or band or of any member of any other tribe or band, or in any other way do them any harm.

ART. IX. There shall be perpetual peace and brotherhood between each and all of said tribes and bands and the Cherokee, Mus-ko-ki, Seminole, Choctaw, and Chickasaw Nations; and the chiefs and head-men of each of the said tribes and bands shall do all in their power to take and return any negroes, horses, or other property stolen from white men or from persons who belong to the Cherokee, Mus-ko-ki, Seminole, Choctaw, or Chickasaw Nation, and to catch and give up any person among them who may kill or steal or do any other very wrong thing.

ART. X. None of the laws of the Choctaws and Chickasaws shall ever be in force in the said leased country so as to affect any of the members of the said several tribes and bands, but only as to their own people who may settle therein; and they shall never interfere in any way with the reserves, improvements, or property of the reserve Indians.

ART. XI. It is distinctly understood by the said several tribes and bands that the State of Texas is one of the Confederate States, and joins this convention, and signs it when the commissioner signs it, and is bound by it; and that all hostilities and enmities between it and them are now ended and are to be forgotten and forgiven on both sides.

ART. XII. None of the braves of the said tribes and bands shall go upon the warpath against any enemy whatever, except with the consent of the agent, nor hold any councils or talks with any white men or other Indians without his knowledge and consent. And the Confederate States will not permit improper persons to live among them, but only such persons as are employed by the Confederate States and traders licensed by them, who shall sell to the Indians and buy from them at fair prices, under such regulations as the President shall make

ART. XIII. To steal a horse or any other article of property form an Indian or a white man shall hereafter be considered disgraceful,and the chief will discountenance it by every means in their power. For if they should not there never could be any permanent peace.

ART. XIV. The Confederate States ask nothing of the Pen-e-tegh-cas, Wichitas, Cado-Ha-da-chos, Hue-cos, Ta-hua-ca-ros, A-na-dagh-cos, Ton-ca-wes, Ai-o-nais, Ki-chais, Shawnees, and Delawares, except that they will settle upon their reserves, become industrious, and prepare to support themselves, and live in peace in peace and quietness; and in order to encourage and assist them in their endeavors to become able to support themselves, the Confederate States agree to continue to furnish them rations of provisions in the same manner as they are now doing, to include, also, sugar and coffee, salt, soap, and vinegar, for such time as may be necessary to enable them to feed themselves. They agree to furnish each tribe or band with twenty cows and calves for every fifty persons contained in the same, and one bull for every forty cows and calves; and also to furnish to al of said tribes and bands together 250 stock hogs, all of which animals shall be distributed by the agent to such persons and families as shall, in his judgment, be most proper to receive them and most likely to take care of them. And they also agree to furnish, for the use of the use of the said tribes and bands, such number of draft-oxen, wagons, carts, plows, shovels, hoes, pickaxes, spares, scythes, rakes, axes, and seeds as may be necessary, in addition to their present supply, to enable them to farm successfully. They also agree to furnish each tribe or band annually with such quantities as the agent shall estimate for, and the superintendent require, of all such articles as are mentioned and contained in the schedule hereunto annexed, marked A; * to be issued and delivered to them, by the agent.

ART. XV. The Confederate States will maintain one agency for the said tribes and bands at the present agency house or some other suitable and convenient location, at which the agent shall continually reside; and they do promise the said tribes and bands that they shall never be abandoned by the agent, and that he shall not be often nor for any long time away from his agency.

ART. XVI. The Confederate States will also employ and pay an interpreter for each language spoken among the said tribes and bands, and also one blacksmith, who shall also be a gunsmith, one striker, and one wagon-maker, for all; all of whom shall reside at the agency; and they will furnish all the people of said tribes and bands who may be sick with medicines and medical service at the agency, where a physician shall be employed to reside for their benefit exclusively. They will also employ for five years, and as much longer as the President shall please, a farmer for each reserve to instruct the Indians in cultivating the soil, so that they may soon be able to feed themselves; and will erect such a number of horse-mills to grind their corn as the superintendent shall consider to be necessary, in order to accommodate all. And the stock and animals to be given to the tribes and bands shall be in charge of the farmers, that they may not be foolishly killed or left to perish by neglect.

ART. XVII. The Confederate States also agree to erect such buildings for the mills, and the blacksmith shops, and houses for the farmers and interpreters, as have been erected among the other Indian tribes, and also to assist the said Indians in building houses for themselves, and in digging wells for water, and opening their lands.

ART. XVIII. The said bands and tribes agree to remain upon their reserves, and not at any time to leave them in order to make crops elsewhere. And if they should leave them the Confederate States shall not be bound any longer to feed them or make them presents or give them any assistance.

ART. XIX. The Confederate States also agree to furnish each warrior of the said tribes and bands who has not a gun with a flint-lock rifle and ammunition, which he agrees never to sell or give away; and the Confederate States will punish any trader or other white man who may purchase one from them.

ART. XX. The Confederate States invite all the other bands of the Ne-um or Comanches to abandon their wandering life and settle within the leased country aforesaid, and do promise them in that case the same protection and care as is hereby promised to said tribes and bands now residing therein; and that there shall be allotted to them reserves of good land, of sufficient extent, to be held and owned by them forever; and that all the other promises made by these articles shall be considered as made to them also, as well as to the tribes and bands now residing on reserves; and that the same present s shall be made them and assistance given them in all respects; and the same things in all respects are hereby also offered the Cai-a-was and agreed to be given them if they will settle in said country, atone for the murders and robberies they have lately committed, and show a resolution to lead an honest life; to which end the Confederate States send the Cai-a-was with this talk the wampum of peace and the bullet of war, for them to take their choice now and for all time to come.

ART. XXI. The Confederate States hereby guarantee to the members of the aforesaid tribes and bands full indemnity for any horses or any other property that may be killed or stolen from them by any citizen of the Confederate States, or by Indians of any other tribe or band: Provided, That the property, if stolen, cannot be recovered and restored, and that sufficient proof is produced to satisfy the agent that it was killed or stolen within the limits of the Confederate States.

ART. XXII. If any difficulty should hereafter arise between any of the bands or tribes in consequence of the killing of any one, of the stealing or killing of horses, cattle, or other stock, or of injury in any other way to person or property, the same shall be submitted to the agent of the Confederate States, who shall settle and decide the same equitably and justly, to which settlement all parties agree to submit, and such atonement and satisfaction shall be made as he shall direct.

ART. XXIII. In order that the friendship which now exists between the said several tribes and bands of Indians and the people of the Confederate States and of the Choctaw and Chickasaw Nations may not be interrupted by the conduct of individuals, it is hereby agreed that if any white man or any Choctaw or Chickasaw injures an Indian of any one of said tribes and bands, or if any one of them injures a white man or a Choctaw or Chickasaw, no private revenge or retaliation shall take place, nor shall the Choctaws or Chickasaws try the shall be tried and punished by the Confederate States; and the life of every person belonging to said tribes and bands shall be of the same value as the life of a white man; and any Indian or white man who kills one of them without cause shall be hung by the neck until he is dead.

ART. XXIV. It is further hereby agreed by the Confederate States that all the Texan troops now within the limits of the said leased country shall hereafter be stationed in forts or garrisons in the said country or be sent into the same, except in the service of the Confederate States and when on the war path against the Cai-a-was or other hostile Indians.

ART. XXV. This convention shall be obligatory on the tribes and bands whose chiefs and headmen signed the same from the same day of its date, and on the Confederate States from and after its ratification by the proper authority.

In perpetual testimony whereof the said Albert Pike, as commissioner with plenary powers of the Confederate States of America to the Indian nations and tribes west of Arkansas, for and on behalf of the said Confederate States, doth now hereunto set his hand and affix and on behalf of their respective tribes and bands, do now hereunto respectively set their hands and affix their seals.

Done at the Wichita Agency aforesaid on this the twelfth day of August, A. D. one thousand eight hundred and sixty-one.

[SEAL.]

ALBERT PIKE,

Commissions of the Confederate States to the Indian Nations and Tribes West of Arkansas.

Ke-ka-re-wa, principal chief of the Pen-e-tengh-ca band of the Ne-um
To-sa-wi, second chief of the Pen-e-tegh-ca band of the Ne-um
Ca-ca-dia, second chief of the Hue-cos
Te-ats, sub-chief of the Hue-cos
O-chi-ras, principal chief of the Ta-hua-ca-ros
Pa-in-hot-sa-ma, war chief of the Pen-e-tegh-ca band of the Ne-um
I-sa-do-wa, principal chief of the Wichitas
A-wa-he, second chief of the Wichitas
A-sa-ca-ra, chief of the Wichitas
Ta-nah, principal chief of the Cado-Ha-da-chos
Tai-o-tun, second chief of the Cado-Ha-da-chos
Cha-wah-un, captain of the Cado-Ha-da-chos
A-he-dat, principal chief of the Hue-cos
Sam Houston, second chief of the Ta-hua-ca-ros
Ca-shao, principal chief of the Ai-o-nais
Jose Maria, principal chief of the A-na-dagh-cos
Co-se-mu-so, second chief of the A-na-dagh-cos
Ke-se-mira, captain of the Ton-ca-wes
Ki-is-qua, second chief of the Ki-chais

John Linny, chief of the Delawares.

Signed, sealed, and copied exchanged in presence of us.

Wm. Quesenbury, secretary to the commissioner
E. Rector, Superintendent of Indian Affairs for the Confederate States
M. Leeper, agent of the Confederate States for the Wichitas and other bands
Motey Kinnaird, principal chief of the Mus-ko-kis
John Jumper, principal chief of the Seminoles
Chilly McIntosh
Israel G. Vore
W. Warren Johnston
W. L. Pike
H. P. Jones
Charles B. Johnston
J. J. Sturm
Wm. Shirley
W. H.Faulkner.

(To the Indian names are subjoined marks.)

ARTICLE SUPPLEMENTARY to the convention between the Confederate States of America and the Pen-e-tegh-ca band of Ne-um or Comanches, Wichitas, Cado-Ha-da-chos, and other bands settled upon reserves, made and concluded at the Wichita Agency, near the False Washita River, on the twelfth day of August, A. D. one thousand eight hundred and sixty-one.

ARTICLE. It being well known to all surrounding tribes and universally acknowledge that, from time immemorial, the Ta-wa-I-hash people of Indians, now called by white men the Wichitas, and of whom the Hue-cos and Ta-hua-ca-ros are offshoots, possessed and inhabited, to the exclusion of all other tribes and bands of Indians, the whole country lying between the Red River and the False Washita, from their junction to the west of the Wichita Mountains, and with the aid of the Ta-ne-I-weh band of the Ne-um held all that country against all comers, and had their villages and fields in the valleys of the Wichita Mountains and upon the creeks, and there cultivated the soil, raised stock, and led an industrious life; all of which facts were known to the commissioner of the Confederate States twenty-nine years ago;

And the United States of America, having, in the year eighteen hundred and twenty, and by subsequent renewals of the grant, ceded the whole of that country to the Choctaws, and having afterward, by patent, conveyed and assured the same to them in fee, and they having made the

Chickasaws joint and equal owners of the same with themselves, whereby the same has been wholly lost to the Ta-wa-I-hash, except such small portion thereof as has been assigned to them by way of reserve, and no compensation whatever has been made from thereof, although they respectfully presented their claim on account of the same to the Commissioner of Indian Affairs of the United States and appealed to that Government for payment of some reasonable price for their said country, to be paid them in such manner as should be most for their benefit and improvement;

And the commissioner knowing that their claim to compensation is a just one, and seeing how poor and helpless they are, and being willing to save them from the necessity of employing persons to urge their claim and of dividing with them what they may receive, but not deeming himself authorized to decide what amount shall be allowed them therefor, nor in what manner it shall be paid:

It is therefore hereby agreed by the Confederate States that the claim of the Ta-wa-I-hash or Wichitas to compensation for their country, between the Red River and the False Washita, shall be submitted to the President for his consideration, who, if he also agrees that it is just, shall determine what amount shall be paid or allowed them in satisfaction thereof, and in what manner that amount shall be paid; and that amount shall accordingly be paid them in such manner as he shall direct.

In testimony whereof the said Albert Pike, commissioner of the Confederate States of America to the Indian nations and tribes west of Arkansas, doth hereunto set his hand, on behalf of the said Confederate States, and affix the seal of his arms.

So done and signed and sealed at Wichita Agency, near the False Washita River, on the thirteenth day of August in the year first aforesaid.

[SEAL.]

ALBERT PIKE,

Commissioner of the Confederate States to the Indian Nations and Tribes West of Arkansas

WM. QUESENBURY,
Secretary of Commissioner.

RATIFICATION.

Resolved (two-thirds of the Congress concurring), That the Congress of the Confederate States of America do advise and consent to the ratification of the Confederate States to the Indian nations west of Arkansas, in behalf of the Confederate States, of the one part, and the Pen-e-tegh-ca band of Ne-um or Comanches, and the tribes and bands of the Wichitas, Cado-Ha-da-chos, Hue-cos, Ta-hua-ca-ros, A-na-dagh-cos, Ton-ca-wes, Ai-o-nais, Ki-chais, Shawnees, and Delasaws, each by its chiefs and headmen, who signed the said articles, of the other part; concluded at the Wichita Agency, near the False Washita the twelfth August, A. D. one thousand eight hundred and sixty-one. And that the Congress also advises and consents to the ratification of the supple same time and place, by the said commissioner on behalf of the Confederate States with the Ta-wa-I-hash or Wichita band of Indians, with the amendments adopted, to wit:

First. Strike out all of Article XIX.

Second. Strike out all of Article XXIV.

Important sites, skirmishes and battles in Indian Territory, 1861-1865

Armstrong Academy: Located Bryan County, 2.5 miles north of Bokchita on State Highway 22, then 2.5 miles east.
- Served as a major Southern Administrative Center and troop assembly point throughout the Civil War. It was here that representatives of the Cherokee, Choctaw, Chickasaw, Creek, Seminole and Caddo formed the United Nations of Indian Territory. Armstrong Academy was re-named Chata Tamaha (Choctaw City) and designated the Capitol of the Choctaw nation.

Backbone Mountain: Located LeFlore County east of state Highway 112, 1 mile south of Pocola.
- Sept. 1, 1863. The 3 hour battle fought on the mountain's summit. Confederate troops under Brig. Gen. William L. Cabell were defeated by Major Gen. James G. Blunt's Union Forces. The battle assured Federal control over Fort Smith and opened the Fort Towson-Fort smith Military Road.

Bayou Menard: Located south of U.S. Highway 62 where it crosses Bayou Menard in northeastern Muskogee County.
- July 27, 1862. Major William A. Phillips' advance troops of the first Federal invasion of Indian Territory during the War Between the States encountered and routed a Confederate force.

Bloomfield Academy: Located Bryan County, 3 miles south of Achille and 1 mile northeast of Hendrix.
- Frequent campsite of the Confederate Chickasaw Battalion during the War. The school opened as a seminary for Chickasaw girls in 1854, used for a hospital and commissary distribution. Extensive footings of the buildings, which burned in 1914, remain.

Boggy Depot: Atoka County, 11 miles west of Atoka, 6 miles east of Wapanucka on state Highway 7, then south 4 miles, now part a State Park.
- Main Confederate Commissary Depot in Indian Territory during the War. Strategically located at the intersection of the Texas Road and the military road between Fort Smith and Fort Arbuckle. The local Presbyterian Church served as a military hospital. 3 miles northeast of Boggy Depot a small skirmish took place on April 24, 1865, 15 days after Lee's surrender at Appomattox. 3 Confederate troopers were killed.

Buck Creek Camp: LeFlore County, 1 mile east of Bokoshe on State Highway 31, then .5 mile south, 2.25 miles east on county roads along the banks of Buck Creek.
- Favorite campsite of the Confederate troops during the war. The First Choctaw and Chickasaw Regiment, CSA, was trained here.

Cabin Creek: Located Mayes County, 3 miles north of Pensacola on west bank of Cabin Creek.
- July 1-2, 1863, first battle. Confederate Brig. Gen. Stand Watie attacked a Federal wagon train where the California Road crossed Cabin Creek. Col. James M. Williams, commanding the federal troops charged across the rain-swollen creek, forced the Southerners to withdraw. Allowed the Federals to re-supply and reinforce Fort Gibson, to maintain their hold on northern Indian Territory.

Cabin Creek: Located Mayes County, 3 miles north of Pensacola on west bank of Cabin Creek.
- Sept. 18-19, 1864, second battle. Gen Watie, with Gen. Richard M. Gano's Texas troops, captured a Federal wagon train worth $1.5 million worth of supplies. Confederates destroyed the disabled wagons and injured mules, returned southward with 130 wagons of food clothing and ammunition. It was a major engagement of the War in the Territory.

Camp Armstrong: Bryan County 3 miles northeast of Bokchito.
- 1862-1865 Confederate Post used as hospital and rest camp.

Camp Brooken: Haskell County, northwest of the junction of State Highways 71 and 9, south bank of the Canadian River.
- 1862, Confederate campsite.

Camp Jumper: Pittsburg County, east side of U.S. Highway 69, 1.5 miles south of intersection with State Highway 113.
- Established by the Confederacy during the War as one of its outposts across Indian Territory. It was named for Col. John Jumper, First Seminole Volunteer Cavalry.

Camp McCulloch: Cherokee County, near intersection of State Highway 82 and U.S. Highway 62.
- 1861, was staging area for the Confederate Campaign to drive O-pothle-yahola and the pro-Northern Indians out of Indian Territory at the beginning of the War.

Camp McIntosh: Caddo County, south side of the Washita River 25 miles north of State Highway 9 and 5 miles west of the Caddo-Grady County line.
- Was westernmost of the 200 mile long Confederate outpost line maintained along the Canadian and Arkansas Rivers. Named for Col. James McQueen McIntosh (no relation to

the Indian McIntosh brothers,) killed at the Battle of Pea Ridge. Occupied intermittently during the War.

Camp Napoleon: Grady County, at Verden along State Highway 62.
- May 26, 1865, meeting between representatives of the pro-Southern Cherokee, Choctaw, Creek, Seminole, Chickasaw, Caddo and Osage Indians and leaders of the Plains Kiowa, Arapaho, Cheyenne, Lipan, Caddo, Comanche, and Anadarko. More than 5,000 Indians attended the meeting, which produced a peace treaty between the Tribes at the close of the War.

Camp Pike: Haskell County, 1 mile northeast of the intersection of State Highways 9 and 2.
- Frequent camping place for Confederate troops.

Camp Ross: Cherokee County, near Ross Cottage, John Ross' home at Park Hill.
- Frequent camping site Confederate Troops.

Camp Steel: LeFlore County, just across the Arkansas-Oklahoma border from Fort Smith.
- 1862, Was Confederate Campsite during the winter.

Camp Wattles: Mayes County, near the mouth of Pryor Creek.
- July, 1862 Campsite used by both Confederate and Federal troops during the War. Established by Union Col. Robert W. Furnas, commander of First Indian Regiment during the first Federal Indian Expedition. Was a base of operations to help the pro-Northern Indians re-establishing control over the Northern part of Cherokee Nation. Shortly after Furnas and his pro-Northern Indian troops were forced to withdraw to Kansas.

Choska: Wagoner County, just east of where State Highway 104 crosses the Arkansas.
- November 9, 1861. Campsite for Col. Douglas H. Cooper's troops after the Battle of Chusta-Talasah.

Chustenahlah: Osage County 4 miles west of Skiatook on State Highway 20 where it crosses Quapaw Creek, then 1 mile north, west side of the county road.
- December 26, 1861. Battle when Confederate Troops commanded by Col. James M. McIntosh intercepted more than 3,500 pro-Northern Creek and Seminole with Opothleyahola.

Chusto-Talasah (Caving Banks): Tulsa County, 5 miles south on U.S. Highway 75 from it's junction with State Highway 20, then 1 mile west and .5 mile south on county roads on the west side of the roadway at the horseshoe bend of Bird Creek.

- November 11, 1961, Battle between Opothleyahola's pro-Northern Creeks and Seminoles and Confederate Col. Douglas H. Cooper's troops.

Concharty: Wagoner County, east of Stone Bluff on Concharty Creek, south of Arkansas River, northeast of US Highway 64.

- Campsite of Confederate Brig. General Douglas H. Cooper's supply wagon train during the battle of Round Mountain. After the battle, troops briefly camped at nearby Spring Hill to rest.

Coody's Bluff: Nowata County, south side of Verdigris River 4 miles from intersection US Highways 169 and 60 on county roads.

- Garrisoned by 500 Cherokee of Col. John Drew during early part of War.

Council Hill: Muskogee County, 2 miles east on US Highway 62 from Okmulgee-Muskogee County line, 4 miles south.

- Headquarters for pro-southern Creek units through the War.

Cowskin Prairie: Delaware County, west of State Highway 10 and north of State Highway 25 intersection.

- June 6, 1862, Site where Brig. General Stand Watie's troops were attacked by Federal force commanded by Col. Charles Doubleday.
- 1863, Pro-Northern Cherokee held National Council, adopted Cherokee Emancipation Proclamation, freeing slaves.

Creek Agency: Muskogee County, 1 mile west of US Highway 69 on Agency Hill.

- October 15, 1863, skirmish between pro-Southern Creek and Cherokee and pro-Northern Cherokee and Osage.

Doaksville: Choctaw County, 1 mile North of Fort Towson on US Highway 70.

- Confederate Capitol of Choctaw Nation 1860-1863, major War supply center.

Fort Arbuckle: Garvin County, 4.5 miles west on State Highway 7 from intersection with I-35 to Hoover, .25 mile north on county road.

- May 3, 1861, two companies Federal Troops withdrew abandoned post. May 5, Texas troops occupied.
- Staging area for Confederate forces in Indian Territory.

Fort Arbuckle on the Arkansas: Tulsa County, north side of Arkansas River 2 miles north State Highway 151 from junction with State Highway 25, east on county road.

- November 11, 1834, abandoned.
- November 1861, some of O-pothle-yahola's pro-northern followers camped among the ruins before Battle of Round Mountain.

Fort Blunt: Muskogee County

- August, 1863, surrounded Fort Gibson, built by Union General William A. Phillips to strengthen Gibson after Federals reoccupied by 6000 Federal Troops.

Fort Cobb: Caddo County, 1.5 miles east of town of Fort Cobb along east bluffs of Cobb Creek.

- May, 1861, abandoned by Federal Troops, immediately occupied by Col. William C. Young and Texas State Troops. About 30 local Indians enlisted, Confederate service, served as guard for nearby Wichita Agency. Abandoned August 1862.

Fort Coffee: LeFlore County, 4 miles north of Skullyville, built on Swallow Rock, overlooking Arkansas River.

- 1838, Abandoned by Federal Troops, became Choctaw Boys Academy,
- 1861- October 1863, occupied by Confederate troops till over run and burned by Federal troops.

Fort Davis (Cantonment Davis): Muskogee County, 1 mile north Bacone College, just east of where State Highway 16 crosses Arkansas River. South side of Arkansas River, 2 miles south of mouth of Verdigris River.

- November 1862, built by Confederates to offset Federal presence at Fort Gibson. Occupied intermittently until December 27, 1862, when Phillip's Federal Command captured and burned the buildings.

Fort Gibson: Muskogee County, in town of fort Gibson, east side of Grand River.

- September 1857, abandoned.
- 1862, Reoccupied by col. Phillip's Federals.

Fort McCulloch: Bryan county, .5 mile south of State Highway 22, 1.5 miles from junction with State Highway 48, 200 yards south of Blue River.

- March, 1862, established by Confederate Brig. General Albert Pike after Battle of Pea Ridge, Arkansas.
- July 21, 1862, Abandoned by Pike, later reoccupied by pro-Southern Troops.

Fort Towson (Cantonment Towson; Camp Phoenix): Choctaw County, just north of US Highway 70 at Fort Towson.

- May 1824, established as Cantonment Towson, abandoned 1829, buildings burned, re-established 1831 as Camp Phoenix due to Choctaw Removal, served as supply depot, and deactivated 1854.
- 1861, occupied by Confederate troops, as Fort Towson, served as regional Headquarters.

Fort Washita, Bryan County, north side State Highway 199, 3 miles west of junction with State Highway 18.

- April 23, 1842, Established.

- May 1, 1861 seized by Confederate forces, served as headquarters for Brig. General Douglas a. Cooper during War, major supply point and hospital facility.

Fort Wayne, (2nd site): Delaware County, 1.25 miles west of Oklahoma-Arkansas border, on State Highway 20 and 4.5 miles south on county roads.

- 1839, established to find healthier climate for troops at Old Fort Wayne (south of present site). Abandoned May 26, 1842.
- July 1861, occupied by Brig. General Stand Watie, served as staging area for Cherokee Mounted Rifles, first unit raised for Confederacy in Indian Territory.
- October 22, 1862 on nearby Beattie's Prairie, Brig. General James Blunt's Federal forces attacked Col. Douglas H. Cooper's Confederate Indians. Gave Federal Army command of Indian Territory north of Arkansas River.

George Washington Caddo's Home: Canadian County, south side of North Fork of Canadian River, 5 miles west of Union City.

- 1864, George Washington Caddo commissioned a major in Confederate Army, authorized to raise Caddo Battalion to prevent raids by Plains Indians into areas occupied by Five Civilized Tribes.

Goodland Mission: Choctaw County, 1.5 miles east on State Highway 2A from junction with US Highway 271.

- Mobilization site for two companies of Second Choctaw Regiment, CSA, during War.

Greenleaf Town: Okfuskee County, 3 miles west of Okemah on state Highway 56 from junction with State Highway 27, 1 mile south on county road.

- August 1861, gathering site for O-pothle-yahola's followers. Old town site was probably west of the road along the creek.
- November 1861, O-pothle-yohola led the Loyal Indians north toward Kansas.

Harris Ferry: McCurtain County, below Harris OK, where State Highway 87 nears Red River.

- Major communications point Indian Territory Confederates and Texas troops during War.

Honey Springs: McIntosh and Muskogee Counties, along Elk Creek on east and west sides US Highway 69 for 1 mile north and one mile south of county line.

- July 17, 1863, Major General James G. Blunt's 3,000 Federal troops assaulted 5,000 Confederate troops deployed along Elk Creek. Confederates, with wet powder that would not fire, were forced out. Broke the power of the Confederacy in Indian Territory for remainder of War.

Iron Bridge: Haskell County, 1.25 miles south of where State Highway 9 crosses San Bois Creek.
- June 16 and 19, 1864, skirmish following Brig. General Stand Watie's capture of J. R. Williams. Bridge built in 1859 by Federal government as part of Butterfield Stage route. Frequently used by Federal and Confederate troops during War.

Pleasant Bluff: Haskell County, northeast edge of Tamaha along Arkansas.
- June 15, 1864, Brig. General Stand Watie ambushed and captured Federal supply steamboat J. R. Williams, hauling supplies from Fort Smith to Fort Gibson. Disabled with cannon fire from bluffs overlooking river, drove it to shore, forced Federal escort to abandon, captured $120,000.00 worth of supplies.

Koweta Mission: Wagoner County, 2.5 miles east on county road from intersection State Highway 52 and Muskogee Turnpike.
- July 1861, seized by Confederates.
- July 1862, Re-occupied by Federal troops.

Locust Grove: Mayes County, south of US Highway 412, 2.5 miles east of Locust Grove.
- July 3, 1862, skirmish, 300 Federals under Col. William Weer surprised Confederate Col. J. J. Clarkson's camp, forcing Clarkson and 110 men to surrender.

Middle Boggy: Atoka County, 1 mile north of Atoka, on North side of Middle (Muddy Boggy) Creek.
- Frequent campsite for Southern troops during War. Local cemetery contains Confederate graves.
- February 14, 1864, some elements of Col. John Jumper's Seminole Battalion, Captain Adam Nail's 1st Choctaw and Chickasaw Cavalry and 20th Texas Cavalry were surprised and defeated by Union force of part of 14th Kansas Cavalry and artillery.

New Springplace: Cherokee county, 1.5 miles southeast of Oaks.
- Site of Moravian Mission, established 1842. Mission buildings burned by pro-Northern Cherokee during War.

Park Hill: Cherokee County Intersection State Highway 82 and Us Highway 62.
- Site of Rose Cottage, Principle Chief John Ross' home. Brig. General Stand Watie burned to ground during War.

Perryville: Pittsburg County, intersection of US Highway 69 and Indian Nations Turnpike.
- Major Confederate Military establishment and supply point during War.

- August 25, 1863, Major General James K. Blunt's Federal forces routed elements of Brig. General William F. Steel's Confederate forces, seized the town and burned the supplies and buildings.

Pleasant Grove Mission; Johnston County. .75 mile west of Emet
- Col. William H. Emory concentrated Federal troops from Forts Washita and Arbuckle in this area at beginning of War.
- May 2, 1861, 2nd Lt. William W. Averell made contact with Emory's column 1.5 miles south junction State Highways 99 and 7 with dispatch from Washington D.C. ordering Emory to withdraw all Federal troops to Kansas.

Pryor Creek: Mayes County, 3.5 miles south of Adair along both sides US Highway 69.
- Battle took place after Confederate victory at Second Cabin Creek commanded by Col James M. Williams.

Round Mountain: Pawnee County, on edge of Lake Keystone, 3.5 miles north on State Highway 48, from where it crosses Pawnee-Creek Counties line.
- November 19, 1861, Col. Douglas H. Cooper's Confederate troops caught pro-northern Creek and Seminole under O-pothle-yohola fleeing to Kansas.

San Bois Creek: Haskell County, along south side of State Highway 9 where it crosses San Bois Creek.
- August 30, 1863, Confederate force encountered advance guard of Major General James K. Blunt's Federals advancing on Skullyville. Running fight followed along 10 miles of road east of San Bois Creek.

Sell's Store: Creek County, 3.25 miles east of Slick where State Highway 16 crosses Brown's Creek.
- Fall, 1861, served as Col. Douglas H. Cooper's headquarters, during search for O-pothle-yahola's Creeks as they fled to Kansas.

Seminole Council House: Pottawatomie County, 3 miles east of Tribbey on county road.
- August 1, 1861, treaty signed between Confederate Brig. General Albert Pike and Principal Chief John Jumper of Seminole.

Skullyville: LeFlore County, along both sides State Highway 9, between Spiro and Skullyville.
- August 31, 1863, Skirmish took place along Fort Towson-Fort Smith Military road, between elements of Major General James K. Blunt's Union force and Brig. General William A. Cabell's Confederate force.

Tahlequah: Cherokee County, junction State Highy51 and US Highway 62, capitol of Cherokee Nation.
- July 1861, Brig. General Stand Watie raised Confederate Flag above the square and declared his intention to fight for the South.

Thioplocco Town: Okfuskee County, 7 miles south, 1 mile east of Okemah on State Highway 27.
- October, 1861, skirmish between pro-Southern and pro-Northern Creek.
- October 1861, Confederate Col. Douglas H. Cooper at the community while chasing O-pothle-yahola's Loyal Indians north to Kansas.

Tullahassee Mission: Wagoner county, 1.5 miles west on State Highway 51B from junction with US Highway 69, then .5 mile north on county road.
- July 1861 occupied by Confederate forces, buildings used for hospitals, barracks, stables.

Tulsey Town: Tulsa County, along banks of Arkansas River, 2.5 miles north of I-44 bridge over the Arkansas in present day Tulsa.
- Well known Creek settlement. Confederate Col. Douglas H. Cooper left his supply train there while his men pursued O-pothle-yahola's followers after Battle of Chustenahlah.

Wapanucka Academy: Johnston County, 2.25 miles north of junction State Highways 7 and 7D, then 1.25 miles east.
- Used as Confederate military hospital and prison during War.

Washita River: Garvin County, along State Highway 193 miles southwest of junction with State Highway 133.
- First Civil War encounter in Indian Territory. Col. William H. Emory's withdrawing column of Federal troops captured vanguard of Col. William C. Young's Texas troops, pursuing Texas Troops. After agreeing to discontinue their pursuit, Texas troops were released and followed at discreet distance behind Federals.

Webber's Falls: Muskogee County, where US Highway 64 crosses Arkansas River.
- April 11, September 9, October 12, 1863. Minor skirmishes, Confederate and Union.
- April 25, 1863, Col. William A. Phillips' Federal troops' surprised meeting of Confederate Cherokee National Council scheduled to convene in Webber's Falls, capturing their supplies and dispersing the delegates.

Wheelock Mission: McCurtain County, 2 miles east of Millerton.
- Quarters and staging area for Confederates several occasions during War.

Wichita Agency: 3 miles north of Anadarko on US 281 from junction with US highway 62, then 5 miles west on county road.
- Established 1859 as first Federal Indian Agency in western Indian Territory.
- August 12, 1861, Site where Confederate Commissioner Albert Pike negotiated treaties with 11 tribes, resulting in 2 treaties.
- October 23, 1863, federally armed force of Delaware, Shawnee, Osage, Seminole, Cherokee destroyed the agency, and massacred pro-Southern Tonkawa camped nearby.

RESOURCES

Dust in the Wind: The Civil War in Indian Territory
By Ethel Taylor, Heritage Books, 2005

M234, roll 232, frames 629-632, Civil War,
National Archives, Washington D.C.

Compiled Service Records of Confederate Soldiers, National Archives, Washington D.C.
M258; Rolls – 77; 78; 79; 81; 82; 83; 84; 85; 86; 87; 88; 89; 90; 91

Compiled Service Records of Union Soldiers, National Archives, Washington D. C.
M109 Roll - 225

Confederate Veteran, Vol. IV, No. 3, Nashville, Tenn., March, 1896.
THE INDIAN TERRITORY 1861 to 1865 by Thomas F. Anderson, Mills, LA

Oklahoma Historical Society, Oklahoma City OK

Chronicles of Oklahoma, Vol. XI, Oklahoma Historical Society, Oklahoma City, OK

National Parks Services, Oklahoma, Arkansas, Missouri

Photos belong to author, unless otherwise stated, courtesy Oklahoma, Arkansas, Missouri Historical Societies, National Park Services.

OFFICIAL RECORDS: Series 4, vol 1, Part 1
Pages 669-687
Confederate States of America - Cherokee

OFFICIAL RECORDS: Series 4, vol 1, Part 1
Pages 445-466
Confederate States of America - Choctaw-Chickasaw

OFFICIAL RECORDS: Series 4, vol 1, Part 1
Pages 426-443
Confederate States of America - Creek

OFFICIAL RECORDS: Series 4, vol 1, Part 1
Pages 513-527
Confederate States of America - Seminole

OFFICIAL RECORDS: Series 4, vol 1, Part 1
Pages 636 - 646
Confederate States of America - Great Osage

OFFICIAL RECORDS: Series 4, vol 1, Part 1
Pages 659-666
Confederate States of America - Quapaw

OFFICIAL RECORDS: Series 4, vol 1, Part 1
Pages 647-658
Confederate States of America - Seneca, Shawnees

OFFICIAL RECORDS: Series 4, vol 1, Part 1
Pages 548-554
Confederate States of America - Comanche

OFFICIAL RECORDS: Series 4, vol 1, Part 1
Pages 542-548
Confederate States of America - Wichita, et. al.

www.ingramcontent.com/pod-product-compliance
Lightning Source LLC
Chambersburg PA
CBHW071132300426
44113CB00009B/947